SOCIAL PSYCHOLOGY

S O C I A L
P S Y C H O L O G Y

Donelson R. Forsyth
Virginia Commonwealth University

Brooks/Cole Publishing Company
Monterey, California

Brooks/Cole Publishing Company
A Division of Wadsworth, Inc.

© 1987 by Wadsworth, Inc., Belmont, California 94002. All rights reserved. No part of this book may be reproduced, stored in a retrieval system, or transcribed, in any form or by any means—electronic, mechanical, photocopying, recording or otherwise—without the prior written permission of the publisher, Brooks/Cole Publishing Company, Monterey, California 93940, a division of Wadsworth, Inc.

Printed in the United States of America
10 9 8 7 6 5 4 3 2 1

Library of Congress Cataloging-in-Publication Data
Forsyth, Donelson R., [date]
   Social psychology.

   Bibliography: p.
   Includes index.
   1. Social psychology. I. Title.
HM251.F635 1986   302   86-17102
ISBN 0-534-06744-1

Sponsoring Editor: *Claire Verduin*
Project Development Editor: *John Bergez*
Marketing Representative: *Bob Podstepny*
Editorial Assistant: *Linda Ruth Wright*
Production Editor: *Ellen Brownstein*
Manuscript Editor: *Barbara Salazar*
Permissions Editor: *Carline Haga*
Interior and Cover Design: *Katherine Minerva*
Art Coordinator: *Lisa Torri*
Interior Illustration: *Vantage Art Inc.*
Photo Editor: *Judy Blamer*
Typesetting: *Omegatype Typography, Inc.*
Cover Printing: *Phoenix Color Corporation*
Printing and Binding: *R. R. Donnelley & Sons, Crawfordsville, IN*
Credits continue on p. 645.

PREFACE

A dictionary definition of a textbook is "a manual of instruction that presents the principles of a subject." But, if that is the case, this book is not a textbook, for it does more than *present* social psychology. Rather, it *teaches* social psychology by encouraging students to look at the world from a social–psychological perspective.

To claim that this book teaches social psychology is hardly daring. Do fish swim? Do birds fly? Do textbooks teach? Sure. My shelves are filled with books that present the facts, findings, theories, and methods of the discipline clearly and comprehensively. However, they sometimes fail to teach students what it means to look at behavior through a social psychologist's eyes: to search for the social determinants of human action; to puzzle over the case of some anomalous social phenomenon; to cast off commensensical explanations when they fail to stand up to empirical tests; to make use of social psychology in their daily lives. Yet, teaching students to take this vantage point should be the primary goal of a textbook on social psychology. Long after they forget that 65% of Milgram's subjects were obedient or the three dimensions of Kelley's attribution cube, students should still be able to look at a social event and say, "Here's how a social psychologist would explain what happened."

■ Organization, Content, and Approach

This overarching goal—to teach students how social psychologists look at the world—shaped the organization, content, and expository style of this book. Looking first at organization, the book is traditionally structured, with chapters dealing with individual processes preceding interpersonal process. The chapters themselves, however, are organized around key themes or concepts that provide readers with a conceptual context for absorbing the information. In Chapter One, for example, Milgram's study of obedience is used to illustrate the interrelationships among all the topics examined by social psychologists and the methods they use in their studies. Summaries and transitions throughout the chapters reiterate the overall theme and the material is organized so that each idea follows logically from the last. This thematic approach illustrates the coherence of a social psychological viewpoint. Students often succeed in memorizing our favorite studies and theories but they don't always come away with an understanding of the foundations of the field. I want them to see how all the studies and theories fit together.

This integrative emphasis also guided the content of the text. Although no book can cover all areas of such a rapidly growing and changing field as social psychology, this text surveys all the traditional topics in the field. The overall approach, however, emphasizes the links between theory, research, and application. As a result, topics such as theory, personality processes, applications, and sex differences are examined throughout the book rather than in isolated chapters. Theory and research are clarified with everyday examples. Applied research is integrated with basic research. Studies of social forces are integrated with studies of individual and personal factors, such as sex differences and personality.

Last, students often attain a better appreciation of the social psychological outlook by applying it in their everyday lives. Students bring with them many kinds of relevant personal experiences and often want answers to questions that they feel are important. When the material is connected to interests they already have, students can learn to understand social psychology more easily. The text, therefore, presents each topic in a way designed to arouse curiosity and motivate study. To answer the question "Why should I, the reader, care?", the discussion emphasizes the impact of social psychology on daily lives and the need to understand practical problems such as aggression and productivity. Through many examples and applications, I try to show that social psychologists study processes that touch virtually all aspects of our social lives.

■ Features

A good textbook includes a number of pedagogical aids. Included in this book are the following:
- Outline to begin each chapter
- Chapter overview, provided in the introduction to each chapter
- Short summaries or implications sections at appropriate places within chapters
- Boxed "Focus" sections (Applications, Controversy, Experiencing Social Psychology, and A Closer Look) to highlight theoretical, research, and applied issues
- Comprehensive summary at the conclusion of each chapter
- Suggested readings at the end of each chapter
- Comprehensive glossary at the end of the book.

For a more complete description of these features, please see "A User's Guide to Social Psychology," p. xvii.

ACKNOWLEDGMENTS

Many people helped me as I struggled to reach these goals. I sincerely thank my fellow social psychologists, scattered across the country, who took time out from their busy lives, to offer hundreds of useful suggestions for improving earlier drafts of this book. They include:

Robin Akert
Wellesley College
Donald Bauman
University of Texas, Austin
Steve Baumgardner
University of Wisconsin, Eu Claire
Gordon Bear
Ramapo College, Mahwah, NJ
Paul A. Bell
Colorado State College, Ft. Collins
Daniel J. Bernstein
University of Nebraska, Lincoln
Arthur Bohart
California State University, Dominguez Hills
Carlton H. Cann
New Mexico Highlands University, Las Vegas
Alfred Cohn
Hofstra University
Francis C. Dane
Clemson University
Joan Fimbel DiGiovanni
Western New England College, Springfield, MA
Howard Garland
University of Texas, Arlington
Jeff Greenberg
University of Arizona, Tucson

William L. Gregory
New Mexico State University, Las Cruces
Kevin D. McCaul
North Daokta State University, Fargo
Stephen G. Misovich
Providence College
Richard Moreland
University of Pittsburgh
Stanley Strong
Virginia Commonwealth University, Richmond
William Carl Titus
Arkansas Technical University, Russellville
Russell Veitch
Bowling Green State University
Robert Zettle
Wichita State University

Rowland S. Miller, of Sam Houston State University, deserves special mention, for he read the entire manuscript and chided me each time I failed to meet his exacting standards. I wish to thank Karl Kelley and Judy Nye as well. They tolerated my time constraints and assisted me in preparing the Teacher's Manual that accompanies this book. I also thank Nancy Murdock for listening to me rave each time I fell prey to writer's block or missed a self-imposed deadline.

I also salute the editorial staff at Brooks/Cole. Despite missed deadlines (euphemistically called "slippages in the schedule"), Claire Verduin provided me with undeserved support over the lifespan of the project. John Bergez, a gifted writer and editor, spent hours carefully teaching me how to write a better textbook. Not only did he show me how to use summaries, transitions, and examples more effectively, but he also helped me understand the difference between a book that presents ideas and a book that teaches ideas. Thanks also go to Ellen Brownstein, my extremely competent production editor, who transformed the manuscript into a book, and the other members of the Brooks/Cole staff: Linda Ruth Wright, Judy Blamer, Katherine Minerva, Carline Haga, Lisa Torri, and Barbara Salazar.

Lastly, I acknowledge the debt I owe all social psychologists, both alive and dead, who have nurtured our science. With sadness, I draw special attention to the contributions of the many great social psychologists who have only recently passed away. As Kurt Lewin explained: "If I see further, it is because I stand on the shoulders of giants." Social psychology is richer for their efforts and poorer for their passing.

Donelson R. Forsyth

BRIEF CONTENTS

ONE   An Invitation to Social Psychology   2

TWO   The Social Self   46

THREE   Social Perception and Cognition   96

FOUR   Attribution   144

FIVE   Attitudes and Prejudice   188

SIX   Attitude Change   240

SEVEN   Personal Relationships   282

EIGHT   Helping Behavior   330

NINE   Aggression   380

TEN   Social Influence   424

ELEVEN   Group Dynamics   470

TWELVE   The Environment and Social Behavior   514

CONTENTS

A User's Guide to Social Psychology   xvii

ONE   An Invitation to Social Psychology   2

The Social-Psychological Perspective   5
Focus 1-1 Experiencing Social Psychology   11
Research Methods in Social Psychology   16
Focus 1-2 A Closer Look   17
Focus 1-3 Controversy in Social Psychology   26
Challenges and Issues in Social Psychology   32
Focus 1-4 Applying Social Psychology   33
Focus 1-5 Controversy in Social Psychology   38
Summary   41
For More Information   43

In Depth The History of Social Psychology   44

TWO   The Social Self   46

The Nature of the Self   49
Focus 2-1 Experiencing Social Psychology   52
Focus 2-2 A Closer Look   57
Focus 2-3 Controversy in Social Psychology   62
Sources of the Self   63
Focus 2-4 Applying Social Psychology   65
Self Processes   72
Focus 2-5 Applying Social Psychology   77
Focus 2-6 Experiencing Social Psychology   80
Focus 2-7 Controversy in Social Psychology   84
Summary   89
For More Information   91

In Depth Sex Roles and the Self   92

THREE Social Perception and Cognition 96

Social Perception 99
Focus 3-1 Experiencing Social Psychology 106
Focus 3-2 A Closer Look 108
Social Cognition 114
Focus 3-3 Controversy in Social Psychology 119
Perceptual and Cognitive Biases 127
Focus 3-4 Applying Social Psychology 128
Focus 3-5 A Closer Look 134
Focus 3-6 Controversy in Social Psychology 138
Summary 139
For More Information 141

In Depth Self-Fulfilling Prophecies 142

FOUR Attribution 144

Attribution Theory 147
Focus 4-1 Applying Social Psychology 150
Focus 4-2 Controversy in Social Psychology 162
Attributional Biases 163
Focus 4-3 A Closer Look 173
Focus 4-4 Experiencing Social Psychology 174
Attributional Theories 176
Focus 4-5 Experiencing Social Psychology 179
Summary 182
For More Information 184

In Depth Attributions and Emotions 185

FIVE Attitudes and Prejudice 188

The Concept of Attitudes 191
Focus 5-1 Experiencing Social Psychology 196
Focus 5-2 A Closer Look 202
Attitudes and Behavior 208
Sources of Attitudes 215
Focus 5-3 Controversy in Social Psychology 218
Focus 5-4 A Closer Look 227
Summary 233
For More Information 235

In Depth Reducing Prejudice through Desegregation 237

SIX Attitude Change 240

Attitudes and Persuasion 244
Focus 6-1 A Closer Look 248
Focus 6-2 Experiencing Social Psychology 257
Focus 6-3 Applying Social Psychology 260
Consistency Theories 261
Focus 6-4 A Closer Look 267
Focus 6-5 Controversy in Social Psychology 272
Summary 275
For More Information 276

In Depth Coercive Persuasion 278

SEVEN Personal Relationships 282

Affiliation 285
Focus 7-1 A Closer Look 288
Focus 7-2 Applying Social Psychology 292
Attraction 295
Focus 7-3 Controversy in Social Psychology 296
Focus 7-4 Experiencing Social Psychology 308
Close Relationships 308
Focus 7-5 Experiencing Social Psychology 311
Dissolution 319
Summary 323
For More Information 324

In Depth Sexual Relationships 326

EIGHT Helping Behavior 330

When Do People Help Others? 333
Focus 8-1 Experiencing Social Psychology 334
Focus 8-2 A Closer Look 339
Focus 8-3 Controversy in Social Psychology 348
Why Do People Help? 350
Focus 8-4 Applying Social Psychology 355
Focus 8-5 A Closer Look 361
Focus 8-6 Applying Social Psychology 365
Summary 372
For More Information 374

In Depth The Sociobiology of Helping 376

NINE Aggression 380

What Is Aggression? 383
Focus 9-1 Experiencing Social Psychology 387
Origins of Aggression 388
Focus 9-2 Applying Social Psychology 390
Focus 9-3 Controversy in Social Psychology 392
Focus 9-4 A Closer Look 400
Focus 9-5 Applying Social Psychology 406
Controlling Aggression 411
Summary 417
For More Information 419

In Depth Competition and Conflict 420

TEN Social Influence 424

Conformity 426
Focus 10-1 Experiencing Social Psychology 430
Focus 10-2 A Closer Look 434
Focus 10-3 A Closer Look 440
Nonconformity 443
Focus 10-4 Controversy in Social Psychology 449
Social Power and Influence 450
Focus 10-5 Applying Social Psychology 455
Summary 462
For More Information 464

In Depth Social Influence in Juries 465

ELEVEN Group Dynamics 470

Social Facilitation in Groups 473
Focus 11-1 Experiencing Social Psychology 478
Focus 11-2 A Closer Look 485
Groupthink 487
Focus 11-3 Applying Social Psychology 497
Leadership of Groups 498
Focus 11-4 Experiencing Social Psychology 502
Focus 11-5 Controversy in Social Psychology 507
Summary 508
For More Information 509

In Depth Polarization in Groups 511

TWELVE The Environment and Social Behavior 514

Territoriality 517
Focus 12-1 Experiencing Social Psychology 519
Focus 12-2 Applying Social Psychology 526
Personal Space 527
Focus 12-3 A Closer Look 532
Environmental Stressors 536
Focus 12-4 Controversy in Social Psychology 541
Focus 12-5 A Closer Look 544
Summary 548
For More Information 549

In Depth Protecting the Environment 551

References 555
Glossary 609
Author Index 619
Subject Index 631

A USER'S GUIDE TO SOCIAL PSYCHOLOGY

Welcome to social psychology. If you are meeting social psychology for the first time, you are about to begin a journey into a new way of looking at yourself and other people. On this journey you will explore the social side of human existence: the way your thoughts, feelings, and actions are influenced by other people. Some of the sights you will encounter along the way may be disturbing: people harming others; people isolated and alone; people failing to reach their potential. Others, though, will highlight the positive side of human action: love, helping people, and working together to achieve important goals. On your travels you will explore both routine, everyday situations and events with far-reaching ramifications for our society and the world at large: violence, cooperation, prejudice, sexism. Linking all of these topics—the negative, the positive, the mundane, and the earth-shaking—is social psychology's fundamental interest in people interacting with other people.

Why should you make this journey? Where will this road take you? One destination is an increased understanding of social psychology's theories, findings, and methods. Once, when I was a neophyte teacher, my enthusiasm for social psychology led me to expect my students to put this goal above all others. I wanted them to learn everything about social psychology. If a social psychology edition of Trivial Pursuit had existed, I would have used it as my final exam. With experience, however, I learned that gaining an overall view of social psychology was more important than learning all the specific details of the field. This book is intended to give you that overall view. It isn't comprehensive, in the sense that it doesn't review all theory and research in social psychology. Rather, it provides a general framework for examining social behavior, while suggesting avenues for more extensive study.

A second reason for studying social psychology is more practical. By gaining an understanding of social interactions and relationships, you may discover answers to problems you now face, or will face in the future. At a personal level, insights gained by the study of human interaction can be applied to your daily life, for social psychologists tend to study processes that we have all experienced. Have you ever wondered why you sometimes let other people talk you into doing things you don't want to do? Why you like some people right off the bat, but dislike other people from the moment you lay eyes on them? Why you have problems maintaining friendships or love relationships? Why you can or can't take charge in groups? Researchers don't have all the answers, but many people gain a deeper understanding of their own actions and interpersonal relations by applying social psychology in their everyday lives.

Social psychology also proves useful in many professional, business, and vocational settings. I am not so unrealistic as to hope that you will decide to revise all your career plans and dedicate your life to social psychology. But no matter what your professional goals, a fundamental knowledge of social interaction should still be helpful. Just about any time people work with other people, social psychological processes shape their actions and outcomes. Because researchers study such phenomena as communication between people, how we perceive and understand each other, leadership and decision-making processes in groups, competition and cooperation, and persuasion, social psychology yields many practical suggestions for improving interpersonal relations in work settings.

Enjoyment is the final reason for studying social psychology. Learning about social interaction should not be painful and depressing, but exciting, satisfying, and even amusing. I must confess that I am embarrassingly fond of social psychology. I don't consider it simply a scientific discipline or my vocation, but a hobby and source of recreation. I am so enthusiastic about the field that I want you not only to learn its principles and findings and to recognize its tremendous practical value, but also to have fun in the process.

Our destinations, then, are knowledge, application, and enjoyment, and this book is the vehicle that will carry us to these goals. Your vehicle has certain standard features that, used properly, will make your journey through social psychology a little easier. This book does not just present social psychology; it teaches social psychology by discussing ideas in a logical framework that gives you a conceptual context for absorbing the information. If you don't use the devices discussed below, your journey into social psychology won't be as smooth as it could be.

Outlines and previews. When you study a new field, it helps to try to organize the information in your own personal way. In fact, as you read each chapter, the material will be more understandable if you can fit each bit of new information into an overall conceptual context. Therefore, you should build an organizational framework before you read the chapter, rather than afterward. To help you accomplish this advance organization, each chapter begins with an outline of the contents. By taking a minute or two to study this outline, you can get a general idea of the way the topics are organized. In addition, the first few pages of the chapter serve as advance organizers by previewing the chapter's contents.

Chapter sections. Be careful not to run out of gas before you reach the end of your journey. One problem with learning by reading is that your motivation dwindles long before you run out of material to read. To guard against burnout, each chapter is broken into three or four major sections. An entire chapter may be too much to read at one time, but the sections within a chapter are easily digestible. Each one stands as a unit, and is followed by a short summary or application that ties the material to the overall theme of the chapter.

Headings and boldface terms. You can also save your energy by taking advantage of the headings and the boldface type that signals the introduction of important concepts. Headings do all sorts of useful things: they warn you about what you are about to encounter, they help you organize the information in the text, and they serve as memory aids when you try to retrieve information. So try to use the headings when you study the material: if you don't actively use them, they can't help much. The major terms printed in **boldface type** are defined in the glossary at the back of the book. Use them to identify critical ideas.

Figures. Visual information, when combined with the verbal information in the text, improves learning. Figures, in particular, serve as "spatial mnemonics": visual devices that aid memory by arranging the material in an organized pattern. Study those figures, because when the time comes to remember the material, you can mentally "see" the material by recalling the figure.

Focuses. From time to time, additional information about the topic under discussion in the text is presented in a special boxed insert. These inserts, which I call "focuses," are of four varieties:

1. A Closer Look: examines in detail a specific point that was only briefly discussed in the text itself.
2. Applying Social Psychology: shows how social-psychological theory, findings, and methods can be used to solve significant social problems.
3. Controversy in Social Psychology: explores current points of disagreement and debate in social psychology.
4. Experiencing Social Psychology: suggests ways to use ideas discussed in the text to understand yourself and others around you.

"Summary" and "For More Information." After reading a chapter, be sure to study the final summary. This section is followed by a list of

sources that you can consult for more information about specific topics that were discussed within the chapter.

"In Depth." A major theory, area of research, or application in social psychology is discussed in depth at the end of each chapter.

I hope that these features will make your journey through social psychology easy, efficient, and enjoyable. Once you open your mind to social psychology, I think you will succumb to its wiles. Again, I warmly welcome you to the field.

SOCIAL PSYCHOLOGY

O N E

An Invitation To Social Psychology

The social-psychological perspective
    The obedience situation
    Responding to authority
    From the social psychologist's perspective
        The social self
        Social cognition and attribution
        Attitudes and interpersonal attraction
        Interpersonal relations and group processes
        The social environment
    Defining social psychology
Research methods in social psychology
    Selecting a research site
    Measurement
        Behavioral measures
        Observation
        Self-report measures
        Nonreactive measures
        Selecting a measure
    Research designs
        Experimental designs
        Nonexperimental designs
        Selecting a research design
    The research process
Challenges and issues in social psychology
    The social psychology of research
        Evaluation apprehension
        Subject roles
        Experimenter effects
    The ethics of research
    The value of research
    Answering the challenge
Summary
For more information
In depth: The history of social psychology

People have been trying to gain a deeper understanding of one another for centuries. In their search for knowledge, they sought wisdom in the writings of great scholars and the prophecies of oracles. They begged their gods for enlightenment and their next-door neighbors for advice. They consulted mystic soothsayers, worldly authorities, and all-knowing experts. They even studied the electrical activity of the brain and searched for unknown psychological mechanisms in hidden territories of the mind.

But in the last 50 years or so, a new viewpoint on human behavior has emerged. This perspective, which is called **social psychology,** lies at the intersection of psychology and other social sciences, such as sociology and anthropology. Like other branches of psychology, social psychology strives to explain why people think, feel, and act the way they do. As *social* psychology, however, the field focuses on *the way other people influence our thoughts, feelings, and actions.* Human beings are a social species. We live our lives in the company of other people. We work together, play together, relax together, eat our meals together, and argue together. If we wish to comprehend ourselves fully, then we must understand how we influence other people, and how they influence us.

What makes social psychology distinctive? What can this explanation of human behavior tell us that other perspectives can't? First, social psychologists view human behavior from a unique vantage point. Because they always search for the social forces underlying our actions, social psychologists notice aspects of our social world that others may not. In a sense, social psychology offers a distinctive way of *looking* at the world. This chapter introduces you to this outlook by examining a rich social situation—obedience to a malevolent authority—from a social-psychological perspective.

Second, social psychology offers a unique way of *studying* the world. Many disciplines, such as philosophy and theology, ask the question "Why do people act the way they do?" Social psychology, unlike these nonscientific approaches, offers answers that can be evaluated by means of scientific methods. Social psychology is as much a way of doing research as a way of thinking about social behavior. This chapter examines these methods briefly before turning to the practical and ethical problems that researchers encounter when human beings are studied scientifically.

The Social-Psychological Perspective

In the early 1960s Stanley Milgram, a social psychologist at Yale University, carried out a series of studies on obedience. Intrigued by people's tendency to yield to the demands of powerful authorities, Milgram tested American subjects' reactions to an experimenter who ordered them to harm a fellow subject. Initially he had planned to conduct similar tests with German subjects, but he soon changed his plans. "I found so much obedience," Milgram explained, "I hardly saw the need for taking the experiment to Germany" (quoted in Meyer, 1970, p. 73; for more information, see Milgram, 1963, 1965, 1974, 1977).

The Obedience Situation

Consider Milgram's experiment from the subject's perspective. Imagine yourself leaving work at five o'clock and driving to the Yale University campus. As you approach the old Romanesque stone building where the Interaction Laboratory is located, you recall that only a week ago you received that flyer in the mail asking for volunteer participants in a scientific study of memory and learning. You sent in your name because you met all the requirements (between the ages of 20 and 50 and not currently enrolled in high school or college), but you are still a little surprised that the researchers called you to schedule today's appointment. Coming to the Yale campus at night is inconvenient, but the study promises to be an interesting experience. Besides, the $4.50 they're paying for the hour's time will be a nice bonus.

Hoping your nervousness doesn't show too much, you enter to find yourself in a scientific-looking laboratory room. A young man in a gray lab coat approaches and asks, "Are you here for the experiment? Fine. I'm Mr. Williams; I'll be conducting the research." The experimenter then gestures to an innocuous-looking man seated in the corner and explains, "That's Mr. Wallace. You are both subjects in tonight's research."

You shake hands with the fiftyish, overweight Mr. Wallace before sitting down. Mr. Williams clears his throat before briskly explaining the study.

> We know very little about the effect of punishment on learning, because almost no truly scientific studies have been made of it in human beings.
> For instance, we don't know how much punishment is best for learning—and we don't know how much difference it makes as to who is giving the

punishment, whether an adult learns best from a younger or an older person than himself—or many things of that sort.

Therefore, I'm going to ask one of you to be the teacher here tonight and the other one to be the learner.

Does either of you have a preference?   [Milgram, 1974, p. 18]

You look at your fellow subject, who shrugs and says no. You do the same. Williams puts two slips of paper into a hat, shakes the hat, and then asks you both to draw one slip. "Mine says 'Learner,' " announces the other subject. Yours reads "Teacher."

At this point you and Mr. Wallace follow Williams into another room, where Mr. Wallace, who is now the learner, is strapped into an "electric chair" (see Figure 1-1). Williams explains that the straps are necessary to prevent excessive movement when the shocks are given; once strapped in, Mr. Wallace will be tied down as tightly as a murderer awaiting execution. Mr. Williams then attaches a wire to Wallace's wrist and says, "This electrode is connected to the shock generator in the next room. And this electrode paste," he adds, "is to provide a good contact and to avoid blisters and burns."

"Are the shocks dangerous?" asks Mr. Wallace.

"No," answers the experimenter. "Although the shocks can be extremely painful, they cause no permanent tissue damage."   [Milgram, 1974, p. 19]

Leaving the learner tied in his chair and ready to receive shocks, you follow Williams into the next room. He asks you to sit in front of a machine labeled:

> Shock Generator, Type ZLB
> Dyson Instrument Company
> Waltham, Mass.
> Output 15 Volts–450 Volts.

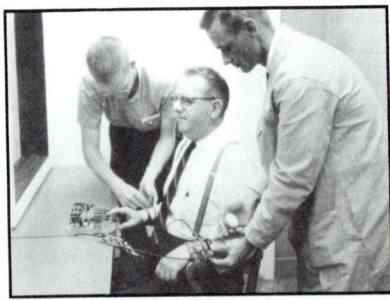 

Figure 1-1   (a) The "teacher" gives a helping hand as the experimenter straps the "learner" into the chair. (b) The experimenter gives the "teacher" a sample shock of 45 volts by pushing down the third lever on the shock generator.

The generator has a row of 30 levers, marked in 15-volt increments beginning at 15 and ending at 450 (see Figure 1-2). The experimenter lets you take it all in, and then explains:

> As the teacher, you will be asked to read a list of word pairs, such as blue–box, nice–day, and wild–duck, to the learner, using this intercom system. Once you have read the entire list to him, you are to test his memory by asking him a series of multiple-choice questions, such as 'blue: sky, ink, box, lamp'; 'nice: rose, wall, duck, day.' The learner communicates his answer by pressing one of four switches in front of him, which in turn lights up one of the four numbered quadrants in the answer box on the top of the shock generator. If the learner answers correctly, then you can move on to the next multiple-choice test question. However, if he gives an incorrect response, he must be given an electric shock. Start at fifteen volts, and increase the shock level one step each time the learner gives a wrong answer. Any questions? Fine. Before we actually begin, we always ask the teachers to experience a sample shock for themselves. So could you roll up your sleeve? Let me attach this electrode. Okay, now I'll flip the switch for forty-five volts and . . . that's an example of the shock the learner will be receiving [paraphrased from Milgram, 1974, pp. 19–20].

Ruefully rubbing your arm as you recover from the sample shock, you begin teaching the learner the list: "blue–box; nice–day; wild–duck," and so on until you reach the end. Then you test his memory with the multiple-choice questions. Before long he misses one of the items.

"No," you explain into the microphone, "the answer is 'duck.' Fifteen volts." As you push down the lever for 15 volts, a small light above it flashes red, a loud buzzing noise fills the room, a series of clicks and

Figure 1-2 (a) The shock generator and (b) a diagram of the generator's control panel. The "teacher" administered a shock by pressing down one of the levers.

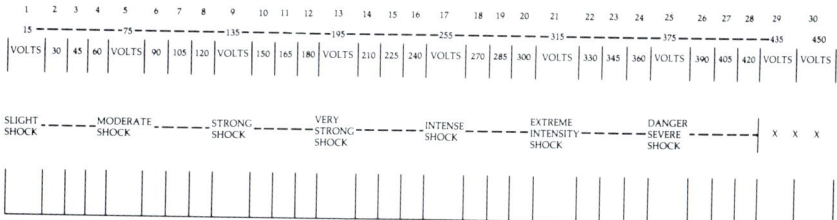

AN INVITATION TO SOCIAL PSYCHOLOGY

switches sound inside the machine, a blue light flashes VOLTAGE ENERGIZER, and the dial labeled VOLTAGE METER swings far to the right. An impressive machine, you think to yourself.

Down the list of questions you go, punctuating each wrong answer with a shock of ever-increasing voltage: 15, 30, 45, 60, and upward. With each step up you become more concerned about the welfare of the learner; after all, the 45 volts that you received seemed painful enough. What would 225 or 270 volts feel like? Finally, as you administer 300 volts for yet another incorrect answer, you hear the helpless learner pounding on the wall.

"I think he's trying to communicate with me."

Mr. Williams looks up from his desk. "Please continue."

"Well, it's not fair to shock the guy. These are terrific volts."

In the same even tone Mr. Williams once more commands, "Please go on. The experiment requires that you continue."

Reluctantly you read the next question, but the learner does not respond. "Mr. Wallace," you ask, "what is your answer?" but the response does not light up on the panel. Turning to the experimenter, you mumble, "Well, that's it." The experimenter, however, sits unmoved in this chair. As you hesitate, he tells you: "Wait five or ten seconds before considering no response as a wrong answer, and then increase the shock level one step each time the learner fails to respond correctly."

Turning back to the microphone, you tell the silent Mr. Wallace, "Wrong. The answer was 'day.' Three hundred fifteen volts." As you press the switch, above the buzzing and clicking you hear a pounding on the wall. Disconcerted by the sound, you once more confront the experimenter.

Teacher: I don't think this is very humane. I can't go on with this.
Experimenter: Please continue. The experiment requires that you continue.
Teacher: No, this isn't right. It's a hell of an experiment.
Experimenter: It is absolutely essential that you continue.
Teacher: The guy is suffering in there. No, I don't want to go on. This is crazy.
Experimenter: You have no other choice, you must go on.
Teacher: But he might be hurt.
Experimenter: As I said before, although the shocks may be painful, there is no permanent tissue damage, so please go on.
Teacher: But the learner doesn't want to continue.
Experimenter: Whether the learner likes it or not, you must go on until he has learned all the word pairs correctly. So please go on.   [Milgram, 1974, p. 32]

Turning back to the control panel, you look at the long row of switches that you have flipped: 15, 30, 45, all the way up to 315. And you look at the switches that remain: 330, 345, 360, and on up to 450. Frozen by indecision, you ask yourself: "What should I do?"

Responding to Authority

Milgram was studying obedience rather than learning; he wanted to understand when and why people follow an authority's orders. Both the experimenter (Mr. Williams) and the learner (Mr. Wallace) were Milgram's accomplices, hired and trained to enact particular roles. The drawing to identify shocker and shockee had been rigged; both of the slips in the hat said "Teacher." The learner's responses were carefully designed to include mistakes, the shock machine hadn't really been connected, and the pounding on the wall at the 300- and 315-volt levels was prearranged. The experimenter's actions were painstakingly rehearsed to create a standard setting for the measurement of obedience. His "manner was impassive, and his appearance somewhat stern throughout the experiment" (Milgram, 1963, p. 373), and he always responded to the subject's questions with the same sequence of "prods":

> Prod 1: Please continue [or Please go on].
> Prod 2: The experiment requires that you continue.
> Prod 3: It is absolutely essential that you continue.
> Prod 4: You have no other choice, you must go on.   [Milgram, 1974, p. 21]

The subjects were both the audience and the actors in Milgram's drama. As audience, they watched as experimenter and confederate played out their parts as authority and victim. Yet, as actors, the subjects were required to obey or disobey. To his surprise, Milgram found that the majority of the subjects he originally studied behaved obediently. As Table 1-1 shows, fully 26 of the 40 subjects (65%) shocked their victims to

TABLE 1-1

Obedience to authority. The percentages reveal several interesting effects. First, all the subjects were obedient, up to a point; no one stopped giving shocks before the 300-volt level was reached. Second, of the subjects who stopped, most refused when the learner first pounded on the wall (at 300 volts) or refused to answer (at 315 volts). Third, once they gave the 315-volt shock, most of the subjects went on to finish the entire sequence.

Shock Level (Volts)	Subjects Who Stopped at This Level	
	Number	Percent
300	5	12.5
315	4	10.0
330	2	5.0
345	1	2.5
360	1	2.5
375–435	1	2.5
450	26	65.0

SOURCE: Milgram, 1974.

the 450-volt level. Even when Milgram modified his original study so that each subject could hear the victim grunting, groaning, and pleading for help when he was shocked, the percentage of completely obedient subjects remained at 65%.

From the Social Psychologist's Perspective

Now that you understand the basic features of Milgram's experiment, try to examine the situation through a social psychologist's eyes. What is it about the experiment that is so fascinating? The surprising degree of obedience shown by the people who served as subjects? The nervousness and anxiety that gripped the teachers as they forced themselves to continue to deliver the shocks? The remarkably diverse reactions of people asked to perform identical actions? The apparent immorality of the subjects recruited by Milgram?

All these questions, and many others, come to social psychologists' minds when they examine Milgram's procedure. Milgram studied obedience in his research, but many more social-psychologically interesting processes, mechanisms, and phenomena are seen in the obedience setting he created. To understand the kinds of questions and topics that make up the field of social psychology, let's revisit the Milgram setting and try to see it as a social psychologist might.

The social self.
If asked, you could rattle off a list of your own characteristics and attributes, for you have a sense of who you are. You possess a personal identity, or **self,** that summarizes your perceptions of your good and bad points, your skills and abilities, and your interests and dislikes. Even though your self is private and personal, it is largely a product of social interaction. To answer such questions as "Who am I?"; "What is my personal worth?"; and "Do people like me?" you must sometimes rely on information provided by other people. Each social encounter provides new opportunities to develop an understanding of your own individual qualities and characteristics (Suls, 1982; Suls & Greenwald, 1983).

What insights does this view of the self yield when applied to Milgram's study? The participants probably viewed themselves in a positive way, as independent, helpful people who would never agree to harm an innocent stranger. Yet when they were told to deliver the shocks, most of them complied. Ellen Langer and her colleagues suggest that the subjects reacted automatically, without thinking about the consequences of their actions (Langer, Blank, & Chanowitz, 1978; Langer & Newman, 1979). Their attention was so focused on carrying out their duties as teachers that they never realized that they were violating their personal standards. In consequence, they obeyed the experimenter (Krebs & Miller, 1985).

Social cognition and attribution. To understand social interactions, researchers must sometimes study processes occurring within each interactant. Many social psychologists are fascinated by **social cognition**—such mental activities as perceiving, judging, reasoning, and remembering, which can influence social behavior (Fiske & Taylor, 1984; Marcus & Zajonc, 1985). This approach assumes that Milgram's subjects were actively perceiving and interpreting everything that happened around them. When Mr. Williams ignored the victim's pleas for help, for example, the subjects may have tried to identify the causes of Mr. Williams' actions. This process is known as **attribution,** as it determines how we ascribe, or attribute, causality to factors in ourselves or the environment (Heider, 1958). Similarly, when you read that 65% of Milgram's subjects were obedient, you probably tried to understand what caused such high obedience rates. Was the pressure really that strong? Were the subjects sadistic, evil people? Was the money so important that people would hurt others to earn it? From an attributional perspective, all of us are intuitive social psychologists, busily trying to understand our social environment by examining the ultimate causes of behaviors and events (see Focus 1-1).

Attitudes and interpersonal attraction. Social psychologists are also interested in the way we evaluate our social world. That these evaluation reactions are often influenced by our **attitudes**—feelings of like or dislike toward an object or event—is a fundamental concept in social psychology

FOCUS 1-1

Experiencing Social Psychology: *If you were a subject in Milgram's study, would you have obeyed?*

If you were to ask ten of your friends if they would have obeyed the experimenter to the 450-volt level, probably all ten would say, "Absolutely not. I'm too independent"; "I wouldn't because I can't stand to see people suffer"; or "No, it would violate my moral code." Unfortunately, however, Milgram's research suggests that at least six of your ten friends would be completely obedient, and that the remaining four would give shocks up to the 300-volt level. In fact, like your friends, you probably think you wouldn't be obedient, when in all likelihood you would give at least 300 volts.

Why do people underestimate their own obedience? According to several researchers, the error stems from some mistaken attributional assumptions. Although the subjects were strongly pressured to obey, many people tend to overlook these kinds of social determinants of actions and to overestimate the causal role played by internal, personal factors. This error results in a tendency to assume that Milgram's subjects were evil, immoral people and that defects in their personalities caused them to give the shocks. And once we blame the subjects for their obedience, we can assume that we ourselves would be able to resist because we don't have defective personalities. Through these intriguing cognitive processes, we succeed in attributing the obedience to the subjects rather than to the situation (Milgram, 1974; Ross, 1977; Safer, 1980).

(McGuire, 1985). Applied to the obedience setting, the concept suggests that subjects' actions may have been mediated by their attitudes toward the experimenter, Mr. Wallace, scientific research, or even Yale University. Most subjects, when later asked why they were obedient, expressed favorable opinions about science and the researcher. They respected Mr. Williams' scientific motives, and therefore felt obligated to continue with the research (Johnson et al., 1981).

Unfortunately for the subjects, however, the learner was a likable person who didn't deserve to suffer. As a result, the subjects acted in a way that ran counter to, or against, their attitudes. When our actions don't match our attitudes, we sometimes experience an aversive psychological distress known as **cognitive dissonance** (Festinger, 1957). To reduce their dissonance, some subjects refused to take any responsibility for their actions; they claimed the experimenter forced them to give the shocks. In one subject's words, "Mr. Williams has the biggest share of the responsibility. I merely went on. Because I was following orders . . . I was told to go on" (Milgram, 1974, p. 50). Others blamed the victim for having volunteered to be the learner, or for being so stupid that he couldn't solve the problems. As Milgram's findings suggest, people's evaluations of themselves are sometimes biased by their feelings and desires.

Social psychologists are also interested in prejudice, a general attitude toward an entire group of people. Would Milgram's findings have varied if the subjects were bigoted whites and the learner was black? If the experimenter was a female and the subjects were sexist males? If subjects were male and the "victim" was a female? Probably. Social psychology's interest in attitudes also extends to the study of liking, friendship, and love. Subjects would probably have responded very differently if the confederate had been a close friend or loved one.

Interpersonal relations and group processes.   Your best friend tries to persuade you to go out bar-hopping the night before a major exam. A club you belong to elects a new leader. You get into an argument with your roommate when she "forgets" to pay the rent. When your car breaks down a good Samaritan stops to help. These everyday situations may seem so commonplace that they don't warrant close scientific study. Yet these are some of the situations that intrigue social psychologists interested in individuals interacting with other individuals. Like chemicals that can dramatically change the color and form of other substances, human beings are the catalysts for many reactions in other human beings. To the social psychologist, if we are to understand people we must understand a wide range of interpersonal processes, including social influence, conformity, group dynamics, altruism, and aggression (Cialdini, 1985; Forsyth, 1983; Moscovici, 1985).

Let us return once more to the Milgram experiment to see how subjects' reactions were influenced by interpersonal relations and group processes.

To begin with a very basic question, we might ask, "What pressures to conform were operating in the obedience situation?" Many people underestimate the impact of social pressures. Social psychologists, however, believe that our actions are often controlled by other people. Consider, for example, the experimenter's *social power*. He could not punish subjects for refusing to give shocks, but they considered him to be a scientific expert. Many also thought that he had the right to demand obedience because he was a researcher at Yale. These situational factors created powerful pressures, which few of the subjects could resist. In subsequent studies Milgram found less obedience when he reduced the experimenter's social power. When, for example, he moved the study from prestigious Yale University to a nearby industrial city (Bridgeport, Connecticut), obedience dropped to 47.5%. And when the experimenter's role was given to an ordinary person who was supposedly also a subject, only 20.0% of the subjects were obedient (Milgram, 1974).

What would have occurred if the teacher had been part of a group of two or three others who blithely went along with the experimenter's commands? Would obedience have been even greater? Or what if the others in the group had refused to administer the electric shocks? Would disobedience then have been the rule rather than the exception?

Social psychologists raise such questions because many of our actions take place in groups: clubs, meetings, teams, work units, military squads, study groups, friendship cliques, and so on. Documenting the importance of group dynamics, Milgram found that subjects were more obedient when they were alone than when they were with others who refused to obey. In the situation shown in Figure 1-3, the subject still gave the shocks, but two other subjects helped with related tasks, such as reading the questions and giving feedback. Only the individual giving the shocks was a real subject, however; the other two were confederates trained to refuse to continue with the shocks at the 150-volt and 210-volt levels, respectively. In this situation, Milgram found that only 10 percent of the true subjects were completely obedient.

Other interpersonal influence processes besides social power, conformity, and group dynamics were also operating in the Milgram setting. A small minority of the participants seem to have been using the shock machine as an aggressive weapon. Feeling that the learner's poor performance reflected negatively on their teaching ability, one subject said, "The only time I got . . . disgusted is when he wouldn't cooperate" (Milgram, 1974, p. 46). Furthermore, just as shocking someone is a form of aggression, refusing to give shocks in the face of strong social pressure can be interpreted as a form of helping behavior or altruism. In contrast to the aggressive subject's reaction, one disobedient teacher answered:

> I do have a choice. Why don't I have a choice? I came here on my own free will. I thought I could help in a research project. But if I have to hurt somebody to do that, or if I was in his place, too, I wouldn't stay there. I

Figure 1-3 When the subject was part of a three-person group, he tended to go along with the other group members. If his fellow group members refused to obey, the subject exhibited similar disobedience.

can't continue. I'm very sorry. I think I've gone too far already. [Milgram, 1974, p. 51]

The social environment.   We interact with each other in specific physical settings and the characteristics of these situations—the location, amount of space available, level of noise, temperature, and so on—influence us in many ways (Darley & Gilbert, 1985). As we noted earlier, by running the study in a scientific-looking laboratory at Yale, Milgram increased the power of the experimenter. Milgram also found that the amount of distance between people in the laboratory setting influenced obedience. In one study, subjects heard the learner complaining about the shock across one of four distances:

1. *Remote:* only a pounding on the wall could be heard.
2. *Voice feedback:* the learner couldn't be seen, but his complaints (grunts, screams, and repeated pleas to be released) could be heard through the wall.
3. *Proximity:* identical to the voice feedback condition, but the learner was in the same room as the teacher.
4. *Touch proximity:* identical to the proximity condition, except that the teacher had to force the learner's hand down onto an electrical plate before giving the shocks.

As Figure 1-4 shows, obedience dwindled as the victim was moved closer and closer to the learner.

Defining Social Psychology

Thomas S. Kuhn introduced the concept of a **paradigm** to describe scientists' shared assumptions about the phenomena they study (Kuhn, 1962, 1970). According to Kuhn, when individuals are trained to be scientists, they learn not only the content of the science—important discoveries, general principles, facts, and so on—but also a way of looking at the world that is passed on from one scientist to another. The paradigm of a science, then, includes both *what* scientists study and *how* they go about their investigations.

Although a detailed understanding of social psychology's paradigm can be developed only over a long period of time and study, we glimpsed elements of it as we probed Milgram's study of obedience. During that analysis we saw that social psychologists are intrigued by people interacting with each other. The effort to understand these interactions leads them to study a range of topics, including intrapersonal processes (the self, cognitions, attributions, attitudes), interpersonal processes (social influence, group dynamics, aggression, altruism), and the social environment (crowding, noise, distances between people). Given the scope of the field, social psychology must be defined in broad terms. Gordon W. Allport proposed that social psychology can be viewed as *"an attempt to*

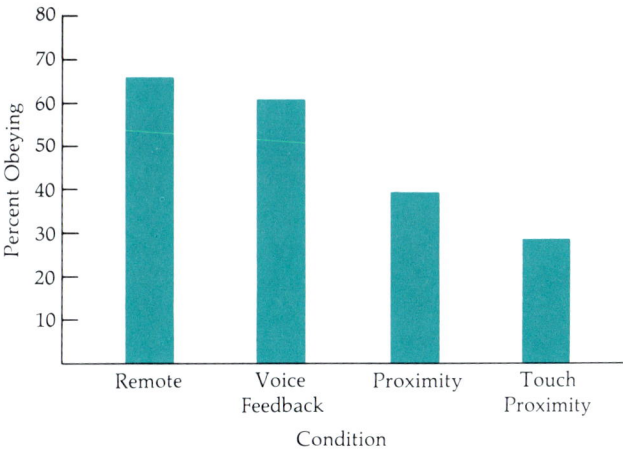

Figure 1-4   Obedience rates across four variations of the Milgram situation. At shorter distances the consequences of the painful shocks became clearer to subjects, who may have felt more responsible for the learner's suffering. When they actually had to touch the victim, only 30% of the subjects were obedient.

TABLE 1-2

Topics in social psychology and chapters in which they are covered. Social psychologists study a wide range of topics, but most can be placed in the categories listed below. The material in this book is generally organized so that we begin with processes that occur within individuals before we move to processes that involve interacting individuals and reactions to the social environment.

Topic	Chapter
An invitation to social psychology	1
The social self	2
Social perception and cognition	3
Attribution	4
Attitudes and prejudice	5
Attitude change	6
Personal relationships	7
Helping behavior	8
Aggression	9
Social influence	10
Group dynamics	11
The social environment	12

understand and explain how the thought, feeling, and behavior of individuals are influenced by the actual, imagined, or implied presence of others" (Allport, 1985, p. 3).

In later chapters we will expand our knowledge of social psychology's paradigm by examining the general areas shown in Table 1-2. The chapters are arranged from the intrapersonal to the interpersonal, for Chapter 2 begins with the social bases of the self and Chapter 12 ends with the social environment. We will also consider certain issues that cut across these general areas, including applications of social psychology, personality processes, and differences between men and women (see Focus 1-2).

Do not, however, overlook the second aspect of social psychology's paradigm. Although we tend to think first of a science's contents—the facts, findings, and theories assembled by investigators—the methods used by scientists when they carry out their research are equally important. To understand social psychology's paradigm, we must consider not only the topics listed in Table 1-2 but also the methods that researchers use to investigate these topics. We turn to these issues in the next section.

■ Research Methods in Social Psychology

All sorts of people use research findings to support their views. Educators who call for improvements in our schools point out that scores on IQ tests have been dropping steadily since the 1950s. Drug firms claim that studies "prove" that their products are effective. Medical experts, drawing on decades of research, warn that smoking cigarettes causes cancer. Women's rights advocates note that, statistically, women are paid less than

---

FOCUS 1-2

A Closer Look: *If two people are placed in the identical social situation, will both react in the same way?*

Although social psychologists look for commonalities in people's reactions to similar settings, they realize that no two individuals are identical. These variations among people, which are generally called **individual differences,** spring from many sources. Some reflect differences in personality traits, dispositions, and temperament. Others can be traced to our unique personal qualities, such as our level of intelligence, self-esteem, or motivation. Physical characteristics, including gender, age, and race, also contribute to differences among people.

Because individuals differ from one another, social psychologists rarely expect everyone to react to a specific situation in exactly the same way (Aronoff & Wilson, 1985; Blass, 1984). For example, 65% of the people in Milgram's study obeyed to the 450-volt level, but 35% did not. Some of these disobedient subjects broke off at the first sign of trouble from the learner, others obeyed until the confederate stopped responding, and still others continued until the shocks reached levels they felt were too dangerous:

> "Surely you've considered the ethics of this thing [extremely agitated]. Here he doesn't want to go on, and you think that the experiment is more important? Have you examined him? Do you know what his mental state is? Say this man had a weak heart." [Milgram, 1974, p. 48]

> "There was I. I'm a nice person, I think, hurting somebody, and caught up in what seemed a mad situation . . . and in the interest of science, one goes through with it. At one point I had an impulse to just refuse to continue with this kind of teaching situation." [P. 54]

> [After the experimenter tells him to continue administering 450-volt shocks.] "What if he's dead in there . . . ? I don't mean to be rude, but I think you should look in on him. . . . Something might have happened to the gentleman in there, sir." [P. 76]

> "I had about eight more levels to pull and . . . he [the experimenter] said, 'Just continue,' so I gave him the next jolt. And then I don't hear no more answer from him, not a whimper or anything. I said, 'Good God, he's dead; well, here we go, we'll finish him.' And I just continued all the way through to 450 volts." [P. 87]

If we take individual differences into account, we can understand these differing reactions. Researchers have found, for example, that people who evidence a generalized respect for the demands of powerful others—*authoritarian personalities*—are more obedient than nonauthoritarians (Elms, 1972; Rigby & Rump, 1979). Similarly, obedience may be linked to moral maturity. In one study, investigators found that advanced moral thinkers tended to disobey the experimenter's orders. In contrast, people who were less morally mature tended to obey (Kohlberg, 1969; Kohlberg & Candee, 1984).

This perspective on social behavior is termed **interactionism** because it assumes that individual differences among people interact with situational factors to determine behavior (Jones, 1985; Snyder & Ickes, 1985). In Kurt Lewin's words, "Every psychological event depends upon the state of the person and at the same time on the environment" (1936, p. 12). He summarized this idea in the equation $B = f(P, E)$: *social Behavior is a function of the Person and the social Environment*. Because interactionism pervades social psychology, in later chapters we will often consider the impact of personality and gender differences on our social behavior.

men for the same work. Social psychologist Stanley Milgram argued that his research indicated most of us would obey a malevolent authority.

The problem you face, as the consumer of these kinds of research-based claims, is that not all studies are created equal. Even though researchers take steps to make certain their studies yield clear conclusions, the perfect scientific study doesn't exist. All studies have both strengths and limitations, so each one must be evaluated with a critical eye. Because you are constantly bombarded by advertisers and advocates who back up their claims with "research findings," learning to recognize these limitations is a valuable practical skill. Although social psychologists are careful to point out the limitations of their studies, others aren't so scrupulous.

What aspects of a study should you take into account when you examine research? Many factors are important, but you may want to begin with the location of the research, the measurements used, and the study's design. Consider Milgram's studies. First, where did Milgram run his research: in the laboratory or in the field? Second, how did he measure obedience? Did he record behavior, carry out observations, or give subjects questionnaires? Third, did Milgram study obedience experimentally, by varying aspects of the situation, or did he study it non-experimentally? These are important questions, for each answer defines the significance and limitations of his research findings. (For more detailed analyses, see Bailey, 1982; Kidder, 1981; Rosenthal & Rosnow, 1984.)

Selecting a Research Site

To study obedience, Milgram carried out a **laboratory study.** Capturing the essence of obedience, he created a miniature social world with an experimenter for an authority, "prods" for orders, and the learner as the innocent victim. Leonard Bickman (1974), in contrast, conducted a **field study** of obedience by manipulating the authority of male experimenters who gave orders to 153 adult pedestrians chosen at random on a street in Brooklyn, New York. Bickman varied the experimenters' authority by dressing them differently; in either a sports coat and tie, a milk carrier's uniform, or a guard's uniform that looked much like a police officer's garb. These experimenters would give the chosen subject one of three arbitrary orders:

1. *Picking up litter.* Pointing to a bag lying on the ground, the experimenter would command, "Pick up this bag for me!"
2. *Dime and meter.* Nodding to a confederate standing near a parking meter, the experimenter explained, "This fellow is overparked at the meter but doesn't have any change. Give him a dime."

3. *Bus stop.* Approaching a subject waiting for a bus, the experimenter would say, "Don't you know you have to stand on the other side of the pole? This sign says 'No standing.'"

Bickman discovered that subjects were more obedient when the experimenter was dressed as a guard rather than as a milk carrier or civilian.

Milgram's laboratory study and Bickman's field study illustrate the contrasting advantages of these two types of research procedures. The strengths of laboratory research stem, for the most part, from the researcher's enhanced control in a lab. Laboratory researchers create the setting they wish to investigate. They can continuously monitor the participants, carefully control the situation, and check for unforeseen processes that may muddy their findings. Unfortunately, laboratory research can often be criticized for sacrificing realism for rigorous control. While the setting may be designed to approximate nonlaboratory situations, subjects are almost always volunteers who are aware that they are participating in a study and that their actions are being scrutinized. In consequence, the results may not hold in less artificial situations.

Field researchers solve this problem by collecting their data in real-world settings. The researchers may introduce manipulations into the setting, but in general they design their research around existing conditions. By taking advantage of ongoing events, field researchers are sometimes able to study extremely powerful social processes that could never be incorporated in a laboratory setting. Because the research is embedded in an existing social situation, however, they may have difficulty controlling aspects of the situation or even locating a naturally occurring situation that will yield useful data. In addition, the fact that the research is conducted in a nonlaboratory setting does not necessarily mean that the findings will hold up in other field settings. Bickman might have drawn very different conclusions, for example, if his study had been conducted in another city, if he had manipulated authority in some other way, or if the experimenters were women rather than men (Mook, 1983).

Measurement

No matter where they carry out their studies, researchers must be able to measure the social processes and phenomena that interest them. Before Milgram could carry out his studies, for example, he had to decide how to measure obedience: behaviorally, through observation, with self-reports, or by relying on nonreactive measures.

Behavioral measures.
Initially perplexed by the question of measuring obedience, Milgram turned the problem over in his mind until his long-standing interest in gadgets and electronics led him to the solution:

tell subjects to give a stranger shocks, and then record the level they reached on the shock generator. Because this method involves direct measurement of behavior, it is termed a **behavioral measure.** Other kinds of behavioral measures are shown in Table 1-3.

Observation. When Milgram supplemented his behavioral data with his own personal description of subjects, he was using **observational methods.**

> Many subjects showed signs of nervousness in the experimental situation, and especially upon administering the more powerful shocks. In a large number of cases the degree of tension reached extremes that are rarely seen in sociopsychological laboratory studies. Subjects were observed to sweat, tremble, stutter, bite the lips, groan, and dig their fingernails into their flesh. These were characteristic rather than exceptional responses in the experiment. [Milgram, 1963, p. 375]

Observation takes many forms, but the basic approach requires an individual who watches and records the subject's actions.

To increase the validity of their observations, researchers sometimes develop systems for objectively defining behaviors. In one study, group members' reactions to their leader's orders were classified in 16 categories by trained observers. The categories included such behaviors as "resisting," "withdrawing," "accepting," "showing dependence," "expressing anxiety," and "expressing depression." This method is often termed **structured observation,** because the observers' perceptions are structured on certain clearly defined categories. While observing the subject, researchers simply note the occurrence and frequency of each of the targeted behaviors (Mann, 1967; see Weick, 1985).

TABLE 1-3

A sampling of measurement methods used by social psychologists.

Method	Example
Behavioral measures	Number of shocks administered; choice when offered one of two toys; running a stop sign
Observational measures	Ratings of the leader's dominance; estimates of subjects' nervousness; counting the number of head nods and eye blinks that occur during a videotaped interaction; watching fellow office workers perform their jobs
Self-report measures	Attitude surveys; rating one's own emotional state; describing a personal experience
Nonreactive measures	Assessing a book's popularity by seeing how many times it has been checked out; using energy consumption as an index of conservation; treating the number of presidential vetoes as an index of power

Participant observation, in contrast, is a special observational method that requires active participation in the social setting by researchers themselves. While imprisoned in the concentration camps at Dachau and Buchenwald during World War II, for example, an investigator used this method to document the high levels of obedience among the prisoners (Bettelheim, 1943). Naturally, when you interpret findings obtained by participant observation you should be careful to remember that the reports could be influenced by the investigator's own feelings about the situation.

Self-report measures. Questionnaires, surveys, and interviews are all **self-report measures** because they ask subjects to describe their personal feelings, attitudes, or beliefs. Milgram's research once more provides an example (Milgram, 1974). To explore his unexpected findings further, he interviewed 137 of his subjects after the shock session. During the interview he asked them to rate their nervousness on a scale from 1 to 13; 1 corresponded to "Not at all tense and nervous" while 13 stood for "Extremely tense and nervous." He concluded from these self-reports that the vast majority of his subjects were moderately to extremely nervous (see Figure 1-5).

Nonreactive measures. Sometimes researchers use measures that have little or no impact on the participants in the research. Often described as "unobtrusive" because they are hidden in the background

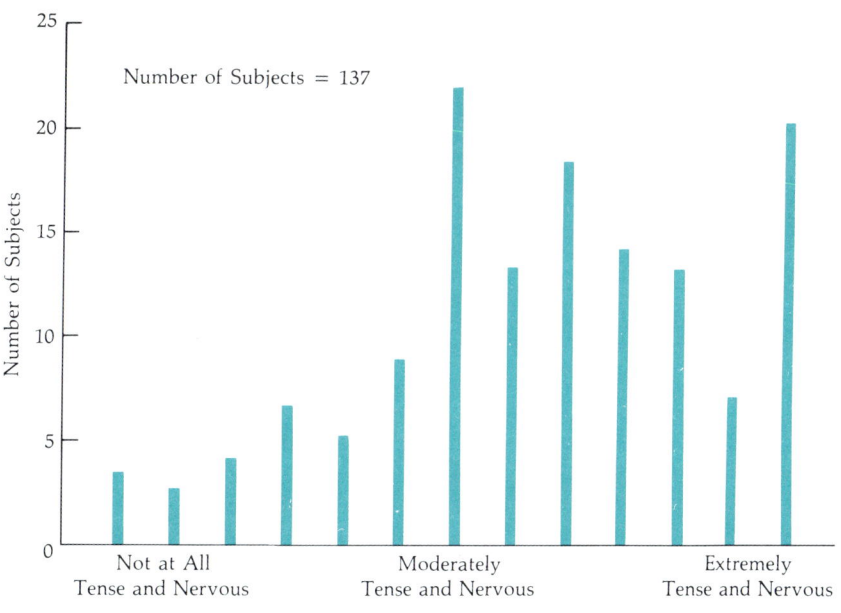

Figure 1-5   Level of tension and nervousness reported by Milgram's subjects.

AN INVITATION TO SOCIAL PSYCHOLOGY

of social settings, **nonreactive measures** are most useful when researchers suspect that subjects' behavior may not be spontaneous if they are aware that their behavior is being investigated. Examples of nonreactive measures include assessing compliance with a local law prohibiting the consumption of alcoholic beverages by sifting through residents' garbage cans (Webb et al., 1981) and measuring obedience to signs prohibiting graffiti by counting the number of messages scrawled on the signs themselves (Pennebaker & Sanders, 1976; Sechrest & Belew, 1983).

Archival analysis is a special type of nonreactive measure that makes use of existing records. Often these records are in public archives—the reports and statistics that are routinely collected by government agencies. Other sources of archival data include old newspapers, personal documents, and the public speeches of politicians. Milgram scrutinized the transcripts of investigations into three wartime instances of obedience to authority: the massacre of civilians at the village of My Lai during the Vietnam War and in the Nazi death camps of World War II, and the mistreatment of Union soldiers imprisoned at Andersonville, Georgia, during the American Civil War. According to Milgram, the soldiers in all these situations stressed the importance of following orders, the fact that they had performed duties required of them, and their lack of responsibility for their actions (see Simonton, 1981).

Selecting a measure. When researchers select a particular measurement method, they must make certain that their methods match their research goals. If investigators want to know about overt behavior or interpersonal processes, both behavioral and observational methods would be excellent choices. With observational methods, however, we look at social behavior through the researchers' eyes. If observers' attitudes and motivations accidentally influence their observations, the results may be biased. In this case, structured observations carried out by uninvolved, highly trained observers will yield more objective information. Self-report methods, in contrast, should be used if researchers are interested in directly measuring intrapersonal processes, such as thoughts, feelings, or attitudes. Unfortunately, these methods assume that people are aware of these intrapersonal processes and are willing to report them. If, for example, people can't gauge their own tendency to obey others, or if they don't want to admit it, then self-report methods may not yield valid information. Furthermore, when direct measures make subjects feel self-conscious, nonreactive measures may be the most appropriate approach.

Thus no one method is better than the others. In some cases researchers should use behavioral or observational methods, but in others a self-report or nonreactive measure may yield more valuable information. In consequence, researchers often use several different types of measures (as Milgram did) or develop specialized measurement tools. Many of these alternative methods are discussed in Chapter 5.

Researchers use a variety of methods to measure social psychological processes.

Research Designs

Suppose you want to know if people who watch violent television programs are more aggressive than people who watch nonviolent programs. So you carry out two studies. In one, you bring people into the laboratory every day for a week. Some subjects are shown only violent television shows and others see only nonviolent shows. After one week, you measure aggressiveness by asking the subjects to give electric shocks to a stranger. In another study, you go into people's homes and ask them to record the programs they watch each week. They also rate the level of their own hostility and anger by means of a questionnaire.

These two studies differ in several ways. One is a lab study and one is a field study. One records obedience behaviorally, the other relies on self-report measurements. The two studies are also based on different research designs. Both studies examine the same question: What is the relationship between watching televised violence and the viewer's aggressiveness? In the first study, you examined this relationship *experimentally* by manipulating aspects of the situation and then measuring the impact of these manipulations. In the other, you examined the naturally occurring *correlation* between television and aggression, but didn't manipulate the situation. This difference between the studies has very important implications.

Experimental designs.
When Milgram first realized that he was obtaining surprisingly high rates of obedience, he quickly began to search for the causes of his subjects' obedience. Identifying these causes required him to *manipulate key aspects of the situation while holding other factors constant*. One factor that seemed to influence the situation was the source of the orders to shock the learner. In Milgram's original study, the experimenter gave all the orders. Were subjects obedient *because* the experimenter was a legitimate authority? What would happen if the orders came from someone who had little or no authority in the setting?

Milgram examined the effects of different sources on obedience by creating three different conditions. In the standard, or control, condition, the experimenter continued to give the orders. In a second condition, the experimenter left the room and another person (actually one of Milgram's confederates) took over the job at the experimenter's desk. Milgram called this the "ordinary person" condition, for the new authority was apparently an ordinary subject. Last, in a rather bizarre variation, Milgram arranged for the learner himself to give the orders to shock. When the learner screamed in pain, the experimenter suggested that the research be terminated. The learner, however, insisted that he was "man enough to take the punishment" and ordered the subject to keep giving him shocks.

Table 1-4 summarizes the three conditions and shows the obedience rates for each. As Milgram anticipated, obedience dropped considerably when an ordinary person gave the orders, and even more when the learner himself demanded to be shocked. In fact, in this final condition all of the subjects refused to continue as soon as the experimenter suggested they stop.

This study possesses the three key features of an **experiment** shown in Figure 1-6. First, Milgram identified the variable he believed *caused* changes in obedience. Any aspect of the situation that fluctuates can be considered a *variable*, but when it is manipulated by the researcher it is called an **independent variable.** In this study the independent variable was the source of the orders. It had three levels: experimenter (control), ordinary person, and learner. Some experiments include several independent variables, but Milgram chose to study only this single independent variable.

Second, all experiments necessarily include one or more variables that are systematically measured rather than manipulated. The investigator wants to know what change the manipulation of the independent variable produces in some other variables. Such variables are termed **dependent variables** because their magnitude depends on the strength and nature of the independent variable. In Milgram's study the dependent variable was obedience, which he measured by recording the exact point at which each subject refused to continue shocking the learner. In essence, then, the independent variable is the hypothesized *cause,* while the dependent variable is the *effect;* Milgram wanted to know whether changes in the source of the orders caused changes in obedience.

Last, Milgram maintained strict control over any other variable that could have had a causal effect on obedience. Otherwise he would not be certain whether observed changes in obedience were produced by the independent variable or by some other factor. To achieve this control, he tried to keep all variables constant except the independent variable, which he himself manipulated. All subjects reported to the same room and were greeted by the same experimenter and learner. They all were promised the same payment, listened to the same story about the purpose of the research, and watched as the confederate was strapped into his

TABLE 1 – 4

Rates of obedience to orders from three sources.

Condition	Source of Orders	Obedience to Source
Control	Experimenter	65%
Ordinary person	A second confederate who takes over for absent experimenter	20
Learner	A learner who asks to be shocked	0

SOURCE: Milgram, 1974.

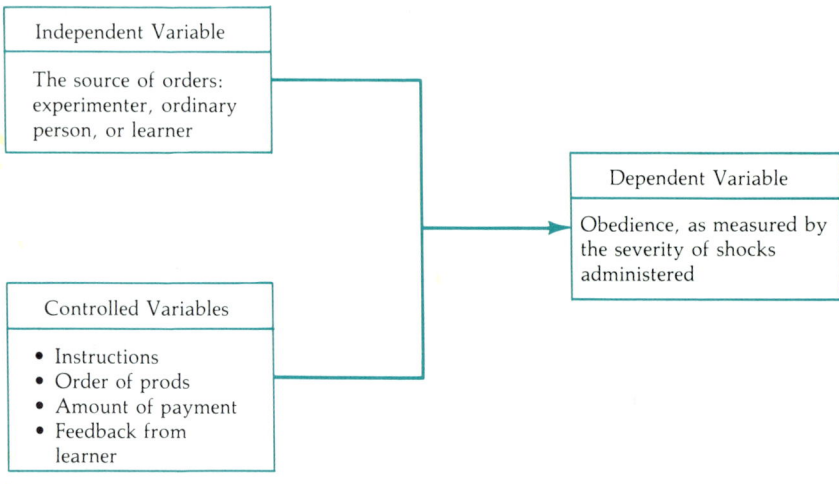

Figure 1-6 Three key features of experiments as seen in Milgram's research. Milgram manipulated the source of the orders (the independent variable), controlled other variables, and then measured obedience (the dependent variable).

chair. They all received sample shocks, sat before the shock machine, and listened for the reaction of the learner.

Milgram also tried to take other variables, such as subjects' occupations and ages, into account. He made certain that each condition contained an equal proportion of skilled and unskilled workers, businesspersons, and professionals, and a proportionate number of 20-, 30-, and 40-year-olds. By matching the conditions he made sure that variables that are associated with occupation and age would have no systematic impact on the dependent variable.

Unfortunately, Milgram's research can be criticized because he did not randomly assign his subjects to the three conditions. As we noted earlier, social psychologists realize that people differ from one another in many ways; some people are naturally more obedient than others, some are friendlier, some are more easily intimidated, some are more assertive, and so on. Because researchers can't hold all these variables constant, they use **random assignment** so that any relevant differences among subjects can be assumed to be spread across all the conditions (see Figure 1-7). Milgram, however, did not randomly assign his subjects to conditions. First he ran all the subjects in the control condition, then he carried out the "learner" condition, and still later the "ordinary person" condition. This procedure leaves open the possibility that some unknown causal factor produced the differences among the three conditions (Cook & Campbell, 1979). Because of this failure to assign subjects randomly to conditions, as well as other limitations in the basic design, some social psychologists have questioned the validity of Milgram's findings (see Focus 1-3).

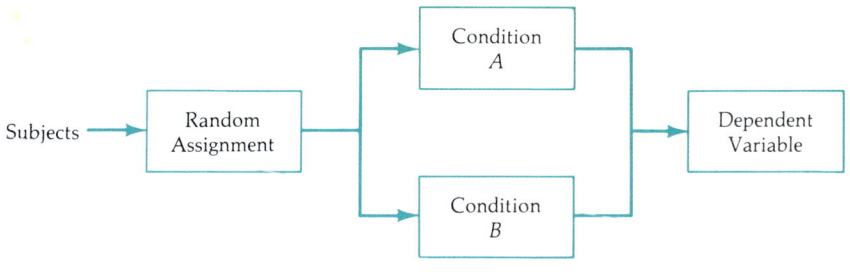

Figure 1-7 In an experiment, the researcher randomly assigns each person from the population of subjects to conditions; by chance, the subject will end up in either condition *A* or condition *B*. This randomization is used to try to distribute all types of subjects evenly across both conditions.

Experimental designs, then, allow researchers to probe causal relationships—to answer questions about the factors that cause us to behave as we do. Many studies carried out by researchers, however, are not experiments. In some cases experimental studies aren't possible; if the researcher can't structure and control the situation, then an experiment will not yield interpretable findings. Also, many important questions don't require a causal answer. Consequently, the social psychologist's research arsenal also includes several nonexperimental methods.

Nonexperimental designs. Many different methods fall under the category of **nonexperimental designs,** but all are similar in that researchers *don't* manipulate an independent variable. Instead, they systematically measure all variables of interest and examine the relationship among the measures. Milgram, for example, wondered if people who felt personally responsible for the learner's misfortune were the ones who were most disobedient. To answer just this question, he asked obedient and disobedient subjects to apportion among the three participants in the research—themselves, the experimenter, and the learner—responsibility for the harm presumably done. As Table 1-5 indicates, defiant subjects allocated more responsibility to themselves (48.4%) than to the experimenter (38.8%). Obedient subjects, however, blamed themselves and the experimenter almost equally. They even gave the learner a little extra responsibility as well.

This analysis relies on a nonexperimental design. Milgram did not manipulate obedience or responsibility. Subjects themselves decided to obey or not to obey and afterward provided their personal judgments about responsibility. Of course, the investigator may believe that one variable *caused* changes in another variable—Milgram may think that feelings of responsibility caused differences in obedience. The investigator can't make conclusive causal inferences, however, without manipulating responsibility.

Nonexperimental studies are generally referred to as correlational studies because the relationship between measured variables is often summarized with a **correlation coefficient** (symbolized by *r*). This statistic measures the strength and direction of the relationship between two variables. As Figure 1-8 indicates, correlations can vary in magnitude from -1.0 to 0.0 to $+1.0$. A correlation of zero would mean that the variables being measured showed no pattern of relationship with each other. Suppose Milgram compared subjects' feelings of responsibility with their level of obedience and found that the correlation between these variables was zero. In this case, knowing how much personal responsibility a subject felt would tell us nothing about how obedient he or she would be. Suppose, however, that the correlation turned out to be 1.0—a perfect positive correlation. This finding would mean that, without exception, the more personal responsibility the subjects felt, the more they obeyed. Finally, suppose the correlation was -1.0. In this case, feelings of responsibility would be negatively, or inversely, correlated with obedience: as personal responsibility increased, obedience decreased. Thus the sign of the correlation (plus or minus) tells us if this relationship is positive (direct) or negative (inverse). If the correlation is positive, then both variables increase and decrease together. If, however, the correlation is negative, then increases in one variable are associated with decreases in the second variable.

FOCUS 1-3

Controversy in Social Psychology: *Are Milgram's findings valid?*

When social psychologists try to assess the validity of any experiment, they generally distinguish between **internal validity** and **external validity** (Campbell & Stanley, 1963; Cook & Campbell, 1979). For a study to be internally valid, the differences between conditions must actually be caused by the independent variable rather than some other variable. External validity, in contrast, "asks the question of generalizability: To what populations, settings, treatment variables, and measurement variables can this effect be generalized?" (Campbell & Stanley, 1963, p. 5).

Milgram's research has been challenged on both counts (Mixon, 1977, 1979; Orne & Holland, 1968; Patten, 1977). Several critics have suggested that subjects were suspicious. Researchers, when conducting laboratory studies, often give subjects a false explanation, or *cover story*, that provides a rationale for the manipulations and measurements. Milgram, for example, told his subjects he was studying learning and punishment. High rates of suspicion would threaten the study's internal validity, for subjects would not think that their obedience was causing any harm. In addition, Milgram may have accidentally varied other factors when he manipulated the independent variable. For example, although he sought to manipulate the source of the orders in one condition by arranging for the learner to ask for shocks, the learner's request may have seemed bizarre; not only did the source of the orders change, but subjects may have concluded that the learner was acting very strangely. Milgram thought that the drop in obedience was due to the low authority of the learner, but in actuality this other variable—the oddness of the learner's behavior—could have been the actual cause of the effect. Factors that vary systematically with the independent variable are called *confounds*, and their unintended intrusion in experiments threatens internal validity.

TABLE 1-5

Percentage of responsibility assigned to the three parties to Milgram's research by disobedient and obedient subjects.

Type of Subject	Number of Subjects	Experimenter	Teacher	Learner
Disobedient	61	38.8%	48.4%	12.8%
Obedient	57	38.4	36.3	24.3

SOURCE: Milgram, 1974.

Between these extremes of $+1.0$ and -1.0 are the intermediate values investigators commonly find. As Figure 1-8 indicates, correlations between $-.2$ and $+.2$ occur when variables are only slightly related to one another. If, for example, the correlation between obedience and feelings of personal responsibility was $-.18$, then the relationship between these two variables would be relatively weak. Knowing how much personal responsibility a subject felt would tell us relatively little about his or her obedience. Larger correlations occur when the variables are more closely related to one another. Remember that, in general, the greater the magnitude of the correlation (the farther it is from zero in

---

Questions concerning external validity have also been raised. Milgram's subjects were volunteers, and evidence indicates that people who volunteer for research behave somewhat differently from nonvolunteers (Rosenthal & Rosnow, 1974). Furthermore, the method used to quantify obedience may have elicited abnormally great amounts of obedience (Gilbert, 1981). By starting with a minor request—to deliver only 15 volts—Milgram may unwittingly have taken advantage of the foot-in-the-door technique. When a large request is prefaced by a small request, people have difficulty refusing the large request (see Chapter 10). Also, the prods used by the experimenter may have been far stronger than the kinds of orders we find in everyday situations.

These criticisms have been answered both by Milgram and by other researchers. When Milgram interviewed many of his subjects after their session, he discovered that fewer than 20 percent reported serious doubts about the cover story. In addition, his findings have been replicated in several different settings, with different subjects and different cover stories, suggesting that his basic conclusions can be generalized beyond his specific conditions (Kilham & Mann, 1974; Mantell, 1971; Martin, Lobb, Chapman, & Spillane, 1976; Milgram, 1974; Shanab & Yahya, 1977; Sheridan & King, 1972; West, Gunn, & Chernicky, 1975).

These findings attest to the internal and external validity of Milgram's research, although the controversy is by no means settled. While some people feel that Milgram's research was too flawed to be valid, others believe that Milgram's experiment is "one of the best carried out in this generation" (Etzioni, 1968, p. 278) because it makes a "momentous and meaningful contribution to our knowledge of human behavior" (Erikson, 1968, p. 279). As we shall discover again and again in later chapters, the beauty of an experiment is sometimes in the eye of the beholder.

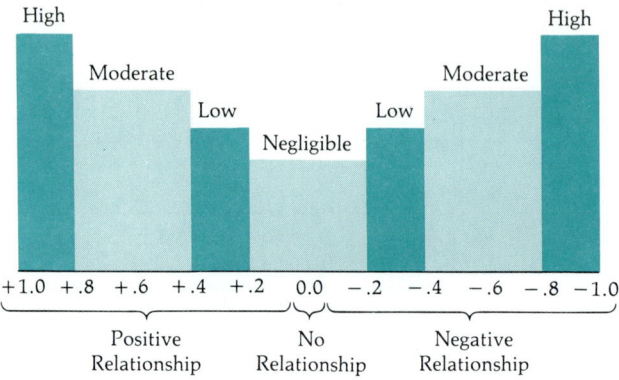

Figure 1-8 Correlations summarize the degree of relationship between two variables. A correlation (or r) near 0.0 indicates that the two variables are not closely related; as the value of r approaches either -1.0 or $+1.0$, the statistic indicates that the variables are closely linked.

either a positive or negative direction), the stronger the relationship between the variables. Researchers can also use statistical tests to determine if the correlations are far enough away from zero to be "significant."

A correlation is a handy way of summarizing the strength and direction of the relationship between two variables. But don't be misled into thinking that correlations demonstrate causality. Consider Milgram's finding that feelings of personal responsibility for the learner's pain were negatively correlated with obedience. It is tempting to conclude that strong feelings of personal responsibility cause subjects to disobey, but the actual relationship may be just the reverse. After administering high-voltage shocks, subjects explained away their embarrassing obedience by claiming they weren't responsible. Thus responsibility doesn't cause disobedience; rather, obedience causes people to deny responsibility. The correlation between these two variables may also be produced by a third variable that the investigator did not take into account. People who are morally immature, for example, may tend to be very obedient, and they may tend to take little responsibility for their actions. In consequence, a significant correlation emerges when obedience and responsibility are measured, even though these two variables aren't causally related. These examples, and those shown in Table 1-6, should convince you that to infer causality from correlational studies is risky at best (Stanovich, 1986).

Selecting a research design. Social psychologists use both experimental and nonexperimental designs in their efforts to understand social behavior. When they wish to investigate a causal relationship, an experimental design is needed. Provided researchers carry out the study properly by manipulating the independent variable, measuring the dependent variable accurately, and controlling any extraneous variables, they can be fairly certain that any changes in the dependent variable were caused by the independent variable. Because experiments yield information about causality, social psychologists rely heavily on this technique: nearly 75% of all studies published in major social psychology journals in the 1970s used experimental designs (Higbee, Millard, & Folkman, 1982).

The experimenter's need to control the experimental situation, however, leads to the major weakness of experimentation: artificiality. Experiments usually require controlled conditions, so they sometimes fail to approximate the complexities of behavior in naturally occurring situations. In such cases, researchers can turn to nonexperimental designs. Correlational studies don't require manipulations and elaborate controls, and they provide precise estimates of the strength of the relationship between variables. They are limited, however, in that they cannot clearly demonstrate causal relationships among variables. They answer such questions as "Are people who watch violent television programs aggressive?" but not "Does watching violent programs cause people to become aggressive?"

TABLE 1 − 6

Correlations and causal inference. Interpret correlational findings with care. No matter how plausible a particular causal inference may be, other interpretations can account for correlational findings.

Correlation	Interpretation A	Interpretation B
Cigarette smoking is negatively correlated with grades in college	Smoking reduces brain power	Anxiety over low grades causes increased smoking
The number of body lice on natives in the New Hebrides is positively correlated with good health	Having a large number of body lice makes one healthy	Lice leave the bodies of extremely ill natives in preference for healthy hosts
The cost of rum is positively correlated with Presbyterian ministers' salaries	Presbyterian ministers buy a lot of rum, so as their salaries increase, the seller raises the price	Inflation over many years has caused both the cost of rum and ministers' salaries to rise
The number of storks in an area of Holland is positively correlated with the area's birth rate	Storks bring the babies	The birth rate is higher in rural areas, where most storks nest
The number of deaths by drowning is positively correlated with the amount of ice cream sold on any given day	People eat too much ice cream, go swimming, get cramps, and drown	People eat more ice cream on hot days, and they are more likely to go swimming (and possibly drown)

SOURCE: Adapted from Huff, 1954.

The Research Process

If you wanted to study the relationship between violence on television and the viewer's aggressiveness, you would be faced with many decisions. As we have seen, you would have either to find a situation that includes the variables you wish to study or to create a laboratory situation. Then you would have to decide among behavioral, observational, self-report, and nonreactive measures. Furthermore, you would have to test your hypothesis by using either experimental or nonexperimental methods.

The importance of research cannot be overemphasized. By collecting information relevant to their hypotheses and questions, social psychologists have succeeded in building and testing conceptual frameworks for understanding human behavior. Milgram's research exemplifies this process. Beginning with a hypothesis about obedience, he worked out a way to measure critical variables and assess their interrelationships. When his subjects obeyed despite their belief that they were causing great harm, Milgram was forced to revise his initial hypothesis in light of the empirical findings. He eventually discovered other variables that were related to disobedience, such as the amount of surveillance by the experimenter, the authority of the individual giving the orders, and the strength of the experimenter's commands. These findings helped Milgram to construct a theory of obedience. This pattern of *hypothesis* → *data* → *hypothesis* → *data* often characterizes progress in scientific research (see, for example, Lakatos & Musgrave, 1970; Manicas & Secord, 1982; Suppe, 1974; Toulmin, 1953).

Because social psychologists study human behavior, their findings also shed light on important social problems. Milgram's research, for example, warns us that people who obey malevolent authorities aren't necessarily spineless and evil themselves. If the pressure to obey is strong, people will yield to it (see Focus 1-4). This focus on people makes social psychology a tremendously useful pursuit, but at the same time it creates unique problems for researchers. How do people react when they know they are being studied by researchers? Are researchers justified in deceiving their subjects? Does social psychology really yield new insights into human behavior? These questions and possible answers are considered in the closing section of this chapter.

■ Challenges and Issues in Social Psychology

Because social psychologists study people rather than rocks, plants, atomic particles, or planets, they run up against challenges and problems that other scientists never encounter. When astronomers focus their telescopes on a passing comet, for example, the comet takes no notice. People, however, sometimes change their behavior when a social psychologist looks their way. Likewise, when physicists examine nuclear particles by exposing a beryllium target to high-energy X rays, they don't have to worry about what will happen to the beryllium. Social psychologists, in contrast, must make certain that no harm befalls the participants in their research. And when astrophysicists tell us that "black holes" occur when matter becomes so dense that light cannot escape its gravitational pull, we don't respond by saying, "Well, that's just common sense." Albert Einstein predicted the existence of black holes, but common sense never did. Yet when social psychologists report that individuals will obey a malevolent authority, listeners often answer, "I already

---

FOCUS 1-4

Applying Social Psychology: *How useful is social psychology?*

Philosophers of science often draw a distinction between **basic science** and **applied science.** In basic research (sometimes called "pure" research), scientists extend our general understanding by testing theoretically important hypotheses. They ask, "Let's compare what is with what should be to see if the theory is adequate." Applied researchers, in contrast, seek information that will prove relevant to some practical problem. They ask, "Let's understand the nature of this problem so we can do something to resolve it" (Bickman, 1981; Bunge, 1974; Forsyth & Strong, 1986).

Social psychology is both a basic and an applied science. Researchers examine general questions dealing with social behavior, but they also explore practical problems that need solution. Milgram, for example, examined basic questions about obedience: Who obeys? What social factors encourage obedience? What emotional processes maintain obedience? However, his studies also yield information on how to prevent excessive obedience; increase individuals' feelings of personal responsibility; warn people about the power of social pressure; remove authorities from the situation. Similarly, studies of attitudes suggest ways to change attitudes through persuasion. By examining productivity in groups, we learn how to increase production. Studies of aggression offer insights into ways to avoid violence.

Remember, however, that social psychology is not simply a body of scientific facts and theories, but also a group of methods for expanding our understanding of social behavior. These methods, too, can be used to solve problems of practical significance (Deutsch & Hornstein, 1975). Such organizations as hospitals, psychiatric treatment facilities, industries, and government agencies often call on researchers to evaluate the effectiveness of their programs. Such *program evaluations* might include a study to determine if a new assembly-line procedure is more efficient than the old one, if new regulations governing the distribution of welfare benefits have reduced the number of fraudulent users, or if special education programs, such as Head Start, lead to increases in students' reading skills (Cook, Leviton, & Shadish, 1985; Wortman, 1983).

Researchers can also create new programs and other innovations through *social experimentation* (Fairweather & Tornatzky, 1977; Riecken & Boruch, 1975; Saxe & Fine, 1981). To study the effects of training on police officers' job performance, for example, one researcher randomly assigned trainees to one of two treatment groups. All trainees took the same courses, but those in the high-stress group trained in a military atmosphere while those in the low-stress group trained in a relaxed, campus-like atmosphere. Because the low-stress subjects outperformed the high-stress subjects in virtually all categories, the program was incorporated in the police department's regular training program (Earle, 1973).

Thus both the content and methods of social psychology are powerful tools for understanding, and possibly solving, practical problems. As you will see, each chapter in this book is filled with applications of social psychology to practical problems. (For more information, see Rodin, 1985.)

knew that." This introduction to the field of social psychology concludes by considering some of the unique challenges facing social psychologists, and the steps they have taken to meet those challenges.

The Social Psychology of Research

Once more, take the place of a subject in Milgram's research. From the moment you enter the lab, you are filled with thoughts and questions about the experiment: "I bet Wallace will learn faster if he gets shocks"; "That experimenter looks like a teacher I had in high school"; "Why did they paint this room such an ugly color?"; "I hope they don't give us any questionnaires to fill out"; "That experimenter must think I'm pretty stupid"; "When will this be over?" Rather than reacting passively as the experiment unfolds, you react socially; you scrutinize the situation, wonder about the reasons for the research, and try to act normally (Adair, 1973; Rosnow, 1981).

The social nature of the research setting can't be ignored. The task of collecting data almost always requires interaction between subjects and researchers, and this interaction itself sets social-psychological processes in motion. Even though the researcher isn't interested in these processes, they can distort subjects' reactions and obscure the meaning of the results. Rather than ignore this problem, researchers have studied the impact of various social-psychological factors on research subjects. These investigations have enabled them to identify biases that sometimes, but not always, color a study's results. Here we will consider three such biases: evaluation apprehension, subject roles, and experimenter effects (Brenner & Bungard, 1981; Miller, 1972a).

Evaluation apprehension.   When people take part in a research project, they often feel that the investigator is evaluating them in some way. Most of us strive to make a good impression when we meet people for the first time, so we behave in a "normal," rational manner. This concern over evaluation is particularly strong in research settings, because people assume that the investigators are insightful appraisers who will notice any flaws they fail to hide. This anxiety-creating concern to appear normal in research is known as **evaluation apprehension** (Rosenberg, 1965). If Milgram's subjects experienced evaluation apprehension, they may have worried about the impression they were making. To appear helpful and "normal," they did whatever the experimenter asked.

Subject roles.   Research participants also behave differently depending on the **subject role** they enact when they enter the study. Some people, for example, try to fulfill the *good subject role* by carefully following instructions and by conscientiously performing all requirements. In their desire to please the researcher by behaving like good subjects, participants have obediently chopped off the heads of live rats with a butcher knife (Landis, 1924), chewed up fried grasshoppers (Zimbardo et al., 1965), immersed their hands in what they believed to be acid (Orne & Evans, 1965), agreed to burglarize a business (West et al., 1975), delivered shocks to a caged puppy (Sheridan & King, 1972), and given apparently lethal shocks to a victim (Milgram, 1974). People who are motivated to be good subjects also try to figure out the purpose of the research. Then they change their responses to confirm the hypothesis they think is being investigated.

In contrast to the good subject role, others may adopt a bad or *negativistic subject role:* they complain that the research is trivial and uninteresting, and therefore refuse to cooperate with the researcher at every turn. Negativistic subjects may even evidence what has been termed the "screw you" effect by actively trying to distort the findings; they respond at random or in other ways that they hope will disconfirm the researcher's hypothesis (Masling, 1966). Negativistic subjects are often very suspicious. They may not actively try to ruin the study, but they can be so intent on discovering the true purposes of the research that they ignore important aspects of the setting and respond haphazardly (see Carlopio et al., 1983; Carlston & Cohen, 1980; Christensen, 1982).

Experimenter effects. Researchers are as human as the people they study, and in consequence they too are sometimes influenced by social-psychological factors. Quite unintentionally, a researcher can let subjects know how they are supposed to respond. A researcher studying cooperation and competition, for example, may accidentally stress the word *cooperation* when giving subjects instructions. The subjects notice the stress and decide that they are supposed to cooperate. Or a researcher studying attitudes may administer the same questionnaire twice, first at the beginning of the study and again at the end. Subjects realize they are being retested, so they assume that a change in their attitudes is expected. These accidental hints are **demand characteristics**—perceptual cues that practically demand responses that will confirm the researcher's hypothesis (Orne, 1962).

A related problem stems from the researcher's expectations about how the study will turn out. Suppose two researchers who are conducting the same experiment expect opposite findings; one experimenter thinks that the subjects assigned to group A will score higher than the subjects assigned to group B, while the second experimenter thinks B will outscore A. According to several studies conducted by Robert Rosenthal, the experimenters' expectations will probably be fulfilled; the group that is expected to perform better will in fact outscore the other group (Rosenthal, 1966, 1969; Rosenthal & Fode, 1963). Although some research suggests that the **expectancy effect** occurs very infrequently, other studies have shown that researchers can unintentionally bias their studies by violating random assignment procedures, by changing their nonverbal behaviors, and by misrecording a subject's responses. Fortunately, many steps can be taken to control expectancy effects. They include automating the role of the researcher, making certain the research personnel are unaware of the hypotheses, and rigorously standardizing the behaviors of the research staff. (Compare Rosenthal & Rosnow, 1984, with Barber, 1976, and Barber & Silver, 1968a, 1968b.)

Because the research situation is fundamentally a social situation, researchers have learned to recognize and cope with biases produced by evaluation apprehension, subject roles, demand characteristics, and expectancy effects. The study of human beings creates a second concern that goes well beyond these practical problems, however. Social psychologists strive to avoid biases that will distort their findings, but they must also design their studies so that the participants are treated in a fair, ethical manner.

The Ethics of Research

You have just finished participating in Milgram's study. You did what you were told. For 30 minutes you punished the learner with powerful jolts of electricity. After you have pushed the lever for 450 volts for the last time, Milgram enters the room. He asks you a few questions. Then he explains that the details of the experiment were withheld from you. The learner is part of the research team. He made mistakes on purpose. He never received a single shock. The story about learning and punishment was a hoax. Your reaction to an authority figure was being examined. You are relieved to learn that Mr. Wallace is fine, but how do you feel about what was done to you?

Studies like Milgram's raise many questions about ethics and human rights. The subjects were misled about the true purposes of the research.

TABLE 1 – 7

Potential risks and benefits in psychological research.

Risks	Benefits
Physical abuse and injury	Advancement of science
Stress, nervousness	Gain in self-insight
Upset brought about by unpleasant self-knowledge	Increased understanding of the scientific process
Loss of self-respect	Monetary payment (in some cases)
Dehumanization	Novel, interesting experience
Legal sanctions (if confidentiality breached)	Increased control over social problems
Mistrust of others	Altruistic satisfaction

SOURCES: Kelman, 1982; Reynolds, 1979.

They were ordered to harm another human being. Many of the subjects were upset by the procedures. Milgrim reports that 14 of the 40 original subjects were seized by fits of nervous laughter, and three subjects experienced "full-blown, uncontrollable seizures" (Milgram, 1963, p. 375). Was Milgram justified, ethically, in carrying out his research?

Moral judgments about social-psychological research are a personal matter; your reactions depend on your own moral beliefs and values. Many researchers, however, evaluate the ethics of research studies by balancing the *risks* that studies create for subjects against the *benefits* to be gained for subjects, society, and science (see Table 1-7). This **risk–benefit approach** has been adopted by the American Psychological Association in its code of ethics, which states that researchers must decide if "there is a negative effect upon the dignity and welfare of the participants that the importance of the research does not warrant" (Ad Hoc Committee, 1973, p. 11). This principle insists that a study is ethical only if its benefits outweigh its costs.

To protect subjects' rights, researchers conduct their research with care and sensitivity. Before a study is conducted, investigators try to predict its costs and benefits. If the cost attached to a study is high, as when participants are deceived about the true purpose of the research (see Focus 1-5), then the investigator must try to develop an alternative method for studying the question. Researchers must also submit their research plans to impartial reviewers before they carry out their research. Often referred to as *institutional review boards (IRBs)*, these reviewers objectively weigh risks and benefits before sanctioning any study involving human participants. (Even IRBs tend to be biased against research that examines sensitive social issues, such as racism and sexism; see Ceci, Peters, & Plotkin, 1985.)

In most studies, subjects are first given a brief but accurate description of their duties in the research and then given the choice to participate or not. This practice is known as **informed consent,** and it serves to remind subjects that they can terminate their participation in the study at any time if they choose to do so. The American Psychological Association guidelines also require that the researchers fully clarify the hypotheses once the study is over. This phase of the research process is typically known as **debriefing,** and it involves reviewing the hypotheses with participants, answering any questions, revealing any deceptions that took place, and removing any harmful effects of the experience. By adopting these and other precautions, social psychologists strive to acquire information about social behavior in ways that will be both scientifically valid and ethically acceptable.

The Value of Research

Milgram justified his research by arguing that his studies uncovered new information about human social behavior. But some critics answered,

"We already knew about obedience. After all, history is filled with people who committed unspeakable horrors simply because they were ordered to do so." Can social psychology defend itself against this criticism? Does research really tell us anything new about human behavior?

Most people are already familiar with the topics that social psychologists study. In fact, through years of interaction with other people you have probably developed your own theories to explain how and why people act the way they do in various situations. It may already have occurred to you that attitudes influence behavior, that people who fail often deny responsibility for their performance, that men like women who play hard to get, and that most people tend to obey authorities.

Unfortunately, these kinds of common-sense assumptions are limited in several ways. First, while they may contain a kernel of truth, they

---

FOCUS 1-5

Controversy in Social Psychology: *Should deception in research be banned?*

Research involving human participants raises many issues. One of the most vigorously debated problems concerns the morality of deception. A survey of 1,188 research reports published over 20 years (Gross & Fleming, 1982) indicated that over 60% of all research studies appearing in the leading social psychological journals involve at least one of the techniques shown in Table 1-8. Milgram's research, for example, required four deceptions: a false cover story, incorrect information about the shock generator, interaction with a confederate, and false feedback about the confederate's pain.

The ethical issues created by deception are not taken lightly by researchers (Kimmel, 1981; Sieber, 1982). Diana Baumrind (1964, 1971, 1985) has argued that deception should be avoided at all costs. She feels that lying and deceiving are not tolerated by people in everyday social situations, and that social psychologists have no right to put themselves above the fundamental moral injunction "Thou shalt not lie." Others point out that habitual deception of subjects will engender distrust and suspicion (Geller, 1982) and that manipulation and deception can lead to the dehumanization of research subjects (Kelman, 1982; Z. Rubin, 1985). Those who adhere to the no-deception position recommend the use of alternative methods, such as naturalistic observation. They also advocate the use of laboratory simulations of social situations. When such simulations use human participants, they are gen-

TABLE 1-8

What kinds of deception occur in research? One survey of 691 studies identified the types of deception listed below. Some studies used more than one form of deception.

Type of Deception	Percent of Studies
False purpose or cover story	81.5%
Incorrect information concerning materials (such as tasks to be completed, questions asked)	42.0
Use of confederate or actor	29.2
False information (feedback) given to participant	17.5
Participant unaware of being in a study	13.7
Two related studies presented as unrelated	9.1
False information about a confederate or other person given	5.3
Participant unaware study is in progress at time of manipulation or measurement	4.1

SOURCE: Gross & Fleming, 1982.

don't apply in all situations to all people. Attitudes influence behavior only in certain limited ways, and in some instances it is the behavior that influences the attitude (Rajecki, 1982). And some individuals—such as teachers and high achievers—take more responsibility for their failures than for their successes (Miller & Ross, 1975). Playing hard to get works only under very specific conditions (Walster et al., 1973). Milgram's studies indicate that most people are obedient, but only in certain situations. Without social-psychological research, these limiting conditions can't be accurately specified.

Second, common sense often rides off in all directions. If a social psychologist tells you that people who fall in love tend to have similar characteristics, the critic can answer, "Of course. Don't birds of a feather flock together?" But what if the researcher found that lovers are often

---

erally referred to as **role-play studies,** for subjects are asked to play the part of an individual in a certain kind of situation. In a role-play study of obedience, for example, subjects would be fully informed about the purposes of the research and the roles they will play. They would, however, be asked "to suspend reality and act spontaneously" by "creating their own roles with full awareness that they are the focus of study" (Geller, 1982, p. 49; see Hendrick, 1977; Krupat, 1977; Mixon, 1977, 1979).

Others defend deception as methodologically necessary (Aronson, Brewer, & Carlsmith, 1985). Although complete openness with participants would ease the investigator's moral dilemma, such openness would limit the internal and external validity of the research. If Milgram's subjects had been fully informed of the purpose of the research, for example, their responses would not have been spontaneous, and the findings would tell us nothing about obedience to authority in real-world settings. The defenders of deception have also criticized the use of role-play research methods, arguing that what people think they will do in a social situation may have little relation to what they actually will do. When Milgram asked individuals to estimate their own and others' obedience in the setting, he found that people predicted that less than one-tenth of 1 percent would obey to the 450-volt level. These responses miss the actual mark of 65% by a wide margin (Milgram, 1977; Miller, 1972b).

Pro-deception forces also offer data that indicate that deception produces none of the harmful consequences suggested by critics (Gerdes, 1979; Milgram, 1974; Smith & Richardson, 1983, 1985). Milgram, for example, discovered that 84% of his subjects were "glad to have been in the experiment"; 80% thought that "experiments of this sort should be carried out"; and 74% indicated that they had "learned something of personal importance" (Milgram, 1974, p. 195). Ethically, social psychologists may judge themselves more harshly than their subjects do (Baron, 1981; Wilson & Donnerstein, 1976).

Ultimately, the debate over deception boils down to a matter of personal moral views. To some people, deception is unethical because it violates fundamental moral principles. To others, deception is allowable if it is necessary to increase our understanding of human behavior. Given these differences, researchers must strive for sensitivity to moral issues rather than perfect consensus on these issues. At minimum, social psychologists must continue to debate and discuss ethical questions to their fullest. Although researchers on opposing sides of an issue may fail to find common ground, their attempts lead to greater understanding of the problems involved, and this in itself is progress (Forsyth, 1981; Forsyth & Pope, 1984).

very different from one another? Then the same critic can reply, "Of course. Don't opposites attract?" Without research, we can't tell which of these two maxims is the more accurate.

Third, common sense may lead us to accept ideas that are erroneous. For example, common sense tells us that

- People feel better if they can blame negative outcomes on factors beyond their control.
- Brainstorming is one of the best methods for making informed group decisions.
- In an emergency, the more bystanders who are present, the more likely you are to be helped.
- Love can't be measured.
- The most important determinant of behavior is one's personality.

Yet research indicates that these statements are, for the most part, inaccurate. Even the most obvious "truths" must be scientifically tested. (See, respectively, Thompson, 1981; Bouchard, Drauden, & Barsaloux, 1974; Latané & Darley, 1970; Rubin, 1973; Mischel, 1984).

Last, we rarely notice when our common-sense ideas are inaccurate because they are protected by *hindsight bias:* our tendency to react to new information by saying, "I knew it all along." After the new quarterback loses the football game, we exclaim, "Why did the coach play him? I knew he wasn't ready!" When we hear about a couple getting divorced, we think, "That's too bad, but you could see it coming a mile away." Looking back at historical events, we can't understand how people could have made such poor choices and decisions. In retrospect, it's perfectly clear that the stock market was bound to crash in 1929 and that Germany could not win World War II. (Of course, it was also once perfectly clear that humans would never visit the moon, or even travel by air.) In fact, now that you know about hindsight bias, you can say to yourself, "That's just common sense; I knew that all along."

Common sense is often useful and often accurate. It organizes our knowledge of people and helps us in our day-to-day lives (Fletcher, 1984). But we need research to test and refine our understanding of people. Through research we can identify the conditions under which common sense is accurate, identify which one of several conflicting beliefs is most accurate, and discard mistaken beliefs that have been too long protected by hindsight bias.

Answering the Challenge

In its brief history social psychology has established a reputation for meeting issues and challenges head on. When researchers realized that their findings could be distorted by evaluation apprehension and other social-psychological processes, they developed ways to deal with these problems. In some cases their methods involved deceiving subjects about the purposes of the research, but once again social psychologists openly examined their procedures and explored alternatives. Also, through research social psychologists have uncovered a wealth of information that extends our understanding of other people—information that supplements and corrects everyday, common-sense notions about the social world. Social psychology is not simply a collection of scientific facts, theories, and methods, but thousands of researchers striving to improve our understanding of one another. Speaking for all my colleagues, I warmly welcome you to our field. (For more information on the history of social psychology, see "In Depth: The History of Social Psychology" at the end of this chapter.)

Summary

The word *social* is used in many ways. Church groups hold socials. We socialize with our friends. Retirees receive social security benefits. Politicians debate socialism. We criticize social climbers. Phys ed teachers give warnings about social diseases. People suffering through hardships are aided by social workers. What links all these usages is the emphasis on people influencing other people. We do not live out our lives in isolation, behaving independently of other people; each of us is enmeshed in a vibrant, complex social world. Researchers in **social psychology** study this social world by examining the way our thoughts, feelings, and actions are influenced by other people.

Stanley Milgram's studies of obedience vividly illustrate both the contents of the field and the methods used in research. To determine how people respond to an authority, he told his subjects to give increasingly severe shocks to another person. The recipient of the shocks was Milgram's accomplice; he did not actually receive shocks, but in some conditions cried out in pain during the procedure. Milgram discovered that 65% of his subjects were maximally obedient.

What does Milgram's research tell us about the content of social psychology? First, to understand the processes that unfold *between* people in social settings, we must sometimes study processes that occur *within* individuals. These intrapersonal processes include our view of who we are (the **self**), our perceptions and understanding of the people around us (**social cognitions**), the way we identify the causes of behaviors and events (**attributions**), and our evaluation of other people, places, and things (**attitudes**). For example, Milgram's subjects may have experienced **cognitive dissonance** when they realized that they had obeyed the experimenter, even though such obedience ran counter to their beliefs. This dissonance may have prompted them to change their attitudes about themselves and the situation.

Second, to comprehend why Milgram's subjects obeyed, we must also take the interpersonal and social environment into account. Milgram's subjects did not wish to harm the confederate, but they were caught in a complex web of social relations and group processes that increased conformity while it discouraged independence. Also, their actions were influenced by the nature of the social environment. Because social behavior occurs in a wide variety of settings, social psychologists study the impact of the social environment on human behavior. Researchers recognize that no two individuals are identical. They generally assume, however, that **individual differences** among people interact with situational factors to determine social behavior. This view, which is known as **interactionism,** is often summarized in the equation $B = f(P, E)$.

Understanding social psychology's **paradigm,** or way of looking at the world, requires more than learning the content of social psychology. Social psychology is not simply a body of scientific facts and theories, but also a way of accumulating information about people. To carry out their research, investigators must generally choose between a **laboratory study** and a **field study.** They also deal with problems of measurement; they can use **behavioral measures** to assess behavior directly, **observational methods** (including **structured observation** and **participant observation**) to describe behavior, **self-report measures** to elicit subjects' own descriptions of their reactions, or **nonreactive measures** to assess behavior indirectly. They may also engage in **archival analysis.**

While many methods have been developed over the years, most researchers opt for either experimental or nonexperimental designs. In **experiments,** the investigator systematically manipulates an **independent variable,** measures a **dependent variable,** and controls other possible causal variables. In general, control is achieved by keeping all potential causes constant except the independent variable and by using **random assignment.** When experiments are properly designed to minimize threats to **internal validity** and **external validity,** they provide better indications of cause-and-effect relationships than nonexperimental designs. **Nonexperimental designs** require no manipulation of variables but instead establish the relationship between two or more measured variables. This strength of the relationship between two variables is often summarized by a **correlation coefficient,** which can vary from -1.0 to 0.0 to $+1.0$. Though these techniques possess unique strengths and weaknesses, experiments are currently the preferred research tool.

Social psychology is both a **basic science** and an **applied science.** As basic scientists, social psychologists construct and test theories that refine and correct our common-sense notions about social life. As applied scientists, they seek solutions to important practical problems. Social psychologists firmly believe that once we understand the social side of our existence, we will understand the essence of human nature.

Milgram's research also illustrates the unique problems that social psychologists, as scientists, face in studying human behavior. Because research involves social interaction among researchers and subjects, investigators must minimize the influence of any biasing social-psychological factors, such as **evaluation apprehension,** the good and negativistic pressures created by the **subject role, demand characteristics,** and **expectancy effects.** They must also take steps to make certain that participants' rights are protected. They must determine the ethicality of the research by weighing risks and benefits, and often they must use special safeguards—such as **informed consent, debriefing,** and **role-play studies**—to avoid deception and to minimize risks to participants.

■ For More Information

1. *Retrospections on Social Psychology,* edited by Leon Festinger (1980), discusses social psychology's past and future as viewed by ten of the most prominent theorists and researchers in the field.

2. *Journal of Personality and Social Psychology* publishes theoretical papers and research reports in three areas of social psychology: attitudes and social cognition, interpersonal relations and group processes, and personality and individual differences. An excellent source of information on the current findings and directions in the field.

3. *Handbook of Social Psychology,* edited by Gardner Lindzey and Elliot Aronson (1985), is a valuable sourcebook of social psychological knowledge. Volume 1 deals with theory and methods; Volume 2 examines specific topics. (Not for the dilettante.)

4. *Obedience to Authority,* by Stanley Milgram (1974), is the best single source of information about his controversial studies. A fascinating view of social behavior presented in an entertaining fashion.

5. *Applied Social Psychology,* by Stuart Oskamp (1984), describes dozens of successful applications of social psychology to practical problems.

6. *Paradigms in Transition,* by Ralph L. Rosnow (1981), reviews the practical and ethical difficulties that face social psychologists and proposes fresh solutions.

7. *Theories of Social Psychology,* by Marvin E. Shaw and Phillip R. Costanzo (1982), catalogs the various theoretical approaches developed by social psychologists.

8. *How to Think Straight about Psychology,* by Keith E. Stanovich (1986), explores the scientific side of psychology in a down-to-earth, amusing style.

9. *A Primer of Social Psychological Theories,* by Stephen G. West and Robert A. Wicklund (1980), provides an overview of the major theoretical frameworks in the field.

IN DEPTH

The History of Social Psychology

Social psychology, as it exists today, is the culmination of a long period of growth and development. If we search back to antiquity, we can find traces of social psychology in the writings of the Greek philosophers Plato and Aristotle, who posed questions concerning humanity's social and political nature. Yet as a scientific discipline, social psychology is not quite one century old, and most of its advances have occurred in the last five decades. Because the social psychology of the 1980s is built on foundations established by theorists and researchers who worked in earlier decades of this century, a brief look at social psychology's historical roots will help us to understand the current state of the field (Allport, 1985).

During the first three decades of this century, social psychologists struggled to define their discipline (Cartwright, 1979). Initially, investigators had difficulty agreeing on appropriate topics for study. The first two textbooks in the field, both titled *Social Psychology* and both published in 1908, surveyed vastly different topics. One, written by a psychologist, focused primarily on instincts (McDougall, 1908). The second, written by a sociologist, was an excursus on crowds and crazes (Ross, 1908). In the early part of this century psychology was dominated by two theories that downplayed the importance of social processes. Sigmund Freud, in his **psychoanalytic theory**, argued that most of our actions are motivated by internal and possibly unknown personality processes; this theory left little room for social determinants of behavior. **Behaviorism** stressed the role of learning through association and reinforcement, and so called into question the need for a social psychology.

Researchers were hampered by the lack of appropriate research tools. Although the first experimental study of a social-psychological process—Norman Triplett's study of the facilitating effect of an audience on children's performance of a simple task—was conducted before the turn of the century, early researchers had trouble translating their ideas into testable hypotheses (see Table 1-9). Without the research techniques discussed in Chapter 1, investigators were forced to rely primarily on description and speculation.

By the early 1930s, however, social psychology was ready to blossom. Investigators, reacting in part to Floyd Allport's influential textbook published in 1924, had narrowed their interests to focus on such topics as attitudes, motivations, and problem solving. They had also developed more precise measurement methods (Thurstone, 1928) and sophisticated experimental procedures (Murphy & Murphy, 1931). These conceptual and methodological advances set the stage for a period of rapid growth that lasted from the mid-1930s well into the 1950s. During this period, dozens of important studies destined to be classic contributions in the field were published. These studies, some of which are listed in Table 1-9, examined phenomena ranging from attitude change to the development of norms to leadership to individual behavior in groups. These remarkable studies, by providing examples of good social psychological research, served as models for a generation of social psychologists (Jones, 1985).

This phenomenal growth continued during World War II. Social psychologists assisted the war effort by examining a range of applied

TABLE 1-9

Prominent events in social psychology, 1897–1959.

Year	Event
1897	Norman Triplett publishes the first laboratory study of a social-psychological phenomenon.
1908	The first two social psychology textbooks are published; both are titled *Social Psychology*.
1924	Floyd Allport emphasizes scientific principles in his textbook *Social Psychology*.
1928	Louis L. Thurstone publishes a precedent-setting paper titled "Attitudes Can Be Measured."
1936	Muzafer Sherif demonstrates that a purely social phenomenon—a social norm—can be created in a laboratory.
1939	Kurt Lewin, Ronald Lippitt, and Ralph White study group members' reactions to leaders who adopt autocratic, democratic, and laissez-faire styles of leadership.
1939	A group of researchers at Yale University publishes data suggesting aggression is caused by frustration (Dollard et al., 1939).
1943	William Foote Whyte uses participant observation to study urban street-corner gangs.
1943	Theodore Newcomb examines the effects of social pressure on attitudes among students at Bennington College.
1953	Researchers at Yale publish the results of a programmatic study of attitude change (Hovland, Janis, & Kelley, 1953).
1954	Gordon W. Allport's timeless analysis of prejudice and stereotyping, *The Nature of Prejudice*, is published.
1954	The first modern edition of the *Handbook of Social Psychology* is published.
1957	Leon Festinger initiates two decades of research on attitude change with the publication of his book *A Theory of Cognitive Dissonance*.
1958	Fritz Heider presents a theory of "common-sense psychology" that provides the basis for all attribution theory and research.
1959	John Thibaut and Harold Kelley publish a general theory of social exchange and interpersonal relations.

topics, including civilian and troop morale, changing attitudes through persuasion and propaganda, improving organization in fighting units, and international relations. Dorwin Cartwright, in reflecting on this period, points out that this applied work completely changed the face of social psychology.

> It opened up new fields of investigation such as organizational psychology, economic behavior, and political behavior. It provided concrete examples of the practical usefulness of social psychology. Most importantly, it fundamentally altered social psychologists' view of the field and its place in society, and established social psychology, once and for all, as a legitimate field of specialization worthy of public support. [Cartwright, 1979, p. 84]

In the years since the end of the war, social psychology has continued to change and grow. As you will discover as you read this book, interest in some topics, such as attitudes, social perception, and group processes, has continued unabated, and new topics have been added. Laboratory experimentation continues to be the preferred tool of the social psychologist, but increasing numbers of researchers are also using nonexperimental techniques and conducting studies in field settings. Applied research, which established a foothold in social psychology during World War II, has become a major force within the field (Reich, 1981). Social psychologists continue to be concerned with social problems as well. The 1980s have seen the field expand its ranks to include growing numbers of women, members of various minority groups, and researchers from countries other than the United States. The field has made remarkable progress during its short history, and we can expect further advances in the future.

T W O

The Social Self

The nature of the self
  The self as known
    The contents of the self-concept
    Self-schemata
    Self-esteem
  The self as knower
    Determinants of self-awareness
    Consequences of self-awareness
  The social self
Sources of the self
  Interpersonal sources
    Accepting feedback from others
    Filtering feedback from others
    Refuting feedback from others
  Behavioral sources
  Cognitive sources
Self processes
  Self-evaluation
    Social comparison
    Self-assessment
  Self-enhancement
    Downward social comparison
    Selective forgetting
    Selective acceptance of feedback
    Compensating for shortcomings
    Self-serving attributions
    Self-handicapping
  Self-consistency
  Self-presentation
    Why self-presentation?
    Monitoring the self during social interaction
    The interpersonal self
Summary
For more information
In depth: Sex roles and the self

We live in an age that encourages self-understanding. Bookstore shelves are stacked with paperbacks promising power and riches to those who "understand the inner self." Articles in magazines and newspapers tout the benefits of self-knowledge with such titles as "Find True Happiness by Becoming the Real You," "Use Self-Analysis to Unleash Your Creative Energies," and "Be the Person You Really Are." And through the miracles of television, radio, and $5.95 cassette tapes, well-known psychologists encourage us to "actualize ourselves," "get in touch with ourselves," and "love ourselves." From all these sources the message rings out clearly: To become a complete, healthy person, you must understand your own self.

It's easy to imagine that your self is something relatively constant and independent of changing situations. Although you may sometimes not be altogether sure you understand who you really are, you undoubtedly have a sense of your enduring qualities and faults, your interests, desires, and ambitions. Moreover, you have a sense that these characteristics don't change much from one day to the next or from one situation to another. Most of us agree with Popeye that "I yam what I yam and that's all that I yam."

Why, then, do social psychologists study the self? Because to a surprising degree *the self is a social creation*. We live out our lives surrounded by other people, and in large part our sense of who we are can be traced back to their direct and indirect influence. Far from being well-defined selves who interact with other well-defined selves, we frequently learn who we are—and alter the way we see ourselves—in the course of interacting with others. The self is not an island unto itself, but an ever-changing result of social interaction.

The self is also an active constituent in social life. No mere foil for powerful social forces, the self influences us in many respects. The way we view other people depends to some extent on the way we view ourselves. The way we act when other people accept us or reject us depends on our evaluation of our self. The impressions we try to create in others' eyes, our actions when we socialize with other people, and even the tasks we set for ourselves are all intimately affected by the self and what the self is doing. Like the director who never takes the stage, but instead guides the actors from behind the curtain, the self is an unseen party to all our social interactions. If we don't understand the self's motives and processes, we're missing a key element as we try to understand what happens when people interact with one another.

In this chapter we will travel down a social-psychological road on a journey to discover the nature of the self. The journey begins with a basic and puzzling question: What is the self? Next we ask: Where does the self come from? How do we acquire our beliefs about ourselves? Finally we'll consider some of the means the self uses to seek its goals, including knowledge, esteem, consistency, and acceptance.

■ The Nature of the Self

Although the legitimacy of the self, as a scientific construct, has been challenged, the evidence of our own senses tells us in no uncertain terms that *something* peers at the world through our eyes, guides our body's movements, and records all our experiences. Whatever this something is called, whether self, consciousness, mind, psyche, or soul, its existence is affirmed each time our introspections discover an inner, personal world (James, 1892/1961).

Why do we feel as if we possess a self? What psychological processes provide the foundation for this sense of identity? According to one view, first suggested by William James nearly a century ago, our sense of self is based on two components (James, 1892/1961). When we direct our attention inward, we encounter the contents of our self: the qualities and characteristics that we believe we possess. This aspect of the self, which James called the *me* or the *known*, is usually termed the *self-concept*. However, if the self-concept is that aspect of your self that is perceived, who is doing the perceiving? Obviously, part of you must guide your attention as you search through the contents of the self-concept. James called this aspect of the self the *I* or the *knower*, but contemporary theorists prefer the term *awareness* (or consciousness; Yates, 1985).

James felt that the me and the I combine to form the self. To understand their functions, think of your self-concept as a personal history that you have recorded over your entire lifetime, a kind of autobiography that catalogs and organizes the many facets of your identity. Each time you acquire new information that you feel defines who you are, you store this information in your self-concept. If the self-concept is a history, however, your self also requires a historian—an active information-processor who selects the data, organizes and records it, and later retrieves it when necessary. In essence, then, your self requires both the known and the knower, the perceived and the perceiver, the history and the historian (Greenwald & Pratkanis, 1984).

The Self as Known

People are constantly forming impressions of other people; such remarks as "Frank is very tall," "Alicia is dynamic," and "Mr. Teupsom is obnoxious" are so commonplace that we scarcely notice them. Yet, just as we form impressions about other people, so we form impressions about ourselves. These perceptions of our own qualities and characteristics comprise the **self-concept:** our private answer to the question "Who am I?" The self-concept does not necessarily describe our true characteristics, but it does summarize and organize our *assumptions* about our qualities. In many cases the self-concept also includes an evaluation of these qualities and attributes. This evaluative component of the self-concept is known as self-esteem (Burns, 1979; Rosenberg & Kaplan, 1982).

The contents of the self-concept.
What kind of information is stored in the self-concept? One simple way of finding out involves asking people to describe themselves in their own words. Consider these two examples:

Nine-year-old: I have dark brown hair, brown eyes, and a fair face. I am a quick worker but often lazy. I am good but often cheeky and naughty. My character is sometimes funny and sometimes serious. My behavior is sometimes silly and stupid and often good it is often funny my daddy thinks. [Livesley & Bromley, 1973, pp. 237–238]

College senior: I am a woman of average intelligence. I am a college student now, but will be graduating soon. When I finish school, I will be getting a job, and getting married. I am a psychology major, but I am pretty disgusted with the university. I am tired of being tied to my mother's apron strings. [Adapted from Kuhn, 1960, p. 42]

Even though these two individuals clearly possess very different views of themselves, their self-descriptions reveal common themes. Both discuss their *physical attributes* ("I have dark brown hair"; "I am a woman"). They also refer to relatively enduring personality *traits* and dispositions. The 9-year-old confesses she is often "lazy"; the college student describes herself as average in intelligence. *Attitudes,* interests, and motivations are also included in the self-concept; we often define ourselves by our likes and our dislikes, as the student did when she said, "I am disgusted with the university." Finally, part of our self-concept includes the *roles* we take during social interaction; the 9-year-old refers to her father, thus assigning herself to the role of daughter, while the college student refers to many roles: psychology major, daughter, wife (Bugental & Zelen, 1950; Kuhn & McPartland, 1954; McGuire & McGuire, 1981).

Notice, too, how both individuals highlight their unique qualities. Although we recognize that we are similar to other people in many ways,

If asked, how would the young man in the center of the group answer the question "Who am I?" According to the distinctiveness postulate, he would probably mention his relatively unique qualities, such as his stature.

our self-concept proclaims our individuality. The 9-year-old may have brown hair just like millions of other people, but she is also cheeky, naughty, funny, and serious: undoubtedly a rare combination in her eyes. Similarly, the college student states that she, like many others, is a psychology major, but then she makes it clear that she is a *disgruntled* psychology major. As these examples indicate, in our own eyes our unique qualities are often more prominent, or *salient*, than our more ordinary qualities. If someone stopped me in the street and asked me to describe myself, I would probably not say "I am an American" or "I am a human being," since these attributes aren't very distinctive. Instead, I would probably describe my more uncommon characteristics, such as my red hair and my interest in social psychology (see Focus 2-1).

Self-schemata. The self-concept does more than just summarize your perceptions of who you are; it also organizes this information. Like the historian who describes past events in terms of recurring themes, the self functions as a specialized memory system that integrates your self-perceptions (Greenwald, 1981; Greenwald & Pratkanis, 1984; Kihlstrom & Cantor, 1984). As one theorist explains, the self-concept is "an organization of parts, pieces, and components [that] are hierarchically organized and interrelated in complex ways" (Rosenberg, 1979, p. 73).

The basic units of this integrated network of data are generally called **self-schemata**: "cognitive generalizations about the self, derived from

THE SOCIAL SELF   51

past experience, that organize and guide the processing of self-related information contained in the individual's social experiences" (Markus, 1977, p. 64; 1980). According to Hazel Markus, a self-schema (*schema* is the singular form; *schemas* or *schemata* are the plural forms) helps us structure all the data about ourselves that we have collected through the years. If the historian who records your self were to file all his or her observations in a large file cabinet, then schemata would be the file folders. Each folder includes information pertaining to one particular aspect of the self, and data are added and deleted with each new experience. Just as a good filing system increases efficiency, self-schemata help us locate the data about ourselves that we need to make decisions or guide our behavior, while ensuring that important information is not lost. Depending on the way your internal historian stores self-information, you may have self-schemata pertaining to any number of traits and qualities, including friendliness, sensitivity, independence, honesty, conscientiousness, and anxiety (Burke, Kraut, & Dworkin, 1984; see Figure 2-1). As "In Depth: Sex Roles and the Self," at the end of this chapter, notes, your beliefs about your masculinity and femininity can also function as schemata.

Self-schemata influence our self-conceptions in many ways. Like letters thrown out by secretaries because the contents don't pertain to any of

FOCUS 2-1

Experiencing Social Psychology: *"Who are you?"*

Take five minutes and write the answer to the question "Who am I?" on a sheet of paper. Imagine that you are giving this information to a complete stranger who knows nothing about you. Be accurate.

William J. McGuire, Claire V. McGuire, and their colleagues believe that you will be selective when you describe yourself. After all, you have been collecting information about yourself for many years, so a comprehensive answer to the question "Who am I?" might take days to record. Therefore, your *spontaneous self-concept* generally includes your most salient attributes—those that stand out more than others. Did you mention your age, your race, or your hometown in your description? The McGuires find that people spontaneously mention these qualities if they are relatively distinctive. If you are a little older or younger than the other students in your classes, you are likely to mention your age in your self-description. Or if you were born in a city, state, or country other than the one where you currently reside, you are likely to mention your birthplace. The McGuires have found similar effects for hair and eye color, height, weight, gender, and race. They summarize their findings in the *distinctiveness postulate:* "a given trait is salient in a person's self-concept to the extent that this trait is distinctive for the person within her or his social groups" (McGuire & Padawer-Singer, 1976, p. 743; McGuire & McGuire, 1981, 1982).

This postulate reaffirms the social nature of the self. Your self-concept stores a vast array of information about your experiences and social relationships. However, qualities that set you apart from other people tend to be more salient than your more ordinary attributes. Thus we are all a bit like Gulliver, who felt very tall when he was in the land of the Lilliputians but very short when he was surrounded by the giants of Brobdingnag. Our answer to the question "Who am I?" changes when the qualities of the people who surround us change.

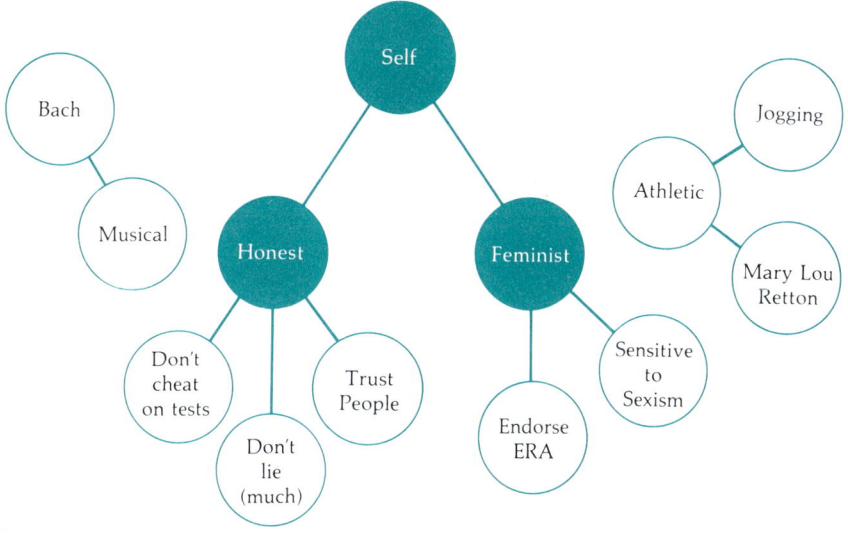

Figure 2-1   In this hypothetical self-concept, only "honest" and "feminist" are schemata; "musical" and "athletic" are not.

the folders in their file cabinets, memories that aren't relevant to our schemata can be lost (Ingram, Smith, & Brehm, 1983; Markus, 1977). Once the self starts a file pertaining to some specific aspect of the self, however, the stored memories are long-lasting (Bellezza, 1984; Rogers, Kuiper, & Kirker, 1977; Rogers, Rogers, & Kuiper, 1979). In one study of this *self-reference effect*, subjects viewed a series of 64 adjectives projected one at a time on a screen (for example, *friendly, ambitious,* and *orderly*). Subjects were asked to decide if various adjectives described either themselves, other people (either Walter Cronkite or their father), or a tree. Later, when subjects were asked to write down all the adjectives they could remember, participants who rated themselves recalled more of the adjectives (Lord, 1980).

These findings offer students some good advice. To improve your memory for unfamiliar terms or concepts, apply the new material to yourself and your own experiences. A note of caution, however: although the self often acts like a historian organizing information, this analogy shouldn't be taken too far. In some respects, the self-concept is decentralized rather than centralized. Williams James (1892/1961), for example, recognized that we have multiple selves, and these selves can be surprisingly independent of one another (Sampson, 1985). Also, our self's organization is shaped in part by the culture in which we live (Gergen, 1984). Indeed, the view of the self as a unified, integrated whole may be peculiar to Western society. Other cultures—those of Bali and Japan, for example—emphasize the unity of all people rather than each person's individuality. As a result, members of such societies don't consider themselves to be unique, autonomous people who exist separately from other people. As one Japanese psychologist writes, "the concept of a self completely independent from the environment is very foreign" to Japan, as that culture tends to view people as embedded in a social context (Azuma, 1984, p. 973). These alternative ways of viewing the self raise many fascinating questions, which social psychologists are just now beginning to examine.

Self-esteem. The historian who is writing your personal autobiography is both author and critic. The self-concept includes generalizations about your qualities and characteristics and also evaluations of these various attributes. Thus you are not just a student, but a *good* student or a *bad* student. You don't have just a face, but an *attractive* face or an *unattractive* face. You possess not merely a self, but a *positive* self or a *negative* self.

This evaluative component of the self-concept, as we have noted, is known as self-esteem. Applied to the entire self-concept, **self-esteem** refers to your general acceptance of yourself, the degree to which you feel you are a person of worth (Burns, 1979, p. 55). If you possess high self-esteem, then you respect, accept, and positively evaluate your self. If, in contrast, you have low self-esteem, then you tend to reject, derogate, and negatively evaluate your self. The questions in Table 2-1 measure general self-esteem, but researchers have also developed ways to assess specific aspects of self-esteem (Fleming & Courtney, 1984; Marsh & Parker, 1984; Marsh, Relich, & Smith, 1983; Shavelson, Hubner, & Stanton, 1976; Wells & Marwell, 1976).

Most of us occasionally experience periods of low self-esteem, when we feel inferior, discouraged, or even worthless. If these feelings persist, they can have serious consequences: anxiety, depression, drug abuse, alcoholism, ulcers, insomnia (see Brockner, 1983). A negative sense of self-esteem can also initiate a vicious cycle of poor performance at work

TABLE 2-1

Measuring self-esteem. Most researchers use self-report methods to assess self-esteem.

1. How often do you feel inferior to most of the people you know?
2. Do you ever think that you are a worthless individual?
3. How confident do you feel that someday the people you know will look up to you and respect you?
4. Do you ever feel so discouraged with yourself that you wonder whether you are a worthwhile person?
5. How often do you dislike yourself?
6. In general, how confident do you feel about your abilities?
7. How often do you have the feeling that there is nothing you can do well?

SOURCE: Fleming & Courtney, 1984, p. 412.

or in school. For students the cycle begins when a low sense of self-esteem leads them to expect to fail an examination. This expectation in turn prompts them to reduce their effort. At the same time, their level of anxiety increases. This combination of low effort and high test anxiety culminates in failure, which the students with low self-esteem then blame on their own lack of ability. The self-perpetuating cycle shown in Figure 2-2 comes full circle (Brockner, 1983; Felson, 1984; see Maruyama, Rubin, & Kingsberry, 1981).

Researchers are currently exploring many alternative ways of breaking the links between low self-esteem and poor performance. One of the most promising of these approaches is based on Albert Bandura's *self-efficacy theory* (Bandura, 1982). According to Bandura, **self-efficacy** is the belief that you can personally produce and regulate your outcomes. Rather than try to bolster individuals' overall feelings of self-esteem, Bandura and his colleagues focus on feelings of self-efficacy in regard to specific tasks. One study manipulated children's feelings of self-efficacy in regard to a math test; some children were given specific attainable goals to work for but others were not. When they were tested later, the children who were working toward attainable goals had higher feelings of self-efficacy, solved more problems on the test, and also were more interested in the test. The vicious cycle was short-circuited (Bandura & Schunk, 1981).

Our feelings of self-efficacy influence many aspects of our social lives, including the careers we pick, the goals we seek in our personal lives, and even our tolerance of pain (Bandura, 1982; Betz & Hackett, 1981; Manning & Wright, 1983; Post-Kammer & Smith, 1985). The very fact that we do evaluate ourselves implies the existence of a second component of

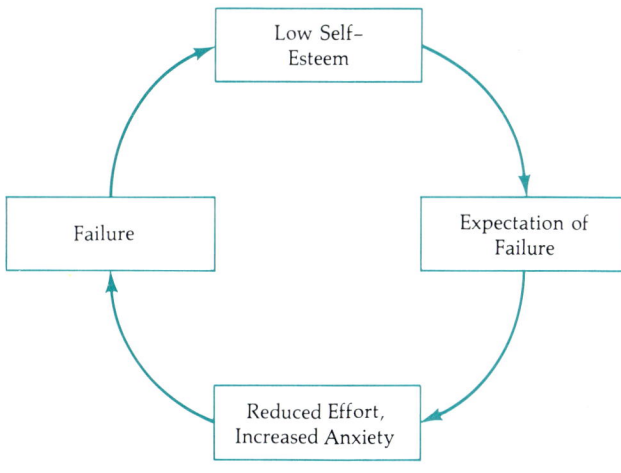

Figure 2-2 The self-perpetuating links between low self-esteem and poor performance.

Self-efficacy is the belief that you can achieve your personal goals, no matter how great the odds against you.

the self that records all the information needed to estimate our chances of success in a given situation. As William James explained, "there must be a knower" to make sense of "all this known" (1892/1961, p. 82).

The Self as Knower

Like a historian reviewing the history she or he is compiling, you can review and examine your inner experiences. If you were to stop reading for a moment, you could describe your feelings, memories, thoughts, and passing fantasies. You could say if you feel tired, hungry, angry, relaxed, or happy. You could also review the contents of your thoughts—your motives, attitudes, plans, ideas, or daydreams—and direct your thinking to concentrate on one of those topics while ignoring all the others. You could even ask yourself questions such as "Who am I?"; "What are my goals in life?"; "What does this paragraph mean?" and consider alternative answers.

When you turn your attention inward to concentrate on the contents of the self, you are in a state known as **self-awareness** (Carver & Scheier, 1981; Duval & Wicklund, 1972). Without self-awareness you could never gain access to your self-concept; you would never, in a sense, know who you were. And you would have difficulty regulating your behavior, for you wouldn't know what your personal standards were or what goals you wanted to seek. Yet despite the importance of self-awareness, you are not always in touch with your self. The world around you vies for your attention, and sometimes wins.

Determinants of self-awareness. Human beings are one of the few species capable of self-awareness (see Focus 2-2), but we don't always use this talent. When we are immersed in a flood of sensory information, our awareness must be selective. At any particular time, we must choose to pay attention to either the self or the external, physical world. Just as

FOCUS 2-2

A Closer Look: *Are human beings the only creatures capable of self-awareness?*

Unlike most animals, humans understand mirrors. When we look at our reflection, we realize that the image is our own. Most other animals, in contrast, react as though the image were another member of their species. Because nonhuman animals can't even be trained to use mirrors for self-examination, many theorists believe they lack a sense of self; they can't recognize their own image because they have no awareness of themselves as an object (Gallup, 1977; Meddin, 1979).

The belief that a sense of self is a uniquely human quality has been challenged, however, by Gordon G. Gallup, Jr. and his colleagues at the State University of New York at Albany. These researchers have discovered that chimpanzees are capable of self-recognition when they are exposed to a mirror. To test for self-recognition, the chimps were placed in a room with a large mirror. At first they acted as if they were seeing another chimpanzee. They greeted the image by bobbing up and down and vocalizing. Over the course of several days, however, the chimps seemed to realize that they were seeing their own image in the mirror. As Figure 2-3 indicates, over a ten-day period the number of social responses dwindled and self-directed responses increased dramatically. The chimps stopped greeting the image and actually began to use the mirror to gain information about parts of their bodies that they couldn't directly observe; they would stare into the mirror, picking bits of food from between their teeth, blowing bubbles, and making faces for their own amusement.

To test for self-recognition more clearly, Gallup went one step further. After anesthetizing the chimps, he painted one eyebrow and one ear with

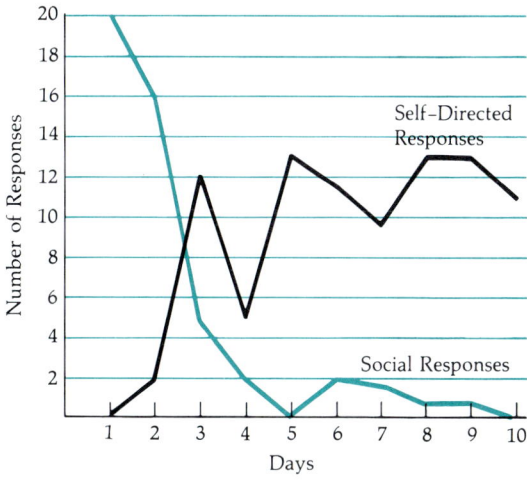

Figure 2-3 Self-recognition in chimpanzees. When Gallup tallied the number of social responses (greeting the mirror image as if it were another chimp) and self-directed responses (using the mirror for self-examination) over ten days, he discovered that social responses decreased steadily while self-examination increased dramatically.

bright red, odorless, nonirritating dye. When the chimps awoke and were placed in a room with a mirror, they spontaneously engaged in self-examination. Unlike unmarked chimps, the painted chimps repeatedly touched and rubbed their dyed ears and brows.

So far, investigators have found evidence of self-awareness only in the great apes: chimpanzees, orangutans, and possibly gorillas. Gallup suggests that porpoises may also be self-aware, but he has yet to devise a way of testing them.

you cannot, in the same instant, see both the faces and the vase shown in Figure 2-4, so you cannot simultaneously focus your attention on both your self and the surrounding environment. When *self-focused*, your attention is concentrated on your inner experiences. If, however, your attention is drawn to the environment—a clock across the room, a radio playing in the distance, or the words on this page—then your awareness is *environment-focused* (Carver & Scheier, 1981; Wicklund, 1975, 1978).

In an everyday situation—sitting in class, conversing with a friend, reading a book in the library—are you likely to be self-focused or environment-focused? To make a prediction, we must take into account the nature of (*a*) the situation and (*b*) your personality.

People tend to become self-focused when they are exposed to environmental stimuli that remind them of their selves. In the classroom you will probably become self-focused if the instructor asks you a question and all the other students turn in your direction. During conversation with a friend your self-focus should increase if your friend asks probing, personal questions. And in the library you will surely become self-focused if a photographer asks you to pose for a picture (Carver & Scheier, 1981; Duval & Wicklund, 1972).

Figure 2-4   The face-vase illusion. Your attention is limited. When you concentrate on the center area of this picture, the vase becomes the "figure" while the surrounding area fades into the background; it becomes the "ground." If you shift your attention to the outer area, the faces become the figure and the vase becomes the ground.

Dispositional factors also influence self-attention, for some people tend to be more self-focused than others; that is, independently of the presence or absence of environmental cues, some of us tend naturally to focus our attention on our self rather than on the situation (Fenigstein, Scheier, & Buss, 1975). Do you tend to

- try to figure yourself out?
- reflect about yourself a lot?
- constantly examine your motives?
- feel concerned about the way you present yourself to others?
- feel self-conscious about the way you look?
- worry about making a good impression?

If you do, your overall level of self-awareness may be higher than most people's. The dispositional tendency to be in a state of self-awareness is generally called **self-consciousness** to distinguish it from self-awareness brought about by situational factors (see Figure 2-5). To the social psychologist the term *self-conscious* literally means "conscious of the self," not a passing state of nervousness or embarrassment.

In sum, researchers believe that we tend to focus our attention on ourselves if something in the situation directs our attention inward. At the same time, any roomful of people will include some who tend to focus on the self more readily than others. Simply knowing what precipitates self-awareness, however, is not enough. We must also consider the consequences of self-awareness: what effect does self-awareness have on our social experiences?

Consequences of self-awareness. When our attention is focused on the environment, the self is like a radio with the volume turned down. Even if we can hear the music, we can't make out the words or recognize the songs. But when we are self-aware, our inner radio plays at high

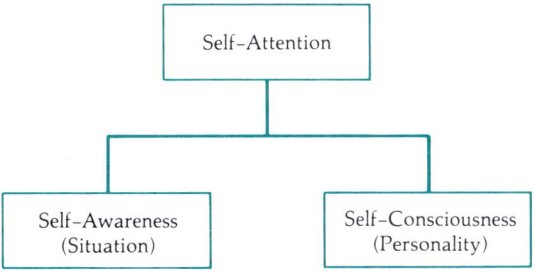

Figure 2-5 The dichotomous self. Researchers have identified several forms of self-attention. Self-attention brought about by situational factors is called self-awareness, while self-attention that stems from general personality characteristics is self-consciousness.

volume, and the self becomes the focal point of our actions, perceptions, and emotions.

If you are self-aware, your behavior tends to reflect your personal tastes and values. Frederick X. Gibbons demonstrated this tendency when he measured male college students' general opinions concerning erotic books, movies, and magazines by asking whether they agreed or disagreed with such statements as "I think laws should be passed preventing the sale of pornography" and "I enjoy reading magazines like *Playboy* and *Penthouse*." One month later he showed these same men pictures of nude women and asked them two questions about each one: "How attractive is she?" and "How exciting is she?" When subjects made their ratings while seated in front of a mirror, their general attitudes toward erotica were correlated with their ratings of the women; the more the subject liked erotica, the higher his ratings of the nudes (especially when the ratings focused on excitement). When the mirror was removed, however, subjects' attitudes concerning erotica were not significantly related to their ratings of the women. Only the self-focused subjects, who were reminded of their personal standards concerning erotica, used these standards to regulate their ratings. Self-awareness and hypocrisy are often antithetical (Gibbons, 1978; Wicklund, 1982).

Self-awareness also tends to make the contents of your thoughts and emotions more accessible to you. Did you, for example, take the SAT test? Do you remember your score? When researchers asked undergraduate men about their scores, most of them remembered doing better than they actually did. The average discrepancy between actual score and self-reported score was about 50 points! If, however, subjects sat in front of a mirror when they reported their scores, the discrepancy dropped to a mere 16 points (Pryor et al., 1977). Self-awareness also intensifies emotional experiences. Michael F. Scheier and Charles S. Carver (1977) first induced good or bad moods in their subjects by having them read elevating or depressing statements. Next, the subjects rated their emotional state while seated in front of a mirror or a blank wall. As Figure 2-6 indicates, self-awareness polarized their moods. Similar effects have been found with stronger emotions, such as sexual arousal and anger (Scheier, 1976; Scheier & Carver, 1977).

These findings raise an interesting implication: self-awareness can be an aversive experience. When we are self-aware, our actions are based on our personal convictions. But if the people around us endorse different values, then self-awareness may earn us rejection (see Focus 2-3). Moreover, when we are self-aware, we confront our weaknesses as well as our strengths. We also take more responsibility for our failures as well as for our successes (Gibbons et al., 1985). In consequence, if we feel that an exploration of our inner experiences will reveal only faults and shortcomings, we tend to avoid self-awareness (Carver, Blaney, & Scheier, 1979; Pyszczynski & Greenberg, 1985). Ignorance *is* sometimes bliss.

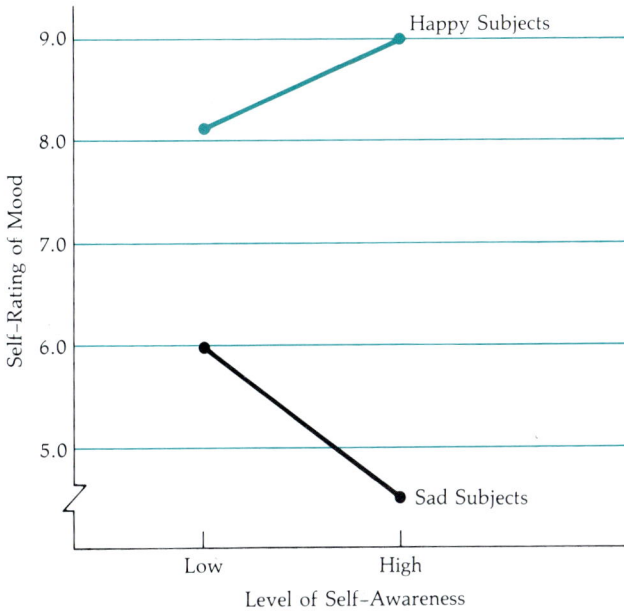

Figure 2-6 Self-awareness intensifies emotions. When seated in front of a mirror, sad subjects felt more negative, while happy subjects felt more positive. The mood ratings can range from 1 (sad) to 11 (elated).

The Social Self

We began our social-psychological journey to the self by considering how your image of who you are is intimately linked to the social world around you. Although we tend to think of our self as a very private place, the self influences and is influenced by each new social experience.

The case of a young girl kept in isolation for 13 years provides tragic but compelling evidence of the social nature of the self. Since infancy, Genie had been locked in a small room by her abusive father. During the day he tied her up in a harness, and at night she slept in a wire-mesh crib with a wooden cover. He fed her—mostly milk and baby food—but she was never clothed or toilet trained. Her father, who killed himself before he could be tried on charges of child abuse, beat her when she was noisy, but never spoke to her (Curtiss, 1977; Pines, 1981).

When Genie was rescued and hospitalized, case workers noticed that she seemed to lack a sense of self. Isolated from other humans, Genie had no opportunity to develop either a personal history or a personal biographer. She had only a fragmented knowledge of her personal qualities (self-concept) and personal worth (self-esteem). She also had diffi-

FOCUS 2-3

Controversy in Social Psychology: *Do we always act on our convictions?*

Francine is a member of a group discussing the role of women in contemporary society. Francine believes that men and women should receive equal pay for equal work and that women should be able to seek any job they desire; the other group members disagree with her. If Francine's attention is focused on herself, will she express her personal view, or will she conform to the opinions of the others?

Francine's self-awareness may generate conflicting tendencies. When Francine is self-aware, she will be more likely to use her personal feelings as standards to regulate her behavior (Carver & Scheier, 1981, 1983, 1984). However, a self-aware Francine may also worry more about the impression she makes on other people. Subjects in one investigation were told to estimate the number of dots presented on a series of slides. To manipulate self-awareness, the researcher had some subjects make their estimates while they watched a live image of themselves played on a video monitor; for others, the screen of the video monitor was blank. When subjects were given information about other people's estimates, they conformed to these estimates more when they were self-aware. Apparently the self-focused subjects looked at themselves from an external, objective vantage point, so they revised their publicly stated opinions to make a better impression (Duval, 1976; see Duval & Wicklund, 1972; Hass, 1984; Stephenson & Wicklund, 1983, 1984).

When will self-awareness encourage personal expression rather than conformity to others' views? One possible answer draws on the distinction between the public self and the private self. The *public self* includes all aspects of the self that other people can readily observe. Blue eyes, Mohawk hairstyles, Boston accents, Levi jeans, and wry remarks are all observable public qualities. The *private self*, in contrast, includes aspects of the self that are experienced subjectively. Feelings of rejection, romantic fantasies, childhood memories, and career aspirations may all be found in the private self. Table 2-2 presents examples of items that assess both private and public aspects of the self (Fenigstein, Scheier, & Buss, 1975). Some environmental stimuli, such as cameras, audiences, and recordings of your own voice, increase public self-awareness. Other stimuli, such as mirrors, create a state of private self-awareness (Buss, 1980; Carver & Scheier, 1981; Fenigstein, Scheier, & Buss, 1975).

According to Charles S. Carver and Michael F. Scheier, when our attention is focused on our public self, we strive to maintain a proper appearance and make a good impression. As a result, we are more likely to conform to others' expectations and opinions. If, in contrast, our attention is focused on our private self, then we strive to make certain our actions and public statements match our private beliefs. If Francine's discussion group is being videotaped, Francine's attention may be focused on her public self; therefore, she will be more likely to conform. If, however, the discussion is taking place in a room with mirrors on one wall, then Francine may become more aware of her private self. In this case, she will probably express her private opinions on the matter. The implications of this distinction between the public and private self are currently being explored (Carver & Scheier, 1981; Scheier, 1980).

TABLE 2-2

Some items from the private self-consciousness and public self-consciousness subscales.

Private Aspects of the Self	*Public Aspects of the Self*
1. I'm always trying to figure myself out.	1. I'm concerned about my style of doing things.
2. Generally, I'm not very aware of myself.	2. I'm concerned about the way I present myself to others.
3. I reflect about myself a lot.	3. I'm self-conscious about the way I look.
4. I'm often the subject of my fantasies.	4. One of the last things I do before I leave my house is look in the mirror.
5. I never scrutinize myself.	5. I'm usually aware of my appearance.

culty gaining access to her internal feelings and experiences: she lacked self-awareness. Without social experiences, the historian cannot collect the information needed to write this autobiography.

As Genie's case makes so tragically clear, the self is social. It is a product of our social experiences and relationships, and it influences our social perceptions and actions. The self also arises from social sources. When Genie began to interact with others, she became aware of herself as an individual. She learned to recognize and write her own name, and she recounted childhood experiences by drawing pictures or constructing simple paragraphs. She also learned to describe herself and her feelings in short, cryptic messages; once while browsing through the shops in the city, Genie turned to her companion and said, "Genie happy."

How did this amazing transformation take place? How did Genie acquire a sense of self? On the next leg of our journey we will see how the self arises from interaction with others.

■ Sources of the Self

Social psychologists view the self as part personal history and part personal historian. But where does the historian collect the information needed to write this autobiography? What are the sources of the self? As you seek an answer to this question, imagine yourself the victim of an accident. When you awaken in the hospital, you have total amnesia; you cannot remember a thing about your past life. Your loved ones show concern, your friends all visit you, your doctors release you, yet your memory doesn't return. During your recovery, what kind of information will you use to rebuild your lost self?

Social psychologists believe that you would rely heavily on social information. First, by watching the way other people respond to you in interpersonal situations, you could draw inferences about your own qualities. If they repeatedly describe you as brilliant, you might eventually come to accept this label yourself. If they seem fearful of you, you might conclude that you were a powerful person. If they treat you with contempt, you might conclude that you were worthless. Second, you could observe your own behaviors while you interact with other people. If you see yourself talking, laughing, and complimenting others, you might conclude that you were a friendly, outgoing person. But if you behave in a critical or hostile manner, you might infer something quite different about your self. You could also turn inward and search for clues to your identity in your cognitions: your emotions, thoughts, desires, and the like. If you feel happy while browsing in the library, you might infer that you were a bookworm. If you remember buying art supplies, then you might conclude that you were an artist.

These three sources of self-information—interpersonal data, behavioral data, and cognitive data—are examined next.

Interpersonal Sources

In important ways, all of us are like amnesiacs who must reconstruct who they are. After all, we aren't born with a clear and detailed sense of who we are. Rather, we learn about ourselves as we go through life, and much of the information we depend upon comes from other people.

Early theorists in both the sociological and psychological traditions stressed the interpersonal foundations of the self (Cooley, 1902; Dewey, 1922; James, 1892/1961; Mead, 1934). According to these theorists, your self-concept is tied to other people's reactions to you. In some cases, other people provide you with direct, explicit information about your personal qualities. A friend may take you aside and tell you that you need to "try to be more sensitive to others' feelings"; a coach may tell you that you are a gifted athlete; a classmate may compliment you on your physical appearance. People also indirectly provide you with self-defining information by responding to you in certain ways. You might begin to think of yourself as a good leader if others were always asking you to take charge of projects, or you might conclude you were entertaining if people always seemed interested in what you had to say. By providing you with both direct and indirect feedback about your personal qualities, people tell you who you are. As one theorist puts it, other people are a mirror that you can use to understand your self:

> . . . as we see our face, figure, and dress in the glass, and are interested in them because they are ours . . . so we perceive in another's mind some thought of our appearance, manners, aims, deeds, character, friends, and so on, and are variously affected by it. [Cooley, 1902, p. 231]

This view has been called **symbolic interactionism** because it assumes that our self-concept is created by our interpretations of the symbolic gestures—words, actions, and appearances—expressed by others during social interaction.

To the symbolic interactionist, the self is built up continually in the course of daily encounters with other people. According to this view, self-definition begins when we take another person's perspective. This process, known as **role taking,** helps us understand how other people perceive us. If a friend compliments you, she may be sincere or she may be buttering you up. If a co-worker criticizes your work, he may be in a bad mood or your work may actually need improvement. To make sense of such symbolic interactions, you must imagine how you would react if you were in their position. By taking the role of the other person you can decide if your friend likes you and if your co-worker thinks your work is flawed.

Next, the information that you gather through role taking is, in some cases, *internalized in your conception of yourself*. Not only do you realize that your complimentary friend likes you, but you also conclude that you are a likable person. If you guess that your co-worker feels your work is below par, you may end up agreeing with his appraisal. Thus you come to know and understand your self by (*a*) imagining how others see you and (*b*) incorporating (or internalizing) this feedback in your own concept of your self (see Focus 2-4).

This view underscores the social foundations of the self. Although you may intuitively believe that the core of your self is fixed and stable, symbolic interactionists believe that your self changes as others' perceptions of you change. Are you then a social chameleon who changes to match the perceptions of the people around you? Not exactly. For one thing, you internalize feedback only from certain people. Also, you don't react passively when other people provide you with feedback. Often you accept only portions of the feedback, and even take steps to correct their mistaken perceptions.

Accepting feedback from others. When we use feedback from other people to define ourselves, we generally rely more on feedback from *significant others*—people (friends, family members, loved ones, peers, leaders) who play particularly important roles in our lives (Hoelter, 1984). The powerful impact of significant others on the self was demonstrated when male college students were asked to rate themselves at the beginning of a semester and again six weeks later. A friend and an acquaintance also rated the men twice. The subjects and their friends didn't agree

---

FOCUS 2-4

Applying Social Psychology: *Is mental illness a myth?*

Symbolic interaction has been applied to a variety of phenomena, including criminality, alcoholism, drug addiction, sexual deviations, and psychological disturbances. Instead of viewing these problems as social or medical diseases that must be cured, symbolic interactionists believe that society creates deviancy by labeling people deviant: by "making the rules whose infraction constitutes deviance," and by "applying these rules to particular people" (Becker, 1963, p. 9). Once people break these rules and society tells them they are deviant, they internalize this societal feedback and actually become deviants.

Consider mental illness. Symbolic interactionists argue that some psychological problems are caused by *labeling*. The process begins when an individual engages in a behavior that society considers bizarre. Society reacts by labeling as deviant both the behavior and the individual who commits it. Because the self is a reflection of the opinions and values of others, the person internalizes the label of deviant. The consequence of the process is the production of an abnormal and stigmatized self in the labeled person. Thus the psychiatric client is

> led into a series of abasements, degradations, humiliations, and profanations of the self. He begins, in other words, some radical shifts in his moral career, a career laying out the progressive changes that occur in the beliefs that he has concerning himself and significant others. . . . In brief, standardized defacement will occur. [Goffman, 1961]

These analyses have led several researchers to suggest that labels and institutionalization should be avoided whenever possible and alternative psychotherapeutic techniques devised to help people cope with the stresses of modern living (Braginsky, Braginsky, & Ring, 1969; Szasz, 1974).

totally, but the discrepancies did become smaller over time. In fact, at the end of the six weeks, subjects' self-ratings were more similar to their friends' initial ratings than to their own. The subjects tended to change their self-ratings to coincide with their friends' ratings; the friends didn't modify their ratings over the period. These findings held only for friends, not for acquaintances, for only friends qualify as significant others (Manis, 1955).

Filtering feedback from others. Before interpersonal feedback can be internalized in your self, it is filtered through your perceptions (see Figure 2-7). Hence your perceptions of others' appraisals may not correspond to their actual appraisals (Felson, 1985). One investigator studied this filtering process by asking football players to describe their personal opinions about their athletic ability and their perceptions of their teammates' ratings of their ability. He discovered that self-appraisals and perceived appraisals were positively correlated ($r = .55$), yet self-ratings and teammates' actual judgments weren't correlated at all (Felson, 1981a). These findings have been replicated in a wide variety of settings: subjects' self-ratings tend to match only their *perceptions* of others' appraisals, not the others' *actual* ratings. Thus, while we may use others as our looking glass, our reaction depends more on the images we see than on the reflections others cast (Shrauger & Schoeneman, 1979).

Refuting feedback from others. What would you do if an acquaintance described you as *submissive* when you always considered yourself to be *dominant?* You probably wouldn't say, "Well, I guess you're right. I must be submissive." Instead, you would try to refute your friend's perceptions while verifying your own view of your self (Swann, 1984). In one study of this process, people who perceived themselves to be either dominant or submissive worked with a partner on a simple task. About

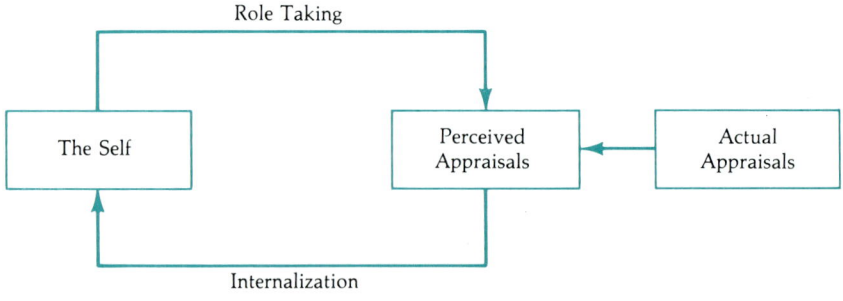

Figure 2-7 The interpersonal origins of the self. According to symbolic interactionism, our sense of self depends upon role taking and internalization. However, our perceptions of these appraisals are more important than the actual appraisals.

TABLE 2-3

Behavioral reactions to social feedback. When objective judges rated subjects on several characteristics related to dominance (commandingness, a tendency to take charge, and so on), they found that subjects who received feedback that was at variance with their self-concept rejected this feedback by exhibiting contrary behavior. The higher the score, the greater the dominance (scores could range from 15 to 75).

	Type of Feedback	
Self-Perception	Consistent with Self-Perception	Inconsistent with Self-Perception
Dominant	36.00	46.29
Submissive	37.20	30.00

SOURCE: Swann & Hill, 1982.

halfway through the session, the partner, who was actually a confederate of the researchers, gave the subject feedback. Some subjects were told that they seemed dominant: "You really seem to be the forceful, dominant type." Others were told they seemed submissive; "You really don't seem to be the forceful, dominant type" (Swann & Hill, 1982).

How did participants react to this feedback? When the feedback clashed with their self-concept, the subjects bent over backward to reassert their dominance or submissiveness (see Table 2-3). Subjects who considered themselves to be dominant but were labeled submissive by the confederate behaved more dominantly. Submissive subjects who thought they had been mistakenly labeled dominant became particularly submissive. When the feedback matched their self-concept, however, the subjects were more reserved in their behavior. As we will see later, we tend to accept feedback from others provided it fits our existing view of who we are (see Figure 2-8).

Behavioral Sources

Hamlet, one of Shakespeare's most tragic characters, has just seen the ghost of his murdered father. The ghost accuses Hamlet's uncle and charges his son to avenge his death. Yet Hamlet cannot bring himself to act.

In an angry soliloquy, Hamlet ponders the meaning of his behavior. He has done nothing to his uncle, who he considers a "remorseless, treacherous, lecherous, kindless villain." Why? What does this shameful inactivity mean? "Am I a coward?" Hamlet wonders. Can it be that "I am pigeon-liver'd and lack the gall to make oppression bitter?" he asks. He admits that his actions seem to suggest cowardice, for otherwise he would already have killed his uncle. But after raging at himself for a time,

"Is it true, Marion, that some of our friends have begun describing me as 'kindly'?"

Figure 2-8 The impact of others on the self. The individual in this cartoon is surprised to find that his friends think of him as kindly, but he may alter his view of himself as a result. Alternatively, he may begin to act very cruelly so that others will realize their mistake.

Drawing by Lorenz; © 1985 The New Yorker Magazine, Inc.

he rejects this conclusion and blames his sloth on the lack of clear evidence implicating his uncle in the crime. Therefore, he devises a plan to trick his uncle into revealing his guilt: he will show his uncle a play that reveals how the murder was committed. This clever resolution of his self-doubt leads him to the famous exclamation "The play's the thing."

Hamlet's quandary highlights a second source of information about your self: *your own behavior*. Like the amnesiac, we sometimes discover information about ourselves by observing what we do. Daryl Bem has developed this idea into a **self-perception theory**. According to Bem, people sometimes "come to 'know' their own attitudes, emotions, and other internal states partially by inferring them from observations of their own overt behavior and/or the circumstances in which this behavior occurs" (1972, p. 2). Common sense tells us that we can discover who we are by ruminating over our private thoughts and feelings. Research, however, indicates that in some cases our access to our internal states is so limited that we are no better off than external observers when it comes to self-understanding (Nisbett & Wilson, 1977; Wilson, 1985). As a result, we must scrutinize our own actions and derive self-knowledge from these behavioral data. Self-perception theory explains why Hamlet accused himself of cowardice; he examined his behavior and explained his actions by calling himself a coward.

Naturally, just as you do not always change your self-definition to match other people's perceptions of you, you don't always base your self-concept on your actions. First, as Bem notes, if factors present in the situation "are the apparent controlling variables of the behavior" (1972, p. 6), then you are unlikely to use your actions as information about yourself. If Hamlet had been unable to attack his uncle, or if other characters had interceded on his uncle's behalf and stayed his hand, then his inaction would not have implied cowardice (Bandler, Madaras, & Bem, 1968). Second, actions are diagnostic only if inner states are "weak, ambiguous, or uninterpretable" (Bem, 1972, p. 2). Hamlet rejected the conclusion that he was a coward because his inner feelings told him that he was brave and strong. He felt certain that he would seek revenge as soon as his uncle's guilt was proved (Brown, Klemp, & Leventhal, 1975; Taylor, 1975). Third, failure to perform a behavior tells us less about ourselves than actual performance of a behavior. If Hamlet had quaked and nervously stuttered whenever his uncle approached, these behaviors would have been strong evidence of cowardice. But Hamlet never showed any of these outward signs; he only failed to act. As researchers have shown, self-perceptions based on nonoccurrences of behavior (failures to act) are not so strong as self-perceptions based on occurrences of behavior (actions) (Fazio, Sherman, & Herr, 1982).

Bem's self-perception theory explains the relationship between our self-concept and our perceptions of our own actions in social settings. If situational factors are not obvious causes of an action, if our internal states are ambiguous, and if an overt action takes place, then we will use our behavior as an indication of our self-concept. Self-perception theory is also relevant to many other social-psychological phenomena, and we will return to it as we examine attributional processes (Chapter 4), attitude change (Chapter 6), and interpersonal attraction (Chapter 7).

Cognitive Sources

Bem emphasized overt behavioral data in his theory of self-perception, but he also noted that we reject behavioral data when they conflict with well-established private self-knowledge. Extending this hypothesis, theorists have recently argued that our *private cognitions*—particularly our thoughts and feelings—constitute a major source of information about the self. As we search for sources of self-information, we do not limit our observations to our overt behavior; we also turn our scrutiny inward to examine our own cognitions—our "subjective experiences that are inherently private and that are available to others only indirectly and insofar as an actor is willing and able to 'communicate' them" (Andersen, 1984, p. 294).

Your ability to base judgments of your self on either internal, cognitive information or external, behavioral data raises an interesting question: When the two sources conflict, which one is more informative? What if you vote for a Republican but think of yourself as a Democrat? What if you feel very hungry but eat like a bird when you sit down to a meal? What if you feel very strongly about saving the environment but never take part in any environmentalist activities? When you seek self-insight, do you rely more on self-knowledge or on overt actions?

In general, evidence indicates that cognitive information tends to triumph over behavioral data when these two sources suggest conflicting conclusions (Chaiken & Baldwin, 1981; Tybout & Scott, 1983). One group of researchers identified subjects who possessed a well-defined personal view of ecology-related issues and subjects who displayed an inconsistent pattern of ecology-related attitudes. Although both groups of people described themselves as pro-environment and pro-conservation, only the first group of subjects defined themselves as environmentalists. Next, the subjects were prompted to recall either pro-ecology or anti-ecology behaviors that they had performed in the past. As Figure 2-9 indicates, this behavioral information had no impact whatsoever on environmental-

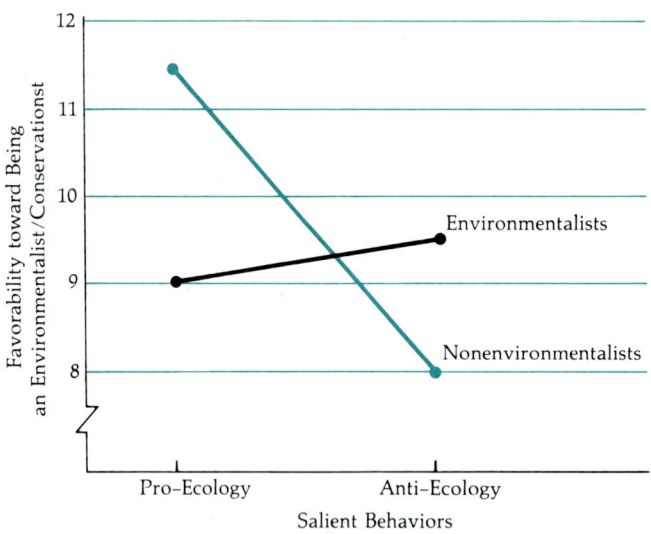

Figure 2-9 The impact of behavioral information on the self-concept. When individuals who unambiguously defined themselves as environmentalists were reminded of their pro- or anti-ecology actions, this behavioral information had no impact on their self-ratings. Individuals with ambiguous self-structures, however, were more likely to base their self-perceptions on their pro- or anti-ecology actions. Scores can range from 1 (unfavorable toward being an environmentalist) to 15 (favorable toward being an environmentalist).
SOURCE: Chaiken & Baldwin, 1981.

ists' self-descriptions. Subjects who lacked clear internal information about themselves, however, were strongly influenced by the behavioral information (Chaiken & Baldwin, 1981).

Research conducted by Susan Andersen and her colleagues also suggests that we tend to assume that cognitions speak louder than behaviors. In one investigation she asked subjects to discuss a number of personal topics, such as career plans, relationships with family and friends, and current conflicts. Before the discussion, one-third of the subjects were told to "emphasize your thoughts and feelings as you describe yourself," a second third were told to "emphasize your overt actions as you describe yourself," and the remaining control subjects were told to present a balanced picture of covert thoughts and feelings and overt behaviors. After the discussion, the subjects were asked if the statements they had made conveyed an accurate and complete impression. As Table 2-4 shows, subjects who focused on covert self-knowledge felt that their statements conveyed more valid information than the subjects who discussed their actual behaviors and those who discussed both behavior and self-knowledge. Thus, in the subjects' eyes, covert self-knowledge triumphed over overt behavioral data (Andersen & Ross, 1984; see also Andersen, 1984; Andersen & Williams, 1985).

These findings explain why most of us feel that no one knows us better than we know ourselves. The self arises from many sources—other people, our own actions, and our cognitions—and only one person has access to the entire gamut of information about you: you yourself. Is it any wonder that even our best friends or closest intimates sometimes misunderstand us? They can't draw on the same sources of information that we can (Bem, 1972).

But does the ability to tap all three sources of the self mean that our view of our self is more accurate than others' views? Not necessarily. While we may be able to draw on more sources of information than other people can, we don't always do so. As Andersen's studies suggest, we

TABLE 2-4

Speakers' ratings of the information conveyed by statements that emphasized thoughts and feelings, behaviors, or thoughts, feelings, and behaviors (scale: 0–100).

Measure	Thoughts and Feelings	Behavior	Control (Both)
Accuracy of information	65.6	51.3	58.8
Completeness of information	55.6	43.1	49.4

SOURCE: Andersen & Ross, 1984.

often overemphasize the value of cognitive data and overlook the useful information contained in our behavior. Also, we aren't always completely objective when we select and weigh information drawn from these three sources. As we will see in the concluding section of this chapter, we tend to ignore certain kinds of information—faults, criticisms, personal inconsistencies, and the like—no matter what the source.

Self Processes

Earlier sections of this chapter unveiled a self that was part history, part historian. As history, your self offers an answer to the question "Who am I?" for it summarizes your perceptions of your qualities and characteristics. As historian, the self extracts information from other people, your behavior, and your cognitions. But how complete is this history, and how accurate is the historian? When we combine information from various sources, how well do we really know ourselves?

This section shows how your self, as an all too human historian, can be pulled in different directions by four processes: *self-evaluation, self-enhancement, self-consistency,* and *self-presentation*. First, your self sometimes strives for valid, unbiased information. You may actually wish to know how you rate as a tennis player, a mathematician, or a lover, so you seek information that will permit you to assess and, if necessary, revise your **self-evaluation**. Second, in some cases you may not wish to know the truth; rather than seek veridical (accurate) information, you may prefer information that confirms your positive opinion of yourself. In such instances, the need for **self-enhancement** overcomes the need for self-evaluation as you strive to view yourself as a good tennis player, an excellent mathematician, or a great lover. Third, because the self is not a blank slate—new information is always integrated with preexisting assumptions about your qualities and characteristics—you sometimes strive to affirm these preconceptions about yourself. When **self-consistency** motivations are strong, you search for data that fit your view of yourself and ignore discrepant information. If you feel you are a bad tennis player or mathematician, then you seek information that confirms this negative preconception, or if you feel you are a great lover, then self-consistency requires you to confirm this positive self-portrait. Last, you must sometimes publicize your private, personal conception of yourself through **self-presentation**. If you want others to share your view of yourself as a semi-pro tennis player, capable mathematician, and superb lovemaker, then you control their perceptions by careful impression management. Thus the self is four historians in one: the accurate historian seeking self-evaluation, the biased historian who rewrites history to achieve self-enhancement, the self-consistent historian who strives to make the data fit initial assumptions, and the theatrical historian who wants to create a particular impression.

Self-Evaluation

*We know what we are,
but know not what we may be.*

—Shakespeare, *Hamlet*, Act IV, Scene 5

Like the history buff who spends long hours consulting all available sources of information before drawing conclusions, you sometimes strive for complete objectivity when you describe yourself. You seek only verifiable data, as if motivated by the dictum "Know thyself." In this process of self-evaluation, you make use of two principal techniques: social comparison and self-assessment.

Social comparison. Diagnostic data about yourself may be acquired in many ways, but you can gain considerable information by comparing yourself with other people. This process, known as **social comparison**, begins when you feel uncertain of some aspect of yourself: your skill on a task, the accuracy of a belief, the appropriateness of your opinions. You might reduce this uncertainty by consulting objective sources of information, but you can also evaluate yourself by drawing comparisons between yourself and others. If you have trouble working the homework problems in your math class, you may become uncertain about your understanding of the course material. So you seek out several classmates and ask them if they, too, are having problems. If they are, then you assume that your difficulties lie in either the teacher or the problems. If, however, all your classmates think the homework is easy, then you may begin to wonder about your own ability (Festinger, 1954; Schachter, 1959).

When do we use social comparison? If you already knew why you were having trouble with the homework problems—perhaps you've always been lousy at math—you wouldn't need the information provided by social comparison. In general, only individuals who are uncertain of some aspect of themselves or the situation engage in social comparison. In confirmation of this tendency, experimental studies have shown that when subjects are placed in an ambiguous situation, they strive to reduce their misgivings by comparing themselves with other subjects (Cottrell & Epley, 1977). Similar findings have been obtained in studies of competitors who evaluated their athletic ability, workers who judged the fairness of their pay rate, and even scientists who appraised the quality of their work (Suls & Miller, 1977). This last finding was obtained by an examination of the number of people scientists thanked when they published the results of their research studies. Drawing on the concept of paradigm introduced in Chapter 1, the researchers identified disciplines with well-defined paradigms (the physical sciences, such as chemistry and physics) and disciplines with less well-developed paradigms (the social sciences, including psychology and sociology). Next they suggested that since uncertainty should be low when assumptions about the discipline and its methods are well established, physical scientists should be less likely to engage in social comparison than social scientists. To test this hypothesis, the researchers studied the acknowledgment footnotes in 633 articles published in leading scientific journals. As they had anticipated, sociologists thanked an average of 2.0 individuals, psychologists thanked an average of 1.2, and researchers in the physical sciences averaged only about 0.5 (Suls & Fletcher, 1983).

Self-assessment. You need not rely completely, however, on social comparison information when you formulate self-evaluations. In some cases you can obtain concrete evidence concerning your skills and abilities by performing diagnostic tasks. This testing process is the basis of Yaacov Trope's **self-assessment** theory. According to Trope, when individuals are uncertain of their attributes, they tend to test themselves by performing tasks that they think will provide the clearest information concerning their abilities.

If you were a subject in his research, you would probably be asked to take a test of some bogus mental ability, such as "integrative orientation." Trope would explain that this ability is very important, but that conventional academic tests fail to measure it accurately. Once your curiosity concerning your own level of integrative orientation was piqued, Trope would ask you to pick the 16 items you wished to take from a bank of items, while also giving you information about the difficulty of the items

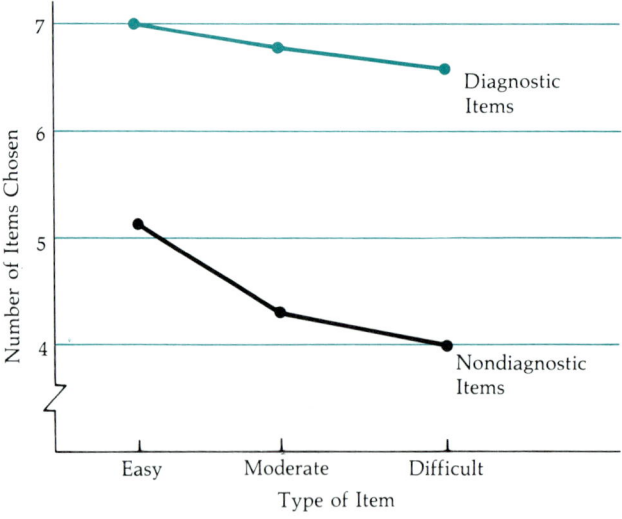

Figure 2-10 Reducing uncertainty by selecting diagnostic items. When Trope asked his subjects to select the questions they wanted to take to measure their intellectual skill, he found that they picked more diagnostic items than nondiagnostic items. The difficulty of the items had little effect on subjects' choices.
SOURCE: Trope & Brickman, 1975.

and how well they measure the bogus skill. This information would identify items that were low, moderate, or high in difficulty, as well as items that were high and low in diagnosticity. The question you would face as a subject: Should you pick easy, moderate, or hard items, and/or diagnostic items or nondiagnostic items (Trope & Brickman, 1975)?

If you responded like the college students Trope and his colleagues studied, you would prefer diagnostic items. Although you might feel anxious and nervous about taking the more difficult items, or embarrassed and unchallenged about taking the easy and moderate items, your need for information about your integrative orientation is so strong that you base your choice on diagnosticity rather than difficulty (see Figure 2-10). In this and other studies, Trope has repeatedly found that when people are uncertain about their abilities, they deliberately test themselves by performing diagnostic tasks (Trope, 1979, 1980, 1983; Trope & Ben-Yair, 1982).

Self-Enhancement

Self-love possesseth all mine eye
And all my soul and all my every part;
And for this sin there is no remedy,
It is so grounded inward in my heart.
  —Shakespeare, Sonnet 62

Through social comparison and self-assessment processes, you can achieve a relatively accurate view of your own traits and abilities. As the lines of Shakespeare's sonnet suggest, however, your need to see yourself in a positive, self-esteem-enhancing light is sometimes stronger than your need for accuracy. As Hazel Markus explains, the "notion that we will go to great lengths to protect our ego or preserve our self-esteem is an old, respected, and when all is said and done, probably one of the great psychological truths" (Markus, 1980, p. 127). Who among us hasn't used one of the six methods examined below to protect and enhance his or her self-esteem?

Downward social comparison.
Self-enhancement mechanisms operate across a range of diverse social settings, but they become particularly evident when you are working to achieve a goal that you personally value. Imagine that you receive B's on the first three tests in math class, but your grade on the fourth test is only a C. Believing that the lower grade could be due to one of two factors—either the fourth test was harder than the others or you just didn't know the material as well—you want to compare your grade with a classmate's grade. Do you seek out Leon, who made A's on the previous tests; Stan, who made B's; or Jerry, who made C's and D's?

If your goal is exclusively self-evaluation, then Stan, the other B student, is the best choice. If you found out that he also got a lower grade, then you would have support for your suspicion that the fourth test was more difficult. If, in contrast, Stan again got a B (or even worse, an A), then his score would suggest that you didn't study enough. Although **upward comparison**—comparing yourself to the higher-scoring Leon—would tell you something about the range of the scores on the test, you gain the most useful information by comparing yourself with someone who is similar to you on some related attribute (such as past test scores). This tendency to select similar others for social comparison is known as the *similarity hypothesis* (Feldman & Ruble, 1981; C. T. Miller, 1984; Zanna, Goethals, & Hill, 1975).

But what if you had studied endless hours for the test? What if you were intensely committed to earning a B in class? What if you felt that a low grade in math meant that you were a worthless person? According to several studies, if comparison with similar others may undermine your self-esteem, you will compare yourself with people who performed more poorly than you did (see Figure 2-11). This process, called **downward social comparison,** was clearly documented in a study in which subjects were told that their personality test scores indicated they possessed maladaptive, hostile attitudes toward their parents. When they were asked to choose a comparison person, 95% of these subjects picked

Figure 2-11 The mirror suggests that self-enhancement can be obtained through downward social comparison, but Ziggy's attributes are so inferior that he must compare himself with nonhuman objects.

someone who scored more negatively than they did. Furthermore, subjects' levels of anxiety decreased after they had an opportunity to examine the other person's score (Hakmiller, 1966).

Most of the available evidence supports the conclusion that we "show a notable preference for self-enhancing comparison" when our self-esteem is threatened (Wills, 1981, p. 249). Furthermore, if we can't make use of downward social comparison because we are the poorest performer, a number of negative consequences may occur. If you receive a C on a test while a friend earns a B, your self-confidence may drop and your feelings of jealousy may increase. To cope with the pain of social comparison you may reevaluate your friendship, disparage and criticize your friend, minimize the importance of the grade, or refuse to help your friend study for subsequent examinations (Salovey & Rodin, 1984, 1985; Tesser & Campbell, 1983). Without downward comparison, we would spend too much of our lives turning green with envy (see Focus 2-5).

Selective forgetting. This season my soccer team lost five of nine games, but only the coach kept careful track of the wins and losses. After the last game the players wanted to celebrate our "winning" season.

FOCUS 2 – 5

Applying Social Psychology: *Do supercopers make other people feel like failures?*

Most of us, at some point in our lives, will encounter challenging obstacles that must be overcome. Someone we love, or we ourselves, may become very ill. We may experience a natural disaster, such as a tornado or flood. We may be injured in an automobile accident or be the victims of a crime. How do we cope with these stressful life events? According to Shelley E. Taylor and her colleagues, we fight back with downward social comparison. By comparing ourselves to others who are experiencing even more severe hardships or those who can't cope with their problems, we can minimize our sense of victimization (Taylor, 1983; Taylor, Lichtman, & Wood, 1984; Taylor, Wood, & Lichtman, 1983; Wood, Taylor, & Lichtman, 1985).

Unfortunately, the media prefer to provide examples of people who are adjusting well to their life crises. These supercopers may convince us that our problems can be overcome, but at the same time our own plight seems more bleak and our coping less effective in comparison with their heroic efforts. Taylor and her associates found, for example, that breast cancer patients who were exposed to supercopers in the media generally felt they themselves weren't coping as well as other people. Because of the negative implications of such comparisons, over 60% of the women compared themselves with those who weren't coping well with their disease (Wood, Taylor, & Lichtman, 1985).

Do these findings offer any suggestions about how we can help people cope with stressful events? First, while supercopers provide encouraging information about the possibility of success, we may be better off if we are exposed to less effective copers. Although dwelling on other people's misfortunes may seem callous, downward social comparison buttresses our self-confidence and helps us cope with adversity. Second, Taylor's findings also suggest that people who are suffering from illnesses or undergoing crises should be given the chance to meet with others who are going through similar experiences. When we interact with people who are in the same boat, we not only acquire valuable information about how to cope with the crisis, but we also increase the likelihood of downward social comparisons.

Because of *selective forgetting*, virtually everyone on the team clearly remembered winning five games and losing only four.

Some negative experiences, such as accidents and funerals, are quite memorable (D. C. Rubin, 1985). Overall, however, our memories of esteem-damaging information—being stood up by a date, failing a course in college, getting fired from a job, losing an important game—tend to fade faster than our memories of positive events—a successful interview, a pleasant first date, achieving the highest average in a course. People usually recall interrupted tasks better than they recall tasks they have completed (the "Zeigarnik effect"); but if they were failing on the interrupted task and succeeded on the completed task, then their recall of the completed task is superior (Greenwald, 1980). Also, when we receive a mixture of successes and failures (as the soccer team did), we tend to overestimate the frequency of our successes while underestimating the frequency of our failures (Vreven & Nuttin, 1976).

The self is usually best served when past failures and shortcomings are forgotten. However, a fascinating exception to this tendency occurs when we want to believe that we are improving over time. When we hope we have changed, all we need to do is remember how bad off we used to be. In one study of this process, college students who wanted to improve their grades took part in a study-skills program. Although the program didn't help them a bit, participants convinced themselves that their skills had improved by exaggerating how poorly they had studied before they joined the program. These findings suggest that when we are trying to change—striving to be thinner, friendlier, sexier, better adjusted, stronger, and so on—but fall a bit short of our goals, we can always say to ourselves, "I may not be perfect now, but I was much worse before" (Conway & Ross, 1985).

Selective acceptance of feedback. The student who fails the test says, "What an ambiguous, invalid test!" The A student replies, "I thought it was an excellent, comprehensive exam." The professor who receives a poor evaluation from the students asks, "What do these kids know about good teaching?" The highly rated professor replies, "Students are excellent judges of quality in teaching." The parent of the child who gets a low score on an intelligence test argues that "IQ scores are meaningless," but the parent of the high-scoring child smiles and says, "Perhaps, but IQ scores do predict academic success" (see Figure 2-12).

These examples all stress our tendency to *derogate the validity of negative feedback while exaggerating the accuracy of positive feedback*. We simply do not believe that negative information is accurate, but wholeheartedly accept the validity of positive feedback. As testimony to the power of this bias, one team of researchers went to great lengths to destroy the credibility of positive feedback by giving subjects one of two tests that purportedly measured their personality. One group was given an impressive, valid-

Figure 2-12 People sometimes refuse to believe negative feedback about themselves.

sounding psychological instrument (the Taylor Manifest Anxiety Scale). Another was asked to complete a patently absurd instrument developed by the humorist Art Buchwald (the "North Dakota Null Hypothesis Brain Inventory"). This test was clearly invalid, for it included such items as "I am never startled by fish," "I think beavers work too hard," and "I would never shake hands with a gardener." Nevertheless, when the subjects later rated the validity of the tests, their judgments were determined by the nature of the feedback. The test that yielded positive information was viewed as more valid than the test that yielded negative information (Collins, Dmitruk, & Ranney, 1977; see Focus 2-6).

Compensating for shortcomings. Few people are successful in everything they do. While I may wish to be a great teacher, a brilliant researcher, an engaging author, and a wonderful spouse, I may fall short of success in some of these endeavors. If I do, however, I can always *compensate for my shortcomings* by reassessing the importance of each role when I formulate my self-definition. If I receive an award for my contributions as a teacher, for example, I can remind myself that good teaching is one of my primary goals. If my spouse divorces me, then I may begin to think: "My career is more important to me than my success in marriage."

We compensate for our shortcomings in many ways. We tend to deemphasize the importance of our negative attributes while emphasizing the importance of our positive ones. If individuals rate themselves on a list of personality traits and identify those that are most important to their self-definition, the important traits are also the positive traits (Lewicki, 1983). Similarly, when individuals indicate (*a*) how bad or good they are in such roles as student, son/daughter, friend, and religious person, and (*b*) the importance of each of these roles for self-definition, the two sets of ratings are correlated (the *r*s ranged from .44 to .78 in Hoelter, 1983). This compensatory tendency helps us survive difficult times, for even in dire straits we can usually find something positive to emphasize: "My business is bankrupt, my parents have disowned me, the love of my life told me I'm a bumbling clod and walked out on me . . . but at least I have my health." And after the game, the losers can console themselves by redefining the importance of winning: "It's not whether you win or lose, but how you play the game."

Self-serving attributions. As we noted in Chapter 1, an attribution is an inference about the causes of behaviors and events. We answer such questions as "Why did this event take place?" and "What caused me to fail this exam?" by formulating attributions.

Although attribution theory stresses the importance of achieving a veridical view of our self and the environment, attributions are often *self-serving:* they protect or enhance our self-esteem by emphasizing our

---

FOCUS 2 – 6

Experiencing Social Psychology: *Are we suckers for positive feedback?*

An entrepreneur once took out advertisements in several newspapers offering readings of astrological charts for a small fee. Rather than bother actually to develop individualized horoscopes, however, he simply sent all of his customers the same general description of their personality and prediction for their future. He received more than 200 letters thanking him for his perceptive, accurate analyses (C. R. Snyder, Shenkel, & Lowery, 1977).

This reaction to the bogus horoscopes stems from our tendency to accept global and ambiguous feedback about ourselves, even if the source of the information lacks credibility. This tendency is known as the *Barnum effect,* in honor of showperson P. T. Barnum; Barnum, whose circuses and theatrical extravaganzas were immensely popular, is reputed to have credited his success to the fact that "there's a sucker born every minute."

To demonstrate the Barnum effect, simply ask someone you don't know very well if you can read their palm, cast their horoscope, or study their handwriting. Next, give them the personality description shown below. Your acquaintance will probably marvel at your insight. And if you want to enhance your believability, make certain that your feedback contains only favorable information. In general, the Barnum effect becomes even stronger when the feedback is primarily positive (Snyder, Shenkel, & Lowery, 1977; compare with Johnson et al., 1985).

> You have a great need for other people to like you and admire you. You have a tendency to be critical of yourself. You have a great deal of unused capacity which you have not turned to your advantage. While you have some personality weaknesses, you are generally able to compensate for them. Your sexual adjustment has presented problems for you. Disciplined and self-controlled outside, you tend to be worrisome and insecure inside. At times you have serious doubts as to whether you have made the right decision or done the right thing. You prefer a certain amount of change and variety and become dissatisfied when hemmed in by restrictions and limitations. You pride yourself on being an independent thinker and do not accept others' statements without satisfactory proof. You have found it unwise to be too frank in revealing yourself to others. At times you are extraverted, affable, and sociable, while at other times you are introverted, wary, and reserved. Some of your aspirations tend to be pretty unrealistic. Security is one of your major goals in life. [Forer, 1949, p. 120]

responsibility for positive, desirable outcomes while minimizing our responsibility for negative, undesirable outcomes. Students who fail a test tend to emphasize the causal role played by the difficulty of the test and bad luck, while successful students point to their exceptional ability and high motivation (Heider, 1958). People who get caught cheating on a test claim they were forced to cheat by situational pressures, while students who don't cheat emphasize their personal moral scruples (Forsyth, Pope, & McMillan, 1985). Individuals whose decisions lead to unpleasant consequences claim that they had no choice in the matter, while they emphasize their freedom of choice when pleasant consequences follow (Harris & Harvey, 1975). The self-serving attributional bias will be examined in more detail in Chapter 4, but the implications of these and similar studies are resoundingly clear: our tendency to take credit for success is self-enhancing, while our tendency to avoid the blame for failure is self-protecting.

Self-handicapping. We sometimes blame our failures on external factors. But do we also occasionally set the stage for self-serving attributions by actively seeking impediments to success? Would a swimmer, worried about an upcoming meet, deliberately cut practices so he could blame a poor showing on his lack of preparation (Rhodewalt, Saltzman, & Wittmer, 1985)? Do people deliberately create stresses in their lives so they can blame their failures on these inhibitory factors (Snyder et al., 1985)? Would a student who thinks she might fail an important test take drugs before the test so she could blame her failure on the drugs (Jones & Berglas, 1978)?

All these examples have been documented by researchers. At present, it appears that people engage in **self-handicapping** by "actively seeking or creating inhibitory factors that interfere with performance" when they think failure is imminent (Arkin & Baumgardner, 1985, p. 170). In one of the earliest demonstrations of this process, college students were led to believe that they would be participating in a "clinical trial" designed to test the influence of two drugs on intellectual performance. The cover story for the study claimed that they would first take a 20-item test of analogies. They would then be given one of two drugs: either Actavil, which would probably improve their intellectual performance, or Pandocrin, which would impair it. Last, they would be given a second 20-item analogy test. In actuality, no drugs were given, for the investigators only wanted to see which one the subjects would choose. As they had anticipated, subjects who didn't think they would pass the second test usually chose the performance-inhibiting Pandocrin. This effect was particularly pronounced among men, a finding that suggests that men may be more likely to handicap themselves than women (Berglas & Jones, 1978, Study 1).

Self-Consistency

To thine own self be true.
—Shakespeare, *Hamlet,* Act II, Scene 1

We have seen that the self is pulled in different directions by somewhat different goals. Whereas the injunction "Know thyself" prompts people to seek diagnostic, veridical self-knowledge, the injunction "Love thyself" encourages self-enhancement. A third injunction can pull us in yet another direction. Just as historians sometimes reach the point where their goals shift from discovering an explanation or set of facts to confirming them, in some instances we seek information that will verify rather than dispute the self-conception we already have. We don't want to discover something new or even something good about ourselves; instead, we want to conclude that, good or bad, we "knew it all along" (Secord & Backman, 1961; Swann, 1983). We seek *self-consistency.*

Like the historian who unintentionally reinterprets "the facts" to confirm a favorite theory, we seek, process, and remember information in ways that confirm our conception of ourselves. To demonstrate our preference for feedback that fits our self-conceptions, investigators gave people who rated themselves as either assertive or nonassertive the chance to seek feedback about their personalities. The information that was offered consisted of 16 items, 8 dealing with assertiveness and 8 with unassertiveness. When subjects selected items to review, they showed a preference for feedback that would confirm their self-conception: asser-

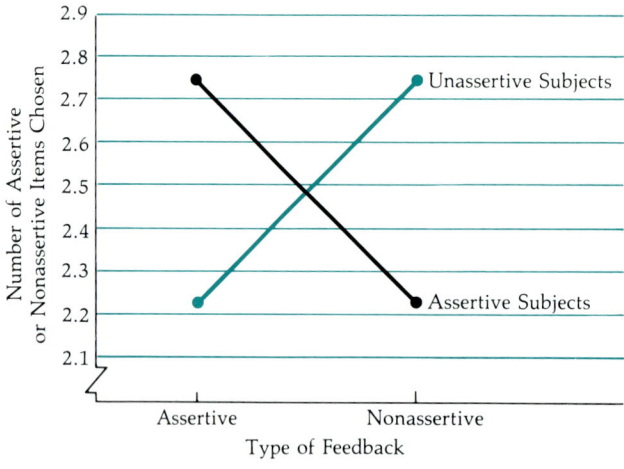

Figure 2-13 Searching for feedback that fits. The two independent variables in this study—(1) the subjects' level of assertiveness and (2) the type of feedback offered—interacted in a crossover pattern. When subjects viewed themselves as assertive, they preferred assertive feedback over unassertive feedback. The reverse tendency was found in unassertive subjects.

tive individuals chose items dealing with assertiveness, while unassertive individuals preferred items dealing with unassertiveness (see Figure 2-13). Similar findings occurred when emotionality served as the personality trait, and when subjects had to pay a small amount of money to gain access to the feedback (Swann & Read, 1981a).

Other studies, notably those conducted by William B. Swann and his colleagues, lend further support to the strength of consistency needs. Swann reports that people have better memories for information that matches their self-conceptions, spend more time studying self-consistent feedback, and "will engage in a wide array of mental gymnastics to dismiss discrepant feedback" (Swann, 1983, p. 44; Swann & Read, 1981b). In fact, Swann argues that self-consistency motives are, in general, more powerful than self-enhancement motives (see Focus 2-7).

Self-Presentation

All the world's a stage,
And all the men and women merely players.
They have their exits and their entrances;
And one man in his time plays many parts.
—Shakespeare, *As You Like It,* Act II, Scene 7

We have seen that people tend to seek veridical information about themselves, but that sometimes they are more receptive to feedback that is positive and consistent with their preconceptions about themselves. Now one last task remains for your personal historian: this stock of private, personal knowledge about the self must be communicated to other people. While we are intimately familiar with our own qualities and characteristics, other people can only catch brief glimpses of our "true" selves. Therefore, in social settings we frequently engage in **self-presentation**: the display of social behaviors that establish, maintain, or refine the impression that others have of us (Goffman, 1959; Schlenker, 1980; Tedeschi, 1981).

The concept of self-presentation (also known as **impression management**) can be traced to many sources, but the works of the social anthropologist Erving Goffman have been particularly influential. According to Goffman, social life is like a series of theatrical performances. Interactants play particular roles, they must strive to maintain their social identities through competent self-presentations, and they are expected to help other interactants to maintain theirs. However, just as we form impressions about others' qualities and characteristics by watching their performances, we realize that our own audience is formulating inferences about us. Therefore, we maintain a particular social identity (or "face") by revealing aspects of the self by means of self-descriptions, body postures, styles of dress, statements of opinions, and the like (Goffman, 1959, 1971).

Goffman's premise was simple—in social situations we actively present our self to others—but the processes he uncovered raise many complex questions. Here we will consider three: Are people always accurate in their self-presentations? Are some of us more adept at self-presentation than others? And how do self-presentations influence our interpersonal relations?

Why self-presentation? Most of us would agree that the politician making a speech and the actor on a talk show are busy trying to project a certain image to the audience; Goffman argued that there is a bit of theater in all social situations. The man who wants everyone to know that he is waiting for a bus rather than just loafing scans the road in anticipation. The woman on her way to lunch who remembers that she left a letter behind on her desk pauses, snaps her fingers, and only then retraces her steps. A student projects an intellectual air by using elegant

---

FOCUS 2-7

Controversy in Social Psychology: *When self-enhancement conflicts with self-consistency, which motive wins?*

All your life you have felt incompetent when dealing with math and numerical computations. In college, however, you perform very well on a math placement test. Will you reject this feedback, as self-consistency theory predicts, or accept the information, as self-enhancement theory predicts?

Some theorists believe that the data support self-consistency theory (Swann & Hill, 1982). They note that in many situations people accept negative, threatening feedback if they have been led to expect negative information. Furthermore, when positive information is unexpected, people are often critical of its validity and accuracy (Deutsch & Solomon, 1959; Feather & Simon, 1971). These theorists also note that many of the self-enhancing mechanisms reviewed earlier (such as downward social comparison, selective memory, and self-serving attributions) are manifested only when people have high self-esteem and show no signs of depression (Pyszczynski & Greenberg, 1985; Tabachnik, Crocker, & Alloy, 1983).

Other theorists, however, favor self-enhancement theory (Jones, 1973). They note that in many instances people show a marked preference for feedback that exceeds their expectations; even individuals who expect to fail and those with low self-esteem are more satisfied after success than after failure. Similarly, no matter how we feel about ourselves, when other people treat us in positive, accepting ways, we tend to like them, while we reject people who treat us in a negative manner (Regan, 1976).

As is so often the case with scientific controversies, greater progress may be achieved if we seek to integrate these two viewpoints. One such attempt at integration has been made by J. Sidney Shrauger. He concluded, after a thorough review of dozens of studies of reactions to feedback, that evaluations that were "consistent with one's initial expectancies were more accurately retained, given more credence, and assumed to result more from one's own abilities than were those which were inconsistent." These predictions of self-consistency held true only at the *cognitive level*, however. When the studies focused on *emotional reactions to the feedback*—"How much was the evaluator liked?" or "Did you enjoy work on the task?"—self-enhancement theory was supported. People clearly disliked the negative feedback and the people who gave it to them, especially if they had negative expectations. Thus, while information that is expected may be viewed as more valid, self-enhancing information is more satisfying (Shrauger, 1975, p. 581).

Through their actions and their public remarks, politicians seek to convince their constituents that they possess the qualities and characteristics prerequisite for effective leadership. In fact, to most Americans, the term *politician* "evokes images of the electioneering role in which every act appears to be carefully calculated" to create a favorable public image (Tetlock, 1985, p. 210).

phrasing when he asks the professor a question. Even in these simple situations, people use impression management to influence others' perceptions.

But why publicize the self? What are the reasons behind all this self-presentational behavior? In some cases, we employ **strategic self-presentation:** we deliberately strive to shape and control others' perceptions of us (Baumeister, 1982; Jones & Pittman, 1982; see Table 2-5). Consider the self-presentations of a man running for reelection to the U.S. Senate (Tetlock, 1981, 1985). While campaigning, he may deliberately use *ingratiation tactics*, such as promises and compliments, to increase his attractiveness (E. E. Jones, 1964; see Chapter 7). The promise "I will cut taxes if I am elected" is often offered to voters, and so is the compliment "You can be proud to be residents of this fine state." The senator may also engage in *self-promotion* by emphasizing his positive qualities in his self-descriptions. He may exaggerate his accomplishments in the Senate and avoid any mention of his shortcomings ("As a result of my efforts, our state received substantially more federal funds than other states"). He may also emphasize his link to other politically successful figures. He may claim that he meets frequently with the president ("Just the other day, during a frank conversation with the president, I . . .") or even arrange for the president to endorse him as a candidate. This tactic is known as *basking in reflected glory* (BIRGing), since the senator, by associating with other successful people, hopes that some of their glory will rub off on him (Cialdini et al., 1976). Should the senator make a mistake of some sort, he can always resort to *excuses*. This tactic reduces or completely eliminates our responsibility for such negative events as failures, blunders, and embarrassing faux pas. When asked why he accepted free transportation from a major defense contractor, the campaigning senator may explain, "I didn't know there were any rules against it." If a heckler asks him why he missed so many subcommittee meetings, he can claim, "My hectic schedule doesn't permit me to attend every meeting" (Snyder, 1984).

Even though individuals sometimes deliberately mislead their audiences through strategic self-presentations, in other cases our public image matches our private self-image quite closely. When you meet someone at a party or in a class, your primary motive may be **authentic self-presentation:** while you may want to make a good impression, you also want the other individual to get to know the "real you." Hence you try to make certain that the public image you create through your self-presentation matches your private image of yourself (Schlenker, 1980). Furthermore, if you feel that your audience is formulating the wrong impression of you, you will intensify your communicative efforts to influence their perceptions of you (Swann & Ely, 1984; Swann & Hill, 1982).

As an active participant in interpersonal settings, you must often choose between strategic and authentic self-presentations. During a job interview, a first dinner with your fiancé's parents, or a chance encounter in a bar, you may want to be "up front" and open, but you also want to establish as attractive a public image as possible. Determining which one of these two motives dominates the other has proven to be a difficult and challenging task for researchers, and some of the answers are still not known. We do know, however, that some factors tend to encourage strategic self-presentation. When the person we are interacting with is very attractive, for example, and the situation calls for a particular social identity, our self-presentations tend to become strategic. Other factors, such as the importance of the attribute to our self-concept, tend to prompt authentic self-presentations. Moreover, as we will see in the next section,

TABLE 2-5

A sampling of self-presentational tactics.

Tactic	Definition	Examples
Ingratiation	Compliments, favors, promises, expressions of agreement designed to increase perceived attractiveness	I just love your hair. Let me help you move next weekend. I like MTV, too.
Self-promotion	Emphasis on competencies and skills through self-descriptions	I got a 4.0 last term. I'm at the top of the tennis ladder. I drive a Corvette.
Basking in reflected glory	Association with people who are admired or successful	My college's team finished number 1. I'm related to Abe Lincoln.
Excuses	Statements that reduce or eliminate responsibility for a negative outcome	I didn't do it. My dog ate it. I lost track of the time.

some of us have a greater tendency than others to present ourselves strategically (Schlenker, 1985; Tedeschi & Riess, 1981).

Monitoring the self during social interaction. Goffman argued that we are all actors in the drama of social life, but some of us are more adept in our performances than others. Poised and tactful, such people always seem to be ready with just the right action or word to set any social situation flowing smoothly. Others, in contrast, seem to disregard the constraints of the situation, and generally do and say whatever is on their minds.

Mark Snyder believes that these variations are caused by individual differences in **self-monitoring:** the degree to which people monitor and regulate their behavior to fit the situation. Some people are high in self-monitoring; they generally "regard themselves as rather flexible and adaptive creatures, who shrewdly and pragmatically tailor their social behavior to fit situational and interpersonal specifications of appropriateness." Low self-monitors, in contrast, "regard themselves as rather principled beings who value congruence between their actions in social situations and relevant underlying attitudes, feelings, and dispositions" (Snyder & Campbell, 1982, pp. 186–187). To measure this difference between people, Snyder developed a 25-item self-monitoring scale. Some representative items are shown in Table 2-6.

These personality differences lead to important differences in the interpersonal realm. Like dedicated actors who spend long hours rehears-

TABLE 2-6

Some representative items from Snyder's self-monitoring scale. For all but the first item, people who agree are higher in self-monitoring.

Category	Example
Concern with social appropriateness of one's self-presentation	At parties and social gatherings, I do not attempt to do or say things that others will like.
Attention to social comparison information as cues to situationally appropriate expressive self-presentation	When I am uncertain how to act in social situations, I look to the behavior of others for cues.
The ability to control and modify one's self-presentation and expressive behavior	I can look anyone in the eye and tell a lie (if for a right end).
The use of self-presentational tactics in particular situations	I may deceive people by being friendly when I really dislike them.
The extent to which one's expressive behavior and self-presentations are tailored and molded to fit particular social situations	In different situations and with different people, I often act like very different persons.

SOURCE: Snyder, 1974, 1979.

ing their lines and making certain they have their parts down just right, high self-monitors have a great deal invested in their self-presentations. Since they strive to make certain their self-presentations match the demands of the situation, they are quite attentive to social cues. When they meet new people, for example, men and women who are high in self-monitoring are more likely than low self-monitors to notice and accurately remember information about the new acquaintances. They are also quicker to form an impression of the people they meet (Berscheid et al., 1976). They will, in fact, go out of their way to acquire information that will help them to guide and manage their self-presentations (Elliott, 1979). And as they think of themselves as flexible, they willingly change their social identities to match the demands of the social situation. If the situation calls for conformity, they tend to be conforming; if it calls for autonomy, they become resolute nonconformists (Snyder & Monson, 1975).

Low self-monitors, in contrast, are more like character actors who tend always to be cast in the same basic role, no matter what the movie or play. They rarely change their self-presentations to fit a situation. Because they act on the basis of their own dispositional qualities—their feelings, attitudes, and self-perceptions—they have little need to pay attention to social cues as guides to action. As a result, their self-concepts appear to be more schematic and accessible. Remember, high self-monitors are scrutinizing the fit between the self and the situation, not just the self. Therefore, it's not surprising that low self-monitors tend to be more aware than high self-monitors of the nature of their self-concept (Snyder & Ickes, 1985).

The interpersonal self. High and low self-monitors view social interaction differently, but is one view better than the other? Is self-presentation a negative form of social behavior that should be avoided?

Most social psychologists believe that self-presentation is neither good nor bad. Although self-presentations can be used to deceive others, they are essential to social interaction. Without self-presentation, you would have difficulty forming impressions of the people around you. You could never establish a public identity for yourself. Nor could you smooth out the little wrinkles that sometimes disrupt the flow of social behavior. By saying "Excuse me" when you step on a stranger's toe, you aren't manufacturing an excuse to get yourself off the hook, only culling a lump from the smooth flow of social interaction. As Goffman explains, self-presentation greases the wheels of social interaction.

Our self-presentations are integrally linked to the other self-processes discussed earlier. First, just as we strive for accuracy when we gather information about our own characteristics through social comparison and self-assessment, we also strive for accuracy when we engage in authentic self-presentation. Second, in many cases strategic self-presentations enhance both our public image and our private self-conception. Self-handicapping, for example, is probably motivated by a desire to project a favorable public image as well as to protect current levels of self-esteem (Arkin & Baumgardner, 1985). When we succeed in creating a certain impression publicly, this impression can be incorporated in our self-concept. The person who describes herself favorably to win others' approval may subsequently experience an increase in self-esteem, just as the person who describes himself in critical terms may experience a loss of self-esteem (Jones et al., 1981; Rhodewalt & Agustsdottir, 1986).

Third, our self-presentations sometimes reflect our need for self-consistency. In one study female college students who were personally committed to a particular career (such as journalism, mathematics, or business) were given bogus feedback indicating that they either possessed or lacked the skills needed to succeed in their areas. How did the women who received information that disconfirmed their self-conceptions react? In their subsequent self-presentations they "corrected" their public image by stressing their abilities and skills. In a follow-up study (this time involving men), the subjects again used their self-presentations to increase their self-consistency, even when inconsistency—the presentation of public images that were inconsistent with their private self-conceptions—would have earned them greater social rewards (Gollwitzer & Wicklund, 1985). Thus, although self-presentational needs can come into conflict with other motives, in many cases self-presentation offers the means of achieving self-evaluation, self-enhancement, and self-consistency (see Tetlock & Manstead, 1985).

■ Summary

Because the self is both a product of and an active participant in social life, social psychologists are currently studying the nature, sources, and processes that influence and are influenced by the self. As William James initially suggested, the self can be viewed as a two-part system. One portion, the **self-concept,** summarizes individuals' perceptions of their personal qualities and characteristics. The self-concept includes **self-schemata**—cognitive generalizations that guide perceptual and cognitive processes—and appraisals of the self's qualities. This evaluative component is known as **self-esteem.** A specific form of self-esteem, **self-efficacy**, concerns individuals' beliefs that they can produce and regulate outcomes. Individuals who are high in self-efficacy are more likely to persist at difficult tasks than are individuals who are low in self-efficacy.

The ability to formulate a self-concept suggests the existence of a second component of the self: awareness or consciousness. Humans' awareness can be focused on either the self or the environment. Environmental stimuli that remind individuals of the self—cameras, audiences, mirrors, and the like—increase **self-awareness,** although some individuals who are high on the personality trait known as **self-consciousness** tend to be more self-focused than others. When we are self-aware, the self plays a larger role in guiding our thoughts, feelings, and actions. If our attention is focused on the public self, we become more concerned with others' impressions of us. Increased awareness of the private self, in contrast, promotes the expression of personal tastes and preferences.

The self-concept appears to be based on information gathered from a variety of interpersonal, behavioral, and cognitive sources. Advocates of **symbolic interactionism** believe that individuals develop an understanding of themselves by imagining how others see them **(role taking)** and then internalizing these perceived appraisals in their self-concept. Significant others, such as family members, friends, and valued peers, are a particularly important source of feedback, but individuals' perceptions of such persons' appraisals have a greater impact on the self than their actual appraisals. Also, people tend to reject feedback that doesn't fit their existing view of the self.

According to Bem's **self-perception theory,** individuals also acquire information about the self by observing their own overt behavior in social situations. Provided actions aren't obviously prompted by the situation and internal states are ambiguous, people assume that their actions are caused by their beliefs, emotions, and other internal states. Evidence indicates, however, that in some cases individuals rely on their private cognitions—particularly their thoughts and feelings—to acquire information about the self.

The self, as an active constituent of social life, seeks a variety of goals, including knowledge (self-evaluation), esteem (self-enhancement), consistency (self-consistency), and acceptance by other people (self-presentation). In the quest for **self-evaluation,** individuals engage in **social comparison** and **self-assessment:** they compare themselves with other people and actively test themselves by performing actions that will yield diagnostic information. **Self-enhancement** involves a different set of processes. To protect or increase feelings of self-worth, individuals often compare themselves with inferiors **(downward social comparison)** rather than superiors **(upward comparison)**, forget their failures, reject negative feedback, compensate for their shortcomings by emphasizing their positive attributes, take credit for success and refuse the blame for failure (self-serving attributions), and seek out impediments that can serve as excuses for future failures **(self-handicapping).** Because **self-consistency** is often as important a motive as self-enhancement, however, individuals will accept negative, threatening information about themselves provided it is consistent with their existing self-conception.

To achieve a fourth goal, **self-presentation,** individuals convey information about the self to others by means of self-descriptions, body postures, styles of dress, and the like. (This process is also known as **impression management.**) **Strategic self-presentations** are attempts to create a public image that others will approve of; **authentic self-presentations** are more accurate. Snyder developed the concept of **self-monitor-**

ing to describe individual differences in self-presentation. People who are high in self-monitoring—the tendency to regulate one's behavior so that it fits a particular interpersonal setting—engage in more strategic self-presentations than low self-monitors. Self-presentation is integrally linked to other motives as well; by presenting themselves to others, individuals can sometimes acquire information about the self, protect their self-esteem, and maintain consistency between their public identity and private self-concepts.

■ For More Information

1. *Attention and Self-Regulation: A Control-Theory Approach to Human Behavior,* by Charles S. Carver and Michael F. Scheier (1981), presents two social psychologists' view of how the self regulates our thoughts and actions.

2. "The Self," by Anthony G. Greenwald and Anthony R. Pratkanis, presents an up-to-date look at the self as a powerful processor of information. This selection is a chapter in Volume 3 of *Handbook of Social Cognition* (Wyer & Srull, 1984).

3. *Encounters with the Self,* by Don E. Hamachek (1978), uses some of the concepts examined in this chapter to explore the link between the self and personal adjustment. An excellent choice for people who want more information on self-improvement.

4. *Psychological Perspectives on the Self,* a three-volume work, includes relatively high-level theoretical papers and literature reviews dealing with many of the topics examined in this chapter. Volume 1 was edited by Jerry Suls (1982), who was joined by Anthony G. Greenwald for Volumes 2 and 3 (1983, 1986).

5. "The Decentralization of Identity," an article by Edward E. Sampson in *American Psychologist* (1985), argues that the self is relatively disorganized, more like a text accumulated haphazardly than like a history written by a single historian. An interesting contrast to the view most social psychologists accept.

6. *Impression Management: The Self-Concept, Social Identity, and Interpersonal Relations,* by Barry R. Schlenker (1980), comprehensively reviews self-presentational processes. Filled with colorful examples and applications to everyday life.

7. *Excuses: Masquerades in Search of Grace,* by C. R. Snyder, R. L. Higgins, and R. J. Stucky (1983), examines how people use excuses to maintain their self-esteem and keep their public images in good shape.

IN DEPTH

Sex Roles and the Self

Most people, when asked to describe themselves, are quick to mention their sex. Indeed, this attribute may be the most fundamental component of the self-concept—an almost inevitable outgrowth of developmental processes that occur in virtually all cultures (Ullian, 1981). As a result, sex is an important social characteristic that is used to define both the self and other people.

The beliefs and expectations about yourself that are based on your biological gender are collectively termed your **sex role.** Traditionally, psychologists and laypersons alike assumed that people generally adopt one of two sex roles: *masculine* or *feminine*. If you adopted a masculine sex role, your self-concept would include such traits as dominance, analyticalness, self-confidence, and forcefulness. If you adopted a feminine sex role, you would be expected to have a yielding, gullible, affectionate, and nurturant self-concept. In fact, femininity and masculinity were viewed as end points of a single continuum of sex roles. Just as temperatures range from hot to cold and sizes are graduated from small to large, people were thought to range from feminine to masculine. And society expected men to be masculine and women to be feminine.

In the mid-1970s, however, a number of researchers, working independently, began to question this assumption (Bem, 1974; Constantinople, 1973; Spence, Helmreich, & Stapp, 1974, 1975). Sandra Bem suggested that masculinity and femininity are separate traits, and that individuals vary in the degrees to which they exhibit feminine and masculine characteristics. Bem also argued that men aren't necessarily masculine and women aren't necessarily feminine. Depending on a host of developmental factors, both men and women can incorporate various degrees of masculinity and femininity in their self-definitions (Bem, 1974, 1979, 1981, 1985).

Bem's conjectures regarding sex roles lead to one particularly startling conclusion. If masculinity and femininity are two separate dimensions that are not strictly dependent on biological gender, then some individuals may be *both* masculine and feminine, while others may not include either dimension in the self-concept. In fact, if for ease of communication we assume that people are either high or low in both masculinity and femininity, then Bem's theory identifies the four types of sex roles shown in Table 2-7: androgynous, masculine, feminine, and undifferentiated.

Bem believes that the sex role you adopt has a telling impact on your self-concept and your

TABLE 2-7

Bem's theory of sex roles. According to Bem, androgynous individuals display both masculine and feminine attributes and characteristics. Sex-typed individuals, in contrast, adopt either the traditional masculine sex role (characterized by ambition, independence, assertiveness, and so on) or the traditional feminine sex role (described as warm, tender, gentle, and so on). Last, some individuals don't describe themselves in either masculine or feminine terms. These individuals are undifferentiated.

Level of Masculinity	Level of Femininity	
	High	Low
High	Androgynous	Masculine
Low	Feminine	Undifferentiated

perceptions of other people. Sex roles may, in fact, function as schemata by organizing the self-concept and regulating the processing of information related to the self. Supporting this view, Hazel Markus and her colleagues have found that people who adopt different sex roles vary considerably in the nature of their self-knowledge. Subjects who adopted a feminine sex role described themselves in more feminine terms, remembered more of their feminine than masculine attributes, and spent less time locating these feminine-oriented memories. Masculine subjects evidenced just the opposite tendency, while androgynous individuals did not favor masculine or feminine attributes in their self-descriptions. Undifferentiated individuals lacked confidence in their self-descriptions. Markus believes that

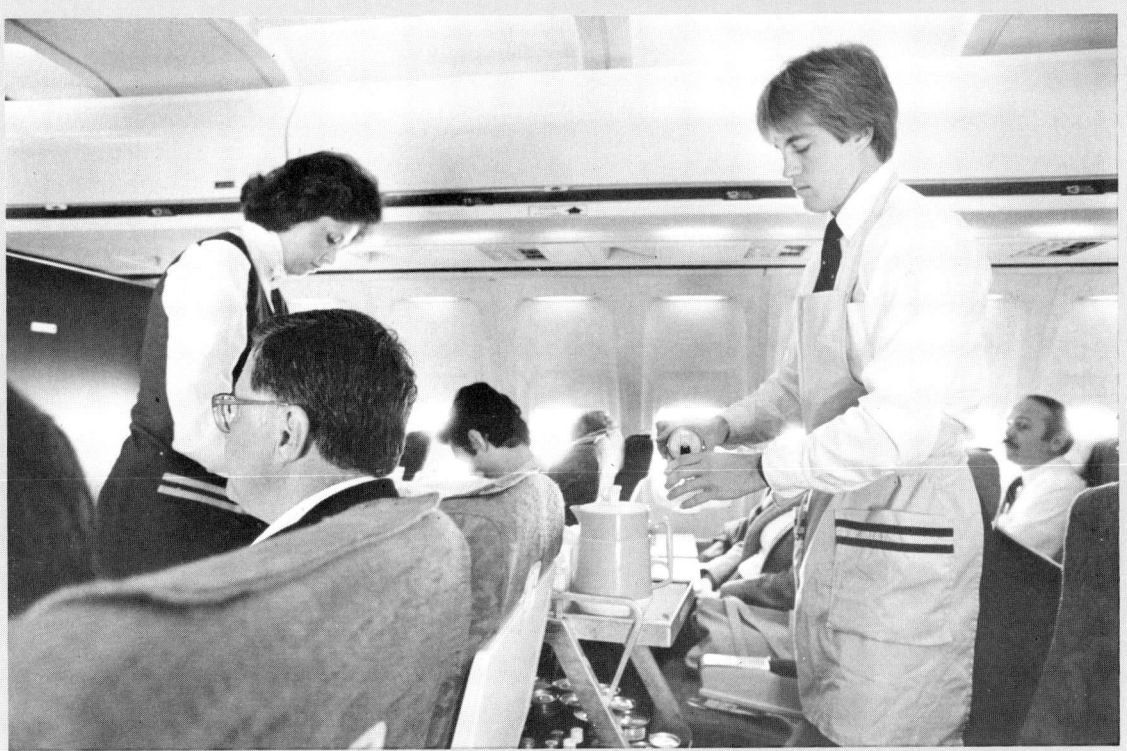

An adrogynous person, whether a man or a woman, possesses skills and abilities that cut across both the traditional masculine sex role and the traditional feminine sex role. An adrogynous man, for example, would be capable of performing a wider variety of tasks than a sex-typed man.

(continued)

IN DEPTH *continued*

undifferentiated individuals may be *aschematic:* their self-concepts include neither masculine nor feminine schemata. At present, however, it is not yet known whether or not androgynous individuals possess both a masculine schema and a feminine schema, or if they, too, are relatively aschematic (Bem, 1981; Markus et al., 1982; Mills, 1983).

Sex roles also influence our perceptions of the world around us. Sex-typed people apparently divide the world up into two mutually exclusive categories, male versus female, and then place items in one of these categories (Larsen & Seidman, 1986). Handwriting becomes "manly" or "womanly" (Lippa, 1977). Some words, such as "butterfly" and "sweater" are viewed as feminine rather than masculine (Bem, 1981). Sex-typed people are also more likely to perceive and react to the people they meet in terms of their biological gender (Bem, 1985; Frable & Bem, 1985) and their physical appearance (Andersen & Bem, 1981).

Although sex roles apparently play a major role in the shaping of the self, some empirical issues concerning the measurement and meaning of androgyny remain unsettled (Myers & Gonda, 1982; Oflofsky, 1981; Spence, 1983, 1985; Tellegen & Lubinski, 1983). And it is not yet known whether or not androgyny is the "superior" sex role. Some studies have found androgynous people to be better adjusted psychologically than sex-typed individuals, to have higher levels of self-esteem, and to appear more flexible. Other studies, however, suggest that these tendencies owe more to masculinity than to femininity or a combination of the two (Taylor & Hall, 1982).

What is clear is that many differences between men and women that were once assumed to be caused by biological factors are in fact determined by social factors. Men aren't destined to be masculine, nor are women destined to be feminine. Rather, our culture creates masculine men and feminine women by convincing us that certain actions and attributes are reserved for males and others for females. The concept of androgyny rejects this view by assuming that masculinity and femininity can be combined in a single, unified self-concept. (Chapter 5 explores sex roles and sexism further.)

T H R E E

Social Perception and Cognition

Social perception
   Nonverbal communication
     Physical appearance
     Kinesic cues
     Paralanguage
     Proxemics
   Verbal communication
     Semantic content
     Expressive content
   From perception to cognition
Social cognition
   Integrating social information
     Unweighted models
     Weighted models
   Organizing social information
     The change-of-meaning hypothesis
     Implicit personality theory
   Cognitive schemata
     Schematic perception
     Schematic memory
     Limits to schematic processing
   Driven cognitive processing

Perceptual and cognitive biases
   Perceptual biases
   Confirmatory biases
     Remembering confirming data
     Seeing confirming data
     Confirmatory hypothesis testing
     Refusing to change our beliefs
     Beyond confirmatory biases
   Heuristics and biases
     Representativeness
     Availability
     Anchoring/adjustment
     Heuristics and errors
   Inferential biases
     Vividness influences interpretation
     Case data overwhelm base rates
     Irrelevant information weakens the effect of relevant information
   Mistakes in understanding
Summary
For more information
In depth: Self-fulfilling prophecies

The truly great detectives of fiction are skilled observers of their fellow human beings. Arsène Dupin, the amateur sleuth of Edgar Allan Poe's *Murders in the Rue Morgue* and *The Purloined Letter*, could anticipate others' thoughts and actions. Television's Columbo, seemingly bumbling in style, solved absurdly complicated crimes by penetrating the murderers' deceptions. And the greatest detective of all, Arthur Conan Doyle's Sherlock Holmes, divined emotions, motivations, and desires at a glance.

Although we marvel at the observational skill of these fictional detectives, their abilities are not unique or even rare. All of us possess the raw talent of a Dupin, a Columbo, or a Holmes; we are all insightful observers of other human beings. When we meet someone for the first time—a professor giving a guest lecture, a stranger standing beside us in line, a newly hired employee at work, or a potential romantic interest at a party—we effortlessly glean subtle clues from their appearance, gestures, words, and behaviors. When talking to acquaintances, we look beyond their words and actions to discover their hidden qualities and characteristics. Even with people we know well we remain ever vigilant, sensitive to new information that will help us test our hunches about their personalities and proclivities (Boice, 1983).

Our detective work is no mere hobby or diversion. If our ability to understand other people were suddenly stripped away, social interaction would probably grind to a halt. We would constantly misinterpret other people's remarks and actions. We might take offense when none was meant, see flirtation in another's boredom, or laugh when others despaired. Our understanding of ourselves would be impaired, for other people are an important source of information about our own characteristics and qualities, as we saw in Chapter 2. Intimate relationships would become impossible, for we could never reach the level of trust and mutual understanding needed for friendship and love. In a sense, everyone in the world would be the same to us. We would be unable to tell the difference between the obnoxious and the nice, a good friend and a cheat, a Mister Rogers and a Frank Burns. Our lives would be an endless series of encounters with strangers (McArthur & Baron, 1983).

Because our quest for information about other people touches so much of our social lives, social psychologists are deeply interested in this detective process. For many years researchers have studied **social perception:** the perceptual processes we use to form impressions of others. These studies, which are reviewed in the first section of this chapter, suggest that social perception, like detective work, requires information. Just as detectives open an investigation by searching for clues, people gather information to form impressions of others. Although this search is guided by many assumptions, expectations, and biases, the perceiver's major goal at this stage of the investigation is the acquisition of information.

After collecting pieces of information that will help us understand the people who populate our social world, we organize them in our cognitions and memories. Like Sherlock Holmes putting each clue in place to solve the mystery, perceivers make sense of their data by forming general inferences about others. In parallel with similar activities among experimental psychologists, social psychologists have recently intensified their study of **social cognition:** the inferential processes underlying our understanding of other people. This emerging view assumes that people are thinking, reasoning organisms, active seekers of information rather than instinct-driven animals or robot-like machines. As we will see in the second section of this chapter, we are not just social animals, but *cognitive* social animals (Baron & Harvey, 1980).

Even the great detectives—the Dupins, Columbos, and Holmeses—made mistakes; they followed the wrong lead, misinterpreted a clue, overlooked a crucial detail. Social perceivers are not immune to error, either. As we will see in the third section of this chapter, our reliance on simplifying shortcuts sometimes creates a variety of inaccuracies, errors, and biases.

■ Social Perception

Do you remember the first day your social psychology class met? In all likelihood, many questions raced through your mind as you waited for class to begin. Will the course be hard? Is the professor a good lecturer? Is this subject boring? Will this teacher grade my work fairly? By the time the class ended that first day, you had formulated tentative answers to all these questions. How did you manage it?

The answer is obvious: by collecting information. Even the greatest detectives of fiction cannot solve crimes without any clues. When they visit the scene of the crime, they gather all manner of information—fingerprints, bloodstains, eyewitness accounts, suspects' statements—

before formulating a coherent account of the crime. Likewise, to gain an understanding of other people, the social perceiver begins by gathering perceptual evidence from many sources, including nonverbal and verbal behavior.

Nonverbal Communication

While scrutinizing your professor's physical appearance and actions, you may have noted that he fidgeted with a piece of chalk as he lectured; that she paced back and forth in front of the class; or that his hair was styled attractively. Because these qualities or actions communicate information without words, they are termed **nonverbal cues.** Although these cues may at first glance seem minor and insignificant, they are profoundly important sources of information concerning others' feelings and emotions. As Sherlock Holmes claimed, "by a momentary expression, a twitch of a muscle, or a glance of an eye," one can "fathom a man's inmost thoughts" (Doyle, 1938, p. 12). Infants communicate nonverbally long before they learn to speak, and evidence indicates that nonverbal cues "provide a qualitative 'script' without which verbal cues cannot be interpreted accurately" (Archer & Akert, 1977, p. 449). Such actions are often displayed unintentionally, so perceivers generally feel that they are more valid sources of information than verbal behavior (Heslin & Patterson, 1982).

Nonverbal information is sent from one person to another over various channels; four of the most important ones are shown in Table 3-1. (1) Any overt *physical characteristic* that we feel tells us something about the person, such as skin color, body size, hairstyle, and even odor, can influence perceptions. So can (2) movements of the body, called **kinesic cues** (*kinesic* means motion) or body language. Gestures, posture, facial expressions, gazing, and touching are usually included in this category. (3) The voice cues that accompany or *para*llel spoken language are called **paralanguage.** Paralanguage is a rich source of information, for it includes the *way* we express ourselves—the intonation of the voice, loudness, pitch, and pauses—as well as distinctive nonverbal sounds, such as laughter, hiccuping, snoring, and uh-huhs. (4) The distances that we maintain between ourselves and others are **proxemic cues** (from the Latin *proximare*, to approach).

Physical appearance.
Like Sherlock Holmes, who took note of the shape of the ears, barely visible tattoos, and calluses to formulate his dramatic revelations, you probably picked up a great variety of data by studying your instructor's physical characteristics. In general, we disregard the warning "You can't judge a book by its cover," for gender, race, age, physique, height, and other visible features all have a tremendous impact on our perceptions (McArthur, 1982).

Take beauty as an example. Although the adage "Beauty is only skin deep" reminds us that physical beauty conveys nothing about the inner person, good looks nonetheless influence our perceptions. Literally dozens of studies of jurors reacting to witnesses, subjects studying photographs, teachers grading students, and interviewers evaluating job applicants underscore the powerful impact of beauty on perceptions. Even when a sexual relationship is not at issue, physically attractive people are generally viewed more positively than less attractive people. Attractive people are seen as more confident, happy, assertive, active, candid, serious, and outspoken than people with average looks (Berscheid & Walster, 1974; Knapp, 1978). Later in the chapter, we will see beauty and other physical attributes activate *stereotypes:* cognitive generalizations about the members of a particular social group or category. In the case of beauty, our perceptions are often based on a *what is beautiful is good* stereotype. We just assume that attractive people possess a range of positive attributes (Dion, Berscheid, & Walster, 1972).

TABLE 3-1

Four nonverbal channels of communication.

Category	Definition	Examples
Physical characteristics	Observable qualities that involve no movements or motion	Body odor Skin color and tone Beauty
Kinesic cues		
Gestures	Actions that convey a specific meaning, illustrate an idea, manipulate the body or an object, or structure interaction	"Thumbs up" (fist clenched, thumb sticking up) Outlining an object's shape Fidgeting with a button Nodding the head
Postures	Positioning of the torso and limbs	Slouching Squatting Arms folded across chest
Facial expressions	Movements of the face	Furrowing the brows Smiling and frowning
Gaze	Movements and focusing of the eyes	Staring or gazing Eye contact with others
Touch	Contact with some part of the body of another person	Pat on the back Slap on the face Kiss
Paralanguage	Vocal cues accompanying spoken language	Tone of voice Mumbling, stuttering
Proxemics	Distance between people	Space between people at a party Seat selections

Your perceptions were probably also influenced by your instructor's style of dress and grooming. Studies conducted in the 1920s that identified clean hair, clean teeth, and pleasant breath as major determinants of a good first impression are still valid today (although norms of appropriate grooming aren't very well defined on many college campuses). The impact of other grooming practices, such as shoulder-length hair on men, crew-cuts on women, vivid artificial hair colors, and even the use of lipstick, perfume, and cologne, varies considerably as fashions wax and wane. In general, however, individuals whose grooming matches the norms of the setting make a more positive impression than individuals who are dressed in a style considered inappropriate (Cash & Janda, 1984; Perrin, 1921).

Kinesic cues. Your body sends many messages to others. When you are on the receiving end of these messages, you can use these kinesic expressions—body stance, pacing, gestures, smiles, frowns, gaze, and so on—to make inferences about others' personality, feelings, and characteristics.

Our hands, faces, and eyes are particularly fluent speakers of body language. According to Paul Ekman, Wallace V. Friesen, and their colleagues, the gestures we make with our hands convey specific messages *(emblems),* clarify our verbal statements *(illustrators),* adjust our body or objects around us *(manipulators),* and regulate social interactions—who speaks next, who enters a doorway first, and the like *(regulators)* (Ekman, Friesen, & Bear, 1984; Johnson, Ekman, & Friesen, 1975; see Table 3-2).

Emblems, unlike many nonverbal cues, tend to be used on purpose; we deliberately choose these gestures to convey a particular message.

TABLE 3–2

Some common types of gestures.

Type of Gesture	Definition	Example
Emblem	A signal, often made with the hand, that conveys a specific meaning	"Thumbs up" (fist clenched, thumb sticking up) The "bird" (middle finger extended)
Illustrator	An action that explains verbal communication but has no meaning alone	Pointing Outlining an object's shape Indicating age with fingers
Manipulator	Touching or rubbing an object or one's own body	Fidgeting with a button Picking the nose Rubbing the eyes
Regulator	An action that structures and organizes interactions	Pointing to next speaker Invitation to enter

How, for example, would you exclaim "All right!" with your hands? Probably by clenching your hand in a fist and extending your thumb upward. Similarly, you probably say "that's crazy" by making a rapid circular motion with your forefinger next to your ear. And anger is expressed in many ways, including the clenched fist and the raised middle finger. Our gestures are so specific in meaning that some researchers feel that they are a form of linguistic communication (McNeill, 1985).

Ekman and his colleagues have found that the meanings of most gestures vary from culture to culture. While the "thumbs-up" gesture used by Roman emperors to spare gladiators means "All right" in the United States, for example, in northern Greece it means "Up yours." The "A-OK" gesture formed when the forefinger and thumb are pressed together to form a circle means "You asshole" in southern Italy, "You're worth zero" in France, and a desire for anal sex in some other parts of Europe. Some cultures have unique gestures that have no meaning to outsiders. The French express "He's drunk" by putting the fist to the nose and then twisting it; the Germans say "Good luck" by balling up their hands into fists (with the thumbs tucked inside) and then making a downward pounding motion. Ekman's studies offer some handy advice to tourists; the next time you travel, be sure to speak as carefully with your hands as with your mouth (see Figure 3-1).

The face is an equally important source of perceptual data. Like gestures, some facial expressions have very specific meanings (Ekman & Friesen, 1975). To most perceivers, yawning means "I'm bored," a wink says "You know what I mean," and a stuck-out tongue conveys rejection. Ekman and Friesen have found that perceivers can consistently identify at least six basic emotions by facial cues alone: happiness, fear, surprise, anger, disgust, and sadness. Extending Charles Darwin's century-old argument that some emotional expressions are understood by people in all cultures, Ekman showed people of various cultures photographs of people demonstrating various emotions. Most subjects easily identified each face as happy, fearful, surprised, angry, disgusted, or sad. When Ekman repeated this study with photographs of unposed, spontaneous displays of emotion, he again found that people could accurately detect emotions, with one exception: in this second study, surprise was sometimes confused with fear (Buck, 1984; Ekman & Friesen, 1975; Izard, 1977). Thus facial expressions, unlike gestures, appear to be a human universal, used in a similar way by people all over the world (see Figure 3-2).

Evidence also indicates that the perceiver's attention is often drawn to the eyes, long recognized as "windows of the soul." *Eye contact* (or gazing) is loaded with social meaning. We express our desire for communication, for example, by signaling with our eyes; when you want to ask a question in class, you try to catch the professor's eye. Conversely, during a discussion your averted eyes tell the professor that you aren't prepared.

Figure 3-1 Talking hands. In 1968 the North Koreans captured an American vessel named the *Pueblo*. The crew members eventually confessed to crimes against Korea, and the Koreans released this photograph as evidence that the confessions had not been coerced. The Koreans didn't notice that three of the men *(front row: far left, far right, and second from right)* displayed the insulting middle-finger gesture. This gesture (known to the Romans as *digitus impudicus*) revealed the American prisoners' contempt for their captors and repudiated their confessions.

Perceivers also make judgments about other people's feelings by observing the amount and direction of their gaze. We generally assume that people who avoid our eyes are embarrassed, ashamed, or disinterested, while a high level of gazing implies involvement, intimacy, attraction, and respect. Perceivers also use gaze as evidence of certain personality traits. In one investigation, people who gazed at subjects only 15% of the time were judged to be cold, pessimistic, cautious, defensive, immature, evasive, submissive, and indifferent. Those who gazed at the subjects 80% of the time were seen as friendly, self-confident, natural, mature, and sincere (Exline & Messick, 1967).

These findings suggest that if you want to make a positive impression when you first meet someone, you should maintain a high level of gaze (see Focus 3-1). Be warned, however, that a constant gaze (a stare) can culminate in negative perceptions. Anyone who has ever tried to stare down someone else knows that humans, like many other animals, communicate aggressiveness and dominance with a stare (Henley, 1977). People describe starers as tense, angry, embarrassed, passive, and unintelligent, and report angry, unfriendly feelings when they are the target

Figure 3-2 Through nonverbal behaviors, we communicate without words.

of a stare (Strom & Buck, 1979). Unless a stare occurs in conjunction with a more positive signal, such as a smile or positive remark, people often respond by terminating the interaction and leaving the general area. Thus eye contact often serves to intensify the dominant mood, whatever it may

FOCUS 3-1

Experiencing Social Psychology: *Are some nonverbal behaviors friendlier than others?*

You have just been introduced to someone you want to impress: a professor in one of your courses, your new boss, a good friend's spouse, a physically attractive stranger. As this person will be basing his or her impression of you on your nonverbal behavior, what should you do to foster a positive image?

Start with the face. Make certain that you look at the other person, use your eyebrows and mouth expressively, and avoid yawns and stares (see Table 3-3). Smiling is especially important, for people who are smiling are usually rated as more attractive than people who aren't smiling, even when raters are told to compensate for the impact of the smile (Mueser et al., 1984). Next, position your body appropriately. Adopt a relaxed (but not too relaxed) posture by turning your head and shoulders in his or her direction, lean forward slightly, and don't slouch. In addition, you may want to adopt an open rather than closed posture by (*a*) keeping your arms hanging down rather than crossed across your chest, (*b*) gesturing outward with your hands rather than clasping them or putting them in your pockets, and (*c*) extending your elbows away from your body rather than pressed against your sides (Mehrabian, 1972). Finally, if the situation makes such a gesture appropriate, a brief touch on the hand, arm, or shoulder is usually favorably perceived (Stier & Hall, 1984).

Why do these nonverbal behaviors usually lead to favorable reactions? According to several theorists, these actions symbolize involvement and friendliness; they seem to say, "I'm interested in what you have to say" (Eibl-Eibesfeldt, 1972; Edinger & Patterson, 1983). Of course, these behaviors should be used only when they match the "display rules" of the situation. Different behaviors are considered appropriate in different situations, and if you violate these implicit norms, you may earn yourself a swift rejection. When you're discussing extremely intimate subjects, for example, a high level of gaze may be inappropriate, so by staring at someone you may ensure your own rejection (Argyle & Dean, 1965). Touching is generally pleasant, but if it's used to demonstrate status or control—as when a high-status man demeans a lower-status woman by putting his arm around her—then touching creates a negative impression (Henley, 1977; Major, 1981). Also, the impact of nonverbal cues sometimes depends on the sex of the sender. Women, for example, were judged more favorably the more they smiled and used facial expressions in one study. For men, facial expressions were unrelated to attractiveness (Riggio & Friedman, 1986).

TABLE 3-3

Positive and negative nonverbal cues.

Positive Behaviors	Negative Behaviors
High eye contact	Low eye contact
Leaning forward	Leaning away
Smiling	Frowning
Moving toward	Moving away
Touching hands	Touching own hair
Broadly smiling	Looking away
Grinning	Sneering
Nodding head	Cold stare
Raising eyebrows	Picking the teeth
Facing forward	Cracking the fingers
Gesturing with hands	Picking at the hands
Showing happiness	Yawning
Open body position	Closed body position
Straightening one's back	Slouching

SOURCES: Burgoon et al., 1984; Clore, Wiggins, & Itkin, 1975; Kudoh & Matsumoto, 1985; Mehrabian, 1972.

be (Ellsworth, Carlsmith, & Henson, 1972; Keating et al., 1981; a detailed review of this research is presented in Argyle & Cook, 1976).

Paralanguage.   Many of our perceptions depend on *how* something is said, rather than *what* is said. For example, when your social psychology professor says, "Aren't we lively today," you know she is sarcastically saying that the class seems bored. When your professor covers material very rapidly, you assume that he is an expert in this particular area. When you ask your professor if the next test is going to be very difficult, her long pause before saying no tells you to expect trouble. In all these cases, you are basing your perceptions on the nonverbal cues that accompany your professor's verbal statements. These cues comprise *paralanguage*, and include such vocal features as pitch, resonance, intensity, and sounds that have no verbal meaning (crying, mumbling, uh-huh, um). Unlike appearance and kinesic cues, which are both visual cues, paralanguage is an auditory cue.

The importance of paralinguistic cues becomes clear when the other verbal and nonverbal communication channels are eliminated experimentally. In one study subjects were exposed to 72 segments of female college students answering one of four different questions. Two of the questions

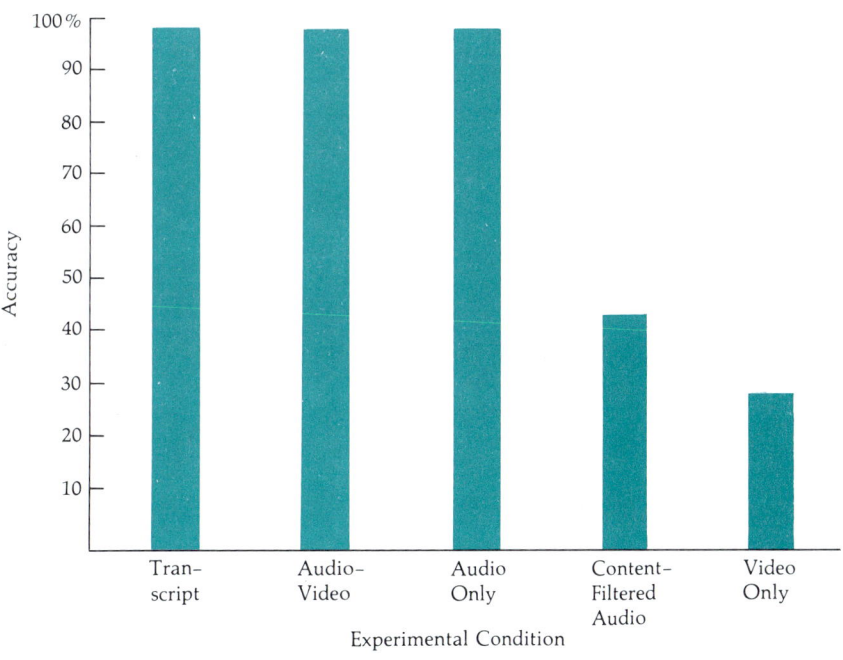

Figure 3-3   Which kind of cue has more impact on your perceptions? Sometimes verbal cues outweigh nonverbal cues, as in this study that rated the accuracy of subjects' perceptions in five experimental conditions.

dealt with positive topics (friendship, happiness) and two with negative topics (dislikes, sadness). The subjects' task: guess what question the woman in each segment was answering (Krauss et al., 1981).

To vary the type of information given to the subjects, the researchers created five experimental conditions.

1. *Transcript only.* Subjects were given a written transcript of each segment but couldn't see or hear the segment.

2. *Audiovideo.* Subjects watched a videotaped recording of each segment.

3. *Audio only.* Subjects listened to a tape recording of each segment.

4. *Content-filtered audio.* Subjects listened to a tape recording of each

---

FOCUS 3 – 2

A Closer Look: *When our words lie, do our bodies confess?*

Before the outbreak of World War II, Adolf Hitler met face to face with British Prime Minister Neville Chamberlain. During that meeting, Hitler claimed that he wanted to avoid war at all costs. He also managed to conceal the fact that his armies were preparing to invade Czechoslovakia. Chamberlain failed to detect these deceptions, with disastrous results (Ekman, 1985).

How could Hitler get away with these bold deceptions? Why couldn't Chamberlain separate truth from falsehood? According to Paul Ekman, Hitler was a "superb performer, easily able to convincingly falsify negative emotions" (1985, pp. 36–37). In addition, because they spoke through translators, Chamberlain lacked access to valuable nonverbal cues that may reveal the truth even when our words are false.

Evidence indicates that when we lie, *our bodies sometimes leak nonverbal cues that signal our deception.* If we aren't careful, as we mutter our falsehoods we may find ourselves moving our hands restlessly or avoiding eye contact. Or we may hesitate before speaking and make unexpectedly long or short

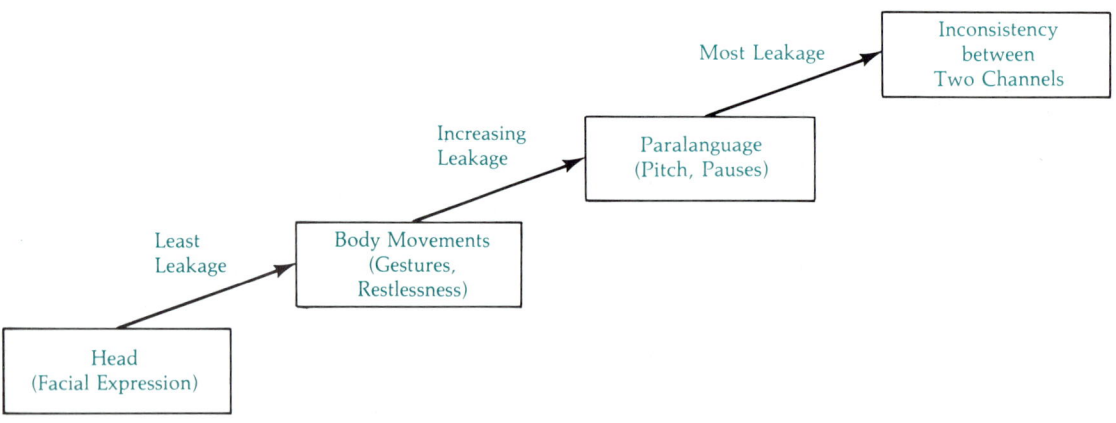

Figure 3-4 The leakage hierarchy. Because nonverbal face and body cues are relatively easy to control, these channels leak the least during deception. Voice cues are more informative, while an inconsistency between two channels (either verbal or nonverbal) is a good indicant of deception.

segment that had been electronically filtered to blur the words but retain the paralinguistic cues. Like muffled conversations heard through a wall, these tapes are not intelligible, but changes in pitch, pauses, tone, and so on can still be detected.

5. *Video only.* Subjects watched a videotape of each segment with no sound track.

Subjects were extremely accurate when they were given the verbal message; they correctly identified the question over 95 percent of the time in the transcript, audiovisual, and audio conditions (see Figure 3-3). When the subjects listened to the filtered tape recording, their accuracy rate dropped dramatically (41.4% correct), but this score was still better

statements. The better the liar, the less nonverbal leakage he or she displays (Harrison et al., 1978; Kraut & Poe, 1980).

Some nonverbal cues, however, are more difficult to control than others. Just as the face is an extremely expressive conveyer of emotional information to others, it is also relatively easy to control when we decide to lie. The gestures that betray us when we lie—nervous body and hand movements—are also fairly easy to control. Our voice tone, however, is more difficult to control, so this paralanguage cue more reliably signals a deceptive statement. These differences in leakage across the various nonverbal channels prompted Robert Rosenthal, Bella M. DePaulo, and Miron Zuckerman to develop the concept of a *leakage hierarchy*. As Figure 3-4 shows, channel leakage increases as we move from the face to the body and then to vocal cues (see Figure 3-5). Lastly, an inconsistency between two channels *(dissynchrony)*, which occurs whenever the channels reveal conflicting information, is the best indicant of deception.

Rosenthal, DePaulo, and Zuckerman conclude that most of us are poor lie detectors, but they offer several useful hints for improving our skills. In general, you should always concentrate on the leakiest of channels (inconsistencies and the voice) rather than on the more secure channels (the body and face). Also, try to begin your analysis by ignoring the content of the communication and focusing your attention on one question: Is this person deceiving me? Only after you settle this question should you search for evidence that reveals his or her true beliefs (Blanck et al., 1981; Rosenthal & DePaulo, 1979; Zuckerman et al., 1982, 1984; Zuckerman, DePaulo, & Rosenthal, 1981).

Figure 3-5 Nonverbal leakage. Paralanguage reveals the clearest evidence of deception, but the cues are usually more subtle than these.
© 1984 by King Features Syndicate, Inc. All rights reserved.

SOCIAL PERCEPTION AND COGNITION   109

than any they could have achieved by random guessing. Their performance in the last condition, in which they could base their responses only on kinesic nonverbal cues, was not much better than chance guessing (32.4%). Thus, even though the tape recording contained no verbal information when it had been filtered, it was still more informative than a silent videotaped recording.

In this study, a picture *wasn't* worth a thousand words; people were more accurate when they had access to audio information rather than visual information. The findings would probably have been different, however, if the women who were observed were discussing more neutral topics, or if they had been answering their questions deceptively rather than truthfully (see Focus 3-2). Researchers now believe that paralinguistic cues sometimes, but not always, provide us with more information than linguistic cues. No one channel gives more information than another in all situations (Ekman et al., 1980; O'Sullivan et al., 1985; Zuckerman et al., 1982).

Proxemics. How would you respond if your professor, on the first day of class, stood directly in front of your chair while she lectured? If he backed away from you when you approached him after class to ask a question? These incidents lead us to the final category of nonverbal behavior shown in Table 3-1: **proxemic cues,** or distancing behavior. The amount of space between people, like so many other nonverbal cues, indicates the level of intimacy or involvement in a relationship. Just as a gaze at too high or too low a level of intensity can be threatening, too little or too much distance between yourself and others can be stressful. The close approach of a stranger or a slight acquaintance, such as your professor, is felt to be overly intimate. Therefore, you would probably withdraw from the situation and form a negative impression of the intruder.

Because proxemic cues, unlike appearance, kinesic, and paralanguage cues, always occur in the context of the physical and social environment, we will examine this topic in more detail in Chapter 12, on the environment and social behavior.

Verbal Communication

Sherlock Holmes typically based his first impressions of people on their outward appearances and nonverbal behaviors, but he sometimes interviewed witnesses and suspects to supplement his collection of clues. Similarly, while such nonverbal cues as physical appearance, kinesic cues, paralanguage, and proxemics influence our perceptions of other people, we don't overlook the perceptual value of information extracted from verbal cues. As the philosopher Ludwig Wittgenstein said, "uttering a word is like striking a note on the keyboard of the imagination" (1965, p. 4).

We gather a great deal of information about others by interpreting their verbal communications, though such messages aren't always as straightforward as they appear. When we listen to another person talk, we are often most aware of the semantic content of the communication—the meanings of the words themselves. Our perceptions are often shaped by the expressive content of the message as well—the interpersonal message behind the words (see Table 3-4). (Stiles, 1978, 1980, and Wish, D'Andrade, & Goodnow, 1980, discuss alternative approaches to verbal communication.)

Semantic content. When people communicate verbally, they use words to convey information. On the first day of the course, for example, an instructor may describe her credentials, background, and interests, and students may use this description to formulate an impression of her. If she says, "I've been teaching for ten years," they may conclude that she is a veteran instructor. If she explicitly proclaims, "I think social psychology is the most important subfield in all the social sciences," they will understand that she likes social psychology. If she says, "I am a warm, sensitive person," the students may say to themselves, "Hey, this one is OK." As these few examples suggest, by interpreting the meaning of a verbal message, we can collect information about other people's attributes, attitudes, and feelings.

Expressive content. Verbal statements also work at a deeper level. They send implicit messages deeper than those conveyed by the semantic content alone. Imagine that at the beginning of the semester you ask the same question—"Do you give make-up tests?"—in five different classes. You receive the following five responses:

Professor A: Yes, I do, but please notify me in advance.
Professor B: I sure do. I realize people get sick sometimes.

TABLE 3 – 4

Two types of verbal cues.

Type of Cue	Definition	Examples
Semantic content	The explicit meaning of the verbal statement	"What is your name?" "I am hungry."
Expressive content	The implicit, interpersonal meaning of the verbal statement	"Can I help you?" (implies warmth, caring) "You will go, won't you?" (implies uncertainty)

Professor C: I guess I can, if you think I should.
Professor D: I already said that I did.
Professor E: Yes, yes, yes. How many times do I have to tell you that? Are you deaf?

At one level, these statements are all identical; they all say yes to the question "Do you give make-up tests?" Clearly, however, these statements vary in expressive content: the connotative verbal indicators of attributes, attitudes, and feelings (Cappella, 1981; Watzlawick, Beavin, & Jackson, 1967).

But how do these five messages differ? What impression does *A* suggest that *B* does not? Why do we react one way to *D* and another way to *E*? Providing a partial answer, researchers have consistently identified at least three themes, or dimensions, underlying perceptions of expressive communications. The first dimension pertains to the *evaluative aspect of the message*. Some messages are positive, implying warmth, acceptance, caring, and friendliness. Others are negative: cold, rejecting, hostile, and unfriendly. Of the five professors, *B* seems positive and caring, while *D* is clearly negative and hostile. The second dimension pertains to *power* or *potency*. At one extreme, some statements emphasize the status of the speaker: his or her ability to control and dominate others. Other statements express a lack of control, weakness, or submissiveness. Of the professors' statements, *A* expresses dominance, *C* submissiveness. Lastly, and with somewhat less empirical consistency, many studies have identified a third dimension: *intensity* or *activity*. This final dimension pertains to the magnitude of the expressed sentiment. *D* is mildly hostile, *E* extremely hostile (Bales & Cohen, 1979; Foa, 1961; Osgood, Suci, & Tannenbaum, 1957; Wish & Kaplan, 1977; compare with Kim & Rosenberg, 1980).

These findings suggest that you implicitly code expressive communications along three dimensions: evaluation (hostile–friendly), power (dominant–submissive), and intensity (mild–intense). These findings also suggest that your perceptions of people are based on these three dimensions. Whenever you meet someone, you tend to ask three basic perceptual questions: (1) Is this person hostile or friendly? (2) Is this person dominant or submissive? (3) How strong are these tendencies? (See Figure 3-6.) As we have seen, you then answer these questions by examining the person's nonverbal and verbal behavior.

From Perception to Cognition

In summary, we are all social sleuths. When we are with other people, we actively collect the information we need to understand their feelings, personalities, behaviors, and thoughts. If, for example, we are introduced to a stranger at a party, we decipher the meaning of her or his nonverbal behaviors: the way he looks, subtle expressions she makes, the tone of

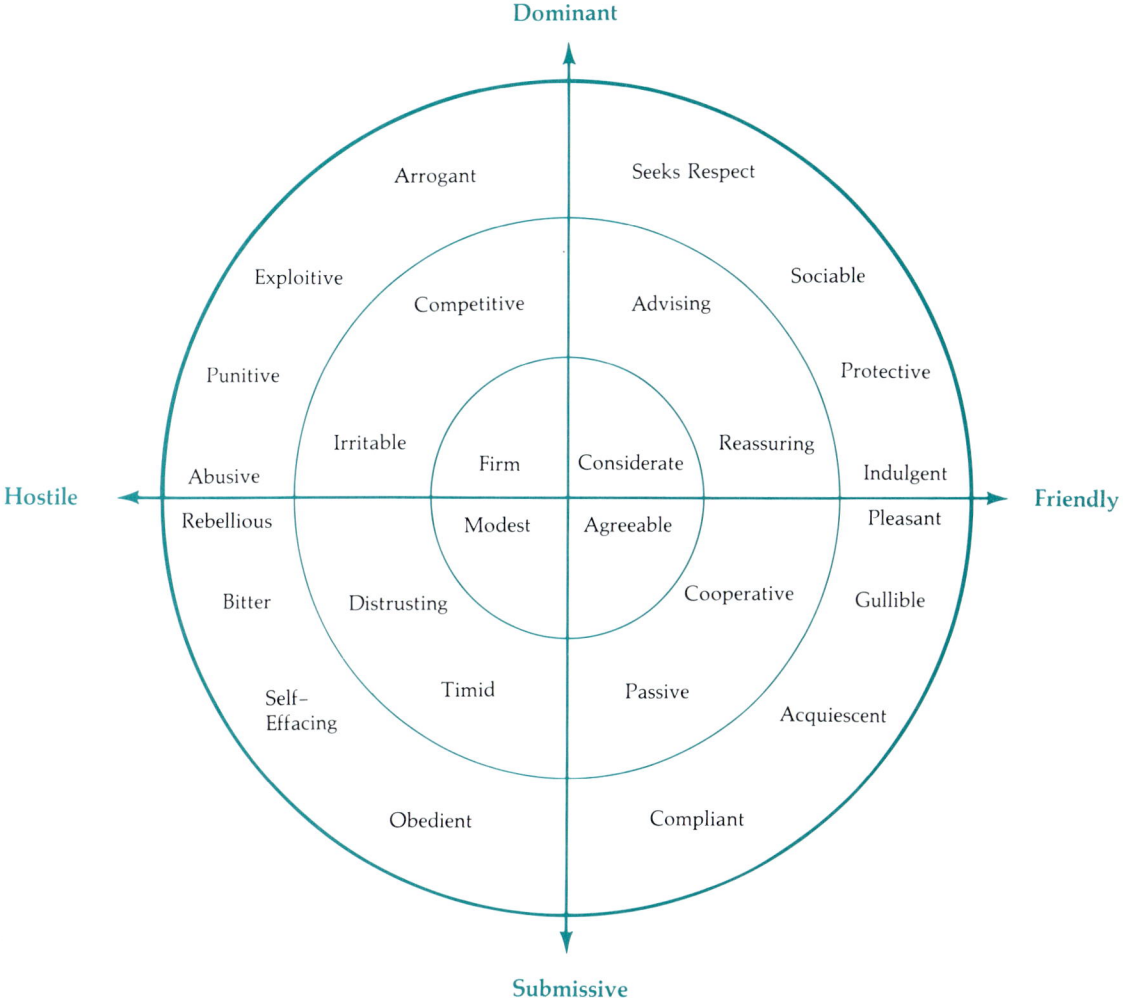

Figure 3-6 The interpersonal circle. The three perceptual dimensions—evaluation, power, and intensity—can be combined to form a circle. Evaluation ranges from hostile *(far left)* to friendly *(far right)*; power ranges from dominant *(top)* to submissive *(bottom)*; and intensity is represented by the distance from the middle of the circle. Locations on the outer edge of the circle are higher in intensity than locations near the center of the circle.

his voice, or even the distance that separates us. We also take note of verbal behaviors, responding to the semantic content of others' words, as well as the expressive content implied by the message.

However, our quest for social knowledge is only beginning once we collect this perceptual information. Although Sherlock Holmes always claimed that "there is nothing like first-hand evidence," the clues mean nothing if they can't be organized in a coherent theory about the crime

During social interaction, we use both verbal and nonverbal behavior to convey information to others. What kind of impression is Billy Martin trying to create in this case? Friendly or hostile? Dominant or submissive? Mild or intense?

(Doyle, 1938, p. 24). Similarly, our perceptions provide us with the raw data that we need, but we must make sense of this information by formulating an overall conception of the individual. At this point in the process, social cognition comes into play.

■ Social Cognition

Suppose we meet a stranger. Our observations tell us that the stranger (*a*) is a man who (*b*) is very handsome and (*c*) friendly (he smiles frequently), but (*d*) talks only about himself. We must organize this information to form an overall impression. Some of his characteristics may prompt a positive reaction: he is handsome and friendly. But why does he talk about himself so much? Is he insecure? No, you conclude, he's too attractive to be insecure. Well, perhaps he is a bit conceited; he is, after all, very attractive. Yes, you conclude, an exaggerated sense of self-importance could certainly account for the data you have collected.

How do we transform our social perceptions into organized social knowledge? How do we construct an overall picture of this person? In some cases, we seem to rely on straightforward combination rules to *integrate* each bit of information to form an overall picture of the person. Like a computer that accepts inputs, performs data-processing steps, and then outputs the information, we routinely collect information, combine it, and form an impression. In other cases, however, the intuitive detective takes over for the rational computer, building impressions that go beyond the available data. Rather than looking at each new person we meet with a fresh, uninformed eye, we use our previously formulated conceptualizations, expectations, and interpretations to *organize* information. This section examines both types of processes.

Integrating Social Information

Imagine that you are thinking of taking a class from either Professor Somm or Professor Menn. When you ask a friend what she thinks of Somm, she says, "He's very intelligent and an OK lecturer." How about Menn? "He's also very intelligent," she says, "but I've never heard him lecture." Who will you pick?

According to **information integration theory,** your choice depends on how you combine, or integrate, this information about Somm and Menn. But how will you achieve this integration? By adding or by averaging? And how will you weight each bit of information? Are all the attributes equally important, or are some (such as intelligence) weighted more heavily than others? Let us consider these alternative approaches, and their consequences, in more detail.

Unweighted models. Several theories predict that people intuitively *add* or *average* pieces of information. These models assume that we begin by evaluating the person's specific characteristics. You may feel that being a man is a neutral characteristic, intelligence is a very positive characteristic in a professor, and "OK lecturer" is a somewhat positive characteristic. In fact, if you were asked to rate each of these attributes on a scale from +3 to −3, being a man would receive a +0 rating, intelligence +3, but OK lecturer only +1.

Once each characteristic is assigned a value, you can either add or average the values to calculate an impression. As Table 3-5 shows, if you add up the values of Somm's and Menn's characteristics, Somm rates +4

TABLE 3−5

Two ways to integrate information: adding and averaging.

Person	Characteristic	Value	Impression	
			Addition	Averaging
Somm	Being male	+0		
	Intelligence	+3		
	OK lecturer	+1	+4	4/3 = 1.33
Menn	Being male	+0		
	Intelligence	+3	+3	3/2 = 1.50

and Menn only +3: you will favor Somm. If, however, you apply the averaging model, Menn wins because the mean, or average, of Menn's two traits is greater than the average of Somm's three traits.

Both the additive and averaging approaches are called **unweighted models**; they assume that each bit of information has an equal impact on your impression. Intelligence, for example, has a higher value than OK lecturer (+3 versus +1), but these traits are weighted equally when they are added or averaged. Some evidence supports the additive model, but the bulk of the research favors an averaging approach. In one well-known study, Norman H. Anderson compared the two models by asking subjects to form an impression of a person who possessed either two or four traits. The two traits were either extremely positive or extremely negative. The four traits included two moderate ones (either negative or positive) and the two extreme traits. As the averaging model predicts, when the moderate traits were added the subjects made less extreme judgments of the individuals. As Figure 3-7 shows, a person who was described as warmhearted and truthful received a higher rating than a person described as warmhearted, truthful, sensitive, and persuasive. Similarly, a person who was spiteful and abusive received a more negative evaluation than a person who was spiteful, abusive, unpopular, and critical (Anderson, 1965; see also Anderson, 1981; Birnbaum, 1974; Gollob, Rossman, & Abelson, 1973; Sloan & Ostrom, 1974; Wyer, 1974; Yamagishi & Hill, 1981).

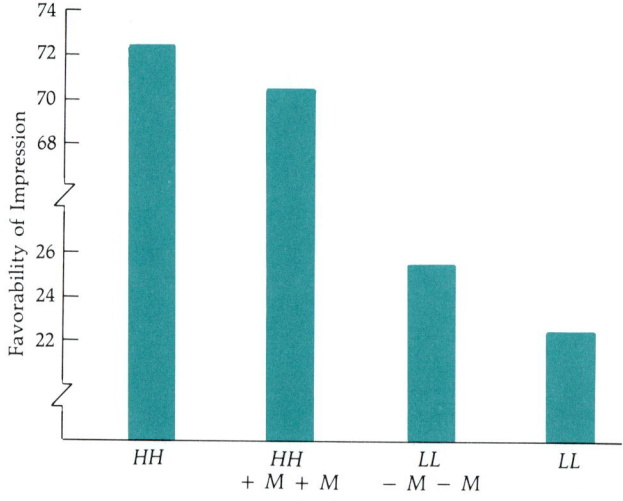

Figure 3-7 Evidence of averaging during information integration. As the averaging model predicts, when two moderately positive adjectives *(+M+M)* were combined with two highly favorable adjectives *(HH)*, subjects' impressions became less positive. Conversely, when two moderately negative adjectives *(−M−M)* were combined with two highly negative adjectives *(LL)*, subjects' impressions became less negative.

Although other portions of Anderson's experiment were less supportive, his study generally suggests that quality, not quantity, counts when we are forming impressions. If you were going to give a piano recital, you should probably perform only two pieces that you knew very well rather than add a third piece that you performed only adequately. Or if two of your three letters of reference for a job are extremely positive while the third is only "above average," send only the positive ones. Similarly, when you prepare an exotic appetizer and a delicious dinner, forgo dessert rather than serve an uninspired one.

Weighted models. An unweighted averaging model describes many types of social judgments, but in some cases one bit of information is stressed more than another. If the piano piece you perform only adequately would challenge a virtuoso, for instance, you may make a better impression by playing it. Similarly, if the above-average letter is written by a famous dignitary, then it may have a much greater impact than extremely positive letters from unknown people.

In these examples, the information is still averaged together, but only after each element has been weighted. To apply this *weighted-averaging model*, imagine that you are asked to form an impression of a professor who is organized, intelligent, and ill-tempered. As before, you begin by assigning a value to each trait (see Table 3-6). Second, you intuitively assign heavier weights to the traits that you think are more important than to the traits you think are less important. If you feel that a bad temper is a particularly important (although negative) trait, you double its weight in relation to the other traits. (Mathematically, weighting simply involves multiplying the value of the trait by its weight, as in Table 3-6.) Third, you average the weighted values together to form an impression. In this example, an impression derived by weighted averaging is less favorable than the impression generated by the averaging of unweighted values.

In support of the weighted models, evidence indicates that some pieces of information influence our judgments more than others. If you were to formulate a judgment of a person who was described as untidy, informal, and murderous, *murderous* is so important that it will overshadow all the

TABLE 3-6

Weighted averaging of information cues.

Cue	Value	Weight	Weighted Value
Organized	+1	1	+1
Intelligent	+3	1	+3
Ill tempered	−2	2	−4
Unweighted average	+2/3 = 0.66	Weighted average	+0/3 = 0

This woman is intelligent, skillful, industrious, cold, determined, practical, and cautious. Given this information, do you think she is sociable or withdrawn? Tactful or secretive? Tolerant or irritable? Witty or cynical? In answering these questions, you rely on your ability to synthesize perceptual information to form a unified impression of a person.

other characteristics (Birnbaum, 1974). The weight associated with each bit of information also seems to depend on:

1. *Extremity*. Some studies suggest that "the weight associated with each element is directly related to its extremity" in value: traits with extreme values carry relatively more weight than traits with more moderate values. As the adjective *intelligent* has the most extreme value (+3; see Table 3-6), it would be weighted more heavily, followed by *ill tempered* (−2) and *organized* (+1) (Manis, Gleason, & Dawes, 1966, p. 404; see Fiske, 1980).

2. *Negativity*. In a surprisingly large number of instances, perceivers tend to weight negative information more heavily than positive information. Because of this tendency to focus on the bad rather than the good, *ill tempered* (−2) may carry added weight (Kanouse & Hanson, 1971; Ronis & Lipinski, 1985).

3. *Salience*. Investigators have repeatedly found that some types of information attract our attention more than others. Vivid, distinctive, or unexpected data are most *salient* perceptually, and hence receive more weight than nonsalient information. If you were expecting an absent-minded, disorganized professor, for example, then *organized* may have been very salient to you (Fiske & Taylor, 1984).

4. *Primacy/recency*. In some cases, the position of the element in the entire set of information influences its weight. A *primacy* effect occurs if information at the beginning of a sequence has a greater impact on our impressions. If, in contrast, the elements at the end of the sequence are more influential, then the process is known as a *recency* effect. In support of the wisdom of "making a good first impression," primacy effects usually overwhelm recency effects. Hence *organized* would receive greater weight than *ill tempered* (Anderson, 1965; Anderson & Norman, 1964).

Anderson believes that, overall, our perceptions of the people around us are based on the weighted-averaging model (see Focus 3-3). However, different people may adopt different cognitive strategies. Some of us may tend to integrate information additively, others may rely on averaging, and still others may both weight and average (Forsyth, 1985). Also, none of the models can explain how the perceiver changes discordant bits of information about another person into an elaborate, richly textured por-

---

FOCUS 3-3

Controversy in Social Psychology: *Do you really know how you think?*

Many people reject mathematical models of impression formation on intuitive, common-sense grounds. After reading about the theories, they rebel, proclaiming, "I'm not a mathematician—I don't use algebra to understand other people!" These people may be right. Some researchers feel that the mathematical models describe the product, not the process. That is, the formulas are powerful predictors of your perceptions, but they don't describe the cognitive processes underlying perceptions.

A second set of researchers, however, firmly endorse these models. They argue that the formulas describe our cognitive processes, but we don't recognize their validity because we aren't aware of these processes. Taking a controversial position on this issue, Richard E. Nisbett and Timothy D. Wilson believe that people have little access to their mental workings. Although we are conscious of our thoughts and feelings, we cannot gain access to the processes that created these cognitive products. We answer such questions as "How did you form your impression of Jill?" and "Why did you make that decision?" by relying on common sense, but our answers may not be particularly accurate (Nisbett & Wilson, 1977).

Consider the following information:

Jill is applying for a job at a crisis intervention center. She is quite physically attractive, and graduated from college with a very good academic record. During her job interview, however, she spilled a cup of coffee, and, in response to a question about personal stresses, described a recent automobile accident in which her pelvis was crushed.

First, form an impression of Jill. How much do you think you would like her? Do you think she would be sympathetic? Intelligent? Flexible in solving problems? Second, what factors influenced your judgments? Her physical attractiveness? Her academic credentials? Her slip with the coffee? Her accident?

When Nisbett and his colleagues asked people to describe the impact of Jill's characteristics on their judgments, the subjects weren't very accurate. Although many said that they liked Jill because of her good academic credentials and her honest description of her automobile accident, their actual evaluations told a very different story; she was actually liked less when she had good academic credentials and had been in an accident. Similarly, subjects said that they weren't influenced by the coffee-spilling incident, but this blunder increased their ratings of Jill's likableness and flexibility (Nisbett & Bellows, 1977).

Nisbett and Wilson's interpretations have not gone unchallenged. Some investigators agree that we may not be aware of our perceptual or memory processes, but argue that our thinking on important matters is accessible. Others have raised statistical objections, while still others have complained that Nisbett and Wilson's hypothesis can't be disconfirmed empirically (Kraut & Lewis, 1982; Smith & Miller, 1978; White, 1980). Although the debate is far from settled, Nisbett and Wilson's argument offers one important lesson: we should not let our intuitions guide our appraisals of scientific theory and research. The theory may not feel right to us, but that doesn't mean that it's not valid.

trait of the person. In many cases, we go beyond integration to organization.

Organizing Social Information

The adding, averaging, and weighted-averaging models explain many cognitive processes, but these mathematical models describe only a part of the total picture. Although the good detective carefully weighs each clue, he or she must draw conclusions that go beyond the content of the clues themselves. As Sherlock Holmes explained, the ideal detective, once "shown a single fact in all its bearings," can "deduce from it not only all the chain of events which led up to it, but also all the results which would follow from it" (Doyle, 1938, p. 253).

Solomon Asch, a pioneer in the field of person perception, examined our ability to go beyond the immediate data by asking college students to form an impression of an "intelligent, skillful, industrious, warm, determined, practical, and cautious" person. Other students were given an identical list, except that *warm* was replaced by *cold*. Although only one word was changed, the two groups of subjects reached startlingly different conclusions. The cold individual was viewed as more unsociable, unpopular, irritable, ungenerous, humorless, and ruthless than the warm person (Asch, 1946).

Asch explained his findings by emphasizing the unity of our impressions. Building on the work of Gestalt psychologists, Asch argued that we organize incoming information to form a unified, integrated whole. Rejecting the assumption that our impression is equal to the average or sum of its parts, Asch assumed that we synthesize the elements to form a unique configuration that goes beyond the content of the individual traits. As the well-known Gestalt dictum argues, the whole is greater than the sum of its parts.

But how do we achieve this integrated view of other people? What do we do when we meet a man who displays many masculine qualities but then cries when he is sad? How do we make sense of a new neighbor who describes herself as warm and friendly but gives only negative, unfriendly nonverbal cues? How do we translate the bits and pieces of information acquired through social perception into a coherent, general conception of the person? Here we consider two possibilities: the change-of-meaning hypothesis and implicit personality theories.

The change-of-meaning hypothesis.
Why did the warm/cold variable have such a dramatic impact on subjects' perceptions? Asch concluded that warmth and coldness were *central traits* in his studies: they "did not simply add a new quality, but to some extent transformed the other characteristics" (1946, p. 264). When the adjective *industrious* was used to describe a warm person, for example, subjects felt that it implied a willingness to work hard to help others, a "desire to accomplish something that would be of benefit." Applied to the cold person, however,

industrious implied *greedy;* the cold industrious person was seen as "ambitious and talented," one "who would not let anyone or anything stand in the way of achieving his goal" (p. 263). In Asch's view, central traits change the meaning of other information available to the perceiver.

To apply Asch's **change-of-meaning hypothesis,** form an impression of Hal, who is unpleasant, cruel, and cold. Now imagine that you have discovered that Hal is also calm and discreet. When you interpret the word *calm,* does it mean poised and serene or cool and calculating? Does *discreet* mean tactful or secretive? Using a similar procedure, Asch found the adjective *calm* meant serene, peaceful, gentle, or tolerant only when it described a kind person. When applied to a cruel person, *calm* was reinterpreted to mean icy, calculating, or shrewd. Transformations like those shown in Table 3-7 have been obtained in other studies (Asch, 1946, Study 5; Hamilton & Zanna, 1974; Zanna & Hamilton, 1977; compare with Kaplan, 1975; Watkins & Peynircioglu, 1984).

The change-of-meaning hypothesis was also supported when subjects formed impressions about a person who possessed two apparently inconsistent traits, such as "sociable and lonely" or "hostile and dependent." Supporting Asch's premise that perceivers strive to organize their impressions to achieve unity, the subjects used various strategies to increase the coherence of their impressions. A sociable lonely person, for example, was seen as "outwardly friendly, but inwardly shy and lonely," and a hostile dependent person was "dependent on his or her parents, but hostile towards everyone else" (Asch & Zukier, 1984; Burnstein & Schul, 1982, 1983; Schul, 1983).

Implicit personality theory. Asch felt that we form more positive impressions of a warm person because warmth is a central trait that influences our interpretation of the person's other qualities. However,

TABLE 3 – 7

Changes in meaning when the same characterization is applied to a warm person and a cold person.

Characterization	Positive Interpretation	Negative Interpretation
Calm	Serene	Calculating
Satirical	Witty	Cynical
Discreet	Tactful	Secretive
Proud	Self-respecting	Conceited
Excitable	Lively	Touchy
Obedient	Cooperative	Submissive
Daring	Courageous	Reckless
Righteous	Virtuous	Dogmatic
Crafty	Clever	Sly
Outspoken	Frank	Blunt

the change-of-meaning hypothesis does not completely explain why central traits influence impressions even when no other traits are present. In one study, Asch gave his subjects just one bit of information: some were told that the person was warm, others that he was cold. Even with this sparse information, subjects tended to describe the warm person, but not the cold person, as generous, wise, happy, and good-looking (Asch, 1946, Experiment 10).

Puzzled by their responses, Asch asked one of his subjects why she rated the warm person so positively. She explained: Warmth "initiates other qualities. A man who is warm would be friendly, consequently happy" (1946, p. 277). Behind these deceptively simple words lurks a set of beliefs about the nature of human beings. This woman's previous experiences with other people had taught her that warmth is generally linked to two other traits: friendliness and happiness. She also believed that coldness implies pessimism and practicality.

Our personal assumptions about the relationships among various traits and attributes are known as **implicit personality theories** (in contrast to explicit personality theories developed by professional psychologists). Like the woman in Asch's research, people assume that certain traits go with other traits. For example, is intelligent Katie industrious or irresponsible? Is skillful Martha persistent or popular? Is irritable Chuck pessimistic or enthusiastic? To answer these questions, you rely on implicit theories about linkages among various personality traits. These intuitive personality theories may tell us that intelligence is linked to industry, but not to irresponsibility; that skill implies persistence, but not popularity; that irritableness goes with pessimism more than enthusiasm. Although different people adopt different implicit personality theories, these beliefs all provide the same cognitive service: they help us turn a small amount of information into a general understanding of the total person (Kim & Rosenberg, 1980; Schneider, 1973; Schneider, Hastorf, & Ellsworth, 1979; Sternberg, 1985).

The social perceiver, equipped with implicit personality theories and making use of the change-of-meaning process described earlier, is a penetrating observer capable of discerning hidden traits and attributes. Although Dr. Watson, Sherlock Holmes's sidekick, was always awed when the great detective made sweeping inferences from a thimbleful of information, our own detective work in everyday interactions is equally impressive. Using only the data we ourselves collect through social perception, we develop detailed and often quite accurate portraits of the people around us (Marsh, Barnes, & Hocevar, 1985).

Moreover, our intuitive theories about other people not only organize their diverse traits but also tie those traits to more general personality qualities. I believe, for example, that people who are friendly tend to enjoy parties. Why? Because, in my implicit personality theory these two characteristics are both related to a more general trait: warmth (the psychologist in me prefers the term *extraversion*, actually). Surpassing an elemental listing of probable relationships among various traits, my assumptions, expectations, and conceptualizations of other people are integrated in a network of cognitive generalizations. This network is known as a **schema**.

Cognitive Schemata

We expect a library to be organized. We wouldn't want to find books about magic, philosophy, math, social psychology, and Moby Dick all mixed together. Instead, books dealing with similar topics should be put close together. Gibbon's *Rise and Fall of the Roman Empire* and an analysis of the American Revolution are both history books: they should be shelved in the same area.

Like books in a library, our perceptions of other people are linked together in an organized system. Just as librarians rely on the Dewey decimal system or a similar system to arrange their collections, we use cognitive structures known as **schemata** to organize and guide the processing of social information. Imagine that you are an executive about to promote one of your employees to a management position. Because you are seeking someone with leadership potential, your perceptions are guided by your schema pertaining to this quality. A schema of this kind is shown in Figure 3-8. It suggests that you think that leaders often possess two fundamental characteristics: they tend to dominate others, and they are also people-oriented (or affiliative). You also think that these general characteristics subsume several more specific personality traits

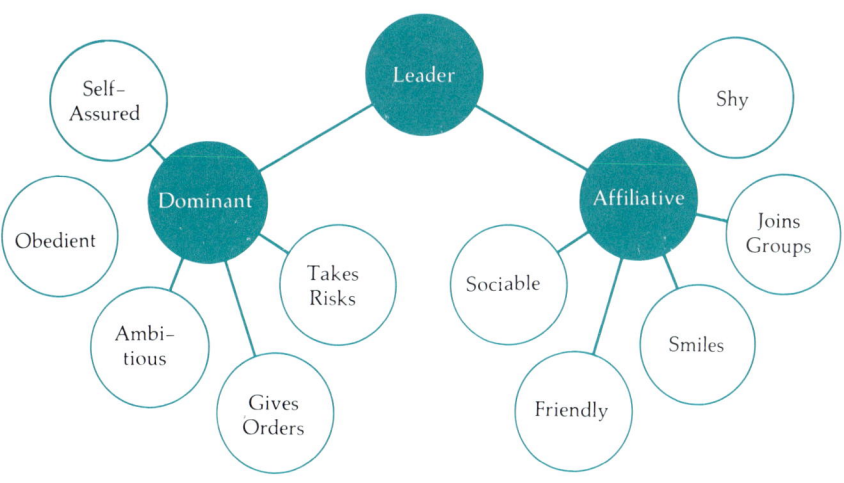

Figure 3-8　A hypothetical leadership schema. In this example, specific traits and behaviors are linked to one of two more global traits—dominance and affiliation—which are in turn linked to leadership.

and behaviors. If one of your employees is self-assured and ambitious, smiles frequently, and works well with others (joins groups), then he or she will probably be your choice (Foti, Fraser, & Lord, 1982).

Schemata organize many kinds of data. As we saw in Chapter 2, our perceptions of our own qualities may be organized by *self-schemata*. Our perceptions of other people may be based on *person schemata* like the one shown in Figure 3-8 (Taylor & Crocker, 1981). Some social psychologists also believe that *stereotypes* are forms of schemata (Hamilton, 1981). In terms of the earlier example, if your employees included men and women and blacks and whites, these gender and racial features could activate an entire set of assumptions about their traits and behaviors. If your stereotype of women, for example, emphasizes submissiveness rather than dominance, then you probably won't select a woman for promotion. As we will see in Chapter 5, stereotypes and prejudice are closely linked.

Once schemata take shape, these conceptual structures begin to drive our impressions. As Susan T. Fiske and Shelley E. Taylor explain, by using schemata we can observe and interpret, remember and forget, infer and judge, "all in ways that fit our expectations about particular kinds of people" (1984, p. 13). Schemata, it seems, are cognitive bullies: they push around our perceptions as well as our memories.

Schematic perception. Antonia Abbey (1982) illustrated the impact of schemata on perceptions in a study of men's reactions to women. Abbey traces the origin of the study to an unpleasant experience she had while listening to a band in a bar. Because the bar was crowded, Abbey and a female companion shared a table with two male strangers. During one of the band's breaks, the four people at the table struck up a conversation. It took very little time for the men to misinterpret the women's friendliness as flirtatiousness, and their own behavior became obnoxious to the women. Somehow the men had detected signs of sexual interest in the women's friendly conversation.

To bring this phenomenon into the laboratory, Abbey asked two college students—one man and one woman—to discuss their experiences in college while a hidden man and woman observed them. Although the couples talked only five minutes and the topic was innocuous, the men still managed to see signs of sexuality in the women's actions. Whether watching or conversing, men tended more than women to interpret the other's behavior as promiscuous and seductive. The conversing men also reported feeling more sexually attracted than the women did, and even rated themselves as more flirtatious. The men's perceptions were apparently shaped by their schemata regarding women and sex. According to Abbey, "men are more likely to perceive the world in sexual terms and to make sexual judgments than women are" (1982, p. 836).

Schemata, it seems, make "possible a certain efficiency and adaptiveness in social cognition," but they sometimes fail to do "justice to the unique qualities of any given individual" (Fiske & Taylor, 1984, p. 13).

Once schemata take shape, they focus our attention on certain traits and behaviors, thereby simplifying (or oversimplifying) our perceptual efforts (Cohen, 1981; Stern et al., 1984). In addition, our schemata influence our perception of incoming information, especially if these schemata are primed or activated before the observations take place (Bargh & Pietromonaco, 1982; Higgins, Rholes, & Jones, 1977). We tend to see what our schemata lead us to expect.

Schematic memory. Schemata may also influence our "person memory" (Fiske & Taylor, 1984; Hastie et al., 1980). Consider a student named Robert who has organized his knowledge of professors in a schema that includes such traits as being absent-minded and intellectual. According to the studies discussed above, as Robert observes an instructor, his attention may be drawn to the professor's actions that are consistent with his schema (Schneider & Blankmeyer, 1983; White & Carlston, 1983). Robert's memory of his observations may also be affected in more than one way. First, he may remember more of his teacher's professorial qualities (being absent-minded, intellectual). Second, he may forget characteristics that are inconsistent with his schema (being athletic, socially skilled). Third, he may complete his schema by "remembering" traits or characteristics that he never even observed (being mature, long-winded).

Limits to schematic processing. Do not assume, however, that schemata always influence our perceptions and memories. In some cases, we aren't ready to use our schema when we process social information. In the years after Robert finishes college, his schema will become less and less accessible to him for use in information processing. Hence, if he meets a professor at a party 30 years from now, this schema may not influence his impressions (Bargh & Pietromonaco, 1982; Higgins, King, & Mavin, 1982; Srull, 1983). Similarly, if no one tells Robert that his new acquaintance is a professor, then his memories will not match a professor schema. In fact, some theorists believe that even if he later discovers this information, his memory will remain unchanged (Bellezza & Bower, 1981; Clark & Woll, 1981; Higgins, Rholes, & Jones, 1977; for an opposing interpretation, see Snyder & Uranowitz, 1978).

Driven Cognitive Processing

Cognitive psychologists often draw a distinction between **data-driven** and **conceptually driven cognitive processes.** Some cognitive processes begin when you receive information about other people and summarize it in a more general form. These summary processes are generally described as data-driven or "bottom-up" cognitions. Others, however, are conceptually driven or "top-down" processes because they are based on your conceptualizations and expectations in regard to other people. These two processes work together to facilitate social understanding.

Let us return to the handsome, friendly man who talks only of himself (see Figure 3-9). The information integration models describe how these four bits of information drive our perceptions. By intuitively adding or averaging them (either with or without weights), we formulate an initial impression. We also consider some higher-order conceptual processes that influence our interpretations. His self-focus may act as a central trait, changing the meaning of his handsome features and frequent smiles. Our implicit personality theory may lead us to make cautious inferences about his other characteristics, and perhaps even to classify him as a conceited person. Thus social cognition is not just a top-down or bottom-

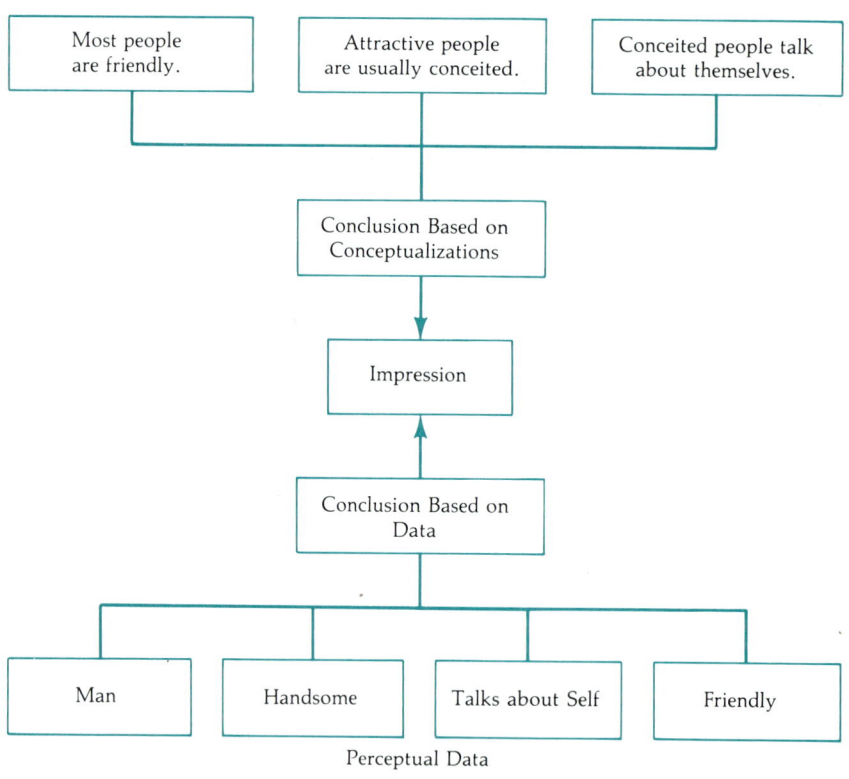

Figure 3-9 Data-driven and conceptually driven cognitive processes work together to select and organize the perceptual information we collect about other people. Our observations of a stranger may yield a generally favorable impression; he tends to talk about himself too much, but otherwise he is attractive and friendly. Our previous experiences with physically attractive people, however, may have convinced us that they tend to be conceited. This assumption, when combined with the observation that the stranger talks about himself, leads to a more negative reaction.

up process, but an up-down process that synthesizes perceptual data in conceptually meaningful frameworks.

■ Perceptual and Cognitive Biases

Despite Sherlock Holmes's claim that the ability to understand other people is quite elementary, we have seen that the process by which social knowledge is generated is active and complex. At a perceptual level, we gather and decipher the social meanings of others' nonverbal and verbal actions to formulate initial impressions. At a cognitive level, we integrate, organize, and structure this information.

In describing these processes, we have emphasized the rationality of social perceivers by comparing them with detectives investigating a crime. Although detectives are capable of brilliant deductions and masterful insights, however, they also make plenty of mistakes: they follow false leads, overlook important clues, and confidently assume their hunches are right even when they are wrong. When we form impressions in everyday situations, we also make mistakes. We are generally accurate observers of our fellow human beings, but we sometimes fall prey to a fascinating array of perceptual and cognitive biases.

Perceptual Biases

Human beings are impressively sophisticated observers, but we aren't infallible. Judgmental tendencies influence the way we see other people, leading to systematic perceptual distortions.

One bias, called the **halo effect,** occurs whenever your overall positive or negative impression of a person colors your perceptions of that person's individual characteristics. As Asch's studies suggested, people who are favorably evaluated are seen as all good, but people who are viewed with disfavor are seen as all bad (Cooper, 1981). The positive halo effect, however, tends to be stronger than the negative halo effect. Lending support to Will Rogers' claim that "I never met a man I didn't like," David O. Sears has documented the **person-positivity bias:** our tendency to evaluate human beings more positively than nonhuman objects. Sears found that we generally give people above-average ratings no matter what the question, particularly when we are judging single individuals rather than members of a group (Sears, 1983).

The **assumed similarity bias** also influences our judgments. When we form an impression of another person, we erroneously assume that he or she is similar to us. If, for example, we like a particular type of music or we consider ourselves to be outspoken, then we assume that the person we are observing also likes this type of music and tends to be outspoken. Assumed similarity is particularly pronounced in regard to characteristics that we have been encouraged to regard as negative. In this case, the bias is termed **projection,** since we tend to project to others those personal characteristics that we feel are socially undesirable (Holmes, 1981; Sherwood, 1981, 1982). Groups of heterosexual men in one study were led to believe that they became sexually aroused when they were shown slides depicting "handsome men in states of undress." Given their sexual preferences, they felt that this arousal was undesirable. In subsequent ratings, the men projected these feelings: they said that others were also sexually aroused (Bramel, 1962, p. 123; see Focus 3-4).

FOCUS 3-4

Applying Social Psychology: *Do our perceptual biases distort performance reviews?*

To increase effectiveness, many organizations carry out *performance reviews:* periodic appraisals of employee performance. Often, much of the review is based on information provided by people who are familiar with the employee's work. The review of a secretary's performance, for example, would be based on his or her boss's answers to a questionnaire that asked about such traits as reliability, initiative, and flexibility. Although these ratings provide critically important information, in recent years researchers in management and organizational psychology have come to recognize that these evaluations may be greatly distorted by perceptual biases (Rice, 1985).

To consider some examples of possible bias, let's look at a performance review system that is familiar to most students: faculty evaluations. Many colleges and universities use student ratings to evaluate their instructors. Although evidence indicates that students are good judges of teaching, their ratings often show telltale signs of halo effects, person positivity, assumed similarity, and projection. First, students who like their professors tend to be uniformly positive in their evaluations, while students who dislike their professors tend to be uniformly negative. Imagine rating a professor who teaches a 400-student lecture class. Although you rate the instructor as excellent on several general items, you should probably give a lower rating on the item "Did the course instructor provide individual help?" After all, you never even saw the instructor outside of class. If a halo effect occurs, however, you will persist in your generally positive ratings.

Second, consistent with the person-positivity bias, most students give their instructors positive evaluations. When Sears examined nearly a third of a million teacher evaluations turned in by students, he found that the professors were rated at 7.22, well above the midpoint of 5 on the 9-point scale. Furthermore, the profs were invariably rated more positively than the course or their professional characteristics (Sears, 1983).

Third, studies suggest that students who perform well in a class—and should therefore feel positive about themselves—generally rate their instructors and fellow students more favorably than students who perform poorly. Although these differential ratings may result from attempts at revenge on the part of students who are doing poorly, they may be brought about by assumed similarity and projection. Students who perform poorly may experience a loss of self-esteem, which they attribute outward so that they downgrade the performance of the instructor (see Marsh, 1980, 1982; Murray, 1983; Sherwood, 1981).

Given that evaluations provide so much useful information in so many different settings, what can be done to increase their accuracy? Social psychologists offer many recommendations. For one thing, evaluators can be trained to recognize and avoid their biases. For another, if evaluators can focus on aspects of performance that are less likely to be influenced by biases—such as nonverbal behavior or very specific verbal behaviors—their judgments are better indicators of true performance (Murray, 1983; other recommendations may be found in Boice, 1983, and Rice, 1985).

The **false-consensus effect** is closely related to the assumed similarity bias. Just as we assume the person we are observing is similar to us, we generally believe that our characteristics and actions are common in the general population. College students who preferred brown bread estimated that over 50% of all other college students preferred brown bread. White-bread eaters fixed the estimate at a more accurate 37% (Ross, Greene & House, 1977; see Mullen et al., 1985).

Confirmatory Biases

Our social cognitions help us sift through and organize a buzzing, blooming confusion of social data. Without some conceptual framework—an assumption, an expectation, a schema, an implicit personality theory—we would spend our entire lives trying to understand other people. These conceptually driven processes, however, sometimes provide this service at a cost: they can bias our conclusions, so that we become oversensitive to information that confirms our initial expectations. As Sherlock Holmes warned: "It is a capital mistake to theorize before you have all the evidence. It biases the judgment" (Doyle, 1938, p. 18). This kind of bias operates in many ways.

Remembering confirming data. As we noted earlier, our recall of information that is consistent with our schemata is often superior to our recall of schema-inconsistent information (Cohen, 1981, 1983; Howard & Rothbart, 1980; Park & Rothbart, 1982). In one study subjects watched a videotape of a woman, identified as either a waitress or a librarian, playing the piano, listening to classical music, drinking beer, watching television, and so on. As predicted, when subjects were asked to recall what they had seen with such questions as "What did the woman drink?" and "What kind of music did she listen to?" they tended to remember those features that were consistent with their stereotypes of librarians and waitresses. If they thought they were watching a librarian, for instance, they remembered that she listened to classical music, but thought that she drank wine rather than beer (Cohen, 1981).

Seeing confirming data. Our beliefs are sometimes so compelling that we unintentionally reinterpret the evidence so that it supports them. Recall, for example, Abbey's (1982) study of college men. Their assumptions about women led them to see sexual invitations where none existed.

Because we sometimes stretch our observations too far, our perceptions may be more biased when we possess a small amount of ambiguous information than when we have none at all! If we know nothing at all about a person, we have no evidence to reinterpret. But give us just a smidgen of information and suddenly our biases have something to work with. In one study of this process, subjects were shown a videotape of a 9-year-old white girl named Hannah. Some subjects were led to believe that Hannah came from a well-to-do family. She was seen playing in a tree-lined park; she lived in a large suburban home, and both parents were college graduates. Other subjects saw a poorer Hannah; she played in a stark, fenced-in schoolyard, her home was in a dilapidated urban neighborhood, and both parents were blue-collar workers with high school educations. Half the subjects saw Hannah take a short achievement test, while the remaining subjects did not see the testing portion of the videotape (Darley & Gross, 1983).

When subjects were asked to judge Hannah's work habits, motivation, maturity, and cognitive skills, they did so only reluctantly if they had not been shown the achievement test segment; after all, they didn't think they should make snap judgments about Hannah's intelligence solely on the basis of her family background. When the videotape included Hannah's performance, however, subjects' biases emerged in full force. Subjects who saw the poorer Hannah gave her lower scores on the test, didn't think she worked as hard, and thought she possessed less cognitive ability. Sometimes a little knowledge is a dangerous (or biasing) thing.

Confirmatory hypothesis testing. Mark Snyder and his colleagues have also shown that when we seek data to test our beliefs about other people, we favor information that confirms our beliefs. In a series of studies, women were given a list of hypotheses about their partners' possible characteristics. Some were given hypotheses that focused on introversion, while others' hypotheses focused on extraversion. Next, subjects were told to form an impression of their partner by asking her questions selected from a standard list. This list included questions that would generally be asked of people who were extraverted ("What would you do if you wanted to liven things up at a party?"; "What kind of situations do you seek out if you want to meet new people?") or introverted ("In what situations do you wish you could be more outgoing?"; "What things do you dislike about loud parties?"). As predicted, the subjects displayed a confirmatory bias. To test the hypothesis that their partner was an extravert, they chose questions that presupposed extraversion. Conversely, to test for introversion, the women chose questions that one would normally ask an introvert. Furthermore, because the biased questioning limited their partners' responses, subjects' expectations were confirmed. They acted as self-fulfilling prophecies—expectations that prompt other people to behave in a way that confirms the expectations (Snyder & Swann, 1978). (See "In Depth: Self-Fulfilling Prophecies," at the end of this chapter.)

Refusing to change our beliefs. Even when we do stumble across evidence that disconfirms our beliefs, we can still be very slow to change our minds. Lee Ross and his colleagues call this recalcitrant revision process **belief perseverance.** If you were a subject in one of Ross's studies, he would first lead you to generate a false belief of some sort. He might give you a false fact, such as "People who enjoy taking risks make good fire fighters," and ask you to write an essay explaining this "fact." Once the false belief was established, Ross would then tell you that the information given you was completely fictitious, manufactured solely for the experiment. But even when the evidence that formed the basis for your belief was discredited, belief perseverance would give your new inference a life of its own: "I realize that you made this information up for this study," you would say, "but I really think it's true that risk takers do make better fire fighters" (Anderson, Lepper, & Ross, 1980; Ross & Anderson, 1982; Ross & Lepper, 1980; Ross, Lepper, & Hubbard, 1975).

Beyond confirmatory biases. As scientists, social psychologists take care to avoid the confirmatory bias. The premise that people seek confirmatory information is so compelling that we tend to overlook studies that disconfirm this hypothesis. Clearly we sometimes fairly test our beliefs, and are capable of casting them off should they prove false. For example, although we tend to seek confirming information if we are trying to place an individual within a global category (such as "alcoholic" or "artist"), we seek disconfirming, surprising data when we are trying to develop an understanding of a single individual (Srull, 1983; Stern et al., 1984). We also tend to escape the restraints of the confirmatory bias if nothing in the situation primes our expectations (Bargh & Pietromonaco, 1982; Schneider & Blankmeyer, 1983), if we feel that the disconfirming evidence will provide important diagnostic information (Trope & Bassok, 1982), when we are motivated to form a clear, unbiased impression of the other person (Erber & Fiske, 1984; Strohmer & Chiodo, 1984), and when the situational information is incongruous (Lingle, Dukerich, & Ostrom, 1983). Thus, while the confirmatory bias is powerful, it is not overwhelming.

Heuristics and Biases

In his first case, *A Study in Scarlet*, Sherlock Holmes rapidly estimated the height of the murderer by applying two rules of thumb, or **heuristics.** First, because "the height of a man, in nine cases out of ten, can be told from the length of his stride," he measured the distance between footprints the culprit had left in the mud. Second, to check his calculation, he noted the position of a message scrawled on the wall, reasoning that "when a man writes on a wall, his instinct leads him to write about the level of his own eyes" (Doyle, 1938, p. 24). Although Holmes's heuristics didn't guarantee a correct answer, they pointed to a possible solution even when the available information was extremely limited.

Social perceivers also use heuristics to reduce their uncertainty about judgments and impressions. In many judgmental settings, we feel uncertain because the data we have don't provide us with sufficient information. When you go to buy a radio, for example, you probably can't judge the quality of the product just by looking it over and listening to it. Therefore, you assume that expensive radios are of better quality than cheaper ones and buy the most expensive radio you can afford (Einhorn, 1980). Conversely, in other situations you may have so much information that you can't possibly integrate it all to reach a decision. You want to weigh all the relevant factors carefully when you buy a new car, select a college to attend, or decide to get married, but you would need weeks or months to think through all the details. To reduce the uncertainty brought about by too much information, you rely on simplifying cognitive rules that reduce the "cost of thinking" (Shugan, 1980).

Heuristics help us process information efficiently and rapidly. Because they are cognition-saving shortcuts, however, they can systematically bias our impressions. For example, estimate the chances that Fred is a social psychologist, given the following information:

> Fred is either a social psychologist or a postal worker. He is married, with two children. He is liberal and ambitious. Fred is also scientifically minded, for he enjoys solving mathematics puzzles, but he is very interested in other people. His major form of recreation is reading.

What are the chances that Fred is a social psychologist?

(a) Greater than 8 chances out of 10.
(b) Between 6 and 8 chances out of 10.
(c) Between 4 and 6 chances out of 10.
(d) Between 2 and 4 chances out of 10.
(e) Less than 2 chances out of 10.

Did you think that Fred is probably a social psychologist? Did you choose fairly high odds—say, greater than 6 chances out of 10? If you did, then you may have relied on several general heuristics identified by Daniel Kahneman and Amos Tversky (Kahneman & Tversky, 1972, 1973, 1984; Tversky & Kahneman, 1973, 1981).

Representativeness. The first heuristic, **representativeness,** helps you choose an interpretation that best fits the available evidence. According to Kahneman and Tversky, to classify Fred as either a social psychologist or a postal worker, you roughly estimated the resemblance between Fred's qualities and your schemata pertaining to the two occupations. If you answered either *a* or *b*, you must have decided that Fred's qualities were more representative of a social psychologist than of a postal worker.

Availability. Did you try to answer the question by recalling various postal workers and social psychologists that you know? This heuristic is known as **availability;** it samples information available in your memory. If all the postal workers you know seem to be nonscientific and uninterested in people, but the social psychologists you know are scientifically minded and people-oriented, then this heuristic may have buttressed your conclusion that Fred is a social psychologist.

Anchoring/adjustment. If you made an initial estimate and then revised it after mulling over the evidence, then you used the **anchoring/adjustment** heuristic. You were asked to estimate the chances that Fred was a social psychologist (not postal worker). Therefore, when you read the description of Fred, you may have set your anchor by thinking to yourself: "Fred is definitely a social psychologist." Then you adjusted this estimate by selecting more conservative odds (such as 6 to 8 chances out of 10).

Heuristics and errors. Representativeness, availability, and anchoring/adjustment helped you process the information available to you and reach a conclusion about Fred. However, you sacrificed accuracy for ease if you decided that Fred was a social psychologist. First, Fred may have some qualities that seem appropriate to a social psychologist, but certainly many postal workers are also scientifically minded, interested in people, and bookish; the personality sketch really doesn't convey much information at all. Second, postal workers far outnumber social psychologists as an occupational group. Therefore, because the personality sketch says so little, a decision based on probability labels Fred a postal worker (see Focus 3-5). Third, if you let the anchor point favoring social psychologist color your judgment, you probably didn't revise your estimate enough. Kahneman and Tversky have repeatedly found that people insufficiently adjust their decisions once they are anchored. As we will see in the next section, heuristics can introduce errors into our understanding of others.

Inferential Biases

This section could appropriately be subtitled "People Infer the Funniest Things," or "Bloopers, Blunders, and Biases in Social Inferences." Although we are impressively sophisticated observers, we make errors. These biases stem in part from our use of the heuristics identified by Kahneman and Tversky. At a more general level, however, they occur because we are just too stingy when it comes to thinking. In Fiske and Taylor's terms, we are *cognitive misers:* we strive to increase our wealth of information about other people, but we can't spare the time or cognitive energy to do so. In consequence, we use "quick and dirty" cognitive processes that "move information through the system quickly, rather than thoroughly" (1984, p. 247). So we make mistakes.

Vividness influences interpretation. We sometimes let vivid but uninformative data steer our inferences. Consider the following situations (adapted from Loftus, 1979, and Reyes, Thomas, & Bower, 1980, respectively):

> Paul is describing an automobile accident he saw this morning.
> *Version 1:* One of the cars ran a stop sign and hit the other car.
> *Version 2:* One of the cars ran a stop sign and smashed into the other car.

Mary is talking about Pat, who got drunk at a party over the weekend.
Version 1: As Pat walked out the door, she staggered against a serving table, knocking a bowl to the floor.
Version 2: As Pat walked out the door, she staggered against a serving table, knocking a bowl of guacamole to the floor and splattering guacamole on the white shag carpet.

Vivid data, by definition, grab our attention: they are novel, interesting, and unexpected. Yet they may yield no more information than less colorful data. In each instance, both versions describe the same case, but the wording of the second version is more concrete and striking. As a result, subjects who read the second version estimate that the car that "smashed" into the other car was traveling faster, and that Pat was drunker when she "splattered" the guacamole.

Why is vivid information so influential? First, as Tversky and Kahneman argue (1974), vivid information may be more available in memory. Second, vivid data may be highly salient to us; if the information captures our attention, we may spend more time examining and processing it (Fiske & Taylor, 1984). Third, some vivid incidents may arouse our feelings and emotions, and these emotions may intensify our reactions to the information (Bower, 1981; Clark, Milberg, & Erber, 1984). (Although one or more of these processes may account for the impact of vivid information, Shelley E. Taylor and her colleagues recommend caution, as the cognitive

---

FOCUS 3-5

A Closer Look: *Can perceivers take advantage of statistical information when they make judgments?*

Sometimes perceivers must become intuitive statisticians to make judgments and decisions. If more students at your school major in psychology than in zoology, for example, probability theory tells you that the roommate you are randomly assigned is more likely to be a psychology major than a zoology major. Or if you flip a coin to see who has to wash the dishes, you realize that heads and tails are equally likely to come up. Similarly, to find out if night classes are easier than day classes, intuitively you would have to compile statistics pertaining to the number of times you got good and bad grades in classes that met during the night and during the day.

Most people aren't great intuitive statisticians. We tend to ignore the basic rules of probability and random events. Too, we commit many errors when we try to assess the degree of relationship, or co-variation, between two outcomes, such as type of class and grades. To understand these errors, test your statistical powers by completing the following problems.

1. Jules is gregarious and literary. Which of the following is more likely?
   (a) He majored in engineering.
   (b) He majored in engineering but later switched to journalism.
2. You flip a coin six times, obtaining the following sequence of tails (*T*) and heads (*H*): *T H T T T T.* On the next flip:
   (a) *T* and *H* are equally likely to come up.
   (b) *T* will probably come up.
   (c) *H* will probably come up.
3. Arie thinks that the use of heuristics causes errors in perception. What kind of outcome does Arie need to test his prediction?
   (a) A heuristics-user who doesn't make errors.
   (b) A heuristics-user who makes errors.

mechanisms that link vivid data to perceptions have not yet been clearly identified; see Fiske & Taylor, 1984; Taylor & Thompson, 1982.)

Case data overwhelm base rates. The power of vivid information is particularly evident when a single vivid case is compared with general summary information (base-rate data). Imagine that you are about to register for a class taught by Professor Green. As you read the results of a recent poll conducted by the student government, you are reassured to find that 75% of 150 students who had taken Green's course rated her above average. When you talk to a friend about your courses, though, he says: "Green. You want to take a course from Green? Are you crazy? My roommate had that course last session, and he hated it. He said she was terrible—disorganized, demanding, and there was no satisfying her. He got a D, after busting his tail all semester." Now what are you going to do? Should you take your friend's advice and avoid Green, or should you listen to the results of the opinion poll?

In such a situation, many people tend to rely more heavily on the concrete anecdotal information (case data) than on information that summarizes a large number of individuals' opinions (base-rate data). Logically speaking, your friend's remarks should slightly alter your judgment, perhaps move your estimate about the class down from 75% (on the basis of the opinion poll) to 70%. However, the vivid anecdote will probably

---

(c) A non-heuristics-user who doesn't make errors.
(d) A non-heuristics-user who makes errors.

Each problem illustrates a different intuitive bias. In answering question 1, the perceiver may be distracted by an assumption that engineers are rarely gregarious and literary. However, a person is less likely to switch from engineering to journalism than to remain in engineering. In fact, to switch from engineering to journalism, you must first major in engineering (Slovic, Fischhoff, & Lichtenstein, 1977).

Question 2 takes advantage of the *gambler's fallacy:* the mistaken idea that an event that hasn't occurred for some time is likely to occur in the near future. Consider gamblers playing dice. To win, they must roll a 7, but they haven't rolled a 7 for ten turns in a row. This string of non-7s, however, only encourages the gamblers, because they think, "It hasn't come up in ten rolls, so by the law of averages, it has to come up now." The dice, however, have no memory; the probability of 7 is always the same, no matter what the outcome has been before. Similarly, although a long series of tails occurred in question 2, these past outcomes don't change the fact that the probability of a head on the next flip is the same as the probability of a tail.

To answer the third question, you must identify the information needed to test the strength of a relationship between two variables. Unfortunately, although people realize that positive covariation information is valuable—for example, finding a heuristics-user who makes errors—they overlook the value of the other types of outcomes. In fact, alternative *a* describes the most informative outcome: if a heuristics-user doesn't make errors, then Arie's hypothesis is incorrect. Although many important perceptual processes depend on our ability to assess covariation between two variables, *our ability to understand covariation is limited* (Beyth-Marom & Fischhoff, 1983; Crocker, 1981, 1982).

overwhelm the statistical base-rate information; you decide to take another course.

Even when the base-rate data are clearly presented and easily interpreted, or when the case is described as very atypical, people continue to rely on the case data. In one study, subjects read a case study of a ne'er-do-well 43-year-old woman who collected welfare for 13 years. Constantly pregnant but never married, she supposedly spent her welfare money on expensive foods and gambling. However, the subjects were also given factual information that disconfirmed the societal myths suggested by the case: the base-rate data explained that 90% of all welfare recipients are off the rolls in four years. Yet when subjects described their feelings about people on welfare, the base-rate information had little influence; the vivid case data prompted a negative reaction, even though they had been told that the case was atypical (Hamill, Wilson, & Nisbett, 1980).

Irrelevant information weakens the effect of relevant information. Complete this simple thought experiment. Let us suppose that a panel of psychologists has developed short personality sketches of 100 successful male professionals. Their sample included exactly 70 engineers and 30 lawyers.

> *Case 1:* You are given no information whatever about an individual chosen at random from the sample. What is the probability that this man is one of the 70 engineers in the sample of 100?
> ____ chances out of 100.
> *Case 2:* Dick is a 30-year-old man. He is married with no children. A man of superior ability and motivation, he promises to be quite successful in his field. He is well liked by his colleagues. What is the probability that this man is one of the 70 engineers in the sample of 100?
> ____ chances out of 100.

When Kahneman and Tversky gave their subjects these problems, they discovered the *dilution effect:* the tendency for irrelevant information to weaken the effect of relevant information. Most subjects got the first case correct. As nothing is known about the person, they relied on base-rate information. The sample consisted of 70 engineers, so they assumed that the chances were 70 out of 100 that a randomly selected individual would be an engineer. When subjects encountered case 2, however, they abandoned the base-rate information. Although they agreed that the personality data were irrelevant, these data diluted the impact of base-rate information. On this question, most subjects estimated the chances were 50 out of 100 (Kahneman & Tversky, 1973; see Kruglanski, Friedland, & Farkash, 1984).

Researchers also believe that irrelevant information can dilute the impact of anecdotal case data. For example, as part of one study, subjects made predictions about a student who was extremely punctual. Because most subjects assumed that punctuality should improve grades, they felt that Henry, who "never arrives late to appointments or meetings," would achieve a grade point average (GPA) of about 3.3. When, however, irrelevant information was added—Henry has a brother and two sisters, he visits his grandparents occasionally, and he goes to sleep around midnight—then subjects felt that Henry's GPA must be closer to 3.0. Apparently the irrelevant information diluted the value of the relevant (Zukier, 1982; see also Nisbett, Zukier, & Lemley, 1981).

Mistakes in Understanding

People make mistakes. We make various perceptual errors. We fail to test our assumptions thoroughly. We let vivid but irrelevant information steer our inferences. We ignore base-rate data that summarize a large number of individuals' opinions and relevant information that is embedded in irrelevant facts. To make matters worse, we have little awareness of our fallibility. We are a little like the endearing but bumbling Scotland Yard detectives in the Sherlock Holmes tales. "It's an open-and-shut case," they announce before proclaiming their erroneous interpretation of the available evidence. Invariably quite confident, the detectives are also invariably quite incorrect.

Some of the earliest studies of social perception demonstrated the tendency to overconfidence by staging "crimes" before large audiences. In the midst of a lecture, an accomplice bursts in, runs to the front of the room, berates, assaults, knifes, shoots, or steals something from the speaker, and then escapes. After the commotion dies down, the witnesses describe the assailant. Accuracy in these situations is influenced by many factors, but distortions are usually very prevalent. Not only do witnesses overlook the assailant's physical appearance, such as hair color and type of clothing, but they also misremember important details of the crime itself; they may recall a weapon when none was used or a shouted curse that was never uttered.

Despite these errors, these fallible witnesses are often very confident of their descriptions. Although we put more stock in the comments of a witness who boasts, "I got a good look at her; I'm absolutely certain she had red hair and wore Nike tennis shoes," studies have shown that confidence isn't correlated with accuracy. In one illustrative study, the witnesses to a staged crime were asked to pick out the perpetrator's picture from a lineup of photographs. The results were sobering: right or wrong, subjects who selected someone from the lineup were very confident that they were correct (Wells & Murray, 1982). These findings should serve as a warning that eyewitness testimony, which plays such a large role in criminal trials, can be misleading. The most confident witness is not always the most correct witness, even when testifying under oath (see Malpass & Devine, 1984, and Wells & Murray, 1984, for reviews; see Focus 3-6).

Why are we so overconfident? Why don't we recognize that our judgments are fallible, that we may be wrong even when we are certain we are right? Our heuristics and cognitive biases undoubtedly contribute to our self-confidence. Since we tend to prefer data that confirm our assumptions, our perceptions are validated more frequently than they are invalidated. In estimating our confidence, we may also rely on an availability heuristic that remembers our successes better than our failures. Our errors are self-erasing.

The *I-knew-it-all-along phenomenon,* or **hindsight bias,** also helps us forget our previous judgmental errors. As we noted briefly in Chapter 1, people often unwittingly change their beliefs about their earlier estimates of events once the events have occurred. For example, when investigators asked subjects to estimate their chances of correctly answering such factual questions as "Which is longer, the Suez or Panama canal?" their estimates of their ability to do so without coaching rose sharply once they

FOCUS 3-6

Controversy in Social Psychology:
Should psychologists warn jurors about eyewitnesses' inaccuracies?

"Is there any doubt in your mind?" asked the prosecutor.
"No doubt," the witness answered.
"Could you possibly be mistaken?"
"No, I am not mistaken," the witness reaffirmed.

On the basis of this witness's testimony, William Jackson was convicted of rape. He spent five years in prison before the police discovered the identity of the actual rapist (see Figure 3-10).

Jackson's case is not unique. Aaron Lee Owens of Oakland, California, spent nine years in prison for two murders he didn't commit. Robert Dillon spent three months and $30,000 trying to clear himself of armed robbery charges. A former Baptist Sunday school teacher was released after serving five years in prison when the actual perpetrator of the crime confessed. And in Seattle, a 31-year-old man spent a year trying to clear himself of a rape charge.

These tragic errors in our justice system highlight the unreliability of our memories and impressions. Although witnesses are generally quite certain their identifications are accurate, their memories can be biased by many factors: the way the police phrased their questions during the investigation; the race of the defendant; the use of photographs for identification before the suspect appears in a lineup; and the age of the witness and suspect (see Wells & Loftus, 1984, for a review). Because of these biases, some psychologists believe that jurors should be warned about the unreliability of eyewitness testimony. Elizabeth F. Loftus, a leading researcher in the area of eyewitness accuracy, advocates the use of psychologists as expert witnesses in some cases. Their testimony could "provide jurors with additional information to better equip them to evaluate the identification evidence fully and properly." Jurors often display *overbelief*—unquestioning acceptance of a confident witness's testimony; the psychologist could remind them of factors that can undermine accuracy (Loftus, 1983a, p. 568, 1983b).

Other psychologists disagree with Loftus (McCloskey & Egeth, 1983a, 1983b). According to their view, expert testimony by a psychologist may be unnecessary; jurors are already supposed to be skeptical. In addition, although some studies suggest that eyewitnesses are unreliable, far more research is needed. These researchers also worry that if the defense hired a psychologist to discredit an eyewitness, the prosecutor might hire a psychologist to support the accuracy of the eyewitness's account.

At present, the issue remains undecided. Although we clearly need to continue to study eye-

knew the correct answer (Fischhoff, 1977; G. Wood, 1978). In a related study, before an election some subjects predicted the percentage of votes each major candidate in a presidential election would obtain. Other subjects provided estimates *after* the election. Even though the postelection subjects were told to forget about the actual election results and base their estimates on their original predictions, they still predicted an outcome closer to the actual results. Unlike foresight, hindsight is 20/20 (Leary, 1982).

■ Summary

The ability to observe and analyze other people may be a remarkable gift, but it is one we have all received. We gather information and form initial impressions through **social perception,** and then transform this infor-

witness accuracy, we may not have time to wait for all the results. In the words of one legalist, "for innocent men and women wrongly accused because of mistaken identifications, expert psychological testimony still offers a beacon of hope" (Frazzini, 1981, p. xx).

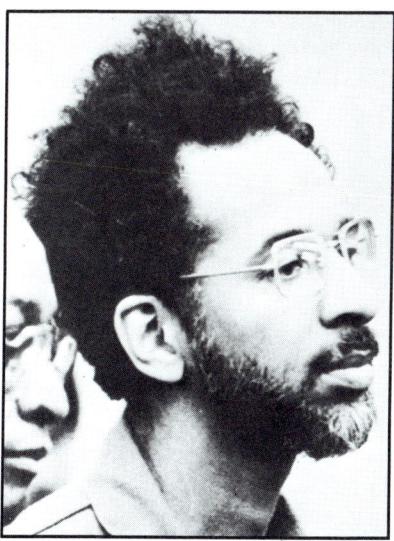 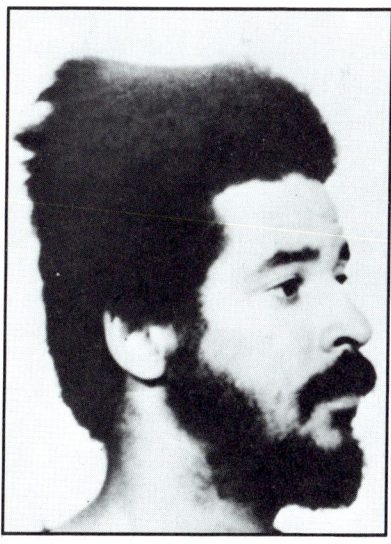

Figure 3-10 William Jackson, pictured at right, spent five years in prison for two rapes. He was released when Dr. Edward Jackson, Jr. (*left;* no relation) confessed.

mation into a coherent picture of the person through **social cognition.** At the perceptual level, we acquire information about the people we meet by taking note of the **nonverbal cues** transmitted by their behavior. Other people's looks (physical characteristics), body movements **(kinesic cues),** the way they express themselves **(paralanguage),** and the distance they maintain from others **(proxemic cues),** all convey information about their moods, emotions, dispositions (such as friendliness or dominance), and even truthfulness. Verbal messages are important sources of information as well, for people reveal their traits and qualities both in the *semantic content* of their words (the words themselves) and in the *expressive content* (implicit meanings associated with the words).

A number of cognitive processes help us organize these perceptual data into a coherent understanding of others' traits and characteristics. According to **information integration theory,** bits of information are combined in processes that resemble adding or averaging, and in some cases one bit of information may be weighted more heavily than another. Solomon Asch's research shows that we also organize our perceptions of other people by changing the meaning of some of the available information. According to Asch's **change-of-meaning hypothesis,** a trait such as calmness is interpreted as serenity when it's attributed to a warm person, but is translated as calculation when it's displayed by a cold person. Our perceptions of other people are also influenced by **implicit personality theories** about the relationships among various traits. These theories help us reach beyond individuals' observed characteristics to make inferences about their unobserved qualities. Last, our perceptions and memories are regulated by **schemata:** networks of cognitive generalizations that organize and guide the processing of social information. Overall, then, our understanding of others is shaped by both **data-driven cognitive processes** and **conceptually driven cognitive processes.**

These perceptual and cognitive processes can lead to mistaken inferences about other people. At the perceptual level, the **halo effect, person-positivity bias, assumed similarity bias, projection,** and **false-consensus effect** all distort our understanding of others. At the cognitive level, confirmatory biases can create a tendency to validate our initial expectations, to remember confirming information, to reinterpret perceptual cues, to test our hypotheses about others selectively, and to hold fast to beliefs even after they have been disconfirmed **(belief perseverance). Heuristics**—cognitive rules of thumb that facilitate the processing of information—include **representativeness, availability,** and **anchoring/adjustment.** These heuristics increase our efficiency, but we sometimes apply them when they aren't appropriate. Vivid but trivial information can also have too great an impact on our perceptions, as can single cases and irrelevant information. If we were aware of these errors, we could be on guard against them. Usually, however, we are overly confident in the accuracy of our judgments. Moreover, even when we do receive feedback that conflicts with our assumptions about others, the **hindsight bias** prompts us to conclude, "I knew it all along."

■ For More Information

1. *The Complete Sherlock Holmes,* by A. Conan Doyle (1938), includes all of the exploits of the greatest social perceiver of them all.

2. *Telling Lies: Clues to Deceit in the Marketplace, Politics, and Marriage,* by Paul Ekman (1985), reviews what we currently know about deception: the nature of lies, the reasons why we lie (and perhaps should lie), and how liars betray themselves nonverbally.

3. *Social Cognition,* by Susan T. Fiske and Shelley E. Taylor (1984), reviews and synthesizes previous theory and research on the cognitive processes perceivers use to understand other people.

4. *Body Politics: Power, Sex, and Nonverbal Communication,* by Nancy Henley (1977), is a scholarly analysis of sex differences and exploitive sexism in nonverbal behavior.

5. *Nonverbal Communication in Human Interaction,* by Mark L. Knapp (1978), is an excellent source of information on all forms of nonverbal behavior.

6. "The Cognitive Perspective in Social Psychology," by Hazel Markus and R. B. Zajonc (1985), provides an insider's view of research and theory dealing with the mental processes that guide our perceptions. This article is a chapter in the *Handbook of Social Psychology* (Lindzey & Aronson, 1985).

7. *Human Inference: Strategies and Shortcomings in Social Judgment,* by Richard E. Nisbett and Lee Ross (1980), offers a fascinating look at the pitfalls and problems human beings encounter when they try to make decisions and judgments about themselves and other people.

8. "Telling More than We Can Know: Verbal Reports on Mental Processes" (*Psychological Review,* 1977) presents Richard E. Nisbett and Timothy D. Wilson's controversial but compelling arguments concerning our inability to gain awareness of our internal cognitive processes.

9. *Person Perception,* by David J. Schneider, Albert H. Hastorf, and Phoebe C. Ellsworth (1979), reviews 50 years of social-psychological research dealing with impression formation.

10. "Quest for Accuracy in Person Perception: A Matter of Pragmatics," by William B. Swann, Jr. (*Psychological Review,* 1984), is a theoretical article that presents an interpersonal view of person perception. Swann's theory is based on the assumption that people use a number of interpersonal strategies to enhance the accuracy of their social perceptions.

IN DEPTH

Self-Fulfilling Prophecies

The **self-fulfilling prophecy** is one of the most intriguing concepts in social psychology. This term was introduced in 1948 by Robert Merton, who speculated that a perceiver's inaccurate beliefs about other people can evoke new behaviors that make the original inaccurate conceptions come true. According to Merton, a vivacious woman who is perceived as boring can become a bore. An honest man who is judged to be a criminal can become a criminal. Perhaps even a dullard who is perceived to be brilliant will become intelligent.

Over the years Merton's thoughts on self-fulfilling prophecies were questioned by social psychologists, but little progress was made toward understanding this puzzling phenomenon. All this changed in 1968, when Robert Rosenthal and Lenore Jacobson published the results of a remarkable study titled *Pygmalion in the Classroom*. The participants in the project were elementary school teachers and their pupils. At the start of the project the teachers were told that some of their students were "late bloomers"—students who display only average abilities during their early years but later make great academic gains. In actuality, the students were selected at random from class rolls. In their abilities they were indistinguishable from their classmates. Yet when the researchers returned eight months later, these "unusual" children had changed. They performed better on a series of tests than students in a control group, and their teachers rated them more positively than the controls. Their IQ scores rose by as much as 30 points.

The Pygmalion study was greeted with skepticism: many people did not believe that expectations could have such powerful effects on students' achievements. The study, however, stimulated hundreds of subsequent investigations. Researchers searched for the Pygmalion effect in educational, industrial, therapeutic, and interpersonal settings. These studies, too, generally found that prophecies are self-fulfilling (Harris & Rosenthal, 1985).

But how does the self-fulfilling prophecy work? What processes enable the inaccurate belief to become true? Researchers are continuing to explore these questions. One possible model is shown in Table 3-8. According to this view, the process begins when the perceiver develops expectations concerning another individual (the target). Next, the perceiver acts on the basis of these expectations. Third, the target person changes his or her behavior to respond to the expectations held by the perceiver. Finally, the target internalizes the dispositions implied by his or her behavior. The prophecy is fulfilled (Darley & Fazio, 1980; Fazio, Effrein, & Falender, 1981).

Table 3-8 also applies the model to the original Pygmalion study. First, the teachers accepted the false information about some of their students. They formed their prophecies. Next, their expectations altered the way they interacted with the students. Many teachers, for example, created a warmer, more positive learning climate for the late bloomers. They also gave late bloomers more feedback about their progress, and even taught them more information (Rosenthal, 1973). Next, the students responded to their teachers' efforts; they asked more questions, worked harder on assignments, and literally learned more. In the final stage, the students altered their self-concepts to match their newly gained academic abilities.

Overall, studies of self-fulfilling prophecies support William B. Swann, Jr.'s **interpersonal model of perception.** According to Swann, social perception is a dynamic interpersonal process. While we tend to think of perceivers as passive observers who simply record their impressions of the people they meet, we actively influence the people we are perceiving. Moreover, the targets of our perceptions play an equally active role in the process. At times we change our identity so that it matches the perceiver's judgment. As we saw in Chapter 2, however, we do not always accept behavioral feedback from others. When perceivers are too far off the mark, we battle for our own view of who we are, and force the perceivers to alter their judgments. We shouldn't forget that the targets have their own prophecies, too (Swann, 1984).

TABLE 3 – 8

A model of the interactional sequence underlying behavior confirmation.

Step	Process	Example
1	Perceiver develops expectations concerning the target	Teachers believe that some of their students are late bloomers
2	Perceiver acts on the basis of this expectation	Teachers show more warmth toward late bloomers, teach late bloomers more material
3	Target person changes his or her behavior in response to perceiver's behavior	Late bloomers learn more, get higher test scores, show improvement
4	Target internalizes the dispositions implied by his or her behavior	Late bloomers redefine themselves as intelligent and as good students

F O U R

Attribution

Attribution theory
    Who makes attributions?
    Why do we make attributions?
        Explanatory attributions
        Predictive attributions
        Self-serving attributions
        Interpersonal attributions
    Where and when do we make attributions?
    What kinds of attributions do we make?
    How do we make attributions?
        Correspondent inference theory
        Self-perception theory
        The cube model
    In summary
Attributional biases
    Biases in self-attributions
        The ubiquity of the self-serving bias
        Why do we make self-serving attributions?
    Observer biases
        Overattribution
        Defensive attribution
        The actor/observer difference
Attributional theories
    Attributions and stressful events
        Learned helplessness
        Mastery orientation and reactions to failure
        Type A personalities and uncontrollable outcomes
    Attributions and psychological health
        Attribution retraining
        Changing attributions through misattribution
Summary
For more information
In depth: Attributions and emotions

The year is 1844. Ignaz Semmelweis, a member of the medical staff of the Vienna General Hospital, is perplexed by the high mortality rates among maternity cases. The death rate is 2.3% in one ward, but in his ward the rate is 8.2%. Some of his colleagues blame the high rate on unknown cosmic forces, but Semmelweis wonders why these mystical causes leave the other ward untouched. Others suggest that overcrowding is the cause, but when the population of his ward dwindles (patients begin to refuse assignment there), the rate remains high. Semmelweis changes the delivery procedures, the routine followed by priests in their visits to the dying, and the examination procedures used by the medical students, but nothing works. He is bewildered.

One day one of Semmelweis's colleagues cuts himself accidentally with a scalpel during an autopsy. Soon he develops the same symptoms of "childbed fever" seen in the mothers. Although the link between microorganisms and infection is not yet known, Semmelweis realizes that unseen "cadaveric matter" from the scalpel must have caused his colleague's illness (and eventual death). From this clue it is only one step to the assumption that the women have been infected by staff members who have gone straight to the delivery room after performing dissections. To test his idea, Semmelweis orders the staff to wash their hands in a solution of chlorinated lime to prevent the spread of infection. His assumption is confirmed: the mortality rate drops dramatically (Sinclair, 1909).

Semmelweis solved his puzzle by searching for causes. We, too, search for the causes of actions and events. When we feel feverish, we wonder, "Am I coming down with a cold?" When a friend treats us harshly, we wonder, "Did I do something to upset him?" When we learn that a married couple is getting a divorce, we ask, "Why are they splitting up?" Like the scientist striving to explain an anomalous observation, a physician seeking the cure for an illness, or an engineer studying the reasons for a bridge's collapse, people in everyday situations constantly form inferences about the causes of behaviors and events. Such inferences are called **attributions.**

Because we are so accustomed to making attributions, we often fail to recognize their far-reaching consequences. They are, for example, a key cog in the perceptual machinery that powers our understanding of ourselves and other people. Would you feel comfortable if you had no idea what caused you to behave the way you do? If you couldn't identify the causes of a friend's anger or your lover's thoughtlessness? Attributions also influence our emotions. Happiness becomes guilt, for example, when we know our income tax refund was caused by cheating rather than legitimate deductions. Attributions may even help us overcome adversity. Just as Semmelweis was able to prevent childbed fever once he diagnosed the cause, through attributions we can identify the causes of problematic aspects of our personal lives. And once we locate the cause, we can sometimes take the steps needed to rid ourselves of the problem.

Social psychologists recognized the tremendous impact of attributions on our social lives in the 1960s. Since that time, researchers have worked long and hard to answer a number of basic questions about attributions. Initially these efforts focused on such issues as: What is an attribution? Why do people search for causes? And what cognitive processes underly our ability to make sense of others' actions? While seeking answers to these queries, researchers discovered that causal attributions aren't always accurate attributions. Like the perceptual and cognitive biases discussed in Chapter 3, attributional biases sometimes distort our conclusions about causality. More recently, however, social psychologists began to apply attributional principles to other areas of social psychology. Researchers studying close relationships, for example, undertook studies of couples' attributions about their arguments. Many practical problems—such as students' loss of motivation in school and psychological adjustment—were also reexamined in the light cast by attribution theory.

This chapter is organized along the lines of these historical researches. First, we explore *attribution theory:* a social-psychological explanation of our perceptions of causality. Second, we consider several *attributional biases:* assumptions and tendencies that shape our causal inferences. Third, we turn to theories that are based on attribution theory, but are focused on specific problems. These *attributional theories* deal with such topics as emotions, motivation, educational achievement, and health.

■ Attribution Theory

In ancient times, two women claimed to be the mother of an infant, and no amount of questioning could identify the liar. So the case was brought before King Solomon, who proposed a simple compromise: the baby would be cut in half, and each woman would receive an equal portion. The first woman accepted Solomon's decision. The second woman, however, was so upset that she withdrew her claim to the child and begged Solomon to turn him over to the other woman.

If you sat on Solomon's throne, would you be able to identify the true mother of the infant? Probably. Like the king, you would judge the two women by interpreting their reactions to the decision. The first woman, by agreeing to the compromise, reveals her deception: why would the child's mother agree to such a deadly bargain? The second woman's behavior, in contrast, offers unambiguous evidence of her sincerity: she cares so deeply for the child that she will give him up in order to save his life. If you attributed her behavior to a parent's love for her child, you are as wise as Solomon; he ruled in favor of the second woman.

King Solomon's truth test illustrates our tendency to make inferences about the causes of other people's actions. As Fritz Heider explained in his insightful monograph *The Psychology of Interpersonal Relations* (1958), in our day-to-day interactions with other people we strive to understand what causes actions and events. Drawing a parallel between the perceiver and the scientist, Heider proposed that people achieve an understanding of the world around them by relying on certain intuitive causal principles. Heider himself was particularly interested in the "common-sense psychology" that we use when we explain other people's actions in terms of dispositional characteristics. Just as King Solomon identified the more loving mother by studying the women's reactions, we make judgments about others' dispositional characteristics—personality traits, attitudes, emotions, and the like—by asking, "Why did he do that?" or "What did she think she was doing?"

In the years since Heider outlined the framework of attribution theory, researchers have sought answers to some very basic questions. Like investigative reporters collecting the basic facts before writing their articles, these investigations have concentrated on the who, why, where, when, what, and how of attributions.

Who Makes Attributions?

Heider's answer to the question "Who makes attributions?" is "Everyone"; to Heider, every person is an intuitive psychologist, formulating attributions about events and behaviors. In support of this assumption, studies of people in everyday social situations have shown that we engage spontaneously in causal thinking. Even when no mention is made of causality, attributional remarks are made by all sorts of people: journalists explaining sporting and political events; members of parole boards discussing the causes of crime; Ann Landers helping the lovelorn understand the origin of their problems; students talking about why they passed a test; gamblers ruminating about their bets; and employees discussing their performance with their employer. Bernard Weiner, after reviewing 17 studies of spontaneous causal thinking, concludes: "there is unequivocal documentation of attributional activity" (1985a, p. 74).

Why Do We Make Attributions?

Jill and Jack get divorced after two years. Sitting alone in her apartment, drinking wine from a glass she received as a wedding gift, Jill wonders why the marriage didn't work out.

Why does Jill ruminate about the causes of her divorce? What purpose is served when we identify the causes of behaviors and events? Although some theorists initially oversimplified the value of attributions, viewing them as just one more way for an individual to form an impression of someone else, we now know that attributions fulfill a variety of functions for the attributor (Forsyth, 1980; Kelley, 1982).

Explanatory attributions. Heider, in his original theory, emphasized the function of **explanatory attributions.** Attributions help us achieve intellectual mastery of our world. Just as scientists develop theories to explain their findings, we formulate attributions to understand our social world. By seeking attributional explanations, Jill can come to understand the factors that undermined her marriage. Without attributional explanations, her divorce would leave her baffled and unsure of herself (see Figure 4-1).

Predictive attributions. Attributions help us predict future actions and events. As Harold H. Kelley (1971a) explains, attributors seek more than simply knowledge; their latent goal is the "effective management" of themselves and their environment. Once Jill understands the causes of her divorce, her future becomes more predictable. If she decides that Jack was primarily to blame, then she can hope to find happiness in the future. If, in contrast, she decides that her flaws contributed to the downfall of the marriage, she can work out ways to avoid similar mistakes

Attributions help us understand our social experiences. If a woman were waiting for a long overdue telephone call from her lover, for example, she would probably ponder the reason why the call could be late. Perhaps he was tied up in traffic. Or had to go out of town on business. Or maybe he has a date with someone else.

Figure 4-1 Why do people make attributions? In some cases, we just feel better if we know the explanation for an event or action.
© 1985 by King Features Syndicate, Inc. World rights reserved.

FOCUS 4-1

Applying Social Psychology: *How do parole boards make their decisions?*

Social psychologists are currently applying their theories and methods to many areas of the criminal justice system. Some researchers are examining the psychological foundations of our laws and criminal codes. Others are asking questions about the legal process itself: How do juries reach decisions? What impact does the judge's instructions to jurors have on their decisions? What is the best way to present evidence so that it has the most impact on jurors? Research in these areas improves our understanding of the legal system and identifies ways in which it can be improved (Monahan & Loftus, 1982).

Studies of parole decisions illustrate the benefits of applying social psychology to the criminal justice system. Consider, for example, a 25-year-old man who is up for parole. At the time of his incarceration, he was unemployed and divorced. He is serving a sentence for murder in the second degree. He and an acquaintance had been talking in a bar when an argument broke out. A push led to a punch. During the scuffle he shot the victim several times. He surrendered himself to police, and pleaded guilty at his arraignment. His conduct in prison has been exemplary. Should this man be paroled?

By reviewing this information about the nature of the crime, the offender's record while in prison, and other personal information, members of the parole board make a prediction about future behavior: Will this individual commit crimes if he is released from prison? According to John Carroll and his colleagues, decisions about parole are based fundamentally on attributions concerning the cause of the crime (Carroll, 1979; Carroll & Coates, 1980; Carroll & Payne, 1977; Carroll & Ruback, 1980; Lurigio & Carroll, 1985). As they review each case, the members of a parole board generally try to decide whether the individual was influenced by situational pressures or whether internal, personal qualities caused the crime. In this case, the man's background and his good record in prison suggest that situational factors prompted the action. Emotional pressures brought about by unemployment may also have contributed to the crime.

Carroll has also found that people who serve on parole boards make decisions somewhat differently from nonexperts. Although both groups tend to agree on the seriousness of the crime, they diverge on predictions of recidivism. Experts, for example, more readily parole someone who has been convicted of murder because they know that murder is a statistical rarity that is often prompted by interpersonal factors. Nonexperts, in contrast, see murder as such an extreme event that they assume the perpetrator is "a murderer" by nature. Experts are also much more likely to base parole decisions on prisoners' records during their incarceration.

These studies illustrate how applied research can be used to advance our understanding of human behavior *and* solve social problems. Carroll's work

in future relationships. Another example of **predictive attributions** comes from the social psychology of law. As Focus 4-1 reveals, decisions about when an offender can be released from prison may sometimes be based on attributional processes.

Self-serving attributions. Heider feels that the attributor is a rational processor of information who attempts to understand and control his or her existence by achieving a veridical perception of reality. He admits, however, that our causal inferences do more than explain and predict. In some situations, we formulate **self-serving attributions:** attributions biased to protect, maintain, or extend beliefs about the self (see Chapter 2). If Jill's attributions are self-serving, she may attribute the divorce to

Attributions and criminal justice. Our jurisprudential system is, in a sense, a formalized system for making attributions about the causes of behaviors and events. For example, in a murder trial the jury must decide if the defendant caused another's death, and also make decisions about intentionality and motive.

lends support to the basic assumptions of attribution theory and also yields useful information about how parole boards operate. Carroll used his findings to develop a set of guidelines for making and monitoring parole decisions, and many of his suggestions have been adopted by his state's parole system. Research such as Carroll's enriches both social psychology and society.

ATTRIBUTION 151

Jack's negative characteristics—his selfishness, insensitivity, demandingness, or undesirable habits.

Interpersonal attributions. People often find themselves in the position of having to describe the reasons for their actions. When motives for behavior are questioned, when actions lead to undesirable outcomes, or when a behavior is misunderstood by others, people try to clarify the causes of their actions. When descriptions of the causes of events are exchanged by two or more individuals, these **interpersonal attributions** serve the function of presenting ourselves as we wish other people to see us.

When Jill discusses her causal perceptions with her friends, she may try to present her case in the most positive light possible. To make certain that they won't think that she is to blame for the divorce, she may describe all the things she did to save the marriage, and all the things Jack did to ruin it.

Where and When Do We Make Attributions?

Although Heider assumed that people routinely formulate attributions about other people, researchers now feel that attributional processes must first be instigated by situational factors. Surrounded by so many behaviors and events that could be studied and explained, we make attributions only when the situation prompts us to do so (Berscheid et al., 1976).

Many researchers believe that attributional processing is switched on whenever the people or objects we encounter attract our attention. Susan T. Fiske and Shelley E. Taylor (1984) have traced attributions back to two properties of the stimulus: vividness and salience. *Vividness* refers to the intensity of the stimulus event. A shout or a tacky Hawaiian shirt are vivid stimuli, and therefore they are more likely to attract our attention than a whisper or a gray sweatshirt. Similarly, we are much more likely to search for causes when the people we encounter possess novel attributes (a physical handicap, for example) or engage in intense behaviors (Fiske, 1980). *Salience* refers to the distinctiveness of the stimulus event in a given context. People who don't fit into a setting—a little girl at an adult party, a lone white person in an otherwise all-black group, a person seated alone when others are in groups—grab our attention and initiate causal analyses. These effects suggest that attributions are often data-driven; they are instigated and guided by the objects that we are perceiving (Bargh, 1984; Fiske & Taylor, 1984; McArthur, 1981; Smith & Miller, 1983; Winter, Uleman, & Cunniff, 1985). (Data-driven cognitive processing is discussed in Chapter 3.)

Attributional processing can also be directly instigated by explicit "why" questions. You may not think twice about why you like a particular song, but if Dick Clark asks you, "Why do you like this song?" you will be forced to come up with an explanation ("It has a good beat, and you can dance to it"). Similarly, if one of your co-workers is a little withdrawn, you may think nothing of it. If, however, somebody asks you to explain why your co-worker is so quiet, then you may begin to search for a satisfactory reason (Enzle & Schopflocher, 1978; Hastie, 1984).

We also undertake attributional analyses when events and actions violate our *expectations*. The world we encounter is usually so predictable and routine that it doesn't puzzle us in the least. To understand it, we need only rely on assumptions based on previous analyses. When we confront the unexpected, however, our attributional machinery is much more likely to be set in motion. What questions, if any, would you ask yourself in each of the following situations?

Situation 1: You consider yourself an above-average tennis player. When you play a match with a friend who is just beginning to learn the game, you win in straight sets.

Situation 2: You put in overtime developing a new marketing strategy for a prospective client. The presentation goes very well, and you are confident you'll get the contract. The client chooses another company.

In situation 1, you probably expected to win. Therefore, after the match you probably didn't think too much about the cause of your success. In situation 2, your failure, because it was unexpected, should have prompted you to ask many attributional questions: Why did this happen? Was there a problem with the presentation? Are my ideas bad? (Weiner, 1985b; Wong & Weiner, 1981).

The instigating impact of disconfirmed expectations on attributional processing has been demonstrated in a variety of settings (Bettman & Weitz, 1983; Clary & Tesser, 1983; Lau & Russell, 1980; Pyszczynski & Greenberg, 1981). In one study, male subjects were first led to believe that they were supposed to form an impression of another person. They then observed an experimenter ask another subject if she would be willing to perform a small favor (fill out a brief questionnaire) or a large favor (complete several hours of personality measures). After the small request, subjects expected compliance; the large request, however, led to an expectation of refusal. The other subject, who was actually a confederate, either agreed to or refused the request, thereby confirming or disconfirming subjects' expectations. Next, subjects were given the opportunity to examine the confederate's answers to some general questions ("What are your hobbies?") or her answers to questions that were related to helping ("Are you the type of person who enjoys doing favors for other people?"). As Figure 4-2 shows, subjects chose more helping-relevant items when their expectations were disconfirmed. Thus actions that take us by surprise instigate attributions, but routine behaviors stimulate little in the way of attributional analysis (Pyszczynski & Greenberg, 1981).

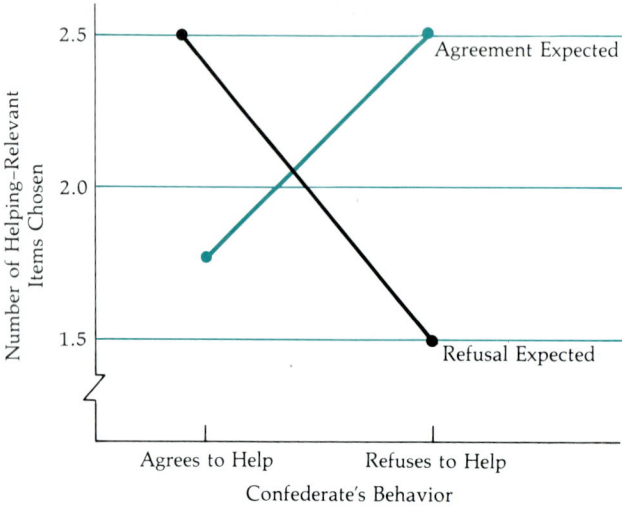

Figure 4-2 Instigating attributions. Subjects' expectations were disconfirmed when (1) they expected helping behavior but the other person (the confederate) refused to help, and (2) they expected a refusal but the other person agreed to help. In both of these conditions, the attributors sought additional information.

What Kinds of Attributions Do We Make?

Many specific attributions have been identified by researchers. To note just a few, students who pass a test sometimes credit good luck, intensive study efforts, the easiness of the test, or their own ability. Alcoholics explain their problem by blaming other people, their own weaknesses, social pressures, loneliness, or boredom. The coach of a winning football team may attribute the team's success to the training program, the skill of the quarterback, or lucky play selection. In any situation, an attributional search is likely to turn up dozens of plausible explanations (Bar-Tal, Goldberg, & Knaani, 1984; McHugh, Beckman, & Frieze, 1979; Weiner, 1980).

Heider noted, however, that explanations differ from one another in certain ways. Imagine that Lukey has just beaten you at horseshoes. When you claim that he was just lucky, he argues that his superior ability helped him win. What is the difference between these two explanations? In Heider's view, specific explanations are linked to more fundamental attributional dimensions. Luck and ability, for example, differ in the *locus of causality*. Ability is an internal causal factor; it is within the individual, for it concerns the person's internal, or dispositional, characteristics. In contrast, situational or environmental factors, such as good luck, are external causes.

Other dimensions may be equally important to consider. Bernard Weiner, for example, has developed a three-dimensional model of attributions based on locus, stability, and controllability (see Table 4-1). Imagine two students who get As on a social psychology test; one thinks, "Wow, all that studying paid off!" but the other concludes, "I really am pretty intelligent." Both are making internal attributions, because effort (studying) and ability (intelligence) are within the person. Their attributions vary, however, along the *stability* dimension. Unstable causes, such as effort, fluctuate over time and situations. Stable causes, such as ability, are relatively enduring. Moreover, their attributions also differ in *controllability*. Some causes, such as our basic level of ability, cannot be modified; they are uncontrollable. Others, in contrast, are controllable. We can choose to work hard or to work very little, so effort is a controllable cause (Weiner, 1980, 1983, 1985b; Weiner & Brown, 1984; see Wimer & Kelley, 1982).

Are these attributional dimensions real? Do people actually organize their causal thinking around them? At present researchers aren't certain, because direct evidence of these dimensions can rarely be obtained. When we want to describe attributions and predict their consequences, however, these dimensions are indispensable. The number of causes that people identify when they explain their actions may be enormous. By taking dimensions into account, we can *describe* the similarities and differences among these attributions. Say we encounter a baseball player and his manager who have just lost a game. The player, Ron Cey, says, "I think we hit the ball all right. But I think we're unlucky." The manager, Tommy Lasorda, says, "It took a great team to beat us." By taking dimensions into account, we can compare these two attributions. Both people think that the loss was externally caused and uncontrollable. Cey, however, thinks that an unstable factor caused the loss, while Lasorda emphasizes a more stable factor (Lau & Russell, 1980; see Elig & Frieze, 1979; Russell, 1982).

TABLE 4-1

Weiner's three-dimensional model of attributions applied in an educational setting.

Locus	Stability	Controllability	Example
Internal	Stable	Controllable	"I always put in a lot of time studying."
Internal	Stable	Uncontrollable	"I have a good deal of ability in this area."
Internal	Unstable	Controllable	"I don't always study, but I did this time."
Internal	Unstable	Uncontrollable	"I was in a great mood when I took the test."
External	Stable	Controllable	"The tutor I hired helped me study."
External	Stable	Uncontrollable	"The teacher gave an easy test."
External	Unstable	Controllable	"I talked a friend into helping me."
External	Unstable	Uncontrollable	"I was just lucky."

In addition, we can better *predict* the consequences of attributions by taking dimensionality into consideration (Weiner, 1985b). Researchers in one study used the dimensions identified by Weiner to predict how students develop expectations about their course grades. Students who had just received their grades on a test were asked if their scores were caused by factors that were internal or external, stable or unstable, and controllable or uncontrollable. The students also predicted how well they would do on future tests in the class. As Weiner's model predicted, students who did poorly on the test and attributed their grades to external, uncontrollable factors (such as the ambiguity of the test) expected to keep right on failing. Successful students, in contrast, were most optimistic about their grades when they attributed their success to controllable factors (such as effort) (Forsyth & McMillan, 1981a).

How Do We Make Attributions?

Researchers have devoted the bulk of their efforts to the question "*How* do we make attributions?" How do we decide whether or not the other people's actions correspond to their private motives and desires? What kinds of information do we consider when identifying the causes of our own actions? How do we separate causes from correlates? Three general attribution models developed by Edward E. Jones, Daryl J. Bem, and Harold H. Kelley offer answers.

Correspondent inference theory.

In 1984 John Z. De Lorean was tried on eight counts of conspiring to purchase cocaine from an undercover agent of the FBI. The prosecutor's evidence included a videotape showing De Lorean smiling into a suitcase filled with cocaine and saying "It's better than gold." Before the jurors were sequestered, however, the judge gave them a specific instruction: if, in their judgment, De Lorean had not been *predisposed* to commit the crime, then he should be acquitted. The jury, after deliberating for 27 hours, found in De Lorean's favor.

Correspondent inference theory, which was developed by Edward E. Jones in collaboration with several other social psychologists, explains the link between the actions we observe and the attributions we subsequently form (Jones, 1978, 1979; Jones & Davis, 1965; Jones & McGillis, 1976). Like the jurors who watched De Lorean on the FBI's videotape, we often see another person performing an action. However, we do not always assume that the action tells us anything about the person's disposition. If we believe this action follows from or corresponds to the person's dispositional characteristics, then we will make attributions (correspondent inferences). If, however, we think that the correspondence between action and disposition is minimal, we won't formulate any attributions. De Lorean's jurors apparently concluded that his actions did not correspond to his dispositions. They felt that the government had entrapped De Lorean and that he was not by nature a drug dealer.

What factors influence correspondence? When do we feel confident that a person's action tell us something about his or her inner characteristics? Of the several variables Jones has examined, *expectations* appear to be particularly important (Jones, 1978). Consider expectations about proper behavior. What do you think about a couple who politely thank their host after a party? Did they really enjoy the party? Or are they just following the norms of the situation? You can't be sure. But what about the couple who tells their host they had a horrible time? These unexpected actions convey considerably more attributional information.

Expectations may also be influenced by the demands of the situation. Compare these two cases:

Case 1: June is applying for a job as a salesperson. She knows that a good salesperson must be able to work well with others. During the interview she says, "I like to be free to do what I want, to work on my own. I usually avoid situations where I have to rely on other people. In fact, one of my favorite summer jobs was working as a forest ranger, because I didn't need to deal with people."

Case 2: April is applying for a job as a computer programmer. She knows that a good programmer must be self-reliant and independent. During the interview she says, "I like to choose my own goals and work on my own. I usually avoid situations where I have to rely on other people. One summer I really enjoyed working as a proofreader, because I didn't need to deal with people."

Who is more independent: June or April?

According to correspondent inference theory, you will probably feel that June is more independent than April. Although both women describe themselves similarly—as loners who are inner-directed and self-reliant—June is applying for a job that requires someone who is outgoing and other-directed. Because this kind of self-description is surprising, you can more confidently assume it corresponds to her actual personality characteristics. Researchers tested this hypothesis by asking subjects to form an impression of a confederate who described himself as inner- or outer-directed when he applied for a job that required interpersonal skills or independence. Subjects' attributions were more extreme when the confederate's self-descriptions ran counter to their expectations (Jones, Davis, & Gergen, 1961).

Self-perception theory. Jones was primarily interested in explaining how we decide if other people's actions tell us something about their private, personal attributes. Daryl J. Bem, in contrast, was more concerned with attributions that we make about the causes of our own behavior (Bem, 1972). As we saw in Chapter 2, Bem assumes that we have no unique insight into our personal dispositions and attributes. Instead, we must make guesses about our dispositional qualities by observing our actions. If we see ourselves working, we assume we like to work. If we eat anchovies, we conclude we like anchovies. This *self-perception process* becomes more complicated when situational factors enter the picture. You may be working because you desperately need the money. You may be eating anchovies because your friends insisted on getting a pizza with anchovies. When your behavior appears to be caused by external factors, you can't draw any inferences from it about your internal motives or desires.

Hypotheses derived from Bem's theory have been supported by a number of studies. Self-perception theory explains, for example, why we sometimes become less motivated to work or study when we are rewarded (Deci & Ryan, 1985). The following folk tale illustrates this process.

> Each day the children harassed the old woman. After school they would play outside her window; if she asked them to be quiet, they only called her obscene names and shouted more loudly.
>
> One day as the children approached, she called to them. "I have grown fond of listening to you play, but my hearing isn't what it used to be. If you will play in front of my window, I will pay each of you fifty cents."
>
> The children laughed at the woman's foolish request, but they agreed to play as noisily as they could. For a week they collected their payment each day after school and raised a tremendous din.
>
> The next week, however, the woman greeted the children with a frown. "Times are hard. I can pay you only a quarter for playing outside my window."
>
> The children complained, but they agreed to her offer. Then, after three days, the woman met them again. "Times are hard. I can only pay you ten cents," she told them.
>
> "Ten cents? That's not enough," they said. And they left her in peace.

This story highlights the difference between **intrinsic motivation** and **extrinsic motivation**. Intrinsic behavior is done for its own sake, for no apparent ulterior motive or goal. People who are intrinsically motivated study for the sheer joy of learning or help others because they find pleasure in doing so. Extrinsic behavior, however, is always a means to some end; when we work for money or study to earn a grade, our actions are extrinsically motivated. As the story of the old woman and the noisy children demonstrates, extrinsic rewards can destroy intrinsic motivation. As Bem explains, we forget our original motivations and assume that external factors are the actual causes of our actions.

This **overjustification** effect has been demonstrated in industrial, organizational, and academic settings (Amabile, Hennessey, & Grossman, 1986; Condry, 1977; Notz, 1975). In one study investigators watched 3-, 4-, and 5-year-old children during their free-play period in nursery school. In the course of these observations they identified the children who liked to play with felt-tip pens (most did; felt-tipped markers have replaced crayons in the hearts of small children). Two weeks later the researchers returned and asked the children to draw pictures with felt-tipped pens for them. One group of children expected and received a reward for their efforts: a colored card with a large gold star, a red ribbon, and the phrase "Good Player Award" in large letters. A second group of children was given an award as a surprise for helping, but had not been told beforehand that they would receive it. A third group of children was simply asked, "Would you like to draw some pictures?" No reward was mentioned or given.

One week later the experimenters again observed the children during their free-play period. As they had anticipated, the children who earlier had been promised a reward for playing with the pens spent only half as much time spontaneously playing with them now. Before the reward, they had spent 17% of their time playing with the pens; now they spent only 9% of their time. The other two groups of children showed no change in the time they spent playing with the pens. Extrinsic rewards, the researchers concluded, "turn play into work" (Greene & Lepper, 1974; Lepper, Greene, & Nisbett, 1973).

The cube model.   I remember covering Harold H. Kelley's **cube model** in my first social psychology class. Although I was confident when I read about the other theories (Heider's common-sense psychology, Jones's correspondent inference theory, and Bem's self-perception theory), I felt a little confused when I read about Kelley's model. Even when I reread the section the next day, I encountered the same result: confusion. So I asked my classmates what they thought about Kelley's model. They, too, confessed to confusion. With growing anger toward the theory, I demanded that our professor explain it. He did, but I still disliked it. Only later did I realize that my rejection of the theory was predicted by the theory itself.

Unlike the theories developed by Jones and Bem, Kelley's theory explains how our attributions about ourselves and other people are based on *covariation*. Covariation is nothing more than the tendency for two things to occur at the same time or in the same place. If each time you drink alcohol you get a headache, drinking and headaches covary. If people who have blue eyes tend to have blonde hair, then blue eyes and blond hair covary. As we discovered in Chapter 1, covariation does not necessarily imply causality. However, Kelley believes that most people ignore this limitation and base their attributions on the **covariation principle:** "an effect is attributed to the one of its possible causes with which, over time, it varies" (Kelley, 1971a, p. 3).

Kelley's theory also assumes that people seek information about covariation from several sources. When I was feeling confused about his theory, for example, I first considered the distinctiveness of my reactions. Did all attribution theories confuse me, or was my reaction to Kelley's theory distinctive? Second, I studied the consistency of my reaction over time. Possibly, if I read about the theory late at night, I was too tired to absorb the information. If, however, I always felt confused when I read about the theory, then my reaction would be very consistent over time. Third,

I gathered consensus information. How did my classmates react to the theory? If they understood it perfectly, then I had only my limitations to blame for my confusion.

These three types of information—distinctiveness, consistency, and consensus—are drawn from the sources Kelley emphasized in his so-called cube theory (Kelley, 1967, 1971a, 1971b). *Distinctiveness*, as the examples shown in Table 4-2 make clear, describes covariation across objects (or "entities"). When distinctiveness is high, we react only when the object is present. When distinctiveness is low, our reaction occurs both when the object is present and when it is absent. *Consistency* refers to covariation over time. Consistency is high when we always react to the object in a particular way, but low when our reaction varies. Lastly, *consensus* information is based on covariation across people. High consensus suggests that the object affects everyone in the same way; low consensus suggests that you are uniquely affected by it. (By the way, are you wondering why the theory is called the cube theory? Well, when Kelley first described these three sources of information, he referred to them as the three "axes" of an attribution "cube." The name stuck. In a recent interview, however, he laments: "In some ways I am not happy

TABLE 4–2

Examples of information high and low in distinctiveness, consistency, and consensus.

Dimension	High	Low
Distinctiveness	Fred is passing all his other courses, but he is failing zoology.	Fred is failing all his courses.
	Ann always feels wonderful when she is with Marc, but only so-so when she's out with Fred or Rudy.	Ann has a good time no matter who she's with, whether it's Marc, Fred, or Rudy.
Consistency	Fred has failed every zoology test he has taken.	Fred has passed some of his zoology tests, but he has failed others.
	Ann has dated Marc five times. Each date has been so much fun that she has decided to date Marc exclusively.	Ann had fun on their first two dates, but lately she has felt bored when she's dated Marc.
Consensus	Everyone is failing zoology.	Some students are doing well in zoology, but others are doing poorly.
	Ann has talked to her friends about Marc. They all say he's wonderful.	Some of Ann's friends like Marc, but others think he's a creep.

that I did it. It was a thought-aiding device, not something I wanted to feature. I should have known that the analogue, being very concrete, would provide the label" [quoted in Harvey, Ickes, & Kidd, 1978, p. 374].)

According to Kelley, attributors emphasize external causes "when evidence exists as to the distinctiveness, consistency, and consensus of the appropriate effects" (1967, p. 196). To apply this prediction, combine the examples in Table 4-2 which are high in distinctiveness, consistency, and consensus. Poor Fred can do little to pass zoology, inasmuch as his failure is caused by external factors. Fred is obviously competent, as he is passing his other courses, but his consistent failure in zoology and the failure of all the other students suggests that the course is extraordinarily difficult (see Figure 4-3). Similarly, Ann's attraction to Marc can be explained by Marc's positive qualities: everyone likes Marc.

But when do people make internal attributions? When is Fred's failure caused by his own inadequacies? When is Ann's attraction to Marc caused by her own personal needs rather than Marc's positive assets? According to research, people make internal attributions when both distinctiveness and consensus are low but consistency is high (Forsyth & McMillan, 1981b; McArthur, 1972, p. 172). Refer once more to Table 4-2. Fred can be blamed for his failure when he is failing all his courses, he has failed all his zoology tests, and other people are managing to pass the course. Similarly, if Ann is indiscriminately attracted to several men, likes Marc on several occasions, and likes Marc even though others think he is a creep, then we would probably conclude that something about Ann (active glands, perhaps) is causing her attraction (see Focus 4-2).

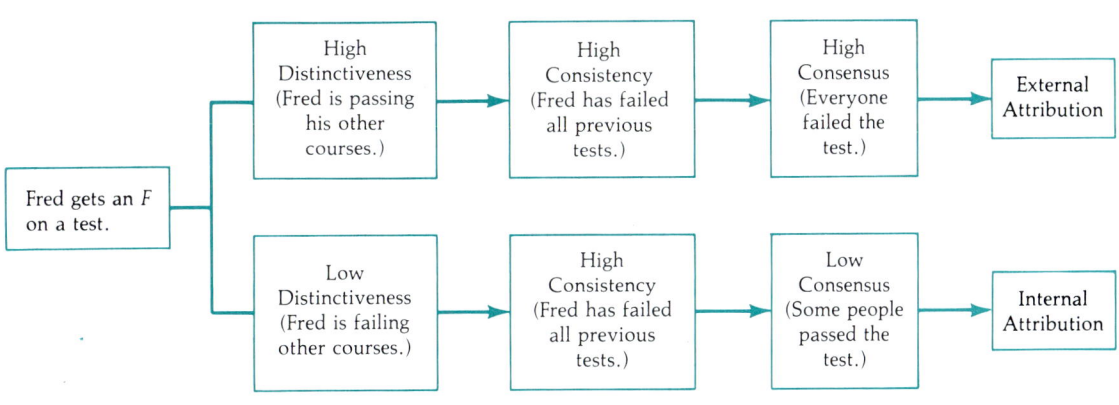

Figure 4-3 An educational example of Kelley's cube model of attributions. Note that consistency is high in both cases, and that the impact of consistency depends on both distinctiveness and consensus information. When consistency is low, factors vary so much over time that the action is attributed to fluctuating situational factors.

In Summary

Without attributions, our social world would seem chaotic, a series of inexplicable events, occurring at random, for no rhyme or reason. But once we formulate attributions, this flood of interpersonal encounters becomes a predictable unfolding of meaningful social life. In the years since Heider discovered this process, researchers have extended his basic ideas by examining a number of fundamental questions.

FOCUS 4-2

Controversy in Social Psychology: *When do people use consensus information?*

Role-play a member of a student judicial committee listening to students who have been caught cheating.

Saul: I admit I cheated on the test, but I've obeyed every other rule in the honor code.
Harvey: I admit I cheated on the test, but I've never cheated on a test before.
Leslie: I admit I cheated on the test, but everyone was cheating.

The committee decides that one of these students must be expelled as an example to other would-be cheaters. Who will you select: Saul, Harvey, or Leslie?

Several studies suggest that the ax may fall most heavily on Leslie (Forsyth & Pope, 1983; Forsyth, Pope, & McMillan, 1985). Although all three committed the same act, Saul emphasized the high distinctiveness of his actions, Harvey pointed out the low consistency of his behavior, while Leslie claimed that her action was high in consensus. Unfortunately for Leslie, of the three types of attributional information, consensus is the weakest. In one of the earliest tests of Kelley's cube model, subjects were given brief descriptions of a person performing such simple behaviors as laughing at a comedian, displaying fear when a dog approached, and performing a task incorrectly. For each description, subjects were also led to believe that distinctiveness, consistency, and consensus were either high or low. In this study, consensus information accounted for only 2.9% of subjects' attributions, while distinctiveness and consistency accounted for 10.2 and 20.0%, respectively (McArthur, 1972).

Richard Nisbett, Eugene Borgida, and their colleagues have argued that the weak impact of consensus information is produced by a flaw in our common-sense psychological thinking. Rather than recognize the informational value of other people's responses in the situation, we tend to rely on our intuitive notions about causality. For example, even if we believe Leslie's claim that "everyone was cheating," we will ignore this information because it violates our intuitive assumptions about moral behavior. This failure to use consensus information parallels the tendency to ignore base-rate data discussed in Chapter 3 (Borgida, 1978; Borgida & Brekke, 1981; Nisbett & Borgida, 1975; Nisbett et al., 1976).

Other social psychologists have challenged these conclusions. These investigators believe that Nisbett and Borgida overstated their case against consensus. In the wake of the initial findings, studies found that the impact of consensus information on attributions depends on many factors, including order of presentation (Ruble & Feldman, 1976; Feldman et al., 1976), the attributors' perspective (Hansen & Lowe, 1976; Hansen & Donoghue, 1977), and the way in which the consensus information is presented (Ajzen, 1977; Wells & Harvey, 1977, 1978; for a review, see Kassin, 1979).

These findings suggest that a middle ground between no influence and strong influence may be the most defensible. As one set of reviewers notes, people don't completely ignore consensus information. Rather, they "use this information, especially under conditions that have been specified in some detail. But they do not use the information precisely—as a computer might" (Harvey & Weary, 1981, p. 50).

Who makes attributions? People do; perceiving causality is a natural and spontaneous process.

Why do we make attributions? For many reasons; attributions explain our social world, predict future events, meet self-needs, and communicate information to other people.

Where and *when* do we make attributions? In many situations, but we are particularly likely to form attributions when we encounter vivid, salient stimuli, when we are asked "why" questions, and when other people or events surprise us.

What kinds of attributions do we form? Our attributions are limited only by our imagination, but researchers feel they vary along such dimensions as locus (internality/externality), stability, and controllability.

How do people reach attributional conclusions? According to Edward E. Jones, we estimate the correspondence between other people's actions and their personal attributes. We formulate self-perceptions after observing our own behavior, says Daryl Bem. And Harold Kelley suggests we draw evidence about covariation from three sources: distinctiveness, consistency, and consensus.

These findings attest to our attributional prowess. We display an impressive understanding of the nature of causality, ourselves, and other people. But just as scientists sometimes run awry with their theories, we, too, sometimes err in our attributions. We are, after all, only human.

■ Attributional Biases

If journalists were writing a feature article on attributions, they might want to concentrate on the basics: who, why, where, when, what, and how. If the journalists were writing a human-interest story, however, they might point out that our attributions aren't always scientifically sound. When the Swiss psychologist Jean Piaget (1934) asked small children why the sun and moon move, one answered: "They follow us about on our walks in order to look at us." When a police officer asked a driver why he was speeding, the man explained, "I just washed my car, and I was trying to blow-dry it." Harold McCluskey, whose body was contaminated by radioactive material in a nuclear accident in 1976, referred to nonphysical causes when explaining his survival: "It's the Creator. Doctors can give you medicine, but only the body does the actual healing, and that's God's work." When a student who had missed 34 questions on a 60-question test was asked about her failure, she explained, "I guessed wrong on a few of the questions." When Orval Wyatt Lyod killed his mother-in-law with an ax in 1981, he claimed that in the darkness of his garage he mistook her for a large raccoon foraging for food.

Although we generally strive to maintain a veridical (accurate) view of our social world, we don't always succeed. The causes that we search for are often ambiguous, so even a systematic search will yield only guesses and conjectures. Moreover, we don't always function as mistake-free attribution machines. As Heider noted many years ago, our perceptions of causality are often distorted by our needs and certain cognitive biases. Here we will consider a few of these distortions, beginning first with inaccuracies that occur when we make attributions about our selves.

Biases in Self-Attributions

Each day's social agenda brings us many opportunities to experience the positive side of social life, and an equal number of chances to find calamity. Your boss praises your work and gives you a bonus. You get a D on a term paper. You tell a joke at a party and no one laughs. Your stocks climb. An attractive stranger smiles at you suggestively. You discover an overdue library book under a pile of dirty clothes. You wreck your car.

Naturally, we often identify the causes of our positive and negative experiences. But in doing so, we display a fascinating tendency to seek out internal causes when our experiences are pleasant and external causes when our experiences are negative. If you ran into another car at an intersection, you would probably attribute your misfortune to the slick road conditions rather than your poor driving skills. If you got an A+ on a test, you would attribute your success to your excellent study habits rather than the simplicity of the test questions. The general tendency to link positive outcomes to personal factors but negative outcomes to external factors is called the **self-serving bias.** As we shall see, it occurs in a wide variety of situations and springs from several interrelated sources.

Attributions help us understand our social world, but they also protect our sense of self-worth from threat. After a collision each driver may try to blame the other driver for the accident rather than take responsibility for having caused the accident.

The ubiquity of the self-serving bias.
Dozens of laboratory studies have confirmed our tendency to take credit for success while dissociating ourselves from failure. When subjects succeeded in their attempts to solve anagrams, win games, or pass tests, they credited their superior intelligence, interest, and motivation. Failing subjects, in contrast, complained about the difficulty of the boring task (Elig & Frieze, 1979; Snyder, Stephan, & Rosenfield, 1976; Forsyth & Schlenker, 1977). When they failed to help a confederate learn a concept, they blamed the confederate; when they succeeded, they accepted responsibility for the confederate's learning (Johnson, Feigenbaum, & Weiby, 1964). When they worked in groups that failed, they denied responsibility for the outcome; when their group succeeded, however, they willingly claimed the credit (Norvell & Forsyth, 1984).

These self-serving attributional biases have also been documented in many field studies. College students, for example, tend to emphasize external factors—such as the difficulty of the test or the teacher's ability—after performing poorly on an examination, but they point to internal factors—such as superior ability and effort—when they achieve a high score (Forsyth & McMillan, 1981a, 1981b). Sports writers, coaches, and players, when explaining wins and losses in professional football games, mention internal factors more often after their team wins than after it loses (Lau, 1984). After a win precipitated by a fluke play (such as a key fumble by the other team), football fans who have placed bets on their team tend to attribute the victory to their team's ability. Losing gamblers, in contrast, emphasize bad luck as the cause (Gilovich, 1983). Candidates for political office who lose the election blame situational factors that they couldn't control: their lack of campaign funds, the voters, or their opponent's visibility. Winners, in contrast, point to their hard work, their personal style, and their campaign strategy when they explain their victory (Kingdon, 1967). Even social psychologists themselves—who investigate self-serving biases—fall prey to the tendency. When their research reports are rejected by a scientific journal, they tend to blame the rejection on external factors, such as the editor, the availability of journal space, luck, and the reviewers. When their papers are accepted, they credit their effort, the soundness of the research design, and their own ability and training (Wiley, Crittenden, & Birg, 1979; see Figure 4-4).

Why do we make self-serving attributions?
These studies lead to one clear conclusion: we tend to take credit for our successes, but avoid the blame for our failures. Researchers have not been content merely to describe this bias, however; they also wish to know *why* these biases occur after success and failure. Imagine that you are sitting in class. The teacher is slow to hand back exams. You patiently wait for yours, wondering if you got an A or a B. At last the professor approaches and hands you your paper. It's marked with a red F. Why would you tend to attribute

Figure 4-4 The self-serving attribution bias. People strive to avoid responsibility for their negative behaviors.

© 1983 by King Features Syndicate, Inc. World rights reserved.

this outcome to external factors, such as the teacher's biases or the ambiguity of the test?

Originally researchers assumed that these biases were motivated by our desire to *protect our self-esteem;* hence the tendency was dubbed a self-serving bias. If you blamed yourself for your failure, then your sense of self-confidence and self-worth would be undermined. Therefore you seek an external factor that can be blamed for your failure. When you succeed, however, you attribute your success to yourself to bolster your sense of self-worth (Bowerman, 1978; Covington & Omelich, 1979).

Although several studies lent support to this explanation, an alternative interpretation was soon suggested. According to this logical, *information-processing* explanation, if outcomes match our expectations, then they are attributed to stable, personal factors. If, however, our outcomes violate our expectations—we expected an A or a B but instead we failed—then we attribute our outcomes to unstable, external factors. Furthermore, in most situations we expect to succeed, as the covariation between our own behavior and positive outcomes is very salient. Hence, if you attributed your failure on the examination to something external to yourself, then you were only logically processing the information available to you; you weren't trying to protect your self-esteem, only to make sense of an unexpected event (Miller & Ross, 1975).

A third explanation of the success-internal/failure-external relationship emphasizes the *interpersonal implications* of attributions. Since you will probably be discussing your grade with the other members of the class, you may be embarrassed by your failure. You hope that others see you as a serious, intelligent person, but if you continually fail examinations, this social image will be threatened. Therefore, to protect your public image, you attribute your poor grades to external factors, while attributing your good grades to your own personal effort or ability (Bradley, 1978) (see Figure 4-5).

Which of these explanations is accurate? Probably all three. In many instances we become so personally involved with our performances that we would experience considerable anxiety if we felt that our inability

Figure 4-5 Self-presentational attributions. Attributions, when verbalized, convey considerable information to others. In this case, the student has probably performed poorly, and so he blames his failure on his teacher. This self-presentational strategy can backfire if the teacher refuses to accept the student's claim.
HERMAN, by Jim Unger. Copyright, 1983, by Universal Press Syndicate. Reprinted by permission. All rights reserved.

made us fail or that random external factors produced our success. In such cases, when ego involvement or need for achievement is high, our attributions may be biased by self-serving motivations (Greenberg, Pyszczynski, & Solomon, 1982; Miller, 1976; Weary, 1980). However, we sometimes need to understand the actual causes of our performance. If you did fail a test in a class, you would need to know how you could avoid another failure in the future. If you simply blamed external factors, then you might continue to fail. Therefore, when you anticipated future tests, your attributions might be based on logical, rational information-processing mechanisms (Wortman, Costanzo, & Witt, 1973). Lastly, when your performances are public, you may wish to make certain that others won't blame you for your failures, but will credit you for your successes. When attributions fulfill an interpersonal, self-presentational function, then you can exclaim, "What rotten luck!" or "The questions weren't clear!" after failure, but "I'm glad I worked as hard as I did!" or "Good, fair test!" after success (Arkin, Appelman, & Berger, 1980; Frey, 1978; Riess et al., 1981; Tetlock, 1981). This functional view of attributions suggests that, depending on the circumstances, all three processes combine to determine attributions after success and failure (Forsyth, 1980; Tetlock & Levi, 1982; Tetlock & Manstead, 1985; see Figure 4-6).

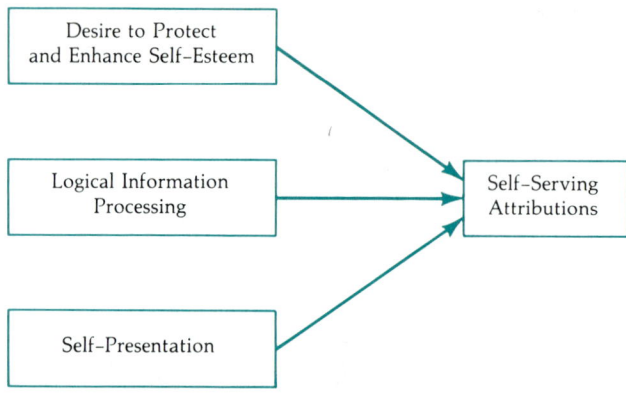

Figure 4-6 The causes of self-serving attributional biases. Although the term *self-serving* suggests that we take credit for success and avoid blame to protect our self-esteem, evidence suggests that several factors combine to influence our attributions.

Observer Biases

Each year thousands of people abandon their everyday routines to join cults. Seemingly without warning, a "normal" son or daughter may decide to join the Unification Church, take up with the Hare Krishnas, or become a Scientologist. Why do you think people become involved in cults of this kind?

When a representative sample of Americans answered this question in 1978 (just after the tragic mass suicide of the People's Temple members in Guyana), dozens of attributional explanations were offered. All of the most frequently mentioned explanations emphasized the dispositional characteristics of the converts. Personal motivations, such as a need for leadership, belonging, or spiritual understanding, were mentioned by many respondents, as were a host of negative characteristics: feelings of hopelessness, gullibility, even mental illness (see Table 4-3). Situational causes were infrequently mentioned. Were those people brainwashed? Were they pressured into joining? Did the cult offer an attractive alternative lifestyle? Most people said no (Gallup, 1978, p. 275).

The tendency to attribute behavior to internal, dispositional factors is not limited to explanations of cultism. On the highway, a fast driver is a "lead foot" rather than someone who is late for an appointment. In the classroom, a student who falls asleep is rude and stupid rather than exhausted by a part-time job. In a store, the sales clerk who pressures you to buy something is pushy, not someone who has just been ordered to increase sales. We constantly underestimate how much people's behavior is influenced by the situations they are facing. This tendency to overestimate the causal influence of dispositional factors while underemphasizing that of situation factors is so pervasive

Hundreds of young members of the Unification Church take their marriage vows in a ceremony conducted by the Rev. Sun Myung Moon. Why did they join this group? Why do they follow Rev. Moon's orders, to the point of marrying whoever they are told to marry?

that Lee Ross calls it the **fundamental attribution error** (Ross, 1977). Although some researchers feel that this focus on dispositional factors is not *the* fundamental error in attribution processing, all agree that the tendency influences many of our judgments of other people. For one thing, the error prompts us to make dispositional attributions even when actions are constrained by the situation. For another, if an accident occurs, we try to fix the blame on one or more of the individuals involved. These two biases are considered in detail below. (Varying views are presented in Harvey, Town, & Yarkin, 1981; Harvey & McGlynn, 1982; and Reeder, 1982.)

Overattribution. The fundamental attribution error exerts its influence on our attributions in a variety of ways. Even when situational causes are obvious, we tend to ignore them. In one study, subjects met briefly with a female consultant to discuss a clinical case. The consultant, who was actually a confederate of the researchers, behaved in either a friendly or an unfriendly manner. Before the discussion, half of the subjects were told that the consultant had been trained to behave in a certain way during the discussion. The experimenter claimed he was testing several consultation methods, so the woman was deliberately trying to be either friendly or unfriendly. The remaining subjects were told that the consultant's actions were spontaneous; that she was just trying to be herself. Surprisingly, when subjects later rated the consultant, they ignored the fact that her behavior was constrained by the situation. As Figure 4-7 indicates, when her behavior was friendly, subjects assumed she was

TABLE 4-3

The percentage of respondents who mentioned various reasons for joining a cult.

Cause	Percentage
Need for leadership or father figure	15%
Unhappiness, feeling of hopelessness	13
Gullibility	13
Need to have a sense of belonging, of community	12
Search for a deeper meaning to life	12
Mental/emotional disturbance	11
Disillusionment with churches	7
Brainwashing	7
Wish to escape from reality	7
Need for something to believe in	6
Insecurity	4
Broken or disorganized home	4
Lack of motivation, ambition, or direction	3
Influence of the devil or false prophets	3
Lack of education	3
Confusion	2
Drugs	2

SOURCE: Gallup, 1978.

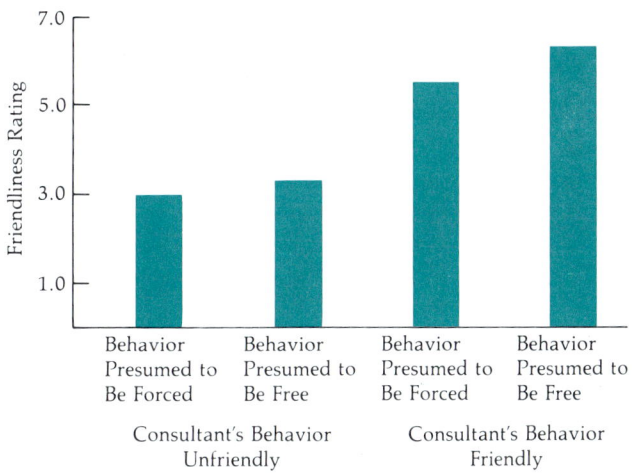

Figure 4-7 Attributions of friendliness. Even when subjects were explicitly told that the other person was forced to behave in a friendly or unfriendly manner, they still attributed her behavior to her dispositional characteristics.

friendly; when she acted unfriendly, subjects assumed she was unfriendly (Napolitan & Goethals, 1979).

E. E. Jones has termed this process **overattribution** because attributions are formulated even though behavior is constrained. In his studies of people attributing attitudes to others, Jones often finds that perceivers use behaviors as evidence of attitudes even when the actions are clearly caused by the situational forces. To examine this process, he asked subjects to read an essay on a particular topic, such as the legalization of marijuana, racial segregation, Fidel Castro's government in Cuba, or abortion. Some subjects were told that the person who wrote the essay was free to take any position on the issue (choice condition), but other subjects were told that the essay writer was assigned a position (no-choice condition). The subjects were asked to estimate the essay writer's true attitude. Invariably people tended to assume that the writers believed what they had written, even when they were told that the writers were only carrying out an assignment. (These studies are reviewed in Jones, 1979.)

Why is overattribution considered a bias? According to Jones, this tendency violates the logic of correspondent inference theory: attributors should realize that actions may not correspond to attributes when the behavior is constrained. But this error occurs consistently in many studies. In fact, Jones once went so far as to arrange for subjects to write an essay setting forth a particular view on a topic and then exchange essays with people in another room. Even though they had just written an essay expressing an assigned position and should have realized that the content of the essay said nothing about the writer's attitude, overattribution still occurred (Snyder & Jones, 1974). The subjects in another study were the ones who made the assignments—they literally told other individuals how to answer a series of questions dealing with abortion. The subjects were the ones who constrained the respondents, but they still assumed the individuals' answers reflected his or her attitudes (Gilbert & Jones, 1986). The only way researchers have found to eliminate overattribution is to have the writer simply copy someone else's essay, or present an essay that is so weak or unenthusiastic that it betrays a refusal to take the assignment seriously (Schneider & Miller, 1975; Snyder & Jones, 1974).

Defensive attribution. Put yourself in the role of an observer listening to a description of an accident.

> Lennie had just bought a car—it was about six years old or so. He and his buddy drove up to Duluth and parked at the top of this hill. Lennie's buddy said Lennie did set the handbrake, but while they were gone the car started rolling. Some camp police who checked the car later said the brake cable was pretty badly rusted and must have broken. Anyway . . . the car really crashed through the window of this store that's right at the bottom. It hit a kid that was standing at the counter and the grocer. The kid was just dazed a little, but the grocer was hurt pretty badly. He was in the hospital all last year. Lennie didn't have any insurance at the time.   [Walster, 1966, p. 76]

Select one: Lennie is (1) not at all responsible, (2) only slightly responsible, (3) somewhat responsible, or (4) very much responsible for the accident.

If you feel that Lennie was completely responsible, the extremely negative outcome of the action may have influenced your attributions of responsibility. According to Elaine Walster, after hearing of a severe accident, observers commonly ask, "Who is to blame?" When she played subjects a tape recording of the Lennie story and asked them to judge his responsibility for the accident on a scale from 1 to 4, she found that they attributed more responsibility to Lennie when the grocer was injured (the version you read) than when the car happened to be deflected from its deadly course by a stump (Walster, 1966). Other studies obtained the same results, even when the actor's intentions, the foreseeability of the consequences, and the justification for the behavior were held constant (Chaiken & Darley, 1973; Phares & Wilson, 1972; Shaw & Sulzer, 1964).

Several factors may combine to increase allocated responsibility for negative actions. First, by blaming someone for an accident, observers assure themselves that a similar misfortune won't befall them. The more severe the accident, the "more unpleasant to acknowledge that this is the kind of thing that could happen to anyone" (Walster, 1966, p. 74). Through such **defensive attribution,** observers insulate themselves from anxiety associated with the recognition that catastrophic events cannot always be avoided (see Burger, 1981; Shaver, 1970a, 1970b). Second, Melvin J. Lerner's **just-world hypothesis** suggests that people "believe that they live in a world where people generally get what they deserve" (Lerner & Miller, 1978, p. 1030). To maintain this belief, we must assume that Lennie was responsible for the harm that was done by his car. In fact, we may even assume that the grocer, who was the victim of the accident, was partly to blame as well (see Focus 4-3). Last, because of the hindsight bias, once people learn about the negative consequences, they unwittingly increase their estimates of the likelihood of the accident. As a result, an unforeseeable accident, when viewed in retrospect, becomes foreseeable (Janoff-Bulman, Timko, & Carli, 1985).

FOCUS 4-3

A Closer Look. *Do we blame victims?*

Following a night class at the University, Judy Wyatt walked across campus toward her car. . . . Less than a block from the victim's car, the defendant accosted the victim and a struggle resulted in which the defendant stripped and sexually assaulted the victim. A passerby heard the victim's screams and phoned the police, who arrived to apprehend the defendant within a few minutes after he had completed his sexual assault. Medical examination indicated that Judy Wyatt had been a virgin prior to this incident.   [Jones & Aronson, 1973, p. 417]

To what degree do you consider the crime to be the victim's fault? Lerner's just-world hypothesis predicts that we sometimes *blame the victim* of a crime for his or her misfortune. Rather than acknowledge that people may suffer unjustly, we assume that victims deserve to suffer because they possess personality flaws or because they behave carelessly or foolishly (Lerner, 1970; Lerner & Miller, 1978). Applied to perceptions of this rape case, Lerner's hypothesis predicts that the crime may threaten perceivers' belief in a just world. If they believe that Judy Wyatt did nothing to provoke her attacker, then they must also conclude that the world is an unjust place where even innocent people are harmed. Therefore, they protect their beliefs by blaming Judy Wyatt for the rape. In fact, when the case was presented to male and female subjects, they attributed *more* responsibility to Wyatt when she was a virgin or a married woman, rather than divorced. Why? Because "the knowledge that innocent, highly respectable females can be raped was particularly threatening to the subjects' belief that the world is just" (Lerner & Miller, 1978, p. 1035).

The victims of many crimes and accidents are blamed for their victimization, but the ramifications of this phenomenon are particularly pernicious for rape victims. The tendency to hold women responsible when they have been raped may be the source of cultural myths that condone rape. Such statements as "Good girls don't get raped"; "Any healthy woman can resist a rapist if she really wants to"; "Women ask for it"; and "When a woman cries rape, you can figure she's been jilted or has something to cover up" all shift blame for the crime to the woman (Burt, 1980). Evidence indicates that this bias also operates in the criminal justice system. Because women are assumed to be responsible for rape, they can be made to feel as if they are on trial for the crime (Brownmiller, 1975). If jurors fall prey to this bias, the rapist is less likely to be convicted (Borgida, 1981). Lastly, a survey of women seeking counseling at rape crisis centers indicates that rape myths are so pervasive that women who have been raped sometimes blame themselves for being attacked (Janoff-Bulman, 1979).

These factors, and many others, conspire to support aggression against women. At present, most rape-prevention strategies focus on what women can do to avoid rape. These methods are undoubtedly useful, but studies of social-psychological reactions to victims suggest that rape will be eradicated only when the social and cultural beliefs that support it are dismantled.

The Actor/Observer Difference

Consider this simple study. Male college students were first asked to explain why they chose their major or why they liked their girlfriend. As expected, they emphasized the positive qualities of the field or the woman: "Psychology is an interesting field," they said, or "Vanessa is a very friendly, outgoing person." Next, they were asked to explain their *best friend's* choices. Now they emphasized their friend's unique dispositional qualities. "He wants to help people," they suggested, or "He has a weakness for blondes" (Nisbett et al., 1973).

The divergence in the two sets of attributions is striking. As we have seen, when we judge ourselves, we often display a self-serving bias. We attribute positive outcomes to ourselves, but we assume that negative outcomes are caused by the situation. But when we make attributions about others, we make a fundamental error: we overemphasize dispositional factors and underemphasize situational factors. Because of these

---

FOCUS 4-4

Experiencing Social Psychology: *What is attributional conflict?*

Conflicts between people are almost inevitable. Even the best of friends and the most compatible lovers run into an occasional problem that must be worked out. In some cases, discussing the cause of the problem helps us to understand one another better and settle our differences. Unfortunately, because many conflicts begin when one person (the actor) does something that irritates the other person (the observer), actor/observer differences can develop. Hence, instead of helping us understand one another better, our attributions only escalate conflicts.

Can you recall an instance when an argument with a roommate, friend, or loved one was prolonged because you disagreed about the cause of each other's behavior? When H. H. Kelley and his colleagues asked 41 dating, cohabitating, or married couples this question, they generated nearly 700 examples. Not too surprisingly, nearly all of the examples involved a negative behavior that angered the observer. When the researchers classified these actions into categories, they ended up with a list of "things you can do to make other people angry":

Figure 4-8 Attributional conflict. Hagar and Helga disagree over the cause of Hagar's complaint. She thinks it's due to his basic personality trait (he's a slob), but he thinks she isn't supportive enough.

© 1985 by King Features Syndicate, Inc. World rights reserved.

opposing tendencies, our attributions about ourselves often differ from our attributions about others.

E. E. Jones and Richard Nisbett call this divergence the **actor/observer difference:** actors (the people who actually perform the behavior) tend to explain their behavior in terms of situational factors, but observers generally emphasize dispositional causes. In discussing the cause of this divergence, Jones and Nisbett note that observers have less information than actors and are less motivated to protect their sense of self-esteem. They also note, however, that the actor and observer see the situation from completely different perspectives. For actors, the environment is salient, so they tend to attribute their actions to external causes. For observers, the actor is salient, so they tend to attribute actions to the actor (Jones & Nisbett, 1971; see Monson & Snyder, 1977, for a review). Whatever the cause of the divergence, as Focus 4-4 makes clear, it can lead to conflict.

---

fail to behave affectionately, display insensitivity, criticize, become excessively involved in outside relationships, behave ineptly, behave irresponsibly . . . the list is lengthy. Although such behavior alone was probably sufficient to create a dispute, Kelley found that the actors and observers disagreed about the causes of these negative actions. During a dispute, actors and observers see the world in very different ways (Passer, Kelley, & Michela, 1978). These sequences typify such attributional conflicts:

Observer: You didn't call me last night.
Actor: I was really busy studying for my test.
Observer: You don't love me anymore.

Observer: Did you remember the dry cleaning?
Actor: Oops. I forgot.
Observer: You're completely irresponsible.
Actor: No, I'm not. I just have a lot on my mind.
Observer: Don't give me that. You just expect me to wait on you.

Actor: I don't want to go to the movies.
Observer: Why do you always decide? You always boss me around.
Actor: No, I don't. I just don't want to go.
Observer: You're so manipulative sometimes.
Actor: Forget it. I'll go.
Observer: I'm not going anywhere with you.

What can you do to avoid attributional conflict? One solution requires *changing your focus of attention*. In several studies, when observers' attention was shifted away from the actor toward the situation, actor/observer differences were minimized (Arkin & Duval, 1975; Storms, 1973; Taylor & Fiske, 1975). To achieve this shift, each party to a conflict should try to see the situation from the other person's perspective. In one study observers were told to empathize with an actor named Margaret:

Imagine how Margaret feels as she engages in conversation. While you are watching . . . picture to yourself just how she feels in the situation. You are to concentrate on the way she feels while conversing. Think about her reaction to the information she is receiving from the conversation. In your mind's eye, you are to visualize how it feels to Margaret to be in this conversation.

When subjects were told to be empathic, they attributed Margaret's behavior more to situational factors than to dispositional factors. These findings, as well as others, lend credence to the idea that empathy helps ease tension between people (D. Regan & Totten, 1975; Stephan, 1975).

Attributional Theories

Social psychologists have expanded our knowledge of attributions along three adjacent research frontiers. First, they have identified processes that were only vaguely implied by Heider's "intuitive scientist" analogy. Second, researchers have documented some fascinating biases in our attributions. Third, most recently investigators have begun to apply attribution theory in such areas as health, psychological adjustment, educational achievement, and loneliness. Several of these attributional theories are reviewed below. We will consider first how attributions influence the way we react to stressful negative events; then we will consider attributions that promote psychological health and reduce stress. "In Depth: Attributions and Emotions," at the end of the chapter, presents an attributional analysis of emotional reactions.

Attributions and Stressful Events

Up to this point we have stressed the benefits of attributions. We found, for example, that our attributions help us make sense of our social world. They also increase our understanding of ourselves and other people. Suppose, though, we experience an extremely negative event—we become very ill, we lose our job, or our marriage becomes filled with conflict. What happens when our causal search tells us that we *cannot* control our outcomes—that the world is, after all, chaotic and unpredictable? Will our attributions, in this case, be adaptive? Studies of learned helplessness, achievement, and individual differences in reactions to uncontrollable events offer an answer to this question.

Learned helplessness.
Martin E. P. Seligman first became interested in maladaptive reactions to stressful events when he was studying learning in dogs. As part of a controlled laboratory study, he trained several dogs to jump over a small partition whenever they received an electric shock. Some of the dogs proved to be extremely difficult to train. Rather than escape the shock by jumping over the barrier, they accepted the shock passively. When Seligman investigated further, he found that the dogs had been used in a previous experiment that involved inescapable shock. As a result of this experience, they had apparently learned that shocks couldn't be avoided. *They had learned to be helpless* (Overmier & Seligman, 1967; Seligman & Maier, 1967).

Seligman based his theory of **learned helplessness** on this insight. According to Seligman, learned helplessness is "the psychological state that frequently results when events are uncontrollable, leading to emotional, cognitive, and motivation debilitation" (Seligman, 1975, p. 9). Initially Seligman assumed that humans experience helplessness whenever their outcomes are independent of their behaviors. However, he and his colleagues eventually reformulated the model to include an attributional component (Abramson, Seligman, & Teasdale, 1978). According to this reformulated view, the *perception* of uncontrollability is more important than uncontrollability itself. If an individual experiences an inescapable aversive outcome but thinks he can control the outcome, then he will not become helpless. In contrast, if a person can control her outcomes but assumes she cannot, then she will become helpless (see Figure 4-9).

Seligman's emphasis on perceived control rather than actual control has been supported in a number of studies (Skinner, 1985). Among subjects exposed to loud noise, for example, those who thought they could switch off the noise experienced fewer harmful aftereffects—even though they never used the switch (Glass & Singer, 1972). A study of people paralyzed by accidents indicated that those who blamed themselves rather than uncontrollable events coped more effectively (Bulman & Wortman, 1977). In a study of rape victims, blaming one's actions ("I should never have walked home alone") rather than one's stable characteristics ("I'm so stupid") led to better coping (Janoff-Bulman, 1979). And on the negative side of the coin, several studies have shown that individuals who adopt an attributional style that emphasizes uncontrollable causes tend to show more symptoms of depression: lack of energy, negative moods, self-condemnation, and withdrawal (Brewin, 1985; Peterson & Seligman, 1984). Taken as a whole, these findings suggest that *perceived control* leads to successful coping with stress, while loss of control leads to helplessness.

Mastery orientation and reactions to failure. Carol Dweck's studies of helpless and mastery-oriented students also lend support to an attributional theory of learned helplessness (Diener & Dweck, 1978, 1980; Dweck, 1975; Dweck & Bush, 1976; Dweck & Licht, 1980; Dweck & Reppucci, 1973; Goetz & Dweck, 1980). In one project fifth-graders were given insoluble problems by one teacher and soluble problems by another teacher. When the teacher who originally gave the insoluble problems switched to soluble problems, a number of children continued to perform poorly; apparently they attributed their earlier failure to the teacher and the difficulty of the problems the teacher assigned and became helpless. Furthermore, the children who evidenced the greatest helplessness were those who blamed their failure on a lack of ability. Students who per-

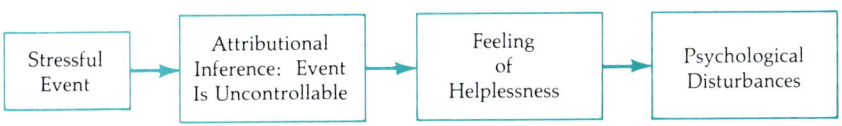

Figure 4-9 Seligman's model of learned helplessness.
SOURCE: Abrahamson, Seligman, & Teasdale, 1978.

formed the best tended to emphasize the causal role played by effort (Dweck & Reppucci, 1973).

In subsequent research Dweck has found that helpless children and mastery-oriented children behave similarly after successes, but when failure occurs they display dramatically divergent reactions. Among mastery-oriented children "effort is escalated, concentration is intensified, persistence is increased, strategy use becomes more sophisticated, and performance is enhanced." When helpless children fail, in contrast, "efforts are curtailed, strategies deteriorate, and performance is often severely disrupted" (Dweck & Licht, 1980, p. 197). In one demonstration of these differences, children who were failing on a cognitive task were told to "think out loud" about what they were doing (Diener & Dweck, 1978). When the researchers examined the content of these verbalizations, they discovered that 52% of the helpless children questioned their ability while none of the mastery-oriented students mentioned ability. In addition, mastery-oriented students emphasized effort and luck more than the helpless students. A subsequent study found that helpless students, when given a series of tasks followed by immediate feedback about success and failure, underestimated their successes, overestimated their failures, and avoided attributing their performances to ability (Diener & Dweck, 1980). These findings, like Seligman's, indicate that attributions play an important role in determining our reactions to stressful events.

Type A personalities and uncontrollable outcomes.   Studies of the **Type A personality** suggest that some individuals experience particularly intense reactions when they feel they can't control their outcomes. The Type A personality was originally documented by Meyer Friedman and Ray H. Rosenman, two cardiologists who were studying the causes of heart disease (Friedman & Rosenman, 1974). Although they began their research by assuming that heart disease was linked to smoking cigarettes, obesity, lack of exercise, and the like, they soon noticed that many of their patients displayed a similar personality syndrome. Aggressive, competitive, and excessively time-oriented, these individuals could justifiably be called workaholics. They set deadlines for themselves, pushed themselves to achieve more and more, and showed almost no sign of patience. Friedman and Rosenman dubbed this constellation of traits the *Type A personality,* and compared it with the low-key, relaxed *Type B personality.*

Type As, as Focus 4-5 explains, are more likely to die of heart disease. In explanation, David C. Glass suggests that Type As spend their lives struggling to maintain control over their environment. Like the mastery-oriented children identified by Dweck, Type As strive to control any stressor they encounter. Thus, although they are more stressed than Bs, they are *initially* less likely to experience helplessness. This advantage is erased, however, if they fail to gain control over the stressor. In this case, Type As display greater learned helplessness than Type Bs (Glass, 1977).

Attributions and Psychological Health

Evidence from a variety of contexts supports the idea that individuals who attribute stressful events to factors they can control cope more effectively than individuals who blame uncontrollable factors. How can these findings be used to promote psychological health and reduce stress? One technique, *attribution retraining*, involves the alteration of individuals' attributions through training. A second method takes advantage of *misattribution* to prompt individuals to shift their attributions from one factor to another.

Attribution retraining.

Attributions in response to stressful events sometimes function as coping mechanisms; they support us as we contend with adversity. Sometimes, however, we fail to take advantage of this shield, and even formulate attributions that exacerbate our distress. In such cases, we may benefit from an **attribution retraining** program that trains us to formulate healthy attributions. Carol Dweck (1975) identified 12 children who showed extremely maladaptive responses after failure: negative expectations about their performance, performance def-

---

FOCUS 4 – 5

Experiencing Social Psychology: *Is your personality Type A?*

Type A individuals display an interesting assortment of qualities. Aside from their competitive, time-oriented, hostile workaholism, they tend to bury their anger, fidget, fear failure, suppress fatigue, drive too fast, and strive to be punctual (Matthews et al., 1977). Most important, they react so intensely to stressors that they increase their chances of dying of heart disease. In one longitudinal study, 63 men who eventually developed heart disease were identified within a larger pool of men who had been classified as either Type A or type B 15 years before the disease developed. As expected, of the men who eventually developed heart disease, 72.6% had been classified as Type A (Matthews et al., 1977).

Because of these implications for your health, it is important to be aware of your Type A tendencies. Although most people can judge their own personalities fairly accurately, you may want to double-check yourself by answering yes or no to the items listed below. These items are only approximate measures of Type A (Friedman and Rosenman prefer interviews), but a score of 8 or more is relatively high. For more information about your reactions to stress, you may want to consult Friedman and Rosenman's book *Type A Behavior and Your Heart.*

1. My everyday life is filled mostly by problems needing solutions.
2. When under pressure or stress, I do something about it immediately.
3. When eating with others, I'm usually the first one finished.
4. When talking to other people, I frequently try to hurry them along.
5. To enjoy myself, I need to win at the sports and games I play.
6. People who know me well think I have far more energy than most people.
7. When I was young, my temper was fiery and hard to control.
8. I prefer to keep at least two projects going at one time so I can shift back and forth from one to the other.
9. I am much more serious about life than most of the people I know.
10. I detest waiting in lines.

icits following negative feedback, and low persistence on difficult tasks. She then trained six of these children to attribute their failures to lack of effort rather than lack of ability. For a 25-day period, these students worked on a series of arithmetic problems while the experimenter-teacher watched. While students were usually told they were doing well, at various intervals the teacher told the student he or she had taken too long to solve the problems. In all cases, however, the teacher then said, "You should have tried harder." The remaining six students were exposed exclusively to success feedback; they were never told they had failed or taken too long.

Dweck measured the students' reactions to negative feedback before the experiment, halfway through it, and again at its conclusion by asking them to solve sets of difficult math problems. As she had predicted, when the students in the control group made mistakes on these problems, their persistence evaporated. The students who had been trained to accept failure and overcome it, in contrast, persisted at these difficult problems, and when they did receive failure feedback they attributed their performance to a lack of effort (see Figure 4-10). These findings lend support to that ever-popular educational maxim "Failure builds character."

A similar approach has proven to be effective with college students. Convinced that students would be more successful if they attributed their outcomes to effort rather than ability, one pair of researchers sought to convince first-year college students that their grades were caused by

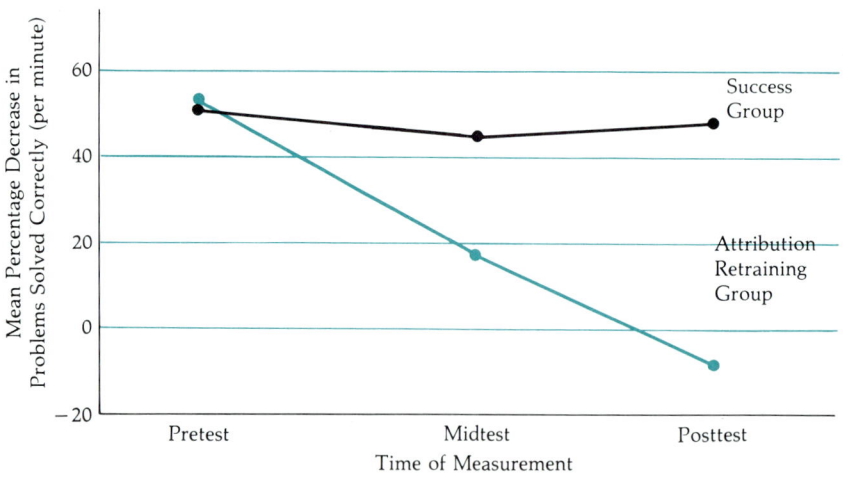

Figure 4-10 The effects of attributional retraining across three testing sessions. When students were taught to attribute outcomes to effort, they persisted at difficult problems. Students who received only positive feedback usually failed.

SOURCE: Dweck, 1975.

unstable rather than stable factors. In a brief presentation, the subjects were told that, on the average, college students improve their grades during their educational careers. They were also shown videotaped testimonials by students who described how their first-year grades had improved over time. The students who received the information were less likely than a control group of students to drop out at the end of their second year; their grade point average improved more markedly; and they performed better on sample items from the Graduate Record Exam (Wilson & Linville, 1982, 1985).

Attribution retraining has also yielded benefits for elderly people living in nursing homes (Langer & Rodin, 1976; Rodin & Langer, 1980), people suffering from severe social anxiety (Forsyth & Forsyth, 1982), and patients recovering from surgery (Langer, Janis, & Wolfer, 1975). Although additional research is needed to identify healthy attributions and define ways to change attributions, the major implication of these studies is clear: some of the negative effects of stressful life events can be reduced when people are helped to formulate attributions that promote healthy psychological functioning (Forsterling, 1985).

Changing attributions through misattribution. When the volcano Mount St. Helens erupted in 1980, a curious attributional phenomenon was noted. The nearby residents experienced considerable stress and hardship, and the cause of their problems was unmistakable: the volcano. As a result, the volcano served as a kind of attributional sponge: bad moods, illnesses, disagreements, and even drunkenness were attributed to the eruption (Newtson & Pennebaker, 1981).

This is an example of **misattribution**: the attribution of an event to a source with which it has little or no connection. Misattribution occurs quite frequently in everyday situations, and researchers have taken advantage of this tendency to develop ways of reducing stress. Michael D. Storms's studies of insomnia provide insight into this process. According to Storms, insomnia is caused by our tendency to attribute a momentary inability to fall asleep to insomnia. Once we decide we are experiencing insomnia, we become more and more aroused, and less and less likely to fall asleep. The more we worry about our insomnia, the worse it gets. Storms calls this escalating attribution process an exacerbation cycle, and believes that it causes a number of stress-related disorders, including insomnia, stuttering, and impotence (Lowery, Denney, & Storms, 1979; Storms & McCaul, 1976; Storms & Nisbett, 1970; Storms et al., 1979).

Storms uses misattribution processes to interrupt this exacerbation cycle. In a study conducted with Richard Nisbett (1970), he gave mild insomniacs pills to take before retiring. All of the pills were inert placebos, but some subjects were led to believe that the pills would relax them, while others were told that the pills would increase their physiological arousal. As predicted, the subjects given the "relaxing" pill took longer to fall asleep than the subjects given the "arousing" pill and control subjects given no pills at all. Although these findings seem to conflict with our intuitions, they make sense if we consider the insomniacs' attributions. When they expected the pill to relax them but still felt restless, they concluded that their insomnia was particularly bad that evening. Hence the relaxing pill contributed to the exacerbation cycle. When, in contrast, subjects thought they had taken an arousing pill, they misattributed their arousal to the pill. This misattribution broke the exacerbation cycle and they fell asleep more quickly.

Subsequent studies suggest that this treatment for insomnia doesn't always work, as people sometimes feel more aroused when they think they have taken an arousing pill, and they don't always attribute their arousal to the pill (see Storms et al., 1979, for a review). In consequence, Storms now recommends less threatening misattribution methods for treating insomnia. In one approach insomniacs were told that their sleep difficulties are caused by their unusually high levels of bodily functioning rather than stress or maladjustment. Once they realize that their inability to fall asleep is "normal," they don't lie in bed worrying about their insomnia. Therefore, the exacerbation cycle is cut short, and they can slowly drop off to sleep.

What conclusions can be drawn from Storms's work and the other investigations of attributions and adjustment that we've considered? Overall, even a cautious reader could conclude that attributions and adjustment are linked in some way. And if we wanted to speculate a bit, we could even identify controllable (and possibly unstable) causes as those most likely to facilitate adjustment. Finally, while much more research is needed, these studies hint at the possibly great impact of attributions on our subsequent actions. Attributional retraining, for example, changes behavior as well as attributions. These findings may prove quite useful in several branches of psychology.

■ Summary

Attributions are inferences about the causes of behaviors and events. Social psychologists believe that to understand ourselves, we must be able to identify what causes our thoughts, feelings, and emotions. And to form accurate perceptions of others, we must know when their actions are caused by their personal qualities and when they are reacting to outside pressures. Just as scientists' theories allow them to explain and predict events, **explanatory** and **predictive attributions** help us explain our social experiences and predict future events. **Self-serving attributions** serve to protect beliefs about the self, and **interpersonal attributions**—those exchanged among individuals—serve a self-presentational function. Moreover, we tend to form attributions when we encounter *vivid* or *salient* stimuli that attract our attention, when we are explicitly asked why an action occurred, and when events and actions violate our expectations.

In any social situation, we may locate dozens of factors that may be the causes of our actions. These factors, however, differ from one another along several key dimensions. Bernard Weiner, for example, emphasizes three dimensions: *locus of causality* (internal/external), *stability* (stable/unstable), and *controllability* (controllable/uncontrollable). By taking these and other dimensions into account, investigators can describe our attributions more accurately and make clearer predictions about the link between attributions and other social-psychological processes.

In the years since Fritz Heider described the attribution framework, other theorists have extended his ideas in several directions. Edward E. Jones's **correspondent inference theory** assumes that we use behavioral data to make inferences only when we feel that the behavior follows from or corresponds to the disposition. Daryl J. Bem, in contrast, concentrates on the attributions we make in regard to our own characteristics. His *self-perception theory* assumes that we make guesses about our inner qualities by noting our behavior. Although this view is counterintuitive, it offers a parsimonious explanation for the **overjustification** effect. Rewards, such as money or prizes, increase our **extrinsic motivation,** but they undermine our **intrinsic motivation** because we forget our original interests. The final major attribution theory, Harold H. Kelley's **cube model,** is based on the **covariation principle:** people attribute an effect to the cause with which it covaries over time. Covariance information is drawn from three sources—*distinctiveness, consistency,* and *consensus*—but people tend to undervalue consensus information.

Several biases systematically distort our causal inferences. When we make attributions about our own actions and experiences, we generally seek out internal causes when outcomes are positive, and external causes when outcomes are negative. This tendency, known as the **self-serving bias,** is probably produced by the need for self-esteem, a tendency to process information logically, and a desire to present oneself in a favorable light. When we make attributions about other people, in contrast, we underestimate how much that person's behavior is influenced by the situation and overestimate the causal influence of dispositional factors. This **fundamental attribution error** leads us to formulate attributions even when behavior is constrained **(overattribution)** and blame others for unforseeable negative consequences **(defensive attribution).** The self-serving bias and the fundamental attribution error combine to generate the **actor/observer difference:** actors explain their behavior in terms of the situation, but observers explain the actor's behavior in terms of dispositional factors.

In recent years social psychologists have developed a number of theories that are based on attributional principles. The findings concerning health and the ability of attributions to help us cope with stressful life events are particularly provocative. M. E. P. Seligman, in his theory of **learned helplessness,** proposes that when we feel we cannot control our outcomes, we experience a range of debilitating consequences, including depression. Carol Dweck, in extending this assumption, has found that mastery-oriented children expend considerable effort to overcome failure, while helpless children simply give up. Also some individuals, known as **Type A personalities,** tend to react very strongly to loss of control. The Type A individual is dominated by a sense of urgency, hostility, and competitive striving, and is more likely than the Type B person to die of heart disease. Findings in all these areas indicate that perceived control leads to successful coping, while loss of control leads to helplessness.

In view of findings that some of the negative effects of stressful life events can be reduced by changes of attribution, social psychologists have sought to modify distressed individuals' causal inferences through **attribution retraining** and **misattribution.** Impressive support for both approaches has been obtained in a variety of settings, illustrating the interdependency of basic and applied research in social psychology.

■ For More Information

1. *Attributions and Psychological Change,* edited by Charles Antaki and Chris Brewin (1982), contains basic theory and review chapters on the applications of attribution theory in clinical and educational practice.

2. "Parole Decisions," by John S. Carroll and Dan Coates (1980), presents a friendly, firsthand account of one researcher's approach to socially relevant research. A chapter in *Applied Social Psychology Annual,* vol. 1 (Bickman, 1980).

3. *Intrinsic Motivation and Self-Determination in Human Behavior,* by Edward L. Deci and Richard M. Ryan (1985), reviews more than 200 laboratory and field studies of intrinsic motivation and integrates the findings in a framework based on the concept of self-determination.

4. *Type A Behavior and Your Heart,* by the cardiologists Meyer Friedman and Ray H. Rosenman (1974), summarizes their research dealing with Type A personalities and heart disease. The book details the nature of Type A behavior and offers useful recommendations on how to control this tendency.

5. *Perspectives on Attributional Processes,* by John H. Harvey and Gifford Weary (1981), is a concise but comprehensive review of the major attribution theories and current trends in research.

6. *The Psychology of Interpersonal Relations,* by Fritz Heider (1958), is a classic tour de force in theory construction, filled with insightful observations.

7. *Attribution: Perceiving the Causes of Behavior,* edited by six of the foremost researchers in the field (E. E. Jones et al., 1971), presents relatively technical theoretical statements dealing with such topics as actor/observer differences, attribution therapy, and causal schemata.

8. *The Psychology of Control,* by Ellen J. Langer (1983), collects in one volume Langer's work dealing with perceived control.

IN DEPTH

Attributions and Emotions

In the late 1800s the psychologist William James offered a radical theory of emotions that stressed the impact of our physiological reactions on our emotional experiences. According to James:

> Common sense says, we lose our fortune, are sorry and weep; we meet a bear, are frightened and run; we are insulted by a rival, are angry and strike. The hypothesis here to be defended says that this order of sequence is incorrect, that the one mental state is not immediately induced by the other, that the bodily manifestations must first be interposed between, and that the more rational statement is that we feel sorry because we cry, angry because we strike, afraid because we tremble, and not that we cry, strike, or tremble because we are sorry, angry, or fearful. [James, 1892/1961, pp. 242–243]

This basic notion—that emotions may follow our physiological reactions rather than precede them—provided the foundation of Stanley Schachter and Jerome E. Singer's **two-factor theory** of emotions. According to Schachter and Singer, before we experience an emotional reaction, two factors must be present. First, some element in the situation must trigger a general, nonspecific arousal. Physiologically, this arousal manifests itself in the form of increased heart rate, tightening of the stomach, and rapid breathing. Second, we must attribute this arousal to a particular emotional experience. In general, this attribution depends upon available situational cues. If we are with an attractive member of the opposite sex, we may label our feelings as love or sexual excitement. If we are arguing with someone, we may conclude we are angry. If we are at a party, we may decide that we are happy or euphoric. Because they assume that "emotional states are a function of the interaction of such cognitive factors with a state of physiological arousal," their approach has been called the two-factor theory (Schachter & Singer, 1962, p. 381; see Figure 4-11).

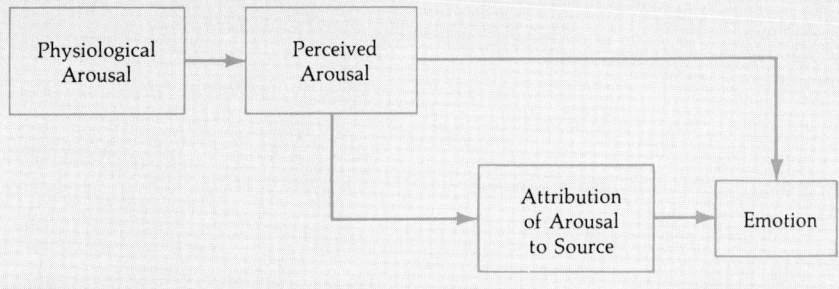

Figure 4-11 The two-factor theory of emotion. According to Schachter and Singer, an emotional experience begins when we experience unexplained physiological arousal. To account for our physical sensations, we identify the cause of our response by relying on environmental cues. Depending upon the results of this attributional search, we assign an emotional label to our experience.

IN DEPTH *continued*

Schachter and Singer tested their theory by manipulating three variables: (1) the degree of physiological arousal, (2) the amount of information subjects had about the cause of their arousal, and (3) the situational cues they would need to define their emotions. Their subjects, all men, were told that the experimenter was interested in studying the effects of a vitamin supplement, Suproxin, on vision. If the subject agreed to take the drug, he was injected with either epinephrine or a placebo. Epinephrine (or adrenaline) was used because it would increase subjects' blood pressure, heart rate, and respiration. Therefore, the subjects who received the epinephrine became physiologically aroused, while those who received the inert placebo did not.

To manipulate subjects' interpretations of their physical experiences, the researcher told some of the epinephrine-injected subjects that though the drug wasn't harmful, they could expect some side effects: they might feel flushed, their hands might shake, and their hearts might pound. Other subjects, however, were given no information at all about the effects of the drug and so received no explanation of the arousal they experienced. When those who had been injected with epinephrine began to feel aroused, they would need to explain their experiences. If they could attribute them to the drug, they should experience no strong emotions. If they had received no warning about the drug's effects, they should interpret their arousal as an emotion.

What kind of emotion would these uninformed subjects experience? Schachter and Singer believed that their reaction would depend on the available situational cues. Therefore, while supposedly allowing time for the Suproxin to take effect, subjects waited with an experimental accomplice for 20 minutes. Subjects were told that the accomplice was also a subject, but he was actually a confederate who was trained to behave in either a euphoric or angry fashion. The euphoric confederate clowned around during the 20 minutes, doodling on scratch paper, playing a game of "basketball" with wadded-up balls of paper, making and flying a paper airplane, building a tower out of file folders, and playing with a Hula Hoop. The angry confederate, in contrast, became increasingly agitated during the 20 minutes. The subjects were asked to complete questionnaires that contained very personal questions. After loudly criticizing questions that requested information about childhood diseases, father's income, and family members' bathing habits and psychiatric adjustment, the confederate flew into a rage at the question "How many times each week do you have sexual intercourse?"

When subjects had not anticipated the physiological arousal, their emotions and behaviors matched the confederate's actions. If, however, subjects were expecting increased heart rate and hand tremors, or if they had received a placebo, their reactions did not parallel the confederate's. (The subjects in a special control condition—people who had been given epinephrine but had been misinformed about its possible effects—also displayed the emotions enacted by a euphoric confederate.)

Subsequent research sometimes replicated and sometimes challenged the two-factor theory. In support of the theory, researchers found that subjects injected with epinephrine before viewing a film comedy laughed more and harder than those given a placebo; subjects given a powerful tranquillizer laughed less (Schachter & Wheeler, 1962). The emotional experiences of people with spinal cord injuries that limit the intensity of their physiological experiences also support the two-factor theory, as do some studies of aggressive and erotic behavior. (Reisenzein, 1983, reviews these studies.)

In addition, Schachter and Singer's *misattribution hypothesis*—the idea that the arousal caused by one factor (such as an injected drug) can be attributed to another factor—has been studied in many settings. As we have seen, studies suggest that insomniacs can sometimes get to sleep faster if they attribute their restlessness to an external, controllable, factor. Several studies of psychological disturbances suggest that such difficulties are sometimes caused by misattributions (Brodt & Zimbardo, 1981). In some cases individuals' emotional responses are influenced by bogus arousal information. In one study male college students were shown a series of slides depicting attractive nude women while their heart rate was supposedly being monitored (Valins, 1966). They had all been told that problems with the equipment would cause their heartbeat to be audible, but in actuality they heard one of two prerecorded tapes, one containing several fluctuations and the other containing a normal heartbeat. Thus some subjects heard their heart rate fluctuate as they watched the women but others did not. As predicted, the men reported greater attraction toward women who had been paired with increases in the bogus heartbeat. (Studies of such phenomena are reviewed in Parkinson, 1985.)

It should be noted, however, that our emotions aren't completely flexible. First, in replications of the Schachter-Singer study, subjects sometimes react negatively when they experience unexplained arousal. Rather than rely strictly on the situation for clues that would help them label their emotions, they tended to be angry rather than happy (Marshall & Zimbardo, 1979; Maslach, 1979). Second, other evidence indicates that arousal may not be a necessary condition for emotions. We may be able to experience happiness or anger even if we aren't physiologically excited (Reisenzein, 1983). Third, the validity of the sequence predicted by Schachter and Singer—arousal → attributions → emotion—has not yet been established (Lazarus, 1984; Zajonc, 1984).

F I V E

Attitudes and Prejudice

The concept of attitudes
    What is an attitude?
        Affect
        Cognition
        Behavior
        Combining the components
    How are attitudes measured?
        Self-report methods
        Attitude scales
        Behavioral measures
        Physiological responses
        The bogus pipeline
    Is one method best?
Attitudes and behavior
    Inconsistencies between attitudes and behavior
    When do attitudes correspond to behavior?
        Availability of the attitude
        Relevance of our attitudes
        Situational factors
    Predicting behaviors from attitudes
Sources of attitudes
    Attitudes are learned
        Mere exposure
        Classical conditioning
        Operant conditioning
        Socialization
        Learning to hate: A summary
    Prejudice as an intergroup attitude
        Intergroup conflict and prejudice
        Social categorization
        Categorization and perceptual biases
        Stereotyping
Summary
For more information
In depth: Reducing prejudice through desegregation

Attitudes are universal. Only some people have a million dollars, blue eyes, social poise, or dandruff, but we all have attitudes. Some of our attitudes focus on political issues: Who do you like for president? What about those Russians? Others are concerned with human rights and social problems: Do you support legalized abortion? What should we do about apartheid—the forced segregation of whites and blacks in South Africa? And still others pertain to personal preferences: Do you like Coke or Coca-Cola Classic? Jazz or hard rock? Our attitudes encompass many topics, but each one illustrates our tendency to react in a positive or negative way to aspects of our social world. We are not just observers and perceivers, but evaluators and critics.

An attitude can pertain to virtually any social object—from abalone earrings and abortions all the way to zoos and zygotes. However, in examining the social psychology of attitudes, we will concentrate primarily on prejudicial attitudes. Society, far from being homogeneous, is made up of many different social groups—blacks, whites, men, women, Catholics, Jews, adolescents, the elderly—and in many cases people develop strong attitudes toward the members of another group. An overall attitude toward a social group is termed **prejudice,** for it causes us to *prejudge* people solely on the basis of their membership in a group or category. Prejudice includes positive biases, but the term has negative connotations. It implies an unfavorable rejection of others that is both unfair and irrational.

Although we will be concentrating on prejudice, do not forget that the questions we raise apply to other types of attitudes as well. Imagine, for example, that we encounter a man who refuses to pay his female employees as much as his male employees. First we might ask: Is this man sexist? His actions seem unfair, but how can we be certain of his attitude? For that matter, how can any attitude be measured? When people express their attitudes, do their words always match their feelings?

If we conclude that the man is sexist, a second question arises: Will this man's sexist attitude always influence his actions? Will he discriminate against women in other ways? Similarly, when does any attitude influence our actions? Do people who prefer Crest always buy Crest rather than Colgate? Do women who demonstrate against abortion always refuse to have an abortion themselves? When and in what ways do attitudes influence our actions?

A third question concerns the origin of prejudice: How did he acquire this biased view of women? Or, at a more general level, how do we acquire any of our likes and dislikes? Why do some people like Coca-Cola Classic whereas others prefer Coke or Pepsi? Why do some people prefer their steak medium well, when others opt for rare? What is the source of our attitudes?

Lastly, once we consider the nature of attitudes, their relationship to behavior, and their causes, we arrive at a final question: Will this man always be prejudiced? When and under what conditions do attitudes change? These important questions are examined at the end of this chapter and in Chapter 6.

The Concept of Attitudes

During everyday conversations, you can hear the word *attitude* used in dozens of different ways. A teacher tells a sulking student that he has "a bad attitude." A boss compliments an employee on her "good work attitude." Coaches commend their players for showing a "team attitude." Although these usages suggest that people have a general understanding of the concept, they also show signs of the same confusion that early psychologists had about attitudes. Are they positive or negative feelings, general mental states, or styles of behavior?

What Is an Attitude?

The term *attitude* has a long history. Originally, painters and sculptors used the word to describe poses that revealed human emotions. When psychologists appropriated the term early in the twentieth century, they applied it to all sorts of mental processes (Nelson, 1939). To some investigators, attitudes pertained primarily to *affective reactions*—feelings or emotional reactions to an object (Katz, 1960; Thurstone, 1928). Others, in contrast, proposed that attitudes were no different from other *cognitions* such as beliefs, values, and knowledge (Chave, 1928). A third group held fast to the original emphasis on *behavior* by defining an attitude as a tendency to behave in a certain way (Campbell, 1950; Green, 1954).

Even today the essential nature of our attitudes remains something of a mystery. Many theorists believe that attitudes involve all three of the elements identified by earlier researchers—affect, cognitions, and behavior. According to this **tricomponent theory,** an *attitude* is (1) an affective feeling of liking or disliking based on (2) beliefs (cognitions) about an object which (3) leads to a readiness to behave in a certain manner (Breckler, 1984; Smith, 1947; see Figure 5-1).

Affect. "I hate whites." "Pete Rose is a great baseball player." "Blacks frighten me." "I like Italian food." "I can't stand pushy women." All of these statements illustrate the emotion in our attitudes: the feeling of liking or disliking that causes us to evaluate an object as good or bad. These emotional reactions make up the *affective component* of an attitude, which can be positive (liking, love, desire, wanting, admiration), negative (disliking, hatred, abhorrence, contempt, rejection), or neutral (ambivalence, uncertainty, disinterest). Many theorists feel that the affective component distinguishes an attitude from all other psychological processes (Fishbein & Ajzen, 1975).

Cognition. The *cognitive component* of an attitude includes various assumptions and beliefs about aspects of our social world. Although our beliefs can be as inaccurate as the affective component is unfair, we feel that these beliefs are supported by objective facts and observations. An American who is prejudiced against Russians, for example, may assume that they deserve this rejection because they are untrustworthy, aggressive, and unintelligent. A prejudiced Anglo may believe that Chicanos are lazy. Such sweeping beliefs about the members of other social groups are generally known as *stereotypes* (Hamilton, 1979).

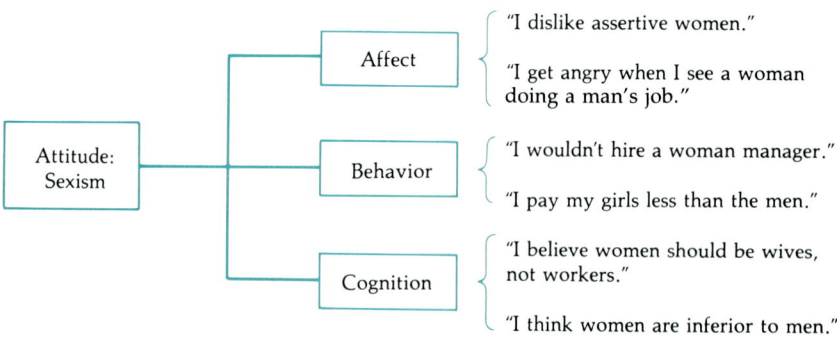

Figure 5-1 The tricomponent theory of attitudes, applied to prejudice against women, defines sexism as an affective feeling of like or dislike based on beliefs (cognitions) about women which leads to a readiness to behave in a certain manner. This tricomponent model emphasizes the so-called *ABCs* of attitudes: Affect, Behavior, and Cognition (Rajecki, 1982).

Behavior. Most social psychologists believe that our attitudes also encompass a *behavioral component*. A sexist man, for example, may quit his job when he is transferred to a department managed by a woman. A prejudiced woman may discriminate against blacks by treating them unfairly. In these two cases, individuals' overt actions are guided by their attitudes. However, the behavioral component of an attitude includes not only overt actions but predispositions to respond in certain general ways. A black racist, for example, could plan to live in a segregated neighborhood and decide to vote only for black candidates in all elections. This readiness to respond is often termed a *behavioral intention* (Fishbein & Ajzen, 1975; Rosenberg & Hovland, 1960).

Combining the components. According to the tricomponent model, attitudes form when all three components—affect, cognition, and behavior—become linked together in an organized structure. In one study based on this assumption, Donald Campbell arranged for white high school and college students to rate five ethnic groups—black, Jewish, Japanese, Mexican, and English—on five scales. To measure affect, he asked the subjects to indicate how much they liked or disliked each group. To measure cognitions, he asked for ratings of each group's competence, morality, and responsibility for social problems. Lastly, he measured behaviors indirectly by asking subjects if they would be willing to interact with members of the groups in a variety of social settings. Campbell discovered that these three components were systematically related to one another. People who disliked Mexicans, for example, also reported many negative beliefs about them and were unwilling to interact with them. In fact, the average of the correlations among the three components was about .50 (Campbell, 1947).

Attitudes link our emotions, cognitions, and behaviors together in an organized structure. In some cases, however, these components are not completely consistent with one another. For example, a person may know that a snake is harmless (cognition), and even agree to touch one (behavior), yet at the same time experience an intensely negative emotional reaction (affect).

Do these findings hold *only* for prejudicial attitudes? Apparently not, for studies of attitudes in regard to ideas and nonhuman objects—including religion, snakes, and contraceptives—also indicate that affect, cognition, and behavior combine to form attitudes (Bagozzi & Burnkrant, 1979, 1985; Breckler, 1984; Kothandapani, 1971; compare with Dillon & Kumar, 1985). These studies also suggest, however, that the three components are not always completely consistent with one another. You may, for example, rationally believe that a black snake is a harmless, attractive creature, yet when one crawls up your leg you may panic. This inconsistency, as we will see in the next section, raises a problem for researchers. On which component should we focus when we try to measure a person's attitude?

How Are Attitudes Measured?

Erving Goffman tells of a visitor to the Shetland Islands who dined with a local family. The visitor complimented his hostess on her fine soup, and she nodded in appreciation. She noticed, however, that her guest ate his soup very slowly and with great deliberation. Because she assumed his actions reflected his true attitudes, she concluded that her guest really didn't like the soup at all (Goffman, 1959).

As this anecdote suggests, attitudes can be measured in a variety of ways. Often we simply ask people to describe their own attitudes directly. Like the Shetland Islander, however, we realize that people's words don't always correspond to their inner attitudes. Bruce may claim to be an avid jogger, yet he may rarely exercise. Yolanda may express contempt for people who watch television, yet she herself watches two to three hours every day. Ray may argue that he is not a racist, yet he may feel uncomfortable when a black man sits next to him on a bus. We can learn a great deal by asking people to describe their own attitudes, but other indices yield important information as well (Dawes & Smith, 1985).

Self-report methods.
In 1928 Louis L. Thurstone published an article titled "Attitudes Can Be Measured." To assess individuals' attitudes, he argued, simply record their answers to one or more questions pertaining to the object. With this simple suggestion, Thurstone laid the foundation for all *self-report measures* of attitudes.

When measuring attitudes with self-report methods, researchers must generally choose between *free-response* questions and *fixed-response* questions. With free-response, or open-ended, questions, respondents must describe their personal viewpoints in their own words. Such questions as "What do you think was the main cause of the inner-city riots of the 1960s?" and "What are the most important problems facing the United States today?" are free-response questions. Fixed-response items, in contrast, offer respondents a choice between two or more alternative

Share your opinion. Using a scale of 1 (worst) to 10 (best) how do you like...

...Q-94's wide variety of music.

[1] [2] [3] [4] [5] [6] [7] [8] [9] [10]

...Q-94's new live stereo concerts.

[1] [2] [3] [4] [5] [6] [7] [8] [9] [10]

...Q-94's elimination of silly DJ chatter.

[1] [2] [3] [4] [5] [6] [7] [8] [9] [10]

...Q-94's concise morning magazine.

[1] [2] [3] [4] [5] [6] [7] [8] [9] [10]

...Q-94's cash giveaways.

[1] [2] [3] [4] [5] [6] [7] [8] [9] [10]

...Q-94's commercial-free music sweeps.

[1] [2] [3] [4] [5] [6] [7] [8] [9] [10]

Additional comments: _____

Name: _____ Age: _____

Address: _____ Zip Code: _____

Telephone Number: _____

Figure 5-2 The way questions are worded and the nature of the alternatives can sometimes bias people's responses. In this case, most of the questions are "loaded." First, each one assumes that the listener already agrees that the station "plays a wide variety of music" and has "eliminated silly DJ chatter." Second, the wording of the questions—such phrases as "silly DJ chatter" and "concise morning magazine"—prompts the listener to respond positively.

answers. "Are you in favor of, or opposed to, the use of busing to achieve racial integration?" and "What soft drink do you prefer: Coke, Pepsi, or Mountain Dew?" are fixed-response questions.

Both types of questions offer unique advantages and limitations. Free-response items are easy to write and give subjects free reign in answering. Before the answers can be analyzed, however, they must first be "coded": the key ideas in the answer must be identified and assigned a numerical value. Also, free-response items are most useful during interviews, because few respondents are willing to write detailed descriptions of their attitudes. Interviewers solve this problem by recording respondents' answers for them, but the presence of an interviewer sometimes distorts

FOCUS 5-1

Experiencing Social Psychology: *How useful are public opinion polls?*

It did not take long for people outside of social psychology to realize that self-report methods could be used to gauge the attitudes and sentiments of the public at large. As early as 1935 pollsters were measuring Americans' attitudes toward politicians, government policies, and products, and by the 1960s public opinion polling had grown into a major industry.

Not everyone, however, agrees that public opinion polls are useful (see Figure 5-3). Critics of polls are quick to recall the infamous polling failures that have occurred over the years. In 1936, for example, the now-defunct *Literary Digest* mistakenly predicted that the Republican candidate, Alfred E. Landon, would easily defeat Franklin D. Roosevelt in the presidential election. And in 1948 most major polls predicted that Harry Truman would lose, yet he handily defeated Thomas Dewey. Some critics also question the impact of polling information on the voter and the validity of sampling techniques.

Advocates of public opinion polls, however, point out that reputable commercial pollsters, such as Gallup, Harris, and Nielsen, are generally accurate to 2.5 percentage points. Furthermore, although basing inferences on a small group of carefully chosen respondents may seem risky, experts note that it's not the size of the sample that counts, but its representativeness. The *Literary Digest* poll failed to predict the winner of the 1936 election even though pollsters sampled the opinions of 2 million voters. The sample, however, was drawn from area telephone books, so the opinions of people who did not own telephones were overlooked—and only the relatively affluent, who tended to vote Republican, could afford a telephone in that Depression year. In the same election, George Gallup successfully forecast the outcome on the basis of a smaller but more representative sampling of American voters.

Given the problems with some polls, you should always examine their results with a skeptical eye. Many kinds of organizations are now conducting polls—newspapers, manufacturers, magazines, television, academic centers, political organizations, commercial pollsters—and not all of them use the appropriate scientific techniques. If the pollsters are trying to generalize their findings to a large segment of society, then the sample should be fairly large; at least 1,500 people is a fair rule of thumb. Furthermore, systematic sampling techniques should be used and questions should be properly worded so that they won't bias responses. Finally, if the poll addresses sensitive or controversial issues, then subjects' responses must be taken with a grain of salt. Like any self-report survey, public opinion polls measure only those attitudes we will publicly reveal; our more private, hidden attitudes may go undetected (Backstrom & Hursh-César, 1981; Slonim, 1960).

subjects' answers to sensitive questions. A racist, for example, may be reluctant to make statements like those shown in Table 5-1 to a black interviewer.

To avoid such problems, many researchers turn to fixed-response items. Such items are more difficult to write, but they can often be administered in the form of a questionnaire. Also, because respondents select one answer from several alternatives, no coding is necessary. Fixed-response items can, however, subtly bias respondents' answers. Faced with an array of alternatives, individuals with no opinion at all on an issue may still pick a position. Also, the nature of the alternatives may lead respondents to answer in a particular way (see Figure 5-2 and Focus 5-1).

Figure 5-3 Critics of public opinion polls believe that they are too often inaccurate. Also, when people hear the results of such polls, their own attitudes toward the issues may be altered. Ironically, one would have to conduct a poll to determine just how much people dislike opinion polls.

Reprinted by permission: Tribune Media Services.

TABLE 5-1

Some free-response items used in a survey of whites' attitudes toward blacks carried out in 1967, when racial tensions were very high.

Respondent 1	Respondent 2
Question: What do you think was the main cause of these disturbances [riots]?	
Agitators. Martin Luther King and Rap Brown and that black bastard Carmichael.	Dissatisfaction. They are dissatisfied with the way they live, the way they are treated, and their place in the social structure of America.
Question: Have the disturbances helped or hurt the cause of Negro rights?	
Hurt. Whites are starting to wise up to what a danger these people can be. They are going to be tough from now on. People are fed up. . . .	They have helped because they have forced white people to pay attention and have brought the subject out into the open and you can't ignore it anymore. . . .
Question: What do you think the city government could do to keep a disturbance from breaking out here?	
Lock up all the agitators and show them we mean business.	Not only promise but actually improve conditions, education, housing, jobs, social treatment. . . .

SOURCE: Campbell, 1971.

Attitude scales. Opinion pollsters often measure an attitude with a single, well-chosen question, but researchers prefer to use **attitude scales:** a series of questions pertaining to a single attitudinal topic. By asking several questions, researchers can have more confidence that the wording of their questions isn't biasing their results. Also, many attitudes are so complex that several items are needed to give a full description of the respondent's perspective. Sexism, for example, may be too complex an attitude to be assessed by the question "Do you favor or oppose equal rights for women?"

Researchers use *scaling methods* to select the items to be included in their attitude scales. Thurstone himself began by asking volunteers to rate a large number of statements about the attitude object on a scale from 0 to 11, where 0 was assigned to an extremely negative opinion and 11 to a very positive attitude. He selected only items that all the judges rated similarly and on which scores varied from very positive to very negative. These items were then presented to the actual respondents in the study, who were told simply to check any item that accurately represented their attitude. He then calculated respondents' attitudes by taking the average of the values of all the items (0 to 11) they endorsed. Figure 5-4 presents a sample of a *Thurstone scale*.

Another scaling method, which predates Thurstone's technique, was based on the concept of social distance: the distances individuals prefer to maintain between themselves and members of other ethnic groups. First suggested by E. S. Bogardus (1925), the *social distance scale* proved to be a useful measure of prejudice, and was the forerunner of a more general measurement method known as a *scalogram* (Guttman, 1950). Table 5-2 presents an example of a social distance scale.

Directions: Put a check mark in the blank if you agree with the item.

_____ 1. Blacks should be considered the lowest class of human beings.   [Scale value = 0.9]

_____ 2. Blacks and whites must be kept apart in all social affairs where they might be taken as equals.   [Scale value = 3.2]

_____ 3. I am not interested in how blacks rate socially.   [Scale value = 5.4]

_____ 4. A refusal to accept blacks is not based on any fact of nature, but on a prejudice which should be overcome.   [Scale value = 7.9]

_____ 5. I believe that blacks deserve the same social privileges as whites.   [Scale value = 10.3]

Figure 5-4   A Thurstone attitude scale. An actual scale would include 10 to 15 items and the scale values (shown in brackets) would not be included (Thurstone, 1931).

A third way of scaling attitudes was recommended by Rensis Likert (1932). With a *Likert scale* the researcher eliminates the need for independent raters by asking respondents to indicate the intensity of their attitudes themselves. As Figure 5-5 shows, on a Likert attitude scale subjects typically indicate degree of agreement with the item on a scale ranging from 1 (strong disagreement) to 5 (strong agreement). Responses to all the items are averaged or summed, and the result is the attitude score.

TABLE 5-2

A sample of a Bogardus social distance scale.

Directions: If you willingly admit members of a group in the specified situation, place a check mark in the blank under the group label.

	Blacks	Jews	Whites	Yuppies
1. To close kinship by marriage	_____	_____	_____	_____
2. To my club as personal chums	_____	_____	_____	_____
3. To my street as neighbors	_____	_____	_____	_____
4. To employment in my occupation	_____	_____	_____	_____
5. To citizenship in my country	_____	_____	_____	_____
6. As visitors only to my country	_____	_____	_____	_____
7. Would exclude from my country	_____	_____	_____	_____

SOURCE: Adapted from Bogardus, 1925, p. 301.

Directions: Indicate degree of agreement by placing the appropriate digit in the blank preceding each item:

1 = strongly disagree   3 = neutral   5 = strongly disagree
2 = disagree   4 = disagree

_____ 1. There is nothing lower than white trash.

_____ 2. It is usually a mistake to trust a white person.

_____ 3. If there is a heaven, it is hard to imagine that there are many white people up there.

_____ 4. The world might be a better place if there were fewer white people.

Figure 5-5 Sample items from a Likert scale measuring prejudice against whites among black students (Steckler, 1957, p. 397).

Behavioral measures. Self-report methods, whether based on single questions or attitude scales, do not always yield clear information about individuals' attitudes. First, they often emphasize the affective and cognitive side of our attitudes but underemphasize the behavioral component. Second, individuals aren't always certain of their own attitudes on issues, so they may have difficulty describing them. Third, people's responses can be influenced by the **social desirability bias:** the tendency to respond to questionnaires and surveys in socially acceptable ways. If, for example, respondents think the researcher would disapprove of them if they expressed racist attitudes, they may express very liberal and egalitarian opinions that in fact they do not hold.

To deal with these problems, investigators often turn to behavioral and physiological measures of attitudes. When Samuel Gaertner and Leonard

Many countries have chosen women to be their leaders, including England (Margaret Thatcher) and the Philippines (Corazon Aquino, see left). U. S. voters, in contrast, have yet to put a woman in the Oval Office.

Bickman wanted to see if blacks and whites are more likely to help members of their own race, they didn't ask people such questions as "If you see a person having car trouble, and that person is black, will you stop to help?" Instead, they assessed a tendency to help directly by using the *wrong-number technique.* They called 1,109 residents of Brooklyn, New York, between 6:30 and 9:30 P.M. and said:

> "Hello. . . . Ralph's Garage? This is George Williams. . . . Listen, I'm stuck out here on the parkway . . . and I'm wondering if you'd be able to come out here and take a look at my car."

When subjects explained that the caller must have dialed the wrong number, "George" continued:

> "This isn't Ralph's Garage? Listen, I'm terribly sorry to have disturbed you, but listen . . . I'm stuck out here on the highway . . . and that was the last dime I had! I have bills in my pocket, but no more change to make another phone call. . . . Now I'm really stuck out here. What am I going to do now? . . .
>
> "Listen, do you think you could do me the favor of calling the garage and letting them know where I am? I'll give you the number. . . . They know me over there." [1971, pp. 219–220]

After hanging up, Gaertner and Bickman waited for the subjects to call the number for Ralph's. The subjects themselves had been identified—on the basis of location of residence, name, and voice characteristics—as either black or white, and the George Williamses who made the telephone calls included seven whites and seven blacks who purposely spoke in a modified southern black dialect. As Table 5-3 indicates, whites evidenced more prejudice than blacks. They helped whites 12% more frequently than blacks, whereas blacks actually helped whites 7% more frequently than blacks.

The wrong-number technique is only one of a wide variety of behavioral measures of prejudice and discrimination. Researchers have inferred attitudes from willingness to serve a racially mixed group in a restaurant; from comments directed at blacks during group discussions; from sig-

TABLE 5-3

Percentages of black and white subjects who helped black and white victims.

	Race of Victim	
Race of Subject	Black	White
Black	60%	67%
White	53	65

SOURCE: Gaertner & Bickman, 1971.

natures on a petition; and from severity of shocks given in an experiment (Crosby, Bromley, & Saxe, 1980). Nonverbal behavior is also a source of information about attitudes, for as we saw in Chapter 3, voice tone, interaction distance, posture, and facial expression can reveal attitudes that are not expressed verbally (Weitz, 1972; Word, Zanna, & Cooper, 1974). As Focus 5-2 notes, behavioral measures of attitudes often find that people don't always live up to their liberal self-reports (Crosby, Bromley, & Saxe, 1980).

Physiological responses. We can also assess attitudes by measuring physiological processes, such as heart rate, respiration, and blood pressure. An early study of prejudice focused on subjects' galvanic skin response (GSR)—changes in electrical conductivity of the skin brought about by minute changes in perspiration. The GSR of white subjects was recorded while the apparatus was being adjusted by either a white

---

FOCUS 5–2

A Closer Look: *Is America becoming less prejudiced?*

Not too long ago racism and sexism were (as the black activist H. Rap Brown said of violence) as American as apple pie. In 1942 most white Americans favored segregated schools and neighborhoods. Little had changed by 1963, when 50.4% claimed they would object if a member of their family brought a black friend home to dinner, 63.6% felt that interracial marriage should be against the law, and 78.2% felt that blacks shouldn't "push themselves where they're not wanted" (see Figure 5-6). Similarly, in the late 1930s most Americans said that they would not vote for a female presidential candidate, even if she were qualified, and that a woman should not work if her husband was capable of supporting her (see Figure 5-7).

Has anything changed since then? According to public opinion polls, yes. As Figure 5-6 indicates, the number of whites who express racist attitudes has dropped substantially over the years. A majority of whites now express a willingness to accept blacks in schools, their homes, neighborhoods, and public office, and even their attitudes toward interracial marriage have mellowed; white racists, once the majority in America, are now the minority (Taylor, 1984). Similar strides have been made in the area of sexism, as Figure 5-6 indicates.

Other evidence, however, is less encouraging. First, when whites are led to believe that their physiological reactions are being monitored by a lie detector, they tend to express more negative stereotypes concerning blacks (Schlenker et al., 1976; Sigall & Page, 1971).

Second, even though people describe themselves as unprejudiced, they often discriminate against blacks and women. Studies of helping behavior (in which the person in need of assistance is either black or white), nonverbal behavior, and aggressive actions in laboratory settings all suggest that when attitudes are measured indirectly, racism again predominates (Crosby, Bromley, & Saxe, 1980). When the white male college students in one study were asked to give electric shocks to a fellow student, angry subjects administered much stronger shocks to black victims than to whites (as in Stanley Milgram's research, the "victims" were confederates and received no shocks). And in a study of nonverbal behavior, the whites who claimed not to be prejudiced turned out to be the least friendly at the nonverbal level when they interacted with blacks (Weitz, 1972).

Third, although opinion polls show that blatant expressions of racism are dwindling, white hostility is still evident in opinions on a number of political

(continued)

assistant or a black assistant. As expected, GSR changed more when the adjustments were made by a black rather a white, although the size of this change dropped with each successive contact (Rankin & Campbell, 1955).

Pupillometrics—the recording of changes in the size of the pupils to measure emotional reactions—is a second physiological index of attitude. Eckhard Hess, the pioneer in this area, supposedly discovered the link between pupil size and emotion while leafing through a book of animal photographs in bed. While Hess was looking at a particularly beautiful photograph, his wife commented that the light must be too dim because his eyes were widely dilated. Hess argued that the light was fine, but later began to wonder if his eyes were betraying his liking for the picture (Rice, 1974). Investigating his hunch, he showed pictures of either landscapes or a female nude to his laboratory assistant. As he had suspected, his assistant's pupils dilated noticeably when he viewed the nude, but

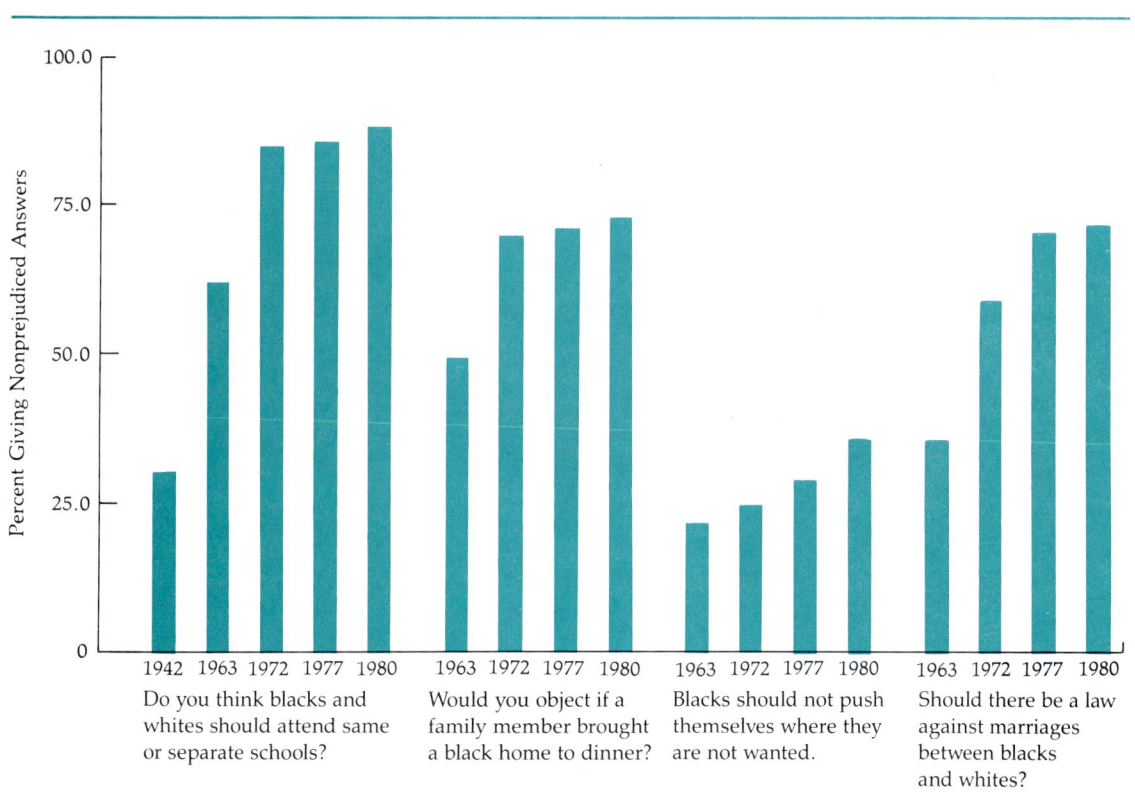

Figure 5-6 Changing patterns in white Americans' attitudes toward blacks.

not when he looked at the landscapes. In subsequent studies, Hess and other researchers discovered that homosexual men's eyes dilated more when they watched nude men than when they watched nude women, that imprisoned child molesters' eyes dilated more when they were shown pictures of little girls rather than mature women, and that individuals experiencing emotional stress showed more changes in pupil size than those who were not stressed (see Figure 5-8 on page 206; these studies are reviewed in Janisse & Peavler, 1974, and Woodmansee, 1970).

Hess's work with pupillometrics, however, also reveals some of the problems encountered when we try to link physiological processes with attitudes. While physiological changes may suggest that the individual is experiencing some sort of emotional reaction, without additional information we can't tell if the reaction is positive or negative. As Hess discovered, pupils don't dilate during positive reactions and constrict during negative reactions; rather, they simply dilate when emotions are

FOCUS 5 – 2   continued

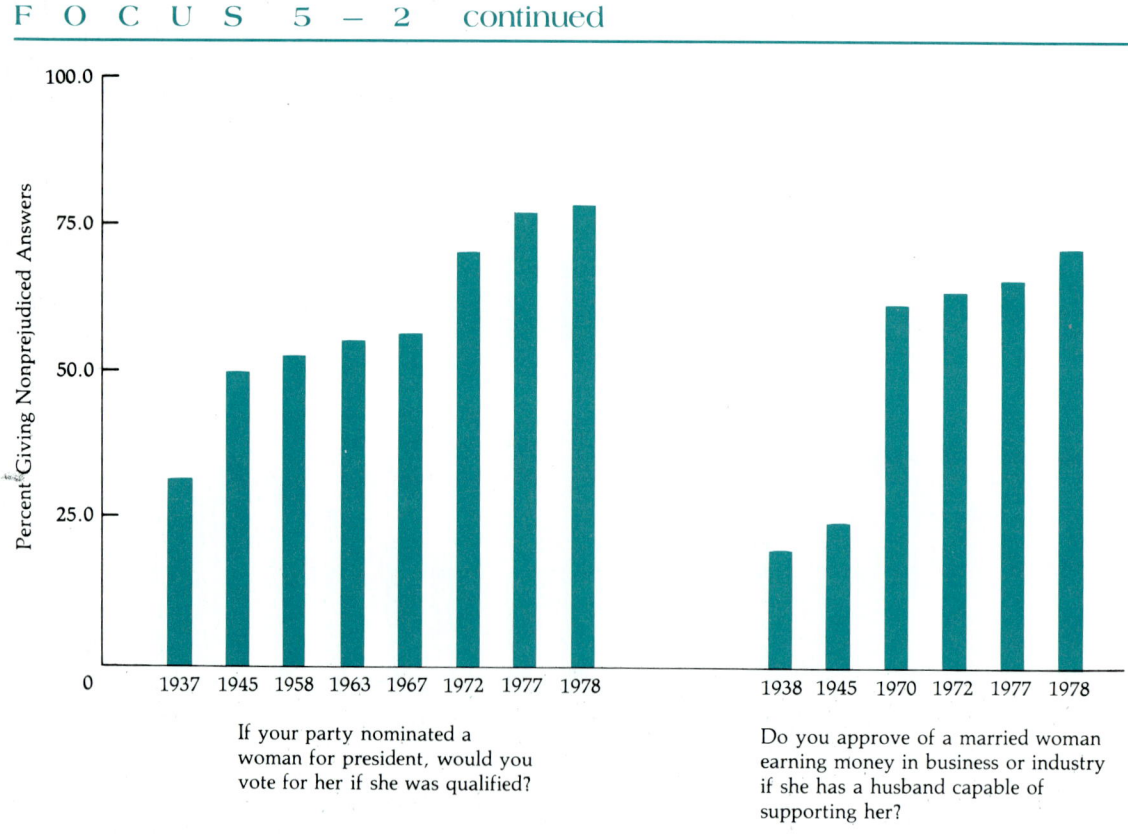

If your party nominated a woman for president, would you vote for her if she was qualified?

Do you approve of a married woman earning money in business or industry if she has a husband capable of supporting her?

Figure 5-7 Changing patterns in attitudes toward women.

strong. In addition, physiological processes are difficult to measure accurately. When women look at a picture of a seminude man, for example, their eyes may dilate more if they focus on the dark background behind the model, but constrict if they focus on the brighter areas of the stimulus. These changes in pupil size may then be mistakenly interpreted as signs of emotional reactions, when they are actually produced by differences in brightness. Our eyes may be windows to our souls, but the view they offer is often hazy.

Other physiological measures suffer from similar problems of interpretation. The *polygraph*, for example, is based on the idea that telling lies creates tension and stress, and this stress can be indicated by increases in heart rate, perspiration, and breathing. Even when a polygraph test is administered by an expert, though, the results are difficult to interpret. Innocent people often become emotionally aroused when they are telling the truth, and habitual liars may remain completely at ease while telling

---

and social issues. Many whites, for example, enthusiastically endorse *principles* of racial and sexual equality, but they do not support programs needed to *implement* those principles. Hence, although they claim to bear no grudge against blacks, many whites oppose busing, government assistance programs, and racial hiring quotas. Along the same lines, few Americans would argue that women are inferior to men, yet many oppose the Equal Rights Amendment and legislation that ensures equal pay for equal work. This "principles-implementation gap" stems in part from a general dislike of government regulations, but it also reflects a lack of commitment to steps needed to achieve egalitarian goals (Institute for Social Research, 1985; Schuman, Steeh, & Bobo, 1985).

Last, blacks continue to report lower levels of satisfaction than whites (Gallup, 1980), as well as feelings of economic, social, and political oppression (Institute for Social Research, 1983a). Even in the 1980s, nearly 30% of all black school children are taught in segregated classrooms and twice as many blacks as whites are unemployed (Meer, 1984). Parallel findings in the realm of sexism suggest that Americans' attitudes toward women have improved over the past decade, but that sexist attitudes persist (Institute for Social Research, 1983b).

In sum, the 1980s have seen both blacks and women on the Supreme Court and the space shuttle, but vestiges of prejudice remain. According to Kenneth B. Clark, a leading social psychologist in the field of racism, modern prejudice is "more complicated and more subtle" (quoted in Winston, 1983). Attitudes are changing, but barriers remain.

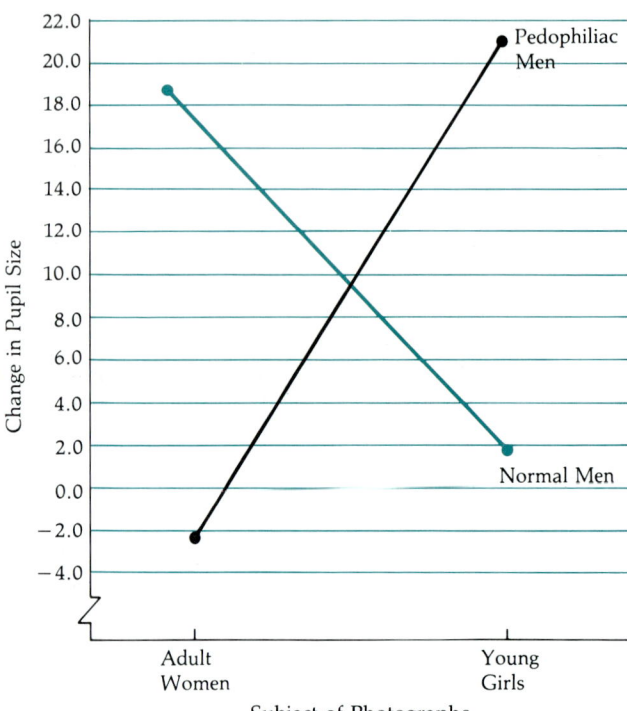

Figure 5-8 Men's reactions to adult women and young girls. In striking support of the value of pupillometrics, investigators discovered that men who had been convicted of molesting children displayed greater eye dilation when they viewed pictures of young girls than when they viewed pictures of adult women (Atwood & Howell, 1971, p. 116).

falsehoods. Even by conservative estimates, polygraph tests are incorrect at least 10% of the time, and the most frequent error is a "false positive": truthful people are erroneously identified as liars. Given these limitations, many experts feel that a polygraph test should never be used as the sole source of evidence concerning truthfulness (Ekman, 1985; Kleinmuntz & Szucko, 1984; Lykken, 1979; Podlesny & Raskin, 1977; Saxe, Dougherty, & Cross, 1983).

The bogus pipeline. Even though polygraph tests can be inaccurate, they often serve as a deterrent to lying. Why lie if the machine is going to catch you? When connected to a "lie detector," individuals tend to make certain their public statements correspond to their private attitudes. The *bogus pipeline* technique takes advantage of this tendency by convincing subjects that the polygraph is a pipeline into their inner thoughts and feelings. In the initial study of this approach, subjects first completed a general questionnaire on their attitudes toward such innocuous issues as movies, sports, and music. Then they were hooked up to a maze of sophisticated equipment that supposedly worked like a lie detector by measuring attitudes physiologically. To convince them that the machine could truly detect their reactions, subjects were asked the same questions that they had completed earlier on the questionnaire. After each question, the machine buzzed momentarily, and then its indicator needle moved to a number ranging from +3 (for strongest agreement) to −3 (for strongest disagreement). In fact, on one item subjects were told to try to fool the machine by concentrating on the attitude opposed to the one they actually held, but even in this case the machine accurately assessed the subjects' true beliefs. Unknown to the subjects, the machine's dials and buzzers were controlled by a confederate in the next room, who had copied the subjects' responses to the original questionnaire (Jones & Sigall, 1971).

These manipulations were intended to convince the subjects that the machine was a direct pipeline into their private attitudes. When connected to the bogus pipeline, individuals do indeed report their attitudes more accurately (Arkin & Lake, 1983; Gaes, Kalle, & Tedeschi, 1978; Gaes, Quigley-Fernandez, & Tedeschi, 1978; see Cherry, Byrne, & Mitchell, 1976, for a critical view). In one study of racial attitudes, white college students rated blacks and white Americans on typical rating scales; other subjects completed the same ratings while connected to the machine (Sigall & Page, 1971). The investigators found little prejudice when standard rating procedures were used, but differences were stronger when subjects' responses were supposedly being double-checked by the machine (see Table 5-4). Once again we see that individuals' publicly expressed opinions aren't always accurate indicators of their private attitudes.

Is One Method Best?

The motorist calls to a man raking leaves in his yard, asking him for directions to a business located acrosstown. The man thinks to himself: Which way is best? She could go down the boulevard. Or she could take the expressway. Or she could take the shortcut down by the river. Unable

TABLE 5 – 4

Average ratings of descriptions applied to white Americans and to blacks by white college students under standard rating conditions and in conjunction with the bogus pipeline. The more negative the score, the greater the disagreement that the description applies to the group. The more positive the score, the greater the agreement that the description applies to the group. [Scale: +3 (characteristic) to −3 (uncharacteristic)]

	Whites		Blacks	
Description	Bogus Pipeline	Standard Conditions	Bogus Pipeline	Standard Conditions
Intelligent	1.7	1.0	0.0	0.5
Stupid	−1.1	−0.1	0.1	−1.0
Physically dirty	−1.7	−1.5	0.2	−1.3
Sensitive	1.5	0.1	0.9	1.6
Lazy	−0.8	−0.4	0.6	−0.7

SOURCE: Sigall & Page, 1971.

to decide, he looks at the motorist and says, "You can't get there from here."

Like the man giving directions, you may be confused by the large number of ways in which attitudes can be measured. However, the answer to the question "How can we measure attitudes?" is not "You can't get there from here." Different methods are best suited for different purposes. Although people sometimes describe their own attitudes too favorably, more often than not self-report methods yield accurate information. Behavioral assessments and physiological measures, too, yield considerable information about attitudes, since their purpose can often be disguised. However, these techniques don't necessarily yield "better" or more accurate information about our attitudes. As we will see in the next section, many factors influence our actions, so the link between behavior and attitude is sometimes an uncertain one.

■ Attitudes and Behavior

Would life without attitudes be possible? Some social psychologists, such as Gordon W. Allport, say no, for "without guiding attitudes the individual is confused and baffled" (1935, p. 806). According to Allport, attitudes touch nearly all aspects of our social lives and "determine for each individual what he will see and hear, what he will think and what he will do." Yet our study of the various ways to measure attitudes revealed that the link between attitudes and actions is sometimes tenuous. An individual who says he supports Ronald Reagan may not vote for him. Someone who likes the color green doesn't buy only green clothes. An acquaintance may claim to be unprejudiced, but she may discriminate against members of other groups. When do our attitudes influence our actions?

Inconsistencies between Attitudes and Behavior

Researchers have been studying the relationship between attitudes and behavior ever since Richard T. LaPiere discovered that prejudicial attitudes aren't always translated into discriminatory behaviors (LaPiere, 1934). Between 1930 and 1932 LaPiere and a young Chinese couple traveled throughout the United States. Although opinion polls conducted at the time indicated that prejudice against Asians was widespread, the trio was turned away from only one establishment out of the 251 restaurants, hotels, and campgrounds they visited. Even more surprising, when LaPiere later sent questionnaires to these same establishments, he found that over 90% of them claimed that they did not serve Chinese. LaPiere's conclusion: attitudes, at least as measured by public opinion polls and questionnaires, don't predict behavior.

In retrospect, LaPiere's study can be faulted on many methodological grounds. He assessed attitudes several months after the behaviors, and during that time the attitudes may have changed. In addition, we have no way of knowing if the person who greeted the Chinese couple was the same person who answered the letter, if responding to a letter asking "Will you accept members of the Chinese race as guests in your establishment?" adequately measures attitudes, or if LaPiere's presence with the couple influenced their acceptability.

At the time, however, his findings sparked a controversy that would last for many years. On the one hand, dozens of studies matched LaPiere's by finding inconsistency between people's attitudes and their behaviors. A replication of LaPiere's work, for example, found that a racially mixed group of women was served in 11 restaurants but was refused reservations in most of the same establishments when they telephoned (Kutner, Wilkins, & Yarrow, 1952). Several other studies, however, reported strong linkages between attitude and behavior. In one project white students first completed a questionnaire measuring racial prejudice (DeFleur & Westie, 1958). Then, as a measure of behavior, subjects completed a "standard photograph release statement" refusing or permitting various uses of photographs of themselves with a black person of the opposite sex; the uses ranged from the very confidential ("Laboratory use, to be seen only by professional sociologists") to the very public ("Use in nationwide publicity campaign advocating racial integration"). Individuals who agreed to less than the average number of uses were labeled high in discrimination, whereas those who agreed to permit wide use of the photos were judged to be low in discrimination. The results indicated that the majority of the subjects acted in accord with their attitudes: 78.3% of the prejudiced individuals also discriminated, whereas 60.9% of the nonprejudiced subjects did not discriminate. Prejudice, in this case, predicted discrimination fairly well. (More comprehensive reviews of these studies may be found in Ajzen & Fishbein, 1977; Liska, 1975; Petty & Cacioppo, 1981; Wicker, 1969; Zanna, Higgins, & Herman, 1982.)

In time, researchers realized that both positions were partially correct. Although attitudes include a behavioral component, many other factors influence our actions as well. Even if you prefer bluegrass music, for example, you may tune your car radio to a hard-rock station to please a passenger. Although green is your favorite color, many other factors—such as quality, price, and availability—will influence your purchase of a car, a house, and clothing. The bigoted individual may not discriminate against members of group X for any number of reasons, including lack of opportunity or fear of retribution. Thus the answer to LaPiere's initial question—"Do attitudes predict behavior?"—was not a simple yes or no, but rather sometimes yes, sometimes no.

When Do Attitudes Correspond to Behavior?

Imagine that you are a sexist man working as a personnel officer in a large company. Today you are interviewing a woman for a junior executive position, and she fulfills all the requirements for the job. Will you hire her?

To answer this question, we need more information about you, your attitudes, and the situation. First, you may be biased against women, but this attitude may not be readily *available* to serve as a guide for your actions. You may, for example, rarely think about your biases, so they simply don't influence the way you act. Second, even if your biases are clear to you, you may decide that they are not *relevant* to the present situation. You may say to yourself: "Personally, I don't think women are as effective as men, but that's beside the point." Third, the *situation* may be so restrictive that your attitudes can't influence your behavior. As we will see below, your male chauvinism may prompt you to reject the job applicant, but many factors—including availability, relevance, and the situation—may weaken the linkage between attitude and behavior.

Availability of the attitude. The television commercial begins with a woman sitting in a restaurant ordering a soft drink. As she waits for her drink, she notices someone across the room drinking vegetable juice. Suddenly she slaps herself on the forehead and exclaims, "I coulda had a V-8!" (see Figure 5-9).

This commercial illustrates the importance of *availability*. According to Mark Snyder, before a person can act on the basis of an attitude, "knowledge of one's general attitudinal orientation must be available to the individual" (1982, p. 112). The woman in the commercial likes V-8 and would have preferred to drink it, but she simply didn't remember her attitude in time to order a V-8. In a sense, we act without thinking of our attitudes.

Several studies support Snyder's argument. Investigators have found, for example, that differences in *self-monitoring* influence the link between

Figure 5-9 This advertisement suggests that we sometimes forget what we like because our attitudes aren't available. If we stop and organize our thoughts, though, our choice will match our true tastes.

attitudes and behavior (Snyder, 1982). As we noted in Chapter 2, individuals who are low in self-monitoring strive to make certain that their actions match their principles, values, and attitudes. High self-monitors, in contrast, prefer to tailor their behavior to each new situation. Only low self-monitors engage in actions and make decisions that are consistent with their attitudes (Snyder & Kendzierski, 1982; Zanna, Olson, & Fazio, 1980).

Some attitudes are also more accessible than others. For example, attitudes formed through direct experience with an object and very extreme attitudes are both more available and more closely linked to our actions (Davidson et al., 1985; Fazio, Powell, & Herr, 1983; Fazio, Sanbonmatsu, Powell, & Kardes, 1986). Also, situational factors sometimes increase the availability of an attitude by drawing our attention to it (Ajzen, Timko, & White, 1982; Borgida & Campbell, 1982; M. Snyder & Swann, 1976). To investigate this process, Mark Snyder and William B. Swann (1976) first measured men's attitudes toward affirmative action programs. Then, two weeks later, these men were asked to formulate a judgment on a court case involving a woman who was suing her employer for sex discrimination. Snyder and Swann found a strong relationship between attitudes and judgments so long as subjects were told to organize their "thoughts and views on the affirmative-action issue." If the investigators did not draw subjects' attention to their attitudes, then no attitude-behavior relationship was found. When subjects were told to organize their thoughts, the correlation between attitudes and judgments was .73. The correlation was only .07 in the control condition.

Relevance of our attitudes. Even if our attitudes are available to us, we may decide that they aren't *relevant* to our actions in this particular situation (Snyder, 1982). Not all attitudes incorporate a well-defined behavioral component.

As with availability, many factors influence the relevance of attitudes to actions. When we become personally involved with an issue, for example, we are more likely to translate our attitudes into action. In one study of this process, investigators polled a group of college students concerning a proposal that would have raised the legal drinking age from 18 to 21. Although 80% of the college students objected to the proposal, substantially fewer were willing to campaign against it by making telephone calls (Sivacek & Crano, 1982). The investigators then split the students into two groups—students under 19, who would be denied alcoholic beverages for two or more years if the proposal passed, and students 21 and over, who wouldn't be affected by the change. The correlation between the students' attitudes toward the proposal and their behavior (as measured by the number of campaign phone calls they volunteered to make) was significant only for the younger students. The attitude-behavior correlation was .61 for the younger students, only .16 for the older students. In other words, the connection between attitude and behavior was much stronger among subjects who had a personal interest in the issue's outcome.

A second factor that influences relevance is the *correspondence* between the attitude and the action. Correspondence, as Icek Ajzen and Martin Fishbein (1977) define it, is the degree to which the attitude and the action focus on identical objects in the same context and at the same time. In LaPiere's study, for example, the object of the behavior was a well-dressed, smiling, English-speaking Chinese couple accompanied by an American professor. The object of the attitude, however, was "members of the Chinese race." Because the attitudinal and behavioral objects were so different (to say nothing of the vast differences in context and time), correspondence was low in LaPiere's study. Hence a nonsignificant correlation between attitude and behavior should have been expected.

Fishbein and Ajzen's assumptions about correspondence have been borne out in a number of studies. In one study a team of researchers assessed subjects' attitudes concerning four issues: the environment, conservation, pollution, and the Sierra Club (an organization dedicated to environmental protection). Five months later the subjects were asked to assist the Sierra Club by writing a letter to the local newspaper, joining the organization and paying dues, and so on. As Figure 5-10 shows, while subjects' attitudes toward the environment, conservation, and

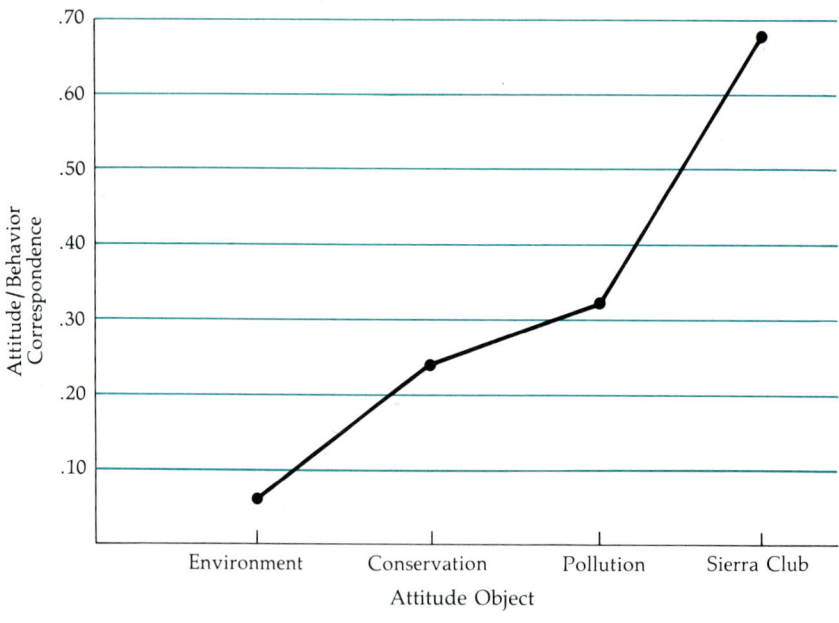

Figure 5-10 The correlation between four attitude objects and willingness to assist the Sierra Club. As Ajzen and Fishbein's concept of correspondence suggests, when the action and the attitude focus on similar objects, the correlation between them becomes stronger (Weigel, Vernon, & Tognacci, 1974).

pollution proved to be poor predictors of behavior, their attitudes toward the Sierra Club itself were highly correlated with their willingness to help the organization (Weigel, Vernon, & Tognacci, 1974). Only this attitude was relevant to the specific action that was being considered.

Ajzen and Fishbein (1977) reported similar findings in their review of previously reported studies on attitude and behavior. They sifted through 109 studies that reported a total of 142 attitude–behavior relations, classifying each finding into one of three categories: low, partial, and high correspondence. As Table 5-5 shows, the attitude–behavior correlations were usually significant (correlations of .4 or more) if correspondence was high. Low correspondence led to nonsignificant correlations.

Situational factors. The sexist personnel officer who wants to put his attitude into action by not hiring the female applicant may find that the situation prevents him from doing so. His company may have an affirmative action policy. His direct superior may be a feminist who would not take kindly to sex discrimination. No qualified male applicants may be available to take the position. In some cases, the situation prevents us from acting in ways that are consistent with our attitudes.

Evidence indicates that the impact of social **norms** on the attitude–behavior relationship is particularly strong (Fishbein & Ajzen, 1975). Norms provide us with guidelines for action, for they are the implicit standards that describe what behaviors should and should not be performed in a social situation. If our attitudes lead to actions that will conform to social norms, then acting out our attitudes poses little problem. If, however, our attitudes call for counternormative behaviors, then we may decide to go against our private feelings to avoid negative social sanctions. One early study of racism, for example, found that most prejudiced whites in a West Virginia mining town discriminated against blacks; they avoided interacting with blacks in social settings, and only 20% of the whites reported having any black friends (Minard, 1952). In the mines, however, attitudes did not predict behavior. Blacks and whites

TABLE 5 – 5

The number of relations between attitude and behavior reported in 109 studies, classified by the level of correspondence and the significance of the findings.

Level of Correspondence	Attitude–Behavior Relation		
	Not Significant	Low or Inconsistent	High
Low	26	1	0
Partial	20	47	4
High	0	9	35

SOURCE: Ajzen & Fishbein, 1977.

worked together without conflict, and 80% of the whites expressed friendship toward blacks.

These findings are understandable if we take into account the difference between the norms of the town and of the mine. The town norms discouraged interracial contacts and therefore promoted a high incidence of discrimination. In the mine, however, work norms emphasized cooperation and productivity, so racial discrimination was discouraged. Hence social norms, rather than attitudes, tended to be the primary determinants of the miners' actions (Campbell, 1963; Green, 1972; Warner & DeFleur, 1969).

Predicting Behaviors from Attitudes

We have seen that our actions don't always follow from our attitudes. Yet this inconsistency doesn't necessarily mean that people are hypocrites who say one thing and do another. Rather, the link between attitude and action depends on many factors, including the availability of the attitude, its relevance to the situation, and the constraints of the situation.

In fact, Ajzen and Fishbein believe that once we take these factors into consideration, we can *predict* behavior from attitudes. According to their *theory of reasoned action* shown in Figure 5-11, attitudes don't cause behavior directly. Rather, attitudes influence our intention to perform the behavior, and then this intention determines the action. Imagine that we want to know if a sexist man will discriminate against a woman who has applied for a job. Unlike other theorists, Fishbein and Ajzen believe that his general attitude toward women may have little to do with his decision to hire this particular woman. Instead, his behavior is determined by his attitude toward the action itself: hiring women. Also, the man's actions will be influenced by his subjective perceptions of the norms surrounding this action. Even though he may have a very negative attitude toward hiring the woman, he may not want to violate social standards that condemn discrimination. Fishbein and Ajzen believe that these two factors—the man's attitude toward the action and his subjective beliefs about norms—combine to form his *behavioral intention*. When will the sexist man plan to reject the woman's application? Only when (1) he does not like hiring women and (2) the norms against discrimination are weak (Ajzen & Fishbein, 1980; Fishbein & Ajzen, 1975).

Studies have yielded considerable support for the theory of reasoned action, suggesting that many kinds of actions—voting, dieting, family planning, career choices—are based on our attitudes (Ajzen & Fishbein, 1980; Davidson & Jaccard, 1979; Pagel & Davidson, 1984; Schifter & Ajzen, 1985). Ajzen and Fishbein's theory provides a strong answer to LaPiere's initial challenge. Granted, not all of our actions are linked to our attitudes. However, once we take into account the nature of the attitude and the situation, then the link between attitude and behavior becomes clearer.

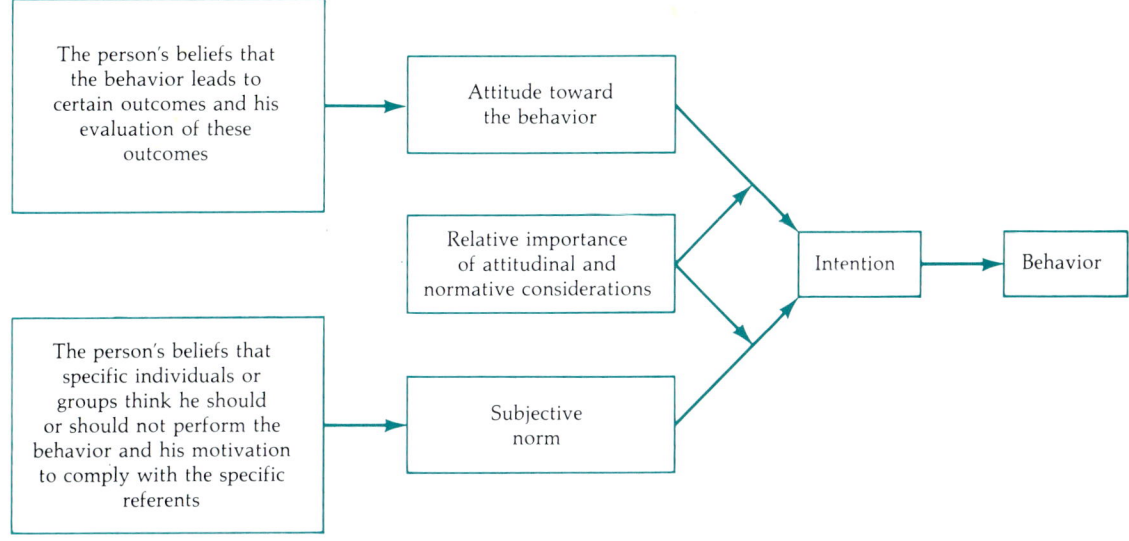

Figure 5-11 The theory of reasoned action. According to Fishbein and Ajzen, human action isn't capricious or haphazard. Rather, humans consider the implications of their actions before deciding if they intend to perform a particular behavior. Two considerations are particularly important: attitudes toward the action itself and perceptions of the norms pertaining to the action. As the figure indicates, these two factors combine to determine behavioral intentions, which then influence actual behaviors.

According to Fishbein and Ajzen, attitudes aren't just consistent with behavior: they *cause* behavior (see Bentler & Speckart, 1981; Kahle & Berman, 1979).

■ Sources of Attitudes

In 1984 some Americans voted for Walter Mondale; many more voted for Ronald Reagan. When a murderer was recently executed in Virginia, hundreds of people massed outside the prison in protest, while across the street hundreds of others gathered to celebrate. A 1983 poll found that 43% of the respondents approved of marriages between whites and nonwhites; 50% didn't; 7% had no opinion (Gallup, 1983).

These phenomena reveal the impact of our attitudes on our social lives. Yet they also illustrate the great diversity of our attitudes. Some people favored Reagan, others Mondale. Some oppose capital punishment, others consider it just. Some people condemn interracial marriage, some approve. Faced with this great diversity, we must ask: Why do some people end up with one set of attitudes while others take an entirely different view? Where do our attitudes come from?

Attitudes Are Learned

Some of our most basic attitudes may be instinctive. The widespread fear of snakes, for example, may spring from our genetic heritage (McGuire, 1985). Such instinctive attitudes are quite rare, however, for we generally acquire our attitudes through experience. We are not born with certain likes and dislikes. Rather, we *learn* to feel and respond to objects in positive and negative ways. In some cases, this learning may take place very gradually as we are repeatedly exposed to an object. Alternatively, our attitudes may form through simple learning processes known as conditioning. Or the people around us may teach us our attitudes through direct and indirect instruction. In any case, we learn to like and love, just as we learn to dislike and hate.

Mere exposure. When the new song first came out, you didn't like it. Now, after you've heard it several times on the radio, you think it's so great you buy the album. When you first attended an integrated school, you didn't care much for the white students. After three years, though, you realize that some of your best friends are white. You aren't much of a basketball fan, but you go to the games because you date somebody who is. After a few weeks, you have been transformed into a basketball booster.

These situations exemplify one of the simplest as well as the most surprising sources of an attitude: **mere exposure** to the object. Although this process runs counter to such revered truisms as "the grass is always greener on the other side of the fence" and "absence makes the heart grow fonder," evidence indicates that if people encounter an object frequently enough, they generally form a positive attitude toward it.

- Correlational findings suggest that words that occur frequently in the English language *(together, good, add, upward)* are generally viewed as more pleasantly toned than words that occur less frequently *(apart, better, subtract, downward)* (Zajonc, 1968).
- When subjects are exposed to nonsense words—such as *iktitaf, afworbu,* and *saricik* once, 5 times, 10 times, or 25 times, their attitude tends to become more positive toward the nonsense words they have heard more frequently (Zajonc, 1968).
- When people are shown a regular photograph of themselves and a photograph developed from a reversed negative, they generally prefer the reverse image. (It corresponds to the image they see of themselves every day when they look in the mirror.) When given the same choice with pictures of friends or loved ones, people prefer the true images over the reverse images (Mita, Dermer, & Knight, 1977).
- In elections involving relatively unknown candidates, individuals who spend the most money on their campaigns (and thereby gain the greatest exposure to the public) generally win. However, when one of

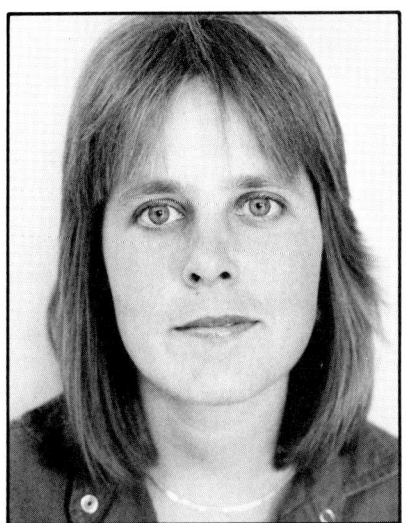 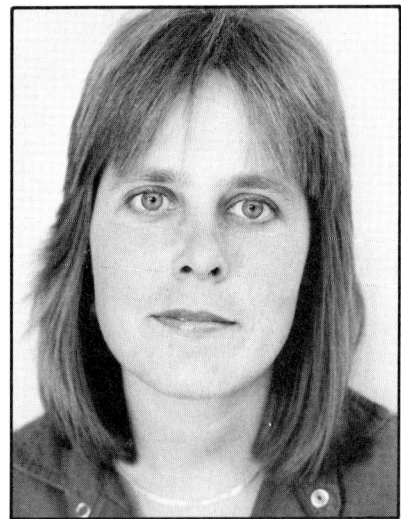

Do you see any differences between these two pictures? The photo on the left is a true image—a picture of the woman as other people see her. The photo on the right, in contrast, is a reversed image; it corresponds to the reversed image the woman would see if she looked at herself in a mirror. Despite the fact that the two photographs seem to be identical, researchers have found that people tend to prefer reversed-image photos of themselves. We see our reversed image each time we look in the mirror, but we rarely see our true image. Because of this repeated exposure, we become more favorable toward the reversed image.

the candidates is well known—either an incumbent or a famous public figure—he or she is far more likely to win the election (Grush, 1980; Grush, McKeough, & Ahlering, 1978).
- Rats who grow up listening to Mozart prefer Mozart's music over Arnold Schönberg's; they will activate a switch that turns on music by Mozart rather than a switch that turns on music by Schönberg. In contrast, rats who listened to Schönberg while growing up prefer Schönberg to Mozart (Cross, Halcomb, & Matter, 1967).

Although the mere exposure effect has been well substantiated, social psychologists are not yet certain why it occurs. Some argue that repeated exposure to an object makes it more recognizable, and that we tend to like things that we recognize. Others argue that the mere exposure effect can occur even when we don't remember ever seeing the object before (see Focus 5-3). In any case, while the underlying mechanism of the mere exposure effect may be unclear, the importance of the phenomenon is not—when we are repeatedly exposed to an object, we often end up liking that object. (I personally find the effect fascinating. But of course I have been exposed to it many times.)

Classical conditioning. Attitudes can also be acquired when a social object becomes associated with pleasant or unpleasant feelings (see Figure 5-13). A television commercial might show a series of scenes that create warm, pleasant feelings—cute puppies playing with little children, baseball players celebrating a victory, young lovers getting engaged, sexy men and women. The people in each scene are all drinking a particular soft drink, and the name of this drink is flashed repeatedly on the television screen. The advertisers are trying to create an association between their product and "feeling good" (Gorn, 1982).

This technique is based on the **classical conditioning** model of learning. As Ivan Pavlov described it many years ago, classical conditioning empha-

---

FOCUS 5-3

Controversy in Social Psychology: *Does recognition mediate the mere exposure effect?*

In the late 1950s the general public was outraged when advertisers began to use *subliminal advertising* to create positive attitudes toward their products. In one case, moviegoers were exposed to the messages "Drink Coca-Cola" and "Eat popcorn" as they watched the film. The messages, however, were *subliminal:* they were presented for such a brief period of time that they were never consciously noticed. Even though the moviegoers were never aware of the messages, the advertisers claimed that sales of Coke and popcorn skyrocketed (see Moore, 1982).

Researchers continue to disagree about the impact of subliminal messages on our attitudes. Some argue that we cannot form an attitude toward an object if exposure to that object is so brief that we are not aware of the object. This view, proposed by Michael H. Birnbaum and Barbara A. Mellers, argues that recognition is the intervening cause, or mediator, that links exposure and liking. As Figure 5-12 shows, the Birnbaum-Mellers model assumes that exposure teaches us to recognize the object, and that objects we can recognize are better liked than unknown objects. If we have heard a song only once, we may not recognize it the second time it's played; but when we hear it for the 201st time, we recognize the song easily. Furthermore, we will probably like the song we recognize more than a song that seems totally unfamiliar to us. Hence exposure causes increased recognizability, which causes increased liking (Berlyne, 1970; Birnbaum, 1981; Birnbaum & Mellers, 1979a, 1979b; Stang, 1974).

Richard L. Moreland and Robert B. Zajonc, in contrast, question the role of recognition because the mere exposure effect still occurs even when subjects can't recognize the attitude object (Moreland & Zajonc, 1977, 1979; Wilson, 1979). In one study subjects wearing stereo headphones listened to a tape-recorded story with one ear and simple melodies with the other. Later, they were unable to identify the melodies they had heard; the story was too distracting. But all the same, they still liked melodies they had been exposed to more than melodies they had never heard before (Wilson, 1979). Similarly, in a related study subjects were shown polygons for so brief a period of time that they couldn't possibly recognize them. In fact, many people weren't sure that anything had been shown to them at all. Yet subjects still preferred stimuli they had been briefly exposed to rather than novel stimuli (Kunst-Wilson & Zajonc, 1980).

Although these findings lend strong support to the Moreland-Zajonc model, they raise many questions as well. First, are the attitudes that we acquire through mere exposure purely affective? Can attitudes exist without any cognitive component, as Moreland and Zajonc suggest? Second, can our attitudes actually be influenced by sensory information that we do not consciously perceive? Studies of subliminal perception generally find that ad-

sizes the link between an environmental cue, or *stimulus*, and the organism's reaction, or *response*. As Figure 5-14 shows, classical conditioning takes advantage of a stimulus-response bond that already exists. No new conditioning is required, for example, to make pictures of sexy men and women evoke positive emotional reactions. The sexy picture is the *unconditioned stimulus* (UCS); the positive reaction is the *unconditioned response* (UCR). During conditioning, the object—in this case, the soft drink—is repeatedly paired with the UCS. After enough pairings, the drink itself becomes the stimulus for a positive reaction. To use Pavlov's terminology, after conditioning the soft drink is the *conditioned stimulus* (CS) and the positive reaction is the *conditioned response* (CR).

vertising messages that are never noticed generally have little or no effect on our attitudes (Moore, 1982). The Moreland-Zajonc model challenges these findings by suggesting that subliminal exposure to *objects* rather than *messages* may increase our liking for those objects. At this point the controversy remains unresolved. The possibility of attitude formation without recognition is intriguing, but more evidence is needed before we can draw any decisive conclusions.

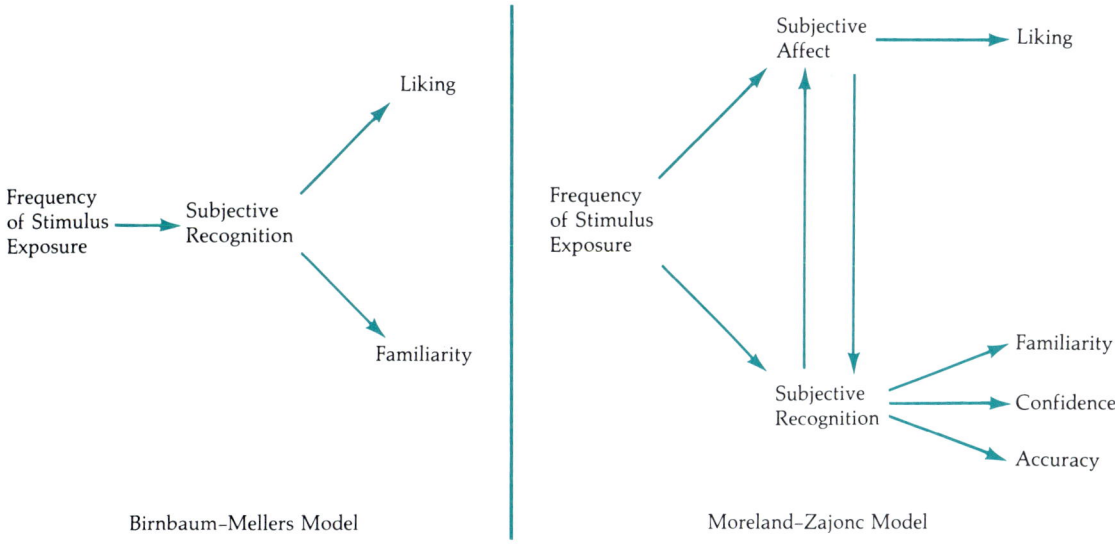

Figure 5-12 Why do we like objects that we have been exposed to repeatedly? According to the Birnbaum-Mellers model, recognition mediates the link between exposure and attitudes. The Moreland-Zajonc model, in contrast, maintains that exposure leads directly to a positive affective reaction.

Figure 5-13 Some advertisements create attitudes through a simple classical conditioning process. Whenever the product is presented to the consumer, it is paired with an object that the viewer already likes. Notice, too, the "face-ism" in the two ads: the billboard featuring the attractive man focuses on his head and upper torso, while the ad featuring the woman shows her entire body.

Researchers aren't yet certain if conditioning effects occur only when people recognize the association (or contingency) between the attitude object and the unconditioned stimulus (see Coleman & Gormezano, 1979; Kahle & Page, 1976; Page, 1969). Overall, however, investigators are convinced that many basic attitudes are formed through this simple conditioning process (Gorn, 1982; Staats, 1975; Staats & Staats, 1958; Zanna, Kiesler, & Pilkonis, 1970). Evidence indicates, for example, that attitudes can form when an object we know nothing about is linked to objects or words that already carry a positive or negative meaning. In one study investigators created attitudes by pairing such nonsense syllables as *yof* and *wuh* with emotionally toned words. Initially *yof* and *wuh* had no meaning at all for subjects; but when *yof* was repeatedly paired with such positive words as *gift, sacred,* and *happy,* people ended up liking *yof*. In contrast, when *wuh* was paired with such words as *bitter, ugly,* and *failure,* subjects eventually acquired a negative reaction to *wuh* (Staats & Staats, 1958).

Operant conditioning.   You are taking part in a survey.

Pollster: Would you mind answering a few questions for me?
You: Not at all.
Pollster: Do you think that mothers with working husbands should seek jobs outside the home?
You: I don't know. I'm not sure.

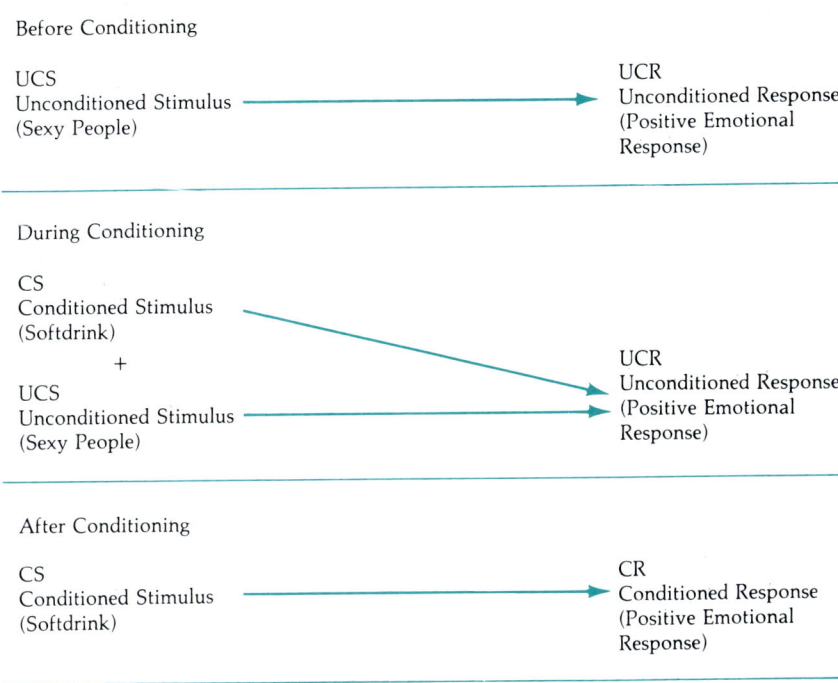

Figure 5-14 Before any conditioning takes place, the unconditioned stimulus (UCS) leads to an unconditioned response (UCR), but the neutral stimulus evokes no response from the person. During conditioning the neutral stimulus is paired with the unconditioned stimulus. Through this process the neutral stimulus becomes the conditioned stimulus (CS); when presented by itself it now evokes a conditioned response (CR).

Pollster: [Pause]. Would you vote for a qualified woman for president?
You: I guess so.
Pollster: OK, good. Do you feel that women are as qualified as men for most occupations?
You: Yes, I suppose so.
Pollster: Very good. Are you in favor of the Equal Rights Amendment?
You: Absolutely.
Pollster: That's great. Thanks for your time.

An innocuous interview? Hardly, for it demonstrates the **operant conditioning** of attitudes. As B. F. Skinner has long argued, when rewards (Skinner calls them *reinforcers*) immediately follow a behavior, that behavior tends to occur more frequently in the future. If the expression of an attitude is immediately reinforced (as when the interviewer said "Good"), then this attitude should be expressed more frequently in the future (Lott & Lott, 1985; Skinner, 1975).

One of the best-known studies of operant conditioning of attitudes was carried out by Chester Insko at the University of Hawaii (Insko, 1965). Insko telephoned students and asked them a series of questions pertaining to Aloha Week, an annual week of recreation held at the university. Half of the students were reinforced with a "Good" each time they expressed a favorable opinion about Aloha Week. When their attitudes were measured one week later in a completely different context, Insko discovered that students whose positive statements had been reinforced expressed more favorable attitudes than students whose negative comments had been reinforced.

Socialization. We learn many of our attitudes in the same way that we learn our language, social norms, and cultural values: through socialization. **Socialization,** which literally means "to make social," teaches us how to interact with other people, what behaviors are expected of us in various situations, and what things are valued in our society. Through socialization we may learn that all people are created equal, but then again we may also learn that Turks are dirty, women are incompetent, Jews are penurious, and blacks are musical.

Society's socializing agents—parents, peers, teachers, relatives, newspapers, books, television, religious groups, and so on—influence our attitudes in many ways. First, these sources may explicitly define, through direct instruction, what is considered good and what is considered bad. Our parents may tell us that certain kinds of people are "not nice" and we should never be seen with them. Our friends may make contemptuous remarks about the members of other ethnic and racial groups (Greenberg & Pyszczynski, 1985). Even the texts of our religion may tell us that "a man . . . is the image and glory of God: but the woman is the glory of the man. For the man is not of the woman; but the woman of the man" (I Corinthians 11: 7–8).

Second, socialization takes place through **social learning.** As Albert Bandura explains, we often learn attitudes by observing and imitating the actions and attitudes expressed by social models, such as our parents and peers. Imagine mom, dad, and daughter eating dinner. During the meal dad remarks that he thinks the Equal Rights Amendment is a communist plot aimed at the destruction of America as we know it. As daughter looks on, mom says, "Yes, dear. Would you like some more potatoes?" According to social learning theory, daughter is likely to express a similar attitude toward the ERA in the future. Unlike classical and operant conditioning, social learning is based on observation of others' actions (Bandura, 1969, 1977).

Bandura notes, however, that the acquisition of the observed behavior depends in large part on what happens to the model immediately after the behavior. Dad was reinforced for his anti-ERA remarks, so daughter should be likely to adopt his position. If mom had risen from the table and said, "That's it! One more chauvinist remark from you and I'll throw you out!" daughter would have learned to avoid her father's behavior. Because the observer doesn't directly experience the consequences, they are called *vicarious consequences*. According to Bandura, learning is more likely to occur when the vicarious consequences are positive than when they are punishing.

Third, socialization occurs as children (and adults) are bombarded by the symbolic cues that subtly define our culture (Sears & Kinder, 1985; Tuchman, 1978). The inferiority of women to men, for example, is a hidden theme in many newspaper stories, advertisements, television programs, and cartoons (see Figure 5-15). Through the newspaper we can learn that the world's affairs are shaped mostly by men. Many advertisements in magazines depict women as subservient to men and overly concerned with their physical appearance. Moreover, photographs of women in magazines often focus on their bodies, while photographs of men tend to center on their faces. This "face-ism" sends the implicit message that women are judged by the shapes of their bodies, while men

"She can't type, but I like to keep her around for a conversation piece."

Figure 5-15   What is the message behind this sexist cartoon? It is an unsubtle reminder that many men consider women to be sexual objects. The men joke that, were it not for her sexual attributes, the woman would not be able to get a job in a business or professional setting.
(Cartoon courtesy of the artist)

are judged by the strength of their ideas (Archer et al., 1983; Akert & Chen, 1984).

Television can also influence our attitudes. Although the content of television commercials has changed in recent years, women are still most often depicted as homemakers. Studies of commercials indicate that women are often portrayed as unintelligent, dependent on male advice, incapable of performing simple tasks, easily persuaded, eager to please men, envious of women who are better cooks or housekeepers, devoted to traditional roles of parenting, and deeply concerned with maintaining their attractiveness (Courtney & Whipple, 1974; Dominick & Rauch, 1972). Television programs themselves present women in an unfavorable light. Men outnumber women 3 to 1 in the world of television (Jennings, Geis, & Brown, 1980); the women who do appear are cast in stereotypic roles: homemaker, secretary, parent (McNeil, 1975); female characters are far more concerned with family than professional goals (Northcott, Seggar, & Hinton, 1975); and victims of violence are usually women rather than men (Gerbner, 1978). Given all these prejudicial cues, it is not surprising that children who are not already sexist tend to become so if they watch large amounts of television (Beuf, 1974; Freuh & McGhee, 1975; Morgan, 1982).

Learning to hate: A summary. Raymond Zyst, a 42-year-old white man, watches as a moving van pulls up to the vacant house next door. Ray wonders what the new neighbors will be like—if they have children, how much money they make, what kind of car they drive, if they will rake their leaves—when suddenly they arrive with the realtor. They are young, well-dressed, and black. Instantly Ray thinks he knows all he needs to know about the new neighbors. He decides to put his house up for sale.

How did Ray become a racist? He wasn't born prejudiced; rather, he learned his racist attitude. Perhaps he grew up in a segregated neighborhood, isolated from contact with blacks, so that exposure processes that would have created a positive attitude were never set in motion. He favors whites simply because he has been exposed to whites over and over again. Alternatively, through classical or operant conditioning processes he may have learned to associate blacks with negative, unpleasant feelings; whites, in contrast, prompt positive, pleasant reactions. Last, his prejudices may reflect his socialization. His parents and friends may have convinced him that blacks aren't as good as whites, and the television programs he watches may portray blacks in a negative light (see Figure 5-16).

Mere exposure, conditioning, and socialization are the sources not only of our prejudices, but of our other attitudes as well. In some respects, however, prejudice is not just one more attitude. Unlike, say, our attitude toward jazz or Ronald Reagan, prejudice is an *intergroup attitude*—a feeling of like or dislike for the members of a social group. Thus to understand

Figure 5-16 Blacks fare no better than women in the treatment they receive on television. Like women, blacks are underrepresented on TV programs (Weigel, Loomis, & Soja, 1980). Some programs—such as "The A-Team"—portray blacks in a stereotyped manner.

BLOOM COUNTY, © 1983, Washington Post Writers Group, reprinted with permission.

the sources of prejudice, we must explore the causes of our intergroup attitudes. We must understand why we tend to favor the members of our own group and reject the members of other groups.

Prejudice as an Intergroup Attitude

In his 1954 book *The Nature of Prejudice*, Gordon W. Allport points out that prejudice is an *intergroup phenomenon*. It is rooted in the basic human tendency to form social groups, and then to favor one's own group over all others. Here we will consider several of the powerful interpersonal processes that are set in motion when two groups collide.

Intergroup conflict and prejudice.

Some whites believe that blacks pose a threat to their way of life. They fear that blacks will move into their all-white suburban neighborhoods and place their children in the neighborhood schools. Whites also realize that blacks want better jobs, and that they may displace white workers. Many blacks, in contrast, believe that whites are striving to maintain the status quo. They feel that whites are trying to keep blacks down, and that most whites don't care what happens to black people (Institute for Social Research, 1983a, p. 7).

These perceptions are consistent with the **realistic group conflict theory** of prejudice (LeVine & Campbell, 1972). According to this view, prejudice can be traced to the realities of direct competition between two groups. When two groups compete for a valued resource, the group that wins does not share the resource with the group that loses. Therefore, the opposing group is seen as a threat, and prejudice soon develops. As Allport remarks, conflict between groups "is like a note on an organ. It sets all prejudices that are attuned to it into simultaneous vibration" (1954, p. 226).

Social categorization.
According to the realistic group conflict theory, people become prejudiced when they feel that other groups pose a threat of some kind. Henri Tajfel, however, argues that prejudice can occur even in the absence of conflict and threat.

Tajfel bases his ideas on the concept of **social categorization:** the idea that human beings tend to classify other people in categories. Through this categorization process, we intuitively segment the world's population into two basic camps: our own group and all the others. We view people in our group (in-group members) more favorably than those outside our group (out-group members). In fact, Tajfel suggests that this **in-group/out-group bias** occurs even when categorization is based on unimportant and irrelevant criteria. If we are women, we favor other women and disfavor men. If we have blue eyes, we are biased against brown-eyed people and prefer blue-eyed people (Tajfel, 1978).

This tendency to reject people who belong to other groups is stronger in some people than in others. Individuals who display characteristics of the **authoritarian personality,** for instance, consistently derogate all out-group members (see Focus 5-4). Tajfel argues, however, that any time categorization occurs, the in-group/out-group bias will emerge. Tajfel has conducted a series of studies in which subjects are assigned to one of two groups on the basis of some unimportant criterion, such as preference in art. Tajfel asks his subjects to indicate privately how a small amount of money should be divided among the members of the two groups. Even though the subjects don't know one another, can't see one another, don't expect to interact with each other, and understand that subjects were assigned to groups on the basis of nothing more significant than a personal preference, they still give extra money to in-group members, depriving out-group members. The tendency to favor in-group members is stronger than the tendency to deprecate out-group members (Brewer, 1979), but Tajfel's conclusion is clear: "the mere perception of belonging to two distinct groups—that is, social categorization per se—is sufficient to trigger intergroup discrimination favoring the ingroup" (Tajfel & Turner, 1979, p. 38; 1986).

Categorization and perceptual biases.
Once we fit people into categories, we no longer look at them as separate individuals with unique qualities. As a result, our perceptions can become biased and unfair (Quattrone, 1986).

Often these perceptual distortions are reflected in in-group members' remarks about the members of other groups. Consider such a remark as "They all look alike." This comment is predicated on the erroneous belief that everyone who is a member of the out-group possesses similar qualities and characteristics. The outgroup is judged to be *homogeneous* (see Table 5-6).

Perhaps as a result of this *out-group homogeneity bias*, people have trouble distinguishing between out-group members (Brigham, 1986; Brigham et al., 1982; Brigham & Williamson, 1979). In a demonstration of this bias, one experimenter asked blacks, whites, Japanese, and Chinese to study 20 photographs of same-race or other-race individuals (Luce, 1974). After one minute, the subjects were shown a new set of pictures and asked to select the ones that had been in the first group. As Figure 5-17 demon-

---

FOCUS 5-4

A Closer Look: *Is there a prejudiced personality?*

In the 1940s a team of researchers gathered at the University of California at Berkeley to investigate the psychological causes of prejudice (Adorno et al., 1950). Disturbed by the flood of anti-Semitism (prejudice against Jews) sweeping Nazi Germany, these researchers asked a simple but fundamental question: Do extremely prejudiced people have unique personality characteristics?

Exploring the personalities of highly prejudiced persons through in-depth interviews, clinical case studies, and questionnaires, the Berkeley researchers soon realized that some individuals simply hated all out-groups; not just Jews, not just blacks, not just communists, but all identifiable out-groups. Furthermore, this rejection of out-groups—or ethnocentrism—was related to a number of personality characteristics that combined to form an overall system of values and beliefs that the researchers labeled *authoritarianism*. To measure these authoritarian characteristics, the Berkeley researchers developed the **F-scale**—*F* because high scores tended toward fascism (Nazism). The F-scale measures nine major personality components (Adorno et al., 1950, pp. 255–257):

- Conventionalism: rigid adherence to conventional, middle-class values. ("Obedience and respect for authority are the most important virtues children should learn.")
- Authoritarian submission: uncritical acceptance of authority. ("Young people sometimes get rebellious ideas, but as they grow up they ought to get over them and settle down.")
- Authoritarian aggression: a tendency to condemn anyone who violates conventional norms. ("A person who has bad manners, habits, and breeding can hardly expect to get along with decent people.")
- Anti-intraception: rejection of weakness or sentimentality. ("The businessman and the manufacturer are much more important to society than the artist and professor.")
- Superstition and stereotypy: belief in mystical determinants of action and rigid, categorical thinking. ("Some day it will probably be shown that astrology can explain a lot of things.")
- Power and toughness: preoccupation with dominance over others. ("No weakness or difficulty can hold us back if we have enough willpower.")
- Destructiveness and cynicism: a generalized feeling of hostility and anger. ("Human nature being what it is, there will always be war and conflict.")
- Projectivity: a tendency to project inner emotions and impulses outward. ("Most people don't realize how much our lives are controlled by plots hatched in secret places.")
- Sex: exaggerated concern for proper sexual conduct. ("Homosexuals are hardly better than criminals and ought to be severely punished.")

The F-scale and the methods used to develop it have been criticized on a number of points. For example, people who are prejudiced but not committed to conservative political beliefs cannot be detected with the F-scale (Rokeach, 1960; this and other criticisms are reviewed in Cherry & Byrne, 1977, and Hyman & Sheatsley, 1954). However, the basic premise of this approach to prejudice—that some attitudes are rooted deeply in the individual's personality—has been supported in a wide range of studies that have linked authoritarianism with prejudice toward blacks (Martin & Westie, 1959), intolerance of ambiguity (Zacker, 1973), childhood experiences (Adorno et al., 1950), preferences for conservative presidential candidates (Lindgren, 1974), obedience to authority (Milgram, 1974), and other important aspects of personality (Harvey, Hunt, & Schroeder, 1961; Rokeach, 1960).

strates, subjects could recognize members of their own group but did much more poorly when they were tested on other groups. In fact, both blacks and Asians had particular difficulty recognizing white faces. Perhaps the "proverbial Chinese laundry man always insists upon seeing the laundry ticket" because "he cannot tell Caucasians apart" (Luce, 1974, p.108).

In many cases, the homogeneity bias is coupled with a tendency to see the in-group as very differentiated. We have a difficult time telling the out-group members apart, but we recognize the unique qualities of each person who is part of our own group. Hence we view our own group as more complex and sophisticated than the out-group. This *in-group/out-group complexity bias* leads us to feel that *"we* are individuals, but *they* are all the same" (Linville, 1982; Linville & Jones, 1980; Park & Rothbart, 1982).

The racially toned phrase—"You seen one, you seen them all"—suggests that one can safely make sweeping statements about the entire out-group after observing one or two of the group's members. If a black is victimized by a white employer, he or she may tend to assume that all whites are racists. Similarly, a visitor to another country who is treated rudely by a passer-by may leap to the conclusion that everyone who lives in that country is rude.

The belief that the behavior of a large number of people can be accurately inferred from the behavior of a few people has been dubbed *the law of small numbers.* In one study of this bias, male students at Rutgers and Princeton watched a videotape of another man making a simple decision, such as choosing to listen to classical music rather than rock (Quattrone & Jones, 1980). To initiate the categorization process, the researchers told some of the observers that they were watching a student from their own college, while others were told that the stimulus person

TABLE 5-6

Four processes at work in social categorization.

Process	*Definition*
Outgroup homogeneity bias	The outgroup is viewed as extremely homogenous
In-group/out-group complexity bias	People conceive of the in-group as more complex than the outgroup
Law of small numbers	People assume that valid judgments about the out-group can be based on observations of a small number of individual out-group members
In-group/out-group extremity bias	People make more extreme judgments of out-group members than of in-group members

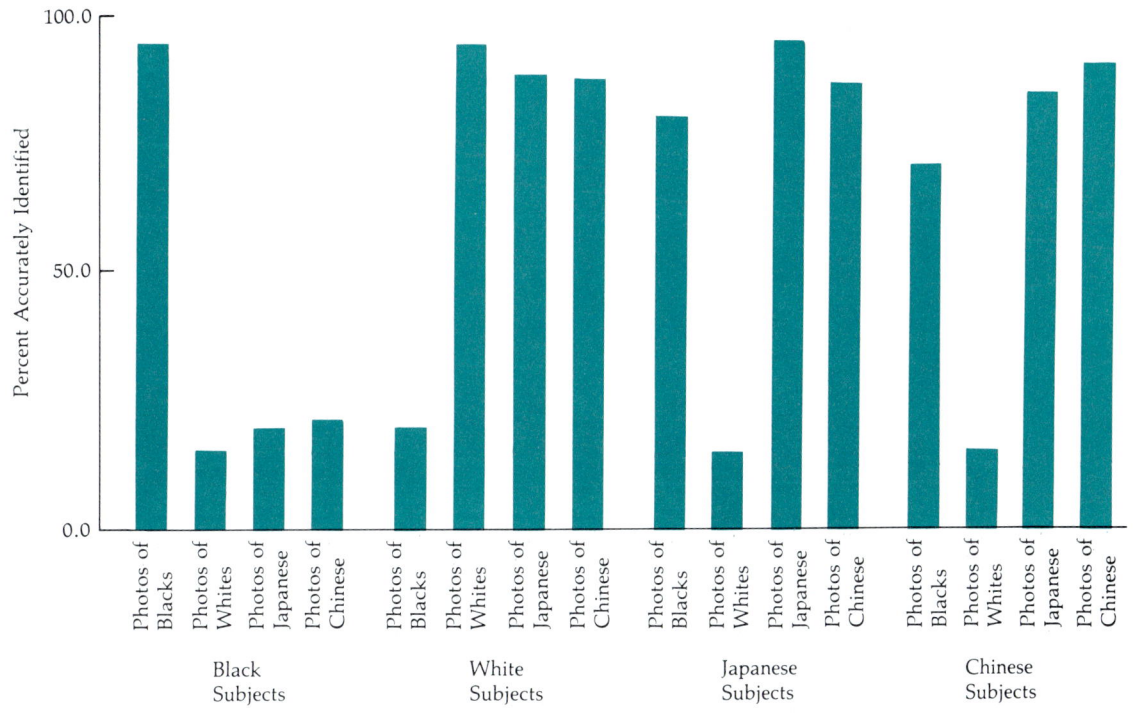

Figure 5-17 The percentage of subjects who correctly distinguished among stimulus persons they had seen previously and novel stimulus persons.

attended the rival university. When the subjects were asked to estimate how many men at Princeton and Rutgers would have made similar choices, they obeyed the law of small numbers when they made judgments about the out-group. They assumed that more students from the rival university would make the same choice as the stimulus person. As Allport concluded, "given a thimbleful of facts, we rush to make generalizations as large as a tub" (1954, p. 9).

A saying popular in the last century and immortalized in many an old Western—"The only good Indian is a dead Indian"—vividly demonstrates a final perceptual bias: the *in-group/out-group extremity bias*. According to this principle, we tend to make very extreme, highly polarized judgments about out-group members, and more guarded, less polarized judgments about in-group members. In one study, college-age men read a brief story about an elderly person or a young person who was described in either favorable or unfavorable terms. As the extremity hypothesis suggests, the member of the out-group—the older person—was rated more positively than the young person when the story was favorable, but more negatively than the young person when the story was unfavorable (Linville, 1982).

You have just met this woman at a party. Can you form an impression of her? Do you think that she is warm and sensitive or cold and blunt? Do you think that she makes decisions quickly or does she procrastinate before committing herself? If given a choice, do you think she would like to go to a movie or to a baseball game? Is she a homemaker or does she work at a bank? Your answers to these questions may have been influenced by your stereotypes about women. Traditionally, stereotypes about the role of women in contemporary society often depict women as warm, sensitive, indecisive, uninterested in sports, and more interested in raising a family than succeeding in a career.

Stereotyping. Categorization also leads to the formation of *stereotypes:* generalizations, or schemata, about the qualities and characteristics of the members of a particular category or social group. Stereotypes of the sexes, for example, may include personality traits assumed to be typical of men and women (see Figure 5-18). Gender stereotypes may also include occupations and social roles that are considered appropriate for men and women (Deaux & Lewis, 1984; R. A. Jones, 1982; A. G. Miller, 1982; Ruble & Ruble, 1982; Stephan & Rosenfield, 1982).

Stereotypes are not intrinsically prejudicial (McCauley, Stitt & Segal, 1980; A. G. Miller, 1982). Like all cognitive schemata, stereotypes summarize large amounts of information about other people, structure our perceptions of others, and reduce the load placed on our fallible memories. For a number of interrelated reasons, however, they often lend support to our prejudices. First, stereotypes are generalizations, and therefore they can easily become overgeneralizations. Although it may be true, for example, that men in general tend to be more aggressive than women in general, this stereotypic belief is inaccurate and misleading when it is applied to all men and all women in all circumstances. Second, some stereotypes *may* include a kernel of truth—that is, they are based on empirically verifiable tendencies in the population being judged.

Whites as Seen by Blacks	Blacks as Seen by Whites	Men as Seen by Men	Women as Seen by Men
Deceitful	Lazy	Aggressive	Affectionate
Sly	Superstitious	Adventurous	Attractive
Intelligent	Ignorant	Ambitious	Dependent
Treacherous	Loud	Confident	Excitable
Dirty	Dirty	Enterprising	Meek
Industrious	Musical	Independent	Sensitive
Lazy	Poor	Loud	Sentimental
Cruel	Stupid	Rational	Submissive
Selfish	Peace-loving	Steady	Talkative
Nervous	Happy-go-lucky	Tough	Weak
Conceited	Religious	Unexcitable	Gentle

SOURCES: Ashmore, Del Boca, & Wohlers, 1984; Stephan & Rosenfield, 1982.

Figure 5-18   Examples of some typical stereotypes

However, they are usually so exaggerated that they are grossly inaccurate (LeVine & Campbell, 1972; Stephan & Rosenfield, 1982). Third, stereotypes are usually evaluative. They suggest that all the members of a particular group have more or less of some positive or negative characteristic. Studies of gender stereotypes, for example, indicate that the characteristics attributed to men are more socially valued than those attributed to women. Hence stereotypes are slanted against women (Ruble & Ruble, 1982). Fourth, many theorists suggest that stereotyping is not a wholly rational activity. Our generalizations about the sexes are too simplistic and inflexible, and they prevent us from seeing the unique characteristics of each person we encounter. Thus, even though our stereotypes help us organize and process information, they exact a cost: they provide a cognitive foundation for our prejudices.

If stereotypes have all these perceptual and cognitive limitations, why do they persist? One explanation suggests that once we acquire stereotypes, they set in motion *confirmatory biases:* perceptual and cognitive biases that affirm the validity of our beliefs. As we saw in Chapter 3, without realizing it we tend to reinterpret ambiguous information about other people until it confirms our stereotypes. In one study junior high school boys were shown drawings of ambiguously aggressive behaviors committed by a black and by a white. Although the actions were identical—only the race of the perpetrator was varied—the subjects felt that the actions committed by the black were "meaner" and more threatening than the identical behavior performed by a white (Sagar & Schofield, 1980). This effect held for both black and white subjects (J. M. Jones, 1983).

Confirmatory biases can also influence our memory, for we tend to remember evidence that confirms our expectations better than disconfirming evidence. In one investigation subjects were led to believe that a particular group of men was more intelligent than most people. They then viewed 50 slides describing behaviors that these men had supposedly performed. Each behavior was associated with a different man, and in each case the man acted in an intelligent manner, an unintelligent manner, or a neutral manner. When their memory of the slides was later tested, subjects overestimated the number of slides that supported their initial expectations and underestimated the number of slides that violated this expectation (Rothbart, Evans, & Fulero, 1979).

This memory bias may explain **illusory correlations: overestimations of the strength of the relationship between unrelated characteristics** (McArthur & Friedman, 1980). To demonstrate how illusory correlations support and maintain our stereotypes, one team of researchers asked subjects to read a series of 24 statements describing the characteristics of an individual who was either an accountant, librarian, doctor, stewardess, salesman, or waitress (Hamilton & Rose, 1980). Half of these statements were designed to be consistent with occupational stereotypes (the salesman, for example, was described as enthusiastic and talkative, while the stewardess was attractive and comforting) while half were irrelevant to the occupational stereotypes. When subjects were later asked to recall the descriptions of the various occupational groups, they recalled more of the stereotype-consistent qualities than of the inconsistent qualities.

Lastly, interpersonal processes also insulate our stereotypes from disconfirmation. When we interact with others, we tend to evoke new behaviors in those persons that are consistent with our stereotype-based expectations. In other words, stereotypes sometimes function as *self-fulfilling prophecies* (see "In Depth: Self-Fulfilling Prophecies," Chapter 3).

The impact of stereotypes on members of the out-group was vividly illustrated by a pair of studies of racial attitudes. In the first study, white male college students interviewed white and black high school students who were interested in joining a team. The interviewers were not aware that the high school students had been trained to give certain answers and behave in a standard fashion. Despite the similarity in their actions, the white interviewers treated black interviewees more negatively than white interviewees: they sat farther away from them, displayed signs of nervousness, and terminated the interviews sooner.

Now the researchers took the situation one step further by asking: How will subjects react when they encounter an interviewer who displays these negative behaviors? All the subjects in this second study were white, but some encountered an interviewer who enacted the negative behaviors identified in the first study. Others met with an interviewer who treated them in a more positive manner. In essence, some of the subjects were treated like whites, while others were treated like blacks.

How did the subjects in the second study respond to these two kinds of treatment? When an independent panel of judges rated their performance, the whites who were treated negatively (the way blacks were in the first study) were judged to be less competent, less confident, and generally less desirable as employees. The whites who were treated like the whites in the first study were rated more favorably. These findings argue that in an actual interview the interviewee will probably live up (or down) to the interviewer's stereotypic beliefs (Word, Zanna, & Cooper, 1974; see also Lord & Saenz, 1985; Skrypnek & Snyder, 1982).

These findings and those discussed earlier in this section, paint a bleak picture. Prejudice is an intensely emotional attitude, yet it appears to be deeply rooted in complex perceptual and cognitive processes. The seemingly harmless tendency for humans to form social groups isn't so harmless after all. Through social categorization, we divide the world up into *us* and *them*. In-group/out-group biases lead us to conclude that *we* are better than *they* are. Our stereotypes reinforce these biases, stand resolute against disconfirmation, and function as self-fulfilling prophecies.

Is there a positive side to the social psychology of prejudice? Perhaps. Although problems remain, real progress has been achieved in the last 30 years. Great strides have been taken to ensure the legal rights of minority groups and women, and abuses that were once common in America are much less common today. By identifying the sources of prejudice, we identify the ways to eliminate it. First, since we learn prejudice during our daily interactions with others, we can unlearn it by reversing the social forces at work in our homes, at school, and in the media. Second, persuasion techniques, which we will consider in Chapter 6, can also be used to undo our antipathies. Third, as "In Depth: Reducing Prejudice through Desegregation," at the end of this chapter argues, biases that create intergroup conflict can be subverted through equal-status contact. Thus there is ground for some optimism. Since social forces create prejudice, social forces can prevent it (Katz, 1978; Stephan, 1985).

■ Summary

Individuals react to the social world in both positive and negative ways. These reactions are guided by *attitudes:* affective feelings of liking or disliking based on beliefs about an object which lead to a readiness to behave in a certain manner. An attitude can pertain to virtually any aspect of the social environment. An attitude toward members of an ethnic, racial, or other group is called **prejudice.** In general, most researchers agree that an attitude has three basic components: a positive or negative affective reaction to the object; a set of cognitions (or beliefs) pertaining to the object; and tendencies to act in a certain way toward the object. This view is known as the **tricomponent theory** of attitudes.

Attitudes can be measured in a wide variety of ways. With self-report techniques, respondents describe their own attitudes by answering free-response questions or fixed-response questions. One special type of self-report method, an **attitude scale,** consists of a series of carefully selected items. Thurstone scales, the social distance scale, and Likert scales are three measures of this type.

When individuals' self-reports may be distorted by the **social desirability bias,** researchers often assess attitudes indirectly by measurement of behavioral and physiological responses. Gaertner and Bickman (1971) used the *wrong-number technique* to measure willingness to help a person who was either black or white. *Pupillometrics* is the measurement of changes in the size of one's pupils as one watches an object. The *bogus pipeline* is a technique by which subjects are convinced that the accuracy of their self-reports is being monitored physiologically. Indirect measures are most useful when individuals strive to describe their attitudes in socially desirable ways. Indirect methods tend to reveal evidence of greater racism than self-report methods.

Do attitudes correspond to behaviors? Although a classic study by LaPiere (1932) suggested that our self-reports about attitudes say little about our actual behaviors, recent research indicates that many factors influence the attitude–behavior relation. First, the attitude must be *available* to serve as a guide for action. The attitude–behavior relation is strongest when people are aware of their attitudes (low self-monitors) and attitudes are easily accessible. Second, the attitude must be *relevant* to action. When we are personally involved in an issue and when the attitude corresponds to a specific behavior, then the attitude–behavior relation becomes stronger. Third, *situational factors*, such as **norms,** work to increase or decrease the bond between attitude and action. Synthesizing these findings, Ajzen and Fishbein's *theory of reasoned action* proposes that attitudes influence behavioral intentions, and that these intentions then determine behavior (Ajzen & Fishbein, 1980).

In most cases, our affective, cognitive, and behavioral responses to social objects are acquired through learning experiences. This learning may take place gradually through **mere exposure:** frequent exposure to an object tends to increase our liking for that object. Alternatively, when an object is repeatedly paired with a stimulus that already creates positive or negative feelings, the object may come to evoke similar feelings. This process is known as **classical conditioning. Operant conditioning,** in contrast, occurs when our behavior is reinforced after we have expressed an attitude or reacted to an object in a certain way. We also acquire our attitudes through **socialization.** Society's socializing agents, such as our parents, peers, teachers, books, television, and religious leaders, may provide us with attitudinal information through direct instruction. Alternatively, we may learn attitudes by observing and imitating their actions and expressed attitudes. Bandura's theory of **social learning** explains this process (Bandura, 1977).

Like other attitudes, racism and sexism result from mere exposure, conditioning processes, and socialization. Prejudicial attitudes, however, are *intergroup attitudes*, so they are also caused by intergroup perceptions and processes. According to **realistic group conflict theory,** prejudice stems from competition for scarce resources. Tajfel (1978) argues that **social categorization** per se is sufficient to produce **in-group/out-group bias.** Individuals with **authoritarian personalities,** as measured by the **F-scale,** are particularly likely to reject out-group members. Social categorization also leads to biased perceptions of others and to *stereotypes:* generalizations (or schemata) about the qualities and characteristics of the members of a social group. Stereotypes are maintained by such confirmatory biases as memory errors and **illusory correlations.** They may also function as *self-fulfilling prophecies* by evoking behaviors that will confirm the original stereotypic belief. Thus, although prejudice is an intensely emotional attitude, it is deeply rooted in the complex perceptual and cognitive processes set in motion by our tendency to classify people in two groups: *us* and *them.*

■ For More Information

1. *Understanding Attitudes and Predicting Social Behavior,* by Icek Ajzen and Martin Fishbein (1980), presents the basic theory of reasoned action. Through examples the authors show how their theory can be applied to predict behavior on the basis of individuals' attitudes.

2. *The Nature of Prejudice,* by Gordon W. Allport (1954), is must reading for anyone interested in the social psychology of prejudice. Although first published more than 30 years ago, the book's theoretical framework for understanding prejudice remains viable today. An excellent integration of theory, case studies, research, and insight.

3. *Survey Research,* by Charles H. Backstrom and Gerald Hursh-César (1981), is an excellent how-to book on opinion polling and survey research. Backstrom and Hursh-César review step by step all the stages of questionnaire design, interviewing, and data analysis.

4. *Sex-Role Stereotypes,* by Susan A. Basow (1980), reviews a number of topics related to gender differences and sexism. The chapters dealing with the sources of sex roles and sex differences and the consequences of sexism are particularly useful.

5. "Attitude and Opinion Measurement," by Robyn M. Dawes and Tom L. Smith, provides an advanced but succinct review of the basic ways to measure attitudes. This section is a chapter in the *Handbook of Social Psychology* (Lindzey & Aronson, 1985).

6. "From Individual Differences to Social Categories: Analysis of a Decade's Research on Gender," an article by Kay Deaux in *American Psychologist* (1984), considers three basic questions about the sexes: (1) In what ways do men differ from women?; (2) What are the psychological implications of sex roles? and (3) Do people perceive and treat women and men differently? This final question focuses on sexism and sex discrimination.

7. *Prejudice and Racism,* by James M. Jones (1972), reviews with a critical eye the social-psychological study of prejudice. Jones places racism in the context of cultural differences between blacks and whites, and suggests steps that can be taken to increase our understanding of racism.

8. *Attitudes: Themes and Advances,* by D. W. Rajecki (1982), reviews some basic ideas concerning attitudes and illustrates the link between attitudes and other areas of social psychology. Taking a thematic approach to the field, Rajecki shows how social psychologists' understanding of various topics has changed over time.

9. *The Psychology of Intergroup Relations,* edited by Stephen Worchel and William G. Austin (1986), includes chapters written by the leading researchers and theorists in the field. Chapters are devoted to such topics as Tajfel's social categorization hypothesis, in-group/out-group perceptual biases, stereotypes, and inaccuracies in the identification of out-group members.

10. Volume 2 of *Consistency in Social Behavior: The Ontario Symposium* (1982), edited by Mark P. Zanna, E. Tory Higgins, and C. Peter Herman, presents papers from a recent symposium held at the University of Waterloo in Canada. The symposium focused on one basic question: When do attitudes and personality traits influence behavior? The 12 papers are most suitable for advanced students.

IN DEPTH

Reducing Prejudice through Desegregation

In 1954 the Supreme Court handed down a controversial ruling in the case of *Brown v. Board of Education of Topeka*. The Court ruled that all laws that required separate facilities for blacks and whites were unconstitutional, for such segregation failed to recognize the equality of races. Forced segregation became unlawful.

In making this historic ruling, the Court relied on evidence supplied by a number of social psychologists. In a brief titled "The Effects of Segregation and the Consequences of Desegregation: A Social Science Statement," Floyd H. Allport, Kenneth B. Clark, Isidor Chein, Stuart W. Cook, and other researchers identified a number of harmful consequences of segregation, including a loss of pride and self-acceptance among blacks (Allport et al., 1953). The statement also argued that equal-status contact between the races would be needed to eliminate the mistaken assumptions and false stereotypes that sustain prejudice. This perspective, known as the **contact hypothesis**, recommended desegregation as the best tool for eliminating prejudice (Cook, 1984).

The Supreme Court mandate took effect slowly, but by the early 1970s a large percentage of the public schools had been desegregated. With desegregation, however, came a growing realization that contact between blacks and whites doesn't always reduce prejudice (Schofield, 1978; St. John, 1975). For nearly every study that reported reductions in prejudice following desegregation, another revealed that desegregation either had no impact on prejudice or actually increased it. One team of researchers found that before their schools were desegregated, black and white children were relatively accepting of those of other racial backgrounds. When desegregation began, however, intergroup attitudes became increasingly negative (Gerard & Miller, 1975; Rogers & Miller, 1981). These findings suggest that intergroup contact is not a panacea for prejudice (Gerard, 1983).

Why doesn't school desegregation always lead to more positive racial attitudes? One possible answer focuses on the *nature* of the contact. Few people would argue that any kind of contact is sufficient to reduce prejudice. If black and white students insult, argue with, physically attack, or discriminate against one another, then certainly such contact should not be expected to yield beneficial effects (Riordan & Riggiero, 1980). Contact under such conditions may actually promote prejudice by providing blacks and whites with information that they can reinterpret to support their biases and stereotypes. Apparently many schools fail to create the appropriate contact situation needed to reduce prejudice (Miller & Brewer, 1984).

Ironically, the social science statement presented in 1954 to the Supreme Court recognized this limitation, for it argued that contact per se is not sufficient to reduce prejudice (Allport et al., 1953; Cook, 1985). These researchers maintained, however, that contact *can* be an effective means of reducing prejudice provided certain preconditions are met. First, the *status* of the individuals who interact in the contact situation must be equal. If, for example, the white students in a school come from middle-class families while the black stu-

(continued)

IN DEPTH *continued*

dents come from lower-class families, these differences in socioeconomic background may create conflicts and tensions. Differences in academic backgrounds and athletic skill can also create rifts between the two groups (Miller, Rogers, & Hennigan, 1983).

Second, the contact should involve informal, *personal interaction* with out-group members rather than superficial contacts. As Thomas Pettigrew (1975) notes, desegregation does not always lead to *integration*. Blacks and whites may attend the same school without interacting with one another. Studies have shown that when a school is first desegregated, contacts between blacks and whites increase, but within a few months the school becomes *resegregated:* blacks interact primarily with blacks, whereas whites interact primarily with whites (Silverman & Shaw, 1973). Also, many school systems compound this problem by grouping students on the basis of their scores on standardized achievement tests. Because of profound differences in educational experiences, whites typically outperform blacks on such tests. As a result, blacks and whites generally end up in different classes, and little contact between groups occurs (Schofield, 1979).

Third, the *norms* of the social situation must encourage friendly, helpful, egalitarian attitudes. Yet in many cases desegregation is mandated by the federal government over the objections of school officials and parents. In this atmosphere of tension and animosity, norms that discourage intergroup conflict often evolve (Stephan & Rosenfield, 1978).

Fourth, the situation must require *cooperative interdependence* in the pursuit of common goals rather than intergroup competition. In one well-known illustration of the disruptive effects of competition on group relations, 22 white 11-year-old boys attending a summer camp were segregated into two groups. When a series of competitions was held, tension between the groups escalated into aggressive encounters. To reduce this conflict, the investigators then staged a series of problems that could be solved only through cooperation. One problem required the boys to locate a leak in the camp's water supply. Another required them to move a truck that apparently had broken down. Each problem prompted the boys to seek *superordinate goals:* goals that could be attained only if the two groups worked together. During and after the pursuit of these goals, animosity between the two groups diminished (Sherif et al., 1961).

Evidence indicates that intergroup contact is much more likely to lead to reductions in prejudice when these four prerequisites are satisfied. In one elaborate study of all four factors, Stuart W. Cook identified highly prejudiced white women through a battery of personality tests. Approximately half of these prejudiced women were assigned to a control condition that received no treatment; the remaining women were hired to "develop a training exercise to be used in industry." For two hours each day for 20 days, they worked with two other women on an experimental task that required them to make complex decisions about a hypothetical shipping business. Both of the other women were part of the research staff; one was black and one was white.

Cook arranged the contact situation to meet the conditions described above. First, the subject and the black confederate were equal in status: they worked in jobs that were equally important and their educational backgrounds were similar. Second, each session lasted two hours, with a lunch break after the first hour. The lunch break provided the black confederate with an opportunity to reveal personal aspects of her life in a friendly, open way. Third, during these lunches both confederates discussed topics dealing with racial equality and desegregation; thus the white confederate had an opportunity to express nonprejudicial attitudes. Last, the task itself could not be solved without close cooperation.

When the subjects rated the black confederate at the end of the study, they were uniformly positive. Moreover, when their attitudes were measured several months later in a completely different setting, many subjects reported more favorable attitudes toward blacks in general. In the original experiment and a subsequent replication, Cook found that 40% of the women in the experimental condition showed a significant reduction in prejudice in comparison with only 12% in the control group. Given the initial strong prejudice of the subjects and the limited amount of contact with blacks (subjects worked with only a single black woman), these results are encouraging (Cook, 1985).

How can these findings be put to practical use? One technique, developed by Eliot Aronson and his colleagues, is known as the *Jigsaw Method* (Aronson et al., 1978). First, the teacher places students in groups containing both blacks and whites. Next, the topic to be studied is broken down into various subtopics. Each subtopic is then assigned to a single student, who must become an expert on his or her assignment. Once the experts master their subunit, they teach what they have learned to the other group members. Aronson and his associates have found that this technique increases motivation and learning while reducing prejudice (Stephan, 1985).

In sum, although many educators initially assumed that desegregation would automatically reduce prejudice, the promise of desegregation remains largely unfulfilled. Despite decades of political and social activism, prejudice and its pernicious consequences persist. The strength of black Americans' personal convictions has helped them cope with these social inequities, but stronger interventions are needed to ensure the effectiveness of current social policies. Desegregating schools is a start, but unless the nature of the contact situation supports egalitarian attitudes, school desegregation will realize only a fraction of its potential. Schools must be integrated rather than merely desegregated.

S I X

Attitude Change

Attitudes and persuasion
  Source variables
    Credibility
    Similarity and attractiveness
  The message
    Speech rate
    Rhetorical questions
    Drawing conclusions
    One-sided versus two-sided communications
    Order of presentation
    Fear and persuasion
  The receiver
    Intelligence and self-esteem
    Gender
    Original attitudinal position
  Understanding persuasion: An application
Consistency theories
  Cognitive dissonance theory
    Consistency versus rationality
    Consistency and choice
    Dissonance and commitment
  Consistency and counterattitudinal behavior
  The evolution of cognitive dissonance theory
    Inconsistency is arousing
    The importance of public commitment
Summary
For more information
In depth: Coercive persuasion

In 1975, few people outside of Georgia had ever heard of Jimmy Carter. In 1976, he was elected president of the United States. In 1968, Joseph R. was arrested at an antiwar demonstration. Now he is a lawyer in New York City. His law firm's largest client is a company that manufactures automatic weapons. In 1974, Patricia Hearst was kidnapped by a revolutionary group that called itself the Symbionese Liberation Army. After two months of captivity, she renounced her former way of life and joined the movement. If asked to name their most cherished possession, children usually pick the stereo or TV set. By adulthood, however, furniture and art objects gain the top spot. And by the time we become grandparents, our most treasured possessions are photographs (Csikszentmihalyi & Rochberg-Halton, 1981).

Attitudes change. Despite our desire to hold fast to our initial tastes and preferences, at times even cherished attitudes must be relinquished. The political candidate who seemed so competent four years ago may fall far short of our expectations. The values that shaped our actions in college may be replaced by the values needed for a successful career. We may run up against arguments that are so powerful that we must rethink our way of looking at the world. When new experiences bring new ways of evaluating important aspects of our lives, our attitudes change.

Many of the forces that cause our attitudes to change were examined in Chapter 5, for the learning processes that lead to the formation of an attitude can also change existing attitudes. Frank, for example, may develop a liking for a cold climate after spending three winters in Vermont. Madge may lose her fondness for Italian food when she comes down with intestinal flu on the same night she treats herself to a large pizza. After watching his favorite movie hero vilify the Russians, Ross may acquire an anti-Soviet attitude. In these examples, newly learned attitudes supplant old attitudes.

Attitude changes can occur in other ways, however. Take U.S. voters' attitudes toward Jimmy Carter. In 1976, he was elected president. By 1980 people were rushing to scrape his campaign stickers off their car bumpers. Why? One answer emphasizes **persuasion:** the communication of facts, arguments, and information calculated to change another person's attitudes. During an election campaign, we receive information from friends, editorials, news stories, and the candidates themselves. If this information convinces us that our attitudes are naive, misguided, or based on mistaken beliefs, then we will abandon them and adopt the recommended position. If, however, we reject these arguments, then we will probably retain our original viewpoint. In 1980, Ronald Reagan's speeches and promises packed more persuasive punch than Carter's.

The first half of this chapter examines the impact of persuasive arguments on our attitudes. Attitude change cannot always be traced back to persuasion, though. People often talk us into adopting new opinions, but our attitudes may also change as a result of internal, psychological processes. Consider the plight of the many Republicans who in 1976 voted for Carter, the Democratic party's candidate. Although Carter may have seemed to be a good alternative to the Republican candidate, for the next four years these Republicans had to live with their choice. When Carter succeeded, they could celebrate their wisdom. But when he faltered, two inconsistent thoughts must have run through their minds: "I am a Republican" and "I voted for Jimmy Carter." How did they cope with the psychological tension that these inconsistent thoughts produced? Many may have rationalized away Carter's weak points and emphasized his strengths. Many others, however, simply changed their attitude toward Carter. In 1980 they returned to the Republican fold by voting for Reagan (Kinder & Sears, 1985).

This view assumes that we are motivated to *maintain consistency*, or harmony, among our various thoughts, beliefs, and attitudes. When our cognitions are consistent with one another, they fit together to form a unified whole. If, however, one cognition is inconsistent with another,

Every four years, voters are asked to put their political attitudes into action by voting for the presidential candidate of their choice. To win votes, candidates use persuasive techniques in their political advertisements, speeches, press releases, and televised debates. In 1980, Ronald Reagan's campaign was more influential than Jimmy Carter's.

then we experience psychological distress. As we will see in the latter half of this chapter, attitude change is one means of reducing such psychological distress.

■ Attitudes and Persuasion

The president's staff awakens her just before dawn and briefs her on the situation. Riots have broken out in the capital city of a South American country. The pro-U.S. government has asked that a peacekeeping force be sent to keep order. The Pentagon feels that a military response is justified, and the president tends to agree.

Over breakfast she discusses the problem with the secretary of state. When he learns that the president is leaning toward a military response, he asks her to reconsider her decision. He admits that U.S. intervention would yield several positive consequences, but he notes several likely negative effects as well. He points to historical examples that argue against military involvement, and suggests several reasonable alternatives. The president pays close attention to his arguments. When he finishes, she questions him to clarify certain points he has made. She then reviews the issues, weighing the Pentagon's position against the State Department's. After discussing several points with her staff, she decides to deny the request for troops (Petty & Cacioppo, 1981).

Why did the president accept the secretary of state's recommendation? According to studies conducted by Carl Hovland and his associates at Yale University, the answer to this question is buried in the three elements that are common to all persuasive settings: the *source* of the persuasive message, the nature of the *message*, and the identity of the *receiver* (Hovland, Janis, & Kelley, 1953). First, consider the source of the persuasive message—the secretary of state. If we were listening to his arguments, we might ask: Is this man an expert on South American politics? Is he a dove? Can we trust him to make an objective decision? Second, the nature of the message is also critical. The secretary of state discussed some of the benefits of a military response before giving his own recommendations. Would a message that mentioned only weaknesses be equally effective? Third, persuasion also depends on who is receiving the message. In the hypothetical scenario, the president initially favored a military response, but she was not committed to this course. Would the secretary have been as successful if the president were intent on a strong show of force (see Table 6-1)?

Source Variables

On any ordinary day you are inundated with persuasive messages from a host of sources. Advertisements urge you to change your hair color, your diet, your smell; newspaper editorials suggest political positions;

movie reviews condemn and acclaim; junk-mail offers fill our mailbox, parents make clear their views, and our friends make suggestions. With all these voices clamoring in your ear, it's no wonder that you tend to listen to some sources more than others. Who do you listen to the most? People who seem credible, people who are similar to you, and people who are attractive.

Credibility. I still remember the cereal box's promise that for only one box top and $1.75, I could be the proud owner of a "self-propelled submarine that dives and surfaces." When the package arrived I filled the bathtub with water, inserted the "propellant" (a tablet of baking soda) in the submarine, and watched. The feebly bubbling submarine slowly sank to the bottom of the tub, where it lay on its side, taking in water and teaching me about credibility.

Most adults, through similar experiences, come to realize that we shouldn't be easily persuaded by claims made by noncredible sources. For example, if we are exposed to a message favoring the further development of nuclear-powered submarines, we are more likely to agree with the message if it is attributed to a well-known U.S. physicist rather than to the Russian newspaper *Pravda* (Hovland & Weiss, 1951). If we listen to a speech arguing for more lenient treatment of juvenile delinquents, we will change our own attitudes more if the source is a court judge rather than a dope dealer (Kelman & Hovland, 1953). We would be more likely to agree with the statement "A little rebellion now and then is a good thing" if it were credited to Thomas Jefferson and not Vladimir Ilyich Lenin (Lorge, 1936). And if we are told that we can get by with far less

TABLE 6–1

Contemporary interest in persuasion can be traced back to the efforts of a team of researchers at Yale University in the 1950s. Although they never developed a formalized theory of persuasion, the Yale Communication and Attitude Change Program identified three basic elements that are common to all persuasion situations: the source, the message, and the receiver.

Source Variable	*Message Variable*	*Receiver Variable*
Credibility (trustworthiness, expertise)	Speech rate	Intelligence
	Rhetorical summary	Gender
Similarity	Drawing conclusions	Initial attitude
Attractiveness	One- vs. two-sided message	
	Order of arguments	
	Appeals to fear	

SOURCE: Adapted from Hovland, Janis, & Kelley, 1953.

"... Do speakers really sound better with 'monster cable'? I can only tell you that in Los Angeles, when asked, 128 out of 150 Ouija boards said 'yes'."

"I don't like to knock a competitor's product, sir, but listening to the Audak HX-7 speaker will make you impotent."

"... Another nice feature is the crossover network, sir. It utilizes heavy gauge wire so the sounds that cross over into the mid-range speaker will have in effect, 'a safe crossing'."

Figure 6-1   Persuasion raises many practical questions. For example, sales personnel must make decisions about how they should make their pitch. Should they present both sides of the argument by admitting that other amplifiers have many good features, or should they just concentrate on their own product's outstanding characteristics? Should they avoid presenting technical information or try to dazzle the customer with facts and figures?
© 1983/1984 C. Rodriguez. Courtesy of the artist.

sleep than we normally get, we tend to agree more with this recommendation if it comes from a Nobel Prize–winning physiologist than if the source is the local YMCA director (Bochner & Insko, 1966).

What makes some sources more credible than others? Research indicates that source credibility is determined by two critical factors: expertise and trustworthiness. Some sources lack credibility because we think they don't know much about the subject being discussed. We may assume, for example, that a taxicab driver is not well informed, not at all an expert. Other sources, however, aren't credible because they can't be trusted to give us unbiased information; like the cereal advertiser, they may be providing us with inaccurate information (see Figure 6-1).

This is not to say that we never believe sources that lack credibility. Even individuals who are typically regarded as untrustworthy—politicians running for reelection, salespersons trying to close a deal, criminals proclaiming their innocence—can be credible sources when they take an *unexpected* stance on an issue (Eagly, Wood, & Chaiken, 1978; Wood & Eagly, 1981). Alice Eagly and her colleagues, for example, exposed subjects to a speech that accused a large company of industrial pollution.

When the speech was attributed to a pro-environment politician who was speaking to a group of environmentalists, subjects questioned the credibility of the source. In contrast, when subjects were told that a political candidate had made the speech while addressing the company's supporters, they felt that the speaker was much more sincere (Eagly, Wood, & Chaiken, 1978). In addition, as Focus 6-1 suggests, sources with little credibility can increase their persuasiveness by capitalizing on the *sleeper effect*.

Similarity and attractiveness. You are in a paint store picking out a brand of paint to use in redecorating your bedroom; you figure you need about three gallons. While you ponder your choice, a clerk walks up and says, "I think brand *A* is the best. I used about three gallons painting my living room and it worked fine." Another clerk, however, suggests brand *B*, explaining, "I used about sixty gallons last month and liked the way things turned out." Which brand will you buy—*A* or *B*?

Surprisingly enough, when the persuasiveness of these two kinds of sources was contrasted in a study actually conducted in a paint store (Brock, 1965), subjects tended to follow the recommendation of the clerk who had used the same amount of paint that they were planning to buy. Although the clerk who had used more of the paint clearly had more experience (and therefore should have been a more credible source), the other clerk was more similar to the subject. Even though the similarity between the clerk and the customer was based on an irrelevant characteristic—does it really matter that they both needed three gallons of paint?—this trivial similarity still made for greater persuasiveness.

In explaining these findings, several investigators have suggested that similarity works by increasing the attractiveness of the source (Simons, 1976). In general, we tend to be attracted to people who are similar to us in some way (Byrne, 1971). In addition, we are more easily persuaded by people we like than by those we dislike (Eagly & Chaiken, 1975; see Figure 6-3 on page 250). If similarity leads to attraction, and attraction leads to greater persuasiveness, it's no wonder that similarity increases a source's persuasiveness (Chaiken, 1979; Horai, Naccari, & Fatoullah, 1974).

The Message

Even communicators with all the right stuff—credibility, similarity, attractiveness—fail as persuaders if they organize and present their arguments ineffectively. Anyone who has ever suffered through a disorganized lecture, listened to a speech that makes no sense, or read an essay that harps on mundane, trivial arguments that are largely irrelevant to the central topic can understand the importance of developing a message that communicates and persuades.

In their basic theory of persuasion, the Yale researchers assumed that the effective message must achieve four goals: First, it must capture the audience's attention, for what is ignored can hardly persuade. Second, the message must be understandable; an audience must comprehend what is being said. Third, the source should strive to make the message convincing enough so that listeners will accept it. Last, the argument must be memorable so that its impact will be long-lasting (Hovland, Janis, & Kelley, 1953).

But how can we create attention-getting, understandable, convincing, and memorable messages? Many alternatives have been suggested.

FOCUS 6–1

A Closer Look: *Should the sleeper effect be laid to rest?*

The **sleeper effect**—a delayed increase in attitude change—was first studied by the Yale group researchers in 1949 (Hovland, Lumsdaine, & Sheffield). Five days after viewing a pro-U.S. film, American soldiers showed little change in their attitudes. Nine weeks later, however, attitude change had occurred, for now the soldiers who had seen the film were more positive than soldiers in a control group who had not seen the film.

Hovland and his colleagues advanced the *discounting cue hypothesis* to account for this surprising effect. Since the soldiers felt that the sponsor of the message—the U.S. Army—was a biased source of low credibility, they tended to discount the information presented in the film. After time had passed, however, the source of the information was forgotten while the information itself was still remembered. Because the cues that originally led the soldiers to question the credibility of the communication were gone, no discounting took place, and the message slowly changed their attitudes.

Subsequent investigators sought to test the discounting cue hypothesis by exposing subjects to messages from credible and noncredible sources and measuring attitudes at different times (these studies are reviewed in Cook et al., 1979). In many of these studies the sleeper effect didn't occur; subjects who listened to a noncredible source showed no increase in attitude change over time. Granted, they were no less positive than subjects who had listened to a more credible source, but this effect occurred because the influence of the highly credible source *decreased* over time. If anything, the findings actually demonstrated a delayed decrease in attitude change—a kind of reverse sleeper effect. These failures to find any evidence of increased attitude change when the source was low in credibility prompted Anthony G. Greenwald and others (Gillig & Greenwald, 1974; Greenwald, 1975) to question the reliability of the effect. In fact, after conducting a series of seven studies that failed to produce a delayed increase in attitude change, Greenwald asked, "Isn't it time to lay the sleeper effect to rest?" (Gillig & Greenwald, 1974).

A group of researchers at Northwestern University answered Greenwald's rhetorical query with a resounding no (Cook & Flay, 1978; Cook et al., 1979; Gruder et al., 1978). These investigators argued that a true sleeper effect could be obtained if several necessary conditions are met (Gruder et al., 1978, p. 1063). First, the message itself must be persuasive enough to produce attitude change. Second, the discounting cue (for example, the low credibility of the source) must be powerful enough to inhibit significantly the attitude change that the message would otherwise have caused. Third, the investigators should make certain that enough time has passed before they measure the attitudes again. Fourth, attitudes should be remeasured before too much time has passed, for otherwise the subjects will forget the original message as well as the source. Fifth, the appropriate statistical tests are needed to detect the effect. When the Northwestern researchers incorporated all these features in a study of the sleeper effect, they obtained the pattern of results shown in Figure 6-2. On the basis of

Speech rate. You have five minutes to persuade someone to major in psychology. What rate of speech should you use?

(a) Slow.
(b) Rapid.
(c) Moderate.

Fast talkers are fairly persuasive. For example, the subjects in one study listened to lecturers who spoke rapidly, moderately fast, or slowly (the

---

this evidence, they concluded that Greenwald's rejection of the sleeper effect was premature. Given the right conditions, we do tend to remember the contents of the communication longer than the source, and in such cases we will show a delayed increase in attitude change.

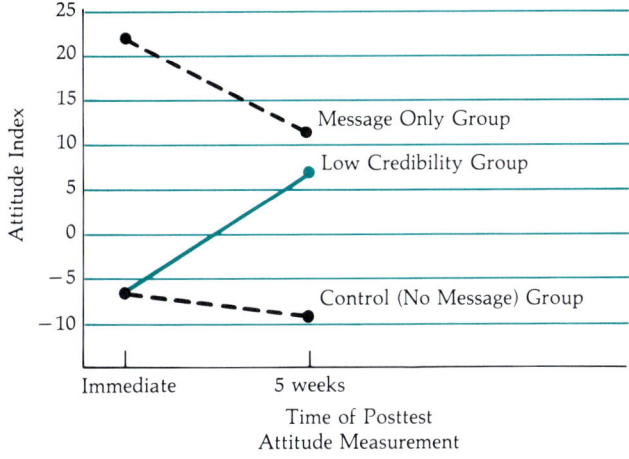

Figure 6-2 When subjects were exposed to a persuasive communication that was described as "false," "inaccurate," and "wrong" (low-credibility condition), they showed no attitude change immediately afterward. Five weeks later, however, their attitudes had changed in the direction of the communication, revealing a sleeper effect. In contrast, the amount of attitude change shown by subjects in the message-only condition dropped considerably over time. Attitude scores could range from −60 (least favorable to advocated position) to +60 (most favorable to advocated position).
SOURCE: Gruder et al., 1978.

Figure 6-3 Manufacturers often select attractive, likable sources in their advertisements for the products.

three rates were 191, 140, and 111 words per minute). The fastest talker was more persuasive than the moderate and slow speakers (Miller et al., 1976). Other studies that have varied the speed of a message electronically without changing its other properties have confirmed the greater persuasiveness of rapid-fire delivery (Apple, Streeter, & Krauss, 1979; MacLachlan, 1979). Why are fast talkers so convincing? Apparently their rapid-fire delivery convinces listeners that they are intelligent and well informed. So long as we don't think they are trying to hide something, fast talkers seem more credible than slow talkers (Miller et al., 1976).

Rhetorical questions. After presenting a powerful defense of your client, which closing statement would be most effective to use during the summation?

(a) "The evidence clearly indicates that my client was acting in self-defense."
(b) "Isn't it clear that my client was acting in self-defense?"

In some cases, ending an argument with a simple summary of the points we have made is more persuasive than a rhetorical question. In other cases, however, ending with a question is more effective. To predict when a rhetorical question is effective, we must consider the listener's cognitive response to the argument.

Cognitive response theory was developed by a team of researchers led by Richard Petty and John T. Cacioppo. It assumes that a persuasive message generates an internal cognitive response that "may agree with the proposals being made in the message, disagree, or be entirely irrelevant to the communication" (Petty & Cacioppo, 1981, p. 225). If the message prompts positive cognitive responses, the listener will be persuaded. A message that leads to negative responses, however, may produce a *boomerang effect:* the listener may become strongly opposed to the advocated position (Cacioppo, 1979; Petty & Cacioppo, 1981; Petty, Harkins, & Williams, 1980; Petty, Cacioppo, & Heesacker, 1981; see also Zillman, 1972; Zillman & Cantor, 1974).

Applying this theory to rhetorical questions, Petty and his colleagues asked college students to listen to a recording advocating comprehensive examinations for all graduating seniors. Four types of speeches were used to manipulate the strength of the argument and the rhetorical style of the messages. In the strong arguments/rhetorical style condition, for example, the message presented many strong arguments and such questions as "Wouldn't instituting a comprehensive exam be an aid to those who seek admission to graduate and professional schools?" while in the weak arguments/regular style condition the supporting arguments were easily refutable and summarized by direct statements. The audiences' involvement with the issue was also manipulated: half of the subjects were told that the proposal was being considered by the president of a distant college (low involvement), while others were led to believe that the new comprehensive exams were being considered for the following year at their own college (high involvement).

Figure 6-4 presents the results of this complex experiment. First, consider the results when people are not personally involved with the topic. According to cognitive response theory, a rhetorical question prompts the listener to respond actively to the message. Thus, when strong arguments are used, rhetorical questions should help. But when the arguments are weak, rhetorical questions will hurt. These predictions were confirmed. But what happens when people are already involved with the issue? In this case, a rhetorical question interfered with persuasion. Since subjects were already paying attention to the message, the question merely distracted them (Petty, Cacioppo, & Heesacker, 1981).

These findings indicate that rhetorical questions should be used with caution. If your audience is apathetic and needs to be roused, they may be effective. But if you already have their attention, then a simple summary is best. (Notice I didn't say, "Isn't it clear that a rhetorical question is most effective when the audience is apathetic and needs to be roused?")

Drawing conclusions. You are trying to convince two friends that, given the current level of unemployment, inflation, and the federal budget deficit, the U.S. dollar should be devalued. How should you end your argument?

(a) Let your friends draw their own conclusions so they don't feel threatened.
(b) Summarize your arguments and point out their implications.

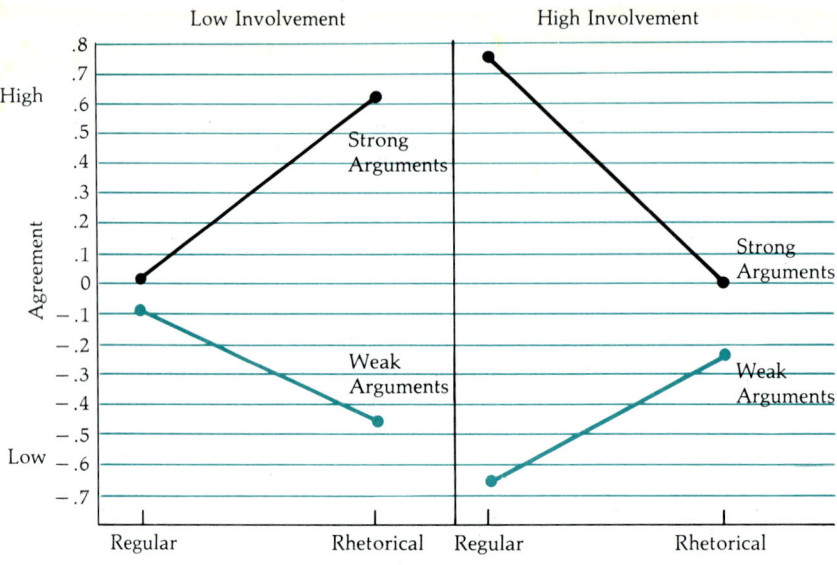

Figure 6-4 As the cognitive response theory of persuasion predicts, rhetorical questions are more effective than regular summaries provided the message presents strong arguments and the audience is not personally involved in the topic under discussion. If the listeners are already involved and your arguments are strong, then a standard summary is more effective.

When issues are complex or your audience shows little interest in what you have to say, drawing conclusions is an effective way of helping the listener understand and remember the persuasive message (Hovland & Mandell, 1952).

Communicators should, however, avoid drawing threatening conclusions, such as "If you agree with me on this issue, then you must vote for me for president"; "In view of the dangers of a nuclear war, you have no choice but to join our antiwar movement"; or "Don't delay! You must act now! Order the Spin-o-matic immediately by calling . . ." Conclusions of this kind may lead to the arousal of **psychological reactance** in listeners—the feeling that their freedom to choose has been threatened or eliminated (Brehm, 1976). Once threatened, a listener may refuse to change or, even worse, move in the opposite direction (a boomerang effect). To demonstrate the consequences of arousing reactance, one investigator exposed subjects to messages with threatening conclusions—such statements as "You have no choice but to agree with me"—or messages with the threatening conclusions deleted. When the subjects initially disagreed with the message, little reactance occurred. When subjects had initially favored the position endorsed in the message, however, a strong boomerang effect was found when freedom of choice was threatened (Worchel & Brehm, 1971).

One-sided versus two-sided communications. In an argument with your prodeception instructor you take the position that social psychologists should stop deceiving their research subjects. How should you present your argument?

(a) Present only the antideception side.
(b) Present both sides.

Many variables influence the effectiveness of one- and two-sided messages, including the audience's level of education, initial attitudes, and familiarity with the issue. Because your teacher is highly educated, already disagrees with your view, and knows there are many different perspectives on the question of deception, you would be more successful if you used a two-sided communication. In general, a one-sided message is best only when the audience is relatively uneducated, already agrees with you, and doesn't know that an alternative position could reasonably be taken (Hovland, Lumsdaine, & Sheffield, 1949).

Order of presentation. You are running for public office, and a debate has been scheduled for broadcast two days before the election; during the debate, the candidates will get 15 minutes each to present their views. Should you present your views:

(a) Second?
(b) First?

Deciding whether to present one's argument before an opposing argument is complicated. Research indicates that people often remember the first argument better than the second—a primacy effect. Yet in other instances the second argument has a greater impact than the first—a recency effect. According to one analysis (N. Miller & Campbell, 1959), timing is crucial. If the audience voted immediately after the speeches, order would be unimportant; both views would be equally well remembered. Conversely, if the audience voted many months after the debate, again no order effects would be found because both messages would have been forgotten. However, if the speeches are given back to back and the vote (or measurement) is taken after a delay of only two or three days (as in the example), then a primacy effect is obtained; the first speech has a stronger impact. Furthermore, to obtain a recency effect there should be a moderately long delay between the first speech and the second speech, and the vote should be taken soon after the second view is presented.

Fear and persuasion. Bob, a close friend of yours, has high blood pressure. Although he knows that high blood pressure can be fatal, and has even made an appointment with a physician, he skipped the appointment and never rescheduled it. How can you persuade him to see a doctor?

(a) Use logical, persuasive arguments.

(b) Use logical arguments, but also frighten him by telling him—in graphic detail—the long-term effects of untreated hypertension.

Motivating listeners to change their attitudes or behaviors by frightening them is effective if the conditions summarized in Figure 6-5 are met (Higbee, 1969; Janis & Feshbach, 1953; Leventhal, Singer, & Jones, 1965; Rogers & Mewborn, 1976). First, the consequences of failure to change the attitude or the behavior must be clearly negative. Second, the listener must believe that the likelihood of these consequences is very great if the message is not accepted. Third, the source must provide a clear and effective means of preventing the negative consequences. If these three conditions are not met, the listener will become defensive and ignore the communication (Rogers, 1975).

For your friend Bob, all three conditions are met, so fear arousal will be an effective method of persuasion. First, the consequences of failure to treat high blood pressure are extremely negative, and they are well known. Second, Bob, like most people, understands that high blood pressure doesn't just go away by itself; without treatment, the likelihood of disability and even early death is very great. Lastly, because high blood pressure generally responds to medication, Bob may be confident that he can avoid the negative consequences if he follows your advice. This three-stage analysis also applies to other health-related behaviors, such as breaking the smoking habit (see Figure 6-6).

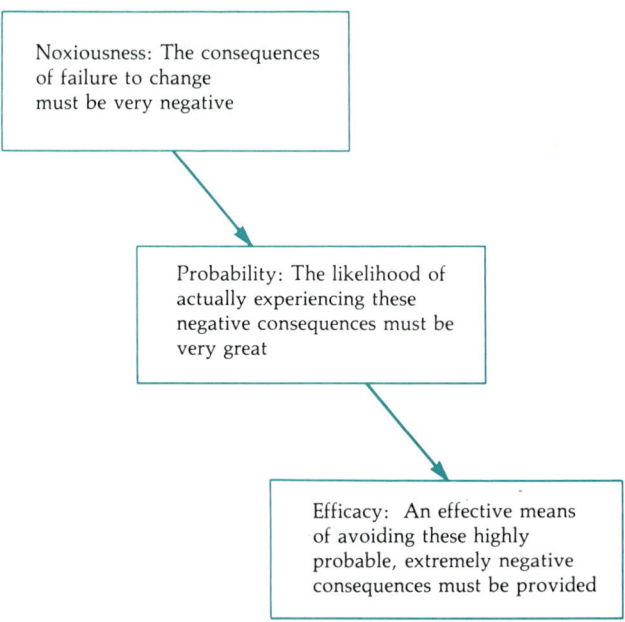

Figure 6-5 Necessary conditions for creating attitude and behavior change through fear arousal.

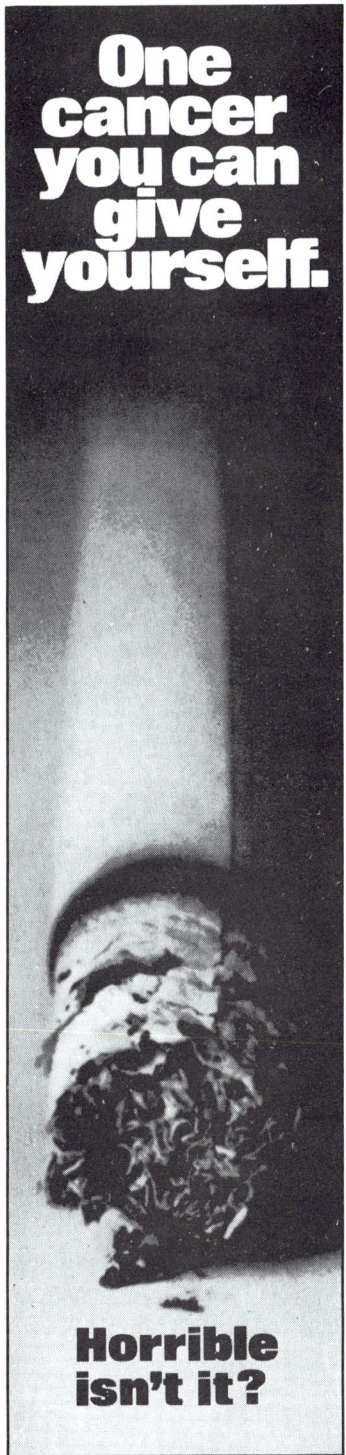

Figure 6-6 The American Cancer Society uses many types of advertising methods to warn Americans about the dangers of smoking. Are messages that arouse fears more effective than milder messages?

ATTITUDE CHANGE

(By the way, *b* was the answer to all of the multiple-choice items in this section. If you got them all correct, you should go into sales, social psychology, or politics!)

The Receiver

We select an excellent source person and carefully design the persuasive message, yet some members of the audience show no change in attitude. Why? Because persuasion does not depend on the source and the message alone, but also on the characteristics of the audience (see Focus 6-2).

Intelligence and self-esteem.
Although wartime research conducted by the Yale group suggested that better-educated soldiers tended to be more persuadable, other studies attested to the negative correlation between intelligence and persuasion (Hovland, Lumsdaine, & Sheffield, 1949; McGuire, 1969). In unraveling this empirical puzzle, William J. McGuire (1968) points out that high intelligence both facilitates and inhibits persuasion. On the facilitation side, the more intelligent audience member shows better comprehension of the message and is more likely to remember it for a longer period of time. On the inhibiting side, more intelligent individuals also have more confidence in their own opinions, so they don't change attitudes without strong persuasive arguments. If these opposing factors cancel one another out, then intelligence will neither increase nor decrease persuadability. The relationship between self-esteem and persuadability seems to follow a similar pattern, for individuals who are high in self-esteem are more likely to pay close attention to the message, but then again, they also have much more confidence in their original attitudes (Petty & Cacioppo, 1981; see also Eagly & Warren, 1976).

Gender.
Why did the snake persuade Eve rather than Adam to try the apple? Did the snake know—on the basis of its very limited experience with humans—that women tend to be more persuadable than men?

Studies of persuasion and conformity in groups substantiate the snake's choice (Eagly, 1978). In her review of 62 persuasion studies that included both men and women, Alice H. Eagly (1978) notes that 82% of the studies reported no differences due to gender, women were more easily persuaded than men in 16% of the studies, and men were more persuadable than women in only 2% of the studies. The differences between men and women, however, are not very large. Moreover, the small differences that were found may have been caused by an overreliance on topics that traditionally interest men more than women (Cooper, 1979; Eagly & Carli, 1981). (Chapter 10 presents more information on sex differences in influenceability.)

FOCUS 6-2

Experiencing Social Psychology: *What kinds of messages influence you the most?*

Advertisements are a form of persuasive communication. In the words of one advertising executive, "advertising is persuasion, and persuasion is . . . an art. Advertising is the art of persuasion" (William Bernbach, quoted in Fox, 1984, p. 251). Advertisers' media include newspapers, television, radio, billboards, and magazines, and their instruments are words and images.

Like artists who adopt particular styles of painting, advertisers tend to approach persuasion in one of two ways. Some take the soft-sell approach by creating a positive *image* for their product. Image-oriented advertisements are often sensory delights. They make use of vivid colors to emphasize the product and highlight the positive effects of using it. Levi commercials, for example, depict interesting people wearing their 501 jeans, and Calvin Klein titillates us with his underwear advertisements.

The hard-sell approach to advertising, in contrast, emphasizes the *quality* of the product. These ads go to great lengths to convince us that the product is the best available, often through the presentation of detailed information about merit, value, and cost. IBM, for example, discusses complex questions about expandability and memory in ads for its computers.

Which kind of advertisement influences you most? Do you pay more attention to a TV commercial that promises a deodorant will enhance your lifestyle, or one that argues the product will keep you dry and odorless? Are you more influenced by an advertisement that shows people relaxing over a beer or one that emphasizes the exacting standards that are used in brewing the product? According to Mark Snyder and Kenneth G. DeBono (1985), the impact of these two types of ads depends on your concern for your social image. Drawing on the concept of self-monitoring discussed in Chapter 2, Snyder and DeBono suggest that people who strive to tailor their behavior to the demands of the situation (high self-monitors) are perfect targets for image-oriented advertising. "Because of their concerns with being the right person in the right place at the right time," they pay more attention to ads that tell them how they can achieve an acceptable image. Low self-monitors, in contrast, prefer to act in ways that are consistent with their personal tastes and preferences. Therefore, they pay more attention to ads that convey information about a product's attributes and quality.

To test this intriguing hypothesis, Snyder and DeBono asked high and low self-monitoring subjects to evaluate image-oriented and quality-oriented advertisements. One advertisement for Irish Mocha Mint coffee depicted a man and woman drinking coffee in a candlelit room. The image-oriented ad included the statement "Make a chilly night become a cozy evening with Irish Mocha Mint." The quality-oriented ad stated: "Irish Mocha Mint: A delicious blend of three great flavors—coffee, chocolate, and mint" (Snyder & DeBono, 1985, p. 589). As anticipated, high self-monitors reacted more favorably to the image ads, while low self-monitors preferred the quality ads. Moreover, as Table 6-2 indicates, high self-monitors reported that they would be willing to spend more money on the product if they were shown an image-oriented ad, while the reverse held true for low self-monitors. As with any form of persuasion, the nature of the message was important, but so were the characteristics of the receiver.

TABLE 6-2

Average amount of money that high and low self-monitors felt they would be willing to pay for a product in response to two kinds of advertisements.

Type of Advertisement	Self-Monitoring	
	High	Low
Image	$3.43	$2.97
Quality	$3.28	$3.50

SOURCE: Snyder & DeBono, 1985, Study 2.

Original attitudinal position. You are very concerned about a friend of yours who smokes two packs of cigarettes a day. When you talk to Alicia about your concern, you discover that she doesn't think smoking is particularly harmful. In fact, on an 11-point scale where -5 is extremely harmful and $+5$ is not harmful at all, she is a $+1$. If you wish to alter this state of affairs, what position should you take during subsequent discussions of the issue? Should you take a very extreme stance (say, a -3) in the hope that the two of you can reach a compromise position that satisfies you? Or should you select arguments that are closer to Alicia's view (say, about 0 or -1) so that you will be sure they won't be rejected out of hand?

Social judgment theory (M. Sherif & Hovland, 1961; M. Sherif & Sherif, 1967; C. W. Sherif, Sherif, & Nebergall, 1965) offers one possible answer to your dilemma. According to this approach, Alicia's own attitude serves as an anchor or standard by which she judges incoming persuasive communications. If the discrepancy between her attitude and your message is small, then *assimilation* will take place: your arguments will be accepted. If, however, the discrepancy between Alicia's attitude and the message is great, then a *contrast effect* will occur; your -3 argument will be seen as very extreme and unreasonable.

As Figure 6-7 indicates, assimilation generally occurs when the message falls in the *latitude of acceptance*. This area includes Alicia's preferred attitudinal position and the surrounding range of opinions on the issue that are still acceptable. A contrast effect, on the other hand, occurs when the message falls in the *latitude of rejection*; opinions that fall in this area are so out of harmony with the receiver's attitude that they are rejected. The buffer area between acceptance and rejection is known as the *latitude of noncommitment*; messages within this range result in neither assimila-

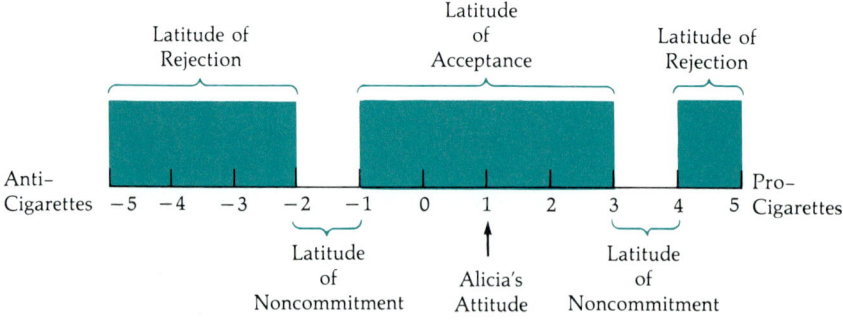

Figure 6-7 According to social judgment theory, all attitudes fall into three categories, or latitudes: acceptance, rejection, and noncommitment. For example, an individual with an attitude of $+1$ on an issue might accept arguments within a range of $+2$ points (from $+3$ to -1), but more extreme arguments beyond this range are likely to be rejected.

tion nor contrast. Thus, if you wish to achieve maximal attitude change, then the discrepancy between your arguments and Alicia's initial attitudes should be as large as possible, but your message must still fall within the latitude of acceptance. Hence a communication advocating a position of -1 would be ideal. Beyond -1, the message would become less and less effective, and if you used an extreme antismoking argument (-5), you might even produce a boomerang effect; Alicia might become even more convinced that cigarettes are not harmful.

Understanding Persuasion: An Application

Imagine that you teach in a high school. Shocked by the prevalence of drug use among your students, you decide to conduct a series of lectures emphasizing the dangers of drugs. Unfortunately, at the end of your program of lectures you discover that the students seem to be even more interested in illegal drugs than they were before. Why? What did you do wrong?

First, consider students' perceptions of the source of the communication. As a teacher, are you a very credible source? What do you, a nonuser, know about the effects of pot, glue, or hard drugs? And can you be trusted to give accurate information about drugs? After all, you are an adult and therefore may be presumed to be biased against anything that appeals primarily to the young, whether drugs, rock and roll, or new hairstyles. Furthermore, inasmuch as your age makes you a dissimilar source, won't students tend to dismiss your information and rely instead on the facts and opinions they get from their peers, who are more similar and more attractive to them?

Second, you may not have put together an effective message. At a fundamental level, your lectures may have been boring, difficult to understand, unconvincing, and unmemorable. For example, your slow rate of speech may have implied that you didn't know what you were talking about. Perhaps after building a weak argument against alcohol use, you closed with the rhetorical question "Now doesn't it make sense that you should never drink booze?" and all the students said no. Similarly, when you presented complex material on the physiological effects of drugs, you forgot to draw conclusions, and even though you know students realize that some people advocate the legalization of marijuana, you presented only the negative side of the argument. Your arguments may not have been organized effectively, and by telling students that "sometimes, in some cases, drug abuse leads to some highly negative consequences," you misused fear appeals.

Third, you may have overlooked the unique characteristics of your audience—their intelligence, self-esteem, and gender. In addition, your arguments may have been too extreme, and hence fell into their latitude of rejection. When you argued against marijuana, for example, you may have created such a contrast effect that your message was viewed as extreme and unreasonable. Hence, when you presented information about more dangerous drugs, these messages were also discounted. In addition, as Focus 6-3 indicates, some of your students' previous experiences with less effective drug lectures may have inoculated them against persuasion.

FOCUS 6-3

Applying Social Psychology: *How can persuasion be prevented?*

Medical inoculations, such as flu shots and smallpox vaccines, work by stimulating the body's natural defense mechanisms. When the organisms that cause the disease are injected into the body in a noninfectious form, the body reacts by building up protective antibodies. Later, if the inoculated individual is exposed to more virulent forms of the disease-causing organisms, the defensive antibodies needed to fight the infection will already be developed, immunizing the individual against the disease.

According to William J. McGuire's **inoculation theory** (1964), resistance to persuasion can also be developed through an inoculation-like process. When the arguments that might be used by a persuasive communicator are presented in a weakened form, receivers defend their beliefs by developing effective counterarguments. When the "immunized" receivers later encounter stronger persuasive messages, they will be less likely to change their attitudes because (1) they have developed cognitive response strategies that facilitate counterarguing and (2) the experience of successfully defending their attitudes against a weak attack has strengthened their confidence in their attitudes.

In one well-known study McGuire attacked subjects' acceptance of several cultural truisms—beliefs that are so widely held by a given culture that they are assumed to be true (McGuire & Papageorgis, 1961). He chose the truisms "You should brush your teeth after every meal" and "Mental illness is not contagious" because he felt that very few of the subjects would ever have been asked to defend these beliefs, so they would have trouble spontaneously generating the counterarguments they would need to refute challenging arguments. Like Pacific islanders who died of measles because their isolation prevented them from developing the necessary defenses, subjects would lack the counterarguments needed to fend off the unexpected attack. As he predicted, McGuire found that subjects who had been inoculated by a series of weak, easily refutable antitruism arguments resisted persuasion more than (*a*) subjects who received no inoculation against a strong attack and (*b*) subjects who had been given only a prepersuasion treatment containing pro-truism information.

McGuire's findings have a number of applications, for they suggest that simply providing receivers with more and more good reasons for their beliefs will not always be an effective way of inducing resistance to attitude change. For example, simply educating small children concerning the negative consequences of smoking cigarettes or taking drugs will not guarantee that they will not later change these attitudes. Inoculation theory suggests that a better approach would be to expose them to the persuasive arguments and pressures they will eventually experience, and then teach them how to refute these arguments and resist these pressures (Evans, 1980).

Inoculation has also been used by advertisers (Bither, Dolich, & Nell, 1971; Szybillo & Heslin, 1973). In one project users and nonusers of a particular product were exposed to refutational advertisements—messages designed to present and then rebut the arguments of competitors—and supportive advertisements—messages that presented only

■ Consistency Theories

Consider Dr. Thomas Armstrong's dilemma. He was sitting in Marian Keech's living room, awaiting the arrival of aliens who called themselves the Guardians. He had met Mrs. Keech several months before, and she convinced him that she could communicate with the Guardians through automatic handwriting; they moved a pencil she held loosely in her hand.

---

the positive characteristics of the product (Sawyer, 1973). As Table 6-3 indicates, when the target product was Bayer aspirin, the supportive appeal mentioned only its positive attributes. The refutational appeal, in contrast, subtly suggested some negative characteristics of Bayer—it's not buffered (like Bufferin) and it doesn't fizz (like Alka Seltzer)—but then belittled these characteristics: "Nothing has ever improved aspirin. Bayer is 100% aspirin." The researcher found that (a) users and nonusers of both the advertised brand and a competing brand were equally influenced by the two types of advertisements; (b) users of only the advertised brand were less likely to switch to a competing brand after a refutational appeal; and (c) users of a competing brand reported stronger intentions to switch to the advertised brand in the refutational condition than in the supportive condition. Thus, overall, refutational ads were generally more effective than supportive ads.

TABLE 6-3

Supportive and refutational appeals used in advertising of four products.

Product	Supportive Appeal	Refutational Appeal
Bayer aspirin	Bayer works wonders. Relax with Bayer. Bayer is 100% aspirin.	Buffer it, square it, fizz it . . . nothing has ever improved aspirin. Bayer is 100% aspirin.
Lava soap	For real dirty hands, reach for Lava—the soap that can really clean.	Lava—world's worst bath soap! Lava users have revolted. They argue that Lava is not only a good soap for hands but for anything else too.
Parker pen	Just one could be all you ever need. At $1.98 it's the best pen value in the world. Up to 80,000 words . . .	Why pay $1.98 for a ballpoint pen? You can get them for 49¢, 69¢, or for free. The kind that skip, stutter, and run out of ink. You pay $1.98 for a Parker, but you never have to buy another.
Renault automobile	Sales are climbing. Renault's new features and fine construction are paying off.	Sure, they save money, but I wouldn't want to take a long trip in one. Foreign cars are easy on the wallet but hard on everything else. Renault is changing all that.

SOURCE: Sawyer, 1973.

Armstrong and his wife joined a small group of devout followers who spent many months studying the Guardians' messages. The messages turned out to be a warning: the planet Earth was about to be destroyed by flood!

The cataclysm was scheduled for December 21, but the Guardians promised to pick up Mrs. Keech's followers at midnight. They gathered in readiness in her living room (Mr. Keech, a nonbeliever, went to bed), bags packed, all metal—zippers, buttons, snaps—removed from their clothing (metal does strange things in flying saucers), passwords all memorized. Unfortunately, midnight came and went with no sign of a flying saucer. The bad news was that Mrs. Keech was wrong when she predicted they would be rescued; the good news was that she was also wrong about the flood.

So how did Dr. Armstrong respond? Did he denounce Mrs. Keech as a fraud? Did he try to contact the Guardians on his own? Did he sew all his zippers back into his clothes? No, he became more committed to Mrs. Keech's teachings. He accepted her rationalization that the tremendous faith and devotion of the group was so impressive that God had decided to call off the flood, and he spread this important message to news reporters. Although the central beliefs of the group had undeniably been disconfirmed, he refused to abandon them. He clung tenaciously to the irrational hope that the space travelers would someday come for him (Festinger, Riecken, & Schachter, 1956).

Dr. Armstrong's reaction to the disconfirmed prophecy becomes explicable if we assume that he wanted to keep all his cognitions (attitudes, beliefs, perceptions) and behaviors consistent with one another. If he admitted to himself that Mrs. Keech was a false prophet, then he would also have to admit that he was wrong in believing in her teachings. Furthermore, he would have no justification for his actions over the previous months: he had quit his job, moved nearly 200 miles to be closer to Mrs. Keech, and alienated his friends and relatives. If, however, he became more firmly committed to Mrs. Keech, then his cognitions and behaviors would all be consistent with one another, and he could avoid the psychological stress that arises from inconsistency.

As Dr. Armstrong's psychological gyrations reveal, the need for **cognitive consistency** is a powerful human motive. Consistency theorists believe that all our attitudes and cognitions are related to one another. In consequence, even though a single attitude—such as Armstrong's devotion to Mrs. Keech—may not make much sense to an uninvolved observer, it fits his other cognitions like the last piece of a puzzle. Moreover, as in Armstrong's case, consistency doesn't always come easily. To achieve harmony among our various attitudes and cognitions, we often must change them until they fit the overall pattern.

A number of theorists have suggested that we change our attitudes in order to maintain consistency among our cognitions (Abelson & Rosenberg, 1958; Heider, 1958; Lewin, 1935; Newcomb, 1953; Osgood & Tannenbaum, 1955). This view is perhaps best elaborated in Leon Festinger's theory of cognitive dissonance (Festinger, 1957).

Cognitive Dissonance Theory

According to Festinger, cognitions that are consistent with one another are *consonant;* they fit together psychologically, with one implying or following from the other. For example, Ed's preference for the color blue is consistent with the fact that his closet contains lots of blue clothes. Juanita's interest in world events is consistent with her habit of watching the nightly news.

Dissonant cognitions, in contrast, clash with one another; they are inconsistent, with one implying the opposite of the other. For example, Chuck's knowledge that he bought his girlfriend a $200 watch for her birthday is inconsistent with the fact that she broke up with him two days later. Similarly, Dr. Armstrong's decision to quit his job to join Mrs. Keech's group was dissonant with Mrs. Keech's failed doomsday prediction.

Lastly, one cognition may simply have nothing to do with another cognition; such cognitions are *irrelevant* to one another. Ed's preference for blue is not related to Juanita's enjoyment of the nightly news. Chuck's romantic woes are irrelevant to Mrs. Keech's failures.

But what do consonance, dissonance, and irrelevance have to do with attitude change? According to Festinger, *dissonance* is an unpleasant psychological state that the individual is motivated to avoid. "Just as hunger is motivating, cognitive dissonance is motivating. Cognitive dissonance will give rise to activity oriented toward reducing or eliminating the dissonance" (Festinger, 1957, p. 70). And while people can reduce their dissonance in many ways (see Table 6-4), one of the most important modes of dissonance reduction is attitude change. For example, an individual who smokes cigarettes despite the dissonance produced by medical evidence linking smoking with cancer may exaggerate the enjoyment derived from smoking; the rejected job applicant may later realize that the job wasn't so hot anyway; and jilted Chuck may realize he was only infatuated with the woman. We avoid the psychological stress produced by cognitive dissonance by changing our attitudes.

Festinger's theory of cognitive dissonance contrasts with the theories of persuasion we examined earlier. Rather than view humans as rational creatures who listen carefully to others' arguments before deciding to change their opinions, Festinger sees us as consistency-seekers who embrace attitudes that ensure our psychological comfort. As a result, we often sacrifice rationality in the pursuit of consistency. Several examples of the triumph of irrationality over reason are examined below.

Consistency versus rationality. Given a choice between a defensible, logical attitude that clashes with our other cognitions and an irrational, unreasonable attitude that meshes with our other cognitions, which will we pick?

In many cases, consistency wins. When Dr. Armstrong's strong convictions concerning the validity of Mrs. Keech's predictions were directly disconfirmed, he still clung to his beliefs. In fact, he rationalized the failure by generating so many additional consonant cognitions that he actually became a stronger believer in the group and began to seek new recruits (Festinger, Riecken, & Schachter, 1956; Hardyck & Braden, 1962).

Daniel Batson (1975) demonstrated a similar triumph of consistency over reason in a study of religious attitudes. First, he split the members of a Presbyterian church group into two groups: strong believers in the divinity of Jesus and people who, while accepting Jesus' teachings, denied his divinity. Batson showed both groups the following bogus newspaper article.

> GENEVA, SWITZERLAND. It was learned today here in Geneva from a top source in the World Council of Churches offices that scholars in Jordan have conclusively proved that the major writings in what is today called the New Testament are fraudulent.
>
> According to the information gained from the unnamed source within the headquarters of the World Council of Churches, Professor R. R. Lowry (author of *The Zarondike Fragments and the Dead Sea Scrolls*), assisted by other scholars, has been carefully analyzing a collection of papyrus scrolls discovered in a cave in the Jordanian desert near where the famous Dead Sea Scrolls were found. Contained within this collection of scrolls, Lowry and

TABLE 6 – 4

Some ways to reduce the dissonance caused by the two cognitions "I smoke cigarettes" and "Cigarettes cause cancer."

Mode of Dissonance Reduction	Description	Example
Change of attitude	Adoption of increasingly positive attitude toward smoking	"I like smoking too much to quit."
Change of behavior	Reduction in smoking	"I've cut down on my smoking."
Addition of consonant cognitions	Adoption of supportive arguments for continuing to smoke	"I don't believe these reports about smoking."
Distortion	Shift in emphasis placed on cognitions	"I don't care how long I live; all that counts is that I enjoy myself."
Denial	Announcement of a change in behavior unaccompanied by any actual change	"I've quit" (puff, puff).

his associates have found letters, apparently written between the composers of various New Testament books, bluntly stating: "Since our great teacher, Jesus of Nazareth, was killed by the Romans, I am sure we were justified in stealing away his body and claiming that he rose from the dead. For, although his death clearly proves he was not the Son of God as we had hoped, if we did not claim that he was, both his great teaching and our lives as his disciples would be wasted!"

Though Lowry initially suspected the authenticity of these scrolls, he was later quoted as saying, "Through radiocarbon dating and careful study of the Aramaic dialect used in writing these letters, I have found it impossible to deny that the manuscripts are authentic. You can't imagine what a struggle this has been; I find no alternative but to renounce my former belief that Jesus Christ was the Son of God. I can no longer be a Christian." [Batson, 1975, p. 180.]

The article had supposedly been "denied publication in *The New York Times* at the request of the World Council of Churches because of the obvious crushing effect it would have on the entire Christian world" (p. 180).

When Batson asked his subjects if their opinions of Jesus' divinity had undergone any change as a result of the article, he found that those who had denied Jesus' divinity became even more doubtful (see Table 6-5). Believers, however, displayed two different reactions. One group of subjects tended simply to reject the dissonant information; they reduced their cognitive dissonance by questioning the veracity of the article. A second group reacted more irrationally. These individuals, despite their reluctant acceptance of the truth of the article, actually intensified their belief in Jesus' divinity. Like the members of Mrs. Keech's group, these subjects emerged "not only unshaken, but even more convinced . . . than before" (Festinger, Riecken, & Schachter, 1956, p. 3). Batson points out the irrationality of this attitude intensification, and applies his findings to the

TABLE 6 – 5

Scores of three groups indicating strength of belief or nonbelief in the divinity of Jesus before and after exposure to presumably disconfirming information [scale: 1 (strongly disagree)–5 (strongly agree)].

Groups	Number of Subjects	Pretest Score	Posttest Score	Type of Change
Nonbelievers	8	3.37	2.91	Lack of belief strengthened
Believers who doubted the information	31	3.97	3.90	No significant change
Believers who accepted the information	11	4.07	4.30	Belief strengthened

SOURCE: Batson, 1975.

problems faced by anyone trying to persuade committed believers to change their attitudes:

> If, on the one hand, the believer does not accept the facts as facts, then clearly one's arguments are without impact. But, on the other hand, if the believer accepts them as true, this may actually drive him into even more fervent adherence to his initial position. [Batson, 1975, p. 184.]

(All the participants in the study were carefully debriefed, and the experiment and the changes it produced were examined in several subsequent class sessions.)

Consistency and choice. We rarely find ourselves in the kinds of predicament that Dr. Armstrong and Batson's subjects experienced. Most of our daily experiences are quite consistent with our central values and beliefs. However, Festinger argued that the same kinds of processes occur in everyday situations whenever we must make a difficult choice.

Imagine that your parents insist that you go to either Ivyleague University or Sunshine Tech. Ivyleague, you realize, has an outstanding academic reputation and a long history steeped in tradition. Tech is a major university located in a sunny climate; it boasts a wide range of social and recreational activities as well as nontraditional educational opportunities. After many sleepless nights spent pondering your decision, you send off your registration materials to Tech, though you still wonder whether you've made the right decision.

We all tend to be reluctant decision makers, especially when the choice is important (selecting a college) and each alternative has much to recommend it (Ivyleague has a better reputation but Tech will be more fun). All the positive aspects of the rejected alternative combine with the negative aspects of the chosen alternative to create distressingly large amounts of cognitive dissonance, and your choice leaves you with the feeling that you've made a tragic mistake. Until, that is, dissonance-reduction processes come to your rescue. Though immediately after the choice you are beset by feelings of regret, given enough time you will begin to justify your decision by discovering new arguments to support your choice (Walster, 1968). Having decided to attend Tech, you may realize that you overlooked some of Tech's positive features: its many excellent academic programs, its location near a large city, and its relatively low tuition. Furthermore, the negative aspects of Ivyleague will become more salient as you note with relief that at Tech you won't be surrounded by preppies and egghead professors. These postdecision justifications result in a *spreading of alternatives* as your attitude toward the chosen alternative becomes even more positive and your attitude toward the rejected alternative becomes more negative.

In an early study of this spreading-of-alternatives phenomenon, Jack Brehm (1956) told college women that if they participated in a study of consumer attitudes toward various products, they would receive one of the products as a gift. The women then rated the desirability of the products, which included records, an art print, a stopwatch, and a radio. To vary the amount of dissonance created by the selection, Brehm established three experimental conditions. In the control condition the women were simply assigned a product; they had no choice, and therefore should have experienced little dissonance. Subjects in the low dissonance condition were given their choice of two gifts, one of which was much more desirable than the other. Because the two choices were already very different in terms of desirability, Brehm felt that such a choice would arouse little dissonance and postdecisional spreading should be minimal. Subjects in the high dissonance condition were asked to choose between two products that were very similar in desirability. As predicted, spreading was much more pronounced when the alternatives were very similar in desirability than when they were dissimilar or when no choice was involved. By inflating the desirability of the chosen product, the women could later reassure themselves that they had made the right decision (see Focus 6-4).

Dissonance and commitment. When the Guardians failed to keep their rendezvous with Dr. Armstrong, his faith in them must have been momentarily shaken. However, he had already invested considerable time, energy, and personal resources in Mrs. Keech's group. These two cognitions—"The group wasn't rescued" and "I am committed to this group"—undoubtedly created cognitive dissonance. By thinking more about the positive features of the group, Dr. Armstrong was able to

FOCUS 6 – 4

A Closer Look: *When does selective exposure occur?*

Like gamblers who become more confident about their bets immediately after they place them (Knox & Inkster, 1968; Younger, Walker, & Arrowood, 1977), Jack Brehm (1956) found that people reduce cognitive dissonance by exaggerating the desirability of the choices they make. In some instances, however, a second dissonance-reduction strategy—**selective exposure**—is also used. After making a decision, people seek out information that is consonant with the choice and avoid dissonant information (Frey & Wicklund, 1978; Wicklund & Brehm, 1976). After deciding to attend Tech, for example, you may spend your time listening to dedicated alumni describe how wonderful the school is, while avoiding a friend who transferred from Tech after a disappointing year.

Although Festinger originally suggested that both types of selective exposure—a search for consonant information and avoidance of dissonant information—were equally likely in any given situation, subsequent studies indicated that the strategy chosen depends on a number of factors. If we think that the information we may get—whether consonant or dissonant—will be easy to refute, then we tend to seek out the dissonant information. If, however, we think the information will be difficult to refute, then we usually selectively seek the consonant information and avoid the dissonant (Frey, 1981). Selective exposure is also strongest when we experience a moderate amount of dissonance (rather than extremely high or low dissonance) over the choice (Converse & Cooper, 1979; Frey, 1982) and when the decision is irrevocable (Brehm & Cohen, 1962).

reduce this dissonance. He had too much invested in it to quit (Teger, 1980).

Researchers investigated this dissonance-reduction process by telling female subjects that they would be allowed to take part in a group discussion of sex (Aronson & Mills, 1959). Some subjects were also told that because only women who could discuss sex without embarrassment were permitted in the group, all prospective members had first to pass an "embarrassment test": they were required to read a series of obscene words and descriptions of sexual interludes aloud to the male experimenter. After passing the bogus test, subjects listened to the group they would be joining through an intercom system. Although they were led to believe that they were eavesdropping on the group members' conversations, the experimenter actually played a tape recording of a discussion that had been deliberately designed to be boring and banal.

By making subjects pass a test that amounted to an initiation before joining a worthless group, the researchers created two inconsistent cognitions: "I worked hard to join this group" and "The group is boring." To escape the dissonance aroused by this inconsistency, the investigators predicted, the women would change their attitude toward the group and come to believe that it was really very interesting. As Figure 6-8 indicates, these changes in fact took place; subjects who had passed the severe initiation became more favorable toward the group than subjects who had been given a mild initiation (reading a series of sex-related but nonobscene words) or no initiation at all. Similar findings have been obtained when strong electric shocks rather than obscene readings were used to manipulate the severity of the initiation into the group (Gerard & Mathewson, 1966).

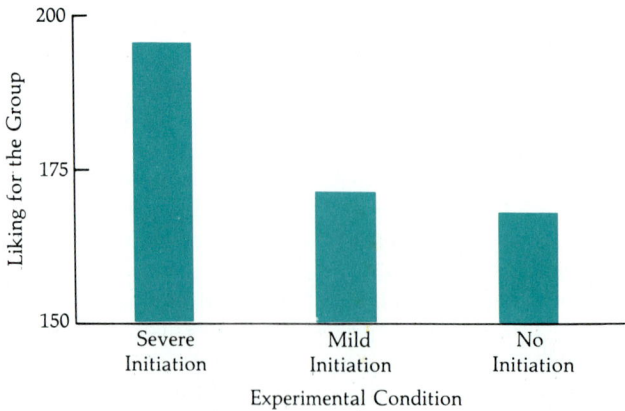

Figure 6-8 Attitudes toward a boring group in three experimental conditions: severe initiation, mild initiation, and no initiation. The highest score possible was 255.

These findings offer a potential explanation for the curious tendency of groups to initiate new members. Initiations demand an investment from inductees, even before they have had a chance to become full-fledged members. These investments may work to bind the initiates to the group, for they become more favorably disposed to it in order to reduce cognitive dissonance. A similar process may bind people to other emotionally involving groups, such as social movements and cults. As the group demands more and more in the way of personal commitment, individuals become more enamored of the group to justify their investment in it. (See "In Depth: Coercive Persuasion," at the end of this chapter.)

Consistency and Counterattitudinal Behavior

We have seen that, given a choice between rationality and consistency, we often choose consistency. Does this preference for consistency extend to our behavior? Harold prefers sports cars, for instance, yet he purchases a station wagon. Susan likes history, but she majors in business. Do such inconsistencies between our attitudes and our behaviors also cause cognitive dissonance?

Leon Festinger and J. Merrill Carlsmith (1959) conducted an intriguing study to answer this question. They began by asking male college students to perform two exceedingly boring tasks: putting 12 spools onto a tray over and over again and turning 48 square pegs a quarter of a turn clockwise. The subjects spent 30 minutes working at each task while the

Initiation rites in college sororities. Fraternities, sororities, and various societies require new members to go through elaborate initiation rites before they can become full-fledged members. These initiations may serve to strengthen the bond between the individual and the group by arousing cognitive dissonance.

experimenter made notations on a sheet of paper. By the time both tasks were completed, subjects had probably formed the cognition "This is the most boring and monotonous experiment imaginable." Next, the experimenter gave subjects a short bogus explanation of the study. Some people, like the subject, he said, performed the task cold, without any explanation. Others were led to believe that the task would be interesting and enjoyable. The experimenter claimed that he was interested in studying the effect of this motivational information on performance.

At the end of the fake debriefing the experimenter hesitated and then added that he would like to hire the subject to play the role of the "fellow who usually meets the waiting subject." Explaining that his regular confederate had been detained, the experimenter offered the subject either $1 or $20 to tell the subject waiting in the next room that the study was interesting and enjoyable, and to remain on call in case he was needed again in the future. Most subjects agreed after a little prodding, and when they were introduced to the waiting subject (who was really the confederate), they described the experiment with such adjectives as "interesting," "enjoyable," and "involving."

This elaborate hoax subtly forced the subject into performing a *counterattitudinal behavior:* an action that was inconsistent with his private attitudes. Although he undoubtedly considered the entire study to be a bore, he voluntarily agreed to tell the waiting confederate that in fact it was interesting. According to Festinger, behaving in such a counterattitudinal manner should create dissonance, but only if the subject was paid $1. As Figure 6-9 indicates, both the $1 and $20 subjects should display the dissonant cognitions "I felt the task was boring" and "I told someone that it was interesting," but the subjects paid $20 had *sufficient justification* for lying about the task; they could think to themselves, "I made a lot of money by telling a little white lie about the study." Because this justification should eliminate their dissonance, Festinger and Carlsmith predicted that they would not change their attitudes. Subjects who were paid only $1, however, had *insufficient justification* for performing the counterattitudinal action. Therefore, they should have experienced dissonance and attitude change.

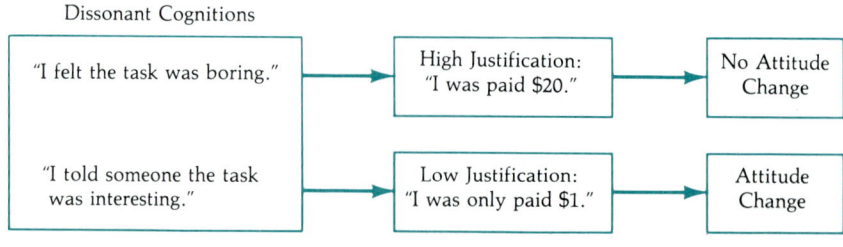

Figure 6-9 The cognitions created through counterattitudinal behavior in the Festinger-Carlsmith experiment.

The results of the experiment are briefly summarized in Table 6-6. Subjects who were paid $1 thought the task was more enjoyable and scientifically important than subjects in the other conditions, and they were also more willing to participate in a similar experiment. As dissonance theory predicted, the subjects who were paid $1, having no justification for their counterattitudinal behavior, experienced the greatest amount of dissonance, which they alleviated by changing their attitude.

Although these findings were initially considered surprising—we generally expect the greatest change in people who are paid the most—remember that the money does not represent a payment or a reward, but a *justification* for behaving counterattributionally. When the justification for an action is great, dissonance is unlikely. When people engage in counterattitudinal behaviors for no good reason, however, dissonance should indeed be great. Money is but one form of justification for behavior; people engage in counterattitudinal actions for all sorts of reasons (Freedman, 1965; Zimbardo et al., 1965; see Focus 6-5).

The Evolution of Cognitive Dissonance Theory

Festinger's theory of cognitive dissonance, by emphasizing the irrational side of our cognitive processes, complements the rational view emphasized by persuasion theorists. We don't always listen to arguments carefully and weigh alternative positions on issues. Sometimes our beliefs become stronger *after* they have been convincingly refuted. We also reduce our misgivings about our decisions by exaggerating the desirability of the alternatives we choose and we value goals and outcomes that we must suffer to obtain. Moreover, when we find ourselves performing counterattitudinal actions, we simply change our attitudes to match our behavior. Was Festinger correct, though, in stressing the importance of cognitive consistency over rationality? Let's conclude our study of this theory by considering several possible answers to this question.

T A B L E 6 – 6

Average ratings of tasks and experiment in three experimental conditions.

	Control	Subject Receives $1	Subject Receives $20
Enjoyablity of tasks[a]	−0.45	+1.35	−0.05
Scientific importance of experiment[b]	5.60	6.45	5.18
Willingness to participate in a similar study[a]	−0.62	+1.20	−0.25

[a]Scale: −5 to +5
[b]Scale: 0 to 10 (0 = "no scientific value"; 10 = "great deal of value")
SOURCE: Festinger & Carlsmith, 1959.

FOCUS 6–5

Controversy in Social Psychology: *Can self-perception theory explain attitude change following counterattitudinal behavior?*

Cognitive dissonance theory often yields counterintuitive hypotheses—they violate our commonsense assumptions about the rationality of human beings. As a result, it takes a little practice to learn to think like a dissonance theorist. Daryl J. Bem (1965), however, doesn't think the effort is worth it.

According to Bem, the attitude changes that people exhibit after they engage in counterattitudinal behavior result from *self-perception* rather than the arousal of cognitive dissonance. As we saw in Chapters 2 and 4, Bem's theory assumes that we infer our attitudes, emotions, and other internal states by observing our own overt behavior. For example, if we observe ourselves sending off an application to Tech rather than Ivyleague, we infer from this behavior that we must like Tech more than Ivyleague. If we diligently prepare to be rescued by people from outer space, we assume that we must believe in the existence of extraterrestrial life. If we work hard to join a group, we infer that we must really like the group. And if we tell someone that a task is interesting, through self-perception we come to believe the task really is interesting (Bem, 1965).

But how does self-perception theory account for the impact of justification on attitude change? According to Bem, individuals are sensitive to external pressures that may influence their actions. If you apply to Tech rather than Ivyleague, but you also know that your parents have promised to give you a new car if you don't go to Ivyleague, then you may not infer that you like Tech all that much. Similarly, if you observe yourself telling someone a task is interesting, why infer a positive attitude toward the task if you know you are telling the lie only because someone has promised to pay you $20? In sum, while self-perception can account for findings obtained in many dissonance experiments, it denies the existence of aversive motivational pressures; people change their attitudes not to reduce dissonance but because they logically infer their attitudes from the overt behaviors.

Each of these opposing interpretations of attitude change has been supported by researchers. For example, though early investigators initially had difficulty predicting precisely when an individual would experience cognitive dissonance, subsequent studies succeeded in identifying a number of conditions that must be met before dissonance is aroused. Furthermore, one of the key assumptions of cognitive dissonance—the notion that cognitive inconsistency creates a negative psychological arousal in the attitude holder—has been supported in recent studies. Both of these advances are examined in the next section.

Self-perception theory, however, has also been supported empirically by simulation studies of counterattitudinal behavior experiments (Bem, 1972). In these investigations observers who read about or watched the procedures used in counterattitudinal behavior studies were able to predict subjects' attitude change, even though as observers they probably experienced none of the psychological arousal hypothesized by cognitive dissonance theory. Also, unlike dissonance theory, self-perception theory can explain why people sometimes change their attitudes after pro-attitudinal action (Kiesler, Nisbett, & Zanna, 1969).

Because both approaches have been empirically supported, some investigators feel that these alternative explanations should not "be regarded as 'competing' formulations but as complementary ones" (Fazio, Zanna, & Cooper, 1977). Although researchers have spent many years striving to disconfirm one theory while confirming another, it now seems that each approach adds another piece to the attitude-change puzzle (compare with Greenwald, 1975; Greenwald & Ronis, 1978; Ronis & Greenwald, 1979). When people are keenly aware of their attitudes—as Mrs. Keech's followers were—we probably need cognitive dissonance theory to explain their intense emotional reactions. When people are performing more routine actions, though, self-perception theory probably offers a simpler account of any attitude change that occurs.

Inconsistency is arousing. Is dissonance the arousing, motivating, dynamic state of tension that Festinger (1957) described in his original theory? Yes, according to recent research (Cooper, Zanna, & Taves, 1978; Kiesler & Pallak, 1976; Steele, Southwick, & Critchlow, 1981; Zanna & Cooper, 1976). One group of researchers secured subjects' agreement to take either a tranquillizer, a placebo, or an amphetamine for research purposes. The subjects were indeed given a placebo, a tranquillizer, or an amphetamine, but all were told that the drug they received was a placebo. They then wrote a counterattitudinal essay favoring the pardoning of Richard M. Nixon (a hot topic at the time). Later, when their attitudes about the pardon were measured on a 31-point scale, tranquillized subjects showed very little change (the mean was 8.6); subjects given a placebo evidenced some change (mean = 14.7); and the highly aroused subjects who had received an amphetamine showed substantial change (mean = 20.2) (Cooper, Zanna, & Taves, 1978). Dissonance and tactics to reduce it, such as attitude change, were also eliminated in a study in which college students drank several beers or mixed vodka drinks after writing a counterattitudinal essay favoring an increase in tuition (Steele, Southwick, & Critchlow, 1981).

Having demonstrated that dissonance is indeed arousing, investigators are currently seeking answers to the question "What is the precise nature of this arousal state?" Although firm conclusions cannot be drawn at present, two distinct possibilities have emerged. On the one hand, the arousal brought about by cognitive dissonance may be intrinsically aversive—a negative, stressful feeling of tension (Higgins, Rhodewalt, & Zanna, 1979; Rhodewalt & Comer, 1979). On the other, dissonance may be arousing, but not always *negatively* arousing; it could be experienced as a positive feeling (Cooper, Fazio, & Rhodewalt, 1978).

The importance of public commitment. Most people pride themselves on their consistency. We awaken each day expecting to act, feel, and think the same way we acted, felt, and thought the day before. Just as we value consistency, however, we also value rationality and logic. We may think ill of people who change their attitudes from one day to the next, but what of those who refuse to change their view in the face of overwhelming counterarguments? People who vacillate on political and social issues may seem uncertain and weak-willed, but is stubborn rigidity an acceptable alternative? As Ralph Waldo Emerson remarked, consistency is a valuable attribute, but a "foolish consistency is the hobgoblin of little minds." If we were to retain our attitudes even though we knew they were based on error or were ill conceived, their usefulness as guidelines for action would be undermined.

When does the need for consistency outweigh our need for reasonable, defensible attitudes? Of the many factors that have been examined by researchers, one of the most important is *public commitment* to our attitudes. If we are the only ones who know how we feel on an issue, we rarely experience cognitive dissonance. If, however, we are publicly committed to a position, then the impact of cognitive inconsistencies becomes much greater.

Many researchers believe that cognitive dissonance may be closely related to our self-presentational needs. As Chapter 2 noted, all of us strive to construct and maintain a particular image of ourselves during social interaction. A young man dining with a woman may present himself as a sophisticate by ordering dinner for his date, insisting on an expensive bottle of wine and speaking French to the waiter. A professor may project an intellectual image by seeming absent-minded, speaking quickly and using obscure terms, and displaying disdain for such non-intellectual activities as sports and television viewing. According to *self-presentation* theory (also known as impression management theory), in such social settings we try to make a particular impression by managing our self-descriptions, actions, and appearances (Goffman, 1959).

Unfortunately, we sometimes find ourselves in awkward situations that threaten to destroy the impressions that we are striving so hard to create. After ordering escargots, for example, our young sophisticate may have to ask the waiter how to eat them; or the professor's intellectual image may be threatened when he is caught watching reruns of "The Love Boat" between classes. Or, as in Festinger and Carlsmith's study, we engage in actions that we never intended to perform. According to

Dissonance is much greater when we act in ways that run counter to our attitudes in public settings. If this woman expresses an opinion in her speech that she doesn't truly believe, she may change her private attitudes. Self-presentation theorists believe that much of the tension produced by counterattitudinal behavior stems from the need for interpersonal, rather than intrapsychic, consistency.

impression management theory, the dissonance in these situations comes from failing to maintain a certain image in public (Schlenker, 1980; Schlenker et al., 1980).

■ Summary

When do attitudes change? In some cases, attitudes acquired through exposure to an object, conditioning, or social learning supplant our earlier attitudes. Often, however, attitude change results from **persuasion**—the communication of facts, arguments, and information calculated to change another person's attitudes.

According to the communication theory of attitude change developed by Carl Hovland and his Yale colleagues, the impact of a persuasive message depends on the *source*, the *message*, and the *receiver*—on who says what to whom. First, sources who are credible, similar to the listener, and attractive tend to be persuasive. Credibility seems to be based on attributions of expertise and trustworthiness to the source, while similarity increases our liking for the source. When we forget the source of the message before we forget the message itself, however, the message can have a delayed effect on our attitudes. This increase in attitude change over time is known as the **sleeper effect.**

The impact of a message on the listener depends on a number of factors, including:

1. *Speech rate.* Rapid speech rates tend to be more persuasive, provided the speaker is viewed as credible.

2. *Rhetorical questions.* Ending an argument with a question rather than a general summary statement is effective when listeners are not already actively involved *and* powerful arguments have been presented. This conclusion is based on **cognitive response theory.**

3. *Conclusions.* Persuasion is greatest when speakers draw conclusions after presenting complex arguments, provided these conclusions do not arouse **psychological reactance.**

4. *One-sided versus two-sided communications.* Evidence indicates that two-sided communications are generally more effective, particularly when the audience is aware of both sides of an argument and disagrees with the speaker.

5. *Order of presentation.* Information presented first generally outweighs information presented second (a *primacy effect*), provided only a short amount of time separates the two messages. As the gap increases, recently presented arguments exert a stronger influence (a *recency effect*).

6. *Fear appeals.* Scare tactics are effective only in very specific situations; for example, when noncompliance will almost certainly lead to negative consequences whereas compliance will almost certainly lead to positive consequences.

Receivers' intelligence, self-esteem, and gender influence their reactions to persuasive messages. In addition, messages that fall within their *latitude of acceptance* tend to be assimilated, as **social judgment theory** predicts. **Inoculation theory** predicts that if the listener has been inoculated against persuasion, little attitude change will occur.

Attitude change also stems from the need for **cognitive consistency.** As Leon Festinger (1957) argues, inconsistencies among our cognitions and/or behaviors lead to an aversive psychological state known as *cognitive dissonance.* To reduce such dissonance, individuals sometimes change their attitudes. These predictions have been supported by a number of intriguing studies. Investigators have found, for example, that we tend to cling to beliefs even after they have been disconfirmed. We also reduce our misgivings about our decisions by exaggerating the desirability of the alternatives we choose, by seeking out information that supports our attitudes (**selective exposure**), and by placing high value on goals and outcomes that we must suffer to obtain. Moreover, as Festinger and Carlsmith (1959) illustrate in their classic study of counterattitudinal behavior, the performance of actions that conflict with our attitudes also creates dissonance. In general, attitude change following such counterattitudinal behavior is greatest when the justification for performing the behavior is low.

In recent years, cognitive dissonance has been tested and extended. As a result of these tests, some researchers now feel that *self-perception theory* is an equally valid explanation of the attitude change that often follows counterattitudinal action. However, self-perception theory cannot account for evidence that indicates that (*a*) counterattitudinal behavior leads to physiological arousal and (*b*) our need for consistency is strongest when we are publicly committed to our attitudes.

■ For More Information

1. *When Prophecy Fails,* by Leon Festinger, Henry W. Riecken, and Stanley Schachter (1956), presents an engaging account of the group that formed around the prophet Marion Keech. While the case study raises some ethical questions, it offers many insights into the experiences that prompted Festinger to develop his theory of cognitive dissonance.

2. "Public Opinion and Political Action," by Donald R. Kinder and David O. Sears (1985), reviews the nature of public opinion, with emphasis on political issues. Questions concerning attitude formation and change are examined throughout the work, but the sections dealing with the antecedents of opinion, media influences, and socialization are particularly useful. This selection is a chapter in Volume 2 of *Handbook of Social Psychology,* edited by Gardner Lindzey and Elliot Aronson.

3. "Attitudes and Attitude Change," by William J. McGuire (1985), another chapter in volume 2 of *Handbook of Social Psychology,* was written for social psychologists and advanced students. Readers who can handle it will find a goldmine of information concerning how attitudes change.

4. *Attitudes and Persuasion: Classic and Contemporary Approaches,* by Richard E. Petty and John T. Cacioppo (1981), takes a state-of-the-art look at attitude change. The book covers all major theoretical perspectives and synthesizes them in a general theoretical framework.

5. *Coercive Persuasion,* by Edgar H. Schein (1961), presents theory and evidence pertaining to the effectiveness of "illicit" persuasion tactics, such as those used by the Chinese during the Korean War. The book also applies concepts derived from the coercive persuasion model to other settings, such as prisons, mental health facilities, and religious communes.

6. *Influencing Attitudes and Changing Behavior,* by Philip G. Zimbardo, Ebbe B. Ebbesen, and Christina Maslach (1977), uses social-psychological theory and research to explain attitude change in everyday settings. Zimbardo and his colleagues also examine extraordinary forms of persuasion, such as interrogation and brainwashing.

IN DEPTH

Coercive Persuasion

Before joining the army at age 19, Joe had lived most of his life in a small town in the Midwest. In high school he was more interested in sports than in his studies but his grades were pretty good. He and Joan had been dating about a year, and they were thinking of marrying when he got out of the army. But when the fighting in Korea escalated, Joe's unit joined the United Nations forces. During a fierce skirmish his position was overrun by North Korean and Chinese troops. Joe was taken prisoner and spent the next eighteen months in a prisoner of war (POW) camp. Finally, in 1953, when the two sides reached an accord, the 3,500 U.S. POWs held by the Chinese were set free. Joe, however, was not among them—he chose to remain in North Korea.

Why did Joe refuse to return to America? Had the Chinese destroyed his attitudes and values through **coercive persuasion**—psychologically compelling techniques designed to change individuals' attitudes against the will? Were these methods so terrifying that no one could resist them?

When Edgar H. Schein interviewed former POWs, he discovered that the Chinese did in fact use systematic indoctrination techniques to alter the prisoners' attitudes. The Chinese referred to the program as *hsi nao*, which literally means "to cleanse the mind." The Americans called it brainwashing. Schein, however, felt that *brainwashing* was much too strong a term, because the methods used by the Chinese were neither unique nor exotic. Rather, the Chinese simply combined many commonplace methods into a single, unified attempt to change attitudes (Schein, 1956, 1961). In his summary of the program, Schein identified three basic phases. First the Chinese sought to disrupt, or *unfreeze,* the POWs' current attitudes and values. The second phase involved *changing* these attitudes to conform with communist doctrine. In the final phase, new attitudes were ingrained with the POWs' overall value system. Schein calls this phase *refreezing*.

The Chinese used physical and social-psychological tactics to unfreeze the men's attitudes. Once captured, many of the men were forced to march for days with very little food or rest. Conditions at the camp were not much better, for they slept in huts with dirt floors, ate mostly cereals and soup, and had no access to medical facilities. These privations, which left them weak and disoriented, were reinforced by disruption of their social relationships. Recognizing the huge benefits of personal and group bonds under such adverse conditions, the Chinese routinely undermined all relationships among the POWs. They disrupted military organization by separating the officers and enlisted men. They broke up any friendships that developed by transferring the men involved. They undermined trust among the prisoners by placing informers in each living area. No religious ceremonies were permitted, and letters from home were withheld so that bonds with loved ones were disrupted. Many of the men became convinced that only letters containing bad news were delivered.

In the second phase, the Chinese relied on both direct and indirect techniques to change the prisoners' attitudes. Each day the POWs attended two- or three-hour "teaching classes" that covered the basic philosophy of communism. The material also included attacks on American values, criticisms of the United Nations, and procommunist propaganda films. Whenever possible the men were also exposed to procommunist testimonials given by fellow POWs: speeches on the benefits of communism, readings of procommunist essays, public confessions to various war crimes. The Chinese repeatedly claimed, for example, that the UN forces were using germ warfare. To convince their prisoners, the Chinese formed a so-called international commission to investigate the problem, and showed movies of staged interviews in which Americans confessed to dropping germ-ladden bombs on North Korea. They also coerced several Air Force officers into visiting each camp and explaining why germ warfare was used.

These direct persuasion tactics were relatively ineffective. The "teachers" were English-speaking Chinese, so their credibility was doubtful. Also, the information about America was often inaccurate and easily refuted. In fact, since the Chinese relied primarily on the works of Mao Tse-tung, men who were familiar with Karl Marx's writings were able to challenge the teachers on the communist principles they were discussing. The testimonials, in contrast, had a great impact on the men. Since they came from fellow POWs, the source was much more credible. These testimonials also undermined social supports for the prisoners' attitudes. When they banded together to reject the communist arguments, this unity reinforced their convictions. The testimonials destroyed this unity.

Just as the direct techniques relied heavily on persuasive methods, the indirect techniques capitalized on the need to maintain consistency among cognitions and behaviors (Festinger, 1957). Time and again the men were coerced into performing procommunist actions. Often these actions were inconsequential, such as copying an essay out of a notebook or answering some questions about life in the United States. Once the men agreed to a minor request, however, a more significant request followed. And the Chinese insisted on some kind of active response, either written or oral. One technique required the men to discuss political questions, such as "Is the aim of the capitalist nations world domination?" After each discussion, the men were asked to write out their answer to the question. If they answered "incorrectly" (by challenging the communist doctrine), the entire group repeated the exercise. Eventually the men decided that little harm could be done if they answered the questions the way their captors wanted. Each small concession led to a slightly larger one, however, until men unwittingly found themselves collaborating with the Chinese. In some cases, such simple methods succeeded in extracting confessions to war crimes and pledges of allegiance to communism. (Chapter 10 contains more information on these social influence techniques.)

The Chinese also tried to create cognitive inconsistencies through interrogation. These sessions could last for days or even weeks as the Chinese questioned the men about their basic values and attitudes. After examining their prisoners' civilian lives in detail, the Chinese would claim that any past problems were caused by flaws in the capitalist system. They described the Korean conflict as a "civil
(continued)

IN DEPTH *continued*

war," and asked the men how they would have felt if a foreign power had intervened in the American Civil War. With these tactics the interrogators often succeeded in convincing the men that U.S. involvement in Korea was inconsistent with principles of fairness.

In the final phase, men who cooperated with the Chinese were asked to make public commitments to communism. They were given jobs to perform around the camp, and they were excused from any unpleasant chores. These men were allowed to form committees that helped run the camp, and they assisted in preparing propaganda leaflets and testimonials. All in all, these tactics sought to provide social supports for the newly acquired attitudes.

How successful was this program of coercive persuasion? Schein points out that at one time or another nearly all of the men performed actions that helped the enemy. *Collaboration* took many forms: prisoners signed petitions protesting the war, made radio appeals, wrote letters home touting the benefits of communism, posed for misleading photographs, made false confessions, ran errands for the Chinese, informed on fellow POWs. The Chinese clearly succeeded in disrupting social relations among the prisoners. Discipline and morale were poor, the men rarely attempted to escape, and disloyalty was rampant (Schein, 1961; Segal, 1954).

The Chinese were less successful, however, in creating long-term change. Of the 3,500 POWs, only 21 voluntarily remained in Korea at the end of the war. Most of the others regained their confidence in America once they escaped the influence of the Chinese. Schein concludes that though the Chinese were effective in the first phase of their strategy—they succeeded in disrupting individuals' value systems—they generally failed to change those attitudes or to refreeze attitudes that they did change. Schein believes that most acts of collaboration resulted from the physical and psychological pressures of imprisonment. Living under constant threat of punishment and even death, the men cooperated in small ways. These actions, however, rarely reflected deep changes in political attitudes. In fact, this firsthand experience convinced many of the men that the communists posed a greater threat to American values than they had originally believed.

Schein's intriguing analysis offers many insights into the social foundations of our attitudes and values. While we often assume that attitudes are very private and personal, they often reflect the beliefs accepted by the groups to which we belong. When we are isolated from these groups, the social supports for our attitudes are cut away. As a result, our attitudes may change (Newcomb, 1943). Once we return to our groups however, we revert to our original attitudinal position. Schein's work and the studies of cognitive dissonance described in Chapter 6 highlight the elasticity of our attitudes. Attitudes may be stretched by attempts at persuasion, but they often snap back.

The concept of coercive persuasion also sheds light on a disturbing contemporary phenomenon: the growth of cults. Many authorities believe that radical religious groups and social movements, such as the Unification Church (Moonies), the International Society for Krishna Consciousness (Hare Krishna), the Divine Light Mission, and the Church of Scientology, use coercive techniques to recruit and retain their members. In accordance with Schein's three-step model, recruits' beliefs are first unfrozen through a series of manipulations: they are deprived of sleep, their diet is altered, and they are persuaded to take part in physically exhilarating activities. Supports for their original attitudes are stripped away when they are isolated from parents and friends. Next, new attitudes are created through a series of lectures and discussions. Often these lectures focus on the teaching of a charismatic leader—a Maharaj Ji or a Sun Myung Moon—who is an extremely effective speaker. Induction into the group proceeds through a series of escalating commitments. Compliance with small requests is followed by greater demands, as was the case with the Korean POWs. Lastly, the emphasis on group living ensures that the newly created attitudes will find strong support within the social group.

Radical groups sometimes succeed in exerting considerable control over their members. The mass suicide of 911 members of the People's Temple at their leader's orders is a case in point. Yet most such attempts at coercive persuasion fail to create long-lasting change among members (Bromley, 1985; Levine, 1984). Interviews with former members suggest that they joined because they were initially attracted to the alternative lifestyle the group offered. They weren't psychologically seduced by special recruitment tactics. And though strong tactics are used to control members' actions, the dropout rate in such groups remains fairly high. By one estimate, 90% of all members leave the group within two years (Levine, 1984). Again, interviews with former members suggest that they became disillusioned with the inconsistency of their leaders' actions, by the group's failure to reach its goals, and by a lifestyle that soon became monotonous. If persuasive techniques were effective, we would expect such groups to retain far more of their members.

Additional research is needed to determine the impact of these groups on their members' attitudes, but at present the available research simply doesn't support the idea that cults brainwash their recruits.

> The lure and power of the new religious groups have been exaggerated. The most telling critique of these groups is not that they capture and enslave innocent youth, but that they ultimately have not been able to provide the answers they had hoped for. [Bromley, 1985, p. 15]

S E V E N

Personal Relationships

Affiliation
   The affiliation situation
      Uncertainty and affiliation
      Fear and affiliation
      Embarrassment and affiliation
   The affiliating personality
      The joiners: People who need people
      The loners: Social anxiety and shyness
   Affiliation: A biological necessity

Attraction
   The power of proximity
   Physical appearance
   Personal characteristics
      Similarity
      Complementarity
   The rewards we receive
      Social approval as a reward
      Social disapproval as punishment
   The economics of attraction

Close relationships
   The two faces of love
   Passionate love
   Companionate love
      Trust and self-disclosure
      Social exchange
      Satisfaction and commitment

Dissolution
   The emotional bases of dissolution
      The loss of passion
      When love turns to anger
   Satisfaction and social exchange

Summary
For more information
In depth: Sexual relationships

Personal relationships are the threads that bind us to other people. We live out our lives enmeshed in these threads, secure in the comfort of long-formed bonds, and striving to make fast the threads of each new relationship. Some seem so strong that we think they will hold us forever. Others are weak—so fragile they can be broken as easily as a strand of a spider's web. But whether long-lasting or short-lived, strong or weak, these threads make up the fabric of your social world. If your life were a patchwork quilt, it would be sewn together by your personal relationships.

We all recognize the importance of relationships in our lives. When asked "What is it that makes your life meaningful?" most people mention their relationships: their friends, lovers, children, and parents (Klinger, 1977). And when people are asked about sources of lasting happiness and satisfaction, "a happy marriage," "a good family life," and "good friends" top the list. Career accomplishments, financial security, and material possessions pale in comparison with our relationships (Campbell, Converse, & Rodgers, 1976).

But personal relationships aren't static; the fabric of your social life is torn and mended and rewoven all the time (Levinger, 1980; Levinger & Snoek, 1972). Consider one strong thread—one long-term relationship—in the social fabric of your life. Whether you have chosen to consider your link to your spouse, your lover, or your best friend, search back through time and recall your first encounter with the stranger who became your intimate friend or lover. Although this first encounter may have seemed uneventful at the time, it set the stage for subsequent developments. Therefore, *affiliation* is our first topic in the study of personal relations, for if human beings didn't affiliate with other human beings, intimate relationships might never have the opportunity to form.

The second phase of personal relationships, *attraction*, begins when a feeling of liking for the other person takes root. You may have met your friend or lover at a crowded party, where many of the other people left

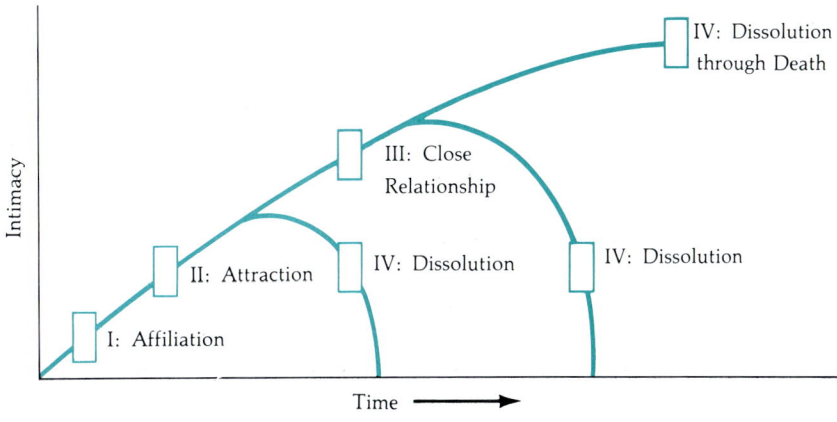

Figure 7-1 The life cycle of three hypothetical personal relationships. Many relationships follow a pattern that begins with affiliation and ends with dissolution. Affiliation sets the stage for the growth of attraction, which then ripens into a close, intimate relationship. In time, however, the relationship may be shattered by either conflict or death.

no lasting impression. Yet something drew the two of you together, and the seeds of a longer, more intimate relationship were sown.

As feelings of attraction deepen, the bond between you becomes a *close relationship*—friendship or love. You become more committed to each other, and you feel you can trust and rely on each other. With trust comes more intimate interaction, the sharing of personal feelings, and a desire to care for the other person. Yet close relationships also bring conflict, strain, and doubt. If these problems can't be managed, then your relationship may enter a final stage: *dissolution*. Your friend becomes a stranger, or your lover becomes an enemy. In this chapter we will chart the growth of our personal relationships from affiliation to attraction to closeness to dissolution (see Figure 7-1).

■ Affiliation

Aristotle, who was as much a social psychologist as a philosopher, proclaimed that humans are social animals by nature. All of us seek solitude from time to time, but we spend much of our lives in the company of other people. We work with other people. We relax with other people. We worship with other people. We eat our meals with other people. We sleep with other people. Humankind is a gregarious species: each of us typically spends between 20% and 60% of our waking hours in the company of other people (Deaux, 1978; Latané & Bidwell, 1977; Wheeler & Nezlek, 1977).

What causes **affiliation?** What prompts us to join together with other members of our species? In part, the motivation comes from without: the situations that we face may be so novel, ambiguous, or frightening that we seek company. However, the need to join with others may also come from within, for some people prefer not to join together with other people. Both factors are examined below.

The Affiliation Situation

What if you lived a life of total isolation? How would you know if you were a success or a failure? How would you learn to appreciate art and music? How would you determine the validity of your political and moral values? How would you assign meaning to everyday events and personal experiences? If you couldn't compare your own opinions, beliefs, and values with those of other people, you could never develop a conception of social reality (Festinger, 1950, 1954).

In ambiguous, novel situations we seek out others because we require information about ourselves and the world around us, and this information is available only from other people. As we learned in Chapter 2, this process is known as *social comparison.* By comparing ourselves to others we can *validate* our existing beliefs. Do you think that Robert Redford is handsome, that abortion is immoral, that social psychology is fascinating, that a woman can be as effective a leader as a man? Through social comparison you can decide whether your reactions are considered correct, valid, or proper. And when we lack sufficient information to form our own judgments, comparison allows us to *construct* entirely new opinions, attitudes, and beliefs (Fazio, 1979).

Other people are an important source of information, but we do not always seek their input. Engaging in social comparison is like asking a teacher a question in a classroom. When you understand the material perfectly, you probably won't need to ask. If, however, you are confused by some of the material, or are afraid you are on the wrong track, then you are more likely to ask questions. Yet even when you need information, you may not ask for it because you are embarrassed to do so. We seek social comparison information when we are *uncertain* about the nature of the situation and when we are *fearful,* but we avoid others when we are *embarrassed.*

Uncertainty and affiliation. Put yourself in the shoes of a subject of Stanley Schachter. One Dr. Gregor Zilstein, who claims to hail from the medical school's departments of neurology and psychiatry, thanks you for agreeing to take part in a study of the physiological effects of electric shocks. Seated in a room filled with electrical equipment, Zilstein explains:

> These shocks will hurt, they will be painful. As you can guess, if, in research of this sort, we're to learn anything at all that will really help

humanity, it is necessary that our shocks be intense. . . . These shocks will be quite painful but, of course, they will do no permanent damage. [Schachter, 1959, p. 13]

As the phrase "quite painful, but will do no permanent damage" runs through your mind, Zilstein asks if you would like to wait your turn in a private room or in a room with several other people. Which room would you select?

Schachter conducted this experiment to see if people affiliate to *reduce their uncertainty* about their social environment. He surmised that his subjects, finding themselves in an ambiguous situation, uncertain about what was happening and what they could expect, would tend to seek out other people so that they could compare their reactions with those of others (see Figure 7-2). As Schachter predicted, when the subjects who expected to receive painful shocks were asked if they wanted to wait alone or with others, 63% chose to affiliate. In contrast, when subjects were told that the electric shocks would "resemble more a tickle or a tingle than anything unpleasant," only 33% chose affiliation.

Schachter summed up his findings with the adage "Misery loves company." He added, however, that if other people know nothing about the situation you face, then there is no reason to affiliate with them. To demonstrate this situation, he again led subjects to expect painful electric shocks and then asked them if they wanted to affiliate or remain alone. Some of the subjects thought that the people they could join were also waiting to receive shocks, whereas others believed that they might join people who "were waiting to talk to their professors and advisors." Schachter felt that if the subjects believed that the others could provide them with no useful information about the situation they faced, then they would have no reason to affiliate with them. As predicted, 60% of the subjects wanted to wait with their fellow subjects, but not a single subject wanted to wait with the nonsubjects. Thus we tend to compare ourselves with people who are similar to us in some way. Or, as Schachter puts it, "misery doesn't love just any kind of company; it loves only miserable company" (p. 24).

Fear and affiliation. The situation created by Schachter didn't simply create uncertainty: it also created fear. The participants wanted more

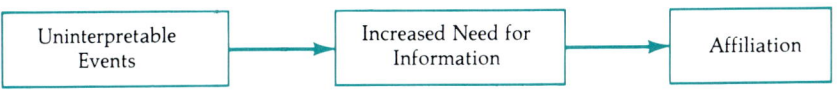

Figure 7-2 People affiliate in order to gain information through social comparison. According to Schachter, (1) uninterpretable events shake our confidence in our own attitudes, beliefs, and opinions; (2) this loss of confidence creates a need for information; and (3) this need can be satisfied through affiliation with others.

than information—they wanted to *reduce their fear* by talking to other people. To explore the link between fear and affiliation, experimenters asked subjects who were waiting for electric shocks if they wanted to wait with people who seemed to be very fearful, moderately fearful, or calm. If subjects wanted to validate their emotions, they should have preferred to affiliate with people who were also fearful. If, however, they wanted reassurance and the chance to reduce their fear, then less fearful comrades would be a better choice. Supporting the idea that misery seeks reassuring as well as miserable company, most of the subjects wanted to wait with less fearful people (Rabbie, 1963; see also Darley & Aronson, 1966; Fazio, 1979; Focus 7-1).

Embarrassment and affiliation. If you have ever committed a social blunder in front of strangers, you have probably felt like crawling under a rock—affiliation was the last thing on your mind. Although we may want information, when other people are watching and evaluating us we may be too embarrassed to seek it out. We sometimes choose to be confused and fearful rather than appear foolish (Rofé, 1984).

To study individuals' reactions to embarrassment, researchers have led subjects to believe that they would have to perform a childish act, such

---

FOCUS 7-1

A Closer Look: *Why do people spread rumors?*

Have you heard that the boss is thinking of laying off half the workers in your department? Did you know some fast-food restaurants put worms in their hamburgers? Someone told me the Navy has photographs of UFOs, but they won't release them for fear of causing a panic. I read someplace that the board of directors of a certain national company are all devil worshipers.

Traditionally, rumors have been viewed as idle gossip or the distorted ramblings of the uninformed. Ralph L. Rosnow, however, believes that this negative reputation is in large part undeserved. Although wild rumors can cause mischief and disruption, Rosnow believes that some rumors are "a reasonable and nonpainful way to obtain needed social comparison information" (Rosnow, 1980, p. 587). Just as threatening situations prompt affiliation, Rosnow argues, "ambiguous or chaotic" situations generate rumors. By passing on rumors, individuals convey information (albeit false information) about the situation. Also rumors often provide reassurance by reinterpreting events in a more positive light. Even bleak, pessimistic rumors may, in the long run, reduce our anxiety by preparing us for bad news (Allport & Postman, 1947; Prasad, 1950).

Rosnow's theory of rumors explains why stressful but ambiguous events are so often the subject of rumor. The accident at the Three Mile Island nuclear power plant, for example, posed a great threat to nearby residents, but it was shrouded in ambiguity. As a result, within days rumors that both exaggerated and minimized the danger began to circulate. Eventually a rumor-control center had to be opened to supply more accurate information to people who had heard that cows were dying, the reactor had melted down, or that a radioactive cloud had been released. Rosnow points out that these rumors may have been factually incorrect, but they gave people a sense of knowing what was happening at a time of great anxiety (Rosnow & Kimmel, 1979). Schachter's subjects affiliated to gain information and reduce fear; the residents around Three Mile Island passed rumors to accomplish these same ends.

as sucking on large nipples and pacifiers. As expected, they expressed a strong desire to remain alone (Sarnoff & Zimbardo, 1961; Teichman, 1973). In a more naturalistic study, experimenters approached college students and asked them to participate in a study of "sexual attitudes." When they arrived for the study, they were told simply to wait for the experimenter to arrive. To create various levels of anxiety and embarrassment, the experimenters varied the contents of the room. In one condition the room contained several electrical devices and information sheets suggesting that the study involved electric shock. In a second condition, the equipment was replaced by contraceptive devices, books on venereal disease, and color pictures of nudes. As predicted, when the room contained fear-provoking equipment, subjects affiliated both verbally and nonverbally. If, in contrast, the room was filled with embarrassing sexual materials, subjects fled. Thus misery may love company, but *embarrassed* misery loves privacy (Morris et al., 1976).

The Affiliating Personality

When President John F. Kennedy was assassinated, Americans grieved in two distinct ways. When researchers asked Americans to describe their reaction to the tragedy, they found that the majority sought solace by talking to others, but about 40% wanted to be left alone (Sheatsley & Feldman, 1964).

To predict affiliation, we must go beyond the situational factors identified by social comparison theorists and consider the personality characteristics of the individuals in the social setting. Even when we face the same situation, different people react in different ways. Some of us seem to seek out social stimulation, whereas others prefer privacy to sociability. While the classification of people in two exclusive categories—"loners" and "joiners"—oversimplifies the intricacies of human nature, researchers have succeeded in identifying personality variables that push people toward other people and other personality variables that pull them apart (see Gangestad & Snyder, 1985).

The joiners: People who need people.

Are you a joiner? When you go shopping, do you prefer to go with others? Do you live alone or with someone else? Do you like to attend public events and join clubs?

Many factors have been linked to individual differences in affiliation. Schachter (1959), for example, was intrigued by *birth order*. Reasoning that children who were born first and only children probably receive greater stimulation and protective guidance from their parents, Schacter speculated that these "first borns" would be more affiliative than "later borns" (Lewis & Kreitzberg, 1979; Zajonc, Markus, & Markus, 1979). Sure enough, when he threatened first and later born subjects with painful or mild electric shocks, he found that birth order did make a difference. As Figure 7-3 indicates, when they expected severe shocks, the first borns were more likely than later borns to affiliate. (Cottrell & Epley, 1977, and Warren, 1966, present divergent views on the strength of the relationship between birth order and affiliation.)

Other researchers have focused on the strength of various needs that make up our personalities. According to this approach, human behavior is guided by a limited number of social drives, or motives, such as the need for achievement, the need for power, and the need for affiliation. When these needs are strong, they exert a pervasive influence on behavior across situations. When they are weak, their influence on actions is minimal (McClelland, 1985).

How can we gauge the strength of these motives? In some cases, the motives can be tapped by traditional self-report methods, such as interviews or questionnaires. Many motivation researchers, however, prefer to use such projective techniques as the Thematic Apperception Test, or TAT (Atkinson, 1958). The TAT requires respondents to write imaginative stories about several ambiguous pictures (see Figure 7-4). The researcher then analyzes the imagery, themes, needs, actions, goals, and other key symbols contained in subjects' stories for evidence of each social motive. The validity of TAT techniques has been questioned by many investigators, but proponents of this method argue that people aren't sufficiently aware of their motivations to describe them accurately through traditional self-report methods (McClelland, 1980, 1985).

Hundreds of studies have focused on the need for affiliation, which is often abbreviated **nAffiliation**. In general, these studies find that people who are high in *n*Affiliation are much more likely to seek out other people

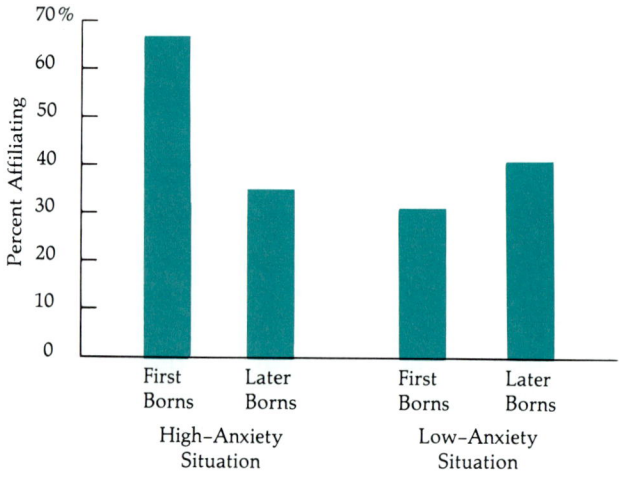

Figure 7-3   When Schachter asked subjects who were waiting for extremely painful shocks or mild shocks if they wanted to wait alone or with others, first borns and only children showed a strong tendency to seek out others, but only when they expected painful shocks.

Figure 7-4 A sample picture from the Thematic Apperception Test (TAT). Social needs are sometimes measured with the TAT. Subjects are shown four or five pictures like this one, and then asked to make up a story that describes what is happening, the relationship between the people in the picture, and the characters' thoughts and interests. Researchers who use the TAT assume that respondents will project their inner motives and needs in the stories they write about the pictures.

than those who are low in nAffiliation, although they also often report higher levels of anxiety in social settings and worry about offending other people (see Table 7-1).

In one study subjects wore electronic pages ("beepers") for one week. Subjects were beeped seven times a day, at random, between 9:00 A.M. and 11:00 P.M. Whenever they were beeped, they completed a short questionnaire explaining what they were doing at the time. Later the investigators counted the number of times the subject was affiliating with others (engaged in conversation or writing letters to other people) or was alone. As expected, nAffiliation score was significantly correlated with affiliative behavior. The correlation was +.41 for both men and women. The implications of these findings are clear: when we join with others, or

TABLE 7-1

Some of the correlates of a high need for affiliation (nAffiliation).

People who are high in need for affiliation tend to:
- Be concerned with "establishing, maintaining, and restoring a positive affective relationship" (Atkinson, Heyns, & Veroff, 1954).
- Watch other people closely in social interactions (Davage, 1958).
- Perceive themselves as compatible with other people (Mehrabian, 1976).
- Join social groups, such as clubs (Smart, 1965).
- Communicate with others in a friendly manner (Exline, 1962; Fishman, 1966).
- Be well liked by others (Mehrabian & Ksionsky, 1974).
- Have high levels of anxiety in social settings (Byrne, 1961).
- Avoid making divisive, offending comments to other people (Exline, 1962).
- Fear rejection by others (McAdams, 1982).

even write to them, we satisfy a basic need. However, this need is greater in some people than in others (Constantian, 1981/1982; McAdams & Constantian, 1983; see McClelland, 1985, for a review).

The loners: Social anxiety and shyness. Henry David Thoreau spent two years secluded at Walden Pond. He would have scored very low in *n*Affiliation, for he felt that

> society is commonly too cheap. We meet at very short intervals, not having

---

FOCUS 7-2

Applying Social Psychology: *How can we overcome the pain of loneliness?*

By joining together with other people, we avoid one of the most distressing experiences known to woman or man: **loneliness.** Loneliness, as the term is used by social psychologists, is not just isolation or being alone. Rather, we experience loneliness when our personal relationships are too few or too unsatisfying (Peplau & Perlman, 1982). In most cases, loneliness occurs because we feel cut off from our network of friends and acquaintances. If you ever moved to a new city, or entered a college located far away from your hometown, the initial **social loneliness** may have caused you to feel unhappy and dissatisfied. **Emotional loneliness,** in contrast, occurs when we lack a meaningful, intimate relationship with another person (Russell et al., 1984; Weiss, 1973). This form of loneliness sets in after a divorce, a breakup with a lover, or repeated failure to develop an intimate relationship with another person. Social and emotional loneliness lead to a common core of negative emotions. When we are lonely, we report feelings of desperation (panic, helplessness, hopefulness, vulnerability), boredom (impatience, uneasiness, anger), self-deprecation (feelings of lack of attractiveness, stupidity, shame), and depression (sadness, emptiness, isolation, self-pity) (Rubenstein & Shaver, 1982).

Loneliness is a significant health problem in the United States. Prolonged periods of loneliness have been linked to such physical illnesses as cirrhosis of the liver (brought on by alcohol abuse), hypertension, and heart disease (Lynch, 1977). Evidence indicates that lonely people are not as healthy as

The shy and lonely. Shy people feel so tense and awkward in social situations that they avoid joining in with others. As a result, they often experience periods of loneliness: feelings of desperation, helplessness, uneasiness, self-doubt, and sadness.

had time to acquire any new value for each other. We meet at three meals a day and give each other a taste of that old musty cheese that we are. . . . Certainly less frequency would suffice for all important and hearty communication. [Thoreau, 1962, p. 206]

Thoreau was a loner simply because he valued his privacy more than contact with other people (Leary, 1983).

In contrast to Thoreau, some people avoid others because they suffer from **social anxiety:** they may desire and value interaction with others,

---

people who are embedded in a network of social relationships (Cohen & Wills, 1985). Loneliness also figures prominently in many mental health problems, such as suicide, depression, anxiety, and interpersonal hostility (Cutrona, 1982; Jones, Freemon, & Goswick, 1981; Peplau, Russell, & Heim, 1979; Weeks, Michela, Peplau, & Bragg, 1980; Wenz, 1977). Loneliness is so commonly reported by individuals suffering from psychological problems that it has been called the "common cold of psychopathology" (W. H. Jones, quoted in Meer, 1985, p. 33).

What causes loneliness? The major precipitating factor is the loss of a loved one. Loneliness is also linked to our perceptions of ourselves and other people. For example, blaming our loneliness on internal, stable factors that cannot be changed—such as basic personality traits or personal faults—exacerbates loneliness, as does the rigid belief that the only cure for loneliness is a satisfying romantic relationship (Cutrona, 1982). Loneliness and shyness go hand in hand, for people who feel that they lack the *social skills* needed to interact effectively with other people often avoid social contacts. Such fears can become self-perpetuating. Once we question our abilities, we may become so guarded in our social actions that we make a negative impression on other people (Jones, Hobbs, & Hockenbury, 1982; Schlenker & Leary, 1982).

Social psychologists have only begun to understand the causes and cures of loneliness, but they do offer some suggestions to people who are suffering through lonely periods in their lives. In general, they warn people to avoid self-destructive reactions to loneliness: passivity, excessive sleeping, overeating, taking tranquillizers, watching too much television, abusing alcohol or marijuana, or workaholism (Rubenstein & Shaver, 1982). Instead, when you feel lonely you should remind yourself that periods of solitude are a normal part of life, and can be used to achieve personal growth and development (Peplau & Perlman, 1982). Other strategies that have been recommended include the following (Rook & Peplau, 1982):

- Try to increase the number of your social contacts by making an effort to talk to people in your classes or next-door neighbors, joining social organizations, or volunteering to help an acquaintance.
- Perform an activity that takes your mind off your troubles, such as going to a movie, exercising, reading a book, writing a letter.
- Improve your physical appearance (buy some new clothes, exercise) or your social skills (learn to dance, join an assertiveness group).
- Talk to a friend or counselor about ways to overcome your feelings of loneliness.
- Remind yourself that the cure for your loneliness may not be the restoration of the loss that caused it. Rather than insist that you need a new romantic relationship to replace a terminated one, for instance, you might try to increase your circle of friends.
- Clearly enumerate all the positive, rewarding relationships you have with other people.
- Revise your personal goals for your social relationships.

but the prospect of meeting other people leaves them feeling anxious and distressed. In many cases, socially anxious people want to make a good impression, but they feel that they lack the skills needed to act in a poised, competent manner. In particular, they feel that the people around them are evaluating them, and that they aren't receiving high marks. Most of us typically experience some anxiety in stressful social situations—when we give a speech, answer questions during a job interview, bumble into a classroom in the middle of a lecture. The highly anxious person, however, reacts negatively to a wide range of settings (Buss, 1980; Leary, 1983; Schlenker & Leary, 1982). In fact, in its most severe form social anxiety is called *social phobia:* "a persistent, irrational fear of, and compelling desire to avoid, situations in which the individual may be exposed to the scrutiny of others. There is also fear that the individual will behave in a manner that will be humiliating or embarrassing" (*DSM III*, 1980, p. 227).

Shyness is one of the most common forms of social anxiety. Philip Zimbardo, who pioneered the social-psychological study of shyness, argues that shy people feel that they cannot interact effectively with other people. Because of these feelings, they experience a number of emotional, physiological, and behavioral symptoms when they encounter other people (Zimbardo, 1977). They tend to report feelings of tension, awkwardness, and discomfort, as well as a fear of social evaluation. They also complain of loneliness (see Focus 7-2). In public settings shy individuals report increases in pulse rate, blushing, perspiration, and "butterflies." They can be identified by their *lack* of social behaviors: their silence in groups, downcast eyes, low speaking voice, and general withdrawal from others. A person who agrees with the statements in Table 7-2 displays many symptoms of shyness (Cheek & Buss, 1981).

TABLE 7-2

Items measuring shyness.

1. I am socially somewhat awkward.
2. I find it hard to talk to strangers.
3. I feel tense when I'm with people I don't know well.
4. When conversing I worry about saying something dumb.
5. I feel nervous when speaking to someone in authority.
6. I am often uncomfortable at parties and other social functions.
7. I feel inhibited in social situations.
8. I have trouble looking someone right in the eye.
9. I am more shy with members of the opposite sex.

Affiliation: A Biological Necessity

When social comparison theorists try to predict affiliation, they tend to ask about the setting: Is the situation ambiguous, anxiety-provoking, or embarrassing? Other theorists, in contrast, look within the person by considering such personality traits as birth order, need for affiliation, and social anxiety. We should not, however, completely deny the *instinctive roots* of affiliation. Across most societies and situations, humans show gregarious tendencies: we live in groups rather than in isolation (Barash, 1982). Like many other creatures, we may be driven together by a herd instinct.

In fact, the human species depends on affiliation for its survival. Although modern medical procedures offer alternatives, the human reproduction cycle usually requires affiliation. Without initial contact, more intimate forms of interaction would be impossible. However, as important as affiliation is to the reproductive success of our species, it is only the first step on this journey. Situational, personality, and instinctive forces may bring two people together, but whether they like or dislike each other is a different issue altogether.

■ Attraction

Theodore Newcomb wanted to know why we like some people more than others. But he didn't want to conduct laboratory studies—too contrived for his tastes. Nor did he opt for field studies—too little control over the situation. Instead, he decided to create his own social microcosm and then watch the attraction process unfold over time.

He carried out his classic studies of interpersonal attraction in the late 1950s. To create his miniature social world, for two years he recruited 17 male students who were transferring to the University of Michigan from other colleges. He offered them free rent in return for completion of a questionnaire each week. All of the men were total strangers to one another when the study began, but four months later they had evolved into an assortment of friends, enemies, and acquaintances (Newcomb, 1960, 1961, 1979, 1981).

Newcomb's findings led him to reject many common-sense notions about the nature of attraction. Whereas poets and romance novelists would have us believe that liking occurs spontaneously and capriciously, Newcomb discovered that interpersonal attraction develops in a predictable pattern. Moreover, when he tested such notions as "familiarity breeds contempt" and "opposites attract," he found that they rarely explained attraction (see Focus 7-3). Instead, he discovered gradual changes in attraction over time. Initially, surface-level factors, such as proximity or appearance, were important. Students who shared a room became very close friends. Physical characteristics, such as appearance and style of dress, also influenced attraction. As time went by, however, more personal factors became important as well. When subjects discovered that others possessed traits and qualities that they valued, their attraction to these others grew stronger. Those who offered others many rewards, such as companionship or social support, were also well liked.

This section traces the growth of attraction through the layers of factors identified by Newcomb. Initially, attraction depends on surface-level factors: we like people who are nearby, or who possess attractive physical qualities. If we peel away this layer, however, we find that personal qualities also count. And when we peel away this layer, we find that, at the most basic level, attraction is a matter of rewards: we like people who provide us many rewards and few costs (Berscheid, 1985; Berscheid & Walster, 1978; Brehm, 1985; Hendrick & Hendrick, 1983).

FOCUS 7-3

Controversy in Social Psychology: *Is the scientific study of personal relationships a worthwhile endeavor?*

Social psychologists have used a wide variety of methods to answer many kinds of questions about personal relationships. Researchers have, for example, identified the basic reasons why human beings tend to gather with other human beings; isolated some of the factors that increase and decrease interpersonal attraction; described the phases of a typical courtship; searched for the sources of dispute in marriage; and documented our everyday conceptions of love. They have even evaluated Dale Carnegie's suggestions about how to win friends and influence people and tested the common-sense notion that playing hard to get wins hearts (E. E. Jones, 1964; Walster et al., 1973).

In recent years, two opposing opinions about the value of these efforts have emerged. One position has been articulated by Senator William Proxmire of Wisconsin. In 1975 he discovered that the National Science Foundation was funding studies of attraction and love. Outraged by the expenditure of public funds on what he felt was useless research, Proxmire held a press conference to insist that "the National Science Foundation put a stop to the Federal version of 'The Love Machine.' " He went so far as to state that "200 million Americans want to leave some things in life a mystery, and right at the top of the things we don't want to know about is why a man falls in love with a woman and vice versa."

Social psychologists, as you might expect, don't agree with Senator Proxmire's claims. First, to critics who say that liking and love can't be understood, they answer that they can. Many puzzles remain unsolved, but even a skeptic must admit that remarkable progress has been made in recent years. Second, to those who say that personal relationships are improper topics for scientific study, social psychologists ask why? Isn't understanding liking or loving as interesting as such venerable empirical problems as "What are the things that look like canals on Mars?" or "Is light a wave or a particle?" Third, critics complain that social psychologists have only confirmed common-sense principles of attraction. Researchers point out that common sense is more often wrong than right in the context of personal relationships. Last, to those who feel that the study of interpersonal relations is a frivolous waste of time and money, experts argue that understanding relationships may be the *most* important goal humans now face. As James Reston, the *New York Times* columnist, puts it, "if the sociologists and psychologists can get even a suggestion of the answer to our patterns of romantic love, marriage, disillusion, divorce—and the children left behind—it could be the best investment of Federal money since Mr. Jefferson made the Louisiana Purchase" (Reston, 1975).

The Power of Proximity

A rejected suitor writes a letter to "Dear Elaine," a social-psychological advice columnist:

> Dear Elaine,
> I have done all I can to win Fred's affections, but he hardly notices me. I am desperate. What should I do?
>
> Rejected Suitor

> Dear R. S.,
> Take advantage of the power of proximity. Move in next door to Fred, and wait. In time, the sheer physical closeness should lead to interpersonal attraction, even if you are an obnoxious person. [Tyler & Sears, 1977]

The impact of close proximity on attraction is remarkable. Although we often think of ourselves as discriminating judges who accept as friends only those who impress us in some way, we generally end up liking people who are nearby. Just as Newcomb found that many roommates ended up liking each other, other investigators have confirmed this *proximity-attraction effect*. For example, when Leon Festinger and his colleagues asked students living in two apartment complexes to identify their friends, most tended to pick nearby neighbors or people who lived in apartments that they passed by daily. Furthermore, people who lived in more centrally located apartments had more friends than those who lived in secluded apartments. The key to popularity was high visibility brought about by close proximity (Festinger, 1951; Festinger, Schachter, & Back, 1950).

Why does physical closeness sometimes lead to emotional closeness? First, proximity removes some of the obstacles that can block the development of interpersonal attraction. We can spend time interacting with people we see frequently without expending much time or energy. Provided these interactions are enjoyable, rather than filled with conflict and tension, our feelings of attraction should grow (Ebbesen, Kjos, & Konečni, 1976; Kenrick & Johnson, 1979; Riordan & Tedeschi, 1983).

Second, because we see our neighbors so frequently, the link between proximity and attraction may be based on *mere exposure*. As Chapter 5 noted, the more frequently we are exposed to social objects, the more we tend to like them. This process also works for people. When exposure to a stranger is varied from high to low, people like the stranger they have seen frequently more than the one they've seldom seen (Brockner & Swap, 1976; Insko & Wilson, 1977; Saegert, Swap, & Zajonc, 1973).

Third, the proximity-attraction effect may be due to our need to maintain consistency among our various cognitions (see Chapter 6). Initially I may not like someone who sits close to me in a class, works at the next desk at the office, or lives in the apartment next door to mine. However, admitting to myself "I dislike Joe" and "I interact with Joe every day" would lead to psychological inconsistency. Hence I change my liking for

Joe to reduce this tension (Arkin & Burger, 1980; Newcomb, 1981; Tyler & Sears, 1977).

Physical Appearance

Folk wisdom may tell us that absence makes the heart grow fonder and familiarity breeds contempt, but evidence indicates that close proximity encourages liking. Similarly, even though we may know that you can't judge a book by its cover, our liking for others can be influenced by their physical appearance. As Chapter 3 noted, we are often drawn to people whose physical attributes we admire or value.

Physical attractiveness, for example, has a tremendous impact on our reaction to another person. We may claim that we ignore another's physical appearance, for we know that "beauty is only skin-deep." Yet, once again, folk wisdom is of little help when we try to understand attraction.

In a ground-breaking study of physical attraction and liking, Elaine Hatfield (formerly Elaine Walster) and her colleagues set up a "computer dance" open to all incoming college students (Walster et al., 1966). To be assigned a date, the students had to pay a fee of $1 and complete a series of questionnaires. The young men and women were led to believe that the questionnaires would be used to match them with a compatible opposite-sex date, but in actuality people were paired at random (with only one stipulation: the man had to be taller than the woman). While they were standing in line to buy tickets and complete their forms, four judges rated their physical attractiveness on a scale from 1 (extremely unattractive) to 8 (extremely attractive).

On the evening of the dance, most subjects met their partners about 8:00, and then talked or danced until a 10:30 intermission. At that time the men and women were taken to different locations, where they completed ratings of their dates. Initially Hatfield and her colleagues assumed that subjects' ratings would be determined by the date's personal characteristics (self-esteem, personality traits, intellectual ability), but these factors mattered very little. The only significant predictor of subjects' reactions was the date's physical attractiveness: the more beautiful or handsome the date, the higher the rating. The correlation between rating and physical attractiveness, as estimated by the objective judges, was .44 for women and .36 for men. And when subjects' own estimates of their dates' looks were used as the index of physical attractiveness, these correlations were even stronger: .78 and .69.

Other researchers have also found that, at least during initial encounters, we tend to like physically attractive people more than unattractive people (Adams, 1981; Berscheid & Walster, 1974). This tendency does not necessarily mean that people are so shallow and insensitive that they base their judgments of others on looks alone. We may seek the company of attractive people because we have learned to associate physical attractiveness with other positive personal traits. As Karen K. Dion, Ellen Berscheid, and Hatfield explain, our judgments of other people are often based on a "what is beautiful is good" stereotype. We just assume that attractive people are more confident, happy, assertive, active, candid, serious, and outspoken than people with average looks. They are also seen as more sexually warm and responsive, sensitive, kind, interesting, strong, poised, modest, sociable, outgoing, and nurturant. Not only are they considered to have better characters, but they are seen as more likely to be socially and professionally successful, to have happy marriages, and to lead fulfilling lives.

The "what is beautiful is good" stereotype gives attractive people an advantage in social situations. Although long-term studies indicate that such people are no more happy or successful than unattractive people, they are more likely to get married (Berscheid, Walster, & Campbell, 1972; Sussman, Gavriel, & Romer, 1983). They also tend to enjoy a more active and satisfying interpersonal life before marriage, and tend to be more skillful in their dealings with other people. Attractive men, in particular, are more assertive than less attractive men and are lower in fear of rejection by others (Reis et al., 1982).

The "what is beautiful is good" stereotype can also act as a self-fulfilling prophecy that turns attractive people into poised, confident extraverts and unattractive people into awkward, withdrawn introverts (see Figure 7-5). In one study, male subjects talked briefly with a woman by telephone. They couldn't see their partner, but they did see her photograph. The pictures, however, were actually snapshots of women who had been previously identified as either attractive (8s on a 10-point scale) or rather unattractive (2.5s on the scale). They were not photographs of their actual partners, who in reality did not vary greatly from one another in physical beauty. As anticipated, the men displayed stereotypic thinking: they rated the partner more positively when they thought she was attractive than when they thought she was unattractive. More important, the women actually behaved more positively when they were talking to men who thought they were attractive. Since the women knew nothing about the pictures, the researchers concluded that the men's behavior varied in accordance with the imagined attractiveness of the women. These behaviors, in turn, evoked more or less friendliness in their female partners. Beauty that was only in the mind of the beholder created actual differences in behavior (Snyder, Tanke, & Berscheid, 1977).

Personal Characteristics

Make a mental list of your three closest friends. Now imagine that someone has asked you to explain why you like these particular people. What will you answer?

Figure 7-5 A prophecy fulfilled. Lucy is so certain that she is unlovable that she overlooks Snoopy's attentions. Her prediction is fulfilled when Snoopy gives up.

© 1972 by United Media Services, Inc. Reprinted by permission.

Most of us, when asked to explain the source of our attraction to others, usually deny the role of proximity and physical appearance. After all, who wants to say, "I like June because she lives next door" or "I date Frank because he has a good body"? Instead, we usually point to their "special" personal characteristics. If you ask me why I like José, I'll say he is friendly. If you ask about Sandy, I'll explain that she has a great sense of humor. And if you ask me why I get along so well with Rich, I'll say I admire his athletic ability.

But why am I drawn to people who are friendly, humorous, or athletic? Why do I consider these particular characteristics to be attractive or admirable? Two basic tendencies generally underlie reactions to others' characteristics. First, we tend to like people who have the same characteristics that we do. Second, we sometimes (but not often) like people with qualities that complement our own characteristics.

Similarity. As soon as Newcomb's subjects got settled in their dormitory, they began to sort themselves into subgroups. In one case, the 17-man group split into two subgroups containing 9 and 7 members (one person was an outcast from both subgroups). It was as if some invisible magnet were drawing certain people together and pulling others apart (Newcomb, 1981).

Newcomb discovered that the magnet was similarity in values, beliefs, and interests. All of the men in one of the cliques were enrolled in the liberal arts college. They all came from cities or suburbs, and they had similar aesthetic, social, theoretical, economic, political, and religious values. Most of the men in the second subgroup were engineering majors who came from small towns in the Midwest, and they, too, shared certain religious and economic values. The outcast had idiosyncratic values and interests that matched those of neither group.

The *similarity-attraction effect*—our tendency to like people who are similar to us—has been confirmed in both laboratory and field situations. Many of the lab studies have used a "bogus stranger" paradigm developed by Don Byrne and his colleagues. After subjects have completed a questionnaire that measures their personal characteristics—attitudes, values, background, personality, and so on—they are shown a copy of a "stranger's" responses to the questionnaire. Although subjects are told that the questionnaire was completed by another subject, in actuality the responses on the questionnaire are tailored to each participant: some people encounter a stranger with very similar characteristics; others are shown a questionnaire containing very dissimilar responses. Subjects then indicate their personal feelings about the stranger and their willingness to work with him or her in an experiment. As Figure 7-6 indicates, the higher the proportion of similar answers given by the "stranger" and the subject, the more favorable the subjects' evaluations (Byrne, 1971; Byrne & Nelson, 1965; Palmer & Kalin, 1985).

These findings have not gone unchallenged. Quite justifiably, many critics have complained that the bogus stranger paradigm forces subjects

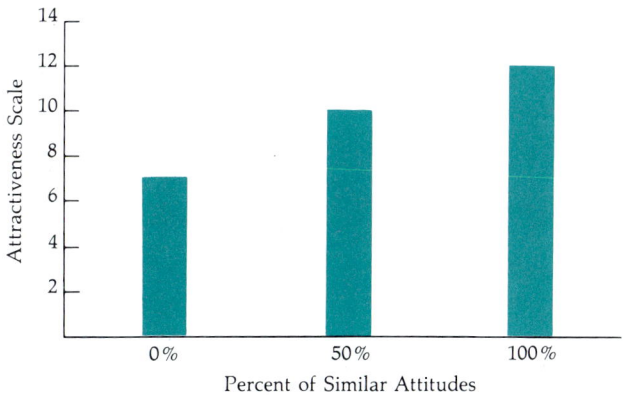

Figure 7-6   The similarity-attraction effect. When subjects rated the attractiveness of a "bogus stranger" on a scale that ranged from 2 (negative) to 14 (positive), they liked a stranger who shared 100% of their own attitudes and beliefs more than someone who shared about 50% of their attitudes. The completely dissimilar stranger—one who had no attitudes in common with the subject—was liked least of all (Gonzales et al., 1983).

to base their attraction ratings on similarity because they have no other information about the stimulus person (Murstein, 1976). Even in nonlaboratory settings, however, similarity promotes attraction. A study of schoolchildren ranging in age from 13 to 18 found that friends shared similar demographic characteristics (age, ethnicity, religion, family income) and liked the same school and recreational activities (Kandel, 1978). When the members of a Reserve Officers' Training Corps identified their friends within the group, they tended to select people with characteristics that matched their own (Davison & Jones, 1976). In presidential elections, voters prefer candidates who adopt positions on issues that are similar to their own (Brent & Granberg, 1982).

Similarity also promotes romantic attraction. When blind dates were arranged between men and women who shared either 33% or 67% of their attitudes, attraction was greater among the high-agreement couples (Byrne, Ervin, & Lamberth, 1970). Married couples also tend to share a variety of personality and attitudinal characteristics (Buss, 1984). Lastly, despite our bias toward beautiful people, our friends and lovers usually match our own level of physical attractiveness. People with average looks may dream of capturing the heart of an extremely attractive person, but they seek out others who are also average in attractiveness (Shanteau & Nagy, 1979).

The impact of similarity on attraction is subtle but powerful. From the very outset, similarity colors our perceptions of others. As soon as we realize we have something in common with someone else, we begin to feel a sense of unity and belongingness (Arkin & Burger, 1980; Darley & Berscheid, 1967; Tyler & Sears, 1977). We also tend to take similarity to be a sign that future interactions will be rewarding and free of conflict (Insko & Schopler, 1972), and we generally assume that people who are similar to us will also like us (Gonzales et al., 1983). Byrne also notes that when other people agree with us, they confirm the accuracy of our beliefs. Hence the discovery of similarity in attitudes, beliefs, and values is a very rewarding experiencing (Byrne, 1971).

We also tend to like similar people because this pattern of attraction is a *balanced relationship*. As Fritz Heider's **balance theory** explains, some relationships are "harmonious"; the elements of the situation all "fit together without stress" (1958, p. 180). Intuitively, we can recognize that the statements "Jim and his best friend, Frank, both like to fish" and "Jill avoids dressing like Alice, whom she hates" describe balanced relationships. Unbalanced relationships, in contrast, " 'do not add up'; they seem to pull in different directions" (p. 180). For example:

> Bob thinks Jim very stupid and a first class bore. One day Bob reads some poetry he likes so well that he takes the trouble to track down the author in order to shake his hand. He finds that Jim wrote the poems.   [p. 176]

This situation is unbalanced because its components are inconsistent. As the triangle at the far left of Figure 7-7 indicates, Bob (whom we will

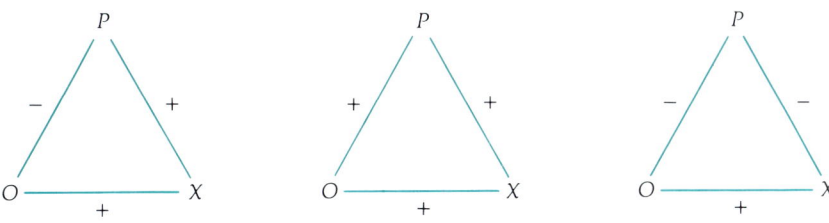

Figure 7-7 Examples of balanced and unbalanced situations. According to Heider, most interpersonal situations contain three basic elements: *P*, the perceiver, whose likes and dislikes are being described; *O*, another person; and *X*, some social object. When these three elements are linked together by either positive or negative relationships, some triads are balanced but others are unbalanced. Triads are balanced if the multiplicative product of the signs is positive (when combined, two negative relationships yield a positive), but unbalanced if the product is negative.

identify as *P*) dislikes Jim (*O*). However, *P* and *O* are similar in that they both like the poetry (*X*). This situation is unbalanced because the number of negative relationships is uneven. If balance is to be regained, the negative relationship must become positive (Bob must decide he likes Jim, as in the center triangle) or one of the positive relationships must become negative (Bob can decide he was wrong about the poetry or Jim can admit he didn't write it). Thus a situation is balanced only when all of the relationships among the three components of the triad are positive or when two of the three relationships are negative while one is positive. In all other cases, the relationship is unbalanced.

Balance theory, like cognitive dissonance theory, predicts that unbalanced relationships create an unpleasant tension that must be relieved by a change in some element of the system. Because disliking someone who is similar to us and liking someone who is dissimilar are both unbalanced situations, we avoid them.

Complementarity. Newcomb's finding that friendships formed between men who were similar to one another in some way lent support to the old adage "Birds of a feather flock together." But what about the idea that opposites attract? Isn't it true that we like people with dissimilar characteristics that complement our own? Wouldn't a highly masculine person want to settle down with a highly feminine person? Wouldn't a dependent, insecure person feel happiest under the protection of a nurturing person? And isn't a masochist the perfect complement for a sadist? According to the concept of *complementarity*, we like people who possess characteristics that fulfill, or gratify, our own personal needs.

When this intuitively appealing notion was tested, researchers once more discovered that everyday assumptions about attraction can be misleading. Among close friends, dating couples, and married pairs, similarity seems to be the rule, while complementarity is the exception. In fact, researchers have been commendably diligent in their search for evidence that supports the complementarity hypothesis. When they first found that complementarity of personality traits failed to promote attraction, some argued that people who have complementary needs should become fast friends. Yet the findings concerning needs are mixed at best; people with mutually satisfying needs aren't necessarily attracted to one another (Meyer & Pepper, 1977). Taking another path, others suggested that complementarity may become more important later in the life cycle of the relationship; similarity may bring people together, but complementarity leads to a long-term relationship. Again, initially promising findings couldn't be replicated by later researchers (Kerckhoff & Davis, 1962; Levinger, Senn, & Jorgensen, 1970). Even an elaborate "pacing hypothesis"—the idea that we seek out people who have interests and characteristics that will stimulate our own personal development—has fared poorly empirically (Buss, 1984). Therefore, at the present time the complementarity hypothesis remains just that: an unconfirmed hypothesis.

The Rewards We Receive

As you plunge a potato chip into the onion dip, your host introduces you to Dale and Pat. During your informal conversation, you discover that Dale recently organized a fund drive for the needy, comes from a very close-knit family, wants to become a social worker, and values honesty and commitment to personal ideals. Pat smiles at you frequently, laughs at your witty remarks, and says that you have "amazing eyes." Who will you like more: Dale or Pat?

If you think that Dale, with all his or her "good qualities," is more attractive than Pat, then you are overlooking a fundamental law of interpersonal attraction, *the reward principle:* we like people who provide us with the maximum number of valued rewards while exacting minimum costs. Dale may possess all the attributes of a saint, but unless Dale rewards you in some way, your attraction to him or her will not grow. Pat, however, has rewarded you with smiles, laughter, and compliments. Pat should win your affection, since "liking for a person will result under those conditions in which an individual experiences reward in the presence of that person, regardless of the relationship between the other person and the rewarding event or state of affairs" (Lott & Lott, 1974, p. 172).

Social approval as a reward.
We receive many kinds of rewards from other people (Brinberg & Castell, 1982; Foa & Foa, 1974). When friends lend you money, do you a favor, buy you lunch, or give you a present, they are giving you tangible, concrete rewards. Even more important are

the social rewards we receive from others. Friends provide you with social support in difficult times. They respect you and admire your personal qualities. They accept and approve of you. These social rewards are so powerful that, in most cases, attraction between people tends to be mutual. When you discover that someone likes you, your initial reaction is to like that person in return. In consequence, most of our relationships are consistent with the *reciprocity principle:* we like people who like us.

Both laboratory and field studies lend support to the reciprocity principle. In a typical laboratory study, subjects may talk briefly to a stranger who later rates the subject in a positive or negative way. As the reciprocity principle predicts, subjects tend to like the positive evaluator but dislike the negative evaluator. (S. C. Jones, 1973, and Shrauger, 1975, review studies of the reciprocity principle.) Researchers have also tested the principle by asking the members of naturally occurring groups—football teams, police squads, classroom groups, and dormitory residents—to identify other group members whom they like. Across these various groups, between 32% and 40% of these choices are reciprocal: if A picks B, then B picks A (Kandel, 1978; Newcomb, 1960; Segal, 1979). Furthermore, when individual differences in "giving" liking (some people just tend to like lots of people, while others dole out their affections in a more reserved fashion) and "receiving" liking (some people are liked by many, while others are liked by only a few) are taken into account statistically, reciprocity is even stronger (Kenny & Nasby, 1980).

We do not always, in all circumstances, like someone who likes us (Mettee & Aronson, 1974). Reciprocity is more likely to occur during the early stages of a relationship (Newcomb, 1979), and friendship tends to be reciprocated more than other forms of attraction, such as respect (Segal, 1979). Also, people with extremely low self-esteem sometimes react negatively when others treat them positively. According to reward theory, people with low self-esteem should be strongly attracted to a positive evaluator, since their need for approval is particularly potent. Balance theory suggests, however, that liking a positive evaluator will create an unbalanced state for people with low self-esteem: P dislikes X (the self), O likes X (P's self), so the only way for P to achieve balance is to reject O (Deutsch & Solomon, 1959; Regan, 1976). While some evidence supports balance theory's predictions, this exception to the reciprocity principle is relatively rare. As Chapter 2 noted, even people with low self-esteem usually like to be liked.

Social disapproval as punishment. If we tend to like people who like us, do we then dislike people who dislike us? Usually, for in most cases disliking begets disliking.

Folklore, again, offers a contrasting view. Socrates, Ovid, the *Kama Sutra,* and Dear Abby all endorse playing hard to get. Rather than reciprocate attraction, remain aloof and show no interest. When Elaine

Hatfield and her colleagues put this common-sense notion to the test, however, they found that playing hard to get did not inspire attraction. In the context of a computer dating center, men were given five folders that supposedly contained background information about their potential dates. Each folder also contained bogus information about each woman's rating of the subject and of four other men. By varying these forms, Hatfield and her associates created three types of women: the hard-to-get woman, the easy-to-get woman, and the selectively hard-to-get woman. The hard-to-get woman rated all the men neutrally; she indicated no great attraction to any of them but was not negative, either. The easy-to-get woman indicated that she liked all the men. The selectively hard-to-get woman indicated that she felt neutral toward all the other men but liked the subject. When the men selected dates, they opted for the selectively hard-to-get woman; they avoided the hard-to get woman (Walster et al., 1973).

Thus, despite the lore surrounding the hard-to-get woman, rejection usually leads to disliking rather than liking. However, one exception to this general tendency has been identified. Imagine that you meet two people, Enrico and Sonny, on five occasions. Each time that you chat with Enrico, he seems warm and friendly, and always says that he enjoys talking with you. Sonny, in contrast, acts cold and unfriendly when you initially meet, but by the fourth and fifth encounters he makes it very clear that he holds you in high esteem. Who will you like better: Enrico, who was always positive, or Sonny, who was initially negative but eventually became positive?

Elliot Aronson and Darwyn Linder believe that approval is nice, but winning approval from someone who is initially negative is particularly rewarding. According to their **gain-loss hypothesis,** a "gain in esteem is a more potent reward than invariant esteem, and similarly, the loss of esteem is a more potent 'punishment' than invariant negative esteem" (1965, p. 156). In a test of this hypothesis, female college students conversed individually with another female subject in seven consecutive sessions. Each subject then listened as the other subject (who was actually a confederate of the researchers) evaluated her. By controlling the confederate's remarks, Aronson and Linder created four sequences of evaluation: all positive, all negative, negative shifting to positive (the "gain" condition), and positive shifting to negative (the "loss" condition). When the subjects evaluated the confederate after all seven sessions, women in the 'gain" condition (negative to positive) were the most positive, while women in the "loss" condition (positive to negative) were the most negative in their ratings (see Figure 7-8; Aronson & Linder, 1965; Mettee & Aronson, 1974).

The hard-to-get phenomenon and the gain-loss hypothesis suggest that in some cases you can increase your interpersonal attractiveness by disliking others. Rejecting people, however, is a relatively risky method of acquiring friends. As Hatfield and her colleagues note, playing hard to

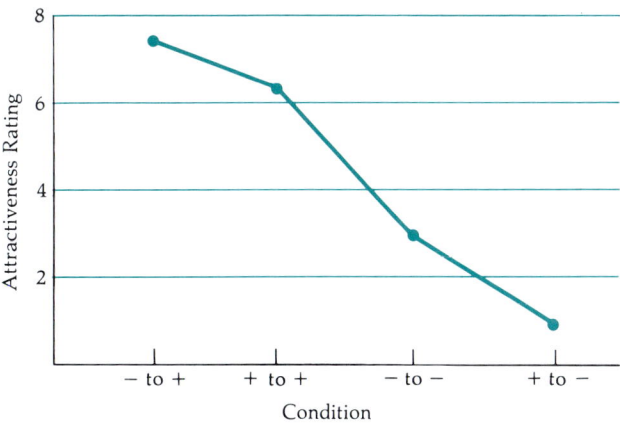

Figure 7-8 The gain-loss theory of attraction. When subjects rated the confederate on a scale of +10 to −10, most of the women gave the confederate a positive evaluation. However, a pattern of negative evaluations shifting to positive evaluations (the "gain" condition) led to more attraction than uniformly positive evaluations. A pattern of positive evaluations shifting to negative evaluations (the "loss" condition) led to a marginally significant reduction in attraction relative to uniformly negative evaluations.

get works only when you reject everyone except the target person. Aronson and Linder's gain-loss theory describes a very rare exception to reciprocity, and several studies have failed to support it (see Brothen, 1977; Sigall & Aronson, 1967; Tognoli & Kiesner, 1972). In consequence, before resorting to rejection, you may want first to try the ingratiation tactics described in Focus 7-4.

The Economics of Attraction

Occasionally social psychologists have confirmed age-old beliefs about liking and disliking. In general, however, adages and folklore aren't much help when it comes to understanding attraction. Does "familiarity breed contempt?" Do we realize that beauty is skin deep? Do opposites attract? Do we like people who play hard to get? No, in every case.

In fact, a simple reward theory accounts for most of what we know about attraction. At least in the initial stages of an interpersonal relationship, we act like shoppers looking for bargains. When we encounter potential partners, we assess their value by enumerating their positive, rewarding features and their negative, costly features. Just as we tend to select the product that offers us the best value for our money, we find people who possess many positive, rewarding characteristics and few negative, costly characteristics attractive. As simple (and as unromantic) as this theory seems, it makes more sense than common sense does.

■ Close Relationships

Close relationships are central to everything we value: our homes, our health, and even our happiness. When our close relationships are disrupted—by conflict, accident, or illness—we experience psychological grief and physical disorder. But when our close relationships are satisfying, we escape the ravages of our impersonal, ever-changing world. Close relationships are vital to our well-being (Hays & Oxley, 1986; Kelley et al., 1983).

What is a close relationship? First, we generally reserve this term for relationships that are based on that strong emotional bond known as *love*. You may like many people—your co-workers, neighbors, and friends—but you don't love them. Rather, our "loved ones" are our best

---

FOCUS 7-4

Experiencing Social Psychology: *How can you get someone to like you?*

Dale Carnegie's book *How to Win Friends and Influence People* was first published in 1937 in an edition of only 5,000 copies. His publishers never expected that a book filled with suggestions for increasing one's likability could be a best seller. But a half century later, the book is still in print, testimony to our common need to be liked and admired by the people around us.

Carnegie is not the only one who can suggest ways to make friends. Edward E. Jones, Camille Wortman, and their colleagues, by drawing on studies that have identified the various antecedents of attraction, also offer some advice on winning friends and making good impressions. Together these suggestions make up *ingratiation theory*, which is a general analysis of the ways people strategically increase their attractiveness in the eyes of others (E. E. Jones, 1964; E. E. Jones & Wortman, 1973).

Talking to a potential romantic partner at a party, meeting a friend's parents for the first time, and lunching with a business client are a few situations ripe for the use of ingratiation. What, for example, should you do when the conversation turns to personal opinions: Whom did you vote for in the last election? What do you think of Bruce Springsteen's new album? Which team are you rooting for this weekend? If you apply the similarity-attraction effect to this situation, the recommendation is obvious: conform to the target's opinion. If the target person likes the Republican candidate, Bruce Springsteen, and the Mets, proclaim that you, too, vote Republican, have all of Bruce's records, and root for the Mets. Or if you don't wish to misrepresent your own opinions, you can still make use of the *opinion conformity* tactic by downplaying your disagreements while focusing the discussion on topics on which you agree.

Through opinion conformity you can increase your attractiveness, but this tactic—like all ingratiation tactics—may backfire if your target realizes that your conformity is an ingratiation ploy. Jones and Wortman label this problem the *ingratiator's dilemma*: "If it is clear to the target person that the ingratiator has something to gain by impressing him, then all these ingratiation tactics are less likely to be effective" (Jones & Wortman, 1973, p. 25). Imagine you are on your way to a movie when you turn to your companion and say, "You're a warm, sensitive person." If your date believes that you are sincere, then this compliment will be rewarding: according to the reciprocity principle, your date should like you more. If, however, your date thinks that you are only trying to butter him or her up, then your date may like you even less.

Sincerity is one of the best ways to escape the ingratiator's dilemma: don't say things you don't mean. As even a sincere compliment can be misinterpreted, however, Jones and his colleagues outline a number of other tactics that can be used to

friends, our lovers, our parents, our spouses, and our children. Second, close relationships are *enduring*. As H. H. Kelley and his colleagues explain, "the close relationship is one of strong, frequent, and diverse interdependence that lasts over a considerable period of time" (1983, p. 287). Thus our close relationships are often intensely emotional, and they endure.

The Two Faces of Love

Love means different things to different people, but for centuries writers, poets, and scholars have drawn a distinction between love as an intense, often sexual need for another person and love as a gradually developing

The intricacies of fledgling personal relationships. The early stages of a personal relationship are often characterized by guarded interactions and polite ingratiation. We avoid behaviors that might create a negative impression, and try to increase our own interpersonal value through the judicious use of ingratiation tactics.

increase the power of a compliment. Avoid seeming too dependent on the target person. If you admit that you haven't gone out with anyone in six months, then your date may think that you have an ulterior motive when you deliver a compliment. Make your compliments positive but plausible. If your date is cold and blunt, don't say, "You're a warm and sensitive person." Instead, compliment your date on some other attribute. In particular, seek an attribute that your date feels is important but that your date is uncertain he or she possesses. As an ingratiation tactic, telling extremely beautiful people they are attractive has little impact: they probably already know it, and other people tell them so all the time. Instead, deliver a compliment that erases their doubts about their own standing on another attribute. As Lord Chesterfield wrote several centuries ago, "very ugly or very beautiful women . . . should be flattered on their understanding, and mediocre ones on their beauty" (Chesterfield, 1774/1901, p. 27).

Opinion conformity, compliments, and other ingratiation tactics are often effective, but they do highlight the seamier side of interpersonal relationships. As Jones and Wortman note, ingratiation tactics are illicit: deceitful, strategic, and manipulative. Intuitively, we tend to see ingratiation as reprehensible, because the people who practice it manipulate others' feelings rather than let them reach their own conclusions. In consequence, Jones and Wortman are careful to explain that when social psychologists study ingratiation, they aren't necessarily advocating this social process. They do point out, however, that "adaptive social life requires a little blarney now and then to mute the impact of disagreement, antagonism, and even love" (Jones & Wortman, 1973, p. 52).

commitment to another person. In one of the most comprehensive historical reviews of the subject, the sociologist John Alan Lee (1977) collected and compared various conceptions of love dating back to Plato's recommendation of sexless love. Aided by a panel of objective raters, he succeeded in identifying the six styles of loving shown in Table 7-3. Note that the first three styles define love as an impassioned emotional experience (Eros, ludus, and mania), while the other three underscore companionship, giving, and interpersonal exchange (storge, agape, pragma). (Hendrick & Hendrick, 1986, also examine these six styles of loving.)

Other theorists have also recognized these two faces of love. Elaine Hatfield and her colleagues, for example, argue that love can be either passionate or companionate. *Passionate love* is an emotion-laden "state of intense absorption in another" (Walster & Walster, 1978, p. 9). People in the throes of passionate love are so fascinated by their partner that their thoughts are disrupted or confused. They may feel an overwhelming need to possess or be possessed by the lover, and find little satisfaction in any other social activities. Passionate lovers desire close physical contact with their partners, including sexual intercourse. *Companionate love*, in contrast, is slow-moving and gradual. It often builds on friendship and respect, and results in a strong mutual commitment. Companionate love is the stuff of long-term relationships. (Similar distinctions are drawn by Davis, 1985; Driscoll, Davis, & Lipetz, 1972; Kelley, 1983; Rubin, 1973).

Passionate and companionate love can occur separately or together (Traupmann & Hatfield, 1981). In fact, the most widely used measure of love, Zick Rubin's "Love Scale," assesses both need for another person and caring (see Focus 7-5). The evidence examined in the next two

TABLE 7-3

Love across the centuries. In different historical eras, love has been defined in a variety of ways.

Name	Style of Love	Characteristics
Eros	Romantic love	The search for the ideal mate, with emphasis on physical beauty
Ludus	Game-playing love	Playing the field; a search for many sexual conquests with little long-term involvement
Mania	Possessive love	Obsessive, jealous, emotionally extreme involvement with the lover
Storge	Companionate love	Slow-developing affection and friendship culminating in a long-term relationship
Agape	Altruistic love	Gentle, caring desire to give to another, without expectation of return
Pragma	Pragmatic love	Practical, rational relationship based on mutual satisfaction

sections, however, indicates that the factors that prompt us to fall passionately in love differ considerably from the factors that contribute to long-lasting, companionate relationships.

Passionate Love

The Romans thought they knew why lovers experience such intense, all-consuming agony and ecstasy. They blamed passionate love on the

---

FOCUS 7-5

Experiencing Social Psychology: *Are you in love?*

If Elizabeth Barrett Browning had asked Zick Rubin her famous question "How do I love thee?" he would have answered: "I count only three basic ways: attachment, caring, and intimacy." Rejecting the idea that love is merely intense liking or sexual need, Rubin wrote a number of statements that dealt with both passionate and companionate love and then asked several hundred heterosexual couples at the University of Michigan to indicate whether each statement described their own love relationships. By examining their responses, he identified three components of love:

Attachment: a strong need to be with the lover. Attachment is a nonsexual form of passionate love, for it implies that the partner is the primary source of personal fulfillment and pleasure (items 1–5 in Table 7-4).

Caring: a desire to help and support the lover. Caring is an altruistic, responsible form of companionate love (items 6–9 in Table 7-4).

Intimacy: a high level of trust and confidentiality achieved in a relationship. Intimacy is also a component of companionate love, for it is based on shared confidences and a willingness to tolerate the partner's negative qualities (items 10–13 in Table 7-4).

Do the items shown in Table 7-4 really measure love? Although the validity of the measure is still being evaluated, initial results are encouraging. Rubin found that people who had high scores on his scale also reported that they were in love with their partner; low scorers weren't so certain of their feelings. He also discovered that when both members of a pair had high scores on the Love Scale, they spent more time gazing into each other's eyes (Rubin, 1973; see also Goldstein, Kilroy, & Van de Voort, 1976). Investigators have shown that scores on Rubins' Love Scale can be used to predict how successful a relationship will be; people who report strong feelings of attachment, caring, and intimacy tend to be more satisfied with their relationship and feel it plays a more significant role in their lives (Sternberg & Grajek, 1984).

If you are interested in discovering what Rubin's Love Scale says about your own intimate relationships, answer the questions shown in Table 7-4; fill in the blank with the name of your loved one. To obtain your overall score, simply sum your answers to the 13 items. A score of 90 is average for college-aged men and women in romantic heterosexual relationships. Recent evidence suggests that people who have particularly high scores on one of the three components of the scale may be experiencing different forms of love. High attachment scores are indicative of general attraction, high caring scores suggest altruistic love, and high scores on intimacy are associated with feelings of friendship (Davis & Roberts, 1985; Steck et al., 1982).

Be warned, however: Completing the questionnaire can be dangerous to your relationship's health. When Rubin and his colleagues asked several hundred couples who were "dating" or "going together" to complete the Love Scale and answer a number of other questions about their relationship, the experience generated some unintended side effects. As the excerpts reported below suggest, some couples reacted in a positive way, but others' reactions were intensely negative (Hill, Rubin, & Peplau, 1976; all quotes from Rubin & Mitchell, 1976).

(continued)

roguish god Cupid, who roamed about shooting people with his gold-tipped arrows. Once wounded, victims became passionately aroused, and consequently fell in love with whomever or whatever they saw next, whether man, woman, or animal. Greco-Roman myth is filled with embarrassing instances of ill-timed shots and unlikely alliances.

FOCUS 7-5 continued

I feel that our participation in the study has made me more aware of how I treat Janet in our relationship. I think at times it has helped me to treat Janet better by being more thoughtful. [p. 19]

I feel that this study brought our relationship close to where it is now. We were forced to look at ourselves honestly and we discussed our differences and problems more openly. [p. 20]

My relationship had been floundering at the time I first took part in the study, and because some of the questions were really soul-searching, I re-examined where we were headed. She was much more serious than I was and I called it off. [p. 19]

I cursed the study for destroying a lot of my fantasies about my boyfriend. [p. 22]

TABLE 7-4

The Love Scale.

Instructions: Indicate your agreement or disagreement with each item as it applies to your boyfriend, girlfriend, husband, or wife. Respond by circling a number from 1 to 9. Number 1 indicates that you disagree completely with the item (Not true at all) and 9 indicates that you agree completely with the item (Definitely true).

1. I feel very possessive toward _____ .	1	2	3	4	5	6	7	8	9
2. If I could never be with _____ , I would feel miserable.	1	2	3	4	5	6	7	8	9
3. If I were lonely, my first thought would be to seek _____ out.	1	2	3	4	5	6	7	8	9
4. It would be hard for me to get along without _____ .	1	2	3	4	5	6	7	8	9
5. When I am with _____ , I spend a good deal of time just looking at him/her.	1	2	3	4	5	6	7	8	9
6. If _____ were feeling bad, my first duty would be to cheer him/her up.	1	2	3	4	5	6	7	8	9
7. I would do almost anything for _____ .	1	2	3	4	5	6	7	8	9
8. One of my primary concerns is _____ 's welfare.	1	2	3	4	5	6	7	8	9
9. I feel responsible for _____ 's well-being.	1	2	3	4	5	6	7	8	9
10. I feel I can confide in _____ about virtually everything.	1	2	3	4	5	6	7	8	9
11. I find it easy to ignore _____ 's faults.	1	2	3	4	5	6	7	8	9
12. I would forgive _____ for practically anything.	1	2	3	4	5	6	7	8	9
13. I would greatly enjoy being confided in by _____ .	1	2	3	4	5	6	7	8	9

There is an element of truth in this myth. According to Elaine Hatfield, Ellen Berscheid, and William Walster's **two-factor theory of love**, *passionate love* is an attributional label used to explain intense physiological arousal (see Chapter 4). The process starts not when Cupid shoots us with an arrow, but when a situational factor makes us feel aroused. Once aroused, we search for a likely cause of our physiological turmoil. If another person who we feel is attractive is nearby, we may attribute our arousal to love. Thus we don't first fall in love and then feel aroused whenever our lover is around. As Figure 7-9 indicates, we first become aroused and then fall in love to explain our arousal (Berscheid & Walster, 1978; Walster & Berscheid, 1974; Walster & Walster, 1978).

Researchers have tested the two-factor theory by first arousing subjects and then exposing them to an appropriate target for passionate love. In one recent study, male college students ran in place for either 15 seconds (low arousal) or 120 seconds (high arousal) to create differences in arousal level. The men were then shown a videotape of a woman whom they thought they would be meeting for a brief get-acquainted talk. For some subjects, the woman wore attractive makeup and form-fitting clothes, her hair was styled, and she spoke energetically. Others, in contrast, saw a videotape of the same woman dressed in ill-fitting clothes, a scarf, and unattractive makeup. In this condition she sniffled and spoke with little enthusiasm. After subjects viewed the videotape, they rated the woman's physical beauty, sexiness, and how much they would like to date and kiss her. As the average ratings shown in Table 7-5 indicate, aroused men reported stronger passion for the attractive woman, weaker passion for the unattractive woman (White, Fishbein, & Rutstein, 1981).

Other studies have yielded similar findings (Cantor, Zillmann, & Bryant, 1975; Dermer & Pyszczynski, 1978; Dutton & Aron, 1974). Men who had just read about a woman's sexual fantasies rated their own lover more positively on Rubin's Love Scale (Dermer & Pyszczynski, 1978). In contrast to men interviewed by a woman while standing on a solid wooden bridge, men interviewed while standing on a suspension bridge

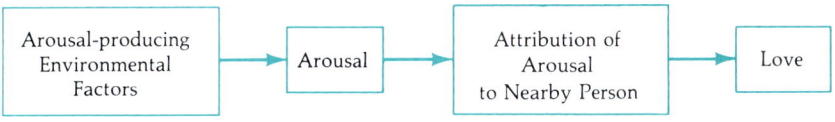

Figure 7-9 The two-factor theory of love. According to Elaine Hatfield and her colleagues, passionate love begins when some environmental event increases our level of arousal. Although the stimulating event is usually a person whom we judge to be attractive, nonromantic stimulants (such as a ride on a roller coaster, the threat of failing an examination, an argument with the boss, or stimulating drugs) are also possibilities. We then search for the cause of our arousal. If another person is nearby, and we feel that he or she has caused our arousal, we may conclude that we are experiencing love.

over a deep gorge showed signs of stronger sexual arousal and were more likely to telephone the interviewer (Dutton & Aron, 1974). Even when nonaroused subjects were led to believe they were experiencing physiological arousal by exposure to bogus information about their heart rate, they showed exaggerated romantic responses (Valins, 1966). The two-factor theory also offers a potential explanation for the so-called *Romeo-and-Juliet effect*. Just as Romeo and Juliet fell passionately in love against their parents' wishes, researchers have shown that the more parents interfere with their children's romances, the more romantically involved their children become. The explanation: the frustration and distress caused by disputes over this romantic involvement can be misattributed to love (Driscoll, Davis, & Lipetz, 1972).

We must be careful to note several conditions that limit the impact of arousal on love. First, the actual cause of the arousal must be ambiguous. A businesswoman traveling by airplane may feel very much aroused during a takeoff in stormy weather, but if she attributes her arousal to fear of flying, she probably won't fall in love with the flight attendant (Kenrick, Cialdini, & Linder, 1979).

Second, Douglas T. Kenrick and his colleagues believe that passionate love is sometimes based on a reinforcement process rather than an attribution process (Kenrick & Cialdini, 1977; Kenrick, Cialdini, & Linder, 1979; Kenrick & Johnson, 1979). Extending the reward model of attraction to love, these investigators point out that lovers provide us with many reinforcers. In particular, in arousing situations loved ones do more than provide a target for our attributions; they also help us reduce our level of arousal. For example, if Kenrick's explanation is applied to the study of men interviewed on solid or frightening bridges, it suggests that the interviewer was better liked on the suspension bridge because she helped subjects reduce their level of fear. Researchers are currently working to determine when passionate love results from reinforcement, as Kenrick suggests, and when it results from a two-factor labeling process, as Hatfield and her colleagues propose (Riordan & Tedeschi, 1983).

TABLE 7-5

Ratings of an attractive and unattractive woman made by men under conditions of high and low arousal. These means are based on four ratings: physical attraction, sexiness, desire to date, and desire to kiss. Ratings could range from 4 (low) to 36 (high).

	Level of Arousal	
	High	Low
Attractive woman	32.4	26.1
Unattractive woman	9.4	15.1

SOURCE: White, Fishbein, & Rutstein, 1981.

In Shakespeare's play, Romeo and Juliet became more passionate the more their family interfered with their relationship. The two-factor theory of love explains this effect; it suggests that the young lovers misattributed the frustration and tension caused by parental interference to romantic love.

These two limitations aside, the two-factor theory offers an intriguing explanation for the emotional tumult and sexual desires that often accompany love (see "In Depth: Sexual Relationships," at the end of this chapter). The theory also highlights our society's tendency to romanticize love. According to Hatfield and her colleagues, the two-factor process works because people assume that arousal and love go together. In America and many other Western countries, love is considered a mysterious and accidental process, something we "fall into" rather than nurture. Movies, television, novels, and poetry describe love as blossoming at first sight, with overwhelming intensity. We are taught that when we feel aroused and a potential partner is nearby, love must be the cause (Averill, 1985; Averill & Boothroyd, 1977; Dion & Dion, 1973).

This conception of love, however, can be misleading. Because we view love as a mixture of emotion and sexual desire, people sometimes assume that a marriage based on passionate love will be successful. Yet too many marriages based on romantic love end in divorce when the fire dies out. As the noted sociologist Willard Waller lamented many years ago:

> It is possibly very unfortunate that people must make one of their most important decisions on the basis of certain delusive emotions of adolescence. There is truth in the ancient proverb, *Amantes amentes,* lovers are mad. And the persons who have the power to excite this madness in others are by no means always the persons with whom it is possible to live happily after the knot is tied.   [Waller, 1938, p. 208]

Waller believed that such a long-term relationship as marriage should be founded on mutual trust, exchange, and commitment rather than emotion. These factors provide the foundation for companionate rather than passionate love.

Companionate Love

Because social psychologists have only recently begun to study companionate relationships, many gaps still remain in our understanding of them (Berscheid, 1985). Despite these uncertainties, however, companionate love appears to be a process that develops gradually over time. Unlike passionate love, which can blossom (and wither) overnight, companionate love must be nurtured. Slowly, and sometimes painfully, individuals must disclose information about themselves so that trust develops. If a relationship is to prosper, both individuals must be willing to contribute to it without asking too much in return. Finally, companionate love requires a commitment to remain in the relationship through thick and thin.

Trust and self-disclosure.

Lightning didn't strike and the earth didn't move when Susan met Pete on his first day at the office. They talked about the weather as they stood by the coffeemaker, avoiding any personal remarks. As the weeks passed, they began to meet for lunch, where they would debate the relative merits of political candidates, swap office gossip, and complain about their work loads. Lunches soon turned into dinners together, and the conversation shifted to personal topics; feelings that they had kept hidden before were now discussed more openly.

The saga of Susan and Pete illustrates the stages of self-disclosure that often characterize growing relationships (Altman & Taylor, 1973). **Self-disclosure,** the process of revealing information about oneself to another person, usually begins with relatively impersonal information. In this *orientation stage,* Pete and Susan were only trying to form a general impression of each other, and possibly to make a good impression themselves. In the *exploratory affective stage,* Pete and Susan began to discuss their personal attitudes and opinions, but carefully avoided intimate topics. About the time Susan and Pete began to date, they had reached the *affective stage;* although a few topics remained taboo, they could now talk about very personal matters. At this point Pete and Susan's relationship hadn't reached the final stage, *stable exchange,* in which all personal feelings and possessions are shared, but it might in time.

This tale also shows how self-disclosure and the growth of intimacy are reciprocally related. Each new self-disclosure deepens the intimacy of the relationship, and this increased closeness then makes further self-disclosures possible. If this gradual cycle of deepening intimacy is disrupted, then the relationship may not mature. If, for example, Susan were to refuse to share personal information after Pete offered his self-disclosures, or if Pete made extremely personal self-disclosures too early in the relationship, the relationship might falter (Chaikin & Derlega, 1974; Wortman et al., 1976; see Figure 7-10).

Do not underestimate the impact of self-disclosure on your relationships with other people. By sharing information about yourself with others you are telling them "I trust you enough to tell you this" (Rempel & Holmes, 1986; Rempel, Holmes, & Zanna, 1985). Also, self-disclosures signal your commitment to the relationship, and encourage self-disclosure in return. As a result, intimacy, self-disclosure, and satisfaction go hand in hand in most close relationships (Berg, 1984; Hendrick, 1981).

Social exchange. Have you ever found yourself wondering about an unlikely couple? Perhaps a man and woman dining at a posh restaurant. The man is strikingly handsome; the woman is his senior by some 15 years, and far less appealing to the eye. Could they be business associates? you wonder. No, they seem to be married to each other. Well, perhaps she is a famous artist, and he was a long-time admirer of her work. No, too farfetched. Perhaps she's just very rich. Yes, that would explain it.

Such incidents illustrate the **social exchange theory** of long-term relationships. According to the reward theory of attraction, we like people who reward us in some way. A close relationship, however, depends on the equitable exchange of rewards between partners. The man's investment in the relationship is his beauty, and we assume that the woman must be able to match this investment with an investment of her own—money, for example. Thus, in exchange for the rewards we receive from our partner, we provide our partner with the rewards he or she desires (Kelley & Thibaut, 1978; Thibaut & Kelley, 1959).

Figure 7-10 Evidence indicates that men's same-sex friendships are less intimate than women's. One reason may be men's tendency to avoid personal self-disclosures (Cozby, 1973). Because men don't share personal information about themselves with other men, their friendships never deepen (Caldwell & Peplau, 1982; Cozby, 1973; Hays, 1985; Hill & Stull, 1981; Reis, Senchak, & Solomon, 1985).

© 1983, Washington Post Writers Group, reprinted with permission.

Social exchange theory explains the sometimes delicate series of exchanges and counterexchanges that characterize the early stages of a relationship. After Pete complements Susan on her appearance, he waits to see if she responds with a show of interest in him. If she does, he may then take another small step forward by asking her to join him for lunch. By agreeing, Susan indicates her willingness to contribute to the relationship. But if she declines, she reveals that she is unwilling to enter into a relationship. Through these small exchanges, individuals gradually work their way up to major investments (Homans, 1961; Huston & Burgess, 1979).

Although the exchange theory of relationships may seem mercenary and calculating, remember that these processes are rarely explicitly acknowledged. Also, the rewards we seek by forming relationships go beyond expensive gifts, sexual gratification, and excitement. By accepting us as close friends or lovers, others show that they approve of us as persons. They also give us social support when times are difficult, care for us when we are ill, and provide us with companionship. Indeed, even the statement "I love you" is a valuable reward that we enjoy receiving. Moreover, in time our exchange relationships may evolve into *communal relationships:* ones in which we seek only to benefit our loved one, with no thought of receiving a benefit in return (Clark, 1984; Clark & Mills, 1979). In such relationships, our pleasure in giving may be the only reward we seek.

Satisfaction and commitment. Harold H. Kelley has recently extended his social exchange theory to include the concept of long-term *commitment* (Kelley, 1979, 1983). He begins by drawing a sharp distinction between love for a person and commitment to a relationship. Love, he argues, is primarily an emotional reaction to another person which typically involves a mixture of "needing, caring, trust, and tolerance" (1983, p. 286). Commitment, in contrast, is the "enduring adherence of persons to their close partners" (p. 313). "A person committed to a relationship is expected to stay in that relationship" (p. 287). Although love and commitment can occur together, love does not necessarily involve commitment; one can fall madly in love with someone yet have no desire to maintain a long-term relationship with that person. Conversely, commitment doesn't necessarily require love; even when love has gone out of a marriage, the relationship may still endure.

Studies of successful long-term relationships also underscore the importance of commitment. In one study, 351 couples married for at least 15 years were asked to explain why their marriages had lasted so long (Lauer & Lauer, 1985). The most frequently offered reasons were "My spouse is my best friend," "I like my spouse as a person," "Marriage is a long-term commitment," and "Marriage is sacred." In a study of college students who were able to maintain a long-term heterosexual dating relationship, satisfaction and commitment to the relationship varied

The development of companionate love. Unlike passionate or romantic love, companionate love is based on mutual trust, commitment, and a willingness to invest in a long-term relationship.

together (Rusbult, 1983). Unfortunately, increased commitment to one relationship also means decreased commitment to others. Hence, as the relationship progresses, contact with other people dwindles and contact with the partner increases. Couples in the later stages of courtship interact with progressively fewer friends, less often, and for shorter periods of time (Lauer & Lauer, 1985; Miolardo, Johnson, & Huston, 1983). Failure to limit other social relationships may be one of the reasons why some relationships never mature or end in dissolution (Surra, 1985). As we all know, not all close relationships last forever.

■ Dissolution

Like the waxing and waning of the moon or the rise and fall of the tides, personal relationships follow a pattern of growth and change. Of all the people you meet, a small number will seem attractive to you. And of those, only a few will become good friends or loved ones. And fewer still will remain good friends and lovers. Why do some of our close relationships endure, while others dissolve?

The Emotional Bases of Dissolution

Strong positive feelings about one's partner are the hallmark of a healthy personal relationship. When we are with someone we love, we experience a range of pleasant feelings: warmth, happiness, satisfaction, and sometimes sexual passion. Over time, however, our emotions may change. They may fade or be replaced by negative, disruptive emotions.

The loss of passion. Earlier discussions of passionate love suggested that the fire of sexual passion tends to dwindle to a flickering afterglow over time. Although initially filled with excitement and passion, romantic love gradually cools. A passionate love relationship is a race against time.

Is this cooling-off process inevitable? Experts aren't certain. Some argue that couples can take steps to keep the passion in their relationships; others are more pessimistic. Ellen Berscheid, drawing on the two-factor theory of love, points out that passionate love requires arousal. If arousal diminishes, then love too must diminish. Moreover, she notes that our physiological makeup is such that we cannot maintain high levels of physiological arousal over a long period of time. "Much as one wishes to hold on to the intensely positive emotions, to retain the euphoric state, there is little that is known about the underlying dynamics of emotion and of its antecedents . . . that suggests this is possible." She concludes that "intense emotion is not maintained—not even intense positive emotion that may be fervently desired, coddled, and encouraged" (1983, p. 158). Therefore, individuals should strive for more moderate but long-lasting emotions, such as comfort, contentment, and affection.

When love turns to anger. In some cases of conflict between partners in a close relationship, positive emotions are not merely lost but replaced by negative, disruptive emotions. Caring becomes hostility, warmth becomes coldness, trust becomes jealousy. The relationship remains passionate, but in an aversive, negative sense.

The emotional climate of dissolving relationships can be seen when the emotional reactions of spouses in distressed marriages are compared to the reactions of spouses whose marriages are not distressed. During everyday conversations, partners in troubled marriages reveal their negative affect by complaining, criticizing, interrupting, insulting, and disagreeing with each other (Birchler, Weiss, & Vincent, 1975). Moreover, while distressed couples continue to divulge intimate, highly personal information about their feelings, these self-disclosures emphasize negative feelings: "I really care deeply for you" becomes "I don't think I can stand to live with you any longer" (Tolstedt & Stokes, 1984). Even when positive emotions are expressed, partners in a distressed relationship rarely respond to them. Instead, they wait for their partner to express a negative emotion, and then reciprocate with an equally negative response (Levenson & Gottman, 1983, 1985). With all this negative affect, it is no wonder that distressed couples get into more arguments than nondistressed couples (Birchler, Weiss, & Vincent, 1975).

When a relationship becomes rife with negative emotions, it becomes less satisfying. Positive feelings are among the most important rewards we receive from others, and when they are cut off, the value of the relationship declines. In terms of social exchange theory, we become dissatisfied with our investment, and therefore may seek divestiture.

Satisfaction and Social Exchange

Relationships grow closer when partners provide each other with the rewards they desire. When the number of rewards we receive dwindles and the costly aspects of our relationship escalate, we become dissatisfied. But does dissatisfaction always lead to withdrawal from the relationship? Let's consider Helen's view of her relationship with Bill. Before they were married, Bill seemed to be exciting and caring. They spent lots of time together, enjoyed the same kinds of activities, and hardly every disagreed. However, almost from the moment they said "I do," things started to change. Nights out on the town became rare events, saved for special occasions. Bill's job took up more of his time, and when he came home from work he rarely did much in the way of household chores. Also, with all the bickering about money, they never seem to be in the mood for sex.

Helen's relationship is not a satisfying one: the rewards she is receiving are too few in comparison with the many costs she must bear. She may remain in the relationship, however, even though she is dissatisfied. She may, for example, feel that she has no alternative to remaining married to Bill. Even if she gets divorced, she may not be able to find anyone who is better than Bill. And she doesn't like living alone. Also, she may feel that she has already put too much into this relationship to let it go. In a sense, she feels a need to recoup her losses. Thus, level of *satisfaction* is not the only factor that determines withdrawal from relationships. According to social exchange theory, we must also consider the value of *alternative relationships* and the magnitude of *investment* in the current relationship (Thibaut & Kelley, 1959; see Figure 7-11).

Several investigators have found that the course of friendship and romantic relationships depends on these three factors (Berg, 1984; Hays, 1985; Rusbult, 1983). Caryl E. Rusbult, for example, charted changes in these three factors over a one-year period. She began her study by recruiting college students who were just becoming involved in a romantic relationship. Then, on each of 12 separate occasions, she asked these men and women to answer a series of questions that tapped perceptions of rewards, costs, satisfaction, alternatives, and investment size. When the final measures were collected, she separated the subjects into three categories: those who remained in their relationships ("stayers"), those who terminated their relationships ("leavers"), and those in relationships ended by the partner's withdrawal (the "abandoned"). As anticipated, stayers reported increases in rewards, satisfaction, and investment over the leavers and the abandoned. Moreover, their costs and alternatives decreased. Leavers, in contrast, reported small increases in rewards but substantial increases in costs. Moreover, satisfaction and investments declined, while their evaluations of alternative relationships became more positive over time. Rusbult concludes, "No wonder they ended their relationship!"

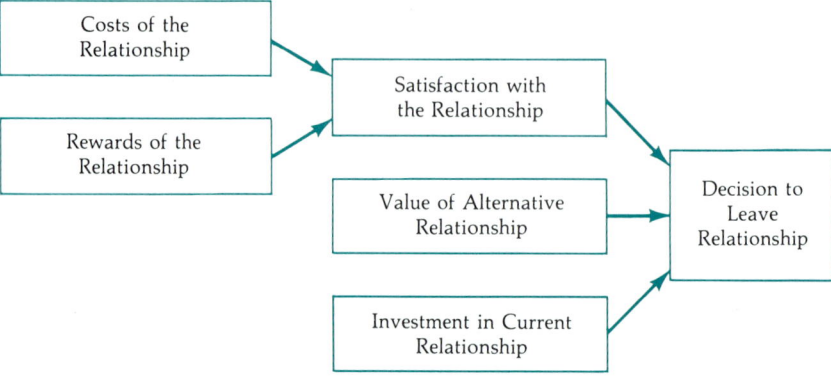

Figure 7-11 Social exchange and relationship dissolution. According to social exchange theory, the balance between rewards and costs determines overall satisfaction with a relationship. However, individuals may remain in unsatisfying relationships if no alternative relationships are available and they feel they have invested too much to withdraw.

How did the abandoned subjects compare with these two groups? Rusbult believes that they were victims of *entrapment:* they had invested so much in the relationship that they couldn't voluntarily withdraw from it. Their costs increased more rapidly than their rewards, so they were dissatisfied. As their alternatives declined in quality, they invested increasing amounts of emotional capital in the relationship. In fact, their investments matched those of the stayers. As a result, they became increasingly committed to their relationship, even though it left them dissatisfied (Rusbult, 1983). Rusbult believes that people who become entrapped in their relationships don't withdraw from them. Instead, they try to improve them, or they just keep hoping that things will improve (Rusbult, Zembrodt, & Gunn, 1982).

Rusbult's findings, and evidence gathered by other social psychologists, offer answers to some long-standing questions about our close relationships. Why do relationships grow cold? Why do people remain in unsatisfying relationships? When do we take steps to improve our relationships rather than leave them? At the present time social psychology offers no pat answers to the question "What can be done to strengthen our personal relationships?" The social-psychological study of close relationships is only in its infancy, and many areas require more study. Yet there are grounds for optimism. As social psychologists continue their love affair with close relationships, our knowledge should continue to grow. Perhaps, in time, solutions to such social problems as marital conflict and divorce will become clear.

■ Summary

Personal relationships follow a pattern of growth and change. Initially, social and personal factors may prompt us to affiliate with others. Next, we become attracted to individuals who possess characteristics we admire or who are similar to us in some way. In time this attraction may ripen into a long-lasting close relationship involving deep friendship or love. Alternatively, the relationship may end in dissolution.

Joining together with members of our own species is known as **affiliation.** This tendency, which is very pronounced in humans, stems from a number of situational, personal, and biological factors. Stanley Schachter's studies illustrate our tendency to seek out other people in order to reduce our uncertainty about social reality and to reduce our fear. Individuals who are "first borns" or only children tend to be more affiliative, as are those who are high in the need for affiliation, or *n***Affiliation.** Embarrassment, however, reduces the likelihood of affiliation, and people who suffer from **social anxiety** or **shyness** also tend to withdraw from contact with others. As a result, they sometimes experience **loneliness.** Loneliness that occurs when our relationships with friends or acquaintances are unsatisfying is called **social loneliness.** Loneliness caused by the lack of a meaningful relationship is called **emotional loneliness.**

Of all the people you meet, a small number will seem attractive to you. Initial attraction depends on surface-level factors, such as proximity and appearance. However, similarity and rewards become increasingly important over time. The following tendencies underlie many of our likes and dislikes:

1. *Proximity-attraction effect:* we like people who live nearby and people we see frequently.

2. *"What is beautiful is good":* we are drawn to people who are physically attractive. This tendency may lead to a self-fulfilling prophecy: because we assume that attractive people are friendly, we treat them in ways that evoke positive responses.

3. *Similarity-attraction effect:* we like people who are similar to us in some way, rather than people who possess qualities that complement our personal needs. **Balance theory** explains the similarity-attraction effect by suggesting that balanced interpersonal relations create less cognitive discomfort than others.

4. *Reward principle:* we like people who provide us with the maximum number of valued rewards while exacting minimum costs. Approval is a potent form of social reward, and most of our relationships are consistent with the **reciprocity principle:** we like people who like us. Disapproval, in contrast, is a powerful punishment, for it almost always leads to disliking. The only documented exception is described by the **gain-loss hypothesis:** initial disapproval followed by approval is more rewarding than invariant approval.

Close relationships are characterized by strong emotional bonds and endurance over a relatively long period of time. Close relationships can be based on passionate love, companionate love, or both. Both forms of love are reflected in the three components of Zick Rubin's Love Scale: attachment (need to be with the lover), caring (desire to support the lover), and intimacy (level of trust and confidentiality).

How does love develop? According to the **two-factor theory of love,** passionate love results from an attributional process. When we experience physiological arousal, we search for a cause of our arousal. If we conclude that another person is the cause, then we experience love. Companionate love, in contrast, develops slowly. Through gradual increases in the intimacy of our self-disclosures, we reveal personal information about ourselves while also demonstrating our trust in each other. Through social exchange, we provide our partner with the rewards he or she desires in exchange for the rewards we ourselves receive. Relationships begin with small exchanges, but gradually work up to more intimate ones. Companionate love also requires a strong commitment to the relationship.

Many factors contribute to the dissolution of a close relationship. Romantic alliances founded on passionate love may expire when the strong emotions that provided the foundation for the relationship cool. Everyday strains and stress can create negative emotional reactions within close relationships. If the emotional climate becomes too negative, the relationship may not survive. **Social exchange theory** suggests that three factors influence the longevity of a relationship: the number of rewards and costs received (or *satisfaction*), the value of *alternative relationships,* and the magnitude of one's *investment* in the current relationship. This theory predicts that individuals withdraw from unsatisfying relationships if alternative relationships are available and if their investment in the current relationship is not too great.

■ For More Information

1. *Intimate Relationships,* by Sharon S. Brehm (1985), is a solid review of theory and research pertaining to attraction and intimacy. Brehm delves deeply into topics considered only briefly in this chapter, including reciprocity, sexuality, equity, and communication.

2. *How to Win Friends and Influence People,* by Dale Carnegie (1937), is a useful guide to techniques for getting along well with others. The book is also filled with insightful observations on the basic nature of our interpersonal relationships.

3. *Our Sexuality,* by Robert Crooks & Karla Baur (1980), is a textbook treatment of the intricacies of human sexual behavior. The authors deal briefly with physiological processes and reproduction, but spend far more time discussing the personal and interpersonal aspects of sex.

4. *Close Relationships,* by Harold H. Kelley and his associates (1983), is a sourcebook of information on the social psychology of long-term relationships. After presenting a general model for understanding close relationships, the book deals with specific topics, including emotions, commitment, and power. This book is written at a relatively high level.

5. *Understanding Social Anxiety,* by Mark Leary (1983), takes a social-psychological look at the anxiety that some people experience in social settings. Leary enumerates the causes and consequences of social anxiety, and makes a number of recommendations for overcoming this problem.

6. *Liking and Loving,* by Zick Rubin (1973), is a lively excursion through the social psychology of interpersonal attraction. Rubin masterfully organizes the findings into a coherent whole, while drawing out implications for everyday life. The book also provides an interesting look at social psychology itself.

7. *The Psychology of Affiliation,* by Stanley Schachter (1959), describes Schachter's pioneering studies of the human tendency to seek out the company of others. The book describes methods and empirical findings that provide the foundations for a contemporary understanding of affiliation. A model of scholarly research.

8. *A New Look at Love,* by Elaine Hatfield Walster & G. William Walster (1978), is a broad summary of recent research on love written by two of the leading experts in the field. In addition to summarizing our current knowledge, the authors offer practical suggestions on how to deal with problems that arise in close relationships.

IN DEPTH

Sexual Relationships

Society's view of sexuality is changing rapidly. The 1950s prescribed the sequence: boy and girl meet; boy and girl fall in love; boy and girl marry; boy and girl raise a family. Sex was an implicit part of marriage, but was rarely discussed in polite circles. But in the 1960s, sexuality became a popular topic in newspapers, in magazines, and on television. It still is. Although some people object to educational programs designed to increase our understanding of sex, most Americans feel that sex education is beneficial. The so-called *sexual revolution* has increased our acceptance of various kinds of sexual activity, including homosexuality and premarital sex (Hunt, 1974). Whereas many sexual topics were once considered taboo, we now discuss sexuality openly and frankly.

Now more than ever, sexuality plays a fundamental role in our personal relationships. Whereas in the 1950s it was not unusual for a couple to postpone sex until after marriage, in the 1980s sex outside of marriage is the rule and abstinence is the exception. This change raises many questions about the impact of sexuality on our personal relationships. Does a close, intimate relationship between two people necessarily involve sex? Does sexual intimacy improve the quality of our relationships? Are sexually intimate relationships more enduring than nonsexual relationships?

Our current conception of love, and romantic love in particular, stresses sexuality. When asked to explain the difference between romantic love and deep friendship, most people mention sexual passion. In most other respects, these two kinds of close relationships are very similar to each other. Good friends and lovers enjoy each other's company, they help each other, and they inspire mutual trust, understanding, and confidence. Only lovers, however, experience strong sexual desire. People in love "want physical intimacy with the partner, wanting to touch and be touched and to engage in sexual intercourse" (Davis, 1985, p. 24). People also realize, however, that sexuality is not the defining characteristic of love. A one-night stand involves sex but requires no love, whereas deep friendship creates companionate love but need not involve sex (Forgas & Dobosz, 1980).

The emphasis on sexuality in our conception of romantic love is reflected in our sexual behavior. For many couples, romantic involvement includes sexual intimacy. In one study investigators charted the sexual development of 430 men and women from 1969, when they were in junior and senior high, until 1979, when they were 23 to 25 years old. The average subject in this study was 18 years old when he or she first engaged in intercourse; 40% of the men and 60% of the women reported that their initial sexual encounter occurred in the context of a steady dating relationship. When the subjects were asked about the reasons for engaging in intercourse, 85% mentioned sex as a way of giving and receiving love and achieving intimacy (Jessor et al., 1983). Similar findings were obtained in the Boston Couples Study, which traced the development and de-

Sexual behavior: The most intimate personal relationship.

(continued)

IN DEPTH *continued*

cline of more than 200 heterosexual relationships over a two-year period. Of these couples, 82% engaged in sexual intercourse (Peplau, Rubin, & Hill, 1977).

The Boston Couples Study also found, however, that some couples do not feel that sexuality is a necessary component of romantic intimacy. By considering when these dating men and women first experienced sex with each other, the investigators identified three types of couples: sexually traditional, sexually moderate, and sexually liberal. *Sexually traditional couples* abstained from sexual intercourse. These couples felt that sex was an important part of marriage, but not of a dating relationship. The sexually traditional women were more religious than the women in the other types of couples, and their career aspirations were more traditional. All of them were virgins.

Sexually moderate couples linked sexuality to intimacy. They refrained from sexual intercourse until they were certain they were in love with each other. For these couples, sexuality was part of a gradual growth in trust, commitment, and intimacy. *Sexually liberal couples*, in contrast, were more permissive. They were more interested in sex per se, and viewed it as a legitimate goal in a casual dating relationship. They engaged in sexual behavior within the first month of their relationship. They felt that sex was an important part of an intimate relationship, but they did not feel that a couple had to be in love before they could engage in sex. For these couples, sex was a means of developing intimacy.

Recent surveys have found that men and women differ in the way they look at sex and romance. Since the 1950s, women have become more accepting of sexual behavior outside of marriage: a survey conducted in 1959 found that 27% of the women considered sexual intercourse without marriage acceptable; by the 1970s, nearly 70% accepted sex without marriage (Skolnick, 1978). The sexes still diverge, however, on the importance they place on sexuality in a personal relationship. Men tend to be more sexually permissive than women (see Table 7-6). They are also more likely to approve of casual sex, sex with many partners, and sex with no strings attached. Women display a more responsible attitude toward sex. More than men they feel that birth control and good communication are both part of mature sexuality. Women also tend to idealize sex more than men (S. Hendrick et al., 1985).

These sex differences may be responsible for disagreements between men and women about sexual activity. In the Boston Couples Study, men were much more likely to mention sex as an important part of a relationship. They also reported more desire for sex than their partners did. In many cases, the woman restrained the couple's sexual activity. When dating couples abstained from sex, 64% of the men reported that their restraint was due to their partner's desire to refrain from sex. Fear of pregnancy and a moral code that opposed premarital sex were other important reasons for refraining from sex.

In sum, the bulk of the evidence indicates that sexuality now plays an important role in the growth and development of our personal relationships. Marriage and sex have always been strongly linked, but in all eras adults have engaged in sexual relationships outside of marriage, too. However, couples vary in the way they incorporate sex in their relationships, and men and women sometimes differ

TABLE 7-6

Mean sexual attitudes of men and women. 1 = strongly disagree; 5 = strongly agree.

Item	Men	Women
I do not need to be committed to a person to have sex with him/her.	3.66	2.18
Casual sex is acceptable.	3.71	2.51
I would like to have sex with many partners.	3.37	1.81
One-night stands are sometimes very enjoyable.	3.90	2.72
Unlimited premarital experience is fine.	3.39	2.49
Birth control is part of responsible sexuality.	4.42	4.55
A man should share responsibility for birth control.	4.21	4.57
Lovers should be able to communicate fully about their sexual relationships.	4.55	4.72
Sex is the closest form of communication between two people.	3.42	3.67
A sexual encounter between two people deeply in love is the ultimate human interaction.	4.33	4.48
At its best, sex seems to be the merging of two souls.	3.80	4.23

SOURCE: S. Hendrick et al., 1985.

in sexual outlook. One final question remains: Does sexual intimacy foster the growth of love?

The evidence on this question is inconclusive. Traditional, moderate, and liberal couples in the Boston Couples Study were equally satisfied with their relationships. This finding suggests that sexual intimacy is not a prerequisite for a happy premarital dating relationship. However, the sexually moderate couples tended to report stronger feelings of love—as measured on Rubin's Love Scale—than the other groups. This difference was particularly pronounced among women who had been virgins before they entered their current sexual relationship. Sexuality, however, was also associated with feelings of guilt and worry over unwanted pregnancy. Thus sex had both a positive and a negative impact on the relationship.

But was sexuality linked to the long-term success of the relationship? After two years, 20% of the couples had married, 34% were still dating, and 46% had broken up. Significantly, sexual type was unrelated to the relationship's success. People who engaged in sexual intercourse were no more likely to remain together than people who refrained from sex. Thus, while sexual intimacy didn't help a relationship endure, neither did it hurt the relationship's chances of success. In conclusion, sex does not appear to be a magic ingredient that guarantees a happy, long-lasting relationship. But neither is it a destructive force that undermines the growth of intimacy and commitment (Brehm, 1985).

E I G H T

Helping Behavior

When do people help others?
  Predicting helping behavior
  The helping situation
    The bystander effect
    Ambiguity of the situation
    Urban versus rural settings
  The people in the situation
    The victim's personal attributes
    The similarity-helping effect
    Men, women, and helping
    Personality traits
  When do people help? A concluding word
Why do people help?
  Deciding to help
    Noticing the event
    Interpreting the event as an emergency
    Taking responsibility
    Identifying a way to help
    The final stage: Helping
  Cost–reward theory
    The costs of helping
    The costs of failure to help
  Helping and emotions
    Misattribution inhibits helping
    Attributions can inhibit helping
    Empathy increases helping
  Moods and helping
    Happiness heightens helping
    Negative moods and helping
  Norms and helping
    The reciprocity norm
    The equity norm
    The social responsibility norm
    Personal norms
  Models of helping: A look back
Summary
For more information
In depth: The sociobiology of helping

Journey back through time to the early morning of March 13, 1964. You, and 38 others, are about to witness a murder.

Watch as Catherine Genovese, "Kitty" to her friends, drives her red Fiat into the parking lot near her apartment in the Kew Gardens section of Queens, New York. She's tired after working late as manager of Ev's 11th Hour Bar, and is probably looking forward to a good night's sleep. But Winston Moseley, who watches patiently as the young woman parks her car, is poised with knife in hand. As Kitty walks to her apartment, she notices Moseley standing in the shadows. In fear and suspicion, she runs. A police telephone box is located down the street. But the box is too far away. Moseley is too close behind. He overtakes her. Without hesitation, he stabs her.

"Oh, my God, he stabbed me! Please help me! Please help me!" she screams. Milton Hatch, one of Kitty's neighbors, throws open his window and calls out, "Let that girl alone!" The lights in other apartments are switched on, other windows are opened, and Moseley backs away into the shadows. But no one approaches. The street remains empty. So he waits as the windows close and the lights blink out. Kitty has dragged herself down the sidewalk and around the corner, but Moseley finds and stabs her once more before fleeing to his car.

Down the street, Moseley waits for the sirens, the lights, and the police. But they never come. Kitty Genovese first screamed at 3:15 A.M. Now, some 20 minutes later, she is still alone, hiding in the stairwell of her apartment building. So Moseley returns for a third attack. He finds her. He rapes her. He stabs her to death.

The police receive the first call from a witness at 3:50. They are on the scene in two minutes, but 37 minutes after the first attack. Catherine Genovese is dead on arrival at Queens General Hospital. Thirty-eight people witnessed the murder, but none of them helped. Only one person even called the police.

Who can hear of the tragic Genovese incident without asking why? Why would people stand by and watch a fellow human cruelly murdered?

Many experts and newspaper readers pointed the finger of blame at the bystanders. Some argued that the onlookers simply didn't want to get involved. Others suggested that the urbanites were cruel and selfish, lacking the moral compunction needed to compel them to act. Still others attributed the tragedy to cowardice or an incapacitating fear of retribution. But these explanations overlook the impact of the social situation on the bystanders. When social psychologists first learned of the circumstances surrounding Kitty Genovese's death, they were as surprised as anyone else. They recognized, however, that giving and receiving help are extremely complex forms of social behavior. To understand why no one helped Kitty Genovese, we can't stop with simplistic explanations. We must systematically study the nature of the interpersonal forces that entrapped the bystanders, leaving them "fascinated, distressed, unwilling to act, but unable to turn away" (Latané & Darley, 1976, p. 310). First we must examine the *when* of helping: When do people help others, and when do they refuse to offer their help? Second, we must understand the *why* of helping: Why do people help others who are in need?

■ When Do People Help Others?

On your way to class, you pass by a car with its lights on. You reach inside and turn them off. When a worker for the March of Dimes asks for a donation, you give her all your change. When an acquaintance in class asks to borrow your notes, you obligingly turn them over to her. You see an elderly man clutch his chest and fall to the ground. You immediately rush to his side and begin emergency first aid.

These actions are all examples of prosocial behavior. In each instance, your actions benefit other people. Perhaps you are late for your next class, you want to use your change to buy a Coke, you need your notes for studying, or you are afraid that the stricken man is severely injured. Nevertheless, you still put the other person's needs before your own. When you perform positive, **prosocial behaviors,** the interests of others become more important than your own. Prosocial behaviors thus contrast sharply with the types of antisocial behaviors to be discussed in Chapter 9. Antisocial actions, such as aggression, rape, and war, harm others. Prosocial actions benefit others.

Many types of behaviors are prosocial: helping in emergencies, cooperating with others, giving to charities, volunteering your time, sympathizing with others, and even common courtesy qualify as prosocial actions (see Focus 8-1). **Altruism,** as described in the story of the good Samaritan, is the most dramatic form of prosocial behavior:

> A certain man went down from Jerusalem to Jericho, and fell among thieves, which stripped him of his raiment, and wounded him, and departed, leaving him half dead. And by chance there came down a certain priest that way: and when he saw him, he passed by on the other side. And likewise a Levite, when he was at the place, came and looked on him, and passed by on the other side. But a certain Samaritan, as he journeyed, came where he was: and when he saw him, he had compassion on him, and went to him, and bound up his wounds . . . and took care of him.   [Luke 10:30–34]

Altruistic behaviors, such as the good Samaritan's, are motivated solely by the other person's need. They are completely unselfish, for the doer expects no reward whatsoever for rendering aid.

Unfortunately, this definition of altruism raises some thorny conceptual problems. First, before we can call someone "altruistic" we must know their motivations. The good Samaritan seems only to want to help a needy person, but he may secretly hope that he will be rewarded for his efforts. If he is motivated by hope of reward, then he is not an altruist. Second, what if the good Samaritan finds great pleasure in helping other people? If he helps others to gain personal pleasure, then he is no longer acting altruistically. Third, some researchers believe that altruism is instinctive. They argue that we are genetically programmed to help others

---

FOCUS 8–1

Experiencing Social Psychology: *How can you help other people?*

When was the last time you helped someone? If you can't recall an instance, you may be overlooking some of the common ways in which we help others. First, helping people doesn't always mean intervening in a serious emergency. Sometimes people need our help in nonserious situations: a friend wants help in moving; a hitchhiker wants a ride. Second, helping can be spontaneous—as when you suddenly decide to stop and help a motorist who has a flat tire—or it can be planned in advance. Benefits, such as the Live Aid concert of 1985, and charity drives are organized forms of helping others. Third, helping can take the form of giving something that you possess to others (donating your time or your money, for example) or performing an action that has positive consequences for others. The differences among various helping situations can be seen in Table 8-1 (Pearce & Amato, 1980):

TABLE 8–1

Differences among various types of helping situations.

Serious	*Nonserious*
Helping to save millions of starving children, assisting victims of an automobile accident, preventing an assault.	Giving change for a phone call, mailing a letter for a friend, handing back tests for the instructor.
Planned	*Spontaneous*
Canvassing for charity, staffing a hotline, chaperoning delinquents on a trip to the zoo.	Helping a lost child, helping a heart attack victim, rescuing a child from a fire.
Doing	*Giving*
Picking up dropped packages, turning off the lights in a parked car, giving cardiopulmonary resuscitation (CPR).	Donating bone marrow, giving money to a panhandler, fixing a meal for some friends.

in certain situations. But if our genes are forcing us to help, can we really say we are ever altruistic? (For a closer look at this argument, see "In Depth: The Sociobiology of Helping," at the end of this chapter.)

To cope with the complexities inherent in the concept of altruism, most social psychologists rely on a less stringent definition in their research. Since the motivations of the helper can rarely be completely known, investigators concentrate on **helping behavior** per se, regardless of the reasons for the helping. After all, even when helping is motivated by greed or some other selfish intention, at least help has been given. If a single individual who wanted to be on television or earn a medal had been among the bystanders who heard her calls for help, Kitty Genovese might have survived the attack (see Bar-Tal, 1976; Gelfand & Hartmann, 1982; Rushton & Sorrentino, 1981; Staub, 1978).

Predicting Helping Behavior

When Kitty Genovese cried out, the 38 bystanders failed to help her. But when John J. Sholly saw an elderly man drowning, he risked his own life to save the man. Sholly was driving across a bridge over the Des Moines River when he saw a man foundering in the water. Realizing the man was drowning, he stopped his car and jumped into the river. Although

Prosocial behavior: actions that benefit other people. Emergencies, like the one shown here, require spontaneous intervention to protect the victim from serious harm. Other situations, in contrast, may require other types of helping: doing a friend a favor, canvassing for charity, donating blood or money, or organizing a benefit are all forms of prosocial behvaior.

he later admitted that his first thought as he plunged toward the bone-chilling water was "Well, dummy, you've done it now. You're going to die," he succeeded in saving the man ("Carnegie Fund," 1984).

Two emergencies—a murder and a drowning—with very different consequences. What was it about these two situations that inhibited helping in one case but promoted it in the other? A glib answer, such as "Big cities make people unfriendly" or "Sholly was a good Samaritan and none of Kitty Genovese's neighbors was" is not enough. To predict when people will help and when they will fail to help, we must take into account both the nature of the situation and the characteristics of the people caught up in that situation. Emergencies are complex social phenomena; they take place in real places and involve flesh-and-blood bystanders and victims. If we ignore either the situation or the nature of the people involved, our analysis will be incomplete (see Figure 8-1).

The Helping Situation

Emergencies are often "strong" situations: they disrupt the ordinary routine of everyday life and prompt us to behave in certain ways (Snyder & Ickes, 1985). But which way does the situation pull us: toward or away from helping? Before we can answer this question, we must ask several others: How many bystanders are present? Is the emergency ambiguous? Where is the emergency located?

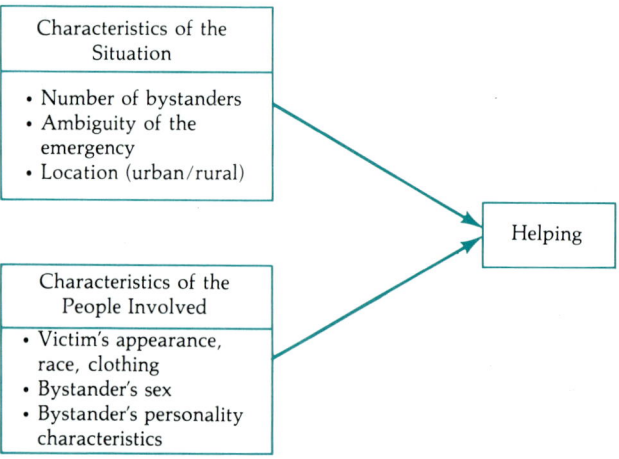

Figure 8-1 When do people help? "Most social psychologists recognize, at least in principle, that it is always the interaction between aspects of people and aspects of situations that gives rise to altruistic" behaviors (Krebs & Miller, 1985, p. 37). Situational factors include the number of bystanders, the ambiguity of the emergency, and the location. The characteristics of both bystander and victim compose the "people" factor.

The bystander effect. When the social psychologists Bibb Latané and John Darley read about the murder of Kitty Genovese, they were struck by the large number of witnesses. Could it be, they wondered, that people are less likely to help if other people are also present in the situation?

To investigate this hypothesis, Latané and Darley created a false emergency in their laboratory (1970). While male college students completed some bogus questionnaires, Latané and Darley pumped white smoke through an air vent into the test room. (The researchers got the idea from the old Camel cigarette sign in Times Square.) Some subjects were alone in the room, but others were part of three-person groups consisting of one subject and two confederates. The confederates pretended to be subjects, but they were trained to ignore the emergency. As the room filled with smoke, they nonchalantly glanced at the vent, shrugged, and went back to their questionnaires. If the subject mentioned the smoke to them, they said merely "I dunno." In a third condition, all three members of the group were actual subjects.

The typical subject who was tested alone left the room to report the smoke within two minutes; 75% reported the emergency within the six-minute time limit. Puzzled, most stared at the vent, went over to get a closer look at the smoke, and finally left the room to seek help. Subjects tested in groups, however, behaved very differently. Only 10% of the subjects tested with the passive confederates ever reported the smoke, and the percentage reached no higher than 15% when all three group members were actual subjects. By the time the six-minute period was up, the room was so smoky that subjects couldn't see the far wall. They coughed and rubbed their eyes, but they stayed at their tables, fanning the fumes away from their papers so they could finish their questionnaires. Latané and Darley had succeeded in documenting the **bystander effect:** people are less likely to help in groups than when they are alone.

However, Latané and Darley's smoke study did not involve helping other people. By helping, the subjects were protecting themselves, as they could have been injured in a fire. Therefore, to approximate a true "bystander situation" more closely, Latané and Darley conducted a second study. Participants were seated in a small room equipped with an intercom system. After they had waited alone for a few moments, the experimenter used the intercom system to explain: "I'm concerned with the kinds of personal problems faced by normal college students under pressure. To gather some general information on this topic, I would like you to discuss some of your personal concerns with five other students." To ensure confidentiality, the experimenter explained all communication would take place by means of the intercom system, so no face-to-face meeting would be necessary. The experimenter said that he himself wouldn't be listening to the discussion.

During the first round of comments, all six subjects gave two-minute descriptions of their school-related personal problems. Only one comment was surprising: one participant admitted that he was subject to seizures, especially when he studied hard or took an exam. When the group began the second round of comments, this person began to sound strange. His statements became increasingly garbled, until finally he complained:

> "I er um think I I need er if I could er er somebody er er er er er give me a little er give me a little help here because er I er I'm er er h-h-having a a a a real problem er right now and I er if somebody could help me out it would it would er er s-s-sure be sure be good . . . because er there er er a cause I er I uh I've got a a one of the er sei—er er things coming on and and and I could really er use some help so if somebody would er give me a little h-help uh er-er-er-er-er c-could somebody er er help er uh uh uh . . . I'm gonna die er er I'm . . . gonna die er help er er seizure er."

With the last word he choked loudly and then lapsed into silence.

Although you may feel certain that you would help in this situation, many of Latané and Darley's subjects did not. The findings shown in Figure 8-2 are consistent with the bystander effect: people help less in groups than when they are alone. While these findings may seem surprising, they have been replicated in approximately four dozen studies of nearly 6,000 people who faced various emergencies alone or in a group.

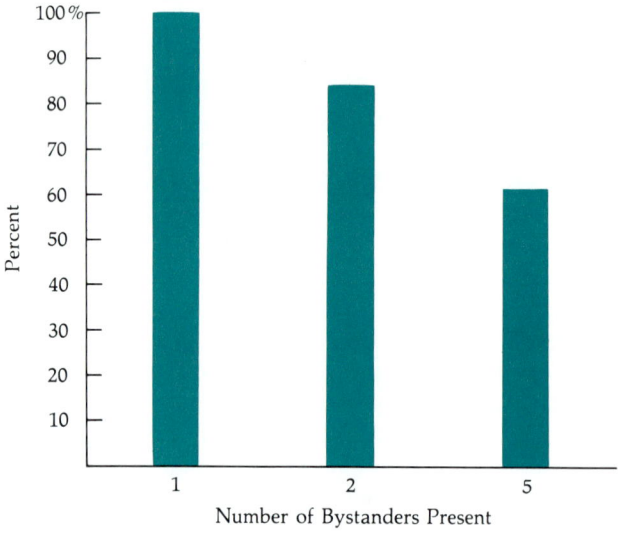

Figure 8-2 The percentage of bystanders who helped a "victim" when they were alone and in groups demonstrates the bystander effect: people are less likely to help in groups than alone. As the number of bystanders who overheard a seizure increased, helping decreased. In fact, all of the single bystanders helped faster: 85% of the subjects who thought they were alone helped before the "victim" lapsed into silence. Only 31% of the subjects in groups responded this quickly.

Across these various studies, about 75% of the subjects tested alone intervened, but only 53% of the subjects in groups helped (Latané & Nida, 1981; see Focus 8-2).

Ambiguity of the situation. About the time that Latané and Darley were documenting the inhibiting influence of bystanders on intervention

---

FOCUS 8 – 2

A Closer Look: *What causes the bystander effect?*

Latané and Darley discovered that bystanders help less in groups than when they are alone. They are careful to point out, however, that the bystanders who failed to help weren't apathetic or afraid to get involved. When subjects witnessed an emergency, many seemed very nervous and worried; their hands trembled, their palms were sweating, and most asked about the victim. To Latané and Darley, the unresponsive bystanders "seemed more emotionally aroused than did the subjects who reported the emergency" (1976, p. 326).

So why didn't they help? Latané and Darley believe that the presence of other bystanders inhibits helping for three basic reasons. The first factor, *diffusion of responsibility,* leaves bystanders feeling that it is not their responsibility to help. "The pressures to intervene do not focus on any one of the observers; instead, the responsibility for intervention is *shared* among all the onlookers and is not unique for any one" (Darley & Latané, 1968, p. 378). Because of diffusion of responsibility, bystanders are even less likely to help if they think that one of the other bystanders has emergency medical training (Schwartz & Clausen, 1970), but more likely to help if they realize that the other bystanders are physically unable to intervene (Bickman, 1971, 1972; Korte, 1970; Ross & Braband, 1973).

Second, because an emergency is such a novel, atypical situation, bystanders often rely on other people's reactions to understand what is happening. Unfortunately, since emergencies are sometimes ambiguous, each nonresponding bystander sends the same inaccurate message to every other nonresponding bystander: "It's OK; no help is needed." This process is known as *informational influence,* since others' responses provide us with information about the nature of the emergency (see Chapter 10).

Third, the bystander effect is also caused by *evaluation apprehension:* onlookers' fear that they will embarrass themselves by doing something inappropriate. Most people prefer to appear poised and "normal" in social settings, and actively avoid doing anything that may lead to embarrassment. In an ambiguous emergency, we look and feel foolish if we offer assistance to someone who doesn't need it. The screams you hear may come from a television set; the owner of the wrecked bicycle may be insulted by your offer of help; the smoke may come from an incinerator. Because evaluation apprehension increases as your audience grows larger, you become socially inhibited (Schwartz & Gottlieb, 1976).

John T. Cacioppo and his colleagues have recently identified a fourth inhibiting factor: *confusion of responsibility.* We sometimes refrain from helping others because we are afraid that onlookers will assume that we are responsible for the victim's suffering. A potential helper realizes that other bystanders try to determine who is responsible for the victim's misfortune when they arrive on the scene of the accident. The potential helper also realizes that the onlookers may assume that anyone who helps is partially responsible for the accident itself. Imagine that you happen on this scene: A man is lying on the ground, a pair of crutches lie nearby, and another person is lifting the man to his feet as several bystanders watch. According to Cacioppo and his associates, you may assume that the helper caused the accident in the first place. Otherwise, why did he help, while the others watched? Thus, bystanders refrain from helping because they don't want to be blamed by other onlookers (Cacioppo, Petty, & Losch, 1986).

in emergencies, Irving M. Piliavin, Judith Rodin, and Jane A. Piliavin (1969) were discovering that people in large groups are sometimes very helpful. Irving Piliavin conceived the study as he rode on a subway in New York City. When an obviously drunken passenger collapsed on the floor of the car, no one moved to help. After Piliavin helped the man to a seat, he realized that the subway could be used as a moving social psychology laboratory for a study of helping.

Over a period of 73 days, the trio of researchers staged 103 accidents on the Eighth Avenue Express. With two observers recording bystanders' reactions, the "victim" would take up a position near a pole in the center of the car (see Figure 8-3). At times he carried a cane and moved as though he were injured or ill. At other times he feigned drunkenness: he smelled of liquor and carried a bottle in a paper bag. In either case, as the train left the station, the victim would stagger and collapse on the floor.

The researchers expected that very few of the bystanders would help. In fact, to provide a positive model of helping, they had another confederate ready to go to the victim's aid. However, the model was rarely needed. On 62 of the 65 trials involving the cane-carrying victim, passengers usually intervened before 10 seconds had elapsed. And while the drunken confederate fared less well, even he received help on 19 of the 38 trials. Lastly, the observers discovered that the more bystanders there were in the victim's immediate area, the more quickly he was helped (see Table 8-2).

How can this reversal of the usual bystander effect be explained? According to Piliavin, Rodin, and Piliavin, when the cane-carrying confederate fell, the bystanders immediately realized he needed help. His cane, faltering gait, and sudden collapse unmistakably signaled *emergency*.

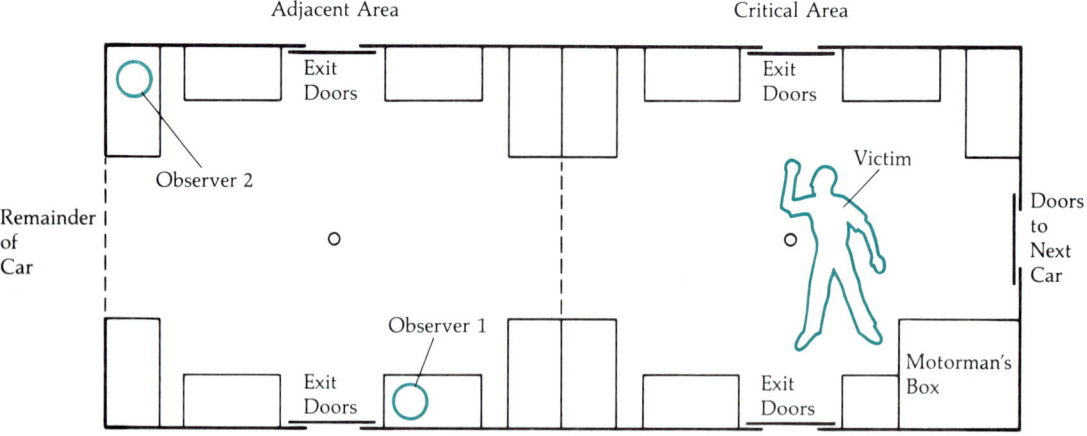

Figure 8-3 The subway study.

Extending their findings, they suggested that the processes discussed in Focus 8-2 inhibit helping only in ambiguous, novel situations. If the bystanders can't actually see the victim, or if they are unsure of the seriousness of the crisis, then diffusion of responsibility, informational influence, evaluation apprehension, and confusion of responsibility combine to block intervention. In unambiguous, face-to-face situations, in contrast, the help-inhibiting processes identified by Latané and Darley are relatively weak.

Russell D. Clark and Larry E. Word tested this hypothesis by manipulating the number of bystanders present *and* the ambiguity of the emergency. Unlike the subway study, this experiment was conducted in a laboratory setting. Told that the study examined sexual attitudes, the subjects (all men) completed a questionnaire while alone, in a two-person group, or in a five-person group. As they worked on their forms, a confederate—dressed as a uniformed maintenance worker and carrying a ladder and venetian blind—passed through the room into the adjacent room. Three minutes later he pushed the ladder against the wall, let it fall to the floor, and then pulled a set of venetian blinds from a 13-foot window. Then he, too, fell to the floor. In the *ambiguous emergency* condition, no extra information was added to the emergency. In the *unambiguous emergency* condition, the confederate groaned sharply when he hit the floor and grunted with each breath. Then he exclaimed, "Oh, my back, I can't move!" and continued to groan (Clark & Word, 1972: Experiment 2).

The amount of helping obtained in the unambiguous emergency was startling. Regardless of the group's size, the groaning victim received help from 100% of the subjects. In the ambiguous condition, in contrast, only 30% of the subjects helped. As Figure 8-4 indicates, people are much more likely to help others in unambiguous emergencies.

These studies of ambiguity suggest that the bystanders at the Kitty Genovese incident may have misinterpreted the situation. They may not have heard her cries clearly, and simply concluded that intervention was

TABLE 8-2

Number of male bystanders in the subway victim's immediate vicinity and average number of seconds between the victim's collapse and bystanders' intervention.

	Elapsed Time	
Male Bystanders	Ill Victim	Drunk Victim
1–3	15	309
4–6	18	149
7 or more	9	97

SOURCE: Piliavin, Rodin, & Piliavin, 1969.

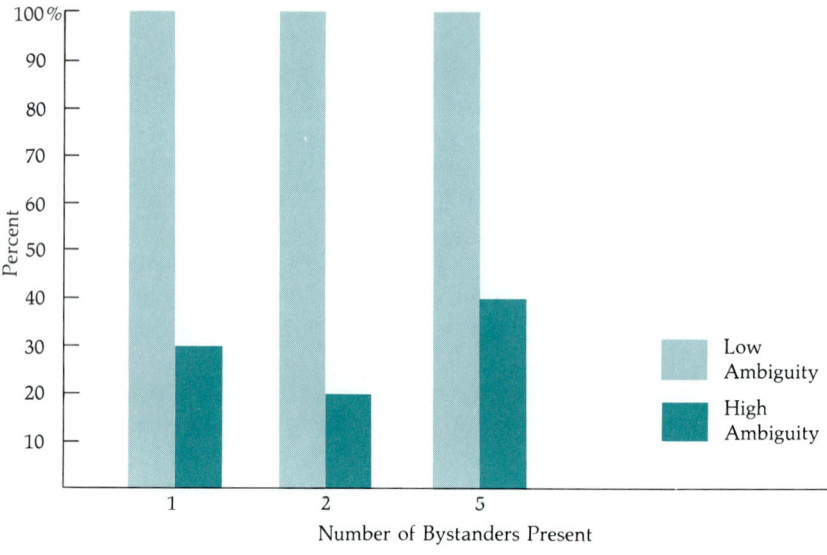

Figure 8-4 The percentage of bystanders who helped a "victim" in situations of low and high ambiguity when they were alone and in groups demonstrates that the bystander effect does not occur when the emergency is unambiguous. When the onlookers were exposed to a clear, unmistakable emergency, they always helped. If the emergency was ambiguous (the victim didn't groan), helping dropped off dramatically.

unnecessary. In the words of one bystander, "We thought it was a lovers' quarrel." In support of this interpretation, only 19% of the people who witnessed a violent staged fight between a man and a woman intervened if the woman screamed, "Get away from me, I don't know why I ever married you!" If, however, the woman clarified the nature of the incident by screaming, "Get away from me, I don't know you!" then 65% of the bystanders helped (Shotland, 1985).

Urban versus rural settings. Before we examine the people (victim and bystander) in the situation, one final situational factor should be considered: location. Many experts on modern society suggest that city life is highly stressful; each day brings unwanted contacts with strangers, great amounts of auditory and visual stimulation, and even threats of physical harm. To cope, residents may avoid personal involvement with others and develop a blasé attitude of indifference. According to this view, people who live in large cities are less likely to intervene in an emergency than people who live in the suburbs and in small towns (Korte, 1978; Milgram, 1970).

Social psychologists have used a variety of field methods to examine the link between urbanism and helping. Showing considerable creativity, investigators typically stage a minor accident or make a small request of passersby in both cities and towns, and then compare the amounts of helping (see Table 8-3). One study used the wrong-number technique to call subjects in Chicago, New York City, and Philadelphia and subjects in small towns outside these cities. In most cases, the small-town residents were more helpful than the city dwellers (Milgram, 1970). In a study using the lost-letter method, 70% of the stamped postcards dropped in small towns around Boston were mailed, compared to only 61% in Boston proper (Korte & Kerr, 1975). Similarly, when researchers deliberately overpaid clerks for small purchases, only 55% of the clerks in cities corrected the mistake, but 80% in smaller towns did so (see Korte, 1978, 1981, for a review).

TABLE 8 – 3

Procedures and applications of field techniques for studying helping behavior.

Technique	Procedure	Application
Wrong number	Subjects are telephoned by a person who is apparently using a pay phone. Claiming to have used his/her last dime in dialing the wrong number, the caller asks the subject to make the call for him/her.	City dwellers are less likely to make the call than residents of rural areas (Milgram, 1970).
Lost letter	Stamped, addressed envelopes are dropped in public areas so they appear to have been lost by the writer before they could be mailed.	Letters dropped in cities are less likely to be mailed than letters dropped in towns (Korte & Kerr, 1975).
Overpayment	After making a small purchase, the customer overpays the clerk by a small amount.	Clerks in towns are more likely to return the overpayment than clerks in cities (Korte & Kerr, 1975).
Sidewalk requests	Small requests are made of passersby; requests include money, name, directions, favorite color.	City dwellers are less likely to name their favorite color than rural dwellers (Amato, 1983).
Stranger at the door	Claiming to have lost a nearby friend's address, a stranger asks to use the telephone to call for more information.	Requester is admitted to more rural homes than urban homes (Milgram, 1970).
Wrong directions	In a public place, a "lost" stranger (a confederate) is given incorrect directions by another confederate.	Bystanders intervene with correct directions more frequently in towns than in cities (Amato, 1983).

One of the most comprehensive studies of urban–rural helping was conducted in Australia by Paul R. Amato (1983). Improving on the methods used in previous studies, Amato studied 55 randomly selected communities with populations that ranged from fewer than 1,000 to more than 3 million (Sydney). In addition, he measured six types of helping: (1) reactions to a serious emergency (Amato, while wearing a bloody bandage on his leg, would fall to his knees with a cry of pain in front of an approaching passerby); (2) responses to the question "What is your favorite color?"; (3) assistance given to a stranger who dropped a stack of envelopes on the ground; (4) donations to the Multiple Sclerosis Society; (5) corrections of wrong directions (see Table 8-3); and (6) refusal to participate in a compulsory census. Even after he controlled for other situational variables—such as the homogeneity of the community, residential stability, and the number of strangers (tourists) who visit the area—he found a significant relationship between helping and population density. People who lived in larger communities were less helpful than people who lived in smaller communities. This finding applied equally to all types of helping with the exception of assistance given someone who dropped a stack of envelopes. This individual received very little help in any community.

Why do urbanites help less? Amato found that helping rates dropped even in relatively small cities (with populations of only 20,000), so overstimulation isn't the answer. More likely, as cities grow larger, the situational forces that block helping become stronger. In larger cities, responsibility is more diffused because more potential helpers are available. Also, since urban bystanders probably don't know each other, they are more likely to misinterpret one another's failure to respond. With more witnesses, evaluation apprehension may also leave bystanders unwilling to get involved. Thus urbanites are inhibited by the nature of the social setting.

The People in the Situation

Unresponsive bystanders are not necessarily callous and coldhearted; rather, situational factors may work to prevent us from helping. However, helping behavior also depends on who is watching and who needs help. We cannot overlook the importance of the people in the situation.

The victim's personal attributes. Consider this simple experiment. Researchers placed a dime on the shelves in telephone booths at Kennedy Airport and Grand Central Station in New York City. They then retreated to a nearby observation point. When an unsuspecting subject entered the booth and used the dime, the experimenters returned. They tapped on the door and said, "Excuse me, I think I might've left a dime in this phone booth a few minutes ago. Did you find it?" When the experimenters were well dressed (suits), they got their dime back 77% of the time.

Informally dressed experimenters (unkempt work clothes) got their dime back from only 38% of the subjects (Bickman, 1974).

If people were all perfect altruists, helping wouldn't depend on such irrelevancies as clothing. But because we often base our initial perceptions of people on their physical characteristics, helping sometimes depends on the victim's personal attributes. Helping becomes more likely if the people who need help are physically attractive (Benson, Karabenick, & Lerner, 1976; Harrell, 1978), if they are dressed attractively (Bickman, 1974; Kleinke, 1977), and if they possess no stigmatizing physical characteristics, such as unattractive birthmarks (Piliavin, Piliavin, & Rodin, 1975), eye patches, or scars (Samerotte & Harris, 1976). Last, women tend to receive more help than men (Deaux, 1976).

The similarity-helping effect. In the study conducted in phone booths in New York City, well-dressed victims received more help than unkempt ones. Most of the bystanders were well dressed, too. Did the researchers discover a tendency to help well-dressed people or a tendency to help people who are similar to us in some way?

To an important degree, the impact of the victim's characteristics depends on the bystanders' personal characteristics. In general, if you feel that others are similar to you in some way, then you will be more likely to go to their aid. This tendency is known as the *similarity-helping effect*, and it parallels the similarity-attraction effect discussed in Chapter 7. Thus birds of a feather not only flock together but also help one another. Similarity may influence helping by creating a feeling of "we-ness" between bystander and victim, so the bystander feels more responsible for helping (Hornstein, 1982; Piliavin et al., 1981).

The similarity-helping relationship has been confirmed in many studies involving such diverse attributes as attitudes, political beliefs, nationality, and race, as well as dress (Dovidio, 1984). In one creative study of similarity in attitudes, researchers clipped two open envelopes together and then dropped them on the sidewalk in a Jewish section of Brooklyn, New York. To manipulate similarity of attitude, the researchers inserted in one envelope a completed opinion poll indicating that the victim was either pro-Israel or anti-Israel. To measure helping, the investigators put a check and a contribution card for the "Institute for Research in Medicine" in the second envelope. If, as the researchers reasonably assumed, the finder favored Israel, the results strongly supported the similarity-helping prediction: 69% of the envelopes in the pro-Israel condition were returned, compared to only 30% of the envelopes in the anti-Israel condition (Hornstein et al., 1971). In a conceptually similar study in the early 1970s, college students—who at the time were presumed to be politically liberal—were less likely to turn off the headlights of a parked automobile bearing bumper stickers touting conservative values (such as "America—love it or leave it") (Ehlert, Ehlert, & Merrens, 1973).

The similarity-helping effect also accounts for some racial biases in helping. Many bystanders help members of their own racial group, but not members of other racial groups. In one illustrative study of racial bias, the drivers of either a 1971 Ford or a 1968 Chevrolet pulled their cars to the side of the road, raised the hoods, and stood next to their cars. When the "victim" of the automotive mishap was white, 94% of the people who stopped to help were white. When the victim was black, 97% of the people who offered assistance were black (West, Whitney, & Schnedler, 1975).

Although discrimination against out-group members isn't always this strong, racial favoritism occurs about 40% of the time (Crosby, Bromley, & Saxe, 1980). In some cases, only whites show greater same-race favoritism (Gaertner & Bickman, 1971; West, Whitney, & Schnedler, 1975: Study 2). Still other researchers find blacks but not whites favoring the members of their own racial group (Wegner & Crano, 1975). And some studies even find a cross-race favoritism, such as whites helping blacks more than whites (Dutton, 1971; Dutton & Lake, 1973; Katz, Cohen, & Glass, 1975). Bystanders appear to favor their own group most frequently when they feel they run no risk in doing so. In many situations, the bystander feels anonymous—the victim can't see the bystander. In such circumstances, whites are much less likely to help a black victim, for there are no social consequences for their prejudicial actions. If, however, bystanders and victim can see each other, then the shield of anonymity is stripped away. In such cases, whites usually help blacks. Apparently even racist bystanders don't want to appear to be prejudiced, so they attempt to disconfirm this negative social image by helping (Dovidio, 1984).

Men, women, and helping.

The heroes of mythology—Odysseus, Perseus, Hercules—were all men. Only men were admitted to King Arthur's Round Table. With few exceptions, comic-book heroes are supermen rather than superwomen (Wonder Woman, an obvious exception, is from a civilization that excludes all males). In 1984, 19 of the 21 U.S. citizens cited by the Carnegie Commission for acts of heroism were men ("Carnegie Fund," 1984).

In legend, fiction, and real-life emergencies, men tend to help more than women. Although exceptions sometimes occur, women help less than men when others are present (Bickman, 1971, 1972; Latané & Darley, 1968; Schwartz & Clausen, 1970). They are also less likely to stop to aid a stranded motorist (Bryan & Test, 1967; Pomazal & Clore, 1973; West, Whitney, & Schnedler, 1975), less likely to give a dime to a stranger (Kleinke, 1977), less likely to relay a telephone message for someone who has dialed the wrong number from a pay phone (Gaertner & Bickman, 1971), and more likely to ignore a victim who collapses on the subway (Piliavin, Piliavin, & Rodin, 1969).

These sex differences may be due in part to the greater risks intervention poses for a woman: she is more likely than a man to be attacked if she stops to aid a stranger in distress. However, sex-role socialization undoubtedly also influences men's and women's reactions to emergencies. Some women may feel that they lack the skills to help when an emergency arises. Men are likely to be better trained to deal with emergencies, especially with mechanical problems, so they are more likely to give assistance. Second, if the bystanders conform to traditional sex roles, then helping may be viewed as a masculine prerogative. The masculine sex role traditionally emphasizes chivalry and bravery, while the feminine sex role emphasizes dependence and passivity. Consider the case of two brothers, John and Terry, who recently helped a woman who was attacked by a man in broad daylight on a Philadelphia street. In describing their heroics, the men explained that they were watching the woman because "she was pretty good-looking." When the man assaulted her, John turned to Terry and said, "Let's get him." He later explained, "There's so much crime, but when you beat up on a woman, I mean, that's it" (Lopez, 1986, p. B-10). Masculinity may provide the "chutzpah" needed for helping.

Helping and masculinity do not always go hand in hand, however. In some cases, individuals who are extremely masculine may not help because they do not wish to appear incompetent (Tice & Baumeister, 1985). However, masculinity proved to be an important determinant of helping in a recent study in which men and women were exposed to a stranger choking on a piece of food. Men, once more, tended to be more helpful than women. This sex difference was most pronounced among sex-typed subjects: masculine men clearly helped more than feminine women. People who possessed both masculine and feminine qualities—androgynous individuals—revealed no sex differences (see Table 8-4).

TABLE 8-4

Percentage of sex-typed and androgynous men and women who helped. The influence of sex was strong among sex-typed individuals: men were more helpful than women. Among androgynous individuals, however, sex differences were minimal. Men gave slightly more direct help, but overall helping rates were equivalent.

Type of Help	Sex-Typed Subjects		Androgynous Subjects	
	Men	Women	Men	Women
Direct	27%	14%	24%	18%
Indirect	12	13	9	20
All help	39	27	33	38

SOURCE: Senneker & Hendrick, 1983.

These findings suggest that as sex-roles change, differences in helping between men and women may become negligible (Senneker & Hendrick, 1983).

Personality traits. The link between personality characteristics and helping has long intrigued social psychologists. As early as 1928, Hartshorne and May, in several volumes titled *Studies in the Nature of Character*, reported some surprising inconsistencies among personality traits and prosocial behavior. These researchers developed 33 ways to measure positive social behaviors—including helping, honesty, and resistance to temptation—and administered these tests to hundreds of children. Across these various tests, some children helped more consistently than others, but the average correlation among the various types of helping was only +.23. The child who agreed to share money with classmates, for example, did not necessarily volunteer to work for the Red Cross or send letters to hospitalized children. In explanation, Hartshorne and May offered the so-called *doctrine of specificity:* prosocial behavior, such as honesty and helping, is situationally specific. The person who helps in one setting may hurt in another.

Despite Hartshorne and May's disheartening findings, social psychologists refused to abandon their search for personality traits that predict helping. As more evidence was gathered with the aid of more valid

---

FOCUS 8-3

Controversy in Social Psychology: *Is the "altruistic personality" a myth?*

Ever since Hartshorne and May offered their doctrine of specificity, social psychologists have argued about the existence of a trait that distinguishes people who help from those who don't help. On one side of the issue stand the situationists, who believe that the emergency setting, and not the bystander's personality, determines helping. In support of their case, they point out that the true altruist—someone who consistently helps other people across a range of situations—is an anomaly. More typically, when individuals are observed in several different kinds of helping situations, they behave inconsistently, sometimes helping, sometimes not (Gergen, Gergen, & Meter, 1972). Furthermore, even though researchers have correlated helping with many different personality traits (including authoritarianism, moral development, Machiavellianism, alienation, autonomy, and trustworthiness), the correlations are usually rather paltry; they average about .30 (Rushton, 1980).

Daniel Batson and his colleagues also point out that the term *altruistic personality* may be a misnomer because it implies that the helper's only motivation is a desire to ease the other person's suffering. In their research they found that certain personality traits, such as self-esteem, feelings of personal responsibility, and empathy, were correlated with helping. But when some of their subjects were led to believe that they could avoid watching the victim suffer, the relationship between personality and helping disappeared. Batson and his associates argue that altruistic individuals aren't truly altruistic—they help others to reduce their own guilt and shame for not helping, not to ease others' suffering (Batson, Bolen, Cross, & Neuringer-Benefiel, 1986).

In contrast, some social psychologists believe that "there is a 'trait' of altruism. Some people are consistently more generous, helping, and kind than

measures of personality and helping, a more optimistic picture began to emerge. Granted, many studies reaffirmed Hartshorne and May's doctrine of specificity: personality didn't predict helping. In other cases, however, people who helped were set apart from nonhelpers by their personality characteristics. Helpful people tend, for example, to be *empathic* people: they have a facility for seeing situations from other people's perspectives (Archer, 1984; Underwood & Moore, 1982). Helpers also tend to be more deeply committed to personal moral standards and values than nonhelpers (Fogelman & Wiener, 1985; Staub, 1978). Individuals who are self-confident also help more, as do those who are less concerned about their own personal safety (Aronoff & Wilson, 1985). Thus personality does influence helping, *sometimes*. As Focus 8-3 notes, however, even someone with an "altruistic personality" may not help when situational forces stand in the way (see Rushton, 1981, for a review).

When Do People Help? A Concluding Word

As you wait for the light to change, your eyes wander to the opposite street corner. There you see a bicyclist brake to avoid a turning car. Her rear wheel locks, the bicycle slides sideways, and she falls roughly to the sidewalk. Legs tangled in the frame of the bicycle, head resting on the

---

others" (Rushton, 1981, p. 66). They note that when multiple measures of personality are taken, the correlation between personality and helping rises markedly. If, for example, several aspects of personality are measured (such as values, moral development, and social responsibility), and then these various measures are combined to form an overall composite, the correlation between this composite score and helping ranges from .40 to .50 (Staub, 1974). Furthermore, interviews with altruists—people who rescued Jews in Nazi Germany during World War II, civil rights workers who participated in the freedom rides of the 1960s, volunteers in community mental health centers—have enabled investigators to identify a number of qualities shared by helpers; a sense of social responsibility, inner-directedness, self-control, flexibility, self-acceptance, empathy, a tendency to take risks, independence, and strong moral values (London, 1970; Rosenhan, 1970).

The final words on this controversy have not yet been written, but once again an integrative approach may best account for the findings. Altruists may exist, but more frequently our actions are shaped by the interaction of personality and situation. In one study, for example, subjects who varied in level of moral maturity overheard a confederate in a neighboring room groaning from severe stomach cramps. As anticipated, subjects who were more morally mature were much more helpful, but only if they had been given permission to leave their room. If the experimenter had told them that the task they were completing was timed and that they could not leave their desks, then they were just as unhelpful as the less morally mature bystanders (Staub, Erkut, & Jaquette, as described in Staub, 1978). Other studies have yielded similar findings, suggesting that helping behaviors, like so many other social actions, are best understood in terms of an interaction between person and situation (Krebs & Miller, 1985).

pavement, the bicyclist lies still for a few moments before slowly raising a hand to her head. Will you help?

Before you say yes, you should realize that, as a bystander watching an emergency unfold, you are caught up in a complex web of interpersonal forces. First, your reaction may be influenced by the characteristics of the situation. According to Latané and Darley (1970, 1976), you will be less likely to help if other people witness the accident: diffusion of responsibility may leave you thinking that someone else should help; you may misinterpret others' ambivalence as a sign that no help is needed; your apprehensiveness about evaluation may drive you away from the potentially embarrassing situation; and you may realize that other bystanders will blame you for the accident if you help. In addition, the ambiguity of the cycling mishap and the location of the accident (such as a college campus, a large city, a small town) will influence your reaction.

Second, the characteristics of the people in the situation—both the victim and you, the onlooker—also influence helping. Without knowing it, you may take note of the cyclist's race, physical attractiveness, and similarity to you before you go to her aid. In addition, your own personal attributes—such as your sex-role identity, your gender, your moral standards—may also influence your reaction. "Will you help?" is a complex question, and it requires a complex answer that takes into account the characteristics of the situation, the victim, and the bystander.

But even if we can predict when you will help, from a scientific viewpoint our analysis remains incomplete. Upon discovering some novel fact or event, scientists often begin by describing the phenomenon through observation and measurement. As their work progresses, they reach beyond the level of description to explain the causes of the phenomenon. When social psychologists first began to study helping behavior, they gathered as much information as they could about the situation and the people involved in it so they could predict when people help and when they do not help. However, they were not content merely to describe helping. Once they understood the complexities of the helping situation, they began to ask *why* people help.

■ Why Do People Help?

As you pass by a middle-aged man on a downtown sidewalk, he pauses in mid-stride. A look of pain floods his face, he folds both arms around his midriff, and he bends over. Head bowed, he staggers to the nearest building. With his back pressed against the wall, he slowly slumps to a sitting position on the ground. You immediately crouch by his side, ask him if he needs help. His speech is incoherent, so you run to a nearby telephone booth and call the police emergency number. You wait by his side until help arrives.

You helped. You saw a person in need and intervened. But why? One answer stresses the decisions you made before you intervened. Questions such as "Is this an emergency?" and "Am I responsible?" must be answered before you can ask "Should I help?" A second approach to helping extends this interpretation by adding an economic element: the calculation of the costs and rewards of helping versus not helping. Did you wonder if you would be rewarded for helping? Did you realize that your conscience would bother you if you walked by the man?

Both of these approaches emphasize your rationality: confronted by an emergency, you examined the situation and decided to help. But what about your emotions? In emergencies, emotions run high. You may have been overwhelmed by a tremendous concern for the man, so you helped. Alternatively, perhaps you were simply in a good mood that day, so you decided to do something nice for somebody. In any case, your emotions and moods influenced your reaction.

A final theoretical perspective assumes that helping, like many other prosocial actions, is governed by social norms. The decisions you make and the emotions you experience are important, but so are the unwritten rules of conduct in the situation.

Deciding to Help

If Bibb Latané and John Darley watched you help the man who fell to the sidewalk, they would conclude that you *decided* to help. They feel that people who witness an emergency make a series of decisions before they actually offer help. Their *decision model* of helping behavior, summarized briefly in Figure 8-5, identifies five basic steps: (1) noticing the event, (2) interpreting the event as an emergency, (3) taking responsibility, (4) identifying a way to help, and (5) implementing the chosen form of help. When bystanders make all five of these decisions, they help; otherwise, they remain uninvolved (Latané & Darley, 1970).

Noticing the event.
Asking yourself "Is something going on here?" is the necessary first step in the helping decision. Sometimes people fail to help just because they never notice that help is needed. When you see a man collapse on the sidewalk, any factor that draws your attention away from his plight reduces the chance that you will help. If your attention is focused on yourself rather than on the situation, for example, then you may not notice his trouble (Gibbons & Wicklund, 1982). Preoccupied by a personal problem—an upcoming test, an argument with a good friend, problems with your job—you pass by the victim without stopping. In addition, if the emergency occurs in a busy section of town, you may be so busy tuning out the environment that you overlook the victim's plight (Korte, 1978).

John Darley and C. Daniel Batson examined this first step in the decision sequence by asking seminary students to give a short speech to some other students. Some had been led to believe that they were late, others were told that they would be right on time if they hurried, and

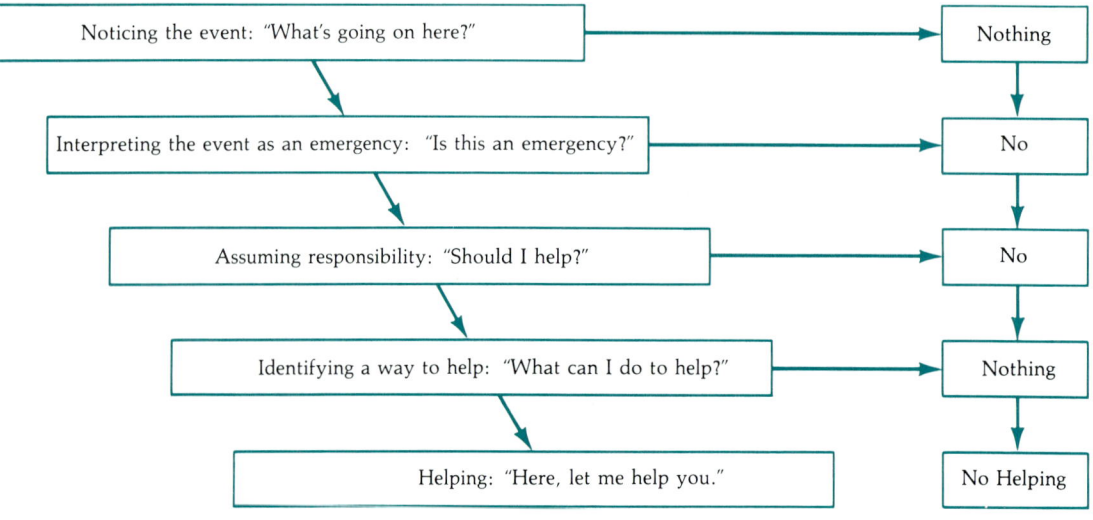

Figure 8-5 The decision model of helping behavior developed by Bibb Latané and John Darley. To help, bystanders must make each of the decisions in the sequence. If the bystanders make a negative response at any point in the sequence, they will not help.

others were given ample time to get to the auditorium where they would give their talk. To reach the auditorium, the subjects had to go down a narrow alleyway. And in that alleyway, slumped in a doorway, was an accomplice of the researchers. Head down and eyes closed, the confederate groaned softly as the lone subject passed by. Remarkably, only 10% of the subjects who thought they were late stopped to help the victim. If they had plenty of time to get to their talk, 63% helped, and 45% of those who needed to hurry helped. The final irony: some subjects were on their way to give a talk on the parable of the good Samaritan, but this reminder of the moral injunction to help others had no influence on their own helping (Darley & Batson, 1973).

In fairness to the participants, Darley and Batson conclude that these deeply religious individuals, hurrying to fulfill a commitment, simply overlooked the victim. When they were interviewed later, most of the subjects recalled seeing someone in the doorway, but they didn't really take any notice of him. These individuals were anything but good Samaritans, but their failure reflects their oversight rather than their lack of concern for others.

Interpreting the event as an emergency. Some of the seminary students in Darley and Batson's study noticed the man lying in the doorway but still failed to stop. When asked why, many gave this explanation: "I thought he was just sleeping off a drunk and didn't need any help." These individuals didn't help because they interpreted the situation as a nonemergency. According to the Latané-Darley decision model, after bystanders notice the event, they ask themselves "Is this an emergency?" If they feel the answer to this question is yes, then they move on in the decisional sequence. If they conclude that the situation doesn't qualify as an emergency, then they will not help.

How do people distinguish between an emergency and a nonemergency? To answer this question, researchers presented subjects with a series of events, and asked them to pick out the emergencies (see Table 8-5 for some examples). When the investigators examined their subjects' selections, they noticed that some emergencies are more easily identified than others. First, events that are perceived to be emergencies tend to occur so suddenly that the victims and bystanders are surprised and unprepared. Second, they also involve an imminent threat of harm to the victim, with the harm escalating as time passes. Third, while the victim can often do nothing to avoid the harm, onlookers or bystanders can ease or avert the crisis by intervening (Shotland & Huston, 1979; see Figure 8-6).

If an event meets all these criteria, then the bystander will probably define the situation as an emergency. And once this decision is made, help becomes more likely. In one study of this key link in the helping process, confederates made requests of students entering or leaving a large campus parking lot. Half of the subjects were exposed to a situation that met the criteria of an emergency: unexpected, escalating harm, with outside help needed. In an emergency situation, for example, the confederate said, "Excuse me. I need some help. I'm a diabetic and I forgot to take my insulin this morning. I'm long overdue. Can you give me a ride home to Boalsburg?" (Boalsburg was about five miles away.) When the

TABLE 8-5

Examples of situations judged to be emergencies, possible emergencies, or nonemergencies.

Emergencies	Possible Emergencies	Nonemergencies
An injured person is bleeding from a cut artery.	A person is lost in woods, shouting for help.	A car door chips other car's paint.
A house is ablaze; inside, people scream for help.	A car is broken down at side of road.	A telethon wants to raise $20 million.
A child is poisoned.	Leaves are burning on a windy day with no one watching.	A car is parked by fire hydrant.
A person lies on ground in shock.	A rock star is in danger of being trampled by fans.	A person scrapes a knee.
A person suffers a heart attack.	An intoxicated friend insists on driving home.	A tramp panhandles.

Figure 8-6 Identifying situations when help is needed. If you saw a jogger fall to the ground and clutch his ankle, would you offer assistance? Your reaction depends, in part, on the way you define the situation: emergency or nonemergency.

situation was a nonemergency, the confederate said, "Excuse me. I need some help. I forgot to take my allergy medicine this morning and it's starting to bother me. Can you give me a ride home to Boalsburg?" As predicted, more people helped in the emergency (64%) than in the nonemergency (45%) (Shotland & Huston, 1979, p. 1830).

Other people help us define situations as emergencies or nonemergencies. Earlier we noted that the bystander effect occurs in part because people misinterpret other people's responses. When you saw the man fall to the ground, you asked yourself, "Is this an emergency?" If no one else was responding, you may have concluded that it wasn't and gone about your business (Latané & Darley, 1976).

Taking responsibility. At this point in the decision sequence you have noticed the man slumped against the wall, and have decided that something is definitely wrong. He isn't drunk, he isn't waiting for the bus: he is injured or ill, and needs help. Now you must ask yourself: "Should I help?"

Unless you feel that you are personally responsible for helping the man, you won't intervene. As we noted earlier in our discussion of the bystander effect, if other people see the man collapse, you may feel less responsible for rendering aid. However, many other variables can increase or decrease feelings of personal responsibility, including friendship, dependence, the number of victims, and the location of the emergency (see Focus 8-4). Responsibility was directly manipulated in one study of groups of children trick-or-treating on Halloween. When the children visited one of the experimental homes, a female experimenter explained that she was collecting candy for hospitalized children who weren't able to go trick-or-treating. In the *control condition*, she pointed to a box on the table and told the children, "Please give them as many as you want by putting the candies in the white box on the table. Then you can leave." In the *one-child-responsible* condition, the experimenter selected one child to be the leader: "I will put you in charge of the group here." Then she told the children to donate as many candies as they wanted. Lastly, in the *each-child-responsible condition*, the experimenter pointed to each child, explaining, "I will be counting on you and you and you . . ." In all conditions, the experimenter left the children alone in the room while a hidden observer recorded their donations (Maruyama, Fraser, & Miller, 1982, pp. 660–661).

FOCUS 8 – 4

Applying Social Psychology: *Does increasing bystanders' feelings of responsibility increase crime prevention?*

Picture yourself on a hot summer afternoon at the beach. As you languish in the sun, a young man spreads a blanket on the sand about five feet from you and turns on his radio. After about two minutes he turns to you and says, "Excuse me, I'm going up to the boardwalk for a few minutes. Would you watch my things?" You say, "Sure," and he vanishes up the beach. A few minutes later a woman walks up to the man's blanket. With no hesitation she grabs the blaring radio and takes off down the beach. What should you do?

When investigators staged this crime at a New York beach, the witnesses were remarkably helpful. Fully 95% of the bystanders who had been asked to "watch my things" intervened by stopping the thief or grabbing back the radio. In contrast, when the victim had said only "Excuse me, I'm here alone and have no matches . . . do you have a light?" before leaving, only 20% of the bystanders intervened when the woman took the radio (Moriarty, 1975). Apparently private citizens will take steps to prevent crime, but only if they feel that intervention is their responsibility.

Other studies suggest that if people realize that crime prevention is their responsibility, then they will be much more likely to act against lawbreakers (Austin, 1979; Bickman & Rosenbaum, 1977; Shaffer, Rogel, & Hendrick, 1975). In one study shoppers waiting in line at a supermarket were exposed to a shoplifter. The thief, who was standing in front of them in the checkout line, stuffed several small items into her purse while the subject looked on. Meanwhile, a confederate with a loaded shopping cart who stood behind the subject said nothing, or made one of two statements:

Low responsibility: Say, look at her. She's shoplifting. She put that into her purse. But it's the store's problem. They have security people here.

High responsibility: Say, look at her. She's shoplifting. She put that in her purse. We saw it. We should report it. It's our responsibility.

When the confederate emphasized responsibility, 72% of the shoppers reported the theft. When the confederate disavowed responsibility, only 32% of the subjects reported the theft. When the confederate said nothing, 41% of the subjects turned in the shoplifter (Bickman & Rosenbaum, 1977).

These findings offer compelling support for crime-prevention programs designed to increase private citizens' feelings of responsibility, such as neighborhood watch groups. The long-term effectiveness of other anticrime programs, such as special methods for reporting crimes, will be enhanced if citizens learn to take responsibility for crime prevention (Klentz & Beaman, 1981).

As responsibility increased from none to one to each child, the trick-or-treaters donated more and more candy. In the control condition, the average contribution was 2.2 candies, but the average rose to 3.3 in the one-child-responsible condition and to 5.0 in the each-child-responsible condition. By the way, before the children left, the experimenter returned to the room and explained that she had found some extra candy. Each child was then rewarded for his or her generosity. In addition, all the candy collected during the experiment was indeed donated to a local hospital.

Identifying a way to help. At long last you are approaching the end of your decision-making sequence. You have noticed the event, interpreted it as an emergency, and feel that it is your responsibility to help. Yet even now, if your answer to the question "What can I do?" is "Nothing," then you will not help.

At this stage in the decision process, experience in emergency settings appears to be one of the primary determinants of helping. If bystanders feel that they possess the skills or abilities needed in the setting, they tend to help. If they think they lack the necessary know-how, they generally fail to intervene. When the emergency involves faulty or dangerous electrical equipment, people experienced in working with electricity tend to help more than those who are untrained (Clark & Word, 1974; Midlarsky & Midlarsky, 1973, 1976). In medical emergencies, as when a person is choking on food or bleeding from a severe wound, bystanders with first-aid training intervene faster than untrained observers (Pantin & Carver, 1982; Shotland & Heinold, 1985). And if a group member is overcome by a seizure, help is much more likely if the bystanders know that they can treat the seizure by giving the victim the medicine he keeps in his pocket (Schwartz & Clausen, 1970).

The importance of competence as a necessary condition for helping receives dramatic support from interviews with real-life good Samaritans. All 32 of the individuals in one study had intervened to prevent a violent crime, such as a street mugging, an armed robbery, or a bank holdup. One of the men had broken up a violent argument between a man and a woman. During the dispute, his jaw was broken by the male assailant. In another emergency, a man entering a grocery store confronted a robber pointing a rifle at the sales clerk. Instantly he disarmed the robber, and was hitting him when the police arrived. In 27 of the 32 cases, the helpers were injured in some way.

When the researchers compared these good Samaritans to a group of randomly selected people who had never intervened in a violent crime, they found that the interveners were far more experienced. Not only had they witnessed more crimes, but they were also better prepared to help in the emergency. As Figure 8-7 indicates, significantly more of the good Samaritans were trained in life-saving, first-aid, medicine, self-defense, or crime prevention (Huston et al., 1981).

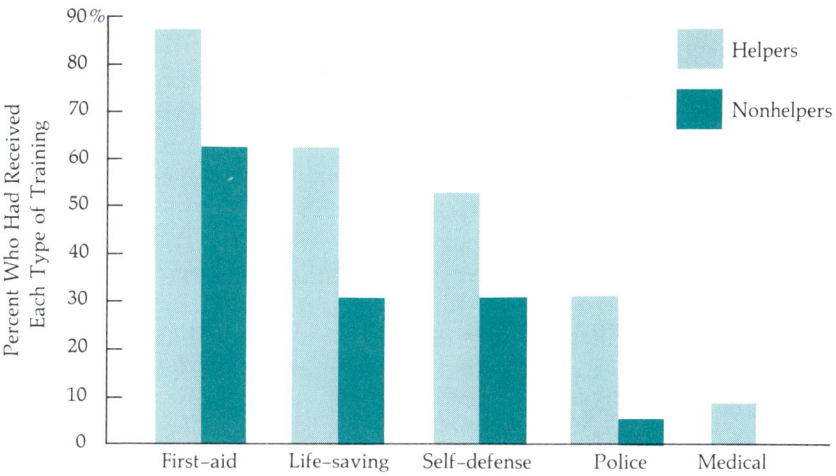

Figure 8-7 When investigators interviewed people who had intervened in violent crimes, they found that helpers tended to be better prepared to cope with the emergency than a matched group of nonhelpers. The helpers also tended to be taller, heavier, and higher in self-rated strength and emotionality than the control group subjects.

The final stage: Helping. With each decision in the sequence, you move closer and closer to the final step: intervention in the emergency. You notice that "something's going on," classify the event as an emergency, take responsibility for providing aid to the victim, and identify a way to help. You are ready to give help. Even at this stage in the sequence, however, you may fail to intervene. The situation may block your response. The man who falls to the ground may refuse your help, or disappear into the crowd before you can reach his side. Or you may be overcome by fear, so you never carry out your decision to help.

Cost–Reward Theory

Most researchers agree that bystanders make decisions about helping. A study conducted by Jane and Irving Piliavin (1972), however, raises questions that the original Latané and Darley theory can't fully answer. While bystanders looked on, a cane-carrying confederate collapsed on the floor of a subway car. In some cases, he just lay on the floor, staring up at the ceiling. In other cases, a thin trickle of stage blood oozed from his mouth. Surprisingly, fewer people helped the bleeding victim. In fact, some people seemed ready to help, but stopped when they noticed the blood. Two teenage girls got up when they saw the man fall, for example, but sat down quickly when one said, "Oh, he's bleeding!"

Why would people be less likely to help the more seriously injured victim? The Piliavins propose that Latané and Darley left out one step in the decision-making sequence: a calculation of costs and rewards. According to the *cost–reward model*, people strive to minimize their costs and maximize their rewards. Once bystanders realize an emergency is occurring, they intuitively calculate (1) the rewards they can expect from helping and (2) the costs that helping may create. In the subway experiment, the bystanders may have identified a number of possible rewards for helping, including thanks from the victim, praise from onlookers, self-praise, and even a monetary reward or a good citizenship award. However, these rewards were offset by many possible costs: lost time, embarrassment, expenditure of effort, danger, fear, and revulsion caused by the sight of blood. When the victim only collapsed, he received help nearly 90% of the time; the costs of helping were low. But if the victim bled, those costs rose and helping dwindled to about 60%. Thus costs—both those of helping and those of failure to help—have a major impact on our reactions in emergencies.

The costs of helping. Many researchers have confirmed the negative relationship between helping and costs. In study after study, as the costs of helping decrease, the probability of helping increases. Darley and Latané manipulated costs by making five different requests of pedestrians in New York City. As Table 8-6 shows, many people helped when the request created few costs, but percentages dropped gradually as the costs rose (Darley & Latané, 1970). In the study of the seminary students hurrying to give a lecture on the parable of the good Samaritan, the time pressures created by Batson and his colleagues may have made helping too costly (Batson et al., 1978; Darley & Batson, 1973). Similarly, in a field study conducted in the subways of New York City, subjects were much less likely to help by correcting the inaccurate directions given by one confederate to another confederate when they feared personal injury or embarrassment (Allen, 1970; see also Borofsky, Stollak, & Messé, 1971; Clark, 1976; McGovern, 1976; Midlarsky & Midlarsky, 1973).

TABLE 8–6

The negative relationship between helping and the costs of helping.

Request	Number of People Asked	Percentage that Helped
"Excuse me, I wonder if you could . . .		
(a) tell me what time it is?"	92	85%
(b) tell me how to get to Times Square?"	90	84
(c) give me change for a quarter?"	90	73
(d) tell me what your name is?"	277	39
(e) give me a dime?"	284	34

SOURCE: Darley & Latané, 1970.

The costs of failure to help. The cost–reward model focuses primarily on the costs of intervention, but in some cases the costs of *failure* to help must also be considered. According to the Piliavins, once bystanders ask themselves, "What are the costs and rewards that I might receive if I help?" they then ask, "What are the costs for me if the victim doesn't receive any help?" (Piliavin & Piliavin, 1972; Piliavin et al., 1981). If you saw a man collapse on the subway and did not help, you might continue to worry about him. You might also feel ashamed and guilty for not helping, and if other people found out about your failure, they might criticize you. In some cities and countries, you can even be convicted of a crime for failure to help. All of these costs of failure to help—empathic worry, shame and guilt, public censure, and prosecution—may combine to prompt you to help.

The cost–reward model, which was recently revised and extended (Piliavin et al., 1981), proposes that the costs of not helping have the greatest impact on bystanders when their personal costs for helping are relatively low. In a test of this assumption, researchers claiming to represent Handicapped Student Services asked college students if they would be willing to serve as a reader for a blind student who had been injured in an automobile accident. To manipulate costs, half of the subjects were told that the blind student was hospitalized in a community clinic several miles from campus, while others were told that the student was in the campus health center. To vary the costs of not helping further, half of the subjects were informed that the student had three major exams in the next week (the costs of failure to help were high) or that he just needed to keep up with his assignments (the costs of failure to help were low). As Figure 8-8 shows, twice as many subjects helped when the costs

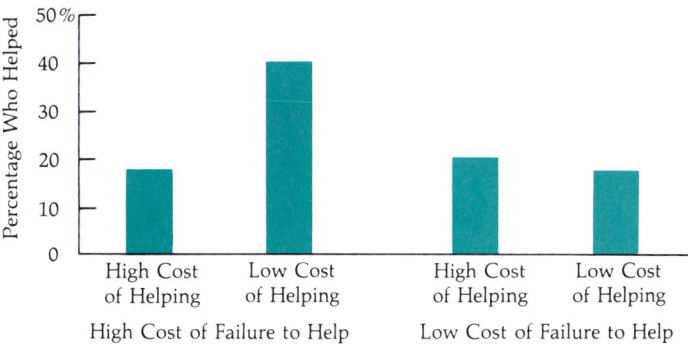

Figure 8-8 Low costs of helping + High costs of failure to help = Helping. These findings support the two basic assumptions of the cost-reward model: First, if the costs of helping are high (subjects have to travel a significant distance to help), people are unlikely to help. Second, provided the costs of helping are low, people are more likely to help if the costs of failure to help are high (the victim's need is great).

of helping were low and the costs of failure to help were high (Clark, 1976: Experiment 2; Piliavin et al., 1981, review other studies that have yielded similar findings).

Helping and Emotions

Both the Latané and Darley decision model and the cost–reward model proposed by Piliavin and her colleagues describe rational bystanders who calmly make decisions and calculate costs and rewards before deciding to help. However, bystanders sometimes ignore their own costs and intervene in very dangerous situations (see Focus 8-5). Indeed, each year the Carnegie Hero Fund Commission honors people who ignore costs as they risk their lives to save others. Consider these cases: David S. Bradford died while trying to save a friend who was drowning; Everett W. Snow was severely burned when he pulled a woman from a burning car; Carl W. Edwards, Jr., was repeatedly stabbed when he prevented the mugging of an elderly man; Edward Franklin Felch and Patrick Joseph McCabe, civilians employed at the Portsmouth Naval Shipyard, saved the life of a sailor who was being asphyxiated by a freon gas leak aboard the U.S.S. *Jack*, but McCabe died as a result ("Carnegie Fund," 1984). What inner forces could have motivated these bystanders to ignore the danger and help?

To answer this question, try to remember the way you felt the last time you witnessed a crisis or emergency: a minor automobile accident, a stranger stumbling on an uneven sidewalk, a child lost in a shopping mall, or even a fictional accident depicted in a television show or movie. Ignore your behavior for a moment and focus only on your feelings. How did you react emotionally when you saw someone else in need?

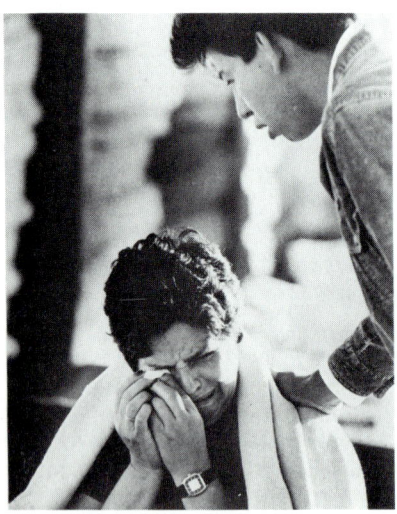

Helping is an emotional response. When we see another person suffering, we often experience intense emotions ourselves. These emotions may prompt us to render aid to the sufferer.

In accordance with an attributional model of emotions (see "In Depth: Attributions and Emotions," in Chapter 4), your emotional reactions may have followed the path outlined in Figure 8-9. First, witnessing another person in need or distress usually causes an increase in general arousal. Your heart beats faster and your blood pressure increases, leaving you

---

FOCUS 8-5

A Closer Look: *When do bystanders engage in impulsive helping?*

The cost–reward model emphasizes the rational side of helping. Its developers admit, however, that people sometimes engage in *impulsive helping*—"rapid, impulsive, noncalculative, 'irrational' helping" behavior—without "going through any very involved conscious decision process" (Piliavin et al., 1981, p. 161). Consider the reactions of subjects in a study conducted by Russell D. Clark and Larry E. Word (1974, Experiment 1). These researchers had found (1972) that virtually all bystanders helped in unambiguous emergencies. To extend these findings, they decided to see if people would be as helpful if the emergency posed a threat to their own well-being. Bystanders-to-be were recruited for the study on the pretense that the researchers were validating a brief paper-and-pencil test of mental ability. As they left the building after their testing session, subjects had to pass by a room filled with complex electrical gadgets and signs reading "Danger: High Voltage." Just as they reached the door of the room, the subjects saw an electrician apparently receive a severe electric shock: a bright light flashed, a dull buzzing sound filled the room, the victim cried out in pain, and he knocked over his equipment as he collapsed on the floor.

Four different conditions were created to vary the ambiguity of the emergency as well as the potential costs of helping. In one condition bystanders faced an unambiguously dangerous situation: the victim lay on several wires and his hand was still in contact with the electrical equipment. In a second condition, nonambiguous and nondangerous, the electrician fell away from the wires and equipment. In the remaining two conditions, the emergency was more ambiguous: subjects couldn't see the electrician clearly, and either they heard him moan (moderate ambiguity) or he made no sound (high ambiguity).

In the nonambiguous situations, the amount of helping was impressive; 53 of the 54 subjects intervened by either directly assisting the confederate or locating others who could help. In contrast, only about 40% of the subjects helped when the emergency was ambiguous. Furthermore, had the electrocution been real, many of the helpful bystanders would have died. Even when they faced a deadly emergency—an unconscious victim still clutching live wires—many subjects grabbed the confederate by his feet and pulled him away from the wires. During a subsequent interview they admitted their mistake, but explained that "at the time they acted so quickly that no consideration was given to the possible harm involved" (Clark & Word, 1974, p. 286). Lastly, and in contrast to the usually observed bystander effect, helping didn't decrease when the subjects witnessed the accident in pairs rather than singly.

How did the subjects react to this stressful experience? Because of the nature of the emergency, Clark and Word carefully debriefed all the subjects in their study. The majority were upset by the experience, but nearly all of them felt better after a thorough discussion of the study. Furthermore, over 90% of the subjects agreed that the research was very valuable, both immediately after their experience and several months later.

Piliavin and her colleagues (1981) believe that arousal is the key to understanding impulsive helping. After reviewing nearly two dozen experimental studies of helping, they note that rapid helping generally occurs when the emergency is serious and the victim's injuries worsen with each passing second. In these situations, the bystanders become so emotionally aroused that they ignore costs and plunge into the dangerous situation.

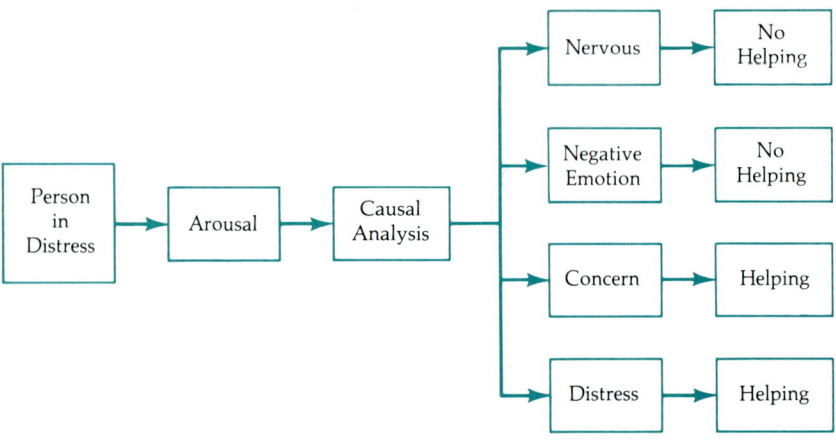

Figure 8-9 An emotion-based model of helping. When we see others in need, we become aroused. To interpret our arousal, we engage in an intuitive attributional analysis of the setting. Depending on the results of this causal analysis, we then experience emotions that either facilitate or inhibit helping.

feeling somewhat stimulated, energized, and possibly tense (Krebs & Miller, 1985; Piliavin et al., 1981). Second, you search for a potential cause for the arousal that you are experiencing. At this point in the process, you may attribute your arousal to your concern for the other person, but you may come up with some other explanation. For example, if you decide that the coffee you drank earlier caused your arousal, you may conclude that you have caffeine jitters. Third, depending on the results of your attribution search, you label your emotion and make a decision about helping. Some emotional reactions, such as *nervousness* or *anger*, will inhibit helping. Others, such as *concern* or *distress*, will increase the likelihood of helping. These various types of emotional reactions are summarized in Figure 8-9 and examined in detail below.

Misattribution inhibits helping. As the model shown in Figure 8-9 predicts, if bystanders attribute their arousal to some extraneous factor, helping is inhibited. Samuel L. Gaertner and John F. Dovidio (1977) examined this *misattribution process* by giving inert pills (placebos) to subjects. The subjects were told that the drugs would improve their performance on a laboratory task, but they could possibly cause a few side effects. Some subjects were told that the pills might increase their heart rate (arousal) and others were told that the pills might give them a headache (nonarousal). Next, while working on the task, the subjects overheard a stack of chairs fall on a woman in the next room. When Gaertner and Dovidio examined the subjects' heart rates and the length of time they waited before helping, they discovered dramatic support for the attributional model. To simplify somewhat, increases in heart rate and speed in helping were positively correlated: people who helped immediately were much more aroused than subjects who were slow to help. Furthermore, subjects who thought they had taken an arousing pill were slower to help than those who took the nonarousing pill; they apparently attributed their physiological state to the pill rather than to the victim's plight. (See Coke, Batson, & McDavis, 1978; Harris & Huang, 1973.)

Attributions can inhibit helping. Even when bystanders attribute their arousal to the victim's misfortune, they may not help. Instead of experiencing an emotion that prompts helping—such as sympathy, pity, empathy, or concern—the onlooker may experience a *negative emotional reaction*, such as anger, disgust, blame, or even hatred. Consider two bystanders who pass by an elderly man lying in a doorway on a cold winter night. The first bystander becomes aroused by the man's plight until she spies an empty wine bottle by his side. Then she thinks: "A drunk. It's his own fault if he freezes to death out here. I won't help." The second passerby, also aroused, thinks: "He's homeless, one of the city's victims. He needs my help." The first bystander refuses to help because she attributes his misfortune to factors within the victim's control. She experiences anger and disgust rather than pity and concern. The second bystander, in contrast, intervenes, for he attributes the victim's problem to factors beyond his control. As this example suggests, if bystanders attribute the victim's problem to an internal, controllable cause, such as lack of effort, poor planning, or bad judgment, then they are unlikely to help. If, in contrast, they attribute the victim's problem to external, uncontrollable factors, then the likelihood of helping is much greater (Meyer & Mulherin, 1980; Weiner, 1980a, 1980b).

Empathy increases helping. A college professor is talking with a student in her office. The student, while pleading with the teacher for postponement of an upcoming test, begins to cry. Reacting to the student's distress, the professor becomes aroused, and attributes this reaction to the student's distress. The teacher helps the student by postponing the test.

Daniel Batson and his colleagues believe that two different motivations may underly the teacher's behavior. First, the teacher may help simply in order to reduce her own personal distress. When she sees the student cry, she, too, feels upset. To erase this distress, she helps the student. Batson describes this reason for helping as *egoistic motivation*, since it is self-serving; this form of helping helps the helper feel better. In contrast, the teacher's behavior may be motivated by *empathy*—an altruistic desire to reduce the distress of the person in need. Unlike the egoistic helper, the empathic altruistic helper is other-serving, for her primary goal is to help the student through the crisis (Batson & Coke, 1981; Batson et al., 1981, 1983; Coke, Batson, & McDavis, 1978; Toi & Batson, 1982).

These two motivations lead to two qualitatively distinct emotional reactions (see Table 8-7). Empathic bystanders describe themselves as concerned, softhearted, compassionate, sympathetic, and moved. Distressed bystanders, in contrast, feel alarmed, grieved, upset, worried, disturbed, or perturbed (Batson et al., 1983). More important, people who experience empathy tend to be more helpful than those who feel personal distress. In a number of studies Batson and his colleagues have shown that bystanders who are told to "imagine how the victim feels" are more helpful than people who are told simply to "observe the situation" (Coke, Batson, & McDavis, 1978; Toi & Batson, 1982). Helpful people are often higher than nonhelpers in *dispositional empathy*—a generalized tendency to take the perspective of other people (Archer et al., 1981; see also Archer, 1984; Batson, Coke, & Pych, 1983). Empathy may also explain why helping behavior steadily increases with age during the first fifteen years of life. Because younger children have not yet developed the cognitive skills needed to take the perspective of another person, they lack the empathic orientation needed for altruistic motivation (Bar-tal, Sharabany, & Raviv, 1982; see Focus 8-6).

Moods and Helping

Emotions play an important role in determining our reactions to emergencies. If we misattribute our arousal to some irrelevant factor or if we blame victims' misfortunes on factors they should have controlled, then we probably won't help. If, however, we feel that our arousal is caused by the other person's distress, then we will probably help. Furthermore, our helping may be motivated by at least two distinct emotional processes: (1) personal distress, which is an egoistic desire to reduce our own anxiety, and (2) empathy, which is an altruistic desire to reduce the other person's suffering.

TABLE 8 – 7

Two emotions mediating helping: empathy and personal distress.

	Empathy	*Personal Distress*
Description	A state in which one experiences the emotions of a person in distress	A state of mental strain experienced at the sight of a person in difficulty
Emotional response	Concern, compassion, sympathy	Alarm, grief, upset, worry, disturbance, perturbation
Type of motivation	An altruistic desire to help another person	An egoistic desire to ease one's own distress

But what about our moods? When we are in a good mood—when things are going well for us and our prospects seem rosy—are we more helpful? And when we get up on the wrong side of the bed, do we take our bad mood out on others by refusing to help them?

Happiness heightens helping. You need a favor. You want to borrow some money from Frank to pay an overdue bill. You missed a class, and you need to borrow some notes from June before the next exam. You want to take a day off from work next week, but you need to get the boss's permission. What is the best time to ask for your favor? (See Figure 8-10.)

Social-psychological research supports the wisdom of the wait-for-a-good-mood ploy. Challenge Frank to a game of tennis, and lose. While he is basking in the "warm glow of success" that follows victory, ask for the favor (Isen, 1970). Don't ask June for her notes on a rainy day. Wait

---

FOCUS 8 – 6

Applying Social Psychology: *Can people become addicted to giving blood?*

What do people receive in return for the blood they donate to community blood banks? Most of these community agencies do not use a credit system, whereby each donor is guaranteed a proportionate amount of blood in the future. Nor do they offer payment of any sort. Instead, giving blood seems to involve only costs: lost time, a little pain, weakness, perhaps even nausea. Moreover, blood donors usually can't be motivated by empathy: they are donating blood to a community agency, so there is no specific victim to empathize with. So why do people donate blood?

Jane Piliavin, Peter L. Callero, and Dorcas E. Evans (1982) believe that many factors prompt people to donate blood the first time: social pressure, guilt, curiosity, embarrassment, shame, whim, and so on. Once they give blood, however, a cycle of strong emotional reactions can create an "addiction" to donating blood. This cycle is best explained by an **opponent process theory** of emotions. According to this model, whenever we experience a positive or negative emotion, after a short period of time we also begin to experience the opposing emotional reaction. If, for example, we discover we have won a million dollars, we will feel happy. However, our emotions will gradually become more neutral as sadder emotions develop that oppose our happiness. The same opponent process occurs if we experience a tragedy. According to the opponent process model, this system works to keep our emotions from becoming too positive or too negative (Solomon, 1980; Solomon & Corbit, 1974).

Piliavin and her colleagues believe that the experience of giving blood initially creates very negative emotions, which soon give rise to positive emotions. As a result, people may become addicted to the pleasure they experience when they give blood. To test their model, Piliavin, Callero, and Evans asked 1,846 donors to complete a questionnaire before and after they gave blood. On the pretest, people who were giving blood for the first time described themselves as uptight, dubious, fearful, skeptical, jittery, regretful, suspicious, angry, defiant, and rebellious. After giving blood, however, they described themselves as relieved, relaxed, self-satisfied, warmhearted, carefree, playful, self-centered, and even egoistic. Moreover, the more times they had given blood, the less intense were their negative feelings. With each visit they experienced less anxiety, but their positive emotions remained strong. For most people, the magic number of visits was four: by the time people had donated blood four times, their positive feelings were so much stronger than their negative ones that they became hooked.

Figure 8-10   Dagwood capitalizes on the "warm glow of success" that follows victory.
© 1985 by King Features Syndicate, Inc. Reprinted by permission.

until the sun is shining; people are usually in a better mood when the weather is pleasant (Cunningham, 1979). Catch the boss just after lunch when she is relaxed and contented (Isen & Levin, 1972). In dozens of studies, researchers have found that momentary happiness heightens helping. After subjects think happy thoughts, receive positive feedback about their skills, find money in phone booths, win games, receive free samples, view pretty pictures, listen to good news, soothing music, or a Steve Martin record, or eat cookies, they become more helpful (Cunningham, Steinberg, & Grev, 1980; Fried & Berkowitz, 1979; Isen, 1970; Isen, Clark, & Schwartz, 1976; Isen, Horn, & Rosenhan, 1973; Isen & Levin, 1972; Manucia, Baumann, & Cialdini, 1984; Moore, Underwood, & Rosenhan, 1973; Veitch, De Wood, & Bosko, 1977; Weyant, 1978; Wilson, 1981; Yinon & Bizman, 1980). A good mood apparently initiates a "loop" of positive thoughts and feelings, which sets the stage for prosocial behaviors (Isen et al., 1978).

Before you rush out and take advantage of the "feel good–do good" effect, be sure to consider these two important limitations. First, if your request is too troublesome, a good mood will not improve your chances of getting help. People try to maintain their good moods, so they probably won't grant your favor if it is too unpleasant (Isen & Simmonds, 1978). Second, make your request for help soon after their happiness-inducing experience, or the good mood may fade away. Immediately after the subjects in one study were given a free sample of stationery, they received a telephone call asking them to relay a message. Helpfulness (and helping) peaked after three or four minutes, then quickly dropped to a very low level (Isen, Clark, & Schwartz, 1976).

Negative moods and helping.   The relationship between bad moods and helping is more complex, and more intriguing as well. Initially, some investigators found that people who were depressed, sad, or unhappy were unlikely helpers. If asked to do a favor or donate to charity, they refused. Other researchers, however, confirmed a "feel bad–do good" phenomenon. Unhappy subjects—people who had just failed a test, seen a stranger receive shocks, reminisced about negative experiences, or imagined a close friend dying of cancer—tended to be *more* helpful (Rosenhan et al., 1981).

Did these researchers, faced with such contradictory findings, give up their attempt to understand the impact of bad moods on helping? Hardly. Rising to meet the challenge posed by these inconsistencies, investigators searched for an overarching explanation that would predict when a bad mood increases or decreases helpfulness. The **negative state relief model** offers one explanation. According to Robert Cialdini and his colleagues, when people are unhappy, they often take steps to change their bad mood into a good mood. Furthermore, having learned that helping others is pleasant and satisfying, sad people sometimes use helping to relieve their sadness (Baumann, Cialdini, & Kenrick, 1981; Cialdini, Darby, & Vincent, 1973; Cialdini & Kenrick, 1976; Manucia, Baumann, & Cialdini, 1984).

Cialdini predicts that people who are in a bad mood will usually help others, for by doing so they help themselves. The model also predicts, however, that sad people will not help if their actions won't make them feel any better. Young children who haven't yet learned that one of the greatest pleasures in life comes from doing for others rather than for oneself don't become more helpful when unhappy; they don't consider helping to be a viable method for achieving relief from their sadness (Moore, Underwood, & Rosenhan, 1973; Rosenhan, Underwood, & Moore, 1974). Sorrowful adults who receive some unexpected money or praise just before a request for help aren't particularly helpful; they have already gained relief from their unhappiness through other means (Cialdini, Darby, & Vincent, 1973). If people believe that their bad mood is highly resistant to change, they won't help; why should they help if such actions won't improve their mood (Manucia, Baumann, & Cialdini, 1984)? And if people are more concerned with their own problems than with those of the other person, then once more they aren't particularly helpful. When bystanders' attention is focused on themselves, they tend to think: "I'm the one who needs help!" (Thompson, Cowan, & Rosenhan, 1980). Thus the negative relief state model predicts that in most cases, sad bystanders spell relief H-E-L-P-I-N-G. However, if the helping → happiness route is obscured, blocked, or too long and difficult to follow, then sad bystanders aren't helpful bystanders.

Norms and Helping

We often encounter people who are seeking charitable donations. A telephone caller asks if you want two tickets to a musical jamboree—it's for a good cause, he reminds you. A magazine ad asks you to "adopt" a hungry child overseas—after all, you have plenty to share. An announcer for your local public radio station thanks you for listening, but reminds you to support the station by sending in a donation. In such situations we often help because we feel we ought to; helping is guided by the norms of the situation.

The reciprocity norm.

In many social situations our actions are based on a **reciprocity norm.** Simply stated, this norm enjoins us to pay back in kind what others give to us. If Norman gives you a birthday gift, then you should give him a birthday present, too. If Janet helps you with your studying, then you should help Janet when she has problems. If you give Venita a ride to class one day, you expect Venita to return the favor in the future. If Juan refuses to help you, then you won't help Juan. Applied to helping, the reciprocity norm suggests that we give to repay past favors and to get favors to be returned at some future date.

Robert B. Cialdini (1985) describes how businesses and charities frequently use reciprocity to increase sales and donations. During the 1970s, for example, many public places were patrolled by Hare Krishnas seeking donations. Initially they weren't very successful; their odd appearance repelled passersby, who usually were unwilling to donate anything more than a scowl. In time, however, the Krishnas increased their success by using a you-owe-me-one sales technique. Before asking for a donation, the Krishnas gave the passerby a gift: a book (the *Bhagavad Gita*, for example), a magazine (*Back to Godhead*, for example), or a flower. Having put the passerby in their debt, they then requested a donation. The power of the reciprocity norm is so great that many people complied.

Like seasoned travelers who have learned to refuse the flowers pressed upon them by Krishnas, some people refuse an offer of help in order to avoid incurring a debt that must be paid back in the future. In one study two-person teams were given two tasks to complete. During a practice session, subjects were led to believe that they would have trouble on task 1 unless they received help from their partner. And while some subjects thought that their partner would probably need help to succeed in task 2, others were convinced that their partner could complete the task without their assistance. As anticipated, subjects were more likely to ask their partner for help on task 1 when they thought they could return the favor during task 2. Other studies supplement these findings by suggesting that people who receive help display intensely negative reactions if they cannot reciprocate that help (Greenberg & Shapiro, 1971; see Bar-tal, 1976, for a review).

The equity norm.

Equity is a norm of justice that defines fair and unfair outcomes of relationships. According to the **equity norm,** a relationship is fair if those involved receive from it a return that is proportional to what they have invested in it. The relationship becomes inequitable when what is given fails to match what is received. Applied to helping, equity theory predicts that people who receive relatively more than they have given will try to give up some of their resources in order to reestablish equity. If, for example, Susan feels her salary is too high, she may donate a portion of it to charity. If Pete can't pay his share of the rent one month, he may feel compelled to do small favors for his roommates (Adams, 1965; Walster, Walster, & Berscheid, 1978).

Equity theory predicts not only when people will help but also the reactions of the recipients of aid (see Figure 8-11). Although we often naively assume that other people want help and will react favorably when it is given, help is a mixed blessing (Fisher, Nadler, & Whitcher-Alagna, 1982). Certainly in some cases, people appreciate receiving help because they feel that, given their inputs and outcomes, they deserve that help. When a wife helps her husband bring in the groceries, for example, he appreciates the help because he has already contributed by going to the store. In other cases, however, helping disrupts the equity of a relationship. When people are given more than they feel they deserve, they feel so uncomfortable that they will try to restore equity in one of two ways: by altering what they put into and take out of the relationship (actual equity) or by distorting their perceptions of these inputs and outcomes (psychological equity). Thus help can lead to a range of negative consequences, including (1) a drop in self-esteem, (2) derogation of the source of help (ingratitude), and (3) exaggeration of one's own misfortunes (see Fisher, DePaulo, & Nadler, 1981, for a review).

Figure 8-11 Why don't they like us? Americans often wonder why the people of other countries that receive substantial aid from the United States display so little gratitude. One explanation relies on the norm of equity. Because recipients of U.S. aid sometimes feel that they have no way of reciprocating the favor and that the United States has some ulterior motive for its help (such as the expectation of military cooperation in the future), they react by derogating the source of the help.

The social responsibility norm. When others depend on us to help them and we know that they cannot reciprocate our help, the **social responsibility norm** shapes our actions. According to this norm, helping people who are in need—the sick, the infirm, the very young, the injured—is a duty that should not be shirked.

The norm of social responsibility explains a curious reaction displayed by some helpers. Kidney donors, for example, despite the medical risks and pain, frequently downplay their own valor (Fellner & Marshall, 1981). The statement of this 60-year-old woman is typical: "People say to me: what a brave thing to do. I say, there was no bravery connected. It was just a thing I had to do" (p. 357). Similarly, an 18-year-old man who donated a kidney to his brother stated: "Some say I'm a very brave person, but bravery had nothing to do with it. Others say I must love my brother a lot, but it seemed like the thing to do at the time" (p. 362). Time and again, donors explain that they simply "had to do it"; the norm of social responsibility compelled them.

The norm of social responsibility doesn't always influence our actions; on occasion we just don't feel obliged to help someone in need. This norm becomes more potent, however, when we feel that the victim is dependent on us. In one study of dependency between the helper and the victim, college students worked in pairs on a simulated industrial task. One subject was assigned the role of worker while the other was to act as supervisor. The researchers created high dependency by telling the workers that the supervisor could win a prize if the people they supervised were highly productive. Although the workers themselves couldn't receive a prize, they still worked harder if their supervisor's outcome depended on their efforts (see Berkowitz, 1972).

The norm of social responsibility also becomes stronger when the victim can't be held responsible for creating his or her problem, when other people model compliance with the norm, and when bystanders are explicitly reminded that helping others is a duty (Berkowitz, 1972; Berkowitz & Connor, 1966; Berkowitz & Daniels, 1963; Berkowitz, Klanderman, & Harris, 1964; Bryan & Davenport, 1968; Paulus, Shaffer, & Downing, 1977). Consider the plight of the Joneses, whose son was striken with cystinosis, a kidney disorder. When their son's kidneys failed, both parents volunteered to be donors, but only the father's kidney was found to be suitable, so he was the donor. Several years later, the son required another kidney. Now his brother volunteered, explaining, "It was no big deal."

The son's willingness to be a donor can be explained through reference to the norm of social responsibility. First, dependency was high: his brother would die without a new kidney. Second, his brother's plight was caused by factors that were beyond his control: he couldn't be blamed for the disease. Third, the mother and father both served as models for helping behavior. Fourth, the family was quite religious, and frequently noted the importance of helping others in need. Hence the son helped (Fellner & Marshall, 1981).

Personal norms. Norms of reciprocity, equity, and social responsibility provide general standards for behavior, but our own personal values and beliefs also guide our actions. For example, person X always stops when he sees a disabled car at the roadside. Person Y never stops to assist stranded motorists, but she regularly donates blood. And person Z doesn't give blood, but she canvasses for the March of Dimes. X, Y, and Z all help, but in ways that are consistent with their own personal norms. X's actions are based on the norm "I should stop to help people who have car trouble"; Y believes "I should donate blood"; and Z feels obligated to raise funds for worthwhile charities. As these examples show, **personal norms** are "situated, self-based standards for specific behavior generated from internalized values" (Schwartz & Howard, 1981, p. 192).

Studies conducted by Shalom Schwartz and his colleagues have repeatedly demonstrated the impact of personal norms on helping (Schwartz, 1968, 1970, 1974, 1977; Schwartz & Fleishman, 1978; Schwartz & Howard, 1980, 1981). Several studies have measured subjects' specific personal norms concerning various actions (such as giving blood, tutoring blind children, and donating bone marrow) and their subsequent willingness to engage in those actions. As expected, people who strongly endorsed a personal norm pertaining to the action were far more likely actually to help in the particular situation. The link between personal norms and helping became even stronger when other variables, such as the tendency to take responsibility for others and awareness of the consequences of one's actions to others, were taken into account (see Schwartz & Howard, 1982).

Models of Helping: A Look Back

To appreciate a beautiful work of art, people often study it from many different perspectives. Similarly, to understand the causes of prosocial behavior, researchers have examined helping from several different theoretical perspectives. First, some look at bystanders as *decision makers*, who help only if all the conditions necessary for intervention are met. Others cast helpers in the role of *cost calculators*, who help others when the costs are low and the rewards are high. A third perspective views bystanders as *emotional attributors*, who seek the causes of their arousal. A fourth view underscores the link between mood and reactions to others, for we are often *happy helpers*. Last, bystanders are *norm followers*, whose offers of help depend on the social rules salient in the setting.

To consider how each view adds to our understanding of helping, let us return to Queens, New York, on March 13, 1964. Why did no one help Kitty Genovese? Some bystanders may have decided that help was unnecessary. Many of her neighbors noticed that something was happening, but only a few thought that they were witnessing an emergency. And fewer still felt responsible for helping, or identified a way to help. Their decision not to help may also have been influenced by the lack of rewards for intervening, and by the high cost of getting involved in another person's problem.

But this view leaves out the emotional and normative side of helping. Many of the bystanders were aroused by the incident, yet they felt no personal concern or distress. Instead, their emotions were more negative. Roused from sleep by noise in the street, they blamed Ms. Genovese for her troubles. Moreover, helping offered them no respite from their bad mood. And what of the norms of the setting? Did they owe Ms. Genovese their help? Would equity be served by a call to the police? Did they feel that it was their personal or social duty to help Ms. Genovese? Apparently not. Norms can encourage helping, but they can discourage it as well.

These factors dispel some of the mystery surrounding Kitty Genovese's death, for they explain the nature of the forces that immobilized the bystanders. They also suggest practical advice should you ever find yourself in need of help. You must "devictimize" yourself. Force the bystanders to make the right decisions. Make the costs of failure to help too great to ignore. Create feelings of empathy in those who are watching. Make it clear that they will feel better if they help. And emphasize the norms that require them to help.

Robert B. Cialdini explains how he once used these methods to gain help when he was involved in an automobile accident. Dizzy after the collision, he watched as cars drove by without stopping. Cialdini writes:

> I remember thinking, "Oh no, it's happening just like the research says. They're all passing by!" I consider it fortunate that as a social psychologist, I knew exactly what to do. Pulling myself up so I could be seen clearly, I pointed at the driver of one car: "Call the police." To a second and third driver, pointing directly each time: "Pull over, we need help." The responses of these people were instantaneous. They summoned a police car and ambulance immediately, they used their handkerchiefs to blot the blood from my face, they put a jacket under my head, they volunteered to serve as witnesses to the accident; one even offered to ride with me to the hospital. [Cialdini, 1985, p. 118]

By destroying the situational factors that inhibit helping, Cialdini was able to secure the help he needed. It is tragic that Kitty Genovese could not achieve the same goal.

■ Summary

In contrast to harmful, antisocial actions, **prosocial behaviors** benefit other people. Prosocial behavior takes many forms, including cooperation, donations to others, sympathy, and aid in emergencies. People engage in prosocial behavior for many reasons. Some prosocial actions may qualify as **altruism,** for the helper is motivated solely by the other person's need. In other instances, helping may be based on selfish motives. Since helpers' motives are difficult to assess, researchers concentrate on **helping behavior** per se—rendering aid to another, no matter what the reason.

When will people help others? Evidence indicates that helping depends on the nature of the situation and the characteristics of the helper and the victim. Dozens of studies have confirmed the **bystander effect:** people are less likely to help in groups than when they are alone. The tragic case of Kitty Genovese illustrates the bystander effect. Even though 38 people witnessed the attack, no one helped her escape her assailant. In explaining this incident, researchers have found that people in groups sometimes experience a reduction in personal responsibility (diffusion of responsibility), misinterpret others' failure to act as evidence that no help is needed (informational influence), become fearful that they will embarrass themselves (evaluation apprehension), and worry that other bystanders will think they caused the victim's misfortune (confusion of responsibility). In some situations, such as unambiguous emergencies and accidents in small communities, these processes are not so powerful. As a result, helping is much more likely.

Our reaction to another person's need for help is also influenced by the victim's characteristics and our own personal qualities. People who possess socially desirable attributes, such as physical beauty, tend to be helped more than less attractive people. So do people who seem to be similar to us in some way (the **similarity-helping effect**). Also, the sexes often react differently in helping situations: women receive more help than men and men render more aid than women. These differences are probably due to sex-role socialization, for women who are androgynous are as helpful as men. Last, personality traits often interact with situational factors to determine helping.

Why do people help other people? According to Latané and Darley's decision model, helping involves five basic steps: noticing the event, interpreting the event as an emergency, taking responsibility, identifying a way to help, and implementing the chosen form of help. A negative decision at any of these steps will prevent a helpful response. Bystanders may also calculate the costs and rewards associated with helping and failure to help. As the **cost–reward model** predicts, in most emergencies people are least likely to help when the cost of doing so is high. Helping is most likely to occur when its cost is low *and* the cost of failure to help is high.

In rare instances, individuals engage in impulsive helping: they ignore personal costs and render aid in dangerous emergencies. Many researchers believe that this form of helping is motivated by emotional arousal. According to this view, when we see others in need, we become physiologically aroused. If we misattribute our arousal to some irrelevant factor, such as our nervousness, then we will not help. Helping is also unlikely when we assign a negative label to our emotion, such as *anger* or *disgust*. Helping becomes more likely when we realize that our arousal is caused by our concern for the other person. In some cases, we may help simply in order to reduce our personal distress (*egoistic* helping). In contrast, we may help because we want to reduce the other person's distress (*empathic* helping). Routine forms of helping, such as donating blood, may also be maintained by the strong positive emotions that arise to oppose the negative emotions associated with the action (the **opponent process theory**). Moods also play a role in producing helping behavior. We tend to be more helpful when we are in a good mood, though bad moods *sometimes* increase the tendency to help. As the **negative state relief model** explains, if we feel that helping others will provide relief from our negative mood, then we tend to help.

Our decision to help another person may also be influenced by a desire to conform to the norms of the situation. These norms include:

1. The **reciprocity norm:** individuals help when they feel they owe others help in repayment for some past assistance.
2. The **equity norm:** help is more likely when individuals feel they have received more than their fair share of rewards from a relationship. People often refrain from helping or refuse to accept help because such assistance will upset the balance of equity in the social relationship.
3. The **social responsibility norm:** individuals render aid because they believe that helping others who are in need is a fundamental social duty.
4. **Personal norms:** some individuals develop their own private values and beliefs about how they should respond to others who are in need.

■ For More Information

1. *Sociobiology and Behavior,* by David P. Barash (1982), provides a textbook overview of sociobiology's theoretical assumptions and empirical findings. Several chapters are devoted to the genetic underpinnings of altruistic actions.

2. *New Directions in Helping: Help-Seeking,* edited by Bella M. DePaulo, Arie Nadler, and Jeffrey D. Fisher (1983), looks at the other side of helping by examining how the person who needs help reacts when help is given and the factors that prompt individuals to seek out help.

3. *Cooperation and Helping Behavior,* edited by Valerian J. Derlega and Janusz Grzelak (1982), contains chapters written by leading experts in prosocial behavior. Many of the chapters deal with altruism and helping behavior; others explore such related issues as cooperation, social traps, and the justice motive.

4. *Morality, Moral Behavior, and Moral Development*, edited by William M. Kurtines and Jacob L. Gewirtz (1984), deals with morality and moral action. This advanced text illustrates the complexities involved in the attempt to predict moral behaviors—such as helping others—on the basis of personality characteristics.

5. *Emergency Intervention*, by Jane A. Piliavin, John F. Dovidio, Samuel L. Gaertner, and Russell D. Clark III (1981), presents an overall framework for understanding helping behavior. The importance of costs and rewards is highlighted, but other variables—such as the number of bystanders present and emotional arousal—are also considered. An excellent resource for the serious student of helping behavior.

6. *Altruism and Helping Behavior*, edited by J. Philippe Rushton and Richard M. Sorrentino (1981), is a collection of original theoretical statements and empirical reviews of the burgeoning literature dealing with helping behavior. The book contains sections dealing with the development of altruism in children, emotional mediators of helping behavior, individual differences in altruism, and reactions to being helped.

7. "The Distinction between Sympathy and Empathy: To Call Forth a Concept, a Word is Needed," by Lauren Wispé (*Journal of Personality and Social Psychology,* 1986), traces the history of the concepts of sympathy and empathy in social psychology. He concludes that helping is more likely to be motivated by sympathy than by empathy.

IN DEPTH

The Sociobiology of Helping

Traditionally, social psychologists have assumed that human social behavior is acquired through experience. We do not instinctively affiliate, help, or harm people; rather, we learn these social behaviors as we mature. Recently, however, an alternative view known as **sociobiology** has emerged to challenge this assumption. Inspired by Charles Darwin's theory of evolution, sociobiology argues that in the last 15 million years the human species has evolved socially as well as physically. Through the process of *natural selection*, individuals who were even slightly predisposed to engage in adaptive social behaviors were the "fittest"—they tended to survive longer and to be more successful in passing their genes along to future generations. Over countless generations, this selection process weeded out individuals who lacked these predispositions, while those who possessed them prospered. Even though these tendencies may not enhance our fitness in today's world, eons spent in harsher environments have left us genetically predisposed to perform certain social behaviors and avoid others (Wilson, 1975).

Evolutionists have long been puzzled by altruistic actions. Ground squirrels, for example, often give alarm calls at the approach of a predator. These calls warn other squirrels to take cover, but they also draw attention to the caller, who is then likely to be killed (Sherman, 1980). Dolphins sometimes stay near an injured dolphin, and will risk their own safety to protect the injured one from a predator (Conner & Norris, 1982). Zebra stallions will attempt to defend colts against attack, even by lions (West Eberhard, 1975). In terms of Darwinian evolution, these actions make no sense. Since altruists expose themselves to greater danger than those who selfishly protect themselves, helping is a disadvantage to personal survival. Individuals who lean toward altruism should be more likely to die than nonaltruists, so their altruistic tendencies cannot be passed on to the next generation. Natural selection should weigh against altruists and favor the selfish individuals who refuse to render aid. So why do animals sometimes engage in altruistic behavior?

The initial solution to this puzzle was offered by the geneticist William D. Hamilton in 1964. Hamilton pointed out that the organism's fundamental goal is not mere survival, or even the survival of its offspring. Rather, the fittest individual is the one that succeeds in passing the maximum number of *genes* on to the next generation. Why, for example, do animals go to all the trouble of breeding and raising offspring? According to Hamilton, parenting is simply an extremely effective means of ensuring the survival of one's genes in a future generation. Caring for offspring may seem self-sacrificing, but these actions are prompted by the gene's "selfish" tendency to seek survival at all costs. Even if the parent perishes while protecting its young, its genes will continue to flourish in its offspring. Thus Hamilton reinterpreted Darwin's famous phrase "the survival of the fittest." To Darwin, the fittest animal is the one that can survive longest. To Hamilton, the fittest animal is the one that maximizes the survival of its genes in future generations. This redefined concept of fitness is known as **inclusive fitness** (Hamilton, 1964).

Parenting, however, is not the only way to enhance the survival of one's genes. Because identical copies of one's genes exist in one's relatives, Hamilton reasoned that a truly selfish gene can further enhance its fitness by helping relatives survive. Ground squirrels, for example, tend to give warning calls only when their close relatives are nearby. A dominant macaque monkey will share food with a subordinate monkey only if the two are close relatives. In many species of insects, workers and soldiers labor to protect the egg-laying queen, but they themselves never produce offspring. Hamilton concludes that these actions may seem altruistic, but they are selfish attempts by the genes to enhance their fitness. Individuals who help close relatives may be risking their lives, but they are also increasing the chances that their genes will survive in their relatives. This process is known as *kin selection*—the evolutionary favoring of genes that prompt individuals to help their relatives, or kin (Maynard Smith, 1964).

The concept of kin selection explains why relatives help one another, but it does not account for the good Samaritan—the person who helps a total stranger. The sociobiologist Robert Trivers has recently suggested that this type of helping may be due to *reciprocal altruism*. Imagine that you are standing on a pier when you hear a drowning man call for help. Would you try to save the man by throwing him a life preserver? Kin selection theory says no, for he is not a relative. Trivers, however, predicts that you will help because you may receive a benefit in return. In this situation, the risk to yourself is minimal—you can save the man without harm to yourself. More important, you may benefit in some way through your action. At least, should you need help in the future and this man is nearby, he will be alive to assist you. Thus self-sacrifice can once again be explained in terms of the logic of the selfish gene (Trivers, 1985).

What implications does sociobiology have for understanding altruistic actions performed by humans? First, sociobiology provides a counterpoint to social psychology's emphasis on learning as the sole means of acquiring social behavior. At the surface level, sociobiology's emphasis on the successful projection of genes into future generations seems to apply only to ancient human societies that struggled to survive. In modern society, most of us can be reasonably certain that our genes will survive in our own offspring, so kin selection is less important. Also, even if we help a stranger, he or she will rarely be nearby when we ourselves require help. However, the current era represents a mere instant in the span of evolution. We may be living in cities, buying our food in supermarkets, and improving our health in hospitals, but these changes are all very recent. According to sociobiology, genetically we are still hunters and gatherers, living in small groups and striving to improve our chances of survival. To understand why we help others, we must understand our evolutionary past.

Second, sociobiology takes a surprisingly
(continued)

IN DEPTH *continued*

positive view of human nature. The theory states that humans are helpful by nature. Granted, our helpfulness is selfish at its root, for it results from natural selection's tendency to favor helping genes over nonhelping genes. Regardless of the reason for our helpfulness, however, the fact remains (sociobiology argues) that we are predisposed to help others.

Last, the concepts of kin selection and reciprocal altruism *may* provide insight into the causes of helping among humans. At the present time, sociobiologists have relied primarily on nonexperimental methods to test their hypotheses, and they have concentrated on nonhuman species. These efforts indicate that altruism is much more common among closely related individuals than among strangers. Species that live in social communities with their close relatives are more altruistic than species that disperse themselves over a wide area. Also, help between unrelated individuals is greatest in social, gregarious species, for only animals that live in groups will have the opportunity to benefit from reciprocated altruism (Barash, 1982).

All of these findings may potentially apply to humans as well as nonhumans. Are we more likely to help our own offspring and our relatives than strangers? Are people in rural areas more helpful than those in urban settings because they are more likely to be related to the victim? Are we more likely to help people whom we recognize because we are more certain that these people will reciprocate our help in the future? Is our tendency to become aroused when we see another person in need the result of a genetic predisposition to empathize with others? Because sociobiology offers a relatively new view of behavior, these and many other questions remain unanswered (Cunningham, 1981; Hoffman, 1981; Ridley & Dawkins, 1980).

N I N E

Aggression

What is aggression?
  Defining aggression
    Aggression as action
    Aggression as intentional
    Aggression as harmful and injurious
  Types of aggression and violence
    Irritable versus instrumental aggression
    Legitimate and illegitimate aggression
    Aggression and violence

Origins of aggression
  A psychodynamic perspective
  Ethology
  Sociobiology
  Motivational approaches
    Aggressive cues
    Arousal and aggression
  Social learning theory
    Overall aggressiveness
    Copying
    Desensitization
    Value-shaping
    Television and aggression: A less than final word
  Normative models of aggression
    The norm of reciprocity
    Emergent aggressive norms
    Norms and deindividuation
  Nature and nurture together: An interaction model

Controlling aggression
  Achieving catharsis without aggression
    Does ventilation work?
    Does displacement work?
    Catharsis: A concluding word
  Undoing aggressive motives
    Controlling arousal
    Incompatible responses
    Remembering mitigating circumstances
  Unlearning aggression
    Modeling nonaggression
    Punishing aggression
  Norms and society

Summary
For more information
In depth: Competition and conflict

Bernhard Goetz is a passenger in a New York City subway. Christmas is just three days away, and the cars are crowded with shoppers and commuters. As the train approaches the Chambers Street station in lower Manhattan, four teenagers approach Goetz. In threatening tones, they demand $5. Goetz's answer: "I have $5 for each of you." He then shoots at the young men with a .38-caliber revolver. All four of the youths are injured, and one, 19-year-old James Cabey, is left partially paralyzed. For nine days Goetz remains at large. Then, on New Year's Eve, he walks into a police station in New Hampshire and confesses to the shootings. He refuses money offered by many sources, preferring to arrange his own bail.

Goetz's actions are by no means unique. With an extensive but sinister arsenal of weapons—teeth, fists, clubs, spears, arrows, swords, guns, cannon, bombs, missiles, and nuclear warheads—humans have been injuring other humans for millennia. Goetz's actions flow from a long tradition of violence among the species *Homo sapiens*.

Yet any act of violence, including Goetz's, raises a number of interrelated questions about aggression. We must first ask, "What is aggression?" Although Goetz clearly injured other people, do we want to label his behavior *aggression?* Surveys of public opinion taken in the months that followed the incident revealed that many people approved of Goetz's actions; they argued that he was justified in attacking the youths. Thus, before we delve too deeply into our analysis of aggression, we must ask: how can aggression be defined, and what forms does it take?

Second, consider the causes of the behavior. How can Goetz's action, and violent behaviors in general, be explained? Some people dubbed him the "subway vigilante" and the *"Death Wish* gunman," calling to mind a Charles Bronson-like figure who haunted the subways in search of muggers to punish. Others felt that his actions were instinctive; that anyone, pushed too far by hoodlums, might react with violence. Still others felt that he was motivated by aggressive racist impulses. The young men

Bernhard Goetz, the so-called "subway gunman." What factors could have prompted this man to shoot four young black men while riding a New York City subway?

were armed not with guns but with sharpened screwdrivers, and any violence on their part was implied rather than explicit: they never threatened Goetz directly. They were black, Goetz was white. No matter what the answer, we want to know what causes aggression. To answer this question we shall consider two general approaches to aggression: theories that stress the instinctive causes of aggression and theories that emphasize its social determinants.

Once we understand the causes of aggression, we will turn to the factors that can decrease it. Goetz's actions led to tragedy, for both Goetz and the four young people he injured. Could this incident have been prevented? Can other acts of aggression, which have become so commonplace in recent years, be eliminated? These questions challenge social psychologists to search for ways to stem the rising tide of violence in contemporary society, and their solutions are examined in the final section of this chapter.

■ What Is Aggression?

Intuitively, you know the difference between actions that are aggressive and actions that are not aggressive. If, for example, Goetz had shot an elderly man who asked him for the time of day, you would certainly consider his actions to be aggressive. If, in contrast, he had explained, "I don't have any money to spare" before turning away, then his actions would seem innocent or even polite.

When we stray from such clear cases as these, the distinction between aggressive and nonaggressive actions begins to blur. What if Goetz had given the teenagers the money, but inside had seethed with rage and fantasized about killing each one of them? What if he had pushed one of the young men away, and the youth had fallen and injured his head? And would Goetz still have been aggressive if he had pulled out his gun, but it jammed so that nothing happened when he pulled the trigger? Your answers to these questions depend on how you define aggression (Johnson, 1972).

Defining Aggression

Social psychologists are still searching for a definition of aggression that successfully distinguishes between acts that are aggressive and acts that are not. If pressed to offer a working definition, however, many would agree that **aggression** is an action performed with the deliberate intention of harming or injuring another person. The key elements in this definition are action, intention, and harm (Berkowitz, 1981a; Stang & Wrightsman, 1981).

Aggression as action.
Gail sometimes experiences strong feelings of hate when she thinks about her boss and Ted fantasizes about attacking and murdering his basketball coach. Are Gail and Ted aggressive?

Although these thoughts and emotions are violent, they do not qualify as aggression. Aggression is often accompanied by strong internal states, such as anger and passion, but *aggression* refers to *behavior*. Aggressive acts can be direct, as when Goetz shot the four youths, or indirect, as when mob leaders tell their thugs to "take care of the problem." Aggression can involve overtly harmful actions (shooting someone) or just the threat of such actions (saying, "Get away or I'll shoot"). In all cases, however, aggression is a form of behavior.

Aggression as intentional.
Before charging Goetz with a crime, the prosecutor must ask a number of questions about his intentions. Did Goetz carry his gun with the intention of using it if necessary? Did he intend only to wound the young men, or was he deliberately trying to kill them? People usually call harmdoers aggressive when they *intend* to inflict harm on others. For example, the clumsy passerby who bumps into us on the sidewalk and the dentist who hurts us by drilling our cavities aren't aggressive, even though they may cause us pain. In contrast, assassins who are poor shots are still aggressive when they pull the trigger and miss their victim because they intended to do harm. Aggression happens not by accident but because one individual intends to harm others (Feshbach, 1971; Tedeschi, Smith, & Brown, 1974).

Aggression as harmful and injurious.
Helping behaviors are prosocial—they lead to positive consequences for others. Aggressive behaviors, in contrast, are antisocial—they expose others to *harmful, aversive consequences*. These aversive consequences include both physical harm, as when someone is attacked, raped, or killed, and psychological injury, such as the effects of threats, insults, and shunning. Remember, however,

that victims' reactions to such consequences vary. If an individual enjoys pain, then someone who satisfies this masochistic need may not be acting aggressively. Aggression involves a victim who is an unwilling participant in the interaction; he or she would rather avoid the consequences that the aggressor inflicts (Baron, 1977; see Figure 9-1).

Types of Aggression and Violence

When she learns that she has been passed over for promotion, Mary Lou gets so angry that she shouts insults at her supervisor. The security guard twists the troublemaker's arm behind his back to control him. Frank, while arguing with his wife, strikes her repeatedly on the face and arms.

These actions all qualify as aggression: they are behaviors, they are intentional, and they are harmful. However, they differ from one another in many respects. Mary Lou's actions flow from her anger, while the security guard is using aggression as a means to an end. Also, the guard may be justified in harming the troublemaker: the troublemaker may have threatened him, so he used force in order to protect himself from harm. Frank's actions, however, are both unjust and unlawful.

Irritable versus instrumental aggression.

The call at home plate is very close, and Billy Martin charges out of the dugout to confront the umpire. Thursting his face within a few inches of the umpire's, Martin waves his hands frantically, shouts, and eventually insults the umpire. When the ump yells, "You're out of the game!" Martin kicks dirt all over the umpire's shoes.

In some cases, aggression is stimulated by our anger and distress. Billy Martin may be genuinely upset by the umpire's call; so upset, in fact, that he loses his temper and becomes aggressive. This form of aggression

Figure 9-1 Is this aggression? Your answer depends on your interpretation of the action. To a social psychologist, aggression is any action that is performed with the deliberate intention of harming or injuring another person.

is generally known as *irritable aggression,* or angry, impulsive aggression. In contrast, sly Billy may be using aggression as an instrument to achieve his own ends, for by strategically displaying an aggressive reaction he hopes to influence the umpire and fire up his players. If he is using aggression to control and influence others, then his behavior is termed *instrumental aggression* (Felson, 1978, 1981b; Tedeschi, Melburg, & Rosenfeld, 1981; Tedeschi, Smith, & Brown, 1974).

Legitimate and illegitimate aggression.

The police officer who uses her nightstick to subdue a violent criminal, the executioner who pulls the switch at the electric chair, and the mugging victim who defends himself by shooting his assailants are all behaving aggressively: they are intentionally harming others. Their actions, however, may be viewed as *legitimate aggression:* harmful actions that are justified by the roles they occupy or their need to protect themselves from harm in a dangerous situation (Tedeschi, Smith, & Brown, 1974).

Our assumptions about an action's legitimacy influence the way we react to aggression. Imagine that you are asked to make a judgment about a barroom brawl. According to the witnesses, Jim instigated an argument over a seat that Robert was saving for his girlfriend. After asking, "Are you looking for a shot in the mouth or something?" Jim took a poke at Robert. He missed, but Robert responded with a punch that ended the discussion. When people evaluated Jim and Robert, most felt that Jim was more aggressive, because his actions were illegitimate. Robert was viewed as less aggressive, for he was only reacting in self-defense. Ironically, Robert, the only person who caused any physical harm, was judged more favorably because people felt his actions were legitimate (Brown & Tedeschi, 1976).

Aggression and violence.

Aggression comes in all shapes and sizes. Relatively mild forms of aggression can be seen in a wide variety of situations. At a football game, two inebriated spectators may push each other; in the shopping mall, a mother may swat her child; in traffic, one irate driver may shout at another driver. These types of aggression are as much a part of social life as more positive forms of behavior (see Focus 9-1).

Unfortunately, our social interactions are too frequently racked by more violent forms of aggression. *Criminal violence* consists of harmful, unlawful actions: assault, aggravated assault, rape, attempted murder, and murder itself. According to statistics nearly 3 of every 100 Americans will be victims of violent crime, and the rates are much higher for some segments of the population (Dodge, Lentzner, & Shenk, 1976). In recent years the public has also become increasingly aware of *domestic violence:* child abuse, spouse abuse, abuse of parents. Tragically, the home, so long considered

FOCUS 9–1

Experiencing Social Psychology: *How aggressive are you?*

People vary considerably in their aggressive tendencies. While some of us are hotheads whose anger can quickly turn into physical aggression, others are more prone to engage in verbal aggression. One method of measuring individual differences in aggression is presented below. To complete this inventory, circle the number (either 0 or 1) to the left of each item to indicate either no or yes.

These items measure your tendency to engage in physical and verbal aggression. To calculate your score for physical aggression, add up the numbers you circled for items 1 to 10. As Table 9-1 suggests, the average score on these items (when the questionnaire was originally devised) is 4.2, but any score between 1.8 and 6.6 is typical of nearly two-thirds of all respondents. To calculate your verbal aggression score, add up the numbers for items 11 to 23. Again, Table 9-1 indicates that 7.2 is an average score, and that most people score between 4.6 and 9.8. Note that, at least on these items, men tend to score higher than women (Buss & Durkee, 1957; see also Biaggio, 1980).

TABLE 9–1

Means and ranges of scores for men and women on physical and verbal aggression.

Type of Aggression	Average Score			Standard Range
	Both Sexes	Men	Women	
Physical	4.2	5.1	3.3	1.8–6.6
Verbal	7.2	7.6	6.8	4.6–9.8

No	Yes	
0	1	1. Once in a while I cannot control my urge to harm others.
1	0	2. I can think of no good reason for ever hitting anyone.
0	1	3. If somebody hits me first, I let him have it.
0	1	4. Whoever insults me or my family is asking for a fight.
0	1	5. People who continually pester you are asking for a punch in the nose.
1	0	6. I seldom strike back, even if someone hits me first.
0	1	7. When I really lose my temper, I am capable of slapping someone.
0	1	8. I get into fights about as often as the next person.
0	1	9. If I have to resort to physical violence to defend my rights, I will.
0	1	10. I have known people who pushed me so far that we came to blows.
0	1	11. When I disapprove of my friends' behavior, I let them know it.
0	1	12. I often find myself disagreeing with people.
0	1	13. I can't help getting into arguments when people disagree with me.
0	1	14. I demand that people respect my rights.
1	0	15. Even when my anger is aroused, I don't use strong language.
0	1	16. If somebody annoys me, I am apt to tell him what I think of him.
0	1	17. When people yell at me, I yell back.
0	1	18. When I get mad, I say nasty things.
1	0	19. I could not put someone in his place, even if he needed it.
0	1	20. I often make threats I don't really mean to carry out.
0	1	21. When arguing, I tend to raise my voice.
1	0	22. I generally cover up my poor opinion of others.
1	0	23. I would rather concede a point than get into an argument about it.

a haven in a heartless world, is now recognized as a setting for routine violence. Evidence suggests that aggression is an integral part of growing up in America: 93% of all adults were spanked during childhood, 31% were punched or beaten, and more than 12% report that they were cut with a knife or threatened by a gun (Mulvihill & Tumin, 1969). Conservative estimates indicate that 1.4 to 1.9 million children between the ages of 3 and 17 will be dangerously abused this year; not just spanked or paddled, but kicked, bitten, beaten, knifed, or shot (Gelles, 1980a, 1980b). And about one-quarter of all American wives have been physically abused at least once by their husbands (Straus, Gelles, & Steinmetz, 1980).

Collective violence—aggressive actions perpetrated by groups such as gangs or mobs—is also a significant social problem in many societies. In its most extreme form, collective violence takes an organized and deadly form: warfare. International violence, or the "use of armed force by a state against the sovereignty, territorial integrity or political independence of another state," continues to threaten the survival of the human species (U.N., 1974).

To make matters worse, the sheer amount of violence in society seems to be mounting. During the period from 1960 to 1975, violent crimes in America increased nearly 50 percent (A. P. Goldstein, 1983). Furthermore, two of the most violent crimes of all, forcible rape and aggravated assault, continued to increase into the 1980s. Violence has escalated even in our public schools, for assaults there increased by 85% in the 1970s, and rapes by 40%. Attacks on teachers also rose dramatically, from 15,000 in 1955 to 110,000 in 1980 (Harootunian & Apter, 1983). Some forms of international violence, such as terrorism, are also increasing. According to the CIA, fewer than 200 acts of terrorism occurred in 1968; in 1980, the number of such acts exceeded 800 (Central Intelligence Agency, 1981). These statistics are sobering and they compel us to search for the underlying causes of aggression in human beings.

■ Origins of Aggression

Since the beginning of recorded history, humans have lived with and died by aggression. Estimates suggest that about 2.6 wars have been fought each year for the last 5,600 years, yielding a grand total of 14,560 wars. During the period from 1820 to 1945, about 58 million people died through violence. In this century alone, nearly one million Americans have been murdered.

Why are humans aggressive? For centuries, scholars and scientists answered this question in one of two ways. Some, like the 17th-century philosopher Thomas Hobbes, argued that humans are naturally vicious creatures. Calling our species *Homo lupus*, or human wolf, he believed that we would quickly murder one another if we were not restrained by civilization. In contrast, others accepted John Locke's *tabula rasa* argument: at birth humans are blank slates on which experience leaves impressions; thus we learn to become aggressive.

Current explanations of aggression still resonate with these two arguments. To the *nature* theorists, aggression springs from our instincts. Psychoanalytic theorists, ethologists, and sociobiologists vary considerably in their methods and emphases, but they all trace aggression back to innate biological factors. The *nurture* theorists, in contrast, generally consider aggression to be a product of learning and the social environment. Humans aren't born aggressive, but become so through experience. Motivational models, social learning theory, and normative models take this approach. After reviewing both nature and nurture theories, we will consider how these two approaches may be integrated to explain aggression.

A Psychodynamic Perspective

June and Sandy, two long-time friends, are commiserating over lunch. "Why don't you find a new job?" suggests June when Sandy complains about her work. Sandy snaps, "Don't tell me what to do." June is confused, and tries to explain that she was just making a suggestion. Sandy responds by saying she's sick of having June always try to push her around and control her. June continues her efforts to placate Sandy, but to no avail. The lunch ends when Sandy says, "Drop dead."

Why did Sandy attack June? To Sigmund Freud, her hostility stems from dynamic psychological forces originating within the **unconscious,** a portion of the mind that actively directs actions and thoughts while remaining hidden from conscious awareness. Freud felt that many primitive urges lurk within the unconscious, but he emphasized two above all others: *eros,* the life instinct, and *thanatos,* the death instinct. While eros propels us toward physical pleasures, such as sex, thanatos propels us toward destruction and violence. Sandy's aggression may stem from a deep-seated hostility toward authorities. When others say or do anything that she interprets as an attempt to control her, she strives to resist them both unconsciously and aggressively. Freud would probably trace Sandy's hostility to childhood experiences involving her parents (Freud, 1961).

Freud thought of hostile impulses in hydraulic terms; he felt that aggression builds up in the unconscious like steam in a broiler. If this psychological steam isn't vented from time to time, the strain on the system can cause psychological disorders. Therefore, healthy people discharge these aggressive urges in a process he called **catharsis.** One way to achieve catharsis is through overt aggression. If aggression is directed outward, catharsis involves the injury of others; an inward aim, in contrast, leads to self-injury (depression, suicide, masochism). However, aggressive urges can also be displaced, or redirected, into more acceptable channels. At an unconscious level Sandy may actually be angry with her boss. Since she could not have released this hostility by physically or verbally attacking her boss without endangering her livelihood, she attacked June instead. Freud argued that all of us, without displacement and self-control, would become as violent as the individuals described in Focus 9-2 (Kutash, 1978).

Ethology

Paul and his girlfriend are sleeping in the bedroom of his apartment when the sound of an overturning chair disturbs Paul's sleep. Suddenly he is wide awake. Hearing someone moving about in the living room, he

---

FOCUS 9-2

Applying Social Psychology: *Do severe psychological disturbances cause violent behavior?*

Case 1. A 30-year-old teacher with no criminal record killed a 7-year-old girl selling Brownie cookies door to door. Infuriated when she couldn't change his $20 bill, he forced her into his basement, where he beat her to death. Described by his mother as a "good, gentle son," in psychiatric interviews he displayed a range of psychological problems, including high anxiety and depression (Revitch & Schlesinger, 1978).

Case 2. By the age of 19, he had raped 12 women and killed 5. In most cases he wore a ski mask and was armed with either a knife or a gun. The attacks were quite brutal; several of the rape-murder victims had been stabbed 20 times. The attacks were motivated by anger and hostility rather than sexuality. When arrested and incarcerated, he was diagnosed as sociopathic, with severe problems dealing with authority and domination (Ressler, Burgess, & Douglas, 1985).

Case 3. Deeply depressed and suicidal, 28-year-old Robert Irwin goes to his girlfriend's house; in his confused state, he decides to kill her. While waiting for her, he strangles her mother and sister and stabs a boarder with an icepick. After the third murder he leaves the house, feeling "as calm as I've been in my life before." Several years before, Irwin had been hospitalized for trying to castrate himself, and was classified as "catathymic" (Wertham, 1978, p. 168).

People kill for many reasons. Some are paid assassins. Others kill while committing another crime, while under the influence of alcohol, or in response to provocation. Some criminologists believe that murder is sometimes caused by mental illness or insanity. In the first case described above, the murderer was raised by an extremely protective mother. Even as an adult, he experienced feelings of hostility, sexual confusion, and loneliness. When he failed to keep these unconscious hostile urges in check, he exploded in violence and aggression. Viewed from this perspective, extremely violent crimes occur when hostile impulses run out of control (Revitch & Schlesinger, 1978, p. 155).

The concept of criminal insanity provides an explanation for inexplicable, random violence. Many psychologists and psychiatrists believe that such crimes can be prevented through psychological treatments that help offenders recover from their "illness." It should also be noted, however, that people who commit violent crimes aren't necessarily sick or insane. In fact, some offenders feign psychopathology in order to escape prosecution for their crimes. Furthermore, most individuals who suffer from psychological problems are not violent, and even when a crime is committed by a disturbed person, his or her problems may not stem from the unconscious processes identified by Freud. Freud's psychodynamic perspective is but one explanation of many (Kutash, Kutash, & Schlesinger, 1978; Scully & Marolla, 1984, 1985; Valzelli, 1981).

leaps from the bed. A low growl begins to form in the back of his throat, and he runs to confront the intruder. By the time he reaches the living room, he is armed with a baseball bat and is shouting incoherently. The unarmed burglar barely escapes through the open window.

Freud would argue that Paul's actions were caused by his unconscious aggressive impulses. **Ethology,** the branch of biology devoted to the study of animal behavior in its natural surroundings, offers a different perspective. According to Konrad Lorenz (1966), many behaviors, including aggression, are instinctive. When birds build nests, ducklings follow their mothers, and cats kill mice, they are carrying out built-in orders that were activated by signals in the environment. Like Freud, Lorenz felt that aggressive drives accumulate within the animal and are released if the pressure becomes too great. However, Lorenz also felt that environmental cues often act to release these aggressive drives. For example, male sticklebacks are highly territorial fish, and will drive away other male sticklebacks. They will not attack, however, if the intruding fish does not have a red underbelly. Apparently this attack response is released by the red coloring of the male's underbelly, for the male stickleback will attack even a block of wood if it has a red mark painted on the bottom (Tinbergen, 1951). The violation of our territory—our house, car, or yard—may be sufficient to release human aggression (see Figure 9-2).

Why are some animals genetically programmed to be aggressive? Ethologists believe that aggression is a highly adaptive response in most species. The strongest, most aggressive animals occupy the top positions in the group's social hierarchy (or, to use ethology's term, the "pecking order"). The control they are able to exercise over food, water, shelter, territory, and mating partners increases their chances of survival. Furthermore, aggression prevents overcrowding by keeping the population from outstripping the available resources and ensures protection of the young. Lorenz reasoned that natural selection would cause the extinction of aggressive species if aggression were harmful. The great frequency of aggression in the animal world testifies to its adaptive value.

Figure 9-2 Aggression as territorial defense. Ethologists such as Konrad Lorenz feel that humans, like most other animals, are instinctively aggressive. If our territory is threatened, for example, we react by attacking the invader. The men pictured here are Afghan freedom fighters. They are displaying the weapons they use in their struggle to drive Russian military forces from their homeland.

Carried too far, however, aggression is maladaptive; the very survival of the species would be threatened if too many members were killed. In consequence, Lorenz postulated the existence of instinctive inhibitions against killing. He observed that most aggressive encounters end when one combatant gives up and displays signs of submission to the victor. Humans, however, seem to lack this instinctive inhibition against killing. Our early ancestors were puny, relatively harmless creatures that lacked the brute strength, sharp claws, massive teeth, and strong jaws needed to kill. Therefore, battles between humans rarely ended in death, so inhibitions were seldom necessary. Once humans discovered weapons, however, our ability to kill far outstripped our ability to respond to cues that turn off aggression. In consequence, we became the only animal that systematically murders other members of its own species: we simply don't know when to stop.

FOCUS 9–3

Controversy in Social Psychology: *Are humans the most murderous animals?*

Ethology bemoans the "loathsome cruelty" of humanity (Dart, 1953; Lorenz, 1966). Only humans engage in pitched battles to the death, for we lack the instinctive inhibitions needed to turn off aggression.

Sociobiologists challenge this position. According to the prominent sociobiologist Edward O. Wilson, murder occurs frequently in many species besides *Homo sapiens,* including tigers, lions, langurs, gulls, macaques, gorillas, and most insects. Infanticide—the killing of infants—is very common in many species. Whenever a male langur monkey takes control of another male's harem, he systematically murders all the infants (Hrdy, 1977). Female ground squirrels sometimes murder their neighbor's infants to make room for their own offspring. Hyenas are habitual cannibals as well, and if the mothers don't protect their young, they are eaten by adults. Conflicts between adults can also end in the death of one of the combatants. When two hyena clans fought over a carcass, for example, the victorious group was not satisfied when the losing group fled. The hyenas chased down the slowest member of the retreating group and killed him. The attackers "bit him wherever they could—especially in the belly, the feet, and the ears. The victim was completely covered by his attackers, who proceeded to maul him for about 10 minutes." The victim was eventually "pulled apart" and eaten by the other hyenas (Kruuk, 1972).

Wilson believes that if an unbiased observer from Mars came to visit Earth and studied humans as just one more animal species, the Martian would probably see very few aggressive actions. Most of the time, in most places, most of us are nonviolent. Only rarely do we perform an action with the intention of deliberately harming or injuring some object or person. He concludes that "there is no universal 'rule of conduct' in competitive and predatory behavior, any more than there is a universal aggressive instinct" (1975, p. 247). He also points out that another aggressive characteristic—hunting and killing other animals for sport—is not unique to humans. Both lions and hyenas sometimes wantonly kill more prey than they can possibly eat. These examples of animal savagery don't justify human aggression. Given the human potential for self-awareness and intelligent action, many naturalists argue that we should be able to control our aggression more successfully than other species (Lorenz, 1966). They do suggest, however, that humans are not the only animals that kill members of their own species.

Sociobiology

Consider the plight of the recently mated male mountain bluebird *(Sialia currucoides)*. When he returns home to his nest, he discovers another male bluebird lurking in a nearby tree. Responding like the jealous husband who finds his wife in bed with another man, the bluebird immediately attacks the interloper. Will he also attack his mate (Barash, 1976)?

Ethologists have trouble predicting the male's reaction, for they cannot specify the environmental cues that may release aggression in this case. Sociobiology, however, offers an intriguing solution to this puzzle. Like ethology, sociobiology is grounded in evolutionary theory and the concept of the survival of the fittest. Sociobiology and ethology differ, however, in their conceptualization of fitness. Ethology, in keeping with classical evolutionary theory, assumes that the fittest animal is the one that survives. Sociobiologists, in contrast, think that the fittest animal is the one that passes its genes on to future generations. As we noted in Chapter 8 ("In Depth: The Sociobiology of Helping"), the ultimate goal of all animals is not merely personal survival, but the survival of their genes. The animal's success in achieving this goal is known as *inclusive fitness*.

Assuming that aggression is a situationally specific action that maximizes the animal's inclusive fitness, sociobiology predicts that the male bluebird will drive off the rival male, for the adulterer poses a great threat to his genetic fitness. He will attack his mate, however, only if her adultery threatens his reproductive potential. If the incident occurs before she has laid her eggs, then his attacks are intense, and he may drive her from the nest. But if no threat exists because she has already laid her eggs, then the male will not attack her (Barash, 1976, 1982).

Sociobiologists reject the notion of a unitary fighting instinct that is automatically touched off by environmental signals. Instead, they hypothesize that humans behave aggressively in some situations because violence and hostility increase our inclusive fitness. Competition, for example, tends to stimulate aggression in humans. For thousands of years humans lived in small hunting-and-gathering groups. By occasionally attacking neighboring groups, humans succeeded in acquiring extra territory, food, and mates. Fighting also occurred within the group to settle disputes. Because more aggressive individuals generally triumphed over those who were less aggressive, aggression emerged as an evolutionarily stable strategy. In consequence, modern-day humans instinctively display aggressive actions when they compete for valued resources (Maynard Smith, 1976; see Focus 9-3).

Motivational Approaches

The day starts off wrong and then gets worse. After oversleeping and skipping breakfast, you get stuck in snarled traffic and are late for work.

The boss ignores your excuses and delivers a long lecture on punctuality. The last straw falls when you go jogging after work. As you cross an intersection, a car nearly hits you before stopping. Your face flushes, your pulse quickens, and you lose control of your temper. A torrent of angry words flows from your mouth: "You stupid jerk! Can't you drive? Pedestrians have the right of way." And when the driver shouts obscenities back at you, you reach over and snap the antenna off the car.

Despite their differences, psychoanalytic theory, ethology, and sociobiology agree that your reaction in this setting is caused by your aggressive instincts. Motivational theorists, in contrast, believe that your actions are stimulated by external, environmental factors. The disruption in your morning routine, the traffic jam, and the lecture from your boss combine to arouse a *motivation,* or *drive,* to engage in aggressive actions. This motive, in turn, prompts you to respond in a hostile way.

One of the earliest analyses of aggression based on motivation was offered by John Dollard, Neal E. Miller, and their colleagues at the Institute of Human Relations at Yale University. These investigators argued that aggressive motives are akin to such basic biological drives as hunger and thirst. Just as we eat and drink to reduce our hunger and thirst, we engage in hostile actions to reduce our aggressive motivations. However, while hunger and thirst are governed largely by biological factors, aggressive motives are triggered by external, social factors. Thus, if your rotten day hadn't motivated you to be aggressive, then you wouldn't have attacked the careless driver (Dollard et al., 1939; Miller, 1941; Miller & Dollard, 1941).

What is the key situational factor that motivates aggression? Frustration, said Miller and Dollard. When external conditions thwart our attempts to reach our goals, we become frustrated. Frustration then arouses an aggressive drive, which surfaces at the behavioral level in the form of (1) an attack on the source of the frustration or (2) displaced aggression aimed at some other person or object. Summarizing their **frustration-aggression hypothesis,** Dollard and his colleagues explained: "The occurrence of aggressive behavior always presupposes the existence of frustration and, contrariwise, . . . the existence of frustration always leads to some form of aggression" (1939, p. 1).

Few social processes are as simple as they first appear, and the link between frustration and aggression is no exception. From its very inception, the frustration-aggression hypothesis required constant modification to fit new findings. First, critics pointed out that frustrating experiences don't inevitably lead to aggression. After oversleeping, fighting a traffic jam, and being reprimanded by your boss, you may feel depressed, fearful, or exhausted rather than hostile (see Baron, 1977). Second, thwarting external factors aren't the only ones that increase our motivation to engage in aggression. A whole host of aversive factors—pain, extreme temperatures, noise, insults, overcrowding, air pollution—have been linked to aggression. Thus, if you are jogging through a noisy,

Environmental factors that can precipitate aggression: annoying noise, traffic jams, overcrowding.

crowded section of town on a hot day while wearing shoes that are too tight, then you may rant and rave at thoughtless drivers even though you aren't frustrated in the least (Berkowitz, 1983; Mueller, 1983).

In retrospect, the frustration-aggression relationship can be considered a special case of the more general motivational model shown in Figure 9-3. This **arousal-aggression hypothesis** predicts that many unpleasant and noxious conditions, including thwarting circumstances, set the stage for aggression. These aversive events create a heightened emotional arousal, which is often subjectively labeled *anger*. This arousal, then, is the motivation that drives the subsequent aggressive actions (see Berkowitz, 1983; Ferguson & Rule, 1983; Zillmann, 1983).

In addition to its broader scope, the revised arousal-aggression hypothesis differs from the original frustration-aggression hypothesis in another critical way. Miller and Dollard hypothesized that frustration is a necessary and sufficient cause of aggression. In other words, frustration always begets aggression, and aggression occurs only when the individual is frustrated. The revised hypothesis, in contrast, argues that aversive events *sometimes*, but not always, prompt aggression. Many times we suffer through days filled with frustrations and irritations without once acting aggressively. Why? Because the link between aversive experiences and aggression depends on many other factors, such as the presence of

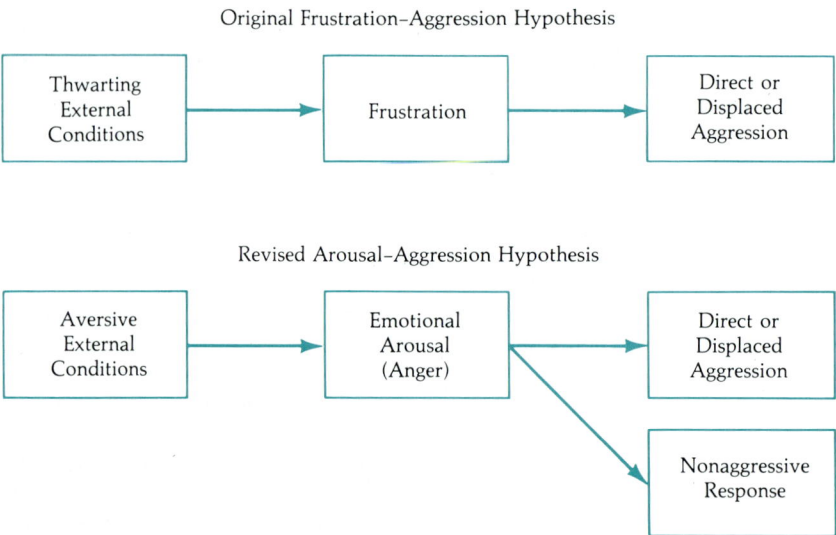

Figure 9-3 The original frustration-aggression model and the generalized motivation model. Originally, researchers assumed that frustration inevitably led to some form of aggression. The revised arousal-aggression hypothesis argues that aversive events lead to arousal, which in turn can prompt aggression, but does not necessarily do so.

situational cues that are associated with aggression and our general level of arousal (Berkowitz, 1981b, 1983).

Aggressive cues. Assume for a moment that you have volunteered to take part in a study of performance and learning. When the second subject scheduled for the session arrives, the experimenter explains that both of you will work on a simple task, take a short break, and then perform a learning problem. Despite your best efforts on the first task, a fairly simple jigsaw puzzle, you fail to find the solution. To make matters worse, the other subject finishes his puzzle quickly and then makes some unclever comments about your competence. To give you a break before starting the next task, the experimenter shows you a short film clip. The seven-minute clip is from the movie *The Champion*, and it depicts a boxer named Midge Kelly (played by Kirk Douglas) taking a very bad beating. When the film is over, you and your partner start the learning task. You take the role of the teacher by delivering electric shocks to the other subject whenever he makes a mistake. Each time he makes an error, you can give shocks that vary from 1 to 10 in intensity. When the other subject makes his first error, you smile to yourself and push the number 4 button on the machine (Geen & Berkowitz, 1967).

As you have probably guessed, the other subject in this study is actually a confederate, and he receives no shocks at all. Furthermore, your failure and his insulting remarks are intentional attempts to anger you. What, however, is the purpose of the film? According to Leonard Berkowitz, the film is an *aggressive cue*. In his view, aversive events (such as your failure at the task and the insults from the other subject) arouse a readiness to respond aggressively, but situational cues must also be present before this arousal is translated into aggressive actions. In consequence, if the film had depicted a track meet, you would have been no more aggressive than control subjects who solved their puzzles and suffered no insults; the aggressive cues needed to pull out aggression weren't present. The results of the actual experiment are shown in Table 9-2. As predicted, the amount of aggression depended both on the magnitude of the aversive events and the presence of situational cues.

TABLE 9 – 2

The number of shocks administered by frustrated, insulted, and control subjects after they watched either a violent film or a nonviolent film.

Condition of Subject	Fight Film	Track Film
Frustrated	4.2	3.4
Frustrated and insulted	5.8	4.1
Control	2.8	3.2

Frustrated, insulted subjects were particularly aggressive when aggressive cues were present in the setting (Geen & Berkowitz, 1967).

Berkowitz and his associates have found that many situational cues can release aggression. For example, angry subjects became aggressive subjects when their target was named Kirk or Kelly (the names of the actor and character in the film clip) or was described as an amateur boxer (see Berkowitz, 1970, for a summary). Weapons are among the most powerful cues for aggression. In one study that used a procedure that was very similar to the teacher-learner paradigm described above, subjects were first given either 1 shock or 7 shocks by the confederate. When it was the subjects' turn to take over the controls of the shock machine, the angry subjects (those who had received 7 shocks) meted out an average of about 6 shocks when a 12-gauge shotgun and a snub-nosed .38-caliber revolver lay next to the shock machine. If the table contained badminton rackets and shuttlecocks or no cues at all, subjects administered significantly fewer shocks: about 4.6. The average number of shocks administered by the unangered subjects ranged from 2 to 3. Berkowitz had documented the *weapons effect:* the presence of weapons makes people more aggressive than they normally would be (Berkowitz & Lepage, 1967).

When Berkowitz published his findings, some researchers suggested that the subjects, skeptical about the presence of weapons in an experimental laboratory, guessed the true purpose of the study (Page and Scheidt, 1971). Berkowitz stands by his original findings, however, and cites other studies that have confirmed the weapons effect (Berkowitz, 1970, 1981c, 1983; Berkowitz & Donnerstein, 1982). For example, Belgian students shown pictures of weapons became more punitive (Leyens & Parke, 1975); college students at a carnival threw more wet sponges at a clown when a gun was visible near the front of the booth (reported in Turner et al., 1977); and drivers were more likely to honk their horns at a stalled pickup truck with a rifle in a gun rack than at one without (Turner, Layton, & Simons, 1975). All in all, these studies argue that the slogan "Guns don't kill; people do" isn't true. Berkowitz explains: "People do have to pull the gun's trigger in order to shoot someone. But to some extent, the weapon can also pull the finger on the trigger" (1981d, p. 3).

Arousal and aggression. When was the last time you lost your temper and acted in a hostile, aggressive manner? A dentist, when asked this question, claimed that he never lost his temper. But when pressed, he recalled an incident that took place while he was exercising after work. He was finishing this workout by lifting weights when another weight lifter accidentally bumped into him. Suddenly enraged, he shouted, "Why don't you look where you're going, asshole? Those weights could have fallen on me!" The incident escalated into a shouting and shoving match. After recounting the incident, the dentist sheepishly admitted, "I guess I overreacted" (Tavris, 1982, p. 169).

If we apply the arousal-aggression hypothesis shown in Figure 9-3 to this incident, the dentist's intense reaction becomes more understandable. Although the trivial irritation wouldn't normally be sufficient to motivate an aggressive action, the dentist was already physiologically aroused. Even though this arousal was produced by his workout and had nothing to do with hostility or anger, the dentist was still in a highly excited state. This energized condition, when combined with an aversive event, prompted an overly aggressive reaction. This process is known as **excitation transfer** (Zillmann, 1983).

Even when our arousal stems from factors that have nothing to do with anger or hostility, it may still fan the fires of aggression. Loud noises, high temperatures, stimulating drugs, physical exercise, and certain types of music can all energize aggression (Zillmann, 1983). As Focus 9-4 notes, even sexual arousal sometimes increases aggression. However, two conditions appear to be necessary for excitation transfer to occur. First, the individual must already be predisposed to engage in aggression. The dentist's exercise-induced arousal, for example, would not have caused him to act aggressively if he hadn't been provoked by the other weight lifter. Second, the true cause of the arousal must be relatively ambiguous. If the angry dentist had correctly attributed his arousal to his exercises, he probably wouldn't have become so hostile. Because he misattributed his arousal to the irritating stranger, his feelings of anger were intensified (Rule & Nesdale, 1976; Zillmann, 1983).

Social Learning Theory

Two kindergartners fighting for a toy punch and kick each other. The young delinquent robs an elderly man at gunpoint. The blitzing linebacker spears the quarterback on the opposing team. Why?

Many processes may be at work, including hostile impulses (psychoanalytic theory), aggressive instincts (ethology and sociobiology), and emotional arousal (motivation models). Such incidents, however, can also be explained by *learning theory*. According to this view, aggression is acquired through experience. Throughout our lives we are rewarded for behaving aggressively. The child who is more aggressive wins the toy. The mugger acquires money. The football player is praised heartily by the coach, his teammates, and the roar of the crowd. In each case aggression is followed by a reinforcer, so it will probably occur more frequently in the future.

Albert Bandura's *social learning theory*, which was introduced in Chapter 5, is one of the most sophisticated approaches to understanding human aggression (Bandura, 1973, 1977, 1983). Like all learning theorists, Bandura emphasizes the concept of reinforcement, for he predicts that people will become more aggressive when their hostile behavior is positively reinforced (rewarded). He also believes, however, that people can learn through observation. The two children who were fighting provided an example, or model, for the other children. Watching them punch each other, their classmates were learning to be aggressive. Similarly, growing up in a rough section of town, the young delinquent may have seen many muggings before he decided to carry one out on his own. By watching game films, the linebacker had many opportunities to learn new ways to hurt the opposition. Thus we acquire aggressive behaviors by imitating the actions of another person who *models* hostile acts.

FOCUS 9-4

A Closer Look: *Do erotica and pornography increase aggression?*

The characters in the movie you are watching on cable television have fallen in love. After several impassioned kisses, they begin to undress each other. Once naked, they slowly sink to the thickly carpeted floor, where they engage in gentle but intense sexual intercourse.

Could watching two people make love possibly make you more aggressive? Yes and no. Erotica—sexual material that is relatively mild and presented in a positive, pleasant way—can actually decrease aggression. Although people vary greatly in their preferences, many of us react positively to this type of material. Thus we become slightly aroused, but our feelings are pleasant and nonaggressive. More intense erotic materials that vividly depict sexual activity may, in contrast, create negative, unpleasant feelings. If we are aroused by pornography—sexual material that is negatively toned—then our sexual arousal may energize our aggressiveness (L. A. White, 1979; Zillmann et al., 1981).

A relatively new form of erotic material, *aggressive pornography*, is even more likely to cause violence. Aggressive pornography graphically depicts a violent, degrading form of sexual activity. In most cases, violence is directed at women or children, who are forcibly raped, beaten, or even killed. This form of pornography has proliferated in recent years, and its consequences may be devastating. Researchers have shown that violent pornography is particularly arousing to known rapists, but that many men who have never committed rape also become aroused when exposed to such films. These effects are particularly pronounced when the victim of the violence seems to enjoy the abuse or to experience orgasm. Men who view such materials are also more likely to accept myths about rape and are more accepting of violence against women. Lastly, watching violent pornography increases the aggressive content of men's sexual fantasies, and in one laboratory study increased their tendency to attack a woman (Abel et al., 1977; Donnerstein, 1983; Donnerstein & Berkowitz, 1981; Malamuth, 1985; Malamuth, Check, & Briere, 1986; Malamuth & Donnerstein, 1982).

These findings are consistent with a motivation model of aggression: the sexual content of the material creates arousal, while the violent content presents cues that further increase the likelihood of aggression. Aggressive pornography also increases violence by modeling hostile, degrading behaviors. When 930 women were interviewed, nearly 10 percent reported an upsetting sexual experience that they felt had been caused by aggressive pornography. One woman reported that her boyfriend tied her up and beat her after getting the idea from a pornographic movie. Aggressive pornography also reinforces a number of prejudices against women (Russell, 1984). According to one source:

> Porn sexually objectifies women. Women feel this degradation. Porn teaches men that women enjoy violence. It eroticizes violence for men. Porn confuses some women into believing they should "experience pleasure through pain." Some men enjoy hurting women physically. It teaches women to endure rape and violence. [Wheeler, 1985, p. 385]

Thus aggressive pornography does not just energize aggression, it actually teaches men new ways to be aggressive, while reinforcing stereotypes of women.

In an early test of this process, Bandura and his associates exposed nursery school children to adults who modeled various types of behavior. Later the children were tested to see if they would imitate the model's actions. In one study some children watched as an adult played quietly with Tinker Toys. Other children watched a violent model attack a plastic Bobo-the-Clown doll.

> The model laid Bobo on its side, sat on it and punched it repeatedly in the nose. The model then raised the Bobo doll, picked up the mallet and struck the doll on the head. Following the mallet aggression, the model tossed the doll up in the air aggressively and kicked it about the room. This sequence of physically aggressive acts was repeated approximately three times, interspersed with verbally aggressive responses such as, "Sock him in the nose . . . ," "Hit him down . . . ," "Throw him in the air . . . ," "Kick him . . . ," "Pow . . . ," and two nonaggressive comments, "He keeps coming back for more" and "He sure is a tough fella." [Bandura, Ross, & Ross, 1961, p. 577]

When the children were mildly frustrated and left alone in the room with Bobo, they were far more aggressive if they had seen an aggressive model than if they had seen a nonaggressive model or no model at all. They had learned to be aggressive by observing aggression (see Figure 9-4).

What would have happened if an experimenter had entered the room and punished the aggressive model for beating up the Bobo doll? According to Bandura, the children would probably not have engaged in aggression, because they would have learned to associate aggression with

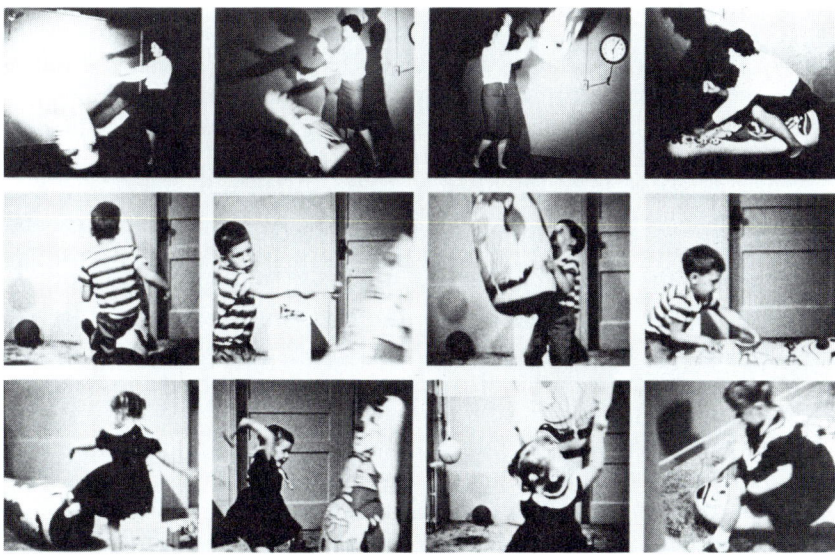

Figure 9-4 Scenes from the Bobo doll studies. Children who watched an adult beat up a Bobo doll acted more aggressively themselves.

punishment. Bandura calls the consequences the model experiences *vicarious consequences,* and he predicts that we are more likely to imitate a model who is rewarded for aggression than one who is punished for it. Children in the Bobo doll study who watched as the model was called a "strong champion" and given candy and soft drinks were more aggressive than children who saw the model punished (Bandura, 1965).

One of the most controversial aspects of social learning theory concerns the role of television as a source of vivid models of aggression. Violence pervades television programming. By one estimate, as many as 80% of all programs depict violence, and the percentage swells to 93.6 when only weekend programming is considered. With the average adolescent currently watching about four hours of television per day, children may witness as many as 13,000 dramatized murders by the time they reach 16 (Signorielli, Gross, & Morgan, 1982). In what ways does this constant diet of mayhem affect us?

Overall aggressiveness.
Bandura's Bobo doll studies suggest that children become more aggressive when they are exposed to an aggressive model, but many critics have pointed out that beating up a plastic doll isn't the same as attacking another living being. A number of studies have answered this criticism by examining actual aggression, either in the laboratory or in the field settings. One pair of researchers randomly assigned children to one of two conditions: some saw a segment of *The Untouchables* which contained a chase scene, two brawls, two shootings, and one knifing, while others saw an exciting sports sequence. Later the children were given the opportunity to aggress against another child by pressing a button marked HURT (the equipment wasn't actually connected, naturally). Those who saw *The Untouchables* pushed the button for a longer period of time. Children exposed to violent programs also tended to behave more aggressively when they played with other children (Liebert & Baron, 1972).

Copying.
Some researchers, including Leonard Berkowitz, believe that viewers sometimes carry out specific types of actions that they have seen on television (Berkowitz, 1984). An 18-year-old high school student, for example, walked into a school for beauticians in Arizona and shot four women and one child. He explained that he got the idea from news stories about Richard Speck, the man who murdered eight nurses in Chicago (Berkowitz, 1970).

A 7-year-old boy was caught sprinkling ground glass into the family's meal. He explained that he had seen somebody kill somebody this way on television, and he wanted to see if it worked (Schramm, Lyle, & Parker, 1961).

In San Francisco, a 9-year-old girl was raped with a bottle by three older girls. The girls told a Park Service officer that four days earlier they seen the movie *Born Innocent,* which depicts the violent rape of an adolescent girl by four other girls using a plumber's plunger (Liebert, Sprafkin, & Davidson, 1982).

Ronald Zamora, 15, killed his next-door neighbor while burglarizing her home. His defense lawyers claimed that his addiction to television had distorted his understanding of reality. An avid fan of most police programs (especially *Kojak*), he said he watched people kill other people all the time on television. He was found guilty of murder and given a life sentence (Liebert, Sprafkin, & Davidson, 1982).

Direct *copying* of specific aggressive actions has been documented in a number of studies. Children who were exposed to an aggressive model in Bandura's Bobo doll studies, for example, not only evidenced a wide range of aggression but mimicked the precise behaviors of the model (Bandura, 1965). Evidence also suggests that reports of spectacular crimes on television and in newspapers, such as the numerous assassinations, hijackings, hostage takings, and cases of murder-suicide, are often followed by increases in similar crimes (see Figure 9-5). Even aggression against oneself, suicide, may occur in imitation of front-page suicides. These findings suggest that the mass media, by giving extensive coverage to acts of violence, may actually promote violence (Bandura, 1983; Berkowitz, 1984; Phillips, 1982; see Figure 9-6).

Desensitization. After watching three hours of car accidents, car chases, murders, battles, rapes, and assaults on prime-time television, how do you react when the late-night newscaster tells you that three suspected drug dealers have been found with their throats cut? Evidence indicates that you may become *desensitized* to real-life violence after prolonged exposure to televised violence. In two studies, children were

Figure 9-5 Mimicking aggressive actions. The shooting of several youths on a New York City subway, given wide coverage by the media, could have served as a model for other vigilantes. Cartoonist Garry Trudeau has suggested that people also copy the aggressive actions of popular movie characters, such as the one played by Clint Eastwood in the *Dirty Harry* films.

© 1985 by G. B. Trudeau. Reprinted by permission of Universal Press Syndicate.

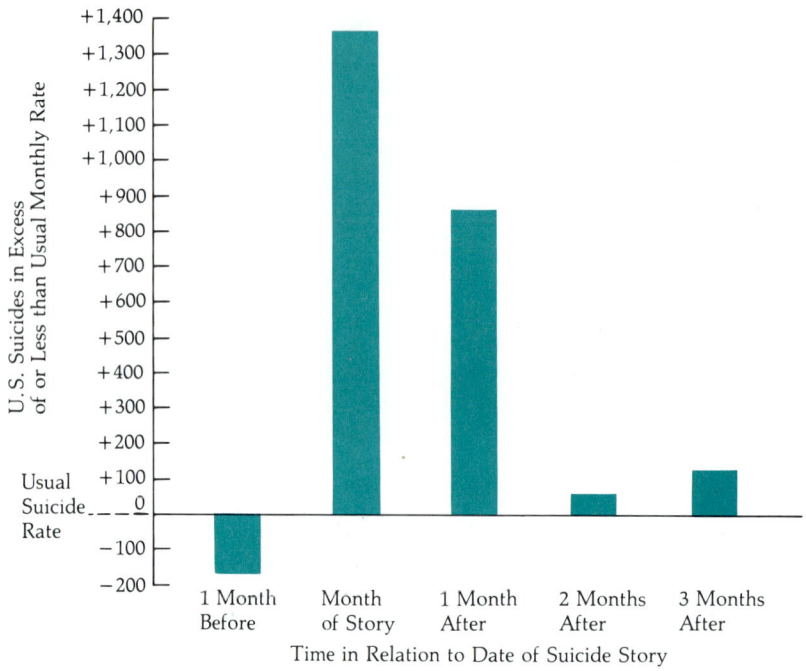

Figure 9-6 If people read about a suicide in the newspaper, are they more likely to kill themselves? To answer this question, one investigator examined the number of suicides in the United States between 1947 and 1968. When suicide rates in the months before and after each of 35 highly publicized suicides were contrasted, the startling increase shown here was revealed. On the average, each suicide story was followed by about 58 copycat suicides.

shown an aggressive film, a nonaggressive film, or no film at all. They were then asked to monitor the actions of two children who were playing in a nearby room. When the two children began to argue and destroy each other's property, the subjects were less likely to intervene if they had just seen a violent movie (Drabman & Thomas, 1974, 1976). Evidence also indicates that people who are exposed to fictitious violence show fewer signs of physiological arousal when they watch scenes depicting real violence (Cline, Croft, & Courrier, 1973; Thomas et al., 1977).

Value-shaping. If aliens from another planet tried to understand our civilization by watching our television shows, they would probably form a distorted view of us. After watching our situation comedies, police shows, detective thrillers, hospital dramas, soap operas, and commercials, they would conclude that the average human being is witty, violent, deceitful, ill, selfish, sexually driven, and vain. Indeed, television seems to shape the viewer's values, so that "the more time one spends 'living' in the world of television, the more likely one is to report perceptions of social reality which can be traced to (or are congruent with) television's most persistent representations of life and society" (Gerbner et al., 1980, p. 14).

Much of this *value-shaping* is related to our views of violence. Since violence plays a major role in TV life, viewers sometimes feel that murder, rape, and assault are routine, commonplace occurrences. To study this distortion, one team of researchers asked 587 adolescents a series of questions about violence in America. Each question was followed by two alternatives, one of which was factually correct while the second was consistent with violence rates in television programming. One item, for example, read: "Think about the number of people who are involved in some kind of violence each year. Do you think that 3 percent of all people are involved in some kind of violence in any given year, or is it closer to 10 percent?" The correct answer was 3 percent; the "television answer" was 10. As Table 9-3 indicates, more of the heavy television viewers selected the television answers. The more television you watch, the more distorted your perception of reality (Gerbner et al., 1979).

Television and aggression: A less than final word. Two scientists are driving by a flock of sheep. One scientist says to the other, "I see

TABLE 9-3

Percentage of heavy and light television viewers who gave "television answers" to questions about violence.

Question	TV Answer	Heavy Viewers (Percent)	Light Viewers (Percent)
How many people are involved in some kind of violence each year: 3% or 10%?	10%	83%	62%
How many people are involved in some kind of violence each week: 1 person out of 100 or 10 people out of 100?	10	73	62
What percent of all people commit serious crimes: 3% or 12%?	12%	88	77
Would you be afraid to walk alone in your neighborhood at night?	Yes	52	46
Is it dangerous to walk alone in a city at night?	Yes	86	79
On an average day, how many times does a policeman usually pull out his gun: less than once a day or more than five times a day?	More than five times	18	6
When police arrive at a scene of violence, how much of the time do they use force and violence: most of the time or some of the time?	Most of the time	56	45
Can most people be trusted, or do you think that you can't be too careful in dealing with people?	Must be careful	62	52

those sheep have just been shorn." The other looks at the sheep for a moment before replying, "On the side facing us, anyway."

This story reminds us never to be too sure we know all the answers. It seems unlikely that anybody would clip sheep on only one side of their bodies, but unlikely things happen every day. Therefore, the skeptical scientist refrained from drawing a hasty conclusion. Similarly, we must remain skeptical about our conclusions concerning television and aggression. Considerable evidence indicates that televised violence and aggression are linked. Bandura found that children behave more aggressively

---

FOCUS 9-5

Applying Social Psychology: *Does watching TV violence cause aggression?*

Since the early 1960s, some social psychologists have argued that violence on television promotes aggression in real-life settings. And for just as long, other social psychologists have argued that television is "not causally implicated in the development of aggressive behavior among children and adolescents" (Milavsky et al., 1982). Which side is right?

Researchers have used a variety of methods to settle this dispute. First, by conducting correlational studies, researchers have frequently found that television viewing and aggression are related. One team of researchers asked more than 700 children to describe their television-viewing habits and the number of times they engaged in such aggressive actions as fighting, delinquency, and disputes with their parents. Other studies have confirmed this study's findings that the more a person watches violent TV programs, the more likely he or she will be to display high levels of aggression (McCarthy et al., 1975).

These findings, however, have been criticized by defenders of television, who note that the correlation between viewed violence and violent actions does not necessarily mean that viewed violence *causes* aggression. It may be that people who by nature are highly aggressive seek out violent programs to view (see Figure 9-7). Or a third variable, such as punitive parental practices, may be causing both increases in aggression and the tendency to watch violent programs. To answer this criticism, researchers also studied the link between television and aggression through experimentation. Some of these studies, such as Bandura's Bobo doll studies,

have been conducted in laboratory settings; others have been carried out in field settings (J. H. Goldstein et al., 1975). In one illustrative study, researchers separated institutionalized delinquent boys into two groups. One group was shown violent films each night for five nights, while the second group was shown only nonviolent films. During the day the boys were observed, and their interactions were objectively coded on level of aggression. Although

Figure 9-7 People who are highly aggressive may seek out violent television programs, while people who are more pacifistic ("sissies") are likely to avoid such programs.

© 1985 by Universal Press Syndicate. Reprinted by permission.

after viewing violence and that adults sometimes copy aggressive actions they have seen on television or read about in the newspapers. Televised violence also reduces our sensitivity to real-world violence, and may distort our perceptions of the world in which we live. All of these findings, as well as those discussed in Focus 9-5, suggest that television *probably* increases the aggressiveness of some viewers. Like the skeptical scientist, however, we must remain open to alternative possibilities. The evidence is strong but not overwhelming (Freedman, 1984).

---

the two groups were equivalent in aggressiveness before the week of films, during that week the boys who were shown the violent films evidenced higher levels of aggression (Parke et al., 1977).

Even these findings, however, can be criticized. Delinquent subjects may be particularly susceptible to the effects of viewed violence. Moreover, some field studies have found that television or movie violence has little or no effect on the observer's behavior (Feshbach & Singer, 1971; Milgram & Shotland, 1973; Singer & Singer, 1980). Furthermore, these brief studies say little about the long-term effects of watching aggression. To deal with these objections, a third approach has been used: longitudinal studies. Leonard Eron and his colleagues, for example, measured the TV violence level and aggressiveness in 875 third-graders in 1960. As the correlational studies suggested, these two variables were correlated ($r = .21$). Ten years later, they tracked down as many of the original subjects as possible (they found 475) and again measured these variables. Somewhat surprisingly, the correlation between the two variables was now only $-.05$. However, when the level of TV violence viewed by the third-graders was compared with the aggressiveness they showed as teenagers, the correlation was .31. These findings suggest that televised violence may have cumulative effects that build up gradually over time (Eron, 1982; Eron et al., 1972; Huesmann, 1982).

What can we conclude from all these studies using all these methods? Although the findings are not clear-cut, they certainly raise troublesome questions about the value of violent television programs. Even a conservative look at the data suggests that televised violence yields few benefits and may be exacting great social costs. Acting on these findings, the American Psychological Association has gone so far as to pass the following resolution:

WHEREAS, the great majority of research studies have found a relationship between televised violence and behaving aggressively, and
WHEREAS, the conclusion drawn on the basis of 25 years of research and a sizable number of experimental and field investigations (NIMH, 1972, 1982) is that viewing televised violence may lead to increases in aggressive attitudes, values, and behavior, particularly in children, and
WHEREAS, many children's programs contain some form of violence,
BE IT RESOLVED that the American Psychological Association (1) encourages parents to monitor and to control television viewing by children; (2) requests industry representatives to take a responsible attitude in reducing direct imitatable violence on "real-life" fictional children's programming or violent incidents in cartoons, and to provide more programming for children designed to mitigate possible effects of television violence, consistent with the guarantees of the First Amendment; and (3) urges industry, government, and private foundations to support relevant research activities aimed at the amelioration of the effects of high levels of televised violence on children's attitudes and behaviors. [Abeles, 1985: Proceedings of the American Psychological Association, pp. 648–649]

Normative Models of Aggression

Sports and aggression often go hand in hand. Baseball games are sometimes marred by bench-clearing brawls. The hard hits of football can turn into late hits and cheap shots. Under the backboards, basketball players jockey for position with nudges, shoves, and elbows to the ribs. And no professional hockey game would be complete without a fist fight or two.

Undoubtedly violence in sports stems from both personal and situational factors (Mann, 1979). Many players often point out, however, that violence is just a part of the game. As one college basketball player explained, "It's OK to try to hurt somebody if it is legal and during the game" (quoted in Bredemeier & Shields, 1985, p. 23). Aggression in sports, and in other settings as well, is *normative:* it is consistent with the implicit standards that regulate social behavior.

The norm of reciprocity.
During the socialization process most of us are taught to control our aggression. While we may realize that violence is one way to achieve our goals, as we grow older we learn that violence is counternormative (Hartup, 1974). Some social norms, however, actually encourage aggression in some situations. One such standard, the *norm of reciprocity,* suggests that we should fight fire with fire (Tedeschi, Smith, & Brown, 1974). In consequence, one of the quickest ways to prompt aggression is to act aggressively. If another student describes one of your opinions as absurd, reciprocity may demand that you call the remark itself absurd. After the lead-off hitter slugs a home run, the pitcher may reciprocate by hitting the second batter with a 90-mile-an-hour fast ball. Or if a wife calls her husband pigheaded, he may feel compelled to say something negative about her. In experimental situations, researchers have found that the easiest way to turn people into aggressors is to make them the target of aggression (Dengerink, Schnedler, & Covey, 1978; Kelley & Stahelski, 1970a; J. W. White & Gruber, 1982). (The tendency for conflict to encourage further conflict is considered in more detail in "In Depth: Competition and Conflict," at the end of this chapter.)

Emergent aggressive norms.
Specific norms that encourage violence and aggression develop in some subgroups. Urban youth gangs, for example, often adopt unique norms that emphasize toughness and physical strength. When conflict arises among members, violence is the preferred means of settling it. When one gang invades another gang's turf, a fight or "rumble" is the normal method of settling the dispute. When gang members need money, they acquire it by committing robberies or muggings. Violence is so strongly ingrained in the normative structure of the group that individuals behave aggressively simply to establish a reputation among their peers. In one study of 69 men who were convicted of violent crimes, approximately 76% claimed to use violence to create a

"tough guy" image (Toch, 1969). Their actions violated society's norms of behavior but they were consisted with the unique norms that had emerged in their particular subgroup (Cloward & Ohlin, 1960; Thrasher, 1927: Yablonsky, 1962).

Norms and deindividuation. A normative approach to aggression argues that some norms keep aggression in check, while other norms encourage specific forms of aggression. What happens when normative constraints are relaxed?

Consider this case. On September 26, 1973, a 27-year-old woman climbed a tower, apparently with the intention of jumping to her death. By the time the rescue squad arrived, a crowd of 300 had gathered at the base of the tower. Rather than assist the rescuers, the onlookers pelted them with rocks while chanting to the woman, "Jump, jump." The woman was eventually rescued, despite the interference of the crowd. (Baiting crowds are analyzed in Mann, 1981.)

Why would people behave so callously? One explanation, offered by Philip Zimbardo, argues that people sometimes lose their sense of personal identity when they are part of a group. Zimbardo calls this process **deindividuation.** According to Zimbardo, when group members become deindividuated, they no longer feel compelled to act in accord with social norms. They also lack self-control and self-regulation, so their actions become highly emotional, impulsive, and atypical. While deindividuation may lead to increasingly positive behaviors, it usually leads to "aggression, vandalism, stealing, cheating, rudeness, as well as a general loss of concern for others" (Zimbardo, 1969, 1975, p. 53; see also Diener, 1980; Prentice-Dunn & Rogers, 1983).

Anonymity is one of the most important determinants of deindividuation. According to Zimbardo, you are more likely to act aggressively when "others can't identify or single you out," and so "can't evaluate, criticize, judge, or punish you." In one test of this hypothesis, small groups of college women were asked to deliver electric shocks to another woman as part of a learning exercise. Some of the women were clearly identifiable to one another; they wore name tags and were introduced to the other group members by name. A second group of women were disguised; they wore large lab coats and hoods over their heads. As predicted, the anonymous women gave more intense shocks than the identifiable women (Zimbardo, 1969). These findings were also obtained in an ingenious field study that was conducted on Halloween. The subjects were 1,352 children who went trick-or-treating at one of 27 experimental homes in Seattle, Washington. To manipulate anonymity, the researchers randomly asked some children to state their names and addresses. Others weren't asked to give their names, and since they were in costume, they should have felt extremely anonymous. Next, the experimenter told the children that they could each have one candy bar. She then left the room while a hidden observer watched to see if the children took extra candy bars or removed any money from a bowl containing pennies and nickels. As Table 9-4 indicates, more children transgressed (by stealing either candy or money) when they were anonymous. The impact of anonymity was greatest, however, when the children were trick-or-treating in groups rather than alone. These findings suggest that the impact of deindividuation is greatest when people are members of groups (Diener et al., 1976).

Nature and Nurture Together: An Interaction Model

We began this chapter by asking how Bernhard Goetz's actions could be explained. Now we have many answers. According to the nature theorists, Goetz's actions can be traced back to innate characteristics that Goetz shares with all members of the human species. From a psychodynamic perspective, his actions stemmed from pent-up hostile urges that demanded an outlet. And to the evolutionists (including both ethologists and sociobiologists), his aggression was a genetically determined reaction to a particular environmental threat. A contrasting perspective traces Goetz's actions to environmental factors. If Goetz felt threatened by the youths, this aversive experience may have created a heightened state of arousal that precipitated his attack. If Goetz had ever seen the Charles Bronson movie *Death Wish*, he might have learned to fight back when threatened by juvenile delinquents. And Goetz may have come from a family and community that favored the use of violence to settle disputes. Thus any one of the six perspectives summarized in Table 9-5 can be applied to explain Goetz's actions.

The nature-nurture controversy is far from settled. Although the instinct models proposed by Freud, Lorenz, and the sociobiologists have been criticized frequently, they yield insights into the personal and instinctive sources of aggression. Similarly, alternatives to motivational, social learning, and normative approaches have been proposed, but these three approaches continue to shed light on aggression.

In time, one of these two sides may win the battle, to be recognized as *the* explanation of aggression. It is more likely, however, that a complete explanation of aggression will recognize that aggression stems from the

TABLE 9 – 4

Percentage of anonymous and nonanonymous trick-or-treaters who transgressed when in groups and alone.

	Anonymous	*Nonanonymous*
In groups	57.2%	20.8%
Alone	21.4	7.5

interaction of biological and social factors. Rather than urge that aggression stems from either nature or nurture, we should recognize that both sets of factors act, both singly and in combination, to influence social behavior. As the sociobiologist David P. Barash explains, both experience and genetic material can influence behavior, but the proportion of the determining factors varies from behavior to behavior and from species to species. To Barash, "behavior is not contained somehow within a gene, waiting to leap out like Athena, fully armored, from the head of Zeus. Rather, genes are blueprints, which code for a range of potential" actions. For some behaviors, this blueprint may be very precise, leaving little room for modification through learning. The genetic foundation for other behaviors may be so general that learning accounts for all of the variability noted (Barash, 1982, p. 30). Thus an interaction model recommends a synthesis of the two views rather than continued championing of one view over the other.

Controlling Aggression

Down through the centuries, countless millions have died not from illness, not from disease, not from accident, but from human aggression. Given the causes of aggression identified in the preceding section, what suggestions do social psychologists offer for controlling violence and hostility?

TABLE 9-5

Six approaches to aggression.

Theoretical Perspective	Type of Model	Source of Aggression	When Does Aggression Occur?
Psychodynamic	Instinct	Unconscious urges	When violent unconscious urges reach high levels
Ethological	Instinct	Natural selection	When environmental cues release the attack instinct
Sociobiological	Instinct	Natural selection	Primarily in competitive situations
Motivational	Learned drive	Arousal or anger	When aversive situational conditions produce arousal
Social learning	Learning	Reinforcement and modeling	When aggression has previously been reinforced in models
Normative	Learning	Conformity to norms or deindividuation	When aggression is consistent with norms or when deindividuation occurs

Achieving Catharsis without Aggression

Both Freud and Lorenz were pessimistic about our chances of eliminating aggression. They believed that hostile impulses build up gradually over time, so that these urges must be discharged eventually. And for Freud, damming up these impulses by keeping them inside is no solution, for unexpressed anger can cause depression, suicide, and other psychological abnormalities (Smyth, 1982). As we noted earlier in this chapter, catharsis—the release and subsequent reduction of aggressive tensions—is inevitable.

Freud was more optimistic about our chances of *controlling* aggression. While acts of violence and aggression are one means of achieving catharsis, we can release our hostile urges in less negative ways. Imagine that you are playing soccer. When the official is looking the other way, a player from the other team deliberately pushes you from behind. Clearly, giving the other player a shove in return will release your aggressive urges, but you can achieve catharsis in other ways. First, you could ventilate your hostility by expressing your anger and annoyance verbally. Second, because hostility can be displaced from one source to another, you could reduce your hostility by playing even harder and scoring a goal. Both of these techniques should lead to catharsis.

Does ventilation work?

Freud's assumption that you can keep your aggressive tendencies in check by venting your anger is consistent with the common-sense idea that "blowing off steam" or "getting it off your chest" will reduce aggressiveness. However, the ventilation process is more complex than Freud and the commonsensible ever imagined. Venting our hostility can leave us feeling better about ourselves, but in many situations anger only heightens our psychological distress. If your boss angers you, for example, shouting at him or her may reduce your tensions, but you are more likely to feel even worse, for now you have to worry about retribution and feel guilty about losing your temper (Konečni, 1975a, 1975b; Konečni, & Ebbesen, 1976).

Ventilation can even backfire completely; by expressing anger you can get yourself even more worked up and hostile. In several studies of children, those who were given the opportunity to vent their anger became more hostile as their personal restraints against aggression were lowered (Feshbach, 1956; Mallick & McCandless, 1966). Also, when retaliation by the target of your anger is possible, the supposedly cathartic act may become the first stage in a series of escalating aggressive interchanges. This spiraling cycle of conflict often occurs in domestic settings. Family violence usually begins with verbal hostilities. Instead of reducing aggression, complaints only fan the flames of conflict. A harsh word from the wife ("You thoughtless, inconsiderate bastard!") may lead to a rebuke from the husband ("You bitch, what do you . . ."), which in turn leads to physical violence (Straus, Gelles, & Steinmetz, 1980). Ventilating anger tends to exercise rather than exorcise hostility.

Does displacement work?

Many theorists, including Freud, believe that unconscious aggressive urges can be *displaced*, or redirected, into more socially acceptable activities. When you punch a pillow, scream in the closet, complain to a friend, play a rough sport, or imagine your enemy's demise, your thirst for aggression is slaked.

Again, however, displacement is no panacea. Although vigorous activities can drain off hostilities, they work only under highly specific conditions. If, for example, you are angry with Mary but displace your hostility by kicking a wall or attacking Mary in your imagination, you probably will gain no relief. In several studies of this limitation to displacement, experimenters mildly irritated subjects by interrupting them while they were trying to count backward from 100 to 0 by twos. Then some subjects were given the chance to vent their hostility by giving the experimenter electric shocks. When subjects' blood pressure rates were compared, the subjects who thought they had harmed the experimenter showed less tension than people who had had no cathartic experience at all. Subjects' blood pressure remained high, however, if they only fantasized about harming the experimenter, or if they were allowed to harm a bystander rather than the irritating experimenter. Displacement simply didn't reduce anger and tension (Hokanson, 1970; Hokanson & Burgess, 1962a, 1962b; Hokanson & Shetler, 1961; Hokanson, Willers, & Koropsak, 1968).

Catharsis: A concluding word.

These findings cast strong doubt on Freud's alternative paths to catharsis. At best, expressing anger or engaging in nonharmful activities can drain hostile impulses, but only under very limited conditions. At worst, anger often heightens hostility and displacement leaves us feeling just as hostile as we were before. Despite Freud's conjectures, people aren't quite like teapots: letting off steam doesn't always decrease the internal pressure (Tavris, 1982).

Undoing Aggressive Motives

Aversive, noxious experiences can, in some cases, arouse a strong motivation to engage in aggressive actions. In consequence, the easiest way to control aggression is simply to avoid all environmental irritants. But for those who can't escape all the hassles that seem to fill our lives, other strategies are needed.

Controlling arousal.

"Count to ten" is an ancient and insightful recommendation for controlling aggression. According to motivation theorists, aversive experiences can create aggression, but arousal mediates the link between aversive conditions and overt hostility. Because a cooling-off period will allow time for your arousal to drop to a more normal level, counting to ten will help reduce impulsive aggression. And if arousal can be controlled, then aggression can be controlled.

Taking a moment to cool off is only one of many ways to control arousal-induced aggression. Drugs that have a calming effect can also reduce aggression in some cases. Studies suggest that marijuana, which is reputed to have mellowing effects on humans, inhibits aggressive actions. Similarly, small amounts of alcohol, which is a depressant, also inhibit aggression. Larger amounts of alcohol, in contrast, tend to increase aggression, apparently because inebriated individuals tend to feel less inhibited when they drink (see Figure 9-8; see Taylor & Leonard, 1983, for a summary). Arousal can also be controlled by avoidance of sources of excitation that can energize an aggressive response. Playing a contact sport, for example, may be a poor choice as an outlet for aggression. Not only will you become aroused, but this excitation may transfer from the athletic context to an aggressive context.

Incompatible responses. The wife tickles her grumpy husband until he starts to giggle. The employee tells his boss a few anecdotes before explaining why the report is late. The handsome man who nearly caused a fender-bender flirts with the woman driving the other car.

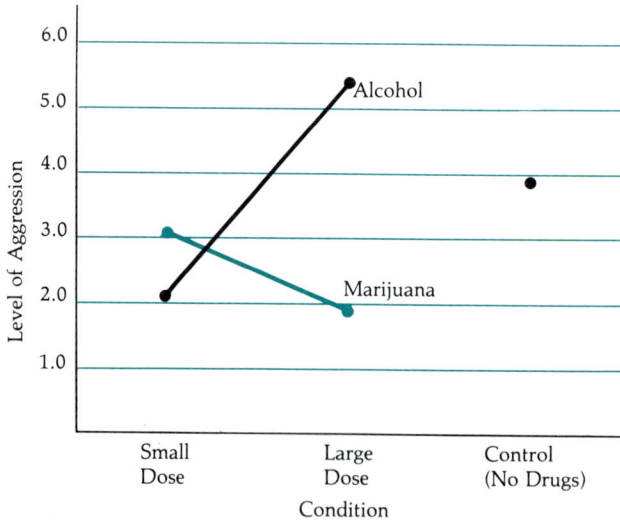

Figure 9-8 The effects of alcohol and marijuana on aggression. Subjects were administered either small or large doses of alcohol or THC (tetrahydrocannabinol, the active ingredient in marijuana). As anticipated, subjects who took THC became less aggressive. In contrast, subjects became more aggressive when they ingested larger quantities of alcohol (Taylor et al., 1976).

According to Robert A. Baron's **incompatible response strategy,** aggression is avoided in such cases by the creation of emotions that are not compatible with anger. The wife short-circuits her husband's anger by making him laugh; the employee undermines anger by creating amusement; the driver relies on mild sexual titillation. As Baron explains (1983, p. 174), any "stimuli or conditions serving to induce responses or affective states incompatible with anger or overt aggression may be effective in deterring such reactions."

Baron demonstrated the effectiveness of the incompatible response technique by giving subjects a chance to deliver electric shocks to a confederate who had angered them. Subjects who were shown a series of amusing cartoons before they delivered the shocks were less aggressive than subjects who saw only neutral pictures of scenery and abstract art (Baron & Ball, 1974). In this study, and others as well, mildly positive experiences tended to undermine aggression. It should be noted, however, that hostile humor or highly arousing sexual material will not reduce aggression because the reactions they tend to generate are compatible with aggression (Baron, 1983).

Remembering mitigating circumstances.

If a friend of yours insults you, you may not get too angry if you know that he or she has just failed an important examination. Although the insult is aversive and possibly arousing, you won't retaliate. Your friend's failure is a *mitigating circumstance*—a background factor that leads you to conclude that the insult was unintentional or unimportant. To a significant degree, when people are told about mitigating circumstances, they often moderate their aggression (see Ferguson & Rule, 1983).

Mitigating information has its greatest impact on us when it is presented before the aversive event even occurs. If the first thing your friend says to you when you meet is "I flunked my test," you will be likely to let the subsequent insult pass. If, however, your friend insults you before talking about the test, this mitigating information may not dam the flow of aggression (Johnson & Rule, 1986; Kremer & Stephens, 1983; Zillmann & Cantor, 1976). In one study of this process, male college students encountered two experimenters. One behaved rudely; he criticized his partner and unfairly accused the subject of making a mistake. The other experimenter, in contrast, behaved politely, and delivered mitigating information by saying, "He's really uptight about a midterm that he has tomorrow." After the session, the subjects encountered a third experimenter who was supposedly evaluating research assistants. When asked if the rude experimenter should be rehired, the subjects were most negative in the control condition, in which no mitigating information was given them. If they had received the mitigating information after being insulted, they still gave the experimenter somewhat negative ratings; he received positive evaluations only when the mitigating circumstances had been explained before the insult. The everyday implications of these findings are clear: if you are going to annoy people, (1) make sure they know it's not your fault and (2) give them your excuse in advance (Zillmann & Cantor, 1976).

Unlearning Aggression

Both social learning theory and normative approaches argue that aggressive behavior is learned through experience. And if aggression is learned, then it can be unlearned.

Modeling nonaggression.
If little Johnny learns to punch his younger brother by watching professional wrestling on television, he can also learn *not* to punch his brother when he sees television characters turn the other cheek. In an experimental study of nonaggressive modeling, angered subjects were asked to give electric shocks to a confederate. While waiting their turn at the shock machine, some of the subjects observed another person either giving shocks (an aggressive model) or not giving shocks (a nonaggressive model). As predicted, subjects who saw a nonaggressive model administered fewer shocks than subjects who saw an aggressive model or subjects who saw no model at all (Baron & Kepner, 1970). Stanley Milgram obtained similar findings in one version of his obedience studies (see Chapter 1). Ninety percent of the subjects who participated with two confederates who modeled disobedience by refusing to comply with the experimenter's commands also refused to shock the learner (Milgram, 1974).

Punishing aggression.
The use of punishment to decrease aggression creates a paradox. Although punishment sometimes effectively eliminates aggression, punishment itself is, in a sense, a form of aggression. Hence it tends to increase feelings of anger, particularly when the punished person thinks the punishment is unfair. Furthermore, people who use punishment are modeling aggression. When the school principal paddles a truant, when a mother spanks her child, when the judicial system executes a murderer, all are saying, "Aggression is a legitimate means to achieve your goals." Hence many experts feel that punishment should be used only as a last resort (see Baron, 1977).

Norms and Society

A final prescription for reducing violence focuses on social norms. In the United States and many other Western countries, violence is not just condoned—it is expected. Our social norms emphasize achievement and victory over others, and aggression is recognized as one means to these ends. Murder and rape are like cheap shots in hockey, just part of the game.

A normative approach to aggression suggests that the rules of the game must change. Although norms resist legislation, steps can be taken to alter the way aggression is judged and evaluated. Educational programs currently being developed can be used to teach children that aggression is a poor means of achieving their goals (A. P. Goldstein & Keller, 1983). Television, which is often blamed for cultivating violence, is now being used to convey messages emphasizing the value of cooperation and nonviolence (Liebert, Sprafkin, & Davidson, 1982). Child-rearing practices can also have a major impact on social norms. One investigator goes so far as to suggest that "if we want to reduce the level of aggression in society, we should also discourage boys from aggression very early on in life and reward them too for other behaviors; in other words, we should socialize boys more like girls" (Eron, 1980, p. 251). Thus, if we wish to eliminate aggression, we must change our society's implicit acceptance of violence as a means of achieving personal goals.

■ Summary

Aggression is an action performed with the deliberate intention of harming or injuring another person. Aggression takes many forms. Irritable or angry aggression involves strong emotional arousal. Instrumental aggression is a less emotional means of manipulating and influencing other people. Aggression is considered legitimate when it is perceived to be justified in the social setting, whereas it is considered illegitimate when it is seen as unjust and unwarranted. Contemporary forms of aggression include such violent crimes as murder and rape, domestic violence, collective violence perpetrated by groups of people, and warfare. Many of these forms of aggression have become increasingly common in recent years.

A number of theoretical perspectives have been developed to explain why humans are aggressive. Several theorists emphasize the biological bases of aggression—they suggest that humans are aggressive by nature. Sigmund Freud's *psychodynamic approach* is based on this assumption. Freud felt that aggression stems from urges that build up gradually over time in the **unconscious. Catharsis,** the discharge of these urges, is often achieved by aggressive behavior. **Ethology** argues that aggression has a biological source, but argues that animals are instinctively sensitive to certain types of environmental cues that serve to release aggressive tensions. Moreover, cues exist to turn off aggression. Lorenz argued that the use of weapons has undermined the effectiveness of these cues in humans. *Sociobiology* also offers a biological view of aggression. Like ethology, sociobiology is based on Charles Darwin's theory of evolution. Sociobiology's concept of *inclusive fitness,* however, argues that the fittest organism is the one that ensures the survival of its genes in future generations. According to sociobiology, aggression is a situation-specific action that maximizes the animal's fitness.

In contrast to Freud's psychodynamic theory, ethology, and sociobiology, social-psychological theories emphasize the impact of situational forces on aggression. *Motivation models* argue that environmental factors heighten the need to be aggressive. The **frustration-aggression hypothesis,** an early motivation theory, argued that thwarting environmental conditions lead to feelings of frustration, and that these feelings of frustration cause aggression. This view has evolved into the **arousal-aggression hypothesis,** which states that (*a*) many aversive environmental factors, such as heat, noise, and failure, can cause physiological arousal, and (*b*) this arousal sometimes leads to aggression. As Leonard Berkowitz's studies of the *weapons effect* suggest, certain social stimuli can function as cues that increase the likelihood that arousal will lead to aggression. Also, physiological arousal caused by nonaggressive stimuli or events, such as a high temperature or pornography, can instigate aggression through a process of **excitation transfer.**

Albert Bandura's *social learning theory* assumes that individuals learn aggressive behavior through reinforcement and observation. In many cases, children are directly rewarded for behaving aggressively. As Bandura's well-known Bobo doll studies show, children also engage in more aggression after observing aggressive acts performed by peer and adult models. One implication of Bandura's social learning theory concerns television: Does watching violence on television cause viewers to become more aggressive? Researchers have found that children who watch violent programs tend to be more aggressive, and they sometimes directly copy types of violence that they have observed. Heavy television viewing has also been linked to reduced sensitivity to real-world violence and to distorted perceptions of social reality. Many (although not all) studies conducted in field settings have also confirmed the link between televised violence and aggression. Most social psychologists feel that violent television programs have harmful consequences.

According to the *normative approach,* aggression is sometimes consistent with the standards of conduct considered appropriate in our society. The norm of reciprocity suggests that violence can be legitimately met with violence, while in some groups unique norms emerge that emphasize aggression and toughness. As norms sometimes keep aggression in check, the removal of such norms can lead to aggression. Philip Zimbardo's theory of **deindividuation** suggests that aggression sometimes occurs when individuals become so submerged in a group that they lose their sense of personal identity. Anonymity and group membership appear to be the key determinants of deindividuation.

How can aggression be controlled? Freud recommended the ventilation of anger to release hostile urges and the displacement of aggression in more socially acceptable actions. Research, however, has failed to confirm the usefulness of these suggestions. Interventions derived from the arousal-aggression model and social learning theory have been shown to be more effective. We can diminish aggression by delaying our reactions until our arousal dissipates, by employing an **incompatible response strategy,** and by accentuating mitigating circumstances. Aggression is also unlearned when children view models who engage in nonaggressive actions. Experts also feel that punishment can temporarily prevent aggression, but that this technique is ineffective in the long run. Lastly, the normative approach argues that aggression can be countered by the elimination of social norms that encourage violence.

■ For More Information

1. *Rape and Sexual Assault,* edited by Ann Wolbert Burgess (1985), studies violence against women from a variety of perspectives. Chapters deal with five basic themes: contemporary attitudes toward rape, victims of rape, family and legal issues, the rapist, and the prevention of rape.

2. *The Resolution of Conflict,* by Morton Deutsch (1973), examines the way in which conflict between people can arise through competition and mistrust. Drawing on his own laboratory studies of subjects' reactions to interdependence, Deutsch offers insights into the causes and consequences of interpersonal conflict.

3. *Aggression: Theoretical and Empirical Reviews,* edited by Russell G. Geen and Edward I. Donnerstein (1982), provides an excellent overview of the field of aggression. The 16 chapters in this two-volume work are written by leading researchers in the field, who provide comprehensive accounts of various aspects of aggression.

4. *Prevention and Control of Aggression,* edited by Arnold P. Goldstein (1983), is a publication of the Syracuse University Center for Research on Aggression. Taking an interdisciplinary approach to aggression, the book presents concrete suggestions for reducing child and spouse abuse, violence in schools, juvenile delinquency, rape, and such forms of international violence as terrorism.

5. *The Early Window: Effects of Television on Children and Youth,* by Robert M. Liebert, Joyce N. Sprafkin, and Emily S. Davidson (1982), takes a close look at the impact of television on our social lives. Liebert and his colleagues explore the link between violent programs and aggression, and also consider television's use as an educational tool.

6. *Anger: The Misunderstood Emotion,* by Carol Tavris (1982), summarizes the social psychology of anger and aggression for the informed lay reader. Filled with interesting anecdotes and commentaries by researchers in the field, the book refutes many common myths about anger. Tavris's treatment of sex differences in anger is particularly insightful.

7. *Working for Peace,* edited by N. Wollman (1985), is a sourcebook of practical psychological tools and techniques that can be used to reduce aggression. The book is aimed at individuals who are involved in the movement for world peace.

IN DEPTH

Competition and Conflict

We cannot expect that all our interactions with others will be smooth and harmonious. Even the best of friends or the closest of lovers experience moments of disagreement, discord, and friction. Inevitably, incompatible activities occur that create **conflict** between us and the people with whom we interact. Conflicts do not necessarily lead to hostility or aggression, but they often shake the foundations of our interpersonal relationships.

Morton Deutsch, who has been studying the causes and consequences of conflict for more than thirty years, believes that many interpersonal conflicts stem from competition. When we cooperate with one another, our success improves others' chances of success. When we compete, however, others must fail if we are to succeed. By striving for our personal goals, we interfere with others' attempts to reach their own goals. By definition, competition creates incompatibility between people, and Deutsch believes that this incompatibility can escalate into interpersonal conflict (Deutsch, 1949a, 1949b, 1973, 1980).

Social psychologists have often used a specialized laboratory technique known as the **prisoner's dilemma game,** or **PDG,** to study the factors that link cooperation, competition, and conflict. This technique derives its name from a tale about two men who are arrested by the police. The suspects are questioned in separate rooms. Although the police are certain that the suspects are guilty, they also realize that without a confession the pair will have to be set free. Therefore, each suspect is told that if he remains silent and his partner confesses, the partner will be released and he himself will receive a sentence of ten years. Alternatively, if he confesses and his partner remains silent, then he will be released and his partner will suffer. If both men confess, both will receive moderate sentences of five years. And should both men remain silent, they will be tried on a minor charge that carries a fairly light sentence of one year.

This situation creates a dilemma for each prisoner. If he confesses, he will end up with either no sentence or a five-year term. By remaining silent, he takes the chance of receiving a one-year sentence or a ten-year sentence. Should he gamble that his partner will remain silent, or give in to the pressure and confess (see Figure 9-9).

In the experimental version of this dilemma, the years are replaced by money or points, and the decision to confess or not becomes a choice between option A and option B (see Figure 9-10). Typically, subjects are seated in separate rooms, and they make their choices simultaneously. After the subjects select either A or B, they are then given feedback about their partner's choice and the amount of money they won or lost. In most cases, subjects choose between A and B a number of times. Each set of choices is called a "trial."

Although the PDG oversimplifies the complexities of conflict, it illustrates the problem that people encounter when they must choose between cooperation and competition (see Wrightsman, O'Connor, & Baker, 1972). Imagine that you are a subject in a study that uses the matrix shown in Figure 9-10. You want to earn $1, and to win that amount you must pick B. But you see that whenever you pick B, your partner loses money. B, then, is the *competitive* choice. Moreover, if you pick B and your part-

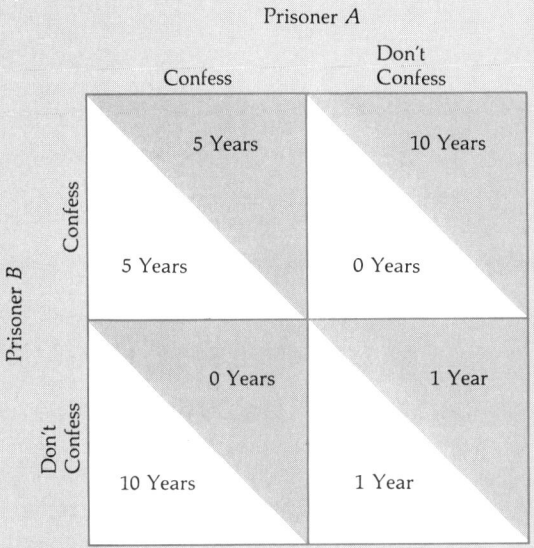
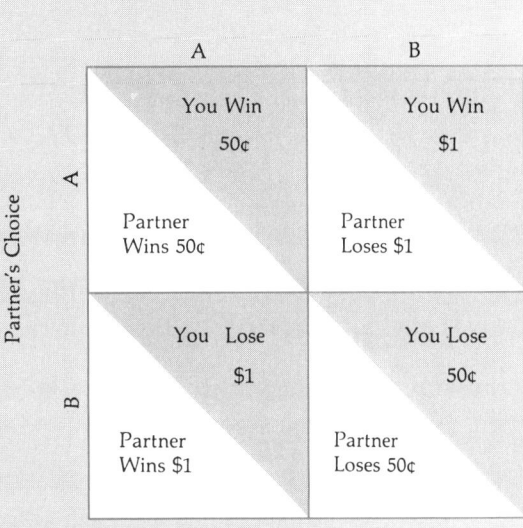

Figure 9-9 The prisoner's dilemma. This chart summarizes the problem faced by two imaginary prisoners. Each prisoner can either confess or remain silent. These choices are shown along the sides of the matrix. The numbers within each cell of the matrix correspond to the outcomes that the two prisoners can receive. In each cell, prisoner A's outcomes are shown above the diagonal line, and prisoner B's outcomes are shown below the diagonal. If, for example, prisoner A confesses but prisoner B does not confess, then A will receive 0 years and B will receive 10 years.

Figure 9-10 A matrix for the prisoner's dilemma game. The subject's task is simple: pick either A or B. In each cell, your outcomes are shown above the diagonal line, and your partner's outcomes are shown below the diagonal. If you choose A and your partner chooses A, for example, you both earn 50 cents. If, however, one of you chooses A and the other chooses B, the one who picks A loses money and the one who picks B wins money. A is the cooperative choice, whereas B is the competitive choice.

ner also picks B, you both lose 50 cents. In other words, if you both make competitive choices, you both lose.

Does option A offer an easy solution to this quandary? Not exactly. A is the *cooperative* choice. If you look at the matrix, you can see that any time you pick A, your partner will earn some money (either 50 cents or $1). What happens if your partner, a stranger you have no way of communicating with, picks B when you pick A? Then you will lose $1 and your partner will earn $1. If you cooperate while your partner competes, you will lose money. Because the PDG creates conflicting pressures to cooperate and compete, it is known as a
(continued)

IN DEPTH *continued*

mixed-motive situation: the motive to cooperate is mixed with the motive to compete.

How do people react when asked to make a choice in the prisoner's dilemma game? In most cases, actions in the PDG follow the *reciprocity principle:* cooperation begets cooperation, while competition begets competition. When people play the PDG with a partner who consistently makes cooperative choices, they tend themselves to cooperate. Those who encounter competitors, however, soon adopt this strategy and they too begin to compete. However, two important qualifications have also been identified by researchers. First, negative reciprocity is stronger than positive reciprocity. That is, a cooperative person who runs into a competitive partner is likely to begin to compete *before* the competitive person begins to cooperate (Kelley & Stahelski, 1970a, 1970b, 1970c). A partner turns into an opponent faster than an opponent turns into a partner.

Second, people sometimes take advantage of people who are unusually cooperative. Imagine that you are taking part in a PDG study. You have gone through five trials, and each time both you and your partner chose A. You cooperated with each other, and won 50 cents each time (see Figure 9-10). Out of boredom or spite or curiosity, however, you decide to compete on trial 6. Your partner continues to cooperate; you win $1, while he or she loses $1. Now, on trial 7, fearful that your partner will pay you back for your competitive choice, you once more pick the competitive option to minimize your loss. Much to your surprise, your partner once again selects A, the cooperative choice. What should you do on trial 8—reciprocate by cooperating, or continue to exploit? Most people choose exploitation. Perhaps a study wasn't needed to verify this point, but the findings do indicate that people are quite ready to take advantage of you if you let them (Shure, Meeker, & Hansford, 1965).

Researchers have also found that the tendencies toward both negative reciprocity and exploitation are caused by the erosion of trust that occurs during competition. The payoff matrix of the PDG makes the exploitation of a cooperating partner a tempting alternative. Recognizing this temptation, subjects sometimes feel that their partners cannot be trusted to make responses that benefit both players. Therefore, they make competitive choices to defend themselves, while they assume that their partner makes competitive choices to exploit their trust. As a result, *mirror-image thinking* occurs: both players assume that their opponent is the competitor who is intent upon winning, while they themselves are only trying to defend themselves (R. K. White, 1977).

Even when they encounter a cooperative partner, subjects are so suspicious that they refuse to reciprocate with cooperation. In one study subjects played a modified version of the PDG against a simulated partner who adopted one of four styles: (1) competitive (maximized personal winnings while minimizing the subject's winnings), (2) cooperative (maximized joint winnings), (3) individualistic (maximized personal winnings but didn't interfere with the subject's winnings), and (4) altruistic (always tried to help the subject win). When asked to describe their partner's motives, subjects were most accurate when the partner adopted an individualistic or competitive style, and least accurate in interpreting cooperation and altruism. They recognized competition when they saw it, but they had difficulty believing that their partners were behaving in a prosocial manner (Maki, Thorngate, & McClintock, 1979; see also Kelley & Stahelski, 1970a, 1970b).

What does the PDG tell us about the causes and consequences of conflict? In our daily lives we constantly encounter mixed-motive situations that force us to choose between competition and cooperation. If we decide to compete, we must realize that our choice will prompt others to compete as well. Cooperation, however, is no guarantee that others will reciprocate. If others interpret your cooperativeness as a sign of weakness, then they may exploit your selflessness. Indeed, to push a competitive partner toward cooperation, you must sometimes show your willingness to compete if necessary. Lastly, conflicts become destructive when they are clouded by misunderstandings and misperceptions. Many of the negative consequences of conflict can be avoided if we simply strive to see the situation from the other person's perspective (Deutsch, 1973).

T E N

Social Influence

Conformity
    When do people conform?
        Breaking unanimity
        The size of the majority
    Why do people conform?
        Informational influence
        Normative influence
        Social pressure
        Fear of dissent
        Mindlessness
        Combining the causes
Nonconformity
    When do people refuse to conform?
        The nonconformist
        The counterconformist
        Sex differences in nonconformity
        Situational supports for nonconformity
    Does nonconformity lead to social influence?
        Idiosyncrasy credits
        Consistency
        Coalition formation
Social power and influence
    Social power
        Reward power
        Coercive power
        Legitimate power
        Referent power
        Expert power
        Combining the five bases
    Social influence tactics
    Specialized tactics
        The foot in the door
        The door in the face
        Low-balling
Summary
For more information
In depth: Social influence in juries

Ancient astrologers had no problem explaining human behavior. They believed that an ethereal fluid flowed down from the planets and the stars to affect human actions. This force, called *influentia*, could be seen at work in countless situations, for it left its mark on the personalities and behaviors of all living organisms. Invisible yet inexorable, influentia was capable of producing an effect without obvious and direct force; it subtly pushed humans in one direction or another without enslaving them.

Social psychologists also believe that our actions are affected by relentless unseen forces, but they trace these forces to other people rather than to the stars. Influence is a social phenomenon, for it derives from the mutual impact of one person on another; other people can change the way we think and act with subtle pressure and power, just as we can change them. To social psychologists this sometimes hidden, sometimes obvious process is not mystical; it is simply social influence.

Social influence occurs in many forms. In some cases, we change our beliefs and behaviors so that they match the beliefs and behaviors of the people around us—we bow to pressures to **conformity**. Other people can sway our opinions, convince us that our beliefs are mistaken, and encourage us to act in some ways rather than others. Influence, however, is a two-way street. If others can change us, then we can change others through **nonconformity**. By refusing to take the majority's outlook, we maintain our own views *and* prompt the majority to reexamine its position. Whether or not the majority or the minority prevails is a question of *power*—who has it and who uses it most effectively.

■ Conformity

Philip G. Zimbardo's Stanford Prison Study underscores the dramatic impact of social forces on our behavior. From a group of 70 volunteers he selected two dozen healthy, intelligent, and psychologically normal men to serve as either prisoners or guards in a simulated prison. The prisoners were "arrested" by uniformed police, booked, and transported to a mock prison that Zimbardo and his colleagues had constructed in the basement of the psychology building at Stanford University. They were sprayed with a deodorant, searched, issued an identification number, and outfitted in a dresslike shirt, heavy ankle chain, and stocking cap. Guards were issued khaki uniforms, billy clubs, whistles, and reflective sunglasses reminiscent of those worn by the guards in the movie *Cool Hand Luke*. The guards were told to maintain security and order in the prison (Haney, Banks, & Zimbardo, 1973; Zimbardo, 1975).

The study was scheduled to run for two weeks, but was terminated after only six days. Why? According to Zimbardo, the subjects became all too immersed in the social situation. The prisoners seemed literally to

TABLE 10–1

What happened in Zimbardo's simulated prison? The behaviors indicated below suggest that the subjects were working hard to conform to the rules of the game. In doing so, they unwittingly slipped into the social roles of prisoner and guard.

Time	Description of Event
Day 1	Prisoners are brought to the "Stanford County Prison."
Day 2	The guards awaken the prisoners at 2:30 A.M. and make them shout out their prison identification number, which is sewn to their shifts.
	The prisoners rebel, remove stocking caps and numbers, and barricade themselves in their cells. Guards counter by hosing them down with a chemical fire extinguisher.
	To prevent rebellious incidents, the guards set up a privilege cell and a solitary confinement cell.
Day 3	Using the bathroom becomes a privilege. After 10:00 P.M. prisoners must urinate in a bucket in their cells.
	Prisoner #8612 is released because of "acute emotional disturbance."
	Visiting day: all parents, relatives, and friends agree to the prison's arbitrary visitation rules.
Day 4	A priest visits the prisoners, encourages them to contact a lawyer or public defender.
	Prisoner #819 is released after breaking down and crying hysterically.
Day 5	Parole board meets; all subjects say that they will forfeit all the payment they have earned as subjects up to this time if paroled.
	Prisoner–guard relations stabilize; prisoners join guards in an attempt to force one subject to end a hunger strike.
	Several factors—the increasing malice of the guards, the depression levels of the prisoners, and the reaction of a colleague to the prisoners' degradation—prompt Zimbardo to consider ending the study.
Day 6	Experiment terminated.

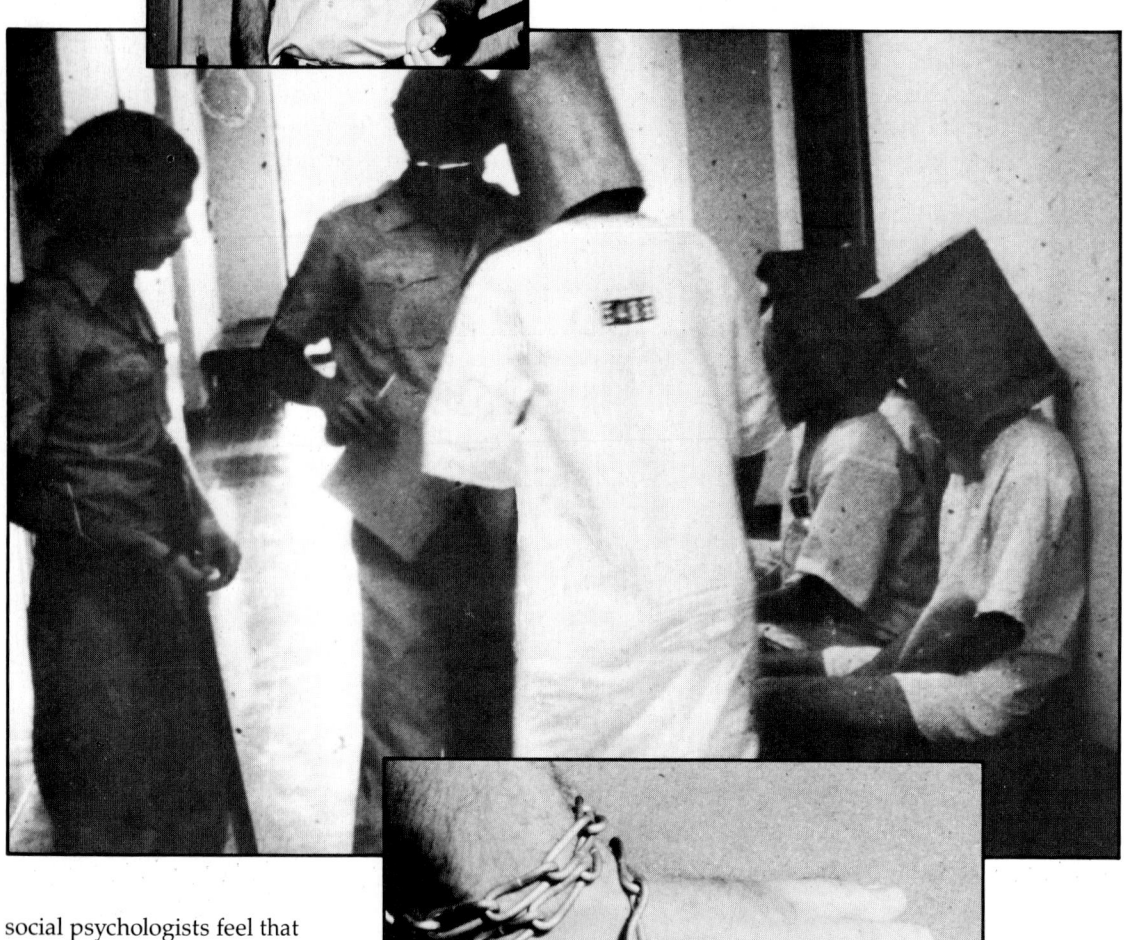

Figure 10-1   Scenes from Zimbardo's Stanford Prison Study. Zimbardo calls this technique for studying social behavior a functional simulation. He admits that his "prison" is very different from a real prison. However, he tried to duplicate the psychological atmosphere of a prison by giving guards reflective glasses and chaining the prisoners. Because he used these procedures, many social psychologists feel that Zimbardo's study tells us very little about the dynamics of social behavior in an actual prison (Festinger, 1980, p. 252).

become prisoners; although some rebelled, the majority became withdrawn and depressed. Several prisoners were released for medical reasons—they suffered severe hysterical reactions, such as uncontrollable crying, disordered thought, and psychosomatic reactions—but even these subjects didn't just say, "I quit this study"; they all asked for *parole from prison!* The guards also changed as the study progressed; many became increasingly tyrannical and arbitrary in their control of the prisoners. They woke the prisoners in the middle of the night and forced them to stand at attention for hours, locked them in a closet, required them to clean toilets with their bare hands, strictly enforced pointless rules, and censored prisoners' mail. Zimbardo confesses that he even found himself sinking too deeply into the role of warden, worrying over possible "prison breaks" and autocratically controlling visiting procedures (see Table 10-1).

What does Zimbardo's study tell us about prisoners and prison life? Not much, for the discrepancies between Zimbardo's simulated prison and real prisons are great (see Figure 10-1). His study does, however, provide us with a dramatic illustration of the power of pressures to conform in social life. Almost from the start, subjects tried to conform to the implicit norms of the situation. A *norm* is a social standard that describes what behaviors should and shouldn't be performed in a social setting. Even though the situation created by Zimbardo was ambiguous, it was not normless. All of the subjects had a general idea of what it meant to act like a prisoner or like a guard. As the study progressed, they became more and more comfortable in their roles. Eventually, to be a guard meant to control all aspects of the prison, and to use force to protect this control if necessary. Prisoners, on the other hand, were supposed to accept this control and try to get through the experience as easily as possible by obeying all the prison's rules. Subjects who refused to obey these norms were pressured by the other subjects until they brought their behavior back in line; nonconformity was not tolerated.

At this point you may be saying to yourself, "I understand that people's actions are sometimes influenced by social pressures, but are these pressures really all that strong?" To answer this question, let's consider some of the situational factors that encourage conformity and discourage independence (see Focus 10-1).

When Do People Conform?

Most of the "prisoners" in the Stanford Prison Study went along with the norms of the situation. Prisoner #416, however, was more rebellious. He went on a hunger strike. In response to this nonconforming behavior, both the guards and the prisoners singled out #416 for punishment. Although his fellow inmates could have supported his rebelliousness, they attacked him verbally with curses, insults, and demands that he eat. The pressure was so great that #416 abandoned his hunger strike. Prisoner #416 had conformed: he changed his behavior in response to social pressure.

When do people yield to social pressure? Solomon E. Asch's pioneering studies of conformity provide a partial answer. Asch began by assembling seven-man groups in a laboratory. He then asked the men to look at two cards like those shown in Figure 10-2; one card contained the "standard" line, while the other card displayed three vertical lines of varying length. The subjects' task was to pick the one line from the second card that was the same length as the standard line on the first card. This comparison process was repeated 18 times, and on each occasion the subjects announced their answers aloud (Asch, 1951, 1955).

Unknown to the subject seated in the sixth chair, all the other participants were confederates; they had been told to choose an incorrect answer on 12 of the 18 trials. On a test trial, for example, the first confederate would glance at the cards and confidently say, "The answer is line one," and this wrong answer would be repeated until it was the subject's turn to answer. Asch wished to see how often the subject would go along with the majority's opinion by repeating the incorrect answer.

FOCUS 10-1

Experiencing Social Psychology: *Are you underestimating the power of social influence?*

Do you find a conformity explanation of Zimbardo's findings surprising? Do you feel that so bizarre an outcome requires an equally bizarre causal explanation? If so, you may be underestimating the power of social norms and conformity pressures. Although we like to think of ourselves as individualists who control our own actions and thoughts, we tend to be rule followers, not rule breakers.

Harold Garfinkel (1967) believes that one of the best ways to discover the power of pressures to conform is to violate an everyday social norm intentionally. He calls these demonstrations *breaching studies*, because they create a gap or breach in the social reality that implicitly guides so many of our actions. To carry out a breaching study, all you need to do is break a common norm of behavior. When you purchase a small object in a store, for example, try to bargain with the salesperson: "I'll give you a quarter for this candy bar, but not a penny more." Or ask several friends to play a game of tic-tac-toe, and during the game erase their mark and replace it with your own. When they challenge your actions, insist that erasures are "just a part of the game." Another method is to refuse to understand common, everyday expressions during conversations with others; if someone says, "How are you?" you answer, "Do you mean physically or psychologically?" Or violate the norm of "civil inattention" by staring at people while riding in an elevator (Goffman, 1963).

Although these norm violations may seem minor, others will probably try to punish you for not conforming. If you refuse to change your behavior, you will probably feel very self-conscious. In one breaching study experimenters asked subway passengers to give up their seats—an unheard-of norm violation for New York city residents. Those who actually succeeded in carrying out the assignment

> felt anxious, tense, and embarrassed. Frequently, they were unable to vocalize the request for a seat and had to withdraw. They sometimes feared that they were the center of attention of the car and were often unable to look directly at the subject. Once having made the request and received a seat, they sometimes felt a need to enact behavior that would make the request appear justified. [Milgram & Sabini, 1978, p. 37]

The social pressure was so intense that many experimenters pretended that they were very ill so that the passengers would understand why they had acted so strangely.

"Can you imagine? At some schools they make you wear a uniform."

We tend to think of ourselves as individualists, free to do, say, and even dress as we want. Yet, we generally conform to the social norms of our group or society.

© 1982 Nick Hobart, PHI DELTA KAPPAN

Judging lines was an easy chore. When subjects worked alone, they rarely made an error. Yet after the confederates had given the same incorrect answer, about one-third of the subjects conformed by also giving the wrong answer. As Figure 10-3 indicates, on the first trial about 20 percent of the 123 subjects agreed with the majority's erroneous opinion. This error rate increased during the next 11 trials, so that the average conformity rate across the session was 36.8%. Only 5% of the subjects conformed on every trial. However, 76.4% of the subjects made at least one blatant error during the experiment.

On the basis of these findings, Asch concluded that "people submit uncritically and painlessly to external manipulation by suggestion," but that "independence and the capacity to rise above group passion are also open to human beings" (1955, p. 32). But when do we choose to conform and when to act independently? According to Asch, our choice is often influenced by the *unanimity* and the *size* of the majority.

Breaking unanimity. In Asch's original study, subjects faced a *unanimous majority:* all six of the confederates agreed on the incorrect answer, leaving the subject alone in his dissent. Because Asch felt that unanimity

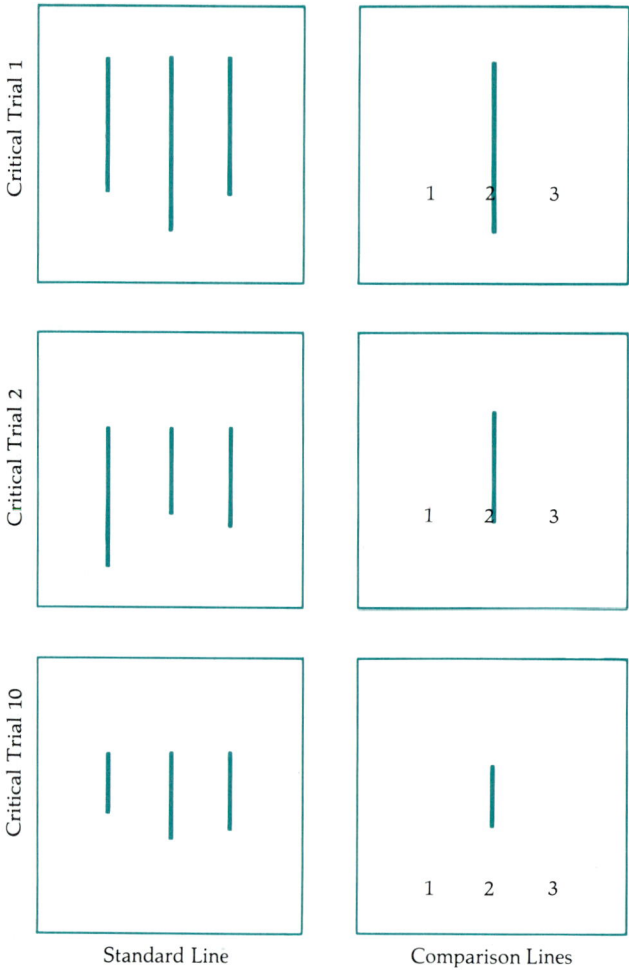

Figure 10-2 Subjects in the Asch conformity study were shown two cards. One pictured the "standard" line, while the second bore three "test" lines. The subjects were to state aloud the number of the line on the second card that matched the standard line in length.

was a critical determinant of pressure to conform, he modified the basic procedure by giving the subject a partner—either a trained confederate or a second uninformed subject. As expected, when someone else disagreed with the majority, conformity rates were cut to one-fourth their previous levels. Thus we can better resist social influence when we have the moral support of an ally.

In fact, even an inaccurate ally helped subjects withstand pressures to conform. In one variation, Asch arranged for some confederates to disagree with the majority but still give an incorrect answer. Again, conform-

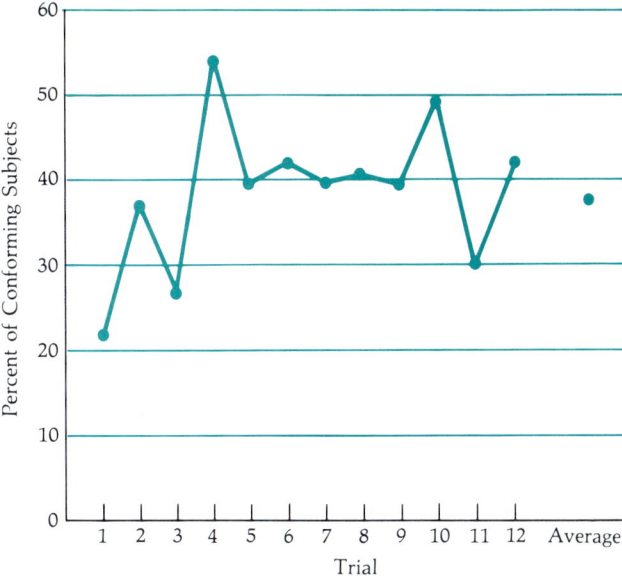

Figure 10-3 Percentage of conforming subjects in the Asch experiment. Subjects' responses can be summarized in two ways. First, on any given trial, one-third of the subjects conformed. The conformity rate averaged across all 12 trials—36.8%—is shown at the far right of the graph. Second, over three-fourths of the subjects conformed at least once during the experiment—76.4% made at least one mistake.

ity rates remained low. Right or wrong, a single dissenting voice breaks the unanimity of the majority. Nonconformists make it easier for others to express conflicting views (Morris & Miller, 1975a).

The size of the majority. Asch also examined a question that continues to puzzle researchers: Does pressure to conform increase as the *size of the majority* increases? By varying the number of confederates, he found that subjects conformed on only 3.6% of the trials if they faced only one opponent. Two opponents, however, increased the percentage to 13.6, while a unanimous majority of three increased conformity to 31.8%. A maximum amount of conformity was found in seven-person groups (37.1%); even a majority of 15 couldn't raise conformity appreciably above this level. These findings suggest that three may be the "tipping point" when it comes to conformity. Subjects who can withstand the pressure of two other people crumble when they face three opponents. Also, beyond three, each added person has a lesser impact on us. As Focus 10-2 explains, a group of 16 people is no more influential than a group of 15 (Knowles, 1983; Latané & Wolf, 1981; Mullen, 1983, 1985; Tanford & Penrod, 1984).

Why Do People Conform?

Picture in your mind a person conforming in the Asch experiment. Who do you see? A pale, nervous sycophant mumbling an answer he knows is wrong? A weak-kneed follower who can't make up his mind without relying on others' opinions? A nearsighted self-doubter who doesn't trust the evidence of his own perceptions?

These images of people who conform are unfair exaggerations. Although the word *conformity* often summons up thoughts of wishy-washy people who are so intimidated by the majority's opinions that they can't stand up for their rights, conformity springs from many sources. Sometimes we conform because we don't want to appear different or are afraid the majority will punish us if we dissent, but in other cases we conform for rational or cooperative reasons. Keeping in mind that conformity can be caused by many factors even in a simple situation like that studied by Asch, let us review several of the more prominent determinants of conformity.

FOCUS 10–2

A Closer Look: *What factors influence social impact in groups?*

During a staff meeting, discussion focuses on whether or not your company should purchase IBM computers or Apple computers. You strongly favor IBMs, but everyone else favors Apples. Will you go along with the group's position or continue to hold out for IBMs?

According to Bibb Latané and Sharon Wolf, the *impact* of the majority on you, the minority, depends on three basic factors: the strength of the individuals in the majority, their immediacy, and the number of people present. To illustrate the assumptions underlying **social impact theory,** they draw an analogy between people and light bulbs. Imagine that you turn on a lamp in an otherwise dark room. Suddenly the room is filled with brightness. The amount of light in the room, however, depends on the strength of the bulb in the lamp: a 25-watt bulb gives just enough light to see by, while a floodlight may reach every corner. The lamp's location is also important. A lamp in one corner may leave the opposite corner of the room in shadow. Also, if we want more light, we can always turn on more lamps. Eventually, however, the room will become so bright that another lamp will make no difference.

In an analogous fashion, your reaction to the Apple devotees depends on their *strength,* or status in the group. If you have just joined the company and are low on the totem pole, then they have more strength than you do. You are a 25-watt bulb surrounded by 100-watt bulbs. *Immediacy* is also important, for people who are physically present in the room will have a greater impact than people who are absent. The accountant may have been unable to attend the meeting, for example, so she sent a message saying she preferred IBMs. Unfortunately, her immediacy is low, since she is not part of the face-to-face group meeting. Last, sheer *numbers* are also critical. How many people oppose you? Four? Eight? Twelve? As with light bulbs, the more people, the greater their impact on you—up to a point. The first light you turn on in a dark room has a greater impact than the hundredth light you turn on. Similarly, the first person who disagrees with you has more impact than the hundredth person added to a majority that disagrees with you. Thus pressures to conform don't increase at a constant rate as more people join the majority. As Figure 10-4 illustrates, "there is a marginally decreasing effect of increased supplies of people" (Latané, 1981, p. 344; see also Latané & Wolf, 1981; Wolf & Latané, 1983; Wolf, 1985).

Informational influence. In familiar, everyday situations you don't need to consult others to make decisions or form opinions; you rely on your own judgment. Sometimes, though, you haven't enough information to respond, so you engage in social comparison; you check to see if your reactions correspond to the reactions of other people present in the setting (see Chapter 2). When you attend a symphony concert for the first time, you may do what others do: clap when they clap, stand when they stand, and shout "Encore!" when they shout "Encore!" Similarly, after ordering an eggroll in a Chinese restaurant, you may look around the room to see if other people are eating their eggrolls with their fingers, forks, or chopsticks. Or if you are supposed to be a prisoner in an odd social psychology experiment, you may see how the other subjects are reacting to figure out what is expected of you. *Informational influence* can be seen in each of these situations. Other people are influencing you by providing information that you can then use in making your own decisions and forming your own opinions.

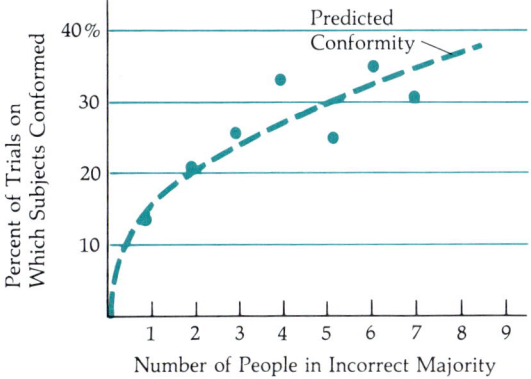

Figure 10-4 The percentage of critical trials in which subjects conformed with majorities of various size. According to Latané and Wolf, social impact increases at a decreasing rate as more and more people join the majority. The dotted line represents this prediction. The data points indicate the amount of conformity found in a study in which the number of people in the majority varied from one to seven (Gerard, Wilhelmy, & Conolley, 1968). Note that the dotted line matches the research findings quite closely.

Researchers have only begun to test social impact theory's predictions, but initial returns are favorable. When Latané reexamined the findings of earlier studies of conformity, he found that they are often consistent with social impact theory. In one study, for example, strength and immediacy were held constant, but the number of people was varied from one to seven. As Figure 10-4 indicates, conformity increased up to a point, but then began to level off (Latané, 1981). The theory has also been used to predict when people will become embarrassed in front of audiences. When subjects were asked to imagine themselves singing "The Star-Spangled Banner," they reported greater nervousness when the audience was high in strength (experts on music) than when its strength was low (tone-deaf college students). Nervousness also increased as the number of people in the audience increased, but only up to a point (Jackson & Latané, 1981). Additional evidence is needed for full evaluation of the theory, but at this time it yields considerable insight into the processes of conformity and social influence. (Jackson, 1986, and Mullen, 1986, examine the strengths and weaknesses of social impact theory.)

Muzafer Sherif (1936) demonstrated the impact of informational influence on our judgments by asking subjects seated in a dark room to estimate the movement, in inches, of a small lighted dot. Unknown to the subjects, the dot remained stationary. Its apparent movement was an optical illusion known as the autokinetic effect: in a dark room, a stationary pinpoint of light will seem to move about because the eye lacks a stable frame of reference. Sherif discovered that after several trials, subjects developed personal expectations about the movement; most estimates ranged from one to ten inches. When they made judgments with others, however, subjects would modify these personal expectations to take into account the others' estimates. As a result (and as Figure 10-5 shows), subjects' judgments became more and more similar until they completely converged during the third session. According to Sherif, subjects were striving to be accurate judges of distance, and so they used the information contained in others' responses to guide their answers. Rather than simply trying to agree with others or being forced into changing their answers by the other group members, subjects were subtly influenced by the information conveyed by the other subjects' responses (Pollis, Montgomery, & Smith, 1975).

Subsequent studies indicated that informational influence was especially important in the autokinetic situation because the judgment task was so ambiguous. Subjects lacked an external standard or experience in the situation, so information obtained from others was critically important. On a less ambiguous, less subjective, or less difficult task, however,

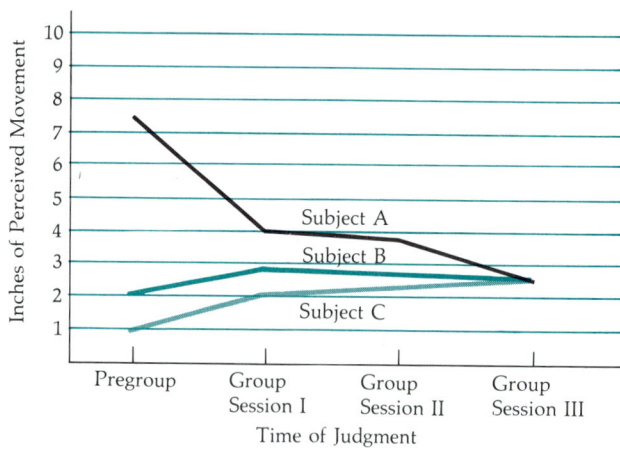

Figure 10-5 The responses of subjects in Sherif's study show increasing convergence of judgments with each session. Although the subjects' private, pregroup judgments differed widely, their judgments tended to converge when they joined with others. This sequence of change is sometimes called a "funnel pattern."

people can use their own values or beliefs rather than rely on others. These findings suggest that informational influence pressures may have been very strong in Zimbardo's prison study; because subjects had never been in such a bizarre situation before, they let other subjects' actions guide their own behavior. Gradually their actions converged—most of the prisoners became docile, whereas the guards (to a lesser degree) became more oppressive and authoritarian. In contrast, informational influence pressures were probably relatively weak in Asch's research, since the problems had such clear-cut answers (Asch, 1951; Coleman, Blake, & Mouton, 1958; Deutsch & Gerard, 1955).

Normative influence.   Some early theorists (Deutsch & Gerard, 1955; Kelley, 1952) drew a distinction between informational influence and normative influence. Informational influence, as we have seen, occurs because others' responses convey information concerning the nature of the social setting and how we should behave. *Normative influence*, in contrast, occurs when we tailor our actions to fit the social norms of the situation. Because norms are not simply external constraints but also internalized standards, we often feel compelled to make certain that we do not violate these rules of behavior. Americans don't drive on the right side of the road, for example, just because everybody else is doing so. Rather, most drivers recognize that this rule must be followed for safety reasons. We conform to many norms because we have internalized them—incorporated them into our own personal system of beliefs and values.

Sherif and other investigators (Jacobs & Campbell, 1961; Pollis, Montgomery, & Smith, 1975; Sherif, 1966) have separated the influence of informational and normative factors by examining the judgmental aftereffects of the autokinetic situation. The gradual changes that occurred in the making of judgments in the presence of others could be attributed to informational social influence—subjects used others' estimates as guidelines. But what would happen when isolated subjects were later asked to make judgments? Would they return to their own idiosyncratic estimates? Or would they continue to base their judgments on the distance norm that their group had developed? As Sherif anticipated, normative influence was found: subjects relied on the group norm even though they were no longer actually in the group setting. They had apparently internalized the norm and did not feel that they should violate it. Sherif was the first researcher to show that a social norm could be created experimentally.

Social pressure.   American society supposedly praises nonconformity and independence. As Ralph Waldo Emerson proclaims, "I must be myself. I will not hide any taste or aversions. . . . I will do strongly before the sun and moon whatever inly rejoices me and the heart appoints" (1926, p. 53). Yet in countless everyday situations the dominant theme is

This man disagrees with the others, but he is the target of strong social pressures that may prompt him to change his beliefs. If he gives in, this change could reflect either compliance—agreeing with others but retaining one's original beliefs—or private acceptance—true conversion to the position endorsed by the majority.

"To get along, go along." Dissent is not rewarded; in fact, it is met with strong pressure aimed at forcing deviants to change their behaviors, beliefs, or attitudes until they match those of the majority. Thus conformity doesn't always result from informational and normative influence, for sometimes we conform because we have given in to direct *social pressure:* social influence tactics designed to persuade, coerce, or otherwise induce us to change our beliefs or behaviors.

Those of us who have found ourselves in unexpected disagreement with a group of people trying to choose a restaurant, pick a movie, nominate a leader, or plan a course of action can sympathize with the confederates in Stanley Schachter's (1951) classic study of the pressures focused on dissenters in small discussion groups. In forming the all-male groups, Schachter made certain that each one contained three confederates: (1) the *deviant*, who was trained to disagree consistently with the majority; (2) the *slider*, who disagreed with the majority at the beginning of the discussion but gradually slid toward agreement; and (3) the *mode*, who consistently agreed with the majority. Schachter was interested in seeing what kinds of pressures would be put on the deviant, and also what effect two other independent variables—the cohesiveness of the group and the relevance of the topic under discussion to the group's goals—would have on conformity pressure.

To gauge the amount of direct social pressure applied to each of these three confederates, Schachter kept track of the number of times each subject spoke to each confederate. When he examined these patterns of communication, he found that the deviant was the target of a barrage of communications as the others tried to reason with him (see Figure 10-6). Also, when Schachter broke the meeting down into ten-minute intervals, he discovered that in most groups the high rate of communication increased throughout the entire session when the target was the deviant, but decreased throughout the session when the target was the slider. Apparently when the group members managed to talk the slider into agreeing, they shifted their efforts to the deviant. Last, when the group was cohesive and the task was relevant, Schachter found evidence of a strong rejection of the deviant by some subjects. Over 75% of the subjects in this condition reached a point where they seemed to give up on the resolute deviant, and therefore stopped communicating with him. All he did was disagree with the others about a matter of opinion; yet in the space of few short minutes he was cast out of the group.

Schachter's findings, and the studies described in Focus 10-3, provide convincing evidence of the lengths to which group members will go to achieve unanimity and consensus. They also make salient the difference between two types of conformity: **private acceptance** and **compliance.** When individuals, through informational and normative influence, personally accept the position advocated by the majority, conformity reflects

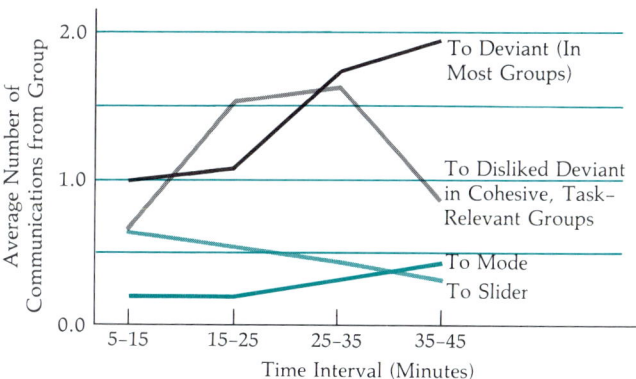

Figure 10-6 Communication patterns. When Schachter looked at how much other group members talked to the three confederates, he discovered that the average number of communications addressed to the mode increased slightly over the session, while communication with the slider decreased. In most cases the deviant received the most communications at all times during the experiment. The only exception to this tendency seemed to occur among subjects in cohesive groups working on a relevant task who disliked the deviant. In this case, communications tapered off toward the end of the session.

private acceptance; the dissenters aren't just going along with the crowd but have actually changed their minds. When conformity results from the majority's pressurings, in contrast, the dissenters may only be publicly agreeing while still disagreeing in private. This type of conformity is usually labeled *compliance*, as it reflects no private change. Most of the conforming subjects in Asch's experiment, for example, were probably complying. They didn't think that the majority was correct, but they didn't want to disagree. A few subjects, however, showed signs of private acceptance. As Asch (1955, p. 33) explains, "among the extremely yielding persons we found a group who quickly reached the conclusion 'I am wrong, they are right.' "

FOCUS 10-3

A Closer Look: *Does all the world love a conformist?*

Although the words "To thine own self be true" may be good advice, they may not help you win many friends. Not only did Schachter discover that we tend to pressure others into conforming to our opinions, but he also found that we dislike those who disagree with us. The group members in his study liked the deviant the least and the mode the most. Furthermore, when the group assigned members to committees, the deviant was saddled with the secretarial chores of the correspondence committee, while the more desirable assignments were reserved for the mode and slider.

Research conducted by John Levine and his associates (Levine, 1980; Levine & Ranelli, 1978; Levine & Ruback, 1980; Levine, Saxe, & Harris, 1976; Levine, Sroka, & Snyder, 1977) has verified that most group members like conformists more than nonconformists. In fact, even a little disagreement with the group is sufficient to limit our likability, for Levine found that sliders—people who change their opinion in the course of discussion—are liked less than people who agree with the majority from the outset (Levine, Saxe, & Harris, 1976). By asking the members of a group discussing a legal case to vote on a recommendation five times, Levine was able to create the six types of sliders, modes, and deviants shown in Table 10-2. When subjects later rated these six types of group members, Levine found that people who never disagreed with the group were liked the most, and those who ended the session still in disagreement were liked the least. As Table 10-2 indicates, even the slider who began by disagreeing with the majority but eventually came around to their side was liked less than the confederate who always agreed with the majority.

Although other investigators have discovered some instances in which these findings don't apply (Alexander & Lauderdale, 1977; Levine, 1980; Morris & Miller, 1975b), in general these results support the strategy of the yes-man or -woman: to be accepted in a group, agree with its members. Although you may earn others' respect by disagreement followed by a gradual increase in conformity, you probably won't win their hearts.

TABLE 10-2

Six types of modes, sliders, and deviants identified by Levine and his associates. The mean attraction score indicates how much each type of person was liked or disliked on an inverse scale of 3 (high) to 21 (low). The lower the score, the more the subject was liked.

Stimulus Person	Initial Position	Final Position	Mean Attraction Score
Mode	Agreement	Agreement	7.2
Slider	Neutral	Agreement	8.7
Slider	Disagreement	Agreement	10.0
Slider	Agreement	Disagreement	13.5
Deviant	Disagreement	Disagreement	16.1
Slider	Neutral	Disagreement	16.4

Fear of dissent.   You go to a party dressed in a dinner jacket or evening gown, and everyone else is in jeans. You think you are ugly because you have one blue eye and one brown eye. While going over a test in class, you shout out the wrong answer; the rest of the class just stares at you. During dinner at an expensive restaurant you belch so loudly that people four tables away turn to look. In the Asch experiment you state that the correct answer is line 2, but the rest of the group chooses line 3.

Elements of informational influence, normative influence, and social pressure are all present in these examples, but these situations also underscore our basic reluctance to appear *deviant*: abnormal, strange, or weird. While we sometimes proudly display our uniqueness and idiosyncrasies (Snyder & Fromkin, 1980), we nonetheless tend to avoid seeming too different from others. Fearful that others may reject or punish us if we disagree, we sometimes take elaborate precautions to make certain that we agree with everyone (Freedman & Doob, 1968; Goffman, 1963).

In retrospect, Asch may unintentionally have created a great fear of deviance in his experiment by choosing such a simple task (Ross, Bierbrauer, & Hoffman, 1976). From the subjects' point of view, the problems were easy and the answer was obvious. Yet they found themselves in disagreement with the group time and time again. Surely they realized that their disagreement must make them look "incompetent, foolish, or even mad" (p. 149). If the task had been more complex or ambiguous, their disagreement could have been explained away in terms of personal whim or low ability. Disagreement on such a simple problem, however, made subjects feel weird, strange, and bizarre. To avoid the negative implications of such deviance, the subjects preferred to conform.

Mindlessness.   Rarely do we find ourselves in such atypical situations as those studied by Zimbardo and Asch. In fact, many situations, such as brushing our teeth, driving our car to class or work, passing an acquaintance on the street, unlocking the door to our home, and preparing for bed, are so routine that we don't need to concentrate on what we are doing. We simply switch on our automatic pilot and respond the way we usually do.

Ellen J. Langer believes that our tendency to respond without thinking things through can lead to *mindlessness,* "a state of reduced cognitive activity in which a person responds to the environment without considering its potentially novel elements" (1982, p. 60). Although mindless people may appear to be processing the relevant information, in actuality they are simply responding on the basis of habit and previously formed discriminations. Like the husband who doesn't notice when his wife has changed her hairstyle, the driver who still stops at the corner long after the stop sign has been replaced by a yield sign, and the bureaucrat who sends your form to the wrong office because she doesn't notice that yours is a special case, when people become mindless they are transformed into creatures of habit.

The concept of mindlessness suggests that people who conform aren't always asking themselves, "Should I agree or disagree?" They aren't even thinking about what they are doing and so conform almost automatically. In one study, for example, Langer and her associates predicted that adults would agree to perform small favors for a stranger provided the requester asked for the favor in a familiar way. To test this prediction, experimenters approached adults using a photocopier at a university library and said: "Excuse me. May I use the Xerox machine?" To manipulate the way the request was made, Langer established three different conditions. In the control condition, no justification for the request was offered. In the second condition, a reasonable excuse was provided: "I'm in a rush." In the third condition, the experimenter offered a senseless explanation: "I have to make some copies." (Of course the requester had to make some copies; why else use the Xerox machine?) The magnitude of the request was also varied: the researcher explained that either five or twenty copies were needed (Langer, Blank, & Chanowitz, 1978; Langer, Chanowitz, & Blank, 1985).

Langer felt that subjects would be shocked out of their mindlessness if the experimenters (1) failed to provide any excuse whatsoever or (2) asked to make a large rather than a small number of copies. If an explanation were offered—even a senseless one—and the favor wasn't too big, Langer felt, subjects would mindlessly conform to the request. As Table 10-3 indicates, these predictions were supported; apparently in some cases people "unwittingly respond to the world as if they were automatons" (Langer, 1982, p. 60; an alternative view is presented in Folkes, 1985).

Combining the causes. These five causes of conformity—informational influence, normative influence, social pressure, fear of dissent, and mindlessness—may all have operated in Zimbardo's simulated prison. Given the uniqueness of the setting, subjects may have relied on the information contained in other subjects' responses. They may also have felt that they were obligated to conform to their roles, since they were

TABLE 10-3

Percentage of subjects in six conditions who conformed by letting the experimenter make copies.

Number of Copies Needed	Reason Offered		
	None	"I'm in a rush"	"I have to make some copies"
5	60%	94%	93%
20	24	24	42

paid participants and wanted to contribute to science. In addition, the guards placed strong social pressures on the prisoners to obey all the rules, while Zimbardo and his staff pressured the guards into conformity. Lastly, the prisoners probably continued with the study because they didn't want to look like quitters who were different from the other subjects, while the guards may have gotten so used to their duties that they mindlessly followed the norms without critically examining them.

These five factors, however, apply to more than just odd, unexpected social actions. In our day-to-day interactions with other people, we constantly modify our behaviors so that they will fit in with the actions of those around us. In ambiguous situations, other people's actions provide us with the social proof we need to make our own choices. If it's OK for them, we assume it must be OK for us (Cialdini, 1985). The guiding influence of norms is often so subtle that we hardly realize that we are obeying them. "Work hard," "Love your family and friends," "Don't walk around naked in public," and "Don't cause pain and suffering" are just a few of the norms that we conform to constantly. And should we fail to match the expectations of those around us, they will be pleased to guide us back to the right path. Often, however, these direct social influence tactics are unnecessary, for we avoid seeming too different from others. And when it comes to everyday routines, we do what we did the day before. We respond mindlessly.

Too much conformity, however, can be destructive. In Zimbardo's study, the subjects and the researcher were transformed when they became too deeply submerged in their social roles of prisoner, guard, and warden. Likewise, if the subjects in Asch's research had been making life-and-death decisions, their choices would have been fatal one-third of the time. Because conformity can blind us to alternatives, it must be tempered with nonconformity.

■ Nonconformity

Despite religious pressures, Galileo insisted that the planets revolved around the sun rather than the earth. Mohandas K. Gandhi, as the leader of the Indian nationalist movement, suffered repeated imprisonment and abuses when he refused to submit to the colonial authority. Sigmund Freud ignored criticisms of this theory of the unconscious mind until it was grudgingly accepted by psychologists. Martin Luther King, Jr., was brutalized and demeaned for advocating racial equality, yet he continued his efforts until his death. The composer Igor Stravinsky was denounced as a musical heretic when *The Rite of Spring* was first performed, but he refused to change a note. Charles Darwin knew that he would be ridiculed and condemned if his research was made public, but he published his *Origin of Species* anyway.

These historical examples demonstrate that the majority doesn't always overwhelm the deviant or minority; sometimes the dissenter, despite all the majority's pressurings, stands firm. These examples also hint at the other side of social influence: the minority's ability to change the majority. The majority doesn't always quash dissent, for sometimes it's the minority that is the influencer and the majority that is influenced (Spitzer & Davis, 1978). Although Asch's findings indicate that the majority can bring powerful and potentially overwhelming pressure to bear upon the minority, other studies have shown that minorities can fight back with pressure of their own.

When Do People Refuse to Conform?

Imagine that you are part of a group responsible for solving a few "simple" word problems. One of the items states: "A man bought a horse for $60 and sold it for $70. Then he bought it back for $80 and again sold it for $90. How much money did he make in the horse-trading business?" (Maier & Solem, 1952). You immediately recognize the correct answer, but before you can say anything several of the other people in your group announce, "This is an easy one: it's ten dollars." You hesitate for a moment, reviewing your reasoning. Could I be wrong? Are they right? Let's see, he bought it for $60, and then . . . No, the answer is $20. Isn't it?

Even when we are certain we are right and others are wrong, voicing our dissent can be difficult. Nonconformity, if it is to occur, requires *supports*. In some cases, these supports come from within. When we read about people who stand firm against the pressure of the majority, we often assume that some inner purpose gives them the strength to remain independent and unchanged. Social settings, too, vary in the amount of support they provide for nonconformity. Nonconformity becomes easier when the setting encourages critical dissent and independence.

The nonconformist.
Some of the earliest systematic studies of individual differences in conformity and nonconformity were carried out by Richard S. Crutchfield. In contrast to Asch's subjects, Crutchfield's sat in individual cubicles containing a series of switches and lights, a system now known as the "Crutchfield apparatus." When asked a question—such as "Which one of the four lines A, B, C, and D is the same length as the stimulus line?"—they answered by flipping the appropriate switch. Although the subjects were led to believe that their answers were being transmitted to the experimenter and the other subjects, in actuality the experimenter simulated the majority's judgments from a master control panel. To test for conformity, Crutchfield substituted incorrect responses on critical trials, and told all the subjects to give their answers last.

Crutchfield found that nonconformists tended to be "self-reliant; independent in judgment; and able to think for" themselves, while conformists were high in "respect to authority, submissive, compliant, and overly accepting" (1955, p. 194). Supporting these findings, other studies indicate that nonconformity is positively related to personality factors that encourage *independence*—such as self-esteem, self-confidence, and expertise on the task at hand—but negatively related to factors that undermine independence: social anxiety, reliance on others for information, authoritarianism, desire for approval, submissiveness, and conventionality. (A detailed review of personality and conformity may be found in Hare, 1976.)

The counterconformist. When psychologists examined soldiers who had been captured by the Chinese during the Korean War, they discovered two very different kinds of resisters (see "In Depth: Coercive Persuasion" at the end of Chapter 6). Some of the prisoners of war reacted like the nonconformists identified by Crutchfield. They rejected the communists' attempts at indoctrination because they simply did not agree with the communists: they were *independents*. Others, however, fought indoctrination because they resisted all forms of authority and influence, regardless of the source. As Edgar Schein explains:

> These men were characterized by a life-long pattern of indiscriminate resistance to all forms of authority, and had histories of inability to get along in the United Nations Army just as they were unable to get along with the Chinese. They openly defied any attempt to get them to conform. [Schein, 1956, p. 166]

Unlike people who dissent because they disagree with the majority and wish to express their own personal views, the anticonformist or **counterconformist** enjoys arguing against any position the majority may adopt (Stricker, Messick, & Jackson, 1970a, 1979b; Willis & Hollander, 1964; Willis, 1970). In a replication of the Asch experiment conducted with alienated college students in Japan, investigators found a surprisingly high level of anticonformity. Although higher amounts of conformity were expected because Japanese society is considered more group-focused than Western cultures, slightly over one-third of the subjects gave incorrect answers on the neutral items (the ones in which the majority gave the correct answer rather than the obviously incorrect response). The subjects were working so hard to disagree with the majority that they deliberately gave wrong answers (Frager, 1970).

Sex differences in nonconformity. For many years, both social psychologists and people outside the field assumed that men tended to be nonconformists and women conformists. Looking back on earlier studies, one researcher wrote: "it has also been well established, at least in our culture, that females supply greater amounts of conformity under almost all conditions than males" (Nord, 1969, p. 198).

Recently, however, Alice H. Eagly and her colleagues have challenged this assumption (Eagly, 1978; Eagly & Carli, 1981; Eagly, Wood, & Fishbaugh, 1981). They note that many of the studies that demonstrated sex differences often stacked the deck against women by using masculine-type tasks. When conformity is tested on neutral problems, few sex differences emerge (Goldberg, 1974, 1975; Javornisky, 1979; Sistrunk & McDavid, 1971). Eagly also argues that researchers may unintentionally bias their studies so that their stereotypes of women and men are confirmed. Without realizing it, investigators tend to "design, implement, or report their studies in a way that results in an egotistical or flattering portrayal of the attributes of their own gender" (Eagly & Carli, 1981, p. 17). As nearly two thirds of the research on conformity has been carried out by men, this own-sex bias has led to an overabundance of studies favoring men over women. After examining earlier research in the light of these two methodological problems, Eagly finds "true" sex differences in only one kind of situation. When people are seated in the same room and must state their opinions aloud, the sexes diverge: men conform less than women. This effect occurs, however, only in face-to-face situations; men and women conform equally when they are anonymous.

What is it about face-to-face situations that brings out sex differences? Eagly suggests that the pressure to conform to stereotypes that postulate the "proper" behavior of men and women may be stronger in public settings. Traditionally, the feminine sex role emphasizes such characteristics as passivity, reliance on others, and a willingness to yield to others. The traditional masculine sex role, in contrast, highlights independence, self-determination, and resistance to influence (Eagly, 1978). If individuals feel that they should behave in a traditional way, then women tend to conform and men tend to remain independent (Eagly, Wood, & Fishbaugh, 1981). Thus nature did not decree that men should be nonconformists and women conformists. If the situation prompts people to act in sex-typed ways, however, men will conform less than women.

Situational supports for nonconformity. What situational factors provide support for nonconformity? Consider the characteristics of juries in America. They meet for only a limited period of time in a highly formal setting, so the group can't become very cohesive. In all but the smallest towns the members of a jury are strangers to one another and don't anticipate any future interactions; they therefore risk little if they fail to make a good impression or win others' friendship. As votes are often taken by secret ballot, jurors can express disagreement with little fear of retribution. The situation is a novel one for virtually all jurors—there are no professional jurors—yet everyone has made judgments concerning right and wrong, guilt and innocence. Juries encourage nonconformity and careful decision making. (We will consider their important social-psychological qualities in more detail in "In Depth: Social Influence in Juries," at the end of this chapter.)

Table 10-4 summarizes the aspects of juries that encourage nonconformity, while also adding some variables that have been identified by researchers. Although the table only samples some of the more frequently studied factors that encourage conformity and nonconformity, it demonstrates that nonconformity cannot be predicted unless the nature of the specific situation is taken into account. Granted, some people may tend to be independents or counterconformists, but if they find themselves in a situation characterized by high cohesiveness, multiple meetings over a long period of time, public responding, and issues that they don't understand, then even the nonconformist is likely to conform (Santee & Maslach, 1982; see Allen, 1975, and Hare, 1976, for reviews).

Does Nonconformity Lead to Social Influence?

Even if you succeed in remaining independent, how can you change others' opinions and actions? If you find that you are the Galileo or Darwin of your group, what can you do to influence the others to adopt your opinion? Researchers offer many possible suggestions; here we consider three prescriptions in detail: (1) preface dissent with conformity; (2) from beginning to end, dissent unwaveringly; and (3) form coalitions with others.

Idiosyncrasy credits. Edwin P. Hollander warns that dissenters who immediately begin by challenging the majority without first earning high status in the group will probably be overruled by the majority. If, however, the dissenters first achieve a high level of status within the group by demonstrating their competence and willingness to cooperate with others, then the majority will be more likely listen to their views. According to Hollander, early conformity to the majority builds up **idiosyncrasy credits**—psychological credits or bonuses ("brownie points") earned by

TABLE 10-4

Situational factors that promote or discourage conformity and nonconformity.

Nonconformity Becomes More Likely If:	*Conformity Becomes More Likely If:*
1. the group members dislike one another, or the group is not cohesive.	1. the group members like one another and the group is highly cohesive.
2. the group meets only once.	2. the group will meet in the future.
3. responses are not made public.	3. responses are made publicly in a face-to-face setting.
4. the issues are complex and allow for a range of opinion.	4. the issues are simple and nonambiguous.
5. the majority opinion is in error.	5. the majority opinion is correct or, at minimum, acceptable.
6. other members of the group disagree with the majority.	6. the majority unanimously favors the solution.
7. the majority members are low in status or incompetent on the task.	7. the majority members are high in status or experts on the task at hand.
8. the majority is small but the minority is large.	8. the majority is large but the minority is small.

contributions to the group. Dissenters can spend these credits later when they take an unpopular position or viewpoint. Without any balance of idiosyncrasy credits, the majority won't tolerate such dissent, and the deviant will be rejected. In support of his model, Hollander found that a male confederate who conformed during the early phases of a group problem-solving session influenced the group members more than a confederate who violated group rules from the very start (Hollander, 1958, 1960, 1961, 1981).

Consistency. Serge Moscovici and his colleagues offer a contrasting recommendation to minorities striving to increase their influence over the majority. Rather than work within the system by prefacing nonconformity with conformity, Moscovici advises, adopt a staunch, unflinching position on the issue from the outset. Moscovici calls this approach **innovation.** He believes that a consistent minority is a "creator of conflicts," an innovator who challenges the status quo of the group by calling for a reevaluation of the issues at hand. When minority members are highly consistent in arguing for their views, they shake the confidence of the majority and thereby force the group to accept a change. To test his theory of change through innovation, Moscovici reverses the typical Asch-style experiment by placing one or two confederates in a group of subjects who are striving to make judgments about colors, political issues, or aesthetic preferences. Quite reliably, Moscovici finds that an unwavering minority can influence the majority's answers. In addition, because the change comes about through conflict processes rather than social pressure, Moscovici argues, it is a deeper, more meaningful change: true conversion to the minority's position rather than mere compliance with someone else's view (Moscovici, 1976, 1980, 1985; Moscovici & Faucheaux, 1972; Moscovici & Nemeth, 1974).

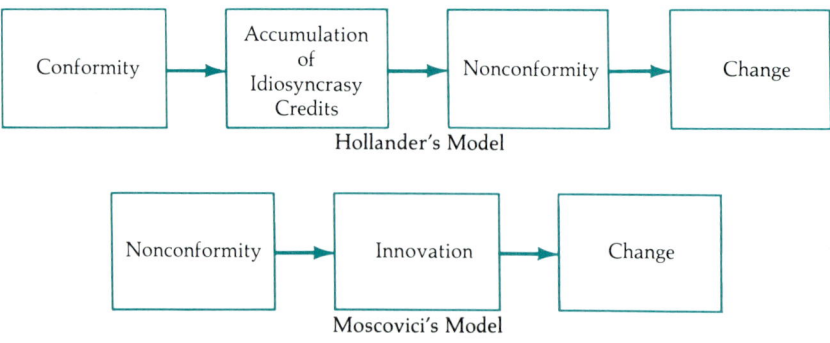

Figure 10-7 Two paths to minority influence: prior conformity and innovation. According to Hollander, you will be most successful as a nonconformist if you preface your disagreement with conformity. Moscovici, however, argues that consistent nonconformity will lead to internal, private change rather than mere public compliance.

Moscovici's advice about consistent disagreement contrasts to some extent with Hollander's recommendations concerning idiosyncrasy credits (see Figure 10-7). Evidence suggests, however, that both strategies can be effective, depending on the situation. In one study researchers contrasted the idiosyncrasy model and the innovation model by asking groups of college students to discuss three proposed ways of reducing university spending: curtailing the school newspaper, raising the prices for admission to athletic events, and increasing tuition. Four of the group members were actual subjects who were generally opposed to these proposals, but each group also included two confederates who took a minority position on all three issues (as Moscovici's innovation model suggests) or on the last issue only (as Hollander's idiosyncrasy credits approach advocates). The investigators found that the minority members influenced the majority no matter which approach was taken. Hollander's approach, however, was more influential in all-male groups (Bray, Johnson, & Chilstrom, 1982). These findings suggest that minorities can reach their goals by taking either of two routes: the direct path recommended by Hollander or the indirect path suggested by Moscovici. Which road is quicker is not yet known (see Focus 10-4; Maass & Clark, 1984; Wolf, 1985).

FOCUS 10 – 4

Controversy in Social Psychology: *Did Moscovici use innovation to change social psychologists' way of thinking about influence?*

For many years Moscovici has argued that the democratic background of social psychology—particularly in North America—is responsible for its emphasis on majority influence rather than minority influence. In a fascinating critique he suggests that most theorists and researchers assume that change comes from within existing social systems rather than from external revolutionary sources; that the victory of the majority is more democratic than the victory of the minority; and that innovation occurs as a result of direct rather than indirect interaction between the majority and the minority. In contrast to this democratic model of social influence, Moscovici's innovation model, which receives its greatest support among European social psychologists, highlights the impact of the minority on the majority and hence is a revolutionary approach to social change (Moscovici, 1976, 1980, 1985).

Ironically, Moscovici's repeated criticisms can be interpreted as a "real-world" application of his model. Moscovici and his European colleagues are minority members of the field of social psychology, for they are outnumbered by North American social psychologists who concentrate on conformity rather than nonconformity. In seeking to change social psychology, Moscovici could have garnered goodwill by conducting a few studies of majority influence before turning to the study of minorities. Instead he has followed the dictates of his own model by never wavering from his fundamental point: that a consistently dissenting minority can change the majority. His method seems to have been effective, for in recent years several theoretical frameworks have been developed to account for both minority and majority influence (for example, Latané, 1981; Tanford & Penrod, 1984), and researchers have begun to explore minority influence in greater depth (for example, Bray, Johnson, & Chilstrom, 1982; Hollander, 1981; Levine, 1980; Ridgeway, 1981, 1982; Santee & Maslach, 1982). Would these changes have come about more rapidly if he had first garnered idiosyncrasy credits rather than consistently dissenting? We can only guess.

Coalition formation. The ten directors of Acme Unlimited are arguing over the merits of a new product. All except Ms. Zimlach oppose the product. Knowing that she faces sure defeat if the issue comes to a vote, Zimlach meets with the board members individually to persuade them to leave the majority camp and join forces with her. If she can win over just one convert, she will have formed a *coalition*—a subgroup within the larger group.

A minority coalition is more influential than a lone individual for several reasons. First, if Zimlach had to face the majority alone, without a single ally, she would probably yield to group pressure; the pressures put on a single dissenter are just too great (Asch, 1955). Second, the more dissenters present in the group—that is, the larger the size of the minority coalition—the more likely the majority will be influenced. One person out of 10 arguing for a decision is easier to ignore than three or four arguing the same point. Third, as she increases the size of her minority coalition, Zimlach will also be decreasing the size of the majority coalition. Whereas the nine individuals united against one may refuse to yield, seven against three may be more uncertain of their position. Because it saps the strength of the majority, a coalition is a surprisingly effective tool of social influence.

But what tactics can Zimlach use to gather recruits for her coalition? How can she persuade others to abandon their comfortable membership in the majority and join her in an uphill fight against large numbers? To solve this problem, Zimlach must make skillful use of her social *power.*

■ Social Power and Influence

In the English language, only a handful of words pertain to love and cooperation, but a vast array of verbs deal with influence. We don't have to coerce people into anything when we can berate, badger, and brainwash them; cajole, convince, coax, and compel them; persuade, proselytize, propagandize, and prevail upon them. We can even wheedle, whine, and wrangle. If our language reveals our preoccupations, then we must be obsessed with power and influence.

Social Power

The human capacity to obey powerful others can be devastating. During World War II, Germans obediently followed Hitler's orders and exterminated millions of Jews. In 1096, Pope Urban II called for all good Christians to free Jerusalem from the "pagans." Literally millions of men, women, and children lost their lives in this bloody "holy" war. In 1978, more than 900 members of the People's Temple drank poison and died when ordered to do so by their spiritual leader, Jim Jones. These three men—Hitler,

In 1978, 900 members of a religious group known as the People's Temple committed mass suicide in a small village in South America. Analyses of the tragedy indicate that the group's leader, Jim Jones, was so powerful that he controlled virtually all aspects of the Temple members' lives—and deaths.

Pope Urban, and Jim Jones—all possessed extraordinary amounts of **social power;** "the capacity to produce intended and foreseen effects in others" (Wrong, 1979, p. 21). They could influence others even when those others tried to resist their influence (Lewin, 1951).

What is the *source* of social power? Why do some people influence us more than others? What can we do to increase our power over other people? John R. P. French and Bertram Raven's theory of power provides a partial answer to these questions. According to French and Raven, people draw power from five key sources: rewards, punishments, status, attraction, and expertise. Those who control these five sources, or *bases*, are powerful, while those who do not are powerless (French & Raven, 1959; Raven, 1965).

Reward power. The influencer who gives or promises rewards to the targets of influence exercises *reward power.* Sometimes tangible, material rewards are given or promised. The supervisor who increases workers' salaries when they raise their productivity and the teacher who gives students extra credit for extra work are both using tangible rewards to influence people. In other instances intangible, social types of rewards, such as approval, compliments, intimacy, agreement, and love, may be used. When you smile at your friends, help them with their course work, or tell them, "You look great today," "You did a great job on that assignment," or "If you help me clean my room, I'll take you to the game tonight," you are using reward power.

Coercive power. The employer demotes a worker to a less desirable position as punishment for poor performance; the teacher tells the class that everyone is going to fail if the exam grades don't improve; in anger, you tell a friend, "You're acting like an idiot," "You're going to wish you were dead if you don't do what I say," or "How would you like a knuckle sandwich?" These examples involve *coercive power* because they are based on threats, warnings, and actual punishment. Tangible threats and punishments include physical abuse, fines, low grades, or firings. Intangible social threats can consist of disapproval, insults, and expressions of contempt.

Coercive power is most effective in changing behaviors when it is applied immediately and without emotion. Even when it is used with care, however, coercive power can have negative side effects (French & Raven, 1959; Podsakoff & Schriesheim, 1985; Raven & Rubin, 1976). We simply do not like people who control us through the use of threats and punishments. We tend to counter coercive influence by avoiding the source altogether, or by resorting to reciprocal aggression (Schlenker et al., 1976).

Legitimate power. Unlike reward and coercive power, *legitimate power* stems from the influencer's recognized right to require and demand the performance of certain behaviors. The employer has a legitimate right to demand a certain level of productivity because of the contractual relationship between employer and employee; the worker has agreed to do a certain job, while the employer has agreed to pay the worker a salary. Similarly, the teacher can insist that students refrain from talking and cheating during exams if both the students and the teacher recognize that these demands are among the teacher's prerogatives. If you and a friend agree to certain rules before deciding to room together, then you have a legitimate right to complain when your friend breaks those rules. Like normative social influence—one of the causes of conformity examined earlier in this chapter—legitimate power arises from an internalized sense of duty, loyalty, obedience, or normative obligation rather than a desire to gain rewards or avoid punishments.

Referent power.   Many of us belong to the same political party as our parents. We purchase the same type of lawn fertilizer as our neighbors. We read the books and magazines that are praised by our best friends. Why? According to French and Raven (1959), people we like, respect, and admire—our parents, neighbors, colleagues—possess *referent power:* their views provide us with important reference points for defining and testing our own beliefs and behavior. The old boss who enjoys the unswerving loyalty of his or her employees may be able to increase productivity simply by looking at a worker. Teachers who are high in referent power—such as the friendly teacher whom all the students like and the tough but well-respected teacher—may be able to maintain discipline in their classes with little apparent effort because the students obey every request. And you can change the attitudes and behaviors of your good friends simply by expressing your attitudes and engaging in certain behaviors.

Expert power.   When we feel uncertain of our own skills and abilities, we often follow the advice of experts and specialists. An employee may balk when asked to perform a routine task in a new way unless the supervisor explains that the recommended change is based on the experience of experts who have found it easier than the old way. Similarly, students may be reluctant to disagree with a teacher who seems to be an expert in his or her field. And when it comes to influencing your friends, you will find it is easier when you tell them "I know what I'm talking about" or "I've been studying this business for several years now." People with special ability based on experience influence us because they possess *expert power.*

Combining the five bases.   The five bases of power described by French and Raven (summarized in Table 10-5) offer a unique way of influencing other people's cognitions and behaviors. In many cases, however, influencers become far more powerful if they employ a combination of these tactics.

The strength of multiple power tactics is evident in many situations. Consider Stanley Milgram's experimental studies of obedience to an authority. As we saw in Chapter 1, Milgram's subjects found themselves facing an extremely powerful authority in the person of Mr. Williams. First, his power to reward was high, because he gave out the payments and because he was an important source of positive evaluations; subjects wanted to win a favorable appraisal from this figure of authority. Second, Mr. Williams used coercive power in his prods. "The experiment requires that you continue"; "It is absolutely essential that you continue"; "You have no other choice, you must go on"—all warn of possible negative consequences for disobedience. Third, many subjects felt that when they agreed to participate in the study they had entered into an oral contract that obliged them to obey. In consequence, Mr. Williams had a legitimate right to control their actions, while the learner had no right to quit the study. Fourth, Mr. Williams also replied on referent power. The subjects respected Yale and recognized the importance of scientific research; so they trusted Mr. Williams to do the right thing. Lastly, very few of the subjects knew much about electricity or its effects in such a situation; because they considered Mr. Williams an expert, they believed him when he said, "Although the shocks may be painful, there is no permanent tissue damage" (Milgram, 1974, p. 21). In sum, Milgram succeeded in constructing a situation in which the authority boasted all five forms of power; reward, coercive, legitimate, referent, and expert. Is it so surprising that he found such high rates of obedience? (See Focus 10-5)

Social Influence Tactics

French and Raven's fivefold theory of power does more than describe the sources of power; it also suggests ways to *use* power to influence others.

TABLE 10-5

French and Raven's five bases of power.

Base	Definition
Reward power	Influence based on positive or negative reinforcers given or offered to the target.
Coercive power	Influence based on punishments or threats directed toward the target.
Legitimate power	Influence based on the target's belief that the powerholder has a justifiable right to demand the performance of certain behaviors.
Referent power	Influence based on the target's identification with, attraction to, or respect for the powerholder.
Expert power	Influence based on the target's belief that the powerholder possesses superior skills and abilities.

According to French and Raven, if you want to change someone's cognitions or behaviors, offer them rewards, threaten them with punishment, emphasize the legitimacy of your request, make certain the target likes, admires, and respects you, and at least try to seem like an expert.

These suggestions, however, only scratch the surface of the vast array of interpersonal strategies that people can use to influence others. In earlier chapters we saw that people often rely on *persuasion* as a means to change attitudes and behavior (Chapter 6). Through *ingratiation* we con-

---

FOCUS 10-5

Applying Social Psychology: *Is psychotherapy applied social influence?*

Some experts feel that the psychological processes that occur in the course of counseling and psychotherapy cannot be explained by social psychological principles. Many psychologists, however, feel that psychotherapy is a form of applied social influence. As the counseling psychologist Stanley R. Strong explains, individuals seek help when they are dissatisfied or frustrated with their current behavior and feel that they can't resolve these problems without assistance. The therapist takes the role of the psychological expert who suggests interpretations of the client's experiences and ways to deal with current problems. Conceptualized as a social influence process, the client's acceptance of the therapist's interpretations or recommendations is a direct function of the client's perceptions of the therapist's power (Strong, 1968, 1982; Strong & Claiborn, 1982).

According to Strong, "successful therapy does not result in clients' simple compliance with the therapists' influence attempts, but in behavioral change that is manifest over a broad range of clients' relationships in their social networks" (1984, p. 17). Therapists generally avoid the use of rewards and coercion to bring about this change. If clients feel that they are merely complying with the therapist's demands, they are more than likely to revert to their original behaviors in everyday situations. Therefore, therapists rely more on legitimate, referent, and expert power. Legitimate power is particularly potent because it springs from the therapeutic relationship itself rather than from the delivery or withholding of valued resources. When individuals follow therapeutic directives because they hope to earn a reward or avoid a punishment, the reason for their behavioral change is transparently obvious. If the therapist is a legitimate authority, however, they strive to change because they personally accept the norms of the relationship. Similarly, when the therapist's status is secured by his or her referent power, clients gain a sense of intrinsic satisfaction from their identification with the therapist. Expert power, though not so influential as legitimate or referent power, also bolsters the therapist's effectiveness.

How do therapists secure their power in the therapeutic relationship? According to a number of studies, therapists make use of three types of cues to convince their clients that they are legitimate authorities, attractive, and competent. *Evidential cues* include primarily nonverbal stimuli, such as age, physical appearance, style of dress, and office location and decor. Therapists try to look the part. *Reputational cues* indicate the therapist's level of experience and expertise, and are provided by degrees, titles, and other professional credentials. Many therapists carefully display their diplomas and certificates so that their clients will know that they have been properly trained. Last, *behavioral cues* include the verbal and nonverbal actions that clients associate with effective interventions. They *act* like therapists. By manipulating these variables, researchers have consistently confirmed the hypotheses of the social influence model: therapists who possess certain characteristics that enhance their expertness, attractiveness, and legitimacy more strongly influence their clients (Corrigan et al., 1980; Heppner & Dixon, 1981).

vince others that we are likable, and that they should follow our suggestions (Chapter 7). Even *aggression* can be considered a social influence tactic; if all else fails, we can control people through coercion and violence (Chapter 9). The social influence tackle box is filled with a wide variety of hooks (Dion & Stein, 1978; Tedeschi, Schlenker, & Bonoma, 1973; Kipnis & Schmidt, 1983).

These hooks, however, are clearly not interchangeable. Ingratiation and aggression, for example, take completely different approaches to social influence. To examine these differences, Toni Falbo and her colleagues asked college students to write essays on the subject "How I Get My Way." Although the students described more than 340 methods that can be used to influence other people, 91% were variations of the 16 basic strategies shown in Table 10-6 (Falbo, 1977; Falbo & Peplau, 1980).

These 16 tactics vary in two important respects. First, some of these methods are more rational than others. Imagine you face this situation: Your social psychology instructor requires a 20-page paper on an approved topic. The paper is due tomorrow and you haven't even picked a topic yet. You have an appointment to see your professor about the situation. What can you do to get the professor to give you an extension? If you tried to reason with your professor by simply stating that you lack the time to do a good job on the paper and need an extension, you would be using a *rational* influence tactic. But if you tried to evade the issue by skipping your appointment and cutting class until you finished the paper, you would be using a *nonrational* method. The 16 methods also vary in directness. If you walked into your instructor's office and baldly stated, "I must have an extension on my paper," you would be using a *direct* method. But if you told your teacher that your paper was stolen, you would be using deceit, an *indirect* method. Figure 10-8 shows how the 16 influence tactics can be classified along these two dimensions.

How will your instructor react if you use one of these various tactics? To answer this question, Falbo arranged for the students who wrote the essays to meet in same-sex groups to discuss "what I plan to get out of college." When the group members rated one another on such factors as friendliness, consideration, and honesty, Falbo discovered that people who had reported the use of rational influence methods were better liked than those who used nonrational methods. Thus, if you used reasoning, compromise, expertise, bargaining, or persuasion to influence your professor, he or she would probably like you more than if you used such a technique as deceit, evasion, or threat.

The type of method you select may say something about your personality. When Falbo studied the relationship between subjects' choice of influence tactic and several personality traits, she found that:

- People who used indirect rational strategies were more concerned with being accepted and liked by the other group members than were those who used direct nonrational strategies.

TABLE 10-6

Definitions of the 16 social influence tactics, and an application to an influence setting.

Strategy	Definition	Application
Thought manipulation	The act or process of making the target think that the agent's idea is the target's own	I get the professor to think that the postponement of the date for the paper is her own idea.
Hinting	The use of covert suggesions	I drop a few remarks about all the work I've had to do lately.
Emotion (target)	An attempt to alter the target's emotions	I try to put him in a good mood by praising his new book.
Deceit	Flattery, lying	I tell him how much I like the course, though I really hate it.
Emotion (agent)	The expression of emotion by the agent	I cry.
Evasion	Avoidance of the person who would disapprove of one's actions	I don't go to class until I finish the paper.
Threat	An indication that negative consequences will occur	I tell her that I'll lodge a complaint against her.
Fait accompli	The presentation of one's desired action as a matter of fact, without avoidance of the target	I just don't turn in the paper until I finish it.
Assertion	An open declaration of one's wishes	I tell her that I need to have an extension.
Persistence	Continuance of one's attempts to influence the target or repetition of a point	I don't leave his office until he agrees.
Simple statement	A matter-of-fact declaration	I simply say, "I need a few more days."
Expertise	A claim to superior knowledge or skill	I claim to know more about the subject than I really do.
Reason	The presentation of a rational argument	I point out the reasons why she should give me an extension.
Compromise	A giving up of a portion of the desired goals by both agent and target	I ask for a three-week extension, then agree to deliver the paper in ten days.
Bargaining	The act of offering something in return for the behavior one wants	I tell him that I'll code data for him if he gives me an extension.
Persuasion	The presentation of convincing arguments	I convince her that I'll be able to do a better job if I have more time.

- People who used indirect nonrational strategies (as opposed to direct rational strategies) tended to accept a Machiavellian, manipulative philosophy in their dealings with others (see Christie & Geis, 1970).
- People who used direct rational methods tended to conform more than those who used indirect irrational methods when they were placed in a conformity situation like that studied by Asch.

Specialized Tactics

I confess to a fear of people who want to sell me something. I'm afraid of their power over me—their ability to sway me, to influence me, to control my behavior by using tactics so subtle that they escape my notice. Once an insurance agent sold me a policy I canceled ten days later. I've purchased stereo equipment that didn't really suit my needs. Once I

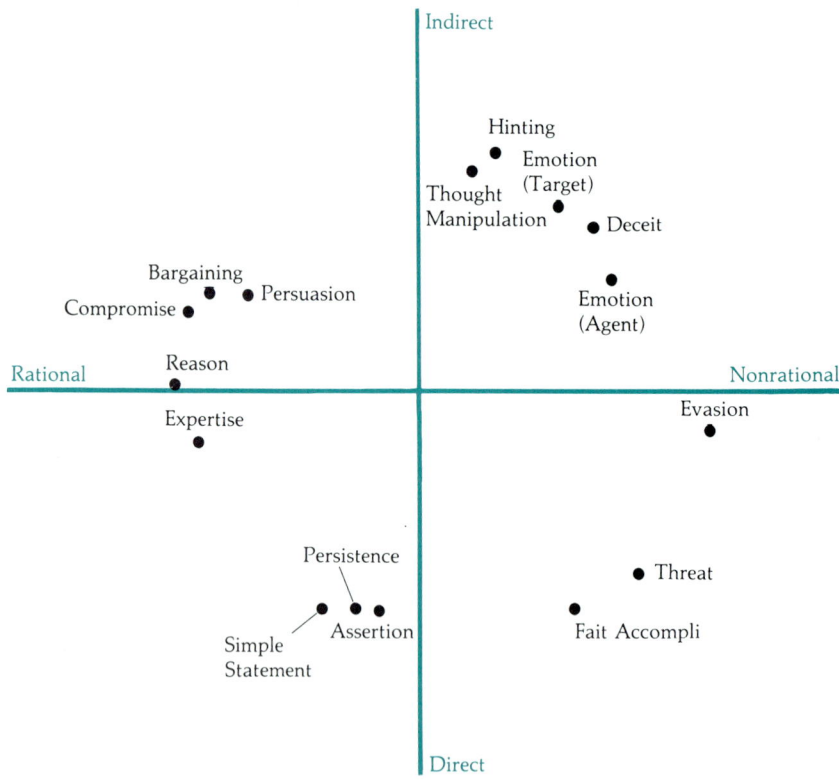

Figure 10-8 Influence strategies. The 16 tactics identified by Falbo can be classified along two basic dimensions: rational–nonrational and direct–indirect. Bargaining, for example, is very rational and somewhat indirect, while evasion is very nonrational and slightly direct.

bought a case of candy bars from a 12-year-old sales whiz. I was putty in her hands.

Studies of sales superstars in a wide range of fields confirm some of my fears by suggesting that some sellers are masters of social influence (Cialdini, 1985; Moine, 1982, 1984). They use not only the influence methods described by Falbo, French and Raven, and other researchers, but more subtle techniques that obscure the pathway that leads their target to the goal they have in mind. To conclude our analysis of social influence, we will review the three indirect tactics summarized in Table 10-7: the foot in the door, the door in the face, and low-balling.

The foot in the door. Have you ever noticed that some panhandlers preface their request for money by asking for the time? That telephone salespeople often begin by asking if you have a few moments to answer some survey questions? That car dealers do all they can to get you to test-drive the car? That organizations in quest of donations sometimes begin by asking if you will sign a petition? That people seeking money for their cults often start by asking you to take a flower as a gift?

Such tactics, advocated by door-to-door salespersons, exemplify the **foot-in-the-door principle.** First get your foot in the door by making some small request that the target can't refuse. Then follow up the initial request with the real sales pitch. In the earliest test of this technique, investigators telephoned women who were homemakers with a small request (Freedman & Fraser, 1966). Claiming to be a pollster for a public service publication known as *The Guide*, the experimenter asked the subject if she would answer some questions about household products.

TABLE 10 – 7

Three indirect influence tactics.

Technique	Basic Form	Example
Foot in the door	First make a very small request that you are certain the target person will agree to; then make the more important request	A door-to-door magazine salesperson asks for a drink of water
Door in the face	First make a very large request that the target will refuse; then make the more reasonable request you really want	A friend asks to borrow your car; when you refuse, he asks for a ride
Low-balling	Get the target to agree to the request before revealing its hidden costs or unexpected lack of benefits	You agree to give someone a ride home, then discover she lives 20 miles away

Influencing others to give. A frank request for a donation to a worthy cause isn't always enough. Sometimes, charities must make use of social influence tactics to goad people into donating.

Once she consented, he asked her a few innocuous questions about household soaps and thanked her for her cooperation. Three days later came the major request. Subjects were recontacted and told that the survey had been expanded: a team of five or six men would visit the subject's home to enumerate and classify all her household products. The men must have the run of the house, so that they could go through all her cupboards and storage places, and the information they collected would be published in *The Guide.*

The researchers discovered that the foot-in-the-door method was very effective: 52.8% of the women who participated in the initial survey agreed to the outrageous second request. In contrast, only 22.2% of the women who were exposed only to the second request agreed. Similar studies have also found that the two requests called for by the foot-in-the-door technique are superior to a single request for many types of behaviors, although a recent review suggests that many factors in the influence setting—such as the gender of the influencer and the amount of time that elapses between the two requests—moderate the power of the foot-in-the-door method (Beaman et al., 1983).

The door in the face. As you walk across campus a student asks you to stop for a minute. Fearing the worst, you listen as the student explains that he is a student counselor in the Youth Counseling Program, and wants to know if you would like to volunteer to help by working as a nonpaid counselor of juvenile delinquents. As a counselor you would have to put in two hours a week for at least two years. Thinking of your other commitments, you immediately answer that you aren't interested. Two years! That's ridiculous! But before you can escape, the student makes another request: Well, would you at least be willing to chaperon a group on a trip to the zoo? It will only take two hours.

If you say yes to the second request, you may be falling victim to the **door-in-the-face technique.** As Robert B. Cialdini describes it, this method reverses the foot-in-the-door approach by prefacing a reasonable request with an initial request that is so extreme that it is sure to be denied. When Cialdini and his associates asked students in the control condition if they would be willing to chaperon juveniles on a trip to the zoo, only 16.7% agreed. When they prefaced this minor request with the major request for two years of volunteer service, they achieved 50.0% compliance (Cialdini et al., 1975).

Cialdini suggests that the door-in-the-face technique may capitalize on a *contrast effect.* Just as lukewarm water will feel colder if you have just had your hand in hot water, the second request seems more reasonable when it is contrasted with the larger initial request. Cialdini suggests that a similar contrast process is at work in many sales settings. If a man tells a salesperson that he wants to buy a three-piece suit and a pair of shoes, the salesperson should show the customer the suit first; a $75 pair of shoes will seem less expensive after he spends $300 on a suit. Similarly, realtors sometimes begin a tour of available homes with a few run-down and overpriced houses so that the other houses they show will seem like attractive bargains.

Low-balling. A final influence tactic depends on inducing the customer to agree to the request before revealing certain hidden costs. In the context of car sales, this **low-balling technique** begins when the dealer offers the customer a bargain on a car. Once the customer agrees—and perhaps even begins the necessary paperwork—the salesperson reveals the hidden costs in a variety of ways. After smoking a cigarette in the backroom, for example, the seller may return and claim that the sales manager refused to allow such a discount; or an extra that the customer thought was included in the quoted price may be added on after the deal has been closed; or the amount of trade-in allowance for the customer's old car may be reduced by the used-car manager. No matter what the method, the goal is the same: induce the target to make a decision before you reveal all the drawbacks. A more commonplace example of low-balling occurs when someone asks, "Will you do me a favor?" and gets us to say yes before revealing what is expected of us.

Low-balling works. In one study a researcher telephoned students to ask if they would be interested in participating in an experiment on thinking processes for extra credit in their psychology class. In the control condition, before asking if the subject was willing to take part the researcher admitted that the sessions were scheduled for 7:00 A.M. In the low-ball condition, however, the researcher omitted this key piece of information until after the subject had agreed or refused to participate. Just as any car salesperson would predict, compliance was greater in the low-balling condition (56%) than in the control condition (31%). Furthermore, when 7:00 A.M. rolled around, the low-ball subjects were more likely than the controls to keep the appointment. Parenthetically, before the subjects were debriefed about the study, they actually participated in the promised study of thinking processes (Cialdini et al., 1978; see Burger & Petty, 1981).

As Cialdini explains, influencers who make use of the foot-in-the-door, door-in-the-face, or low-ball technique are exploiting our tendency to respond without considering our options. In a hurry to get on with our lives, we often react to others' requests automatically. Each of these techniques commits us to a course of action that we never even stopped to consider. In a sense, they amount to psychological jujitsu. Just as martial arts experts use their opponents' weight and momentum against them, these techniques push us into psychological motion and then take advantage of our momentum. To escape these traps, Cialdini recommends wariness—fight the urge to respond automatically to these influence techniques. Remember to base your choices on your own best interests (Cialdini, 1985).

■ Summary

Social influence occurs when one person changes his or her beliefs or behavior in response to social pressure. Zimbardo's prison study provides a vivid illustration of social influence, for the subjects engaged in bizarre behaviors for no apparent reason. Closer inspection of the situation, however, reveals that subjects who failed to fulfill the roles of prisoner and guard were pressured by other subjects until they brought their behavior back into line.

Individuals often change their beliefs or behaviors to conform to the beliefs and behaviors of the people around them. In his pioneering studies, Solomon Asch used a line-judging task to assess individuals' tendencies to agree with others' mistaken judgments. On an average trial, over one-third of the subjects conformed and over 75% of the subjects conformed at least once during the study. **Conformity** is greatest when the majority is unanimous and contains at least three members. Conformity increases as more members are added beyond three, but at an ever decreasing rate. **Social impact theory** explains these findings by suggesting that conformity depends on the strength, immediacy, and number of individuals in the majority.

Conformity is caused by the following five factors:

1. *Informational influence:* we use other people's reactions to evaluate our own beliefs and guide our actions.
2. *Normative influence:* we strive to make certain that our actions are consistent with social standards.
3. *Social pressure:* we yield to direct influence techniques, such as persuasion and coercion.
4. *Fear of dissent:* we prefer to project an image of normality rather than deviance.
5. *Mindlessness:* we sometimes fail to consider the implications of our actions and therefore respond automatically.

Informational and normative influence often lead to **private acceptance** of the majority's view, while social pressure, fear of dissent, and mindlessness result in **compliance.**

Conformity is not inevitable, however. **Nonconformity** is seen in individuals who resist the pressure to conform. Two types of nonconformists have been identified. *Independents* publicly express ideas that are consistent with their personal standards, regardless of the pressure to conform. **Counterconformists,** in contrast, deliberately express ideas that clash with the dominant view, simply to opppose that view. Women conform more than men, provided the situation involves face-to-face interaction. In addition to these personal characteristics, a number of situational factors can provide support for nonconformity.

If minorities manage to resist the majority's pressuring, they sometimes succeed in influencing the majority. According to the concept of **idiosyncrasy credits,** minorities who preface dissent with agreement are more influential than minorities who consistently disagree. The concept of **innovation,** in contrast, recommends unwavering adherence to one's position. In all likelihood, both approaches are effective. Minorities also influence majorities through *coalition formation.*

Social power is the capacity to change other people's behaviors and beliefs. According to John French and Bertram Raven, people draw their power from five sources: rewards and promises (*reward power*), threats and punishments (*coercive power*), status and position (*legitimate power*), attraction and respect (*referent power*), and skill and ability (*expert power*). Often these bases of power are supplemented by a variety of tactics, such as persuasion, coercion, reasoning, bargaining, and deceit. These tactics vary in directness and rationality. Individuals may also make use of indirect influence techniques that take advantage of our tendency to conform unthinkingly. Influencers who use the **foot-in-the-door technique** preface a large request with a small one. The **door-in-the-face technique** reverses this sequence: after receiving a very large request, people tend to comply with a small request. The influencer who uses the **low-balling technique** extracts a commitment from the target person before revealing its hidden costs.

■ **For More Information**

1. *Influence: Science and Practice,* by Robert B. Cialdini (1985), is an exceptionally well-written excursus on the techniques that compliance professionals—salespersons, advertisers, charity workers, and panhandlers—use to influence us in our daily lives.

2. *Inside the Jury,* by Reid Hastie, Steven D. Penrod, and Nancy Pennington (1983), presents a detailed social-psychological analysis of communication, influence, and decision making by juries.

3. *The Powerholders,* by David Kipnis, (1974) examines the "metamorphic" effects of power for both the powerful and the powerless.

4. "The Psychology of Social Impact," by Bibb Latané (*American Psychologist,* 1981), presents a relatively nontechnical analysis of the basic principles underlying this mathematical model of power and influence in social interaction.

5. "Hidden Impact of Minorities: Fifteen Years of Minority Influence Research," by Anne Maass and Russell D. Clark III (*Psychological Bulletin,* 1984), reviews all the evidence bearing on Moscovici's theory of minority innovation and influence.

6. *Obedience to Authority,* by Stanley Milgram (1974), provides an authoritative explanation of why we obey and disobey others.

7. *Power: Its Forms, Bases, and Uses,* by Dennis H. Wrong (1979), reviews theories of social power developed by both psychologists and sociologists. Wrong focuses primarily on conceptual issues.

IN DEPTH

Social Influence in Juries

Societies that follow the British legal tradition settle questions of guilt and innocence by submitting them to a jury. As early as the 11th century, the neighbors of a person accused of wrongdoing in England were asked to weigh the evidence and render a verdict. In theory, the jury is the "finder of fact"—a group of representative citizens who can objectively decide if a law has been broken and punishment is warranted (Kadish & Paulsen, 1975). Because juries lie at the core of our judicial system, researchers have recently intensified their efforts to understand their dynamics and their effectiveness (see Hastie, Penrod, & Pennington, 1983; Simon, 1980).

How do juries make decisions? According to Reid Hastie and his colleagues, the *deliberation process* generally follows the steps outlined in Figure 10-9. The group's first task involves the setting of procedures for voting and discussing the issues. In some cases, a head juror ("foreman") must also be elected at this time. Once the agenda has been set, the jurors discuss the evidence that was presented during the trial and record, openly or by secret ballot, their initial preferences for the verdict. Over 30% of all juries reach complete consensus on the very first ballot, so their task is finished at this point (Penrod & Hastie, 1980). More frequently, however, the jury members disagree with one another. To resolve this disagreement, a consensus-seeking process is initiated. During this phase of the deliberation, the group may ask the judge for instructions and request additional information concerning the evidence. The group spends most of its time, however, discussing points favoring the two possible verdicts. This process eventually leads to agreement on a verdict. A hung jury—one that is unable to agree on a verdict—occurs in only about 6% of all cases (Kalven & Zeisel, 1966).

Although the jury situation is deliberately structured to provide support for nonconformity, the verdict favored by the majority of the jurors *before deliberation* usually corresponds to the jury's final verdict. If the majority favors guilt when the first vote is taken, in 90% of cases the jury will eventually return a verdict of guilty. If, in contrast, the majority of the jurors favor innocence, a not-guilty verdict is reached in 86% of cases. Interviews with jurors and studies of mock (simulated) juries created for research purposes indicate that juries reach consensus by pressuring the members of the minority. Staunch minorities can sometimes resist this influence, but their success is determined largely by the number of their members. As Solomon Asch's studies revealed (1955), a lone dissenter will generally change his or her vote, but as the minority swells in size, its power increases dramatically. In fact, a computer model that simulates jury deliberations assumes that a three-person minority in a standard 12-person jury will be relatively weak, but a four- or five-person coalition will be fairly stable and influential (Penrod & Hastie, 1980).

Evidence also indicates that much of the pressure is applied by the jurors of higher status. Fred Strodtbeck and his colleagues documented this bias by recording communication patterns in simulated juries. Enlisting the cooperation of the court, Strodtbeck repeatedly selected 12 individuals from the pool
(continued)

IN DEPTH *continued*

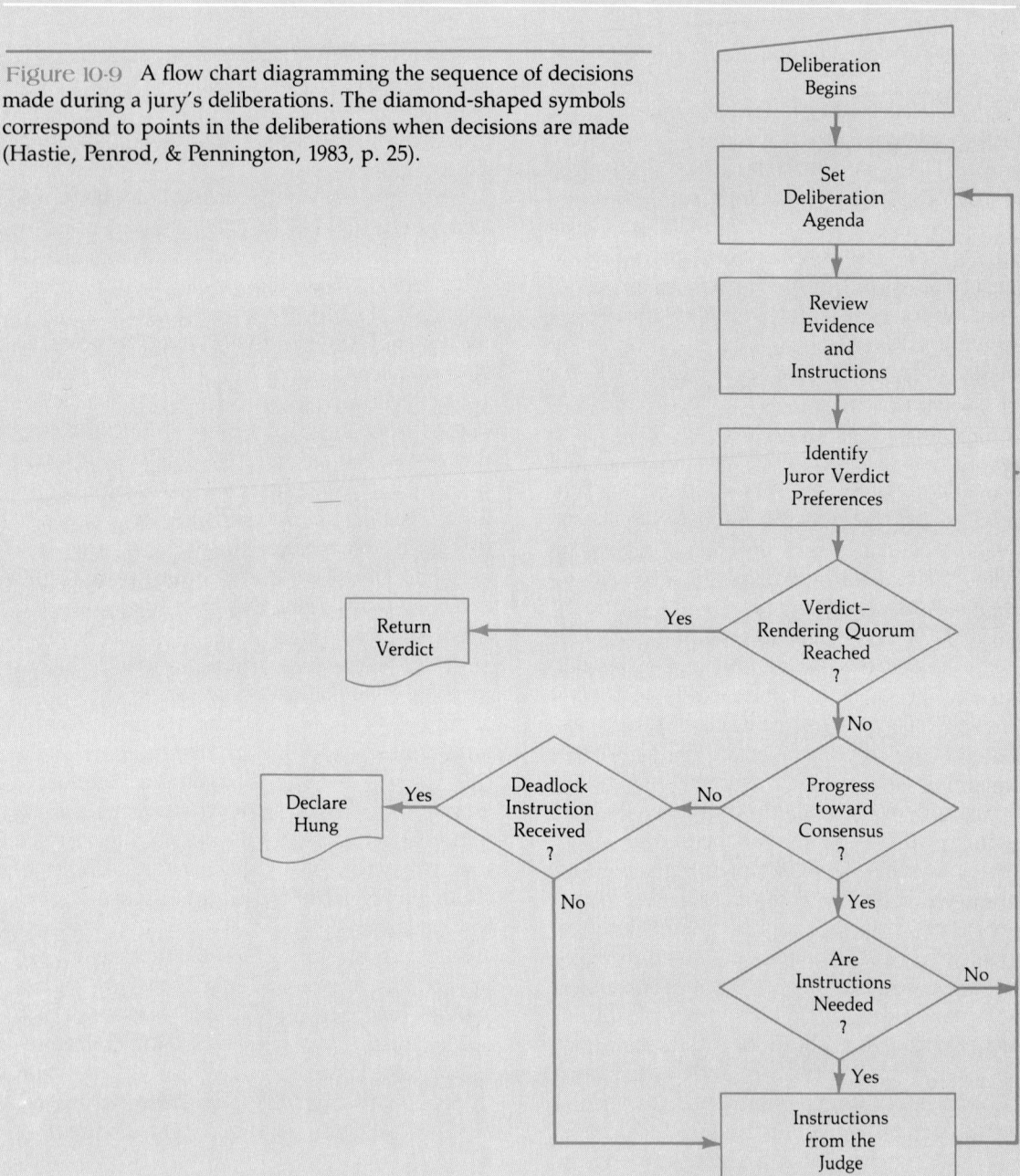

Figure 10-9 A flow chart diagramming the sequence of decisions made during a jury's deliberations. The diamond-shaped symbols correspond to points in the deliberations when decisions are made (Hastie, Penrod, & Pennington, 1983, p. 25).

of eligible jurors, simulated the pretrial interview process used to eliminate biased jurors, and assembled the group in the courtroom. A bailiff then played a tape recording of a trial and asked the group to retire to a jury room to decide upon a verdict. Except for the use of the tape-recorded trial, the groups were treated just like actual juries (Strodtbeck & Hook, 1961; Strodtbeck & Mann, 1956; Strodtbeck, James, & Hawkins, 1957).

Strodtbeck and his associates found that jurors with certain qualities tended to exert stronger influence in the groups. People with higher-paying jobs, such as professionals and proprietors, talked more than those who had lower-paying jobs. The higher status individuals also provided more leadership within the group; the lower status individuals tended to follow their direction. In fact, a central core of high-status members generally dominated the group discussion. This core accounted for as much as 70% of the jury's communications. Their effectiveness as influencers became apparent when Strodtbeck compared the group's verdict to the juror's predeliberation preferences. The correlation between high-status jurors' predeliberation preferences and the jury's final decision was .50. For low-status jurors, the correlation was only .02. Sex differences were also apparent: women joined in the discussion less frequently than men and were more likely to express agreement with the majority (James, 1959; Strodtbeck, James, & Hawkins, 1957).

Do these social influence processes change appreciably when juries are smaller? Researchers raised this question in response to the 1970 Supreme Court ruling on six-person juries. In the case of *Williams* v. *Florida* (1970), Williams sought to have his conviction overturned on the grounds that the jury had included only six persons. The Supreme Court ruled, however, that a jury did not necessarily require 12 members. The justices concluded that six should be sufficient to "promote group deliberation, free from outside attempts at intimidation, and to provide a fair possibility for obtaining a representative cross-section of the community" (p. 100). The high court's decision sparked a widespread revision of jury systems throughout the country.

Researchers, however, have identified a number of important changes that occur when juries are reduced in size (Saks, 1977). First, larger juries tend to deliberate for a longer period of time than smaller juries. Second, communication is more evenly distributed in smaller groups, because no central core of jurors dominates the discussion. Third, pressure to conform may be greater in smaller juries. On the one hand, Asch's studies indicate that conformity rates remain essentially constant once the group includes four members. However, the dissenting juror has a lesser chance to find an ally in a six-person group than in a 12-person group. The Supreme Court assumed that a 5-to-1 vote in a six-person jury was equivalent to a 10-to-2 vote in a 12-person jury. At the psychological level, however, these two situations differ dramatically. When the vote is 10 to 2, the dissenter faces the majority with an ally. When the vote is 5 to 1, the juror faces the majority alone. Thus, while pressures to conform are equally

(continued)

IN DEPTH *continued*

strong in six- and 12-person juries, the supports for nonconformity are weaker in six-person juries.

Researchers aren't yet certain if these differences between six- and 12-person juries lead to differences in conviction and acquittal rates. Jurors participate more in small groups, and smaller groups are more efficient. However, dissenters may be able to form coalitions more easily in larger groups. Although preliminary evidence suggests that these advantages and disadvantages balance each other in the long run, additional research is needed before any firm conclusions can be reached (Saks, 1977).

Although many questions concerning juries remain unanswered, applications of social psychology to juries have already proven to be particularly informative. First, researchers have been able to test many theoretically interesting hypotheses by studying the interchanges between minorities and majorities in juries. Studies such as Asch's represent an important first step in understanding conformity, but theories must also survive when they are tested in nonlaboratory settings. Second, by examining juries, social psychologists have contributed directly to our understanding of an important social issue. Many of the questions that courts must settle, such as the debate over the six-person jury, can be answered through research. By documenting the interpersonal processes underlying human behavior in groups, we can evaluate and even improve our current methods of making legal decisions.

E L E V E N

Group Dynamics

Social facilitation in groups
    Early experiments and puzzling findings
    Dominant and nondominant responses
    Why does social facilitation occur?
        Arousal
        Evaluation apprehension
        Distraction and conflict
    Testing the three theories
    Productivity losses in groups
        The Ringelmann effect
        Avoiding losses in productivity
Groupthink
    Symptoms of groupthink
        Overestimation of the group
        Closed-mindedness
        Pressures toward uniformity
        Defective decision-making strategies
    Causes of groupthink
        Cohesiveness
        Isolation
        Biased leadership
        Decisional stress
        Polarization
        Combining the causes
    Avoiding groupthink
        Removing the causes
        Alleviating the symptoms
Leadership of groups
    Traits versus situations
        The trait approach
        The situational approach
        Beyond situationism: Interactionism
    Fiedler's contingency theory
        Two leadership styles
        Leadership effectiveness
        Evaluating the theory
Summary
For more information
In depth: Polarization in groups

Everyone had gone: the secretaries, the mailroom clerks, the young executives, the janitors, the assembly-line workers. They'd collected their last paychecks, cleaned out their desks and lockers, turned in their ID cards, and gone home. After four years of steadily growing losses, the Murdock Computer Company had folded.

To understand his failure, Louis Murdock made an appointment to see Pat Smith, the president of Advanced Products, Inc. API manufactured the same line of products as Murdock's bankrupted company, but API had grown increasingly successful during the same years in which Murdock's company was fading away. Murdock wondered what magic made API a success.

"There's nothing magical at all about what we do here at API," Smith said when Murdock described the purpose of his visit, "but we do have a unique philosophy about how a company should be organized. Instead of thinking of our employees as individuals who must be managed to maximize their usefulness, we think of API as a collection of **groups**. And by taking the dynamics of these groups into account, we ensure that API will be a successful business.

"Let me give you some examples. Wouldn't you have difficulty explaining a child's actions if you ignored his or her family? Wouldn't an athlete's behaviors seem enigmatic if you overlooked the nature of the team? Aren't the dynamics of an elementary school classroom puzzling when you fail to recognize the teacher's leadership qualities? Of course. In the same fashion, we feel that we can achieve a true understanding of our employees only by taking into account their membership in the interdependent groups that make up API. We try always to remind ourselves that human beings are social creatures whose actions are influenced by the other members of their groups."

Murdock wasn't very impressed by this advice, and said so. "What you're saying is neither new nor unique. Much of what we did in my company—from manufacturing our products to solving production problems to making corporate decisions—occurred in groups, and we worked hard to keep them organized and operating efficiently. Are you saying that our groups were incompetent?"

Smith was diplomatic. "No, of course not. But groups are complex, and even well-informed executives can fail to capitalize on all of the advantages of groups, or avoid all their disadvantages. But look, the practical implications of this emphasis on groups aren't very clear when we try to discuss it in the abstract. Why don't I have someone show you around here so you can see how we put these ideas into practice? Come along and I'll introduce you to Bob Marks. He'll show you our assembly plant."

■ Social Facilitation in Groups

Mark's office overlooked the floor of the assembly room, where workers were soldering electronic components onto the circuit boards of small computers. Again, Murdock wasn't impressed. "The setup seems pretty typical," he commented.

Marks agreed. "It is. But our system is unique in a few subtle and important ways. First, as you can see, our workers are organized in small clusters, six to a group. [See Figure 11-1] Second, the workers within each cluster are all doing different things. Some install one part, others are responsible for another component. Third, nearly all the workers' stations face inward, so that everyone can look up and see everyone else in the group. The last station is the only exception: this step in the assembly is carried out by one person in a small room."

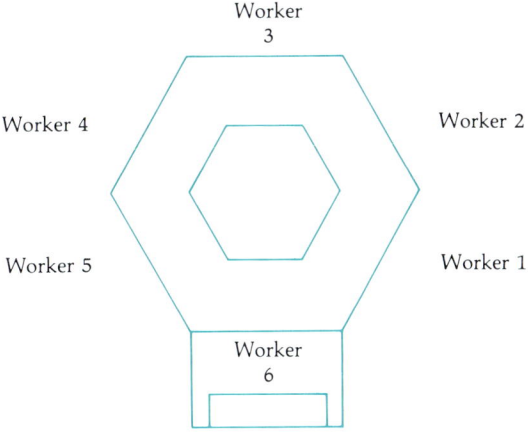

Figure 11-1 An assembly-line cluster layout. In this hypothetical arrangement, five employees work in a group. The sixth member of the team works in isolation.

"Well, that's a little different from my system," admitted Murdock, "but why perform some tasks in groups and others in isolation? Does it make any difference if people work in the presence of others or if they work alone?"

Marks answered enthusiastically. "Of course it makes a difference! Haven't you ever heard of social facilitation?"

Early Experiments and Puzzling Findings

The question raised by Murdock—do people work more efficiently when other people are present?—was first studied by Norman Triplett in 1897. Triplett was intrigued by the improved race times of bicyclists when they competed against other cyclists. Comparing records from bicycle races, Triplett discovered that people cycled an average of 32.6 miles per hour when they were competing with other racers, 31.0 miles per hour when they were paced by another cyclist, and only 24.0 miles per hour when they were racing alone and unpaced.

Some observers at the time felt that these differences were caused by a phenomenon known as drafting: the lead cyclist creates a partial vacuum that pulls followers along while also breaking down wind resistance. Triplett, however, attributed the faster race times to social-psychological rather than physical forces. Basically, he believed that the presence of others leads to psychological stimulation that enhances performance. To test his hypothesis, he conducted one of the first laboratory studies in the field of social psychology. He eliminated the possibility of drafting by arranging for 40 children to play a game, in pairs or alone, that involved turning a small reel as quickly as possible. As he had anticipated, he found that the children turned the reel faster when they played the game in pairs than when they played alone. Triplett had succeeded in experimentally verifying a phenomenon that we now know as **social facilitation:** the enhancement of an individual's performance when that person works in the presence of other people.

Researchers soon began to extend Triplett's findings. Initially, it seemed that social facilitation occurred only during *coaction*—when people were working on similar tasks. Before long, however, researchers found evidence of social facilitation in the presence of a *passive audience*. One early researcher discovered that people could lift more weight when they were being observed by another person (Meumann, 1904). This effect was discovered accidentally when the researcher made an unscheduled visit to his laboratory one night while a subject was busy lifting weights as part of an exercise study. The subject had been working in private at peak efficiency for several days, but he surpassed his previous levels when the experimenter was watching. As most weight lifters and exercise enthusiasts know, the presence of others can enhance performance.

Investigators also discovered that social facilitation is not a uniquely human phenomenon; puppies, chickens, mice, rats, monkeys, armadil-

The facilitating effects of other people. In some situations, the presence of other people improves our performance. These other people can either be watching us, as in this case, or they can be performing similar tasks in the same general vicinity (coaction).

los, ants, opossums, and even cockroaches are among the species that show signs of increased performance in the presence of other members of their species (Cottrell, 1972). In one coaction study the investigator painstakingly measured the excavation efforts of 36 ants working to build nests alone or in groups of two or three. In line with studies of humans, each ant began to work sooner and moved more earth when it worked in the presence of other ants than when it worked alone (Chen, 1937). Similarly, hungry chickens were given food in isolation or in the presence of observing chicks who watched through a clear plastic barrier. The chicks pecked 84% more often before an audience than in isolation. If the "observing" chick was dead, however (the experimenter propped a chick's corpse against the plastic partition), no social facilitation occurred (Tolman, 1968).

Occasionally a researcher reported completely contrary findings: the presence of others actually detracted from performance. For example, college students' written arguments opposing passages from philosophical works were of poorer quality when the students wrote them in a group than when they worked alone (Allport, 1924). In another study students needed more practice to learn a list of nonsense words when they were being watched by an audience than when they worked alone (Pessin, 1933). Subjects also made more mistakes in solving multiplication problems with either an audience or a coactor than when they were alone (Dashiell, 1930).

Why do coactors or audiences sometimes inhibit rather than facilitate performance? Social psychologists were troubled by this question for many years, until Robert B. Zajonc offered a compelling explanation based on the difference between dominant and nondominant responses (Zajonc, 1965, 1980).

Dominant and Nondominant Responses

When Robert Zajonc (1965) surveyed the conflicting social facilitation findings generated over the preceding six decades, he realized that previous studies had failed to draw a distinction between dominant and nondominant responses. **Dominant responses** are well-learned or instinctive behaviors that the organism has practiced and is primed to perform. **Nondominant responses,** in contrast, are novel, complicated, or untried behaviors that the organism has never performed before or has performed only infrequently. Zajonc noted that in some studies, subjects needed to perform only dominant responses to do well on the problems they faced; lifting weights, bicycling, and eating rapidly, for example, all require dominant responses. Subjects in some other studies needed to perform nondominant responses to succeed. When they attempted to solve mathematics problems or memorize lists of words, for example, subjects had to learn to give nondominant responses.

Applying this distinction to social facilitation, Zajonc hypothesized that the presence of others increases our tendency to perform dominant responses and decreases our tendency to perform nondominant responses. Therefore, if the dominant response is the correct or most appropriate response in that particular situation, then social facilitation occurs; people will perform better when others are present than when they are alone. If the task calls for nondominant responses, however,

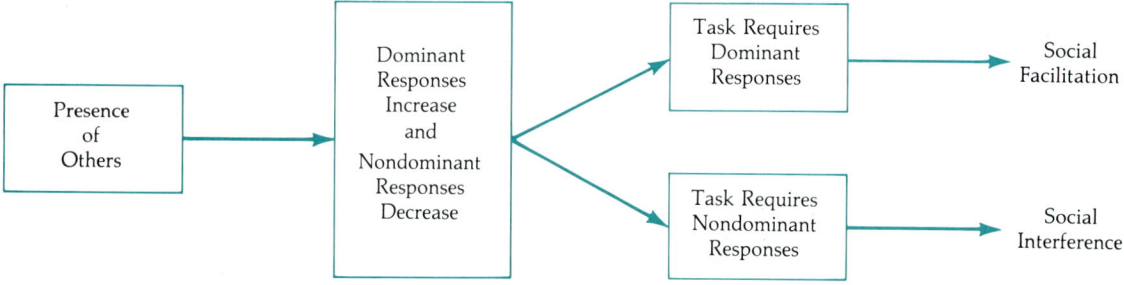

Figure 11-2 Social facilitation of dominant and nondominant responses. According to Zajonc, the presence of others increases the likelihood that the organism will emit dominant responses. Therefore, if the dominant response is the appropriate answer in the situation, the presence of others is facilitating. If, however, the situation calls for a nondominant response, the presence of others will interfere with performance.

then the presence of other people constitutes social interference (see Figure 11-2). Imagine that you must memorize some pairs of words. If the pairs are common associations, such as *blue–sky* or *clean–dirty,* then the dominant response is correct. If you hear *blue* or *clean,* the word *sky* or *dirty* is likely to pop into your head very quickly. Hence your performance will be better if other people are present. If, however, you are trying to learn some very uncommon associations—such as *blue–rutabaga* or *clean–discombobulation*—then you are required to make a nondominant response, and an audience will hurt more than help.

Zajonc demonstrated this distinction in a clever study of cockroaches (Zajonc, Heingartner, & Herman, 1969). As anyone who has surprised a roach in the kitchen late at night knows, cockroaches run from bright lights. Therefore, Zajonc designed two mazes with a start box near a light and a goal box hidden from the light. One of the mazes was extremely simple—just a straight runway from the start to the goal. The second maze was more complex: the roaches had to turn to the right to reach their goal. If Zajonc's explanation of social facilitation and interference is accurate, when other roaches are present the roaches should perform more efficiently in the simple maze than in the complex one. As Table 11-1 indicates, the results matched these predictions perfectly. When the cockroaches were tested in the simple maze, they escaped the light more quickly in pairs than alone. In the complex maze, however, they escaped more quickly alone than with another cockroach. In a similar study, Zajonc and his colleagues placed observer roaches in small plastic cubicles located around the mazes. As in the coaction study, the presence of an audience facilitated performance of the simple task but interfered with performance of the complex task.

Why Does Social Facilitation Occur?

Once we take into account the type of response needed in the situation—either dominant or nondominant—social facilitation becomes more predictable. If you are only a beginner at tennis, say, your serve will probably suffer from the presence of an audience or another player. But if you have practiced your serve so often that it is a well-learned, dominant response,

TABLE 11–1

The average number of seconds taken by the cockroaches to escape from the bright light in Zajonc's research.

Task	Alone	Coaction
Simple	40.6	33.0
Complex	110.4	130.0

SOURCE: Zajonc, Heingartner, & Herman, 1969.

then an audience or coactor will probably improve your performance. Similarly, if you are preparing for a test, you may perform better if you do your initial studying in isolation but practice your answers in a group (see Focus 11-1).

A recent review of 241 studies of social facilitation involving nearly 24,000 human subjects found that facilitation occurs primarily in association with simple tasks that require dominant responses (Bond & Titus, 1983). But what causes social facilitation? Why does it make a difference that a task requires dominant or nondominant responses? Although social psychologists have not fully answered these questions, three processes have been extensively examined: arousal produced by (*a*) mere presence, (*b*) evaluation apprehension, and (*c*) distraction and conflict.

Arousal. Zajonc (1965, 1980) believes that arousal mediates, or acts as the intervening causal link between, the presence of others and task performance. Zajonc's approach, diagrammed in Figure 11-3, assumes that the mere presence of other people should be sufficient to produce *physiological arousal.* These other people may or may not have the slightest interest in what we are doing. They may merely be occupying the same physical area that we do, or they may be watching us very closely. No matter. Zajonc conjectures that humans, as well as many other species, become more aroused and alert when others are present. Once aroused, they tend to perform more dominant responses and fewer nondominant responses. Provided dominant responses are appropriate for the task at

FOCUS 11-1

Experiencing Social Psychology: *Do we learn more efficiently in groups or alone?*

Do you like to prepare for your examinations in study groups—informal gatherings of students who are supposedly learning and reviewing course material? If you do, maybe you should reconsider your strategy.

Study groups have some advantages. If you are missing notes, if you don't understand certain topics or aren't sure what material to study, then exchanging ideas and explanations with your classmates can be helpful. If you are trying to learn new material in these study groups, though, the presence of other people will work against you. In fact, Robert Zajonc (1965, p. 274) recommends that students study "all alone, preferably in an isolated cubicle," until they feel that they know the course content very well. Otherwise, the presence of others will interfere with overt and covert practicing of material, retention, and understanding (S. M. Berger et al. 1981, 1982).

Once you have learned the material thoroughly, the presence of others should prove helpful. If students have studied so much that the correct answers are now dominant responses, according to Zajonc, they should take their "examinations in the company of many other students, on stage, and in the presence of a large audience." Such a setting can facilitate the performance of correct responses and increase the student's grade. Zajonc's analysis also lends support to a favorite professorial rebuttal to students who complain that they don't have enough time to finish their tests: "You have plenty of time if you know the material well."

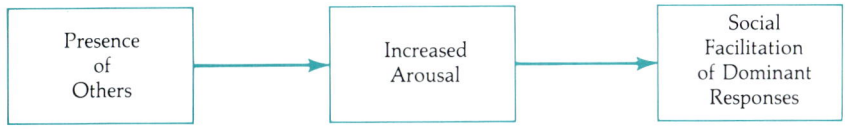

Figure 11-3   Zajonc's explanation of social facilitation argues that arousal is the key variable mediating the relationship between the presence of others (either an audience or coactors) and performance on simple tasks that require only dominant responses.

hand, arousal will improve performance. If nondominant responses are needed, however, this arousal will lead to decrements in performance. Zajonc believes that this tendency to become aroused when other people are present is an unlearned, innate reaction.

Evaluation apprehension.   Imagine yourself reciting a well-memorized poem while standing before a group of fellow students. All the students are seated with their backs to you, however, and are listening to rock music through individual headphones. Your audience is paying no attention to you; they have no idea if you are doing a good or bad job.

According to Nickolas B. Cottrell (1972), the audience wouldn't help your recital in this situation because the mere presence of other people isn't sufficient to produce social facilitation. Cottrell agrees with Zajonc that we perform dominant behaviors better when we are aroused and nondominant behaviors better when we aren't aroused. Unlike Zajonc, however, Cottrell believes that we become increasingly aroused only when the other people present are a source of negative or positive evaluations. Through experience with coactors and audiences, we come to expect observers to evaluate us as they observe us. In consequence, like subjects who are worried about the impression they are making on the experimenter (see Chapter 1), we often experience *evaluation apprehension* when others are present. Figure 11-4 summarizes Cottrell's perspective: first comes evaluation apprehension, then arousal, and then social facilitation.

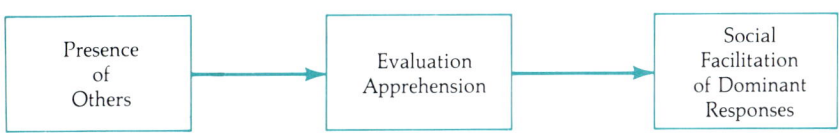

Figure 11-4   Cottrell's explanation of social facilitation argues that evaluation apprehension mediates the relationship between the presence of others (either an audience or coactors) and performance on simple tasks that require only dominant responses.

Distraction and conflict. As early as 1904 investigators noted that working in the presence of an audience or coactors can be *distracting* (Meumann, 1904); our attention is divided as we try to concentrate both on the task and on the audience's or coactors' reactions. Glenn S. Sanders and his colleagues (Sanders, 1981a; Sanders & Baron, 1975; Sanders, Baron, & Moore, 1978), however, believe that distraction has positive as well as negative consequences. On the negative side, distraction interrupts our concentration on the task at hand and reduces the amount of time we can spend working. On the positive side, when we are distracted we experience cognitive conflict as we try to attend both to our task and to the other people at the same time. This conflict increases our level of motivation; we work harder to try to overcome the effects of the distraction.

The balance between these positive and negative consequences determines the impact of others on task performance. If the task is so simple that the increase in motivation outweighs the decrements caused by distraction, then social facilitation will occur. But if the task is so complex that the increase in motivation is unable to offset the negative consequences of distraction, then the presence of others will lead to decrements in performance. This distraction/conflict model is shown in Figure 11-5.

Testing the Three Theories

Researchers have tested these three theories in a number of experiments (Geen, 1980, 1981; Sanders, 1981a; Zajonc, 1980; see Table 11-2). In an ingenious unobtrusive test of Zajonc's arousal theory, Hazel Markus (1978) examined the impact of an audience on both dominant and non-dominant responses. After telling subjects that the study would start in

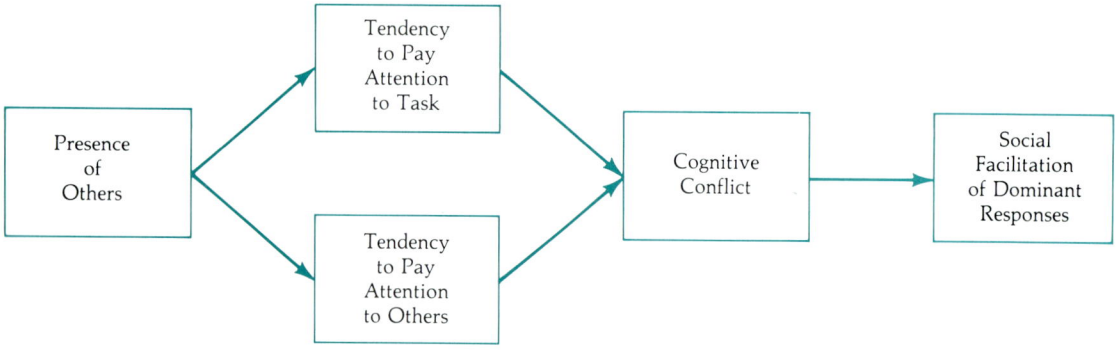

Figure 11-5 The distraction/conflict model of social facilitation. According to Sanders, when others are present, attention is divided between the task being performed and the people who are present. These competing tendencies lead to cognitive conflict, which helps performance on simple tasks but undermines performance on complex tasks.

a few minutes, she explained that she wanted to make sure that all of the subjects were dressed in the same way. So she asked each one to put on a lab coat, a pair of large socks, and a pair of shoes that they would find in the next room. The subjects didn't realize it, but an observer recorded the amount of time they took to take off their shoes and socks and don the experimental clothing.

By asking the subjects to perform these tasks, Markus succeeded in measuring both dominant responses (taking off and putting on their own shoes) and nondominant responses (putting on and taking off a pair of large socks, a pair of shoes, and a lab coat that tied in the back). To manipulate the presence of others, she had the subjects perform these various actions alone, under the gaze of an attentive observer, or in the presence of an incidental observer who sat with his back to the subject, absorbed in his work on a piece of equipment.

The results of Markus's study are shown in Table 11-3. As Zajonc's theory predicts, when the task called for dominant responses, subjects took the most time alone and the least time when an attentive audience was present. In contrast, when they performed novel actions they worked fastest alone and slowest when either type of audience was present. If you look closely at the data presented in Table 11-3, however, you will note a slight but significant deviation from the findings predicted by Zajonc's theory. According to Zajonc, the mere presence of other people should be sufficient to produce arousal. As Table 11-3 shows, however, the strongest effects were found when the audience was looking directly at the subjects. These findings are consistent with Cottrell's theory, if we assume that the attentive audience created evaluation apprehension. Sanders' theory can also explain the findings: the attentive audience was a greater distraction. Zajonc's theory cannot easily account for these findings.

Markus's findings, and those of several other studies, suggest that all three processes implicated by the theorists—arousal produced by the mere presence of an audience, evaluation apprehension, and distraction

TABLE 11-2

Three possible explanations of social facilitation processes.

Theory	Mediating Processes	Source
Zajonc's arousal theory	The mere presence of others increases arousal	Unlearned
Cottrell's evaluation apprehension theory	The presence of others increases arousal only when individuals also experience evaluation apprehension	Learned
Sanders's distraction/conflict theory	The presence of others causes distraction, attentional conflict, and increased motivation	Not specified

leading to conflict—play a role in social facilitation (Cottrell, 1972; Geen, 1981; Markus, 1981; Sanders, 1981a, 1981b). In some cases—especially those involving innately fixed behaviors such as eating and drinking—the arousal sparked by the mere presence of others may be sufficient to produce social facilitation. In other situations, social facilitation effects may become pronounced only if the audience can see and evaluate the subject's performance. Lastly, the presence of others can be distracting (Baron, Moore, & Sanders, 1978), and if the task is a simple one, the conflict caused by this distraction may cause increments in task performance. Rather than eliminate any of the theories, we should recognize that an adequate conceptualization of social facilitation must take into account all three processes.

Productivity Losses in Groups

As Bob Marks and Louis Murdock were nearing the end of their discussion of the assembly room procedures, Murdock asked, "Do you train your new workers in groups?"

"No," Marks replied. "We put them in clusters only after they've practiced their assembly skills so often that they've become dominant responses. And because the final step in the assembly process is very complex—all circuits must be double-checked by the troubleshooter—it's carried out in isolation. By using a group-centered assembly process for the tasks that require dominant responses and an isolation booth for the task that requires nondominant responses, we maximize our production efficiency."

"I see now how social facilitation affects performance," Murdock said, "but I still have a question. In your clusters, each person adds one more component to the total product, so they can't directly compare their own performance with what the others are doing. Wouldn't your workers have more evaluation apprehension if they were all doing the same thing?"

TABLE 11-3

The average number of seconds required for subjects to perform two tasks in three conditions. As expected, subjects took off their own shoes and socks (dominant task) faster than they put on the unfamiliar clothes (the nondominant task). And they performed the dominant task even more rapidly if an observer was present. When they turned to the task that required nondominant responses, the presence of an observer slowed them down.

Type of Response Needed	Alone	Incidental Audience	Attentive Audience
Dominant	16.46	13.49	11.70
Nondominant	28.85	32.73	33.94

SOURCE: Markus, 1978.

"That's a good point," answered Marks. "But if everyone was doing the same thing, we'd have trouble keeping track of who was responsible for each component. We'd know which group assembled the product, but we couldn't tell which person added which part. And we have to be able to identify the inputs of each member of the group or all the advantages of social facilitation will be wiped out by a negative process that undermines group productivity. Have you ever heard of the Ringelmann effect?"

The Ringelmann effect. Many years ago a French agricultural engineer named Max Ringelmann used a tug-of-war procedure to study group performance. When he arranged for individuals and groups to pull on a rope attached to a pressure gauge, he discovered that the amount of pressure exerted by the group increased as people were added to the group; the bigger the group, the stronger the group. He also noted, however, a mysterious loss of individual strength as the group grew larger. As Figure 11-6 suggests, an average individual working alone was able to exert about 63 kilograms (kg) of pressure. Therefore, two people working together should be able to exert 126 kg (63 kg + 63 kg), three people should pull 189 kg (63 kg + 63 kg + 63 kg), and so on. Ringelmann's groups, however, regularly fell below this level of production. Dyads managed to pull only about 1.9 times as much as one person, triads only 2.5 times as much, and eight-person groups a woeful 3.9 times the individual level. Even though the task was a simple one, the presence of other people led to inferior performances (Steiner, 1972). This

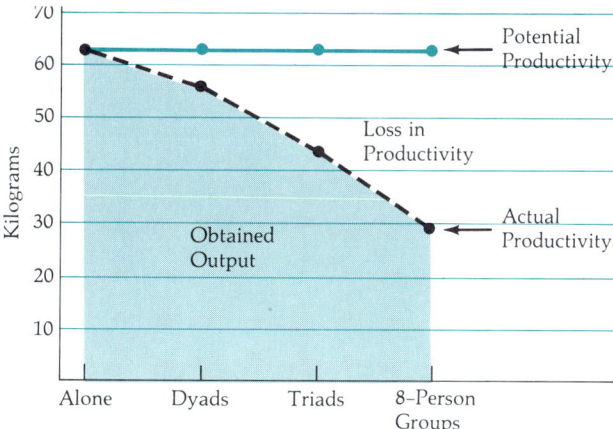

Figure 11-6 The Ringelmann effect. If individuals in groups were able to pull as much as they did in isolation, the potential productivity should be directly proportional to group size. As Ringelmann discovered, however, most groups rarely reach this level of performance. In fact, the larger the group, the greater the discrepancy between potential productivity and actual productivity.

intriguing tendency for individuals to become less productive as group size increases is known as the **Ringelmann effect.**

What causes the Ringelmann effect? Many researchers now feel that two interrelated processes combine to create a loss in productivity in groups (see Focus 11-2). The problem stems in part from *coordination losses.* When people must work together as a unit, they can have trouble coordinating their individual activities and contributions, so they never reach the maximum level of efficiency. Three people on a tug-of-war team, for example, invariably pull and pause at slightly different times, so their efforts aren't perfectly coordinated. In consequence, they are stronger than a single person, but not three times as strong (Harkins & Petty, 1982; Steiner, 1972).

Losses in productivity in groups are also caused by **social loafing,** the "reduction of individual effort exerted when people work in groups compared to when they work alone" (Williams, Harkins, & Latané, 1981, p. 303). If an instructor asks a group of students to be responsible for preparing a group report on a certain topic, some of the group members may feel that others can pick up the slack. In consequence, they don't put much effort into the project, and the overall productivity of the group is diminished (see Figure 11-7; Jackson & Williams, 1985).

Avoiding losses in productivity. Social loafing has been documented on collective tasks of many types, including tasks requiring physical exertion, perceptual judgments, and even cognitive effort (Ingham et al.,

Figure 11-7 Many hands make light the work. Evidence indicates that the inefficiency of some work groups goes beyond problems of coordination. As the number of group members increases, people tend to expend less and less effort—a process known as social loafing.

FOCUS 11-2

A Closer Look: *What causes the Ringelmann effect?*

Have you ever not bothered to clap at the end of a play or performance because you assume everyone else is making enough noise already? Or at sporting events, do you sometimes give just a few halfhearted rahs because the other spectators are cheering wildly?

These everyday examples of the Ringelmann effect inspired a series of studies conducted by researchers at Ohio State University (Harkins, Latané, & Williams, 1980; Williams, Harkins, & Latané, 1981). After telling their male subjects that the study would address "the effects of sensory feedback on the production of sound in social groups," the researchers asked them to shout as loudly as they could while alone, in dyads, or in six-person groups. All of the subjects wore blindfolds and headsets, which played a loud stream of noise that masked any noise made by other group members. As expected, individual productivity was lower in groups. When subjects were tested alone, they averaged a rousing 9.22 dynes per square centimeter (about as loud as a pneumatic drill). Furthermore, two- and six-person groups generated more noise than subjects working alone, but the productivity of each individual subject dropped. In dyads, each subject worked at only 66% of capacity, and in six-person groups at 36%. This drop in productivity is represented by the dashed line in Figure 11-8 (Latané, Williams, & Harkins, 1979, Experiment 2).

The Ohio State researchers weren't interested simply in demonstrating that people cheer less in groups than alone. They also wanted to verify experimentally that the Ringelmann effect was caused by two separate processes: coordination losses and social loafing. To separate these two processes they tested noise production in "pseudogroups": subjects were led to believe that either one other subject or five other subjects were cheering with them, but in actuality they cheered alone (the blindfolds and headsets made this deception possible). Thus any loss of production in these conditions couldn't be due to coordination problems, because no other group members were shouting; any decline in pro-

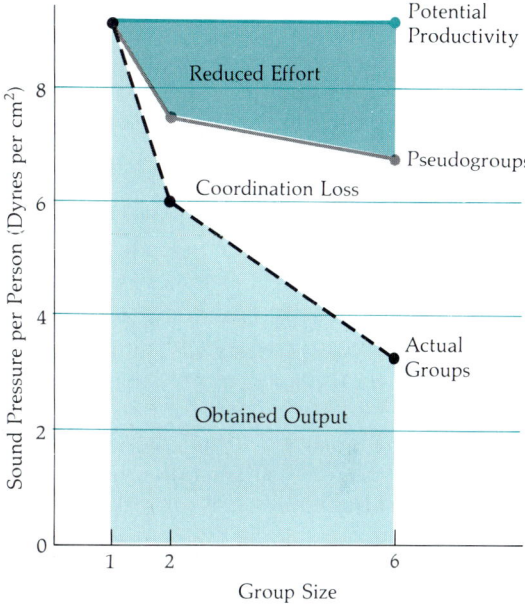

Figure 11-8 The amount of sound produced per person when subjects were alone, in dyads, and in six-person groups. The shaded area below the dotted line represents the amount of noise produced by people in the three conditions. The area between the solid line marked "pseudogroups" and the dashed line represents losses due to faulty coordination. The area above the solid line signifies losses due to social loafing.

duction could be attributed only to a reduction in effort—in other words, social loafing.

Figure 11-8 reports the results of this study. As the two-factor explanation of the Ringelmann effect predicts, part of the loss of productivity was due to coordination losses and part to social loafing. If subjects thought that one other person was shouting with them, they shouted only 82% as intensely, and if they thought five other people were shouting, they reached only 74% of their capacity. These findings suggest that even if work groups are so well organized that virtually all losses due to faulty coordination are eliminated, individual productivity may still lag because of social loafing.

1974; Latané, Williams, & Harkins, 1979; Petty, Harkins, & Williams, 1980; Petty et al., 1977). Given the scope of the problem, investigators have begun to explore ways to reduce the harmful consequence of group membership.

Increasing identifiability—making certain each individual member's contribution to the group project can be clearly identified—has proven particularly effective in several studies (Kerr & Bruun, 1981; Williams, Harkins, & Latané, 1981). In one project subjects were asked to shout as loudly as they could alone, in pairs, or in groups of six. Extending the research discussed in Focus 11-2, the investigators established three experimental conditions: (1) an actual group, in which all the subjects shouted at the same time; (2) a pseudogroup, in which subjects were led to believe that others were shouting, but in actuality they were cheering alone; and (3) a pseudogroup/identifiable condition, identical to the other pseudogroup condition except that subjects were led to believe that their individual contributions could be identified (Williams, Harkins, & Latané, 1981, Experiment 1).

The results shown in Table 11-4 attest to the power of increased identifiability. As in previous research, when subjects shouted in actual groups, they reached only a small fraction of their potential. In dyads, they worked at only 59% of their peak efficiency, and in six-person groups their productivity dropped to 31%. Their increased performance in the pseudogroups indicates that part of this loss in productivity was due to coordination problems, but Table 11-4 also indicates that the subjects were still working at 60 to 70% of their peak efficiency. When they knew their inputs were identifiable, however, the discrepancy between potential and actual performance was virtually eliminated as the subjects achieved well over 90% efficiency.

These findings suggest that identifiability is an effective means of reducing social loafing, even if group members only think that their

TABLE 11-4

The impact of identifiability and group size on social loafing. Overall, subjects expended less effort when they worked in groups. In actual six-person groups, they averaged only 31% of their potential productivity. The loss in productivity was very small, however, when subjects thought that their personal performance was being monitored (pseudogroup/identifiable condition).

	Group Size	
Condition	Two	Six
Actual group	59%	31%
Pseudogroup	69	63
Pseudogroup/Identifiable	98	92

SOURCE: Williams, Harkins, & Latané, 1981, Experiment 1.

individual inputs are known. Identifiability thus provides the basis for the assembly room procedures described earlier. Rather than have all the group members perform the same task and then collect all the finished products in a common receiving area, the hypothetical Advanced Products, Inc., made each worker responsible for a specific task so that his or her contribution to the group's product was easily identifiable. By using these methods, the company effectively eliminated the social loafing component of the Ringelmann effect.

■ Groupthink

After thanking Marks for the tour, Murdock hurried to keep his appointment with Arthur Shaver, vice-president for product development. As he entered Shaver's spacious office, he noticed a plaque on the wall:

*Madness is the exception in individuals
but the rule in groups.
—Nietzsche*

"The quote exaggerates," said Shaver, "but it serves to remind us that strange things can happen when people make decisions in groups. I firmly believe that groups offer many advantages over individuals when it comes to solving problems and formulating decisions, but they can go awry if steps aren't taken to monitor their effectiveness. Groups are sometimes more effective than individuals, but not always."

"I know exactly what you mean," Murdock said. "The board members of my company seemed to work together like a well-oiled machine. We always reached complete agreement on all decisions, we settled issues quickly and efficiently, and we never squabbled among ourselves. We were such a close-knit group that our discussions were always cordial and uneventful. There was never any competitiveness or disharmony. After each meeting we'd congratulate ourselves on our excellent decisions, for we never doubted that our products would be successful. Yet somehow our decisions led to failure after failure."

Shaver frowned. "Your group displayed many of the symptoms of a debilitating process known as groupthink. The group members try so hard to agree with one another that they make mistakes they'd avoid if they were deciding things alone."

Symptoms of Groupthink

Irving Janis (1982, 1983) began his studies of decision-making groups after reading historical accounts of the advisory committee that planned the invasion of Cuba at the Bay of Pigs in 1961. This group included some of the most brilliant political minds in the United States, yet the group made mistake after mistake. His interest piqued (and challenged by his teenaged daughter, who insisted that social-psychological factors couldn't possibly explain the failure), Janis conducted extensive case studies of the groups described in Table 11-5. Each of these military or governmental groups included top-quality personnel; most had been picked for their intelligence, their dedication, and their outstanding decision-making skills. Yet when they gathered together in a group, something happened. To paraphrase Carl Jung, the individually clever heads became one big nincompoop.

Janis concluded that the members of these groups experienced **groupthink,** a distorted style of thinking that renders group members incapable of making a rational decision. According to Janis (1982, p. 9), groupthink is "a mode of thinking that people engage in when they are deeply involved in a cohesive in-group, when the members' strivings for unanimity override their motivation to realistically appraise alternative courses of action."

To Janis, groupthink is a disease that infects healthy groups, rendering them inefficient and unproductive. And like the physician who searches

TABLE 11-5

Six fiascoes attributable to groupthink among U.S. government and military officials and their advisers.

Year	Group	Fiasco
1941	Senior advisers to Admiral H. E. Kimmel: 20 captains, vice-admirals, and other executive naval officers	Concentrated on Pearl Harbor's importance as a training base to such an extent that it was left unprotected
1950	President Truman's policy-making group, including the Joint Chiefs of Staff, and members of the National Security Council	Authorized the crossing of the 38th parallel during the Korean War, which prompted a counterattack by China
1961	President Kennedy's ad hoc advisory committee, including the secretaries of state and defense, Joint Chiefs of Staff, and top CIA officers	Planned the disastrous Bay of Pigs invasion
1965–1968	President Johnson's Tuesday Lunch Group, consisting of White House staff members, the chairman of the Joint Chiefs, the CIA director, and several cabinet secretaries	Consistently advocated increasing U.S. involvement in Vietnam, including aerial bombardment of Hanoi, defoliation, escalated ground fighting
1972–1973	President Nixon's White House staff, including John Dean, John Ehrlichman, Charles E. Colson, and H. R. Haldeman	Decided to cover up the activities surrounding the Watergate break-in by destroying evidence and bribing the burglars

for symptoms that distinguish one disease from another, Janis has identified a number of symptoms that occur in groupthink situations. These danger signals, which should serve to warn members that they may be falling prey to groupthink, include overestimation of the group, closed-mindedness, pressures toward uniformity, and defective decision-making strategies.

Overestimation of the group. Groups that have fallen into the trap of groupthink are actually planning fiascoes and making all the wrong choices. Yet the members usually assume that everything is working perfectly. According to Janis, the tendency to *overestimate the effectiveness of the group* is due partly to two types of illusory thinking: (*a*) illusions of invulnerability and (*b*) illusions of morality. Nixon's White House staff, for example, was certain that Nixon, with all his power and resources, could easily dispose of any problems that might arise as a consequence of the Watergate break-in. Furthermore, transcripts of the famous Nixon tapes indicate that the group felt that the coverup was a morally appropriate action; that bribes, lies, and deception were permissible because their purpose was to protect the president.

Closed-mindedness. Group members caught in groupthink become *closed-minded*. Instead of remaining open to alternatives, they work together to rationalize, or explain away, any misgivings or opposing views. They also tend to view anyone who opposes them in a negative, stereotyped way. For example, the naval advisers and officers responsible for the protection of the U.S. Pacific Fleet based at Pearl Harbor received many warning signals indicating the possibility of a Japanese air attack, but they managed to dismiss them all through rationalizing and stereotyping. They convinced themselves that weak little Japan would never dream of attacking the powerful U.S. fleet; that the Japanese would concentrate on easier targets located thousands of miles from Hawaii; that the Japanese didn't have the courage to gamble their fleet of aircraft carriers in such a bold attack; that the Japanese lacked the military know-how and expertise to carry out such an attack successfully. All of these rationalizations lulled the navy into a false sense of security.

Pressures toward uniformity. As Chapter 10 noted, conformity is a natural and necessary aspect of a group's dynamics. But in groupthink situations, *pressures to conform* become overwhelming. Each individual member of the group experiences a personal reluctance to disagree. Even members who begin to question the group's decision privately will hide their misgivings when they discuss the issue openly. Group members also become increasingly intolerant of dissent. In fact, some of the group members may adopt the role of *mindguard*. Janis coined this term to refer to self-appointed vigilantes who try to shield the group from information that will shake the members' confidence in themselves or their leaders.

Through self-censorship, pressuring dissenters, and mindguarding, the group develops an atmosphere of *unanimity.* Although every single person may privately disagree with what is occurring in the group, publicly everyone expresses total agreement with the group's policies.

Janis finds many of these symptoms in the ad hoc committee that advised President John F. Kennedy on the Bay of Pigs invasion. Although many of its members discerned loopholes in the invasion plan, they remained silent during the meetings because they didn't want to make waves. Furthermore, whenever disagreement did occur, it was quickly quashed by the rest of the group members, who urged the dissenter to work with the group rather than against it. In addition, several of the group members—including then Secretary of State Dean Rusk—acted as mindguards by diverting controversial information from the group and by taking potential dissenters aside and pressuring them to keep quiet. Almost from the very start of the discussions the group seemed to be in agreement on the plan. A "curious atmosphere of assumed consensus" characterized each session (Schlesinger, 1965, p. 250), as members just went through the motions of group deliberation and discussion.

Defective decision-making strategies. The decisions made in groupthink situations can be described in many ways, none of them complimentary. Such words as *fiasco, blunder, failure, error, misfire,* and *débacle* are fair descriptors, for groupthink leads to decisions that are so inadequate that they seem to court disaster.

Janis notes that these fiascoes are a logical outgrowth of the *poor decision-making strategies* so symptomatic of groupthink. In Kennedy's advisory group, discussion focused on two extreme alternatives—either endorse the Bay of Pigs invasion or abandon Cuba to communism—while ignoring all other potential alternatives. In addition, the group lost sight of its overall objectives as it became caught up in the minor details of the invasion plan, and failed to develop contingency plans to follow should the original tactics fail. Lastly, the group actively avoided any information that pointed to limitations in their plans, while seeking out facts and opinions that buttressed their initial preferences. The group members didn't make a few small errors; they committed dozens of blunders.

Causes of Groupthink

You probably belong to at least one group that must make decisions from time to time. You may belong to a community association that needs to choose a fund-raising project; a union or employee group that needs to ratify a contract; a family that must discuss your future. Could these kinds of groups experience groupthink? Yes, if the causal factors specified by Janis are present. Here we review five of the most important factors: cohesiveness, isolation, leadership style, stress, and group polarization.

Cohesiveness. In physics, the strength of the molecular attraction that holds particles of matter together is known as cohesiveness. Similarly, a group's **cohesiveness** is the strength of the relationships linking the members to one another and to the group itself. In a cohesive group, such as the board of Murdock's defunct computer company, members express strong liking for one another and for the group as a whole. They are proud to identify themselves as group members and defend the group against criticism. Close-knit, unified, and high in esprit de corps, a cohesive group suffers little from turnover or intragroup conflict (Cartwright, 1968).

Members of cohesive groups are usually much more satisfied than members of noncohesive groups. Janis believes, however, that there is a danger in extreme cohesiveness. When cohesiveness intensifies, so does its members' tendency to accept the group's goals, decisions, and norms without reservation. Conformity pressures also rise as members become reluctant to say or do anything that goes against the grain of the group, and the number of internal disagreements—so necessary for good decision making—decreases. In fact, evidence indicates that anyone who does manage to disagree with the rest of the members of the group that is high in cohesiveness is likely to be ostracized (Cartwright, 1968; Schachter, 1951). Janis (1982, p. 176) admits that noncohesive groups can also make terrible decisions, "especially if the members are engaging in

The cohesiveness of social groups. Some groups, such as sports teams, work units, or this military police unit, are more cohesive than others. The members of such groups express strong liking for the group, proudly identify themselves as members, and often defend the group against criticism.

internal warfare," but they do not fall prey to groupthink. Only in a cohesive group do the members refrain from speaking out against decisions, avoid arguing, and strive to maintain friendly, cordial relations with one another at all costs.

Isolation.   Many military, industrial, and governmental groups work in secret. They avoid leaks by maintaining strict confidentiality, working only with people who are members of their group. The government advisors who planned the Bay of Pigs invasion believed that only a surprise attack would succeed, so they insulated themselves from any outside contacts. Unfortunately, their *isolation* limited the amount of information available to the group and prevented any type of consultation with independent experts. Although military analysts who were not included in the group could have provided fresh insights and useful criticisms of the plan, their input was avoided. The group's isolation from important sources of information resulted in a poor plan that was never rigorously tested.

Biased leadership.   Leaders can also contribute to the growth of groupthink. A *biased leader* who exerts too much authority over the group members can increase conformity pressures and railroad decisions. Many groups follow a rigid protocol that gives the leader considerable control over the group discussion. The leader determines the agenda for each meeting, sets limits on discussion, and can even decide who will be heard. A biased leader can discourage dissension by expressing his or her own views at the very outset, and by urging the group to strive for agreement rather than critical discussion.

President Lyndon B. Johnson's actions as the leader of his advisory committee on Vietnam War strategies provide many examples of biased leadership. He was committed to escalating the Vietnam War, and met each Tuesday with military experts to consider strategy and select targets for bombing. Johnson controlled the discussion at all meetings, and expressed his own views forcefully and unwaveringly. He refused to allow the group to discuss deeper issues—such as ways to achieve peace through negotiation—and called dissenters such names as "my favorite dove" or "Mr. Stop-the-Bombing." Johnson also forced Secretary of Defense Robert McNamara to resign from his post because he continually disagreed with the group's policies; Johnson felt that McNamara was undermining the unity of the group.

Decisional stress.   As Janis notes, most of us experience *stress* when we must make an important decision. Important choices—such as which college to attend, which house or apartment to buy or rent, which car to buy, whom to marry—are made reluctantly, and only after we have suffered through days and nights of worry, anxiety, and uncertainty (Janis & Mann, 1977).

To reduce the stress of decision making, we make use of a number of coping mechanisms. We sometimes procrastinate for so long that we avoid the decision entirely. Or we make an arbitrary decision and then rationalize our choice. Or we deny responsibility for our choice by delegating the decision to someone else. Unfortunately, these tendencies can actually be stronger when people make major decisions in groups than when they decide alone. The insecurity of each individual can be minimized if the group quickly chooses a plan of action, with little argument or dissension. Then, through collective discussion, the group members can rationalize their choice by exaggerating the positive consequences, minimizing the possibility of negative outcomes, and concentrating on minor details while overlooking larger issues. Naturally, these stress-reduction tactics increase the likelihood of groupthink (Callaway, Marriott, & Esser, 1985).

Polarization. Common sense suggests that groups tend to be more conservative than individuals; that, faced with a choice between risky and cautious alternatives, groups prefer caution. Research indicates, however that groups' decisions tend to be more extreme than individuals'. Groups don't urge restraint—instead, they *polarize* our opinions.

Imagine you are a member of a group that has generated ten possible solutions to a problem. Some of the solutions are risky; although they will yield tremendous gains if they are successful, the likelihood of failure is high. Other solutions are cautious; they will yield only small gains, but they are much more likely to be successful. Still other solutions fall near the midpoint of the risk-caution continuum; these moderate solutions will yield some benefits, but they pose some risks as well.

In this situation, **group polarization** will probably occur. As Figure 11-9 demonstrates, the group will shift away from the midpoint of the continuum toward either the risky or caution pole, with the direction of

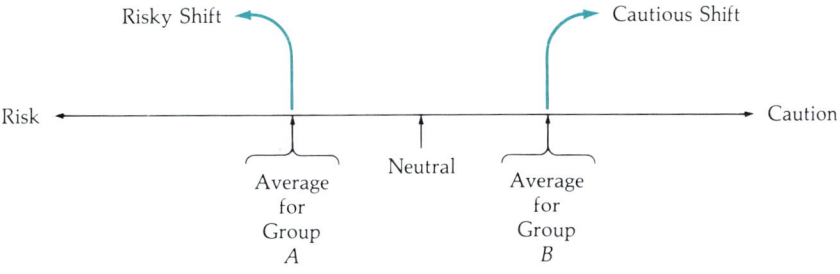

Figure 11-9 Polarization in groups. If the average of the group members' prediscussion opinions is closer to the risky pole (group *A*), then a risky shift will occur. A cautious shift occurs when the group's average prediscussion opinion is closer to the cautious pole (group *B*).

polarization depending on the average of the individual group members' opinions before the group discussion. If the average choice of the group members' prediscussion choices is closer to the risky pole (group *A* in Figure 11-9), then a *risky shift* should occur: the group should settle on a solution that is riskier than the average of the prediscussion choices. If, however, the average of prediscussion choices is more cautious (group *B* in Figure 11-9), then a *cautious shift* should take place: the group should advocate greater caution. Such polarization also applies to postdiscussion judgments made by group members. If the members are later taken aside and asked to make their judgment in private, their opinions usually remain polarized (Myers & Lamm, 1976).

Groups experiencing groupthink are ripe for polarization. The members are not initially neutral—they lean toward caution or risk. Hence, when they gather together in a group, their initial preferences become polarized, and they end up making decisions that are too risky or overly cautious. Polarization is examined in more detail in "In Depth: Polarization in Groups," at the end of this chapter.

Combining the causes. Janis maintains that you need not worry too much if one of these factors operates in your group; you will probably manage to avoid groupthink. For example, if the executives of Murdock's company had been highly cohesive but had held their meetings in public under the leadership of an impartial leader and had experienced little decisional stress, they probably wouldn't have fallen into groupthink. When two or more of these factors are present, however, groupthink becomes likely.

John A. Courtright (1978) tested this hypothesis by manipulating two potential causes of groupthink: cohesiveness and decisional stress. He told some groups of college students discussing the question "What is the best method for recruiting new students to the university?" that their groups were cohesive, while others were led to believe that their groups were not cohesive. In addition, some groups worked under stress: they were told that they must hurry and decide on one good idea through cooperative discussion (the "limiting" condition). Courtright told other groups that they had plenty of time to discuss the issue and that "the best solutions usually come from vigorous competition among a large number of incompatible ideas" (the "freeing" condition). A final condition was added to serve as a control: these subjects were given no instructions about how they should make their decisions.

Courtright's study supports Janis's belief that two or more causal factors must be present before groupthink will occur. As Table 11-6 indicates, highly cohesive groups evidenced signs of groupthink only when decisional stress was high. In this condition, the disturbing lack of disagreement among group members suggests that they were avoiding conflict by seeking concurrence. In fact, highly cohesive groups disagreed the most in the freeing condition, less in the no-instruction condition, and least in the limiting condition; the opposite pattern was found, to a lesser extent, in the groups that were low in cohesiveness.

Analysis of the quality of the groups' solutions also indicated that the worst solutions came from highly cohesive groups working under time and discussion limits. These findings lend support to Janis's prediction (1982, p. 245) that "we expect high cohesiveness to be conducive to groupthink only when certain additional determining conditions are present," such as isolation, biased leadership, or decisional stress.

Avoiding Groupthink

Figure 11-10 summarizes Janis's theory of groupthink. Janis assumes that a large number of group and situational factors contribute to the development of groupthink, but he emphasizes high cohesiveness above all other causes. Janis believes that once a group falls prey to groupthink, various symptoms of faulty group process begin to surface, including overestimation of the group's effectiveness, closed-mindedness, strong pressures toward uniformity, and faulty decision-making strategies. The process culminates in a fiasco.

Steps can be taken to reduce the likelihood of groupthink. The group situation can be structured in ways that reduce or eliminate the potential causes of groupthink—cohesiveness, isolation, biased leadership, and stress. And even if all the factors that precipitate groupthink are present, steps can be taken to reduce its symptomatic consequences. Some strategies for achieving these two interrelated goals are reviewed below.

Removing the causes. Janis doesn't recommend reducing the cohesiveness of the group as a means of limiting groupthink. As he notes, the impact of cohesiveness on group processes can be either negative or positive, depending on other characteristics of the group and setting. He does, however, recommend several methods for dealing with the other causes of groupthink. First, to reduce isolation, people who are not

TABLE 11-6

The average number of disagreements in cohesive and noncohesive groups working under freeing and limiting conditions of decisional stress and with no instructions.

Degree of Cohesiveness	Decisional Stress		
	Freeing	Limiting	No Instructions
High	6.38	2.19	4.38
Low	4.44	6.63	4.00

SOURCE: Courtright, 1978.

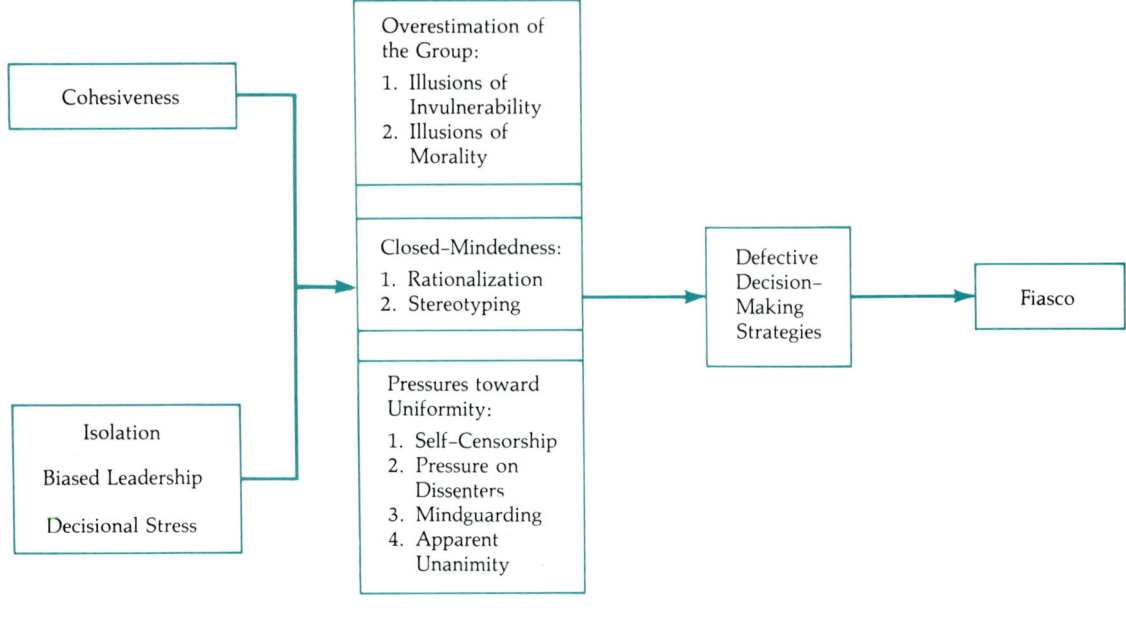

Figure 11-10 Irving Janis's theory of groupthink.

members of the decision-making group should be periodically invited to meetings and encouraged to give their opinions and criticisms of plans. Also, group members should feel free to discuss the decision with trusted subordinates who aren't members of the group. Second, leaders must strive to remain impartial. They must make it clear that they expect the group members to argue and criticize and should state their own preferences only after all voices have been heard. Third, although decision-making, by its very nature, tends to be stressful, groups can reduce this stress and avoid polarization by allowing sufficient time for full discussion and routinely holding "second chance" meetings—review sessions held after the final decision is made but before the plan is put into action. Janis recommends that these second-chance meetings be held in different, more relaxed settings, citing as precedent the decisional techniques of the ancient Persians. History claims that they made all important decisions twice: once when sober and once when drunk.

Alleviating the symptoms. Even if groupthink's causes cannot be directly attacked, its symptoms can be treated. First, Janis stresses the importance of eliminating overconfidence by cataloging and reviewing the in-group's limitations and, if relevant, the out-group's strengths. Second, as a safeguard against closed-mindedness group members should devote a sizable block of time to "surveying all warning signals from the rivals and constructing alternative scenarios of the rivals' intentions" (Janis, 1982, p. 268). Third, to reduce conformity pressures the

FOCUS 11-3

Applying Social Psychology: *Enhancing creativity through groups.*

How can potato chips be packaged so they take up less space? Why is a family like an ocean? What other products besides tea could be packed in bags? List as many possible uses for cardboard boxes as you can. How would the world be different if everyone had six fingers instead of five?

To solve these kinds of problems, individuals must be able to generate a variety of potential solutions. Rather than restrict their focus by concentrating on only one or two solutions—as is so typical in groupthink situations—the problem solver must pursue the creative and innovative while avoiding the routine and traditional. Many organizations—governments, businesses, industry, schools, and so on—rely on groups when they seek creative answers.

Many methods have been developed to enhance creativity through group interaction. One of the most famous, **brainstorming,** is based on the four rules shown in Table 11-7: expressiveness, nonevaluation, quantity, and building (Osborn, 1957). Brainstorming encourages group members to generate as many ideas as possible without worrying if these ideas are good or bad. Ideas can be analyzed later, but during the brainstorming phase all ideas, no matter how half-baked or bizarre, should be expressed. Quantity counts more than quality.

Evidence indicates that brainstorming stimulates creativity, but only in some conditions. On the positive side, the sheer presence of others may be stimulating (Ruback, Dabbs, & Hopper, 1984), and the interchange of ideas may lead to the discovery of novel solutions that individuals working alone would never have imagined. On the negative side the studies of social loafing described earlier imply that people may not work so hard when they are members of an interacting group. In fact, some studies have shown that when people are asked to generate creative ideas in isolation, they devise more solutions than people working in groups (Bouchard & Hare, 1970; Bouchard, Barsaloux, & Drauden, 1974).

How can brainstorming be improved? First, training in creative problem solving is essential; if the group members simply sit down and brainstorm without discussing the four rules shown in Table 11-7, their efforts will probably be less than satisfying (Bouchard, 1972a). Second, recording ideas individually, after the group session, helps control social loafing (Philipsen, Mulac, & Dietrich, 1979). Third, in some cases a skilled discussion leader is essential (Bouchard, 1972b; Gordon, 1961; Prince, 1975). Group members must sometimes be stimulated before they become creative. Last, creativity takes time and energy. When ideas begin to dwindle, group members shouldn't try to hurry along to a new topic.

TABLE 11-7

The rules of brainstorming.

Rule	Content
Expressiveness	Express all ideas that come to mind, no matter how strange, wild or fanciful. Do not be constrained; freewheel whenever possible.
Nonevaluation	Ideas shouldn't be evaluated during the idea-generation stage. All ideas are valuable, and criticism is unwarranted.
Quantity	The more ideas, the better.
Building	All ideas belong to the group, so group members should feel free to modify, extend, and draw on others' proposals.

group leader should (*a*) establish an atmosphere of open inquiry in which criticism, debate, and dissension are the norm rather than the exception; (*b*) break the group down into subgroups, which work independently on the decision; and (*c*) ask one or more group members to play the role of devil's advocate by consistently criticizing the ideas and suggestions raised by others.

Fourth, the group should always try to use effective decision-making strategies. Even before beginning deliberations, for example, the group members should plan the process they will be using to arrive at a decision. Problem-solving groups rarely devote much time to this issue—they generally jump immediately to the question under discussion. Unfortunately, the more time the group spends in strategy planning, the more likely it is to make a good decision (Hackman & Morris, 1975; Hirokawa, 1980, 1984). In addition, the group members should generate as many alternative solutions to the problem as they can, perhaps by using such techniques as brainstorming (see Focus 11-3). Lastly, all these alternatives should be fairly and painstakingly reviewed before one is chosen as the solution to the problem.

■ Leadership of Groups

Murdock was feeling a little depressed. After listening to Shaver describe the symptoms, causes, and consequences of groupthink, Murdock realized that he and his executives could serve as prime examples of the process. And later, as he watched Shaver conduct a problem-solving meeting—the group generated dozens of creative uses for one of the company's new computer products—he began to dread his next and final appointment. If he could learn so much from two of API's junior executives, what would Smith, the president of the company, have to teach him about leadership?

"I'd be a fool if I claimed to be an expert on leadership," Smith announced as soon as Murdock was seated. "Although leadership—like sex and child rearing—is found in all human societies [Lewis, 1974], it's been called the most misunderstood phenomenon on earth [Burns, 1978]. When one individual influences and motivates others who are striving to attain the group's goals and their own, we call the process leadership, but our ability to define it doesn't mean we understand it."

Murdock was learning, but not quickly enough. "I agree that leadership is complex, but I think my years of experience have taught me the difference between a leader and a follower. Energy, toughness, and dominance all go into good leadership, and the man with all those qualities is bound to be a success."

"So you think only energetic, tough, dominant *men* make good leaders?" said Ms. Smith with a smile. "Naturally, I disagree. I believe a leader's success depends as much on the situation as on personal characteristics."

Traits versus Situations

Scholars down through the centuries have debated the controversy that entraps Murdock and Smith. In the 19th century the historian Thomas Carlyle argued that famous figures in history—Alexander the Great, Napoleon, Cleopatra, Julius Caesar, Catherine the Great—possessed certain characteristics that destined them to be great leaders. To Carlyle, leadership was a quality that exists in some people and not in others. He advanced the *great-leader theory* of history (he called it the "great man theory"), which argued that the success and failure of nations and empires are determined by the skills and abilities of their leaders (Carlyle, 1841; Simonton, 1980).

Leo Tolstoy, the Russian novelist, argued that great leaders, far from shaping history, are themselves shaped by *situational forces* beyond their control. Rejecting the idea that leaders are geniuses with unique characteristics, he proposed that the "spirit of the times"—the Zeitgeist—destines them either to succeed or to fail (Tolstoy, 1869/1952).

These two perspectives—Carlyle's great-leader theory and Tolstoy's Zeitgeist approach—survive today in two models of leadership: the trait approach and the situational approach.

The trait approach.

When social psychologists began their scientific studies of leadership, they initially endorsed the *trait approach*. Adopting a scaled-down version of Carlyle's great-leader theory, most felt that the ability to lead others must be related to measurable personality, intellectual, and physical characteristics. Therefore they searched for these mysterious leadership traits by giving a wide assortment of psychological tests and measures to effective leaders, ineffective leaders, and followers. Unfortunately, these studies yielded mixed results. Granted, leadership ability did seem to be correlated with certain qualities and characteristics. Outstanding leaders tended to be more achievement-oriented, adaptable, alert, energetic, responsible, self-confident, and sociable than poor leaders and followers; they were also taller, more intelligent, older, and heavier. However, the correlations between these characteristics and leadership ranged from only .20 to .30, suggesting that other factors also play a causal role in determining leadership effectiveness (Bass, 1981; Gibb, 1969; Stogdill, 1974).

The situational approach.

The failure to discover powerful linkages between personality and leadership led researchers to reconsider Tolstoy's Zeitgeist model. This *situational approach* argues that leadership is determined by a host of variables operating in the leadership situation, including the needs of the group members, the availability of resources, and, most important, the type of task to be performed. If a group is about to disintegrate because of heated conflicts among the members, for example, the effective leader will be someone who can improve the group's interpersonal relations (Katz, 1977). Similarly, if individuals possess skills that facilitate performance on task X but undermine performance on task Y, then they are likely to emerge as effective leaders only if the group is working on task X (Stogdill, 1974). Thus, rather than assume that Fred, who is an outstanding leader in his SWAT team, will also be an outstanding leader in an aerobics class, situationalism suggests that the leader must fit the setting.

Beyond Situationism: Interactionism

Situationism avoided some of the pitfalls that ensnared the trait view of leadership, but even this approach proved too simplistic. First, most forms of situationism emphasized the fit between the leader and the group's task, but ignored the fit between leaders and their followers. Second, this approach overlooked the possibility that while the situation may favor one individual over another, leaders often modify their behavior to fit the situation, or change the situation to fit their own needs. Third, the situationist model suggests that leadership is static, when evidence indicates that leadership involves continual change (Hollander, 1978, 1985).

An **interaction model of leadership** avoids some of these limitations by taking into account the reciprocal relationships among the leader, the situation, and the group members (Barrow, 1977; Cartwright & Zander, 1968; Hollander, 1985). According to this model (shown in Figure 11-11), these three elements interact: each variable in the system can potentially influence and be influenced by every other variable in the system. Hence, rather than assume that leaders simply exert authority over their followers, the interactionist model views leadership as a mutual social relationship between leader and group members. Leaders are influenced also by the nature of the setting, but they can influence the setting or adjust their own behavior accordingly. The model views leadership as a fluid, dynamic process, involving continual adjustments among the three elements. In consequence, while the nature of the setting and group members' characteristics may prompt the emergence of leaders with certain characteristics, other factors may determine whether or not these individuals perform effectively as leaders or retain the endorsement of their followers (see Focus 11-4).

Fiedler's Contingency Theory

"I think I understand the advantages of an interactional approach," Murdock said after reviewing Table 11-8, "but I'm having trouble applying

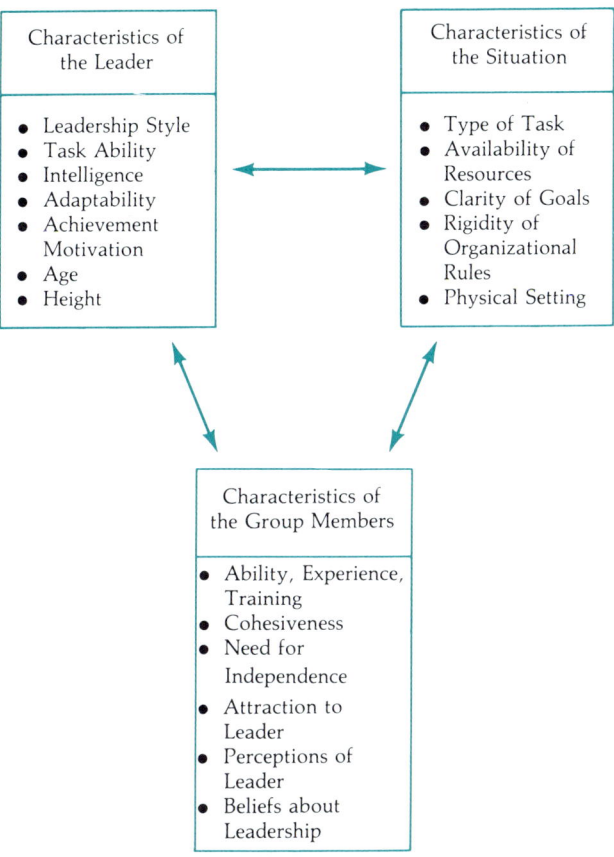

Figure 11-11 A schematic representation of an interactional approach to leadership. According to this view, the characteristics of the situation interact with the attributes, behaviors, and perceptions of the leader and followers (such as those suggested here) to influence the leadership process.

the theory in a specific situation. For instance, at one point before my company folded the productivity of the research division fell considerably. The fellow who was running that division was a real go-getter—a company man ("Company person," Smith interjected) who emphasized results and stressed the attainment of specific goals—but for some reason his subordinates disliked him. Does interactionism tell me what I should have done to improve the situation?"

Smith explained: "Leadership problems don't have simple solutions because many variables have to be taken into consideration. In the last few years, though, a number of specific interaction theories have been developed that suggest ways of improving leadership effectiveness. I can't review them all, but let me describe one in detail. **Contingency theory,** which was developed by Fred Fiedler, is an interaction model that assumes leaders' effectiveness is contingent on their leadership style and the favorability of the situation."

Two leadership styles. Although leadership requires many different skills and behaviors, empirical evidence continually attests to the fundamental importance of two key variables: *task orientation* and *relationship orientation*. As early as 1948 theorists noted that many leaders fulfill two

---

FOCUS 11-4

Experiencing Social Psychology: *Who would you pick to be your leader?*

The instructor of one of your courses randomly assigns all the class members to five-person groups. These groups must complete a project within three weeks, and each group member will get whatever grade the group project earns. Your group's members are shown in Figure 11-12. Person A is very familiar with the topic of the project, and offers excellent suggestions. B is very friendly and makes certain everyone is satisfied with the group's decisions. C misses most of the meetings. D typically sits at the head of the table and talks more than the rest of the group members. Excluding yourself, who would you predict would emerge as your group's leader? Can you predict *leadership emergence*?

As the interactionist approach shown in Figure 11-11 suggests, leadership processes are influenced by many situational, personal, and interpersonal factors. However, the processes that determine which individual in the group will assume the leadership role depend primarily on group members' perceptions (Berger et al., 1977; Berger, Wagner, & Zelditch, 1985; Calder, 1976; Green & Mitchell, 1979). When your group begins its discussion, you will treat each group member's actions and characteristics as evidence attesting to the presence or absence of leadership ability. If someone in the group matches your intuitive definition of a leader, then you will probably allow that individual to lead. This approach draws on the concept of schema, discussed in Chapter 3 (Foti, Fraser, & Lord, 1982).

Because leadership emergence is strongly influenced by the group members' perceptions, common-sense assumptions about leadership can influence this process. Studies suggest, for example, that of all the people in our fictitious group, D is the most likely to become the leader. Although A may be the most qualified because she possesses more task-relevant skills, if the group members are prejudiced against female leaders, then A may not be allowed to lead. Studies suggest that many people erroneously assume that men make better leaders than women (Jacobson & Effertz, 1974; Rosen & Jerdee, 1973, 1978), even though the available evidence indicates that men and women share equally in leadership skill (Brown, 1979). Furthermore, although good leadership often calls for the skills displayed by B, evidence also indicates that group members devalue interpersonal skills when they select leaders (Carbonell, 1984; Forsyth et al., 1985).

C clearly doesn't deserve the leadership role, for his attendance record betrays a lack of interest in the group (Fisher, 1980). But why select D? First, D looks older than the others, and group members often assume that age, experience, and leadership ability go hand in hand (Stogdill, 1974). Second, in our culture the head of the table is so strongly associated with leadership that we naturally assume that the person who sits there is the group leader (Nemeth & Wachtler, 1974). Third, evidence also indicates that many group members associate talkativeness with leadership (Burke, 1974; Stein & Heller, 1979). In fact, it doesn't really matter if D's comments are helpful or valuable to the group, for people seem to be more influenced by the sheer quantity of participation than by its quality. Thus D will probably emerge as the leader for reasons that have little to do with leadership ability.

functions in groups: they help the group perform assigned tasks and they promote smooth interpersonal (sometimes called socioemotional) relations among members (Benne & Sheats, 1948). In the early 1950s, studies conducted at Ohio State University found that group members' perceptions of their leaders were often based on these same two dimensions (Halpin & Winer, 1952). During this period, investigators who were developing a method of coding group behavior (see Chapter 1) discovered

Figure 11-12 Who would you pick to be a group leader?

that most actions could be classified as either task-oriented or relationship-oriented (Bales, 1958). Recent studies similarly suggest that the leadership role includes two fundamental components: task orientation (defining problems for the group, establishing communication, making evaluations, planning activities, coordinating group members' efforts) and relationship orientation (boosting morale, increasing cohesiveness, reducing interpersonal conflicts, providing emotional support) (Kerr et al., 1974; Lord, 1977).

Fred Fiedler's leadership theory (1978, 1981) extends these findings by arguing that most leaders lean toward one of these two orientations: some tend to be task-oriented, while others tend to be relationship-oriented. To assess this tendency, he asks people to rate the person they least prefer to work with on a series of adjective pairs such as *pleasant–unpleasant, friendly–unfriendly,* and *nasty–nice.* People who get high scores on this **least preferred co-worker (LPC) scale** are assumed to be relationship-oriented; after all, they even rate the person they don't like to work with positively. Low LPC scorers are assumed to be task-oriented. (If you find this method of measuring leadership style rather odd, you are not alone. This scale has generated considerable controversy and debate; see Rice, 1978a, 1978b, 1979; Schriesheim, Bannister, & Money, 1979; Schriesheim & Kerr, 1977.)

Leadership effectiveness. Which leadership style is more effective: task or relationship? According to Fiedler, it depends on the three interrelated group and situational factors shown in Table 11-9: *Leader-member relations* (which can be either good or bad), *type of task* (either structured or unstructured), and *leader's power* within the group (either strong or weak). To simplify somewhat, Fiedler predicts that when all of these factors are favorable—for example, relations are good, the task is structured, and the leader occupies a powerful position within the group—or extremely unfavorable, the task-oriented leader will perform most effectively. In contrast, the relationship leader should be more effective in

TABLE 11-8

The fundamental assumptions of the three approaches to leadership.

Perspective	Guiding Assumption
Trait approach	Individuals' traits predispose certain people to emerge as effective leaders.
Situationism	Situational factors cause people with certain characteristics to emerge as effective leaders.
Interactionism	Situational factors, the leader's traits and behaviors, and followers' characteristics and perceptions interact to determine who emerges as an effective leader.

moderately favorable or moderately unfavorable situations. The precise predictions of the theory are shown in Figure 11-13.

Consider two professional baseball teams called the Punks and the Rockers. Both coaches have strong positions of power because they can decide who plays and who doesn't and they can kick people off the team. The task is highly structured because everyone knows what he needs to do to play baseball effectively. However, the leader-member relations differ on the two teams. The Punks' coach enjoys very positive relations with the players, whereas the Rockers' coach and players don't get along. As Figure 11-13 shows, the model predicts that the Punks will perform best if their coach is task-oriented, while the Rockers need a relationship-oriented coach.

Evaluating the theory. Like most theories, Fiedler's approach to leadership possesses both weaknesses and strengths. On the negative side, some studies have failed to support the theory (Graen, Orris, & Alvares, 1971; Vecchio, 1977), and (as noted above) the LPC method of measuring leadership style has been questioned. In addition, because Fiedler relies heavily on nonexperimental data, we cannot be certain that leadership style or the favorability of the situation *cause* increases or decreases in the leader's effectiveness. Lastly, several critics have complained about the lack of theoretical justification for the predicted relationships (Ashour, 1973a, 1973b; McMahon, 1972). Leadership style and the favorability of the situation jointly determine leadership effectiveness, but the underlying reasons for this relationship are unclear. Although Fiedler's recent work suggests that highly favorable situations may prompt leaders to change their leadership behaviors (1978, 1981), such fundamental questions as "Why does the relationship-oriented leader perform poorly in a highly favorable setting?" and "Do task-oriented individuals actually behave that way in a leadership situation?" remain unanswered.

TABLE 11-9

The three variables that determine the favorability of the leadership situation.

Variable	Definition	Conditions
Leader–member relations	The extent to which the leader is accepted by the group members	Good vs. poor
Task structure	The degree to which the group has clear tasks to perform and verifiable goals to accomplish	Structured vs. unstructured
Position power	The amount of power and authority inherent in the group's leadership position	Strong vs. weak

SOURCE: Fiedler, 1978.

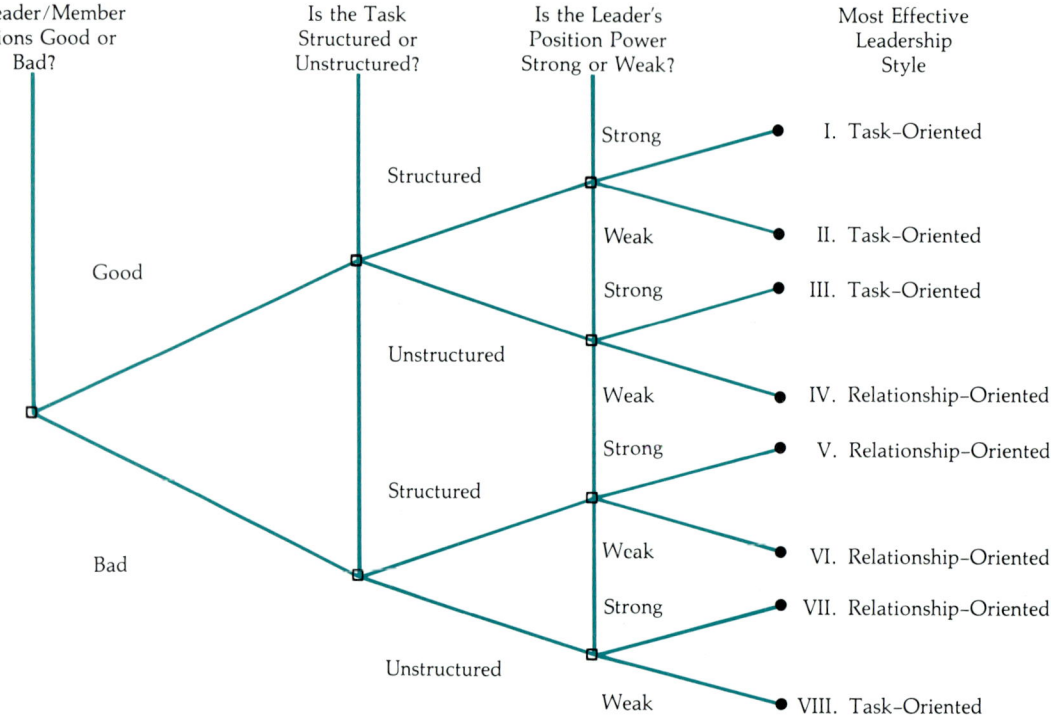

Figure 11-13 A tree diagram of the predictions of Fiedler's model. Start at the left-hand side of the tree and follow the direction associated with each answer to the three questions. The terminal nodes, numbered I through VIII, correspond to eight possible leadership situations. The top three situations (I–III) are highly favorable, the middle four situations (IV–VII) are moderately favorable or moderately unfavorable, and the last situation (VIII) is unfavorable. The most effective theoretical leadership mode in each situation is shown at the right.

On the positive side, a leadership training program derived from the theory (LEADERMATCH) has proven useful (see Focus 11-5). The theory has been tested in more than 300 studies, most of which support Fiedler's predictions (Peters, Hartke, & Pohlmann, 1985; Strube & Garcia, 1981). A study of male cadets of the U.S. Military Academy at West Point created leadership situations that varied from highly favorable to highly unfavorable. To manipulate leader–member relations, some leaders were assigned followers who disliked them, while others were assigned more affectionate subordinates. These groups worked on both structured and unstructured tasks, and the leader's position of power was either strong or weak (leaders could evaluate their subordinates only in the "strong" position power condition). When the performance rates of the groups led by cadets who scored high or low on the LPC scale were compared, the results supported the predictions summarized in Figure 11-13: Groups led by a task-oriented leader outshone relationship-led groups in the extremely favorable and unfavorable situations, while the reverse was generally true in the moderately favorable settings (Chemers & Skrzypek, 1972; Shifflet, 1973).

Smith and Murdock were saying goodbye. "All in all," Murdock admitted, "I suppose I underestimated the intricacies of groups and interpersonal relations. I just never realized that social forces count as much as internal, psychological factors. I saw my employees as individuals who

---

FOCUS 11 – 5

Controversy in Social Psychology: *Leadership throughout the group's life cycle.*

Paul Hersey and Kenneth Blanchard (1976, 1977) have challenged Fiedler's contingency theory on several issues. First, they argue that leaders need not be either task-oriented or relationship-oriented. Rather, they assume that leaders can be low or high in their task orientation, and simultaneously low or high in their relationship orientation. Thus, rather than argue for two basic types of leaders, Hersey and Blanchard view leadership as a fourfold typology (see Figure 11-14).

They also disagree with Fiedler's suggestions for training group leaders. In the LEADERMATCH program, Fiedler teaches group leaders to change the group situation to fit their particular leadership style. If task-oriented leaders find themselves in a disadvantageous group situation, for example, they should change the situation until it matches their style. Hersey and Blanchard, in contrast, recommend that leaders adapt their style until it fits the particular situation. To be specific, they argue that groups require different things from their leaders at various stages of their development. As Figure 11-14 shows, newly formed groups require a high-task/low-relationship leader to get them organized and motivated (quadrant 1). As the group matures, however, leaders should change their behavior to become more relationship-oriented (quadrant 2) and, still later, less task-oriented (quadrant 3) and less relationship-oriented (quadrant 4). Although the evidence that has been collected is not sufficient to determine which of these two opposing views—Fiedler's LEADERMATCH concept or the Hersey-Blanchard life-cycle approach—is more effective, Blanchard's application of his theory to management in business settings (termed "one-minute management") has become immensely popular (Blanchard & Johnson, 1981).

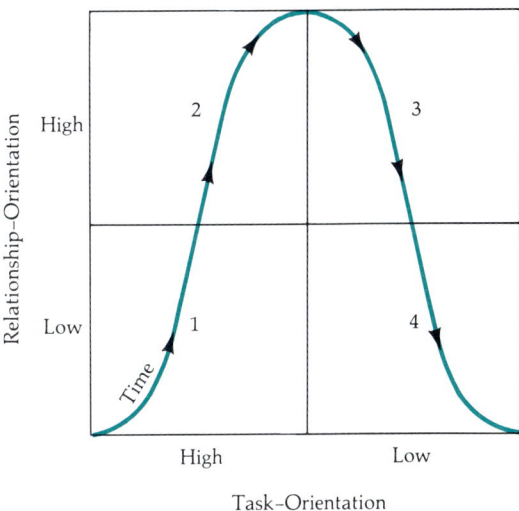

Figure 11-14 The Hersey-Blanchard life-cycle theory of leadership. According to this theory, leaders must be flexible. When the group first forms, they must use a quadrant 1 style of leadership (high task and low relationship), but change over time to other styles of leadership as the group matures. The curve that passes through each quadrant represents change over time.

were sometimes influenced by other individuals, but I overlooked the powerful impact of groups. I just assumed that a hard-working employee would be productive in any setting—whether alone or in a group. That a cohesive group would make good decisions, even under great pressure. That a person who could organize and direct other people would be a successful leader, no matter what the situation. If I'd realized that the situation counts as much as the person, I think I'd have done some things differently."

"I'm glad I've been some help to you," Smith answered. "Our knowledge of group dynamics is still full of gaps and uncertainties, but all the same, we know a lot more about how people behave in groups today than we did twenty years ago. Groups aren't necessarily good or bad. They help us raise our level of productivity in some settings and lower it in others. Some groups make informed creative decisions, but others plan out fiascoes. And a leader who succeeds in some settings can fail in others. Because leaders are made, not born, I'd like to suggest that you visit our personnel office. You could learn even more about leadership if you came to work for us."

■ Summary

Social behavior is often group behavior. Clubs, friendship cliques, work groups, military units, teams, classrooms, and assembly lines are all **groups,** for each of these social settings requires interaction among two or more individuals. Such interaction has many aspects, including task performance, decision making, and leadership.

As early as 1897, social psychologists recognized that individuals sometimes work more efficiently when other people are present. This tendency, known as **social facilitation,** occurs when others are working nearby (coaction) and when others (an audience) are watching us work. In large part, whether or not social facilitation occurs depends on the type of task being performed. The presence of others facilitates the performance of simple tasks requiring **dominant responses,** but interferes with performance on complex tasks requiring **nondominant responses.** Many theories have been developed to explain social facilitation. Zajonc's arousal theory argues that the mere presence of others automatically leads to arousal, but other theorists feel that individuals become aroused only when they experience evaluation apprehension or distraction. In all likelihood, several processes combine to determine task performance when others are present.

The presence of others undermines performance if the **Ringelmann effect** occurs. When individuals are pooling their efforts to create a single product, they often become less productive as the size of the group increases. This tendency is caused by coordination problems and by **social loafing,** the reduction of individual effort when people work in a group. To avoid social loafing, individuals' contributions to the group effort must be identifiable.

Groupthink is a strong concurrence-seeking tendency that interferes with effective group decision making. Irving Janis believes that this process is responsible for many fiascoes and blunders perpetrated by groups. The *symptoms* of groupthink include overestimation of the group's effectiveness, closed-mindedness, strong pressures toward uniformity, and defective decision-making strategies. Turning to the *causes* of groupthink, Janis predicts that **cohesiveness** is a necessary condition for groupthink; that is, groupthink occurs only in highly cohesive groups where pressures to conform are strong. Groupthink is also likely to occur in isolated groups, if the leader is biased, and if the group experiences stress. If **group polarization** occurs, the group may make more extreme decisions. How can groupthink be avoided? Janis recommends either treating the symptoms or removing the ultimate causes. Groups should avoid isolation and the leader should remain impartial and minimize stress. Also, the group should avoid overconfidence, close-mindedness, and conformity pressures. Effective decision-making strategies, such as **brainstorming,** also reduce the group's vulnerability to groupthink.

Leaders play a key role in determining a group's effectiveness. Early theorists generally took either a trait or a situation approach to leadership, but most modern theorists have adopted the **interaction model of leadership,** emphasizing the interaction of the leader's and the group members' characteristics and the nature of the situation. Fred Fiedler's **contingency theory,** for example, predicts performance by considering the leader's style of leadership and the favorability of the leadership setting. Like many other leadership theorists, Fiedler argues that leaders perform two basic functions in groups: They help the group members successfully complete their tasks while maintaining positive interpersonal relations within the group. Fiedler, however, believes that most leaders emphasize one of these goals more than the other, and assesses this orientation with the **least preferred co-worker (LPC) scale.** By taking into consideration the leader-member relations, task structure, and the leader's power, Fiedler predicts that task-oriented leaders (low LPCs) are more effective in situations that are either extremely unfavorable or extremely favorable, while relationship-oriented leaders are more effective in intermediate situations. Fiedler's theory has been supported in many settings. Alternative theoretical perspectives suggest that effective leaders modify their style to fit the demands of the situation.

■ For More Information ■

1. *SYMLOG: A System for the Multiple Level Observation of Groups,* by Robert F. Bales and his associates (1979), sets forth a general theory of group structure and a technique for observing interaction in small dis-

cussion groups. This high-level book illustrates the complexities encountered in the study of ongoing group interaction.

2. *The One-Minute Manager,* by Kenneth Blanchard and S. Johnson (1981), illuminates the leadership process by describing one man's search for the principles of effective leadership. Although the solutions oversimplify somewhat, this entertaining book is an outstanding example of how social psychology can be applied in business settings.

3. The two-volume *Small Groups and Social Interaction,* edited by Herbert H. Blumberg, A. Paul Hare, Valerie Kent, and Martin F. Davis (1983), contains chapters written by leading experts in the field of group dynamics for social psychologists and professionals in related fields.

4. *Group Dynamics: Research and Theory,* edited by Dorwin Cartwright and Alvin Zander (1968), contains many of the recognized classic works in the field of group dynamics. Cartwright and Zander's introductory remarks about groups and group processes offer many insights into groups.

5. *An Introduction to Group Dynamics,* by Donelson R. Forsyth (1983), is an introductory textbook on groups. Chapters deal with group formation, conflict, decision making, groupthink, and leadership.

6. *Victims of Groupthink,* by Irving Janis (1982), takes a sober look at the pitfalls of group decision making and recommends many ways to avoid groupthink. Excellent reading for anyone who regularly takes part in groups that make important decisions.

7. *Groups: Interaction and Performance,* by Joseph E. McGrath (1984), examines three fundamental group processes: the consequences of group activity for the group's members, the nature of interpersonal behavior in groups, and group productivity and task performance.

8. *Making Groups Effective,* by Alvin Zander (1982), examines the many factors that can undermine and increase human performance in groups. Drawing on his important studies of group productivity, Zander offers dozens of useful suggestions for improving groups.

IN DEPTH

Polarization in Groups

For centuries people assumed that groups exert a moderating, subduing effect on their individual members. The common belief was that if some radical members advocate a plan of action that seems too risky, the group gently steers them toward more cautious solutions. Conversely, when conservative members take an extremely cautious stance on issues, then the group steps in to suggest a bolder solution. As a result, groups were thought to be more moderate decision makers than individuals.

In the early 1960s, however, social psychologists began to question this assumption. By asking individuals to make judgments alone and then in groups, they found a surprising shift in the direction of greater riskiness after group interaction (Stoner, 1961; Wallach, Kogan, & Bem, 1962). In one landmark study, male and female college students responded to 12 story problems in which a hypothetical individual had to choose between one of two possible courses of action. In each story, the alternative that offered the more desirable rewards was also the course of action least likely to be carried out successfully. One story, for example, described a male electrical engineer who had a very secure job with many benefits. While attending a convention, he was offered a job with a newly founded company. His salary at the new job would be much higher, but the company might fold in the near future. Subjects were asked: "What would the probability of success have to be before you would advise the character in the story to choose the riskier course of action?"

Subjects completed this "choice dilemma questionnaire" at the very start of the experiment, once while part of a group of four or five other subjects, and again while alone. Some subjects also completed the questionnaire once more several weeks after the session. When answers were compared, the researchers found that the subjects generally advocated riskier decisions in groups than as individuals. Moreover, this group shift carried over when they gave their private choices following the group discussion. This change was dubbed the **risky shift** (Wallach, Kogan, & Bem, 1962).

In the decade from 1960 to 1970 researchers carried out hundreds of studies of the risky shift in groups. Occasionally investigators reported the opposite tendency: groups shifted in the direction of *caution*. For example, when the early risky-shift researchers examined the amount of postdiscussion change revealed on each item of the choice dilemma questionnaire, they frequently found that group members consistently advocated a less risky course of action than did individuals on one particular item (Wallach, Kogan, & Bem, 1962). And by 1969, researchers reported evidence of individuals moving in *both* directions after a group discussion, suggesting that both cautious and risky shifts occur (Doise, 1969; Moscovici & Zavalloni, 1969).

Researchers eventually realized that risky shifts after group discussion are part of a larger, more general process. When people discuss issues in groups, they tend to decide upon a more extreme course of action than would be suggested by the average of their individual judgments. The direction of the shift, however, depends on the group members' original viewpoints. As David G. Myers
(continued)

IN DEPTH *continued*

and Helmut Lamm explain (1976, p. 603) "the average postgroup response will tend to be more extreme in the same direction as the average of the pregroup responses." Group discussion intensifies judgments, and thus *polarizes* them (Myers, 1982). For example, before the subjects in one study conducted in France joined groups, they reported positive opinions of their own government but negative opinions about Americans (Moscovici & Zavalloni, 1969). After discussion, they became even more favorably disposed toward their government and even more negative toward Americans. Similarly, evidence indicates that if prejudiced persons discuss racial issues with other prejudiced individuals, their attitudes become even more negative. Conversely, if mildly prejudiced persons discuss racial issues with other mildly prejudiced individuals, they become less prejudiced (Myers & Bishop, 1970).

Why does group polarization occur? Initially a variety of explanations were proposed. Some researchers endorsed the *leadership hypothesis:* individuals with more extreme opinions exercise more influence over the group members because of their greater persuasiveness, confidence, assertiveness, and involvement in the discussion. Other investigators, in contrast, felt that shifts were due to *familiarization.* As individuals discuss problems with others, they become more familiar with the issues. As familiarity increases and uncertainty decreases, subjects are more willing to advocate extreme alternatives. A third approach traced polarization to *diffusion of responsibility.* Drawing on studies of helping behavior, some theorists suggested that group members take less personal responsibility for the negative consequences of their decisions when in groups, so they feel comfortable endorsing more extreme solutions. Overall, however, the bulk of the evidence lends support to the *cultural value hypothesis.* When individuals discuss their opinions in a group, they shift in the direction that they think is consistent with the values of their culture. If they feel that risk is valued, then they become riskier after a discussion. If, in contrast, they feel that caution is culturally valued, a cautious shift occurs (Clark, 1971; Myers & Lamm, 1975, 1976).

Precisely how cultural values are translated into group shifts is not yet clearly understood.

Some theorists feel that shifts occur because group members are able to generate many more arguments favoring the valued position. For example, if the group is answering the choice dilemma questionnaire, group members generate more arguments favoring risk than favoring caution. According to this *persuasive-arguments hypothesis*, the group persuades itself as it develops more arguments favoring the initially preferred pole (Burnstein & Vinokur, 1973, 1977; Vinokur & Burnstein, 1974, 1978). Second, the shift may be due to *social comparison* and *self-presentational processes* (Goethals & Zanna, 1979; Myers & Lamm, 1976; Myers, 1978). According to this approach, during group discussion people actively compare themselves with others. Through social comparison, they discover that while they agree with the other group members, some members of the group have stronger (or more extreme) attitudes than they do. Not to be outdone, group members then begin to endorse more extreme positions. For example, individuals who consider themselves to be risk-takers may find that they are cautious in relation to the others in the group.

Therefore, they shift their choices in a riskier direction. In all likelihood, both processes underlie choice shifts (Stasser, Kerr, & Davis, 1980).

In their quest to understand polarization processes, social psychologists have generated a wealth of information about the impact of the group on the individual. Early studies of polarization relied too heavily on artificial, uninvolving decisions. Recent studies, however, have linked polarization processes to a variety of significant interpersonal processes. Evidence indicates, for example, that during intergroup conflict polarization leads to more extreme reactions to the members of other groups, and thus promotes tension and aggression (Semmell, 1976). Polarization has also been documented in groups making judgments in legal cases, for juries shift toward guilt or innocence depending on the distribution of predeliberation opinions on the verdict (Kaplan & Schershing, 1981). The analysis of polarization in groups significantly increases our understanding of groups and attests to the long-range value of both laboratory and field research methods.

T W E L V E

The Environment and Social Behavior

Territoriality
    The nature of human territories
        Controlling access to territories
        Marking territories
        Defending territories
    The functions of territories
        Territories as social organizers
        Territories as privacy maintainers
    Territoriality and residential satisfaction
Personal space
    How much space in personal space?
        Personal characteristics
        Others' characteristics
        Interpersonal relations
        Situational factors
    Reactions to invasions of personal space
        Invasion and arousal
        Can invasions be positive?
Environmental stressors
    Crowding
        Overload
        Loss of control
        Attributions
        Interference
        Staffing
        Combining the five factors
    Noise
        Turning sound into noise
        Adapting to noise
        Noise and social behavior
    Temperature
Summary
For more information
In depth: Protecting the environment

For the moment, you are a rat. You live with 80 other rats in what should be rat paradise: a series of four interconnected pens. Each pen contains a drinking fountain, a feed hopper, and a "highrise," a five-nest burrow that can be reached by a spiral staircase. You have plenty of food to eat, water to drink, and other rats to mate with; you should be happy.

But there is trouble in paradise. The available space comfortably houses between 50 and 60 rats, and you feel a little cramped living here with 80. This crowding wouldn't be too severe—20 rats to a pen—except that two of the biggest males have captured the two pens that can be reached by only one ramp. They spend most of their time dozing at the base of the ramp, waking at the approach of interlopers, whom they attack and drive away. These males keep a harem of about ten females in their pens, and they have forced the rest of the rats into the remaining two pens. During feeding periods, as many as 60 rats crowd around the food hopper.

How do you react to this overcrowding? If you are a male rat, you have an outside chance of becoming one of the dominant rats with a harem. But even the dominant rats behave abnormally: they spend almost all their time defending their turf, they virtually ignore their harems and offspring, and they show an odd propensity to bite the tails off all the other rats, even the pups. Still, they are better off than the nondominant males. Some of you have become withdrawn; you spend much of your time in the burrows, ignoring the other rats, even the females. Others of you have lost the ability to distinguish between appropriate and inappropriate sexual partners, and try to mount males, females who are not ready to mate, and even sexually immature rats. You may become one of the "probers" (Calhoun, 1962). Probers are hyperactive and hypersexual males who constantly search for sexually receptive females. As a prober you sometimes foray into one of the defended zones in search of females, but you quickly retreat when challenged. You also violate courtship rituals by attacking females in their burrows. If you are a prober, you are also a cannibal: you eat baby rats.

If you are a female rat and live in a harem, your life is fairly normal. You can mate, build a nest in the burrow, and raise your young in peace. If you live in one of the two overcrowded pens, however, you are repeatedly raped by gangs of probers. You are quite likely to die giving birth. If you survive, you are a poor mother. You fail to build a nest for your young, protect them from danger, or nourish them. Ninety-five out of 100 pups born in one of the crowded pens die before they reach maturity.

You are not a rat, though. You are a human being. But like the rats studied by John B. Calhoun (1962), you are sometimes profoundly influenced by your social and physical environment. Like the dominant rats, you probably have established a territory that you consider to be your property. Your territory may consist of your home, a reserved parking space, a chair in a classroom, or a certain spot at the beach, but you defend it with as much energy as a rat defending his pen. Similarly, you probably like to maintain a certain amount of space between yourself and others when you interact with them, and when this distance is too small, you feel crowded. If crowding is prolonged—as in Calhoun's study and in some urban areas—it can have many negative consequences: illness, counternormative behavior, and negative emotional states. Lastly, your actions, like those of the rats in the four pens, take place in a physical context, and the layout and design of this environment influence your behavior. To try to understand your behavior without taking into account the place in which it is performed would be like trying to understand the behavior of Calhoun's rats without knowing that they were living in a small, experimental enclosure.

In this final chapter we will examine the *relationship between our social behavior and the environment.* The field is broad; indeed, entire disciplines, such as human ecology, environmental psychology, demography, and ethology, examine environment-behavior relationships. Here we will focus on aspects of the social and physical environment that can profoundly influence our interactions with others: territoriality, personal space, and environmental stressors, such as crowding, noise, and extreme temperatures.

■ Territoriality

Who would not be proud of the tremendous advances human beings have made in a scant ten thousand years? We have developed writing, systems of trade, and complex forms of social organization. We have built huge cities, developed transportation and communication networks, and reshaped the land. We have nurtured the development of art, created beautiful music, and written powerful prose and poetry. We have even visited our planet's moon.

Yet, when it comes to territoriality, our actions follow an ancient pattern. Like so many other members of the animal kingdom, we still establish areas that only we can use and enjoy, and we strive to protect these places when others intrude. We erect doors to keep people out, post signs to warn them to keep away, hang curtains so they can't see in, and establish penalties to impose on them if they enter. Like wolves patrolling their home range, birds defending their nests, monkeys howling warnings to intruders, or rats guarding the ramp leading into their pens, humans are territorial creatures. In consequence, to understand social behavior fully, we must understand the nature and function of our territories.

The Nature of Human Territories

A **territory** is a specific area that an individual or group of individuals claims and defends for personal use. While territoriality varies from place to place and from culture to culture, it usually involves three interrelated processes: controlling access, marking the boundaries, and defending against intrusion.

Controlling access to territories.
When people establish a proprietary claim to a place, they usually strive to control access to it: they alone decide who is allowed to enter. When a gang establishes its turf in the inner city, the members make certain other gangs don't intrude. Similarly, when people buy a new home or move into a new apartment, they often install locks and elaborate burglar alarms to prevent break-ins. Even in prisons, hospitals, dormitories, and other institutional settings, residents strive to establish who may enter their room, sit on their bed, or use their bathroom.

Although we try to control access to all our territories, controllability is more important for some areas than for others. You probably insist on deciding who sleeps in your bed, but you are less concerned about who parks their car on the street in front of your house or who walks across your college's campus. To explain these varying reactions, Irwin Altman draws a distinction between primary, secondary, and public territories. According to Altman, control is highest for *primary territories*, areas that are maintained and "used exclusively by individuals or groups . . . on a relatively permanent basis" (Altman, 1975, p. 112). Any place that you feel belongs exclusively to you or your group—a dorm room, a chair in a study area, a rented parking space, a home, a private office—can be considered a primary territory.

Individuals maintain only a moderate amount of control over their *secondary territories*. These areas are actually located in public settings—restaurants, streets, parks, college campuses—but because the occupants use the area on a regular basis, they come to consider it theirs. In neighborhood bars the regular customers often develop a preference for particular stools and tables, and will ask intruding strangers to move. College students often become very territorial about their chairs, to the extent they always sit in the same place during each class period (see

Focus 12-1). Because these territories are established through regular use rather than legal ownership, the occupant cannot always mount a successful defense when others intrude.

Our control over *public territories* is even more limited. While occupants can prevent intrusion when they are physically present in the situation, they cannot expect to control access after they leave. A telephone booth, a restroom stall, a spot on the beach, a seat at a bar, or a space at a parking meter is "yours" while you are using it, but it becomes the next user's territory when you leave.

FOCUS 12 – 1

Experiencing Social Psychology: *Can a chair in a classroom become a territory?*

How would you react if you went to your social psychology class and found someone sitting in your seat? Would you retreat to some other area of the room? Challenge the person's right to sit in the chair? Politely ask the person to move to another location? Sit in the closest available chair?

According to research, students frequently develop proprietary feelings about particular areas of the classroom. Not only do they habitually sit in the same chair during each class session, but they defend these territories against invasion and use by others. Territoriality is more pronounced in the center areas of the classroom than at the periphery (Haber, 1980).

Although you may think that you select a seat in the classroom at random or arbitrarily (to be near the door or a potential romantic target, for instance), some theorists believe that your choice of territory betrays your relationship to the instructor, your peers, and the university as a whole. In your social psychology class do you typically sit in the front, back, side, or central area of the classroom? According to Gilda Moss Haber, the closer you sit to the front, the more you identify with the professor rather than your peers. If you sit far to one side of the room, you identify with neither the professor nor your peers. Haber has also shown that in American classrooms, in both predominantly black and white universities, whites tend to sit at the center of the room while blacks and foreign students sit in the peripheral areas (the front rows, back rows, and sides) (Haber, 1982; see Table 12-1).

Studies also indicate that the location of your territory can even influence your grades in the course. Students in the center and front areas earn higher grades and participate more than students who sit at the rear of the room (Knowles, 1982; Sommer, 1969). Some evidence indicates that these differences are found because the more talkative or more interested students choose central territories (Levine et al., 1980, 1982); other studies underscore the impact of ecological factors, such as proximity to the instructor (Stires, 1980, 1982). In fact, in one very old study conducted at a university that assigned students to their seats alphabetically, students in the front rows scored 3% to 8% lower than students in the central areas, while students in the rear rows scored 10% lower than the central students. The moral of this study should be clear: to achieve higher scores, sit in the center of the classroom (Griffith, 1921).

TABLE 12 – 1

Haber's theory of classroom seating choices.

Identification with Instructor	Seat Area Chosen	
	High Peer Identification	Low Peer Identification
High	Center area	Front rows
Low	Back rows	Sides

SOURCE: Haber, 1980.

Marking territories. The male poodle urinating on every rock, bush, fire hydrant, and tree in an area and the homeowner posting a "No trespassing" sign are both marking their turf—identifying territorial boundaries by erecting or leaving indicators that announce their spatial claims. Many species use bodily wastes or secretions from scent glands for markers; humans tend to rely more on walls, fences, and signs ("Do not enter," "Occupied"), as well as more subtle devices: a coat left on a chair, a hedge around a plush lawn, a beach towel spread out on the sand, a nameplate on a door.

Why do we mark our territories? In part, we use markers to prevent territorial invasions. In one study of the effectiveness of markers in libraries and study areas the researchers placed various objects on the table in front of unoccupied chairs (Sommer, 1969). As shown in Table 12-2, when the objects were personal and valuable (a sport coat, notebooks, and pen), the chairs were never occupied during the entire two-hour observation period. Less personal markers, however, reserved the space for a shorter period of time. In a similar study personal markers again effectively held a chair in a crowded bar, although masculine markers (a sport coat and small briefcase) tended to be more effective than feminine markers (a jacket and a flowered book bag) (Shaffer & Sadowski, 1975).

Markers fulfill not only a *protective* function (by keeping others out) but also a *personalizing* function: they provide occupants with a means of expressing aspects of their personalities, interests, and values. To demonstrate this function, Altman and his colleagues recorded and classified the territorial markers used by first-year students living in dormitories at the University of Utah (Hansen & Altman, 1976; Vinsel et al., 1980). Although many of the markers found in dorm rooms were primarily

We often mark our public territories with books, newspapers, and articles of clothing.

academic in nature (schedules of classes, syllabi, calendars), others highlighted the occupants' religious and political values, athletic and sports interests, and entertainment preferences. Women had a greater tendency than men to decorate their space with markers emphasizing personal relationships (photographs of family and friends); men's markers tended to be more sports- and school-oriented.

Altman and his colleagues also discovered an intriguing relationship between territorial marking and continuation in school. By comparing the markings of students who left at the end of their first year ("dropouts") with the markings of students who were still at the university one year later ("stayins"), Altman discovered that dropouts evidenced less diversity in their markings. While the stayins tended to display items related to a variety of topics, the dropouts' markings were all concentrated in one topic. A typical stayin's room contained posters, schedules, postcards, and plants; a typical dropout's wall was completely covered by pictures of rock groups. Dropouts also displayed more items related to their family and hometown (photographs of high school friends, drawings by siblings), while stayins displayed more items related to the university and the surrounding area (campus and city maps, pictures of local recreational sites). The investigators concluded that dropouts marked with less diversity "because they chose to reveal only a few facets of themselves to others. Furthermore, their decorations symbolized a lack of commitment to the university and community" and a "greater commitment to their past life and to their parents and friends" (Vinsel et al., 1980, p. 114). Thus dropouts' markers broadcast their uncertainty about their new territory, while stayins used their markers to stake out their territorial claims.

Defending territories. When others ignore our markings and seek to usurp our control over access to an area, we can either surrender our territory and withdraw or defend our turf through threatening nonverbal behaviors (the "Please get out of here" look, the "frozen stare"), polite and not-so-polite requests ("Please leave" or "Get out!"), physical interventions (the gentle shove or little push), or all-out aggressive attacks.

TABLE 12-2

The mean number of minutes (during a 2-hour period) that passed before a territory was invaded.

Condition	Control (No Marker)	Randomly Scattered Magazines	Neatly Stacked Magazines	Jacket, Notebooks, and Pen
Minutes	20	32	77	120

SOURCE: Sommer, 1969.

Evidence indicates that primary territories are usually defended rather than abandoned, but that the invasion of a public territory usually results in withdrawal (Sommer, 1969).

Studies also attest to the *home field advantage:* when opponents fight over turf, the defender usually triumphs over the intruder. Case studies of street gangs indicate that defending groups usually succeed in repelling invading groups, apparently because they are more familiar with the physical layout of the area and have access to necessary resources (Whyte, 1943). A study of the aggressive encounters between patients on a psychiatric ward indicated that patients dominated others when they were on their own territories (Esser, 1970). Similarly, college students working with another student on a cooperative task spend more time talking, feel more "resistant to control," and are more resistant to influence when they are in their own room rather than their partner's room (Edney, 1975; Conroy & Sundstrom, 1977; Taylor & Lanni, 1981).

The strength of the home field advantage has also been demonstrated in studies of athletic events: on the average, the home team is likely to outperform the visiting squad, especially when it is supported by cheering and booing fans (Greer, 1983). An important exception to this general tendency occurs when the pressure to win becomes too great. According to Roy Baumeister and his associates, in key games athletes can become so concerned with winning that they perform below their level of expertise. When they are playing before their home audience, these pressures are intensified. In common parlance, the team chokes. To study this home field *disadvantage,* Baumeister studied the records from professional baseball's World Series games from 1924 to 1984. Because the victor of the Series must win four games out of seven, Baumeister reasoned that the home field would be an advantage in the early games, when the pressure is relatively low. In the last game of the series, however, the pressure to win becomes too great when the team is playing at home, so playing at home creates a disadvantage. As predicted, the home team won 60.2% of the first two games of the series but only 40.8% of the last game. Studies of other sports yielded similar findings, leading Baumeister to conclude that fans who demand a victory can cheer their team on to ruin (Baumeister 1984, 1985; Baumeister, Hamilton, & Tice, 1985; Baumeister & Steinhilber, 1984).

The Functions of Territories

We have seen that human beings, like so many other species, establish proprietary orientations toward specific areas. Although territorial behavior depends largely on the type of territory we have established—either primary, secondary, or public—territoriality usually involves controlling access, marking off boundaries, and defending our preserves when others encroach. In fact, some theorists believe that these fundamental processes have remained unchanged for thousands of years.

The stability and pervasiveness of territoriality in contemporary society raise an interesting question: Why do modern men and women continue to engage in this ancient form of behavior? Perhaps when our ancestors lived in simple hunting-and-gathering societies they needed to control their food sources against encroachment by others (Altman & Chemers, 1980), but increased industrialization and improved agricultural methods have lessened the average person's dependence on the land. Yet as a species humans remain quite territorial. Why?

Territories as social organizers.   One explanation of the continued territoriality of humans emphasizes the important functions territories still serve in contemporary society. Julian Edney, a leading investigator of human territoriality, believes that they regulate and organize many forms of social behavior (1976). Because we have primary territories, we know from one day to the next where we can sleep and relax, and where we can locate friends and loved ones. They also provide us with a place to leave our possessions (comedian George Carlin defines a "home" as a "place to leave our stuff while we're out looking for more stuff"), store our food, and interact with others. Secondary territories allow us to routinize our actions across a number of social situations, while public territories regulate our interactions with other people who also wish to use the space. Territories serve as *social organizers*.

The organizational function of territories becomes most evident when territoriality is disrupted. In one field study of territoriality in a cottage at a boys' rehabilitation center, investigators systematically recorded territoriality (consistent use of particular areas within the cottage) and incidents involving conflict and aggression over a ten-week period (Sundstrom & Altman, 1974). During the first five weeks of the study, the boys maintained fairly well-defined territories; the more dominant boys controlled the most desirable areas, while the less dominant boys were left with the lower-quality areas. During this period such disruptive behaviors as disobedience, fighting, and stealing were minimal.

This tranquility was shattered when two of the most dominant boys in the group were transferred out of the cottage and two new members were added. For the next three weeks the boys seemed to be striving for control of the choicest territories, and in consequence the incidence of fighting and other forms of disruptive behavior rose dramatically. In the final few weeks of the study, territories again began to emerge, and with them came reductions in conflict and misbehavior.

Territories as privacy maintainers.   Altman (1975, 1976) points out that territories are also useful in *maintaining privacy*. He argues that our notions of privacy depend on the balance between desired privacy and achieved privacy. As Figure 12-1 shows, if we are subjected to more contact with others than we want, we will seek greater isolation. If, in contrast, we have too little social contact, we will actively seek out others.

According to Altman's model, individuals will be satisfied only when their level of achieved privacy equals their level of desired privacy.

Territories can therefore be used to make "adjustments of self-boundaries to permit various levels of contact with others" (Altman, 1975, p. 31). In the study of dormitory residents described earlier, the investigators identified a number of territorial techniques used by students to strike a satisfactory balance between achieved and desired social contacts. To increase social contact, the average student used 4.3 of the strategies shown in Table 12-3. The most popular methods included leaving one's territory to visit a neighbor, inviting a neighbor into one's own territory, telephoning someone, and going to a public area. The students used an average of 3.8 of the strategies shown in the table to avoid interactions, including closing off their primary territory by shutting the door, retreating to a secluded, quiet territory, and tuning out distracting noise. Unfortunately, not all of the students were adept at using these various mechanisms to maintain privacy. Dropouts reported using fewer contact-seeking and contact-avoiding strategies than stayins, and they also rated those they used as less effective. Dropouts seemed to be using the wrong mechanisms to manipulate their level of privacy. While stayins used music to increase social contact, for example, dropouts used loud music to drown out other sounds. In addition, dropouts who sought social contact tended to go to the lounge areas, despite the fact that these lounges were notoriously poor places to meet people (Vinsel et al., 1980).

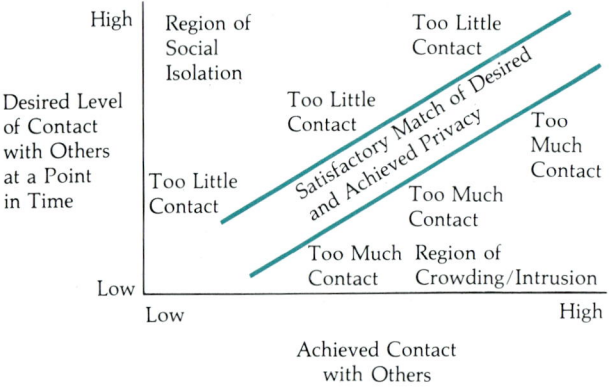

Figure 12-1   Altman's model of privacy. Altman believes that privacy depends on the successful matching of desired interpersonal contact and achieved interpersonal contact. For example, if you experience an average number of contacts with others but desire very little contact, you will seek greater privacy. In contrast, if you desire considerable contact and experience only an average amount, you will seek to limit your privacy.

Territoriality and Residential Satisfaction

Although territoriality is an ancient form of behavior, territories still fulfill important human needs. As we have seen, they organize our social interaction and also help us maintain our privacy. Given their continuing usefulness to humans, researchers have recently begun to explore the negative consequences when people *cannot* maintain territories. If territories fulfill important social functions, how do people react when they reside in an area that they cannot territorialize?

Andrew Baum, Stuart Valins, and their associates (Baum & Valins, 1977; Baum, Harpin, & Valins, 1975; Baum & Davis, 1980) have carried out a number of studies of individuals' reactions to living in areas that foster territoriality and areas that cannot be territorialized effectively. In their studies of college students, they compared reactions to traditional dorms and suite-style dorms. In the traditional dormitory a long corridor provides access to each room, and certain areas—bathroom and lounges—are shared by all the floor residents. In the suite-style dorm, two or three bedrooms are clustered around a common lounge and bathroom.

TABLE 12-3

Percentage of students living in university dormitories who reported using various privacy-maintaining mechanisms.

Mechanism	Percentage
Contact-Seeking Mechanisms	
Opening door to room	64%
Going to student union	22
Phoning someone	74
Visiting others' rooms	71
Attracting others with music	21
Using bathroom at busy time	10
Inviting people to own room	64
Studying in a busy place	30
Going to dorm lounge	70
Contact-Reducing Mechanisms	
Shutting door to room	92
Finding quiet place	62
Arranging room for privacy	16
Tuning out noise to study	52
Going for walk alone	49
Using bathroom at quiet time	12
Preparing for bed in quiet place	16
Tuning out noise to sleep	59
Using loud music to cover noise	19

SOURCE: Vinsel et al., 1980.

Baum and Valins found that the lack of secondary territories in the traditional dormitory had a number of negative consequences. Residents in these dormitories tended to feel crowded, complained of their inability to control their interactions with others, and emphasized the lack of privacy in the dormitory. Suite residents, in contrast, developed deeper friendships with their suitemates, worked with one another more effectively, and even seemed friendlier when they interacted with people outside the dormitory setting. Baum and Valins concluded that these differences stemmed from the corridor residents' lack of control over their living area. Although they frequently used the bathrooms, lounges, and hallways, they could not claim these areas as secondary territories. In consequence, they were less satisfied with their living environment.

Studies of isolated groups and elderly city dwellers also underscore the importance of territories. When pairs of male volunteers lived in small, isolated rooms for several days, researchers noted that the groups who experienced the most anxiety, stress, and withdrawal either overused or

---

FOCUS 12-2

Applying Social Psychology: *Creating defensible spaces in our cities.*

Urban planners and architects strive to design safe, low-cost, and easily maintained housing for low-income urbanites, but too often their plans ignore social-psychological factors. The massive Pruitt-Igoe housing project in St. Louis included many features that designers believed would reduce crime and vandalism—open areas between buildings, special vandalism-resistant lighting fixtures, tiled walls designed to discourage graffiti—but within a few years the project was a ruined wasteland. Many of the 2,762 apartments were vacant, crime and vandalism were rampant, and most residents lived in constant fear of attack. The project was eventually torn down (Yancey, 1971).

What went wrong at Pruitt-Igoe? According to the architect and urban planner Oscar Newman (1972, 1980), low-income housing should always include **defensible space:** semipublic areas surrounding the apartments that residents can territorialize. Although Pruitt-Igoe residents maintained primary territories within their apartments, they could not defend any secondary territories within or around their building. So many people lived in each building that residents couldn't be distinguished from outsiders, who moved freely through the buildings by using the undefended stairwells. The areas between the buildings included no barriers or other territorial markings, and the height of the buildings made surveillance of these areas impossible. In addition, some features of the project—window gratings, unpainted cinder block walls, and lack of landscaping—only served to remind residents that they lived in a low-income "project" that its builders expected to be vandalized.

Newman recommends several ways to increase the defensibility of spaces. First, boundaries must be established to give residents control over hallways, lobbies, and nearby streets and playgrounds. Second, residents must be able to maintain surveillance over these semipublic areas. Third, the design of the building must foster positive, protective attitudes. Fourth, if possible, the project should be built in a low-crime area. These recommendations have stimulated considerable controversy, but several field studies have supported the basic concept. In one study Newman compared two housing projects built side by side in New York City. The newer project, Van Dyke, was built in 1955 along the same lines as Pruitt-Igoe: mostly large, 14-story buildings separated by open spaces. The Brownsville project

underused their territories. In contrast, the dyads that functioned well in this unique situation used territoriality processes to regulate their privacy and interpersonal relations effectively (Altman, 1977; Altman & Haythorne, 1967; Altman, Taylor, & Wheeler, 1971). Among elderly women territoriality is similarly associated with feelings of control and safety (Normoyle & Lavrakas, 1984). Given these findings, some experts argue that builders and city planners should design living areas so that they can be easily territorialized (Taylor & Brower, 1985; see Focus 12-2).

■ Personal Space

What is the dimension that influences so many of our social interactions but remains hidden and unnoticed? Space, according to the anthropologist Edward T. Hall (1966). Although we rarely pay much attention to the distance that we maintain between ourselves and other people, personal

was eight years older and featured six-story X-shaped buildings with some three-story wings. Occupants entered the Brownsville buildings at the central core, where open staircases were located (see Brower, Dockett, & Taylor, 1983; Brown & Altman, 1983; Taylor, Gottfredson, & Brower, 1980, 1984).

Newman discovered that the Brownsville buildings were far more defensible than the Van Dyke's. Each entrance was used by only a small number of families, and anyone approaching it could be observed from dozens of windows. The open stairways were easily monitored by residents, who let their children play in the hallways and on the landings. Residents even left their doors ajar to "keep an eye on the place." This greater defensibility was associated with stronger bonds between neighboring families, a more positive attitude toward the police, and lower crime and maintenance rates (see Table 12-4). Although this study was strictly correlational and should be interpreted with caution, these findings, along with many others, have reshaped designers' thinking about the importance of territories, and have also been incorporated in many anticrime programs, such as Neighborhood Watch.

TABLE 12-4

Number of crimes and maintenance jobs required in two urban housing projects.

Incident	Van Dyke	Brownsville
All crimes	1,189	790
Felonies, misdemeanors, and offenses	432	264
Robberies	92	24
Malicious mischief	52	28
Other	613	474
All maintenance jobs	3,301	2,376
Maintenance jobs other than glass repair	2,643	1,654
Nonglass jobs per unit	1.47	1.16
Full-time maintenance staff	9	7
Elevator breakdowns per month	280	110

SOURCE: Newman, 1972.

space profoundly influences our social relations. If you doubt the accuracy of this statement, try the following demonstration. Go to a public place; sit next to someone; slowly move closer and closer; note the effects. Do not be surprised if your target reacts with anger, suspicion, and flight, for you are committing a social offense: you are violating someone's personal space.

Leslie A. Hayduk defines **personal space** as "the area individuals maintain around themselves into which others cannot intrude without arousing discomfort" (1983, p. 293). Sometimes likened to an invisible bubble or electrical field, our personal space completely surrounds us, although it tends to be smaller behind our backs than directly in front of us. Like our territory, our personal space is an area to which we strive to control access, and when violations do occur, we experience discomfort and try to reestablish control. Unlike our territory, however, our personal space is portable—it moves along with us from place to place—and is not usually marked in any detectable way.

How Much Space in Personal Space?

Our analysis would be quite simple if human beings' personal space requirements were equal and constant; if, for example, everyone liked to keep about 25 inches between themselves and others no matter what the situation. Clearly, however, the size of one's personal space varies over time and across situations; two inches may be just right in one setting but stressfully close in another. In reviewing some of the factors that influence the size of personal space, we will focus on the four sets of variables shown in Figure 12-2: individual factors, characteristics of the other interactant, interpersonal relations, and situational factors. We cannot hope to cover all the known determinants of personal space, but we can consider several variables in each category below (see Hayduk, 1978, 1983, for an excellent review and analysis).

Personal characteristics.
As Figure 12-2 shows, our need for personal space depends in part on our *personal characteristics and qualities* (Hayduk, 1983). Despite some inconsistencies in the data, studies of demographic factors indicate that black Americans stand farther apart than white Americans, that women require less space than men, and that children's zones are smaller than adults' (Aiello & Thompson, 1980; Giesen & McClaren, 1976; Severy, Forsyth, & Wagner, 1979). Similarly, individuals with "abnormalities"—such as violent prisoners, schizophrenics, and emotionally disturbed children—seem to have relatively large personal space zones (Gilmour & Walkey, 1981), as do individuals with certain personality characteristics (Altman, 1975).

One of the most interesting individual determinants of personal space differences is culture. According to Edward T. Hall (1966), many of our distance norms are specific to our particular culture or subculture. We learn what distance is "proper" in various situations, and are surprised

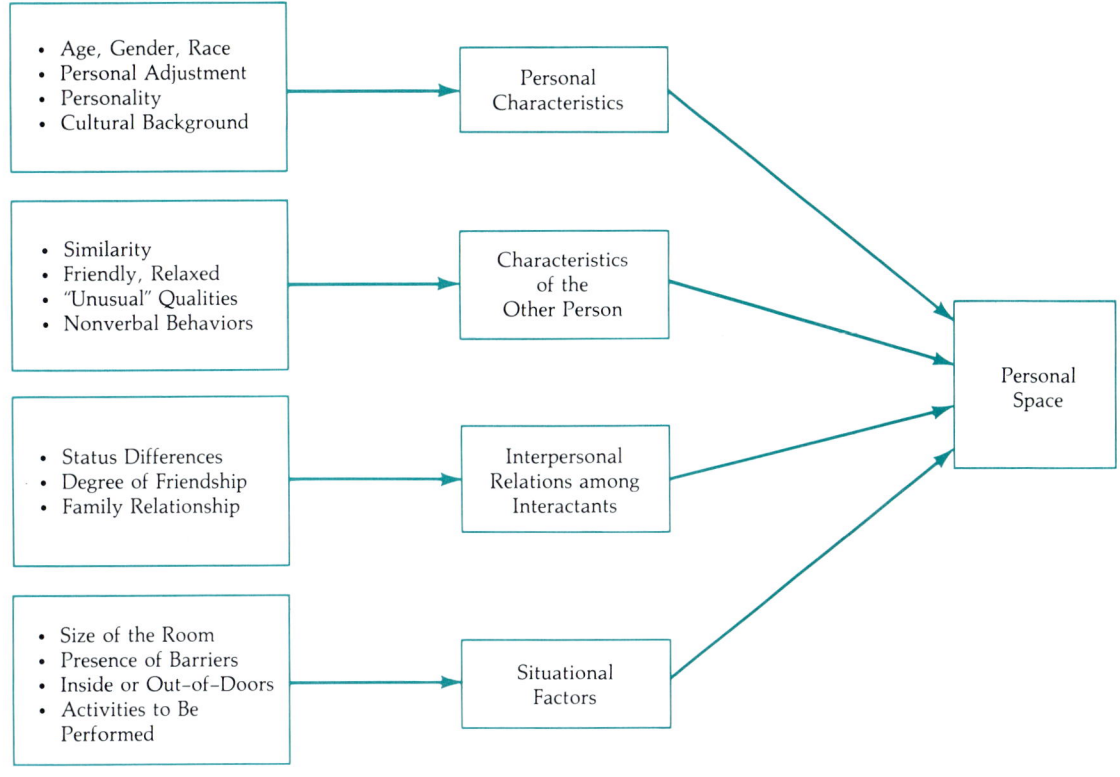

Figure 12-2 Determinants of personal space. Your spatial requirements are influenced by a variety of factors, including your personal characteristics, the characteristics of the other interactant, your relationship to the other person, and the nature of the situation.

when we find that other countries and cultures have established very different norms. Hall recounts one amusing incident when he was sitting comfortably in an almost empty hotel lobby. Suddenly, for no apparent reason, a total stranger walked up and stood so close to his chair that he could hear the man breathing. Hall refused to abandon his chair despite this invasion, and the stranger stood there until he was joined by several other people. At this point Hall realized that the stranger was Arabic, and that his behavior was consistent with his cultural beliefs about space. In Arabic countries, personal space zones are quite small and open to invasion, particularly in public areas.

In explaining cultural differences in personal space, Hall draws a broad distinction between contact and noncontact cultures. According to Hall, people who grow up in *contact cultures* of the Mediterranean, Middle East, and Latin America learn to prefer strong sensory involvement with others and so seek direct social contact whenever possible. Residents of such *noncontact countries* as the United States, England, and Germany try to limit their spatial openness with others. Hall notes that the French maintain very small personal spaces in trains, buses, cafés, and even their homes, and that they increase their involvement with other people by using more direct body postures and eye contact (see Chapter 3). In consequence, when Americans visit Paris, they are sometimes shocked to find a stranger approaching so closely that he or she touches them, breathes in their face, and stares right into their eyes. Furthermore, when they attempt to protect their invaded personal space, the Parisian interprets their retreat as a lack of good manners.

Others' characteristics.   The size of our personal space is also affected by the qualities and characteristics of the person or persons we are approaching. We tend to maintain smaller personal spaces when we interact with people who seem to be similar to us in race, age, and even attitudes (Fisher, Bell, & Baum, 1984), but again the findings are not completely consistent. Our personal zones also shrink when we interact with people who seem friendly, pleasant, cooperative, and relaxed (Altman, 1975), but they expand when we believe that the other person is unusual in some respect. For example, studies reviewed by Altman indicate that individuals remain at greater distances when they interact with someone who has some visible physical disability, such as extreme obesity or the loss of a limb. We also strive to isolate ourselves from individuals who are socially stigmatized, such as the mentally handicapped.

The interactant's nonverbal behaviors can also influence the size of our personal zone. If we feel uncomfortable because the other person maintains more eye contact than we feel is appropriate, we sometimes compensate by increasing our personal space (Patterson, 1975, 1976, 1982). These adjustments are consistent with an *equilibrium model of personal space,* which argues that interactants maintain a preferred level of intimacy by adjusting such nonverbal behaviors as personal space, body orientation, and eye contact. If we feel that more intimacy is needed but our partner is not maintaining much eye contact, we may respond by moving closer to the person. In contrast, if our partner is discussing extremely intimate topics while staring at us, we may compensate by moving farther away (Argyle & Dean, 1965). Through such continual adjustments we can keep the intimacy of our interaction at the level we desire (Burgoon, 1978, 1983).

Interpersonal relations.   As logic and experience suggest, the type of relationship linking interactants plays a particularly significant role in determining personal space. A study of 562 U.S. Navy personnel ranging in rank from enlisted personnel to captain indicated that subordinates conversing with superiors required more space than conversing peers (Dean, Willis, & Hewitt, 1975). In addition, many studies suggest that we require less space when we are with friends than when we are with strangers or mere acquaintances. This effect occurs in both same-sex and mixed-sex dyads, but it is more pronounced in women (Hayduk, 1983; see Focus 12-3).

Situational factors. Many situational factors influence personal space, including room size (M. White, 1975), the presence of physical barriers (Baum, Riess, & O'Hara, 1974), and location indoors or outdoors (Pempus, Sawaya, & Cooper, 1975). Hall (1966) notes that interpersonal distances vary with the type of behavior in which interactants are engaged. Rather than assume that a single zone of personal space exists, Hall proposes the four *interpersonal zones* shown in Table 12-5. If the situation calls for intimate behaviors—sex, kissing, handshakes, slow dancing, or even boxing—then interactants' personal space zone is generally quite small, zero to 18 inches (see Figure 12-4). In less intimate but somewhat personal situations, such as friendly conversations or individual therapy, the zone ranges from 18 inches to about 4 feet. In social situations, distances range from 4 to 12 feet. Purely public situations—lectures or speeches—require more than 12 feet. (Altman & Vinsel, 1977, offer evidence bearing on the validity of Hall's zone theory.)

Reactions to Invasions of Personal Space

Although our personal space is unmarked and invisible, we still object when people enter it without our permission. Keeping appropriate distances between ourselves and others is one way of controlling our social interactions, so we fight to maintain desired distances between ourselves and others. On the other hand, sometimes a violation of our personal space can be quite enjoyable.

TABLE 12-5

Hall's zones of interpersonal distance.

Zone	Distance	Activities
Intimate	Touching to 18 inches	Sex, massage, comforting, handshakes, dancing, wrestling, boxing
Personal	18 inches to 4 feet	Casual conversation, automobile travel, parties, walking
Social	4 to 12 feet	Dining, business meetings, interactions with strangers
Public	12 feet or more	Lectures, addresses, plays, recitals, sports events

SOURCE: Hall, 1966.

Invasion and arousal. Many studies of invasions of personal space have documented the negative consequences of spatial encroachment (Knowles, 1980). When confederates approached too closely to people studying in libraries (Sommer, 1969), sitting outdoors (Felipe & Sommer, 1966), standing on escalators (Harris, Luginbuhl, & Fishbein, 1978), or walking down the street (Konečni et al., 1975; R. J. Smith & Knowles, 1978), the targets displayed a number of negative reactions, including reduced eye contact, shifts in body posture, verbal rebukes, and withdrawal from the situation.

Studies have shown that violations of our personal space can be stressful. When others approach too closely, we experience heightened physiological arousal: our heart rate and blood pressure tend to increase, we breathe more quickly, and we sometimes perspire more (Aiello, Epstein, & Karlin, 1975; Evans, 1979; Walden & Forsyth, 1981). One of the more creative—if ethically controversial (see Koocher, 1977)—investigations of the arousal properties of personal space invasion was conducted in a

---

FOCUS 12-3

A Closer Look: *Do men and women differ in spatial needs?*

In contrast to common stereotypes of the two sexes, men tend to be more spaced out than women. Across a number of studies using a variety of measurement methods, women's personal spaces have tended to be smaller than men's (Hayduk, 1983). Women allow others to get closer to them than men do, and they approach other people more closely. Women also take up less space by sitting with arms close to their sides and by crossing their legs, while men enlarge their personal space by assuming expansive, open positions (Mehrabian, 1972). Even when walking, female students minimize their space by carrying their books in both arms, resting the edges against the stomach and chest (Jenni & Jenni, 1976). Men, in contrast, usually carry their books in one arm, with the edges resting on the hip or side of the leg.

The sexes also show other interesting differences in the use of space. While research indicates that our personal zones are smaller when we are interacting with close friends, this relationship between distance and attraction may be due entirely to women's preference for proximity. In one study of same-sex pairs, researchers first photographed pairs of adults as they walked along a city street and then asked the couples to describe the nature of their relationship (Heshka & Nelson, 1972). When the researchers later calculated personal space sizes by examining the photographs, they discovered that women needed less space when they were with close friends, but that men's spatial needs were unrelated to intimacy. Similarly, a study of mixed-sex dyads indicated that the reduced distance separating interacting friends was due largely to the fact that the women moved closer to the men; the men stayed where they were (Edwards, 1972).

Men and women also respond differently when their personal space is invaded, although the point of attack makes an important difference. In one study conducted in a library, male and female confederates sat adjacent to or across from same- or opposite-sex subjects (Fisher & Byrne, 1975). When one researcher later approached the subjects and asked them to rate the confederate, men were most negative when the intruder sat *across from them*, while women were most negative when the intruder sat *beside them*. In a second study, when the investigators recorded the placement of books and belongings on library tables, they found that men erected more barriers against adjacent invasion. As Figure 12-3 indicates, women tended to place their belongings in front of the adjacent chairs, while men placed their belongings in front of adjacent

men's restroom (Middlemist, Knowles, & Matter, 1977). Building on physiological research demonstrating that individuals take longer to begin to urinate and urinate for a shorter period of time when they feel stressed or aroused, these researchers unobtrusively recorded the length of time before men began to urinate and the length of time they urinated across three experimental conditions: alone, moderate interpersonal distance (a confederate used the rightmost urinal when the subject was at the leftmost urinal), and close interpersonal distance (a confederate used the urinal next to the subject). As predicted, delay of urination increased from 4.9 seconds in the control (alone) condition to 6.2 seconds in the moderate distance condition and to 8.4 seconds in the close distance condition, while duration decreased in the same conditions. Stressed by a too-close companion, the men started more slowly and finished more quickly. As women's restrooms almost always provide privacy, this work has not been replicated with women.

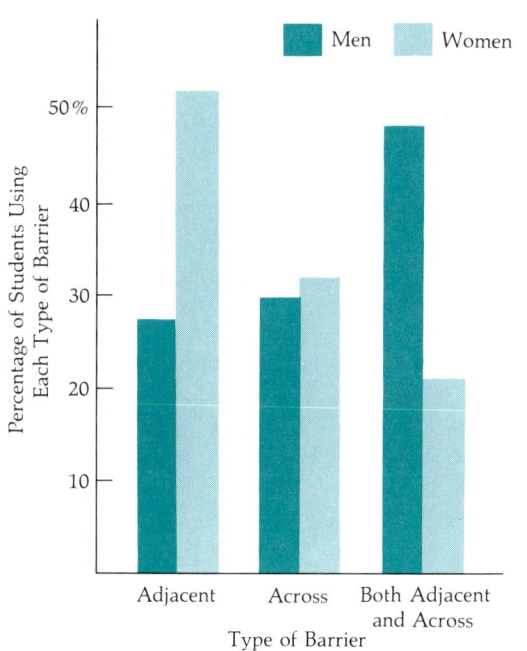

Figure 12-3 Sex differences in protecting personal space. Women are more protective of adjacent seating positions, while men are more likely to defend adjacent and opposite seats.

chairs *and* chairs across from them. In a related study, however, men showed signs of greater discomfort than women when the intruder was a man who approached them from the rear (Harris, Luginbuhl, & Fishbein, 1978).

Women are more likely to withdraw when their space is invaded, while men are more likely to stand their ground. In one study of near-collisions of men and women on a public sidewalk, the woman moved out of the man's way 63.2% of the time, the man moved out of the woman's way 15.8% of the time, and both moved 21.0% of the time (Henley, 1977). This weaker resistance to spatial invasion may explain why people more willingly invade the personal space of a woman than of a man (Reiss & Salzer, 1981).

As Hayduk (1983) noted after reviewing 110 studies that measured men's and women's personal space needs, sharp and consistent differences between the sexes are not always observed. Furthermore, in discussing the source of these differences, Hayduk emphasized the role played by socialization over biology. Women tend to be more affiliative than men, more positive toward others, and more concerned about maintaining positive interpersonal relations with others. In consequence, as women are drawn closer to others psychologically, they are also drawn to them physically.

Figure 12-4 Hall's four interpersonal zones. According to Hall, interpersonal distances are dependent on the type of behavior being performed by interactants: (*a*) intimate, (*b*) personal, (*c*) social, and (*d*) public.

Can invasions be positive? Although these findings indicate that invasion of personal space is a negative experience, other findings suggest that such invasions may have a positive side. If the intruder is a close friend, a relative (Willis, 1966), or an extremely attractive stranger (see Figure 12-5), invasions are interpreted as positive experiences. Similarly, if target persons believe that the other person is attempting to initiate a friendly relationship (Murphy-Berman & Berman, 1978) or needs assistance (Baron, 1978), they tend to react positively rather than negatively.

To account for these diverse findings, recent theoretical models argue that our reaction to invading others depends on *cognitive labeling*. According to this view, closeness leads to arousal, which can be either stressful or pleasurable depending on our interpretation of the invasion. If we believe that the invader has encroached on our space because she or he is rude or manipulative, our reaction will probably be negative. But if we attribute the encroachment to positive factors—such as the invader's desire to become more intimate or friendly with us—then we may react more favorably (Knowles, 1980; Patterson, 1976).

This cognitive labeling process was well demonstrated in one study when the experimenter interviewed single subjects while seated either six or 30 inches away. After the interview, the experimenter gave the subject either a very positive evaluation or a very negative evaluation. As predicted, when the experimenter behaved in an unfriendly manner by criticizing the subject, the personal space invasion was interpreted negatively; subjects not only reported less liking for the experimenter (see Figure 12-6) but also complained that the study was uninteresting and unenjoyable. Positively evaluated subjects, in contrast, liked the space-violating experimenter the most, and also described the study in more positive terms. Thus close distances may work to intensify our feelings and emotions (Storms & Thomas, 1977, Experiment 3).

Figure 12-5 Invasions of personal space can sometimes be pleasurable.

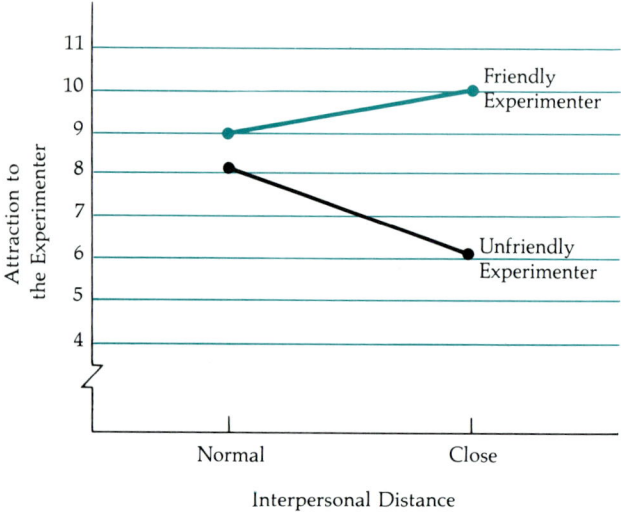

Figure 12-6 Positive and negative reactions to invasions of personal space. When they were separated by a normal distance, subjects liked the friendly experimenter slightly more than the unfriendly one. When their personal space was violated, subjects expressed more extreme liking or disliking. The attraction ratings could vary from 1 to 13, with higher scores indicating greater liking.

■ Environmental Stressors

We live in an ever-changing, ever-stimulating environment. For 24 hours each day, whether awake or asleep, we are bombarded by a flood of information about events unfolding in the surrounding environment. Some of these environmental events are so mild that they slip by without our awareness; some are so positive that they fill us with pleasure; still others are **stressors**—"environmental events or forces [that] threaten an organism's existence and well-being" (Baum, Singer, & Baum, 1982, p. 15).

Environmental stressors directly influence the nature and quality of our social interactions. Social behavior takes place in a physical context, and the particular properties of that environment shape our actions. If you are trying to work with a group of people on a project, for example, your interactions may be hampered if the space that is available doesn't fit your needs. If you meet someone for the first time at a noisy party, you may be unable to make any kind of impression over the din of the music. And when people unexpectedly find themselves in uncomfortably hot or cold environments, they often display a variety of negative interpersonal behaviors, including anger, irritability, and discomfort. To understand social behavior we usually need to consider the people in the place rather than the place itself. However, when we become crowded, when noise reaches high levels, when the temperature is too high or low, then the physical environment begins to control our social interactions.

Crowding

Consider the following settings: a sold-out football game; a party with 40 guests given in a two-bedroom apartment; a psychology class held in a large auditorium; a bar that closes its doors at 10:00 P.M. when the occupancy limit is reached; a beach packed with row after row of attractive sunbathers.

These are all high-density situations: a large number of people are packed into a relatively small area. Just because the density is high, however, we should not assume that the interactants will necessarily feel crowded. Most social psychologists, adopting a distinction explored by Daniel Stokols (1972), use the term **density** to refer to a physical condition that is determined by the number of individuals present in a given area, while **crowding** is a psychological condition that occurs when people think that density is too high. Although density may be high at the football game or the beach, the interactants may not feel the least bit crowded. In contrast, if the students in the large auditorium expected a smaller class or the customers at the bar feel that the service is too slow, then they may feel crowded even though the density level is much lower.

In recent years investigators have identified a number of factors that determine when individuals in high-density situations will experience the subjective psychological state we call crowding. Although we cannot exhaustively review all important factors, five seem particularly critical: degree of overload, controllability, attributions, interference, and staffing.

Overload. As density increases, people are exposed to more and more inputs from their surrounding environment. Although human beings can handle a high level of sensory stimulation, in some settings—such as a busy city street, a shopping mall packed with holiday shoppers, or the floor of a stock exchange—the stimulation is so great that we experience psychological **overload**—an excessive number of inputs that come so rapidly that the information cannot be processed effectively. When overload occurs, we tend to feel crowded and stressed, and usually respond by using one or more coping mechanisms to eliminate excessive environmental stimulation. Residents in such large cities as New York, for example, might avoid the overload brought about by high density by ignoring all but the essential information about their environment, following strict habits as they move about the city, avoiding contact with strangers, or withdrawing from the setting whenever possible (Milgram, 1970; Saegert, 1978). Similarly, studies of crowding in high-density, corridor-style dormitories indicate that students who use screening strategies that avoid overload are better adjusted than those who do not (Baum et al., 1982).

Loss of control. As Chapter 4 noted, when people feel that important events and outcomes in their lives are *uncontrollable*, they experience a variety of negative psychological and emotional consequences (Thompson, 1981). The concept of controllability suggests that high-density situations are stressful because they undermine our sense of control over our own personal behavior, our ability to understand and process information, and our choices and decisions (Schmidt & Keating, 1979). Andrew Baum and his associates have spent many years studying crowding in dormitories. As we saw earlier, territoriality, privacy, and overload all influence adjustment to dormitory living, but students' "expectations for maintaining control over social experiences in the residential setting" seem to lie at the heart of the crowding–stress relationship (Baum & Davis, 1980, p. 474). Baum and his colleagues discovered that after "tripling"—the assignment of three students to a room designed for only two—one of the roommates is often rejected by the other two (Aiello, Baum, & Gormley, 1981). Baum found that the isolated roommates believed that their lives in the dormitory were uncontrollable; they complained about their inability to regulate interactions or change "the way things are," and also reported negative expectations about future opportunities to gain control in the dormitory (see Table 12-6). A higher percentage of the rejected triples (43%) also reported experiencing problems while living in the dormitory than triples who weren't rejected (23%) and students living in double-occupancy rooms (21%) (Aiello, Baum, & Gormley, 1981; Baum & Davis, 1980; Baum & Valins, 1979).

Attributions. Research conducted by Stephen Worchel and his colleagues attests to the impact of *causal attributions* on crowding (Worchel, 1978; Worchel & Teddlie, 1976; Worchel & Yohai, 1979). Building on studies

TABLE 12–6

Mean ratings of perceived control reported by dormitory residents (1 = low control, 5 = high control).

Measure	Type of Resident		
	Double Occupancy	Tripled (Not Rejected)	Tripled (Rejected)
Control in dormitory	2.70	2.94	2.14
Ability to regulate interactions	2.48	2.75	1.52
Change the way things are (in general)	3.97	3.99	3.07
Expected control in dormitory	2.62	2.59	1.80

SOURCE: Aiello, Baum, & Gormley, 1981.

that have shown that we tend to become physiologically aroused when others approach us too closely, Worchel suggests that the cognitive label we assign to this arousal determines our reactions to high-density situations. If we attribute this arousal to the excessive closeness of others, then we will label the experience "crowding." If, however, we attribute the arousal to some other source—such as fear of being attacked, anxiety over bad news, or job tension—then we will not feel crowded. In one laboratory study of this hypothesis, Worchel arranged for the members of five-person groups to sit very close together or comfortably far apart (Worchel & Yohai, 1979). He then told the subjects that they would be exposed to subliminal noise to see if inaudible sounds influenced their performance on several tasks. Actually the subjects were never exposed to noise; this cover story allowed Worchel to manipulate their attributions about the causes of their arousal. Reasoning that subjects seated close together would feel less crowded if they could attribute their arousal to some other causal factor, he told one-third of the subjects that the noise might cause stressful, uncomfortable side effects. Another third of the subjects was told that the noise should be relaxing, and the final third was given no explanation of the effects of the sound. When subjects' reactions in these three groups were compared (see Figure 12-7), the investigators discovered that subjects who attributed their arousal to

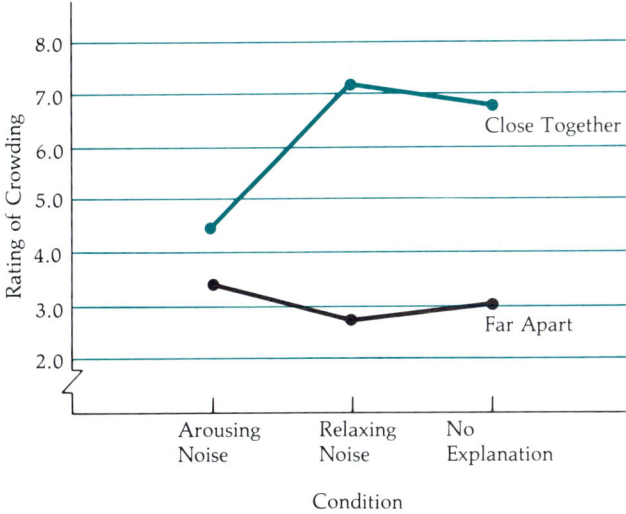

Figure 12-7 Perceptions of crowding and attributions. Subjects seated close together generally reported feeling more crowded than subjects seated far apart. The important exception, however, occurred when subjects were led to believe that the subliminal noise would have arousing side effects. These subjects felt no more crowded than those seated far apart (1 = not crowded, 10 = very crowded).

the fictitious noise rather than the high density felt less crowded than the other subjects.

Interference. Some high-density settings don't seem crowded because all the people present are able to accomplish their various tasks and achieve their goals without *interference*. In a field study of reactions to a street fair, investigators discovered that visitors who were interested in making purchases or looking at exhibits felt more "bothered by the number of people" than those who were more interested in people-watching, entertainment, and social interaction (Morasch, Groner, & Keating, 1979, p. 225). Similar findings have been obtained in laboratory studies (Heller, Groff, & Solomon, 1977; McCallum et al., 1979; Paulus et al., 1976; Sundstrom, 1975).

Staffing. According to the ecological psychologist Allan Wicker (1979), a given number of people is optimally efficient for any particular setting (see also Barker, 1978). If the requirements of the setting match the number of people present, then the setting is *optimally staffed*. If too many or too few people are present, however, the setting is overstaffed or understaffed, as the case may be. Many amusement parks, fast-food restaurants, limited-access highways, airports, and bars are designed to handle a large number of people, so even when density reaches high levels, these settings don't seem crowded. If very few users are present in these settings, though, they seem empty and underutilized.

Combining the five factors. To understand how these five factors can combine to influence reactions to high-density settings, imagine a male college professor driving into a large city for a social psychology conference. As he drives closer and closer to the heart of the city, he is exposed to so many unfamiliar surroundings, sights, and people that he begins to feel overstimulated (overload). To cope, he concentrates on finding his way to his hotel, but he misses his exit and gets lost (loss of control). As his distress mounts, he searches for a cause of his arousal (attribution), and quickly finds an obvious source: the city with its crowded highways, sidewalks, and skyline. His reaction is further intensified when a minor accident blocks the entrance to the hotel (interference), and he discovers the parking garage is completely filled (overstaffing). Given this combination of factors, the professor will probably feel very crowded in this high-density setting.

What would happen to this person if he experienced this type of environmental stress repeatedly over a prolonged period of time? Would he, like the rats studied by Calhoun, begin to display negative effects of high density, such as increased irritability, aggressiveness, and withdrawal? Focus 12-4 considers the impact of prolonged crowding on humans.

FOCUS 12-4

Controversy in Social Psychology: *Does crowding cause social pathology?*

In the early 1960s researchers studying crowding in animals reported some dramatic findings. They discovered that the mass migrations of lemmings (small furry rodents found in Scandinavian mountain regions) which frequently continue on into the sea, where vast numbers of them drown, occur when the animals become overcrowded (Dubos, 1965). When the number of deer living on an island in Chesapeake Bay grew too large for the available space, they died by the scores (Christian, 1963; Christian, Flyger, & Davis, 1960). Similarly, Calhoun (whose studies were described at the beginning of this chapter) argued that overcrowding may cause pathological behavior in rats: disrupted courtship rituals, aberrant sexual behaviors, heightened aggressiveness, and failures in parenting. Calhoun coined the term *behavioral sink* to describe overcrowded living conditions that "aggravate all forms of pathology that can be found within a group" (1962, p. 143).

Scientists were quick to note the parallels between Calhoun's behavioral sink and our own urban habitats. On the basis of findings generated by animal researchers as well as early sociological theorizing, these researchers suggested that many problems associated with urban living—crime, juvenile delinquency, vandalism, rioting, mental and physical illnesses—are caused by overcrowding. To test this social pathology hypothesis, researchers calculated the correlation between the number of people living in an area of a city and the number of problematic social behaviors reported by the residents. Unfortunately, while these findings (see Table 12-7) generally supported the social pathology hypothesis, the high- and low-density areas that were studied varied in so many other ways—such as amount of police protection, community services, educational level, stability, and income—that the causal relationship between density and pathology was obscured. When these other variables are taken into account statistically, the correlations noted in Table 12-7 tend to disappear (Freedman, 1973; Galle, Gove, & McPherson, 1972).

Because of these interpretational difficulties, in recent years investigators have sought to study the harmful effects of crowding in new and creative ways. Researchers have gained greater control over extraneous variables by studying the effects of residential crowding in such settings as prisons, hospitals, naval ships, dormitories, and laboratory groups. These studies (reviewed in Paulus, 1980, and Fisher, Bell, & Baum, 1984) have succeeded in tying high density to a number of negative processes, but experts continue to argue about the inherent negativity of crowding. Many contemporary theorists note that while crowding is stressful, human beings have learned to cope effectively with it (Baum, Singer, & Baum, 1982). Hence crowding results in social pathology only when people fail to cope satisfactorily. Jonathan Freedman, in contrast, has advanced a *density-intensity hypothesis* that argues that high-density situations only intensify whatever is already occurring in the setting (Freedman, 1975, 1979). If cities were pleasant and trouble-free, then crowded cities would be even more pleasant. If the urban environment is unpleasant, then crowding will serve to intensify its unpleasantness. Although research has not yet fully evaluated either of these arguments, at present we can cautiously conclude that the social pathology hypothesis, at least in its boldest form, is probably an exaggeration.

TABLE 12-7

Some representative correlations between urban density and symptoms of social pathology.

Symptom	Correlation
Infant mortality rate	.32
Incidence of tuberculosis	.70
Incidence of venereal disease	.83
Illegitimate birth rate	.50
Admissions to mental hospitals	.74
Juvenile delinquency	.63
Welfare rates	.37
Suicide	.04

SOURCE: Freedman, 1973.

Noise

Noise is any sound that is unwanted. Sound results from changes in air pressure detected by the sensory organs of the ear; noise results from the judgment that the incoming auditory message is unpleasant, unwanted, and irritating. Thus one person's sound may be another person's noise. If you turn up your stereo so high that the plaster on the ceiling starts to crack, the sounds you are generating may be music to you but noise to your angry neighbor. Noise is in the ear (and brain) of the listener.

Turning sound into noise. When does a sound become a noise? First, and perhaps most obvious, the greater the sound's volume, the more likely it will be considered noise. Sounds in the range of 0 to 50 decibels (dB) are very soft, and generally produce little irritation for the listener, while sounds over 80 dB may be bothersome enough to be called noise (see Table 12-8). Of course, a 30-dB whisper in a movie theater may still prompt a "Please be quiet," while a 115-dB rock concert may evoke considerable pleasure (for reviews, see Cohen, 1980; Cohen & Weinstein, 1981).

Second, research conducted by David Glass, Jerome Singer, and their colleagues suggests that unpredictable, uncontrollable sounds are more irritating than continuous sounds that can be controlled (see Figure 12-8). As the subjects in one study were working on several tasks, they were exposed to nine-second bursts of loud, unidentifiable noise (110 dB) (Glass, Singer, & Friedman, 1969, Experiment 2). Half of the subjects

TABLE 12-8

Decibel levels of various sounds and their effects on hearing.

Decibels	Sound	Effect on Hearing
0	Breathing	Hearing threshold
10	Pin dropping	Barely audible
30	Whisper at 15 feet	Very quiet
50	Light traffic in the distance	Quiet
70	Freeway at 50 feet	Difficult to hear conversation at normal volume
90	Heavy truck at 50 feet	Hearing damage after 8 hours
110	Dance floor in a disco	Difficult to hear a shout from more than 6 inches away
130	Jet taking off at 200 feet	Maximum limit of amplified speech
140	Planes landing on aircraft carrier deck	Painfully loud

SOURCE: Turk, Turk, Wittes, & Wittes, 1974.

were shown small buttons attached to their chairs, and were told that they could terminate the noise simply by pressing the switch; the remaining subjects received no such instructions. The subjects were asked not to use their buttons (and none did), but the knowledge that a means of controlling the noise was available to them served to reduce its aversiveness. Subjects with buttons rated the noise less irritating and distracting than did the other subjects. Glass and his colleagues noted that a researcher working down the hall from their laboratory was also irritated by the noise; he complained, "I can't stand hearing that noise anymore. It's not so much the loudness as not knowing when it's going to come on" (1969, p. 205).

Annoyance also depends on your attitudes and beliefs about the noise and its source. If you were awakened at 3:30 A.M. by your neighbor's loud music, your irritation would be great if you (*a*) disliked your neighbor, (*b*) felt that your neighbor was uncaring and thoughtless, (*c*) believed that the music was unnecessarily loud, and (*d*) thought that the disruption of your sleep would impair your health or reduce your efficiency the following day (Cohen, 1980).

Adapting to noise. Glass and Singer, in their initial studies of people working on various types of cognitive and mathematical tasks, discovered few debilitating effects of noise. Although subjects showed signs of stress when they were first exposed to the sounds, most were able to overcome the irritating effects of the noise and continue working effectively. However, Glass and Singer soon discovered that this adaptation process could prove psychologically costly. As they experimented with highly unpredictable and uncontrollable noises (see Focus 12-5), they realized that

Figure 12-8 Personal headphones offer one way to gain control over the sounds in our environment. Evidence even indicates that joggers experience less stress if they listen to music as they run (Miller & Tejwani, 1984).

"individuals expend 'psychic energy' in the course of the adaptive process," and thus are "less able to cope with subsequent environmental demands and frustrations" (Glass, Singer, & Pennebaker, 1977, p. 134). Later investigations have sought to catalog these aversive aftereffects of exposure to noise, which include increases in physical illnesses (headaches, heart disease, allergies, and digestive disorders), infant and adult mortality rates, mental illnesses, interpersonal conflict, and even impotence (Cohen, 1980). The magnitude of these aftereffects is not yet known.

A team of researchers led by Sheldon Cohen has found some disturbing effects of noise in young children. These investigators began by identifying children who attended schools located in the air corridor of the Los Angeles International Airport. Owing to the close proximity of the airport, noise levels in these schools often reached 95 dB; during a typical schoolday, flights passed overhead every 2.5 minutes. When these children were compared with students living in quieter areas of Los Angeles, the investigators found that they had higher blood pressure, were less likely to solve a nine-piece jigsaw puzzle, and were more likely to give up before the allotted time for the task had expired. These differences were

FOCUS 12–5

A Closer Look: *Why can't I find any negative aftereffects of noise?*

Gerald Gardner (1978) first noticed the problem in 1975. As part of a course in environmental psychology, he arranged for students to replicate Glass and Singer's studies of the aftereffects of noise. Using standard methods, he first exposed the college student subjects to 100-dB bursts of predictable or unpredictable noise or silence. Then he measured their error rates on a simple proofreading task. Unfortunately, although he had successfully replicated Glass and Singer's findings in three studies conducted in 1973 and 1974—the subjects made more errors after listening to unpredictable noise—in two studies conducted in late 1974 and 1975 he failed to find any negative aftereffects.

Gardner was initially perplexed by this sudden reversal in findings, but soon hit upon an explanation. The first three studies were all conducted before the implementation of new federal guidelines for research involving human beings. Although subjects were treated fairly, none of them completed an informed consent agreement—a formal statement indicating that they understood the nature of the procedures and their rights as subjects. Consent forms were used in the final two studies, however, and they emphasized that the subjects were free to withdraw from the experiment at any time without penalty.

Gardner belatedly realized that the new consent procedures may have increased subjects' feeling of control over the noise, thereby eliminating its negative aftereffects. To test this possibility, he replicated his earlier studies one more time. Half of the subjects were given consent forms to sign and the others were not. As he had anticipated, the subjects who had not been given consent forms experienced negative aftereffects, but those who signed the forms indicating their control of the situation did not. These findings suggest that our efforts to protect subjects' rights can sometimes eradicate the very phenomena we are attempting to investigate. Fortunately, recent evidence suggests a solution: investigators discovered that informed consent doesn't interfere with subjects' reactions if the phrase "If at any time you feel that you wish to discontinue your participation you have only to inform us; all procedures will stop immediately" is deleted (Dill et al., 1982).

most pronounced among children who had lived in the noisy area for three or more years, and were not erased when noise levels were reduced (as part of a settlement of a lawsuit filed against the airport). These findings clearly argue against undue exposure of children to excessive environmental noise (Cohen, Glass, & Singer, 1973; Cohen et al., 1980, 1981a, 1981b).

Noise and social behavior. Before considering a final source of environmental stress—temperature—we should note the negative impact of noise on prosocial and antisocial behavior. Noise not only reduces altruism (see Chapter 8) but also increases aggressiveness, especially when the individual has been angered by the victim (Donnerstein & Wilson, 1976, Experiment 1; see Chapter 9). Related research suggests, however, that the impact of noise on aggression is reduced when people believe that the noise can be controlled (Donnerstein & Wilson, 1976, Experiment 2; see Figure 12-9).

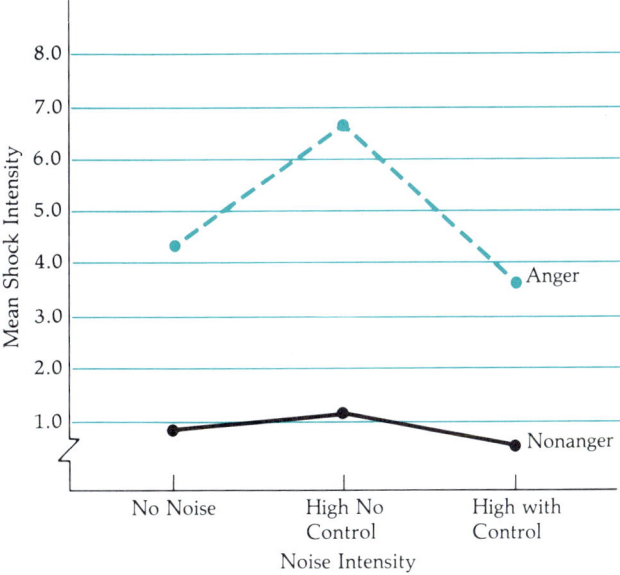

Figure 12-9 The impact of controllable and uncontrollable noise on aggression. Subjects who had been given either one shock (nonangry) or nine shocks (angry) by the experimenter's male accomplice were told to shock the accomplice each time he made a mistake on a bogus learning task. Although angry subjects generally delivered more intense shocks (no shocks were, of course, actually delivered), they chose particularly strong shock levels when they were exposed to loud bursts of uncontrollable noise.

Temperature

Until that often-imagined time in the distant future when all humans live in climate-controlled habitats, people will be exposed to extremes of temperature. Although our technology has brought increased protection from thermal stress, we cannot always keep as cool or as warm as we would like.

Unfortunately, very little is currently known about the influence of temperature on social behaviors. Without argument, extreme temperatures are stressful, but many factors influence our reactions to more moderate thermal stressors. Humidity, air pressure, and wind all influence our body's ability to adjust to temperature extremes, as do the clothes we wear and the type of activity we engage in. In addition, if we are acclimatized to heat or cold, or believe that the temperature is controllable or nonstressful, then the thermal effects may be minimal. Thus, while research (and everyday experience) tells us that high and low temperatures are uncomfortable, their impact on our social behavior depends on a number of interrelated physiological, psychological, and situational factors (Bell, 1981; Bell & Greene, 1982).

The impact of temperature on one form of social behavior has been examined more closely than others: aggression. Our common-sense notions about aggression are reflected in such expressions as "hot under the collar," "flaring tempers" and "that burns me up." In fact, when the U.S. Riot Commission searched for the causes of the racial violence that occurred in 1968, it concluded that high temperatures were to be blamed. The commission warned city officials to expect trouble when long, hot summers heat the spirits and tempers of urban populations.

Although this "long, hot summer" explanation of collective violence is intuitively appealing, Robert A. Baron has proposed that extremely high temperatures actually work to reduce violence. Baron came to this conclusion after conducting a series of laboratory studies in which aggression was measured by shocks delivered by subjects to a confederate (Baron, 1972; Baron & Bell, 1975, 1976). Initially he believed that his subjects would deliver more intense shocks when the temperature in the room was in the mid-90s than when it was in the low 70s, but in these studies the high-temperature group was less aggressive. He concluded that uncomfortable heat leads to two somewhat incompatible reactions: it does produce a negative affective reaction that can increase anger, but it also produces a strong desire to escape from the noxious environmental setting. Thus the heat-stressed subjects were angry, but they were so uncomfortable that their primary concern was to finish the experiment as quickly as possible.

These experiments led Baron and his colleagues to conclude that aggression is linked to temperature in a *curvilinear relationship.* Although moderate increases in temperature will prompt increased aggression, at extremely high levels the need to escape from the heat will reduce aggression. In an archival test of this hypothesis, Baron identified 102 instances of serious collective violence that occurred in the United States between 1967 and 1971 (Baron & Ransberger, 1978). As Figure 12-10 shows, the frequency of these disorders rose with the temperature through the mid-80's, but then fell sharply as the temperatures soared into the 90s.

Although several other studies lend support to Baron's curvilinear hypothesis (Baron, 1976; Bell & Baron, 1981; see Baron, 1978), some investigators feel that the relationship between heat and aggression is *linear.* In other words, aggression doesn't drop off at high levels, as Baron suggests, but continues on in a straight line. At present, the issue is the subject of much heated debate (Anderson & Anderson, 1984; Carlsmith & Anderson, 1979).

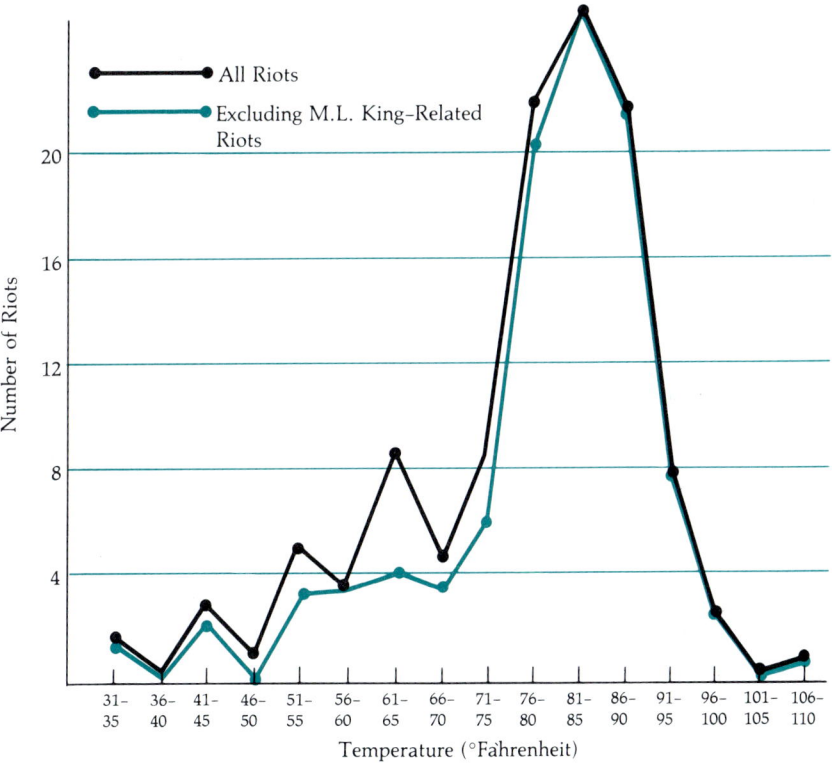

Figure 12-10 The link between temperature and aggression. According to Baron, these findings indicate that riots become more likely as the temperature rises, but only up to a certain point. Once the temperature rises above 85°F, the likelihood of violence drops. Note also that, in order to assess the possible impact of Dr. Martin Luther King's death on this relationship, Baron plotted two functions: one including all riots, and one excluding those that protested the assassination. The two analyses yielded similar patterns.

Although researchers do not agree on the precise nature of the relationship between aggression and temperature, at minimum the available evidence indicates that heat can exacerbate our aggressive tendencies. In fact, all the evidence drawn from studies of crowding, noise, and temperature suggests that environmental events often exert negative influences on our social lives: they make us more aggressive, critical, angry, and aggressive. Thus, one solution to this social problem lies in improving the quality of our environment. As "In Depth: Protecting the Environment," at the end of this chapter, argues, a crowded, noisy, uncomfortable environment threatens our well-being. Therefore, we should begin today to take steps that will lead to a healthier environment tomorrow.

■ Summary

Because social interactions occur in a physical setting, our behavior is often profoundly influenced by such environmental factors as territoriality, interpersonal distance, crowding, and noise. A **territory** is an area of controlled access that is usually marked and defended against intrusion by others. According to Irwin Altman, humans maintain primary, secondary, and public territories, but control is most important in primary territories. Territorial markers function to prevent invasion, and they allow us to express our personal values as well. When our territories are invaded, the home field advantage usually gives us the edge over the intruder.

Territories serve multiple functions for humans, for they organize social behavior and help us maintain our privacy. Hence we tend to be more satisfied when we live in a residence that we can territorialize in some way. Some theorists feel that increases in the amount of semipublic area surrounding one's residence (**defensible space**) lead to decreases in vandalism and crime.

During social interaction, we strive to keep a comfortable distance between ourselves and others. This distance is known as **personal space.** Unlike territories, which are always specific to a particular geographic location, our personal space moves with us. However, we defend our personal space against intrusion as we do our territories. Our personal space needs are influenced by several factors, including:

1. Personal characteristics: age, gender, race, personality, and cultural background. For example, children, women, whites, and people raised in "contact cultures" require less space than adults, men, blacks, and people raised in "noncontact cultures."
2. Others' characteristics: age, gender, race, similarity, and nonverbal behaviors of our partners in the interaction.
3. Interpersonal relations: type of relationship between interactants. Friends, for example, stand closer together than acquaintances.

4. Situational factors: room size, type of task to be performed, location. Hall identifies four personal space zones that vary in accordance with the intimacy of our activities: intimate, personal, social, and public.

Men and women tend to use space differently. Women approach others more closely than men, require less space when interacting with friends, and associate intimacy with side-by-side seating arrangements. Women are more likely to withdraw when their personal space is violated. Both men and women, however, react to violations of personal space with defensive behaviors. Evidence indicates that violations of personal space lead to physiological arousal, but the consequences of this arousal vary depending on individuals' interpretations of the intrusions.

Aspects of our environment, including overcrowding, noise, and uncomfortable temperatures, can lead to stress. These **stressors** not only threaten our well-being but also influence the way we interact with others. **Crowding,** a psychological condition that occurs when **density** is too high, has been linked to five separate processes: psychological **overload,** loss of control, attributional labels, interference among interactants, and overstaffing. It is not yet known if overcrowding invariably leads to psychological and behavioral problems in humans.

When is unwanted sound labeled **noise?** When it is loud, unpredictable, and uncontrollable, and your attitudes and beliefs about the source are negative. Despite the annoyance noise creates, evidence indicates that humans gradually adapt to loud noises, but at a cost. Children who attend schools in noisy areas, for example, display reduced intellectual ability and elevated blood pressure. Noise has also been linked to increases in aggression and decreases in altruism.

Extremes in temperature also influence our social interactions. Evidence indicates that we perform less effectively at very high and low temperatures. Although aggression and violence may be linked to high temperatures, at present the precise nature of this relationship is not known. Researchers have identified both a curvilinear and a linear relationship between rising temperatures and violence.

■ For More Information

1. *The Environment and Social Behavior,* by Irwin Altman (1975), reviews basic studies of personal space and territoriality and organizes these topics within an original theoretical framework based on the concept of privacy.

2. *Environmental Problems/Behavioral Solutions,* by John D. Cone and Steven C. Hayes (1980), proposes a series of behavioral interventions that can be used to increase behaviors that are environmentally protective and decrease those that are environmentally destructive.

3. *Environmental Psychology,* by Jeffrey D. Fisher, Paul A. Bell, and Andrew Baum (1984), provides a textbook introduction to the study of the reciprocal relationships between humans and their environment.

4. "Personal Space: Where We Now Stand," by Leslie A. Hayduk (*Psychological Bulletin,* 1983), painstakingly reviews and synthesizes hundreds of studies of interpersonal distance, crowding, and personal space.

5. *Personal Space,* by Robert Sommer (1969), takes an entertaining look at interpersonal distancing processes from one researcher's viewpoint.

6. *An Introduction to Ecological Psychology,* by Allan W. Wicker (1979), is an excellent overview of one of the oldest approaches to the relationship of the environment and behavior. A particularly useful source of information on staffing (or "manning") theory.

IN DEPTH

Protecting the Environment

The "tragedy of the commons" illustrates the negative consequences when people seek immediate personal gains at the risk of long-term social losses. In simpler times, families grazed small flocks of sheep and other animals in a common pasture. So long as the families in the village kept only a few animals in the "common," everyone benefited: the villagers, the sheep, and even the pasture. Often, however, some families would increase the size of their herds. Another sheep or goat made life easier, and the extra animals cost no more to feed. But as more and more animals were added to herds, the common became overcrowded. The herds stripped the common of its grass, and the pasture was ruined (Hardin, 1968).

Adding extra animals made life easier in the short run, but eventually the villagers paid the price for their selfishness. As John Platt explains, the tragedy of the commons is an example of a **social trap:** a situation in which an action that is personally advantageous is damaging to society as a whole. In contemporary times, we no longer fall prey to the social trap of the tragedy of the commons, for all commons have already been destroyed. Our own social traps prompt us to act in ways that are environmentally destructive: littering, cutting down forests, erecting gaudy billboards, running all-terrain vehicles through wilderness areas, polluting the air, dumping sewage into streams, turning up thermostats in winter, driving gas-guzzling cars. We act in what we perceive to be our own best interests, ignoring the long-range impact of our selfishness (Edney, 1980).

We often seek technological solutions to our environmental problems. If we are running out of coal to fuel our power plants, we turn to nuclear energy. If rivers are being polluted, we develop better waste-treatment facilities. If cars are polluting the air, we improve their exhaust systems. Social psychologists, however, feel that technology solves only part of the problem. Although scientific advances will undoubtedly continue to play a major role in solving our environmental problems, we must also consider social-psychological solutions. We must discover ways to discourage environmentally destructive behaviors while we promote environmentally constructive behaviors; littering and polluting must give way to energy conservation and recycling (Cone & Hayes, 1980).

Educational programs aimed at increasing public awareness of environmental issues offer one means of achieving this goal. Beginning in the 1970s, many public utilities and oil companies launched massive information campaigns designed to reeducate Americans about conservation. Similarly, federal agencies sought to foster proecology attitudes toward littering, pollution, and conservation through various types of educational programs. Unfortunately, although these interventions increase our knowledge of environmental issues, they don't always lead to changes in our behaviors. Several studies have shown that individuals who expressed great concern for the environment didn't necessarily engage in positive forms of environmental action (O'Riordan, 1976). Leonard Bickman found that 94% of the nearly 500 people he interviewed expressed a positive attitude toward

(continued)

IN DEPTH *continued*

Saving the environment from destruction. Social psychologists are currently exploring ways to discourage such environmentally destructive behaviors as littering, polluting, and wasteful consumption.

cleaning up litter; yet when they left the interview situation, only 1.4% of the subjects picked up the litter that Bickman had planted in their path. Most assumed it was somebody else's responsibility.

Researchers have also found, however, that steps can be taken to increase the correspondence between attitudes and behaviors (Burn & Oskamp, 1984; Pallak & Cummings, 1976; Pallak, Cook, & Sullivan, 1980). In one longitudinal study of energy conservation, investigators manipulated homeowners' commitment to energy-saving actions. After giving subjects information about energy conservation, the interviewer asked them to sign a pledge that they would try to reduce the amount of energy they used to heat their homes. Some subjects were led to believe that their names would be released to the news media at the end of the study (public commitment), while others were told that their names would be kept confidential (private commitment). At the end of one year, the subjects who had publicly committed themselves to conservation were found to have used less heating fuel (natural gas), than the subjects in the private commitment condition. In fact, the subjects in the latter condition used as much energy as homeowners who had received no information about conservation at all (Pallak, Cook, & Sullivan, 1980). These findings suggest that educational programs designed to foster proenvironmental attitudes can be effective tools provided special care is taken to ensure the link between attitudes and behaviors.

Researchers have also sought to change environmental behavior directly through the use of prompts, reinforcements, and feedback. These three techniques are all based on learning theory, for they assume that we acquire our behaviors through reinforcement (see Chapter 5). *Prompts* are situational cues that convey information about appropriate behavior. Signs, for example, are often used to remind us to "help keep our community clean," "turn off the lights when you leave," and "keep off the grass." To be effective, they should be polite; a sign that is too demanding, such as "You MUST NOT litter," can actually lead to more littering by creating feelings of reactance (Reich & Robertson, 1979). Prompts are also more effective when they encourage actions that are fairly easy to perform (Geller, 1981).

Researchers have also made use of *reinforcement* principles by administering desirable rewards to individuals each time they engage in an environmentally constructive action. All sorts of incentives have been used to encourage proecology actions, including raffle tickets, monetary payment, decals that say "I conserve energy," and social approval (Geller, Winnett, & Everett, 1982). Reinforcement also takes more subtle forms. When we receive money back from our deposit on a soda bottle, pay less on our heating bill, or drive in a commuter traffic lane because we have three passengers in the car with us, our behaviors are being reinforced.

Positive effects have also been obtained by giving people *feedback* about their level of energy consumption. Like prompts, feedback tells individuals when they need to conserve. And because feedback gives people informa-
(continued)

IN DEPTH *continued*

tion about how close they are to their goals, it also functions as a reinforcer. Thus feedback is among the most powerful of all learning techniques for decreasing energy consumption. In one elegant field study of feedback, researchers asked the owners of identical homes if they would participate in a study of energy conservation. In some homes, a small device that monitored the operation of the air conditioner and the outside temperature was installed by the family telephone. A blue light on the device flashed whenever the outside temperature fell below 68°F and the air conditioner was running. Thus the device signaled the homeowners to shut off their air conditioning and open their windows. If they complied, the device rewarded them by shutting off the light. Some households were also given a chart that summarized their energy conservation efforts. Three days a week for a month a research assistant read the family's electric meter and charted the amount of energy they had "conserved" and "wasted" (Becker & Seligman, 1978). When the energy consumption rates were examined, investigators found that households with the signaling device had reduced their electricity consumption by over 15%. The chart also helped somewhat, resulting in a 9% reduction.

Educational programs and learning techniques are but two of many methods that researchers are currently exploring in their efforts to eliminate the social traps that encourage short-term gain at the expense of long-term losses to society. Educational programs increase our awareness of the long-range implications of our selfish actions. Such learning techniques as prompts, reinforcement, and feedback directly attack the short-term benefits of environmentally destructive behavior by reminding us that an action that seems to be rewarding at the moment will soon bring us many costs. Although social psychologists are only beginning to develop the tools needed to create long-term change, the preliminary results are promising. Questions of energy conservation are bound to become more important in the future as resources are drained and the need for conservation becomes more critical. We can only hope that we can effect large-scale changes in our responses to our environment before it's too late.

REFERENCES

Abbey, A. (1982). Sex differences in attributions for friendly behavior: Do males misperceive females' friendliness? *Journal of Personality and Social Psychology, 42,* 830–838.

Abel, G., Barlow, G., Blanchard, D. H., & Guild, D. (1977). The components of rapists' sexual arousal. *Archives of General Psychiatry, 34,* 895–903.

Abeles, N. (1985). Proceedings of the American Psychological Association, 1985. *American Psychologist, 40,* 621–653.

Abelson, R. P., & Rosenberg, M. J. (1958). Symbolic psycho-logic: A model of attitude cognition. *Behavioral Science, 3,* 1–13.

Abramson, L. Y., Seligman, M. E. P., & Teasdale, J. D. (1978). Learned helplessness in humans: Critique and reformulation. *Journal of Abnormal Psychology, 87,* 49–74.

Adair, J. G. (1973). *The human subject: The social psychology of the psychological experiment.* Boston: Little, Brown.

Adams, G. R. (1981). The effect of physical attractiveness on the socialization process. In G. W. Lucker, K. A. Ribbens, & J. A. McNamara, Jr., (Eds.), *Psychological aspects of facial form.* Ann Arbor, Mich.: Center for Human Growth and Development.

Adams, S. (1965). Inequity in social exchange. In L. Berkowitz (Ed.), *Advances in experimental social psychology* (Vol. 2). New York: Academic Press.

Ad Hoc Committee on Ethical Standards in Psychological Research. (1973). Ethical principles in the conduct of research with human participants. Washington, D.C.: American Psychological Association.

Adorno, T. W., Frenkel-Brunswick, E., Levinson, D., & Sanford, N. (1950). *The authoritarian personality.* New York: Harper.

Aiello, J. R., Baum, A., & Gormley, F. (1981). Social determinants of residential crowding stress. *Personality and Social Psychology Bulletin, 7,* 643–644.

Aiello, J. R., Epstein, Y. M., & Karlin, R. A. (1975). Field experimental research in human crowding. Paper presented at the Annual Meetings of the Eastern Psychological Association, New York.

Aiello, J. R., & Thompson, D. E. (1980). Personal space, crowding, and spatial behavior in a cultural context. In I. Altman, J. F. Wohlwill, & A. Rapoport (Eds.), *Human behavior and environment* (Vol. 4). New York: Plenum.

Ajzen, I. (1977). Intuitive theories of events and the effects of base-rate information on prediction. *Journal of Personality and Social Psychology, 35,* 303–314.

Ajzen, I., & Fishbein, M. (1977). Attitude-behavior relations: A theoretical analysis and review of empirical research. *Psychological Bulletin, 84,* 888–918.

Ajzen, I., & Fishbein, M. (1980). *Understanding attitudes and predicting social behavior.* Englewood Cliffs, N.J.: Prentice-Hall.

Ajzen, I., Timko, C., & White, J. B. (1982). Self-monitoring and the attitude-behavior relation. *Journal of Personality and Social Psychology, 42,* 426–435.

Akert, R. M., & Chen, J. (1984). Gender display: The incidence of facial prominence in print and television media. Paper presented at the Annual Meeting of the Eastern Psychological Association, Baltimore, Md.

Alexander, C. N., Jr., & Lauderdale, P. (1977). Situated identities and social influence. *Sociometry, 40,* 225–233.

Allen, H. (1970). An exploratory study into bystander intervention and helping behavior in the subway. Unpublished doctoral dissertation, New York University.

Allen, V. L. (1975). Social support for nonconformity. In L. Berkowitz (Ed.), *Advances in experimental social psychology* (Vol. 8). New York: Academic Press.

Allport, F. H. (1924). *Social psychology.* Boston: Houghton Mifflin.

Allport, F. H., et al. (1953). The effects of segregation and the consequences of desegregation: A social science statement. *Minneapolis Law Review, 37,* 429–440.

Allport, G. W. (1935). Attitudes. In C. Murchison (Ed.), *Handbook of social psychology.* Worcester, Mass.: Clark University Press.

Allport, G. W. (1954). *The nature of prejudice.* Reading, Mass.: Addison-Wesley.

Allport, G. W. (1985). The historical background of modern social psychology. In G. Lindzey & E. Aronson (Eds.), *Handbook of social psychology* (Vol. 1, 3rd ed.). New York: Random House.

Allport, G. W., & Postman, L. J. (1947). *The psychology of rumor.* New York: Henry Holt.

Altman, I. (1975). *The environment and social behavior.* Monterey, Calif.: Brooks/Cole.

Altman, I. (1976). Privacy: A conceptual analysis. *Environment and Behavior, 8,* 7–29.

Altman, I. (1977). Research on environment and behavior: A personal statement of strategy. In D. Stokols (Ed.), *Perspectives on environment and behavior.* New York: Plenum.

Altman, I., & Chemers, M. M. (1980). *Culture and environment.* Monterey, Calif.: Brooks/Cole.

Altman, I., & Haythorne, W. W. (1967). The ecology of isolated groups. *Behavioral Science, 12,* 169–182.

Altman, I., & Taylor, D. A. (1973). *Social penetration: The development of interpersonal relationships.* New York: Holt, Rinehart & Winston.

Altman, I., Taylor, D. A., & Wheeler, L. (1971). Ecological aspects of group behavior in social isolation. *Journal of Applied Social Psychology, 1,* 76–100.

Altman, I., & Vinsel, A. M. (1977). Personal space: An analysis of E. T. Hall's proxemics framework. In I. Altman & J. F. Wohlwill (Eds.), *Human behavior and environment: Advances in theory and research* (Vol. 1). New York: Plenum.

Amabile, T. M., Hennessey, B. A., & Grossman, B. S. (1986). Social influences on creativity: The effects of contracted-for-reward. *Journal of Personality and Social Psychology, 50,* 14–23.

Amato, P. R. (1983). Helping behavior in urban and rural environments: Field studies based on a taxonometric organization of helping episodes. *Journal of Personality and Social Psychology, 45,* 571–586.

Andersen, S. M. (1984). Self-knowledge and social inference: II. The diagnosticity of cognitive/affective and behavioral data. *Journal of Personality and Social Psychology, 46,* 294–307.

Andersen, S. M., & Bem, S. L. (1981). Sex typing and androgyny in dyadic interaction: Individual differences in responsiveness to physical attractiveness. *Journal of Personality and Social Psychology, 41,* 74–86.

Andersen, S. M., & Ross, L. (1984). Self-knowledge and social inference: I. The impact of cognitive/affective and behavioral data. *Journal of Personality and Social Psychology, 46,* 280–293.

Andersen, S. M., & Williams, M. (1985). Cognitive/affective reactions in the improvement of self-esteem: When thoughts and feelings make a difference. *Journal of Personality and Social Psychology, 49,* 1086–1097.

Anderson, C. A., & Anderson, D. C. (1984). Ambient temperature and violent crime: Tests of the linear and curvilinear hypotheses. *Journal of Personality and Social Psychology, 46,* 91–97.

Anderson, C. A., Lepper, M. R., & Ross, L. (1980). Perseverance of social theories: The role of explanation in the persistence of discredited information. *Journal of Personality and Social Psychology, 39,* 1037–1049.

Anderson, N. H. (1965). Averaging versus adding as a stimulus combination rule in impression formation. *Journal of Experimental Psychology, 70,* 394–400.

Anderson, N. H. (1981). *Foundations of information integration theory.* New York: Academic Press.

Anderson, N. H., & Norman, A. (1964). Order effects in impression formation in four classes of stimuli. *Journal of Abnormal and Social Psychology, 69,* 467–471.

Antaki, C., & Brewin, C. (Eds.). (1982). *Attributions and psychological change.* New York: Academic Press.

Apple, W., Streeter, L. A., & Krauss, R. M. (1979). Effects of pitch and speech rate on personal attributions. *Journal of Personality and Social Psychology, 37,* 715–727.

Archer, D., & Akert, R. M. (1977). Words and everything else: Verbal and nonverbal cues in social interpretation. *Journal of Personality and Social Psychology, 35,* 443–449.

Archer, D., Iritani, B., Kimes, D. D., & Barrios, M. (1983). Face-ism: Five studies of sex differences in facial prominence. *Journal of Personality and Social Psychology, 45,* 725–735.

Archer, R. L. (1984). The farmer and the cowman should be friends: An attempt at reconciliation with Batson, Coke, and Pych. *Journal of Personality and Social Psychology, 46,* 709–711.

Archer, R. L., Diaz-Loving, R., Gollwitzer, P. M., Davis, M. H., & Foushee, H. C. (1981). The role of dispositional empathy and social evaluation in empathic mediation of helping. *Journal of Personality and Social Psychology, 40,* 786–796.

Argyle, M., & Cook, M. (1976). *Gaze and mutual gaze.* Cambridge: Cambridge University Press.

Argyle, M., & Dean, J. (1965). Eye contact, distance, and affiliation. *Sociometry, 28,* 289–304.

Arkin, R. M., Appelman, A. J., & Burger, J. M. (1980). Social anxiety, self-presentation, and the self-serving bias in causal attribution. *Journal of Personality and Social Psychology, 38,* 23–35.

Arkin, R. M., & Baumgardner, A. H. (1985). Self-handicapping. In J. H. Harvey & G. Weary (Eds.), *Attribution: Basic issues and applications.* New York: Academic Press.

Arkin, R. M., & Burger, J. M. (1980). Effects of unit relation tendencies on interpersonal attraction. *Social Psychology Quarterly, 43,* 380–391.

Arkin, R. M., & Duval, S. (1975). Focus of attention and causal attributions of actors and observers. *Journal of Experimental Social Psychology, 11,* 427–438.

Arkin, R. M., & Lake, E. A. (1983). Plumbing the depths of the bogus pipeline: A reprise. *Journal of Research in Personality, 17,* 81–88.

Aronoff, J., & Wilson, J. P. (1985). *Personality in the social process.* Hillsdale, N.J.: Erlbaum.

Aronson, E., Brewer, M., & Carlsmith, J. M. (1985). Experimentation in social psychology. In G. Lindzey & E. Aronson (Eds.), *Handbook of social psychology* (Vol. 1, 3rd ed.). New York: Random House.

Aronson, E., & Linder, D. (1965). Gain and loss of esteem as determinants of interpersonal attractiveness. *Journal of Experimental Social Psychology, 1,* 156–172.

Aronson, E., & Mills, J. (1959). The effects of severity of initiation on liking for a group. *Journal of Abnormal and Social Psychology, 59,* 177–181.

Aronson, E., Stephan, C., Sikes, J., Blaney, N., & Snapp, M. (1978). *The jigsaw classroom.* Beverly Hills, Calif.: Sage.

Asch, S. E. (1946). Forming impressions of personality. *Journal of Abnormal and Social Psychology, 41,* 258–290.

Asch, S. E. (1951). Effects of group pressure on the modification and distortion of judgments. In H. Guetzkow (Ed.), *Groups, leadership, and men.* Pittsburgh: Carnegie Press.

Asch, S. E. (1955). Opinions and social pressures. *Scientific American, 193(5),* 31–35.

Asch, S. E., & Zukier, H. (1984). Thinking about persons. *Journal of Personality and Social Psychology, 46,* 1230–1240.

Ashmore, R. D., Del Boca, F. K., & Wohler, A. J. (1984). Gender stereotypes. In R. D. Ashmore & F. K. Del Boca (Eds.), *The social psychology of female-male relations: A critical analysis of central concepts.* New York: Academic Press.

Ashour, A. S. (1973a). The contingency model of leadership effectiveness: An evaluation. *Organizational Behavior and Human Performance, 9,* 339–355.

Ashour, A. S. (1973b). Further discussion of Fiedler's contingency model of leadership effectiveness. *Organizational Behavior and Human Performance, 9,* 369–376.

Atkinson, J. W. (Ed.). (1958). *Motives in fantasy, action, and society.* Princeton, N.J.: Van Nostrand.

Atkinson, J. W., Heyns, R. W., & Veroff, J. (1954). The effect of experimental arousal of the affiliation motive on thematic apperception. *Journal of Abnormal and Social Psychology, 49,* 405–410.

Atwood, R. W., & Howell, R. J. (1971). Pupillometric and personality test score differences of female aggressing pedophiliacs and normals. *Psychonomic Science, 22,* 115–116.

Austin, W. (1979). Justice, freedom, and self-interest in intergroup conflict. In W. G. Austin & S. Worchel (Eds.), *The social psychology of intergroup relations.* Monterey, Calif.: Brooks/Cole.

Averill, J. R. (1985). The social construction of emotion: With special reference to love. In K. J. Gergen & K. E. Davis (Eds.), *The social construction of the person.* New York: Springer-Verlag.

Averill, J. R., & Boothroyd, P. (1977). On falling in love in conformance with the romantic ideal. *Motivation and Emotion, 1,* 235–247.

Azuma, H. (1984). Secondary control as a heterogeneous category. *American Psychologist, 39,* 970–971.

Backstrom, C. H., & Hursh-César, G. (1981). *Survey research* (2nd ed.). New York: Wiley.

Bagozzi, R. P., & Burnkrant, R. E. (1979). Attitude organization and the attitude-behavior relationship. *Journal of Personality and Social Psychology, 37,* 913–929.

Bagozzi, R. P., & Burnkrant, R. E. (1985). Attitude organization and the attitude-behavior relation: A reply to Dillon and Kumar. *Journal of Personality and Social Psychology, 49,* 47–57.

Bailey, K. D. (1982). *Methods of social research.* New York: Free Press.

Bales, R. F. (1958). Task roles and social roles in problem-solving groups. In E. E. Maccoby, T. M. Newcomb, & E. L. Hartley (Eds.), *Readings in social psychology.* New York: Holt, Rinehart & Winston.

Bales, R. F., Cohen, S. P., & Williamson, S. A. (1979). *SYMLOG: A system for the multiple level observation of groups.* New York: Free Press.

Bandler, R. J., Madaras, G. R., & Bem, D. J. (1968). Self-observation as a source of pain. *Journal of Personality and Social Psychology, 9,* 205–209.

Bandura, A. (1965). Influence of model's reinforcement contingencies on the acquisition of imitative responses. *Journal of Personality and Social Psychology, 1,* 589–595.

Bandura, A. (1969). *Principles of behavior modification.* Stanford, Calif.: Stanford University Press.

Bandura, A. (1973). *Aggression: A social learning analysis.* Englewood Cliffs, N.J.: Prentice-Hall.

Bandura, A. (1977). *Social learning theory.* Englewood Cliffs, N.J.: Prentice-Hall.

Bandura, A. (1982). Self-efficacy mechanism in human agency. *American Psychologist, 37,* 122–147.

Bandura, A. (1983). Psychological mechanisms of aggression. In R. G. Geen & E. I. Donnerstein (Eds.), *Aggression: Theoretical and empirical reviews* (Vol. 1). New York: Academic Press.

Bandura, A., Ross, R., & Ross, S. (1961). Transmission of aggression through imitation of aggressive models. *Journal of Abnormal and Social Psychology, 63,* 575–582.

Bandura, A., & Schunk, D. H. (1981). Cultivating competence, self-efficacy, and interest through proximal self-motivation. *Journal of Personality and Social Psychology, 41,* 586–598.

Barash, D. P. (1976). The male response to apparent female adultery in the mountain bluebird, *Sialia currucoides:* An evolutionary interpretation. *American Naturalist, 110,* 1097–1101.

Barash, D. P. (1982). *Sociobiology and behavior* (2nd ed.). New York: Elsevier.

Barber, T. X. (1976). *Pitfalls in human research.* New York: Pergamon.

Barber, T. X., & Silver, M. J. (1968a). Fact, fiction, and the experimenter bias effect. *Psychological Bulletin* (Monograph Supplement), *70,* 1–29.

Barber, T. X., & Silver, M. J. (1968b). Pitfalls in data analysis and interpretation: A reply to Rosenthal. *Psychological Bulletin* (Monograph Supplement), *70,* 48–62.

Bargh, J. A. (1984). Automatic and conscious processing of social information. In R. S. Wyer & T. K. Srull (Eds.), *Handbook of social cognition* (Vol. 3). Hillsdale, N.J.: Erlbaum.

Bargh, J. A., & Pietromonaco, P. (1982). Automatic information processing and social perception: The influence of trait information presented outside of conscious awareness on impression formation. *Journal of Personality and Social Psychology, 43,* 437–449.

Barker, R. G. (Ed.). (1978). *Habitats, environments, and human behavior: Studies in ecological psychology and ecobehavioral sciences from the Midwest Psychological Field Station, 1947–1972.* San Francisco: Jossey-Bass.

Baron, R. A. (1972). Aggression as a function of ambient temperature and prior anger arousal. *Journal of Personality and Social Psychology, 21,* 183–189.

Baron, R. A. (1976). The reduction of human aggression: A field study of the influence of incompatible reactions. *Journal of Applied Social Psychology, 6,* 260–274.

Baron, R. A. (1977). *Human aggression.* New York: Plenum.

Baron, R. A. (1978). Aggression and heat: the "long hot summer" revisited. In A. Baum, J. E. Singer, & S. Valins (Eds.), *Advances in environmental psychology* (Vol. 1). Hillsdale, N.J.: Erlbaum.

Baron, R. A. (1981). The "costs of deception" revisited: An openly optimistic rejoinder. *IRB: A Review of Human Subjects Research, 3,* 8–10.

Baron, R. A. (1983). The control of human aggression: A strategy based on incompatible responses. In R. G. Geen & E. I. Donnerstein (Eds.), *Aggression: Theoretical and empirical reviews* (Vol. 2). New York: Academic Press.

Baron, R. A., & Ball, R. L. (1974). The aggression-inhibiting influence of nonhostile humor. *Journal of Experimental Social Psychology, 10,* 23–33.

Baron, R. A., & Bell, P. A. (1975). Aggression and heat: Mediating effects of prior provocation and exposure to an aggressive model. *Journal of Personality and Social Psychology, 31,* 825–832.

Baron, R. A., & Bell, P. A. (1976). Aggression and heat: The influence of ambient temperature, negative affect, and a cooling drink on physical aggression. *Journal of Personality and Social Psychology, 33,* 245–255.

Baron, R. A., & Kepner, C. R. (1970). Model's behavior and attraction toward the model as determinants of adults' aggressive behavior. *Journal of Personality and Social Psychology, 14,* 335–344.

Baron, R. A., & Ransberger, V. M. (1978). Ambient temperature and the occurrence of collective violence: The "long hot summer" revisited. *Journal of Personality and Social Psychology, 36,* 351–360.

Baron, R. M., & Harvey, J. H. (1980). Contrasting perspectives on social knowing: An overview. *Personality and Social Psychology Bulletin, 6,* 502–506.

Baron, R. S., Moore, D. L., & Sanders, G. S. (1978). Distraction as a source of drive in social facilitation research. *Journal of Personality and Social Psychology, 36,* 816–824.

Barrow, J. C. (1977). The variables of leadership: A review and conceptual framework. *Academy of Management Review, 2,* 231–251.

Bar-Tal, D. (1976). *Prosocial behavior: Theory and research.* Washington, D.C.: Hemisphere.

Bar-Tal, D., Goldberg, M., & Knaani, A. (1984). Causes of success and failure and their dimensions as a function of SES and gender: A phenomenological analysis. *British Journal of Educational Psychology, 54,* 51–61.

Bar-Tal, D., Sharabany, R., & Raviv, A. (1982). Cognitive basis of the development of altruistic behavior. In V. J. Derlega & J. Grzelak (Eds.), *Cooperation and helping behavior.* New York: Academic Press.

Basow, S. A. (1980). *Sex-role stereotypes.* Monterey, Calif.: Brooks/Cole.

Bass, B. M. (1981). *Stogdill's handbook of leadership.* New York: Free Press.

Batson, C. D. (1975). Rational processing or rationalization? The effect of disconfirming information on a stated religious belief. *Journal of Personality and Social Psychology, 32,* 176–184.

Batson, C. D., Bolen, M. H., Cross, J. A., & Neuringer-Benefiel, H. E. (1986). Where is the altruism in the altruistic personality? *Journal of Personality and Social Psychology, 50,* 212–220.

Batson, C. D., Cochran, P. J., Biederman, M. F., Blosser, J. L., Ryan, M. J., & Vogt, B. (1978). Failure to help when in a hurry: Callousness or conflict. *Personality and Social Psychology Bulletin, 4,* 97–101.

Batson, C. D., & Coke, J. S. (1981). Empathy: A source of altruistic motivation for helping? In J. P. Rushton & R. M. Sorrentino (Eds.), *Altruism and behavior.* Hillsdale, N.J.: Erlbaum.

Batson, C. D., Coke, J. S., & Pych, V. (1983). Limits on the two-stage model of empathic mediation of helping: A reply to Archer, Diaz-Loving, Gollwitzer, Davis, and

Foushee. *Journal of Personality and Social Psychology, 45,* 895–898.

Batson, C. D., Duncan, B. D., Ackerman, P., Buckley, T., & Birch, K. (1981). Is empathic emotion a source of altruistic motivation? *Journal of Personality and Social Psychology, 40,* 290–302.

Batson, C. D., O'Quin, K., Fultz, J., Vanderplas, M., & Isen, A. M. (1983). Influence of self-reported distress and empathy on egoistic versus altruistic motivation to help. *Journal of Personality and Social Psychology, 45,* 706–718.

Baum, A., Calesnick, L. E., Davis, G. E., & Gatchel, R. J. (1982). Individual differences in coping with crowding: Stimulus screening and social overload. *Journal of Personality and Social Psychology, 43,* 821–830.

Baum, A., & Davis, G. E. (1980). Reducing the stress of high-density living: An architectural intervention. *Journal of Personality and Social Psychology, 38,* 471–481.

Baum, A., Harpin, R. E., & Valins, S. (1975). The role of group phenomena in the experience of crowding. *Environment and Behavior, 7,* 185–198.

Baum, A., Riess, M., & O'Hara, J. (1974). Architectural variants of reaction to spatial invasion. *Environment and Behavior, 6,* 91–100.

Baum, A., Singer, J., & Baum, C. (1982). Stress and the environment. *Journal of Social Issues, 37(1),* 4–35.

Baum, A., & Valins, S. (1977). *Architecture and social behavior: Psychological studies of social density.* Hillsdale, N.J.: Erlbaum.

Baum, A., & Valins, S. (1979). Architectural mediation of residential density and control: Crowding and the regulation of social contact. In L. Berkowitz (Ed.), *Advances in experimental social psychology* (Vol. 12). New York: Academic Press.

Baumann, D. J., Cialdini, R. B., & Kenrick, D. T. (1981). Altruism as hedonism: Helping and self-gratification as equivalent responses. *Journal of Personality and Social Psychology, 40,* 1039-1046.

Baumeister, R. F. (1982). A self-presentational view of social phenomena. *Psychological Bulletin, 91,* 3–26.

Baumeister, R. F. (1984). Choking under pressure: Self-consciousness and paradoxical effects of incentives on skillful performance. *Journal of Personality and Social Psychology, 46,* 610–620.

Baumeister, R. F. (1985). The championship choke. *Psychology Today, 19(4),* 48–52.

Baumeister, R. F., Hamilton, J. C., & Tice, D. M. (1985). Public versus private expectancy of success: Confidence booster or performance pressure? *Journal of Personality and Social Psychology, 48,* 1447–1457.

Baumeister, R. F., & Steinhilber, A. (1984). Paradoxical effects of supportive audience on performance under pressure: The home field disadvantage in sports championships. *Journal of Personality and Social Psychology, 47,* 85–93.

Baumrind, D. (1964). Some thoughts on the ethics of research: After reading Milgram's "Behavioral study of obedience." *American Psychologist, 19,* 421–423.

Baumrind, D. (1971). Principles of ethical conduct in the treatment of subjects: Reaction to the draft report of the Committee on Ethical Standards in Psychological Research. *American Psychologist, 26,* 887–896.

Baumrind, D. (1985). Research using intentional deception: Ethical issues revisited. *American Psychologist, 40,* 165–174.

Beaman, A. L., Cole, C. M., Preston, M., Klentz, B., & Steblay, N. M. (1983). Fifteen years of foot-in-the door research: A meta-analysis. *Personality and Social Psychology Bulletin, 9,* 181–196.

Becker, H. S. (1963). *Outsiders.* New York: Free Press.

Becker, L., & Seligman, C. (1978). Reducing air-conditioning waste by signaling it is cool outside. *Personality and Social Psychology Bulletin, 4,* 412–415.

Bell, P. A. (1981). Physiological, comfort, performance, and social effects of heat stress. *Journal of Social Issues, 37,* 71–94.

Bell, P. A., & Baron, R. A. (1981). Ambient temperature and human violence. In P. F. Brain & D. Denton (Eds.), *Multidisciplinary approach to aggression research.* New York: Elsevier/North-Holland Biomedical Press.

Bell, P. A., & Greene, T. C. (1982). Thermal stress: Physiological, comfort, performance, and social effects of hot and cold environments. In G. W. Evans (Ed.), *Environmental stress.* London: Cambridge University Press.

Bellezza, F. S. (1984). The self as a mnemonic device: The role of internal cues. *Journal of Personality and Social Psychology, 47,* 506–516.

Bellezza, F. S., & Bower, G. H. (1981). Person stereotypes and memory for people. *Journal of Personality and Social Psychology, 41,* 856–865.

Bem, D. J. (1965). An experimental analysis of self-persuasion. *Journal of Experimental Social Psychology, 1,* 199–218.

Bem, D. J. (1972). Self-perception theory. In L. Berkowitz (Ed.), *Advances in experimental social psychology* (Vol. 6). New York: Academic Press.

Bem, S. L. (1974). The measurement of psychological androgyny. *Journal of Consulting and Clinical Psychology, 42,* 155–162.

Bem, S. L. (1979). Theory and measurement of androgyny: A reply to the Pedhazur-Tetenbaum and Locksley-Colten critiques. *Journal of Personality and Social Psychology, 37,* 1047–1054.

Bem, S. L. (1981). Gender schema theory: A cognitive account of sex typing. *Psychological Review, 88,* 354–364.

Bem, S. L. (1985). Androgyny and gender schema theory: A conceptual and empirical integration. *Nebraska Symposium on Motivation, 32,* 179–226.

Benne, K. D., & Sheats, P. (1948). Functional roles of group members. *Journal of Social Issues, 4(2),* 41–49.

Benson, P. L., Karabenick, S. A., & Lerner, R. M. (1976). Pretty pleases: The effects of physical attractiveness, race, and sex on receiving help. *Journal of Experimental Social Psychology, 12,* 409–415.

Bentler, P. M., & Speckart, G. (1981). Attitudes "cause" behaviors: A structural equation analysis. *Journal of Personality and Social Psychology, 40,* 226–238.

Berg, J. H. (1984). Development of friendship between roommates. *Journal of Personality and Social Psychology, 46,* 346–356.

Berger, J., Fisek, M. H., Norman, R. Z., & Zelditch, M., Jr. (1977). *Status characteristics and social interaction.* New York: Elsevier.

Berger, J., Wagner, D. G., & Zelditch, M., Jr. (1985). Introduction: Expectation states theory: Review and assessment. In J. Berger & M. Zelditch, Jr. (Eds.), *Status, rewards, and influence.* San Francisco: Jossey-Bass.

Berger, S. M., Carli, L. C., García, R., & Brady, J. J., Jr. (1982). Audience effects in anticipatory learning: A comparison of drive and practice-inhibition analyses. *Journal of Personality and Social Psychology, 42,* 478–486.

Berger, S. M., Hampton, K. L., Carli, L. L., Grandmaison, P. S., Sadow, J. S., Donath, C. H., & Herschlag, L. R. (1981). Audience-induced inhibition of overt practice during learning. *Journal of Personality and Social Psychology, 40,* 479–491.

Berglas, S., & Jones, E. E. (1978). Drug choice as a self-handicapping strategy in response to noncontingent success. *Journal of Personality and Social Psychology, 36,* 405–417.

Berkowitz, L. (1970). The contagion of violence: An S-R mediational analysis of some effects of observed aggression. *Nebraska Symposium on Motivation, 18,* 95–135.

Berkowitz, L. (1972). Social norms, feelings, and other factors affecting helping and altruism. In L. Berkowitz (Ed.), *Advances in experimental social psychology* (Vol. 6). New York: Academic Press.

Berkowitz, L. (1981a). The concept of aggression. In P. E. Brain & D. Denton (Eds.), *Multidisciplinary approach to aggression research.* New York: Elsevier/North Holland Biomedical Press.

Berkowitz, L. (1981b). Aversive conditions as stimuli for aggression. In L. Berkowitz (Ed.), *Advances in experimental social psychology* (Vol. 15). New York: Academic Press.

Berkowitz, L. (1981c). How guns control us. *Psychology Today, 15*(6), 11–12.

Berkowitz, L. (1981d). *When the "trigger" pulls the finger.* Washington, D.C.: American Psychological Association.

Berkowitz, L. (1983). The experience of anger as a parallel process in the display of impulsive, "angry" aggression. In R. G. Geen & E. I. Donnerstein (Eds.), *Aggression: Theoretical and empirical reviews* (Vol. 1). New York: Academic Press.

Berkowitz, L. (1984). Some effects of thoughts on anti- and prosocial influences of media events: A cognitive-neoassociation analysis. *Psychological Bulletin, 95,* 410–427.

Berkowitz, L., & Connor, W. H. (1966). Success, failure, and social responsibility. *Journal of Personality and Social Psychology, 4,* 664–669.

Berkowitz, L., & Daniels, L. R. (1963). Responsibility and dependency. *Journal of Abnormal and Social Psychology, 66,* 664–669.

Berkowitz, L., & Donnerstein, E. I. (1982). External validity is more than skin deep: Some answers to criticisms of laboratory experiments. *American Psychologist, 37,* 245–257.

Berkowitz, L., Klanderman, S. B., & Harris, R. (1964). Effects of experimenter awareness and sex of subject and experimenter on reactions to dependency relationships. *Sociometry, 27,* 327–332.

Berkowitz, L., & Lepage, A. (1967). Weapons as aggression-eliciting stimuli. *Journal of Personality and Social Psychology, 7,* 202–207.

Berlyne, D. E. (1970). Novelty, complexity, and hedonic value. *Perception and Psychophysics, 8,* 279–286.

Berscheid, E. (1983). Emotion. In H. H. Kelley, E. Berscheid, A. Christensen, J. H. Harvey, T. L. Huston, G. Levinger, E. McClintock, L. A. Peplau, & D. R. Peterson, *Close relationships.* New York: Freeman.

Berscheid, E. (1985). Interpersonal attraction. In G. Lindzey & E. Aronson (Eds.), *Handbook of social psychology* (Vol. 2, 3rd ed.). New York: Random House.

Berscheid, E., Graziano, W., Monson, T. C., & Dermer, M. (1976). Outcome dependency: Attention, attribution, and attraction. *Journal of Personality and Social Psychology, 34,* 978–989.

Berscheid, E., & Walster, E. (1974). Physical attractiveness. In L. Berkowitz (Ed.), *Advances in experimental social psychology* (Vol. 7). New York: Academic Press.

Berscheid, E., & Walster, E. (1978). *Interpersonal attraction* (2nd ed.). Reading, Mass.: Addison-Wesley.

Berscheid, E., Walster, E., & Campbell, R. (1972). "Grow old along with me." Unpublished manuscript, University of Minnesota.

Bettelheim, B. (1943). Individual and mass behavior in extreme situations. *Journal of Abnormal and Social Psychology, 38,* 417–452.

Bettman, J. R., & Weitz, B. A. (1983). Attributions in the boardroom: Causal reasoning in corporate annual reports. *Administrative Science Quarterly, 28,* 165–183.

Betz, N. E., & Hackett, G. (1981). The relationship of career-related self-efficacy expectations to perceived career options in college women and men. *Journal of Counseling Psychology, 28,* 399–410.

Beuf, A. (1974). Doctor, lawyer, household drudge. *Journal of Communication, 25,* 142–145.

Beyth-Marom, R., & Fischhoff, B. (1983). Diagnosticity and pseudodiagnosticity. *Journal of Personality and Social Psychology, 45,* 1185–1195.

Biaggio, M. K. (1980). Anger arousal and personality characteristics. *Journal of Personality and Social Psychology, 39,* 352–356.

Bickman, L. (1971). The effect of another bystander's ability to help on bystander intervention in an emergency. *Journal of Experimental Social Psychology, 7,* 367–379.

Bickman, L. (1972). Social influence and diffusion of responsibility in an emergency. *Journal of Experimental Social Psychology, 8,* 438–445.

Bickman, L. (1974). Clothes make the person. *Psychology Today, 8(4),* 48–51.

Bickman, L. (1981). Some distinctions between basic and applied approaches. In L. Bickman (Ed.), *Applied social psychology annual* (Vol 2). Beverly Hills, Calif.: Sage.

Bickman, L., & Rosenbaum, D. P. (1977). Crime reporting as a function of bystander encouragement, surveillance, and credibility. *Journal of Personality and Social Psychology, 35,* 577–586.

Birchler, G. R., Weiss, R. L., & Vincent, J. P. (1975). Multimethod analysis of social reinforcement exchange between maritally distressed and nondistressed spouse and stranger dyads. *Journal of Personality and Social Psychology, 31,* 349–360.

Birnbaum, M. H. (1974). The nonadditivity of personality impression. *Journal of Experimental Psychology* (Monograph), *102,* 543–561.

Birnbaum, M. H. (1981). Thinking and feeling: A skeptical review. *American Psychologist* (Comment), *36,* 99–101.

Birnbaum, M. H., & Mellers, B. A. (1979a). Stimulus recognition may mediate exposure effects. *Journal of Personality and Social Psychology, 37,* 391–394.

Birnbaum, M. H., & Mellers, B. A. (1979b). One-mediator model of exposure effects is still viable. *Journal of Personality and Social Psychology, 37,* 1090–1096.

Bither, S. W., Dolich, I. J., & Nell, E. B. (1971). The application of attitude immunization techniques in marketing. *Journal of Marketing Research, 8,* 56–61.

Blanchard, K., & Johnson, S. (1981). *The one-minute manager.* New York: Berkeley Books.

Blanck, P. D., Rosenthal, R., Snodgrass, S. E., DePaulo, B. M., & Zuckerman, M. (1981). Sex differences in eavesdropping on nonverbal cues: Developmental changes. *Journal of Personality and Social Psychology, 41,* 391–396.

Blass, T. (1984). Social psychology and personality: Toward a convergence. *Journal of Personality and Social Psychology, 47,* 1013–1027.

Blumberg, H. H., Hare, A. P., Kent, V., & Davis, M. F. (Eds.). (1983). *Small groups and social interaction.* New York: Wiley.

Bochner, S., & Insko, C. A. (1966). Communicator discrepancy, source credibility, and opinion change. *Journal of Personality and Social Psychology, 4,* 614–621.

Bogardus, E. S. (1925). Measuring social distance. *Journal of Applied Sociology, 9,* 299–308.

Boice, R. (1983). Observational skills. *Psychological Bulletin, 93,* 3–29.

Bond, C. F., & Titus, L. J. (1983). Social facilitation: A meta-analysis of 241 studies. *Psychological Bulletin, 94,* 265–292.

Borgida, E. (1978). Scientific deduction—evidence is not necessarily information: A reply to Wells and Harvey. *Journal of Personality and Social Psychology, 36,* 477–482.

Borgida, E. (1981). Legal reform of rape laws. In L. Bickman (Ed.), *Applied social psychology annual* (Vol. 2). Beverly Hills, Calif.: Sage.

Borgida, E., & Brekke, N. (1981). The base-rate fallacy in attribution and prediction. In J. H. Harvey, W. J. Ickes, & R. F. Kidd (Eds.), *New directions in attribution research* (Vol. 3). Hillsdale, N.J.: Erlbaum.

Borgida, E., & Campbell, B. (1982). Belief relevance and attitude-behavior consistency: The moderating role of personal experience. *Journal of Personality and Social Psychology, 42,* 239–247.

Borofsky, G. L., Stollak, G. E., & Messe, L. A. (1971). Sex differences in bystander reactions to physical assault. *Journal of Experimental Social Psychology, 7,* 313–318.

Bouchard, T. J. (1972a). Training, motivation, and personality as determinants of the effectiveness of brainstorming groups and individuals. *Journal of Applied Psychology, 56,* 324–331.

Bouchard, T. J. (1972b). A comparison of two group brainstorming procedures. *Journal of Applied Psychology, 56,* 135–138.

Bouchard, T. J., Barsaloux, J., & Drauden, G. (1974). Brainstorming procedure, group size, and sex as determinants of the problem-solving effectiveness of groups and individuals. *Journal of Applied Psychology, 59,* 135–138.

Bouchard, T. J., Drauden, G., & Barsaloux, J. (1974). A comparison of individual, subgroup, and total group methods of problem solving. *Journal of Applied Psychology, 59,* 226–227.

Bouchard, T. J., & Hare, M. (1970). Size, performance, and potential in brainstorming groups. *Journal of Applied Psychology, 54,* 51–55.

Bower, G. H. (1981). Emotional mood and memory. *American Psychologist, 36,* 129–148.

Bowerman, W. R. (1978). Subjective competence: The structure, process, and function of self-referent causal attributions. *Journal for the Theory of Social Behavior, 8,* 45–75.

Bradley, G. W. (1978). Self-serving biases in the attribution process: A reexamination of the fact or fiction question. *Journal of Personality and Social Psychology, 36,* 56–70.

Braginsky, B. M., Braginsky, D. D., & Ring, K. (1969). *Methods of madness: The mental hospital as a last resort.* New York: Holt, Rinehart & Winston.

Bramel, D. A. (1962). A dissonance theory approach to defensive projection. *Journal of Abnormal and Social Psychology, 64,* 121–129.

Bray, R. M., Johnson, D., & Chilstrom, J. T., Jr. (1982). Social influence by group members with minority opinions: A comparison of Hollander & Moscovici. *Journal of Personality and Social Psychology, 43,* 78–88.

Breckler, S. J. (1984). Empirical validation of affect, behavior, and cognition as distinct components of attitude. *Journal of Personality and Social Psychology, 47,* 1191–1205.

Bredemeier, B. J., & Shields, D. L. (1985). Values and violence in sports today. *Psychology Today, 19(10),* 23–32.

Brehm, J. W. (1956). Post-decision changes in desirability of alternatives. *Journal of Abnormal and Social Psychology, 52,* 384–389.

Brehm, J. W. (1976). Responses to loss of freedom: A theory of psychological reactance. In J. W. Thibaut, J. T. Spence, & R. C. Carson (Eds.), *Contemporary topics in social psychology.* Morristown, N.J.: General Learning Press.

Brehm, J. W., & Cohen, A. R. (1962). *Explorations in cognitive dissonance.* New York: Wiley.

Brehm, S. S. (1985). *Intimate relationships.* New York: Random House.

Brenner, M., & Bungard, W. (1981). What to do with social reactivity in psychological experimentation? In M. Brenner (Ed.), *Social methods and social life.* New York: Academic Press.

Brent, E., & Granberg, D. (1982). Subjective agreement with the presidential candidates of 1976 and 1980. *Journal of Personality and Social Psychology, 42,* 393–403.

Brewer, M. B. (1979). In-group bias in the minimal intergroup situation: A cognitive-motivational analysis. *Psychological Bulletin, 86,* 307–324.

Brewin, C. R. (1985). Depression and causal attributions: What is their relation? *Psychological Bulletin, 98,* 297–309.

Brigham, J. C. (1986). Race and eyewitness identifications. In S. Worchel & W. G. Austin (Eds.), *Psychology of intergroup relations* (2nd ed.). Chicago: Nelson-Hall.

Brigham, J. C., Maass, A., Snyder, L. D., & Spaulding, K. (1982). The accuracy of eyewitness identification in a field setting. *Journal of Personality and Social Psychology, 42,* 673–681.

Brigham, J. C., & Williamson, N. L. (1979). Cross-race recognition and age: When you're over 60 do they still "all look alike?" *Personality and Social Psychology Bulletin, 5,* 218–222.

Brinberg, D., & Castell, P. (1982). A resource exchange theory approach to interpersonal interactions: A test of Foa's theory. *Journal of Personality and Social Psychology, 43,* 260–269.

Brock, T. C. (1965). Communicator-recipient similarity and decision change. *Journal of Personality and Social Psychology, 1,* 650–654.

Brockner, J. (1983). Low self-esteem and behavioral plasticity: Some implications. In L. Wheeler & P. Shaver (Eds.), *Review of personality and social psychology* (Vol. 4). Beverly Hills, Calif.: Sage.

Brockner, J., & Swap, W. C. (1976). Effects of repeated exposure and attitudinal similarity on self-disclosure and interpersonal attraction. *Journal of Personality and Social Psychology, 33,* 531–540.

Brodt, S. E., & Zimbardo, P. G. (1981). Modifying shyness-related social behavior through symptom misattribution. *Journal of Personality and Social Psychology, 41,* 437–449.

Bromley, D. G. (1985). Cult facts and fiction. *VCU Magazine, 14(2),* 10–15.

Brothen, T. (1977). The gain/loss concept and the evaluator: First some good news, then some bad. *Journal of Personality and Social Psychology, 35,* 430–439.

Brower, S., Dockett, D., & Taylor, R. B. (1983). Residents' perceptions of site-level features. *Environment and Behavior, 15,* 419–437.

Brown, B. B., & Altman, I. (1983). Territoriality, defensible space, and residential burglary: An environmental analysis. *Journal of Environmental Psychology, 3,* 203–220.

Brown, D., Klemp, G., & Leventhal, H. (1975). Are evaluations inferred directly from overt actions? *Journal of Experimental Social Psychology, 11,* 112–126.

Brown, R. C., Jr., & Tedeschi, J. T. (1976). Determinants of perceived aggression. *Journal of Social Psychology, 100,* 77–87.

Brown, S. M. (1979). Male versus female leaders: A comparison of empirical studies. *Sex Roles, 5,* 595–611.

Brownmiller, S. (1975). *Against our will: Men, women, and rape.* New York: Simon & Schuster.

Bryan, J. H., & Davenport, M. (1968). *Donations to the needy: Correlates of financial contributions to the destitute.* Princeton, N.J.: Educational Testing Service.

Bryan, J. H., & Test, M. A. (1967). Models and helping: Naturalistic studies in aiding behavior. *Journal of Personality and Social Psychology, 6,* 400–407.

Buck, R. (1984). Emotion development and emotion education. In R. Plutchik & H. Kellerman (Eds.), *Emotions in early development.* New York: Academic Press.

Bugental, J. F. T., & Zelen, S. L. (1950). Investigations into the self-concept—the W-A-Y technique. *Journal of Personality, 18,* 483–498.

Bulman, R. J., & Wortman, C. B. (1977). Attributions of blame and coping in the "real world:" Severe accident victims react to their lot. *Journal of Personality and Social Psychology, 35,* 351–363.

Bunge, M. (1974). Towards a philosophy of technology. In A. C. Michalos (Ed.), *Philosophical problems of science and technology.* Boston: Allyn & Bacon.

Burger, J. M. (1981). Motivational biases in the attribution of responsibility for an accident: A meta-analysis of the defensive-attribution hypothesis. *Psychological Bulletin, 90,* 496–512.

Burger, J. M., & Petty, R. E. (1981). The low-ball compliance technique: Task or person commitment? *Journal of Personality and Social Psychology, 40,* 492–500.

Burgess, A. W. (Ed.). (1985). *Rape and sexual assault, a research handbook.* New York: Garland.

Burgoon, J. K. (1978). A communication model of personal space violations: Explication and an initial test. *Human Communication Research, 4,* 129–142.

Burgoon, J. K. (1983). Nonverbal violations of expectations. In J. M. Wiemann & R. P. Harrison (Eds.), *Sage annual reviews of communication: Nonverbal interaction* (Vol. 11). Beverly Hills, Calif.: Sage.

Burgoon, J. K., Buller, D. B., Hale, J. L., & deTurck, M. A. (1984). Relational messages associated with nonverbal behaviors. *Human Communication Research, 10,* 351–378.

Burke, P. A., Kraut, R. E., & Dworkin, R. H. (1984). Traits, consistency, and self-schemata: What do our methods measure? *Journal of Personality and Social Psychology, 47,* 568–579.

Burke, P. J. (1974). Participation and leadership in small groups. *American Sociological Review, 39,* 832–842.

Burn, S. M., & Oskamp, S. (1984). Increasing community recycling with persuasive communication and public commitment. Unpublished manuscript, Claremont Graduate School.

Burns, J. M. (1978). *Leadership.* New York: Harper & Row.

Burns, R. B. (1979). *The self-concept: Theory, measurement, development, and behavior.* London: Longman.

Burnstein, E., & Schul, Y. (1982). The informational basis of social judgments: The operations in forming an impression of another person. *Journal of Experimental Social Psychology, 18,* 217–234.

Burnstein, E., & Schul, Y. (1983). The informational basis of social judgments: Memory for integrated and nonintegrated trait descriptions. *Journal of Experimental Social Psychology, 19,* 49–57.

Burnstein, E., & Vinokur, A. (1973). Testing two classes of theories about group-induced shifts in individual choice. *Journal of Experimental Social Psychology, 9,* 123–137.

Burnstein, E., & Vinokur, A. (1977). Persuasive arguments and social comparison as determinants of attitude polarization. *Journal of Experimental Social Psychology, 13,* 315–332.

Burt, M. R. (1980). Cultural myths and supports for rape. *Journal of Personality and Social Psychology, 38,* 217–230.

Buss, A. H. (1980). *Self-consciousness and social anxiety.* San Francisco: Freeman.

Buss, A. H., & Durkee, A. (1957). An inventory for assessing different kinds of hostility. *Journal of Consulting Psychology, 21,* 343–349.

Buss, D. M. (1984). Toward a psychology of person-environment (PE) correlation: The role of spouse selection. *Journal of Personality and Social Psychology, 47,* 361–377.

Byrne, D. (1961). Anxiety and the experimental arousal of affiliation need. *Journal of Abnormal and Social Psychology, 63,* 660–662.

Byrne, D. (1971). *The attraction paradigm.* New York: Academic Press.

Byrne, D., Ervin, C. F., & Lamberth, J. (1970). Continuity between the experimental study of attraction and real-life computer dating. *Journal of Personality and Social Psychology, 16,* 157–165.

Byrne D., & Nelson, D. (1965). Attraction as a linear function of proportion of positive and negative reinforcements. *Journal of Personality and Social Psychology, 1,* 659–663.

Cacioppo, J. T. (1979). Effects of exogenous changes in heart rate on facilitation of thought and resistance to persuasion. *Journal of Personality and Social Psychology, 37,* 489–498.

Cacioppo, J. T., Petty, R. E., & Losch, M. (1986). Attributions of responsibility for helping and doing harm: Evidence for confusion of responsibility. *Journal of Personality and Social Psychology, 50,* 100–105.

Calder, B. J. (1976). An attribution theory of leadership. In B. M. Staw & G. R. Salancik (Eds.), *New directions in organizational behavior.* Chicago: St. Clair Press.

Caldwell, M. A., & Peplau, L. A. (1982). Sex differences in same-sex friendship. *Sex Roles, 8,* 721–732.

Calhoun, J. B. (1962). Population density and social pathology. *Scientific American, 206(2),* 139–148.

Callaway, M. R., Marriott, R. G., & Esser, J. K. (1985). Effects of dominance on group decision making: Toward a stress-reduction explanation of groupthink. *Journal of Personality and Social Psychology, 49,* 949–952.

Campbell, A. (1971). *Whites' attitudes toward black people.* Ann Arbor, Mich.: Institute for Social Research.

Campbell, A., Converse, P. E., & Rodgers, W. L. (1976). *The quality of American life.* New York: Russell Sage Foundation.

Campbell, D. T. (1947). The generality of a social attitude. Unpublished doctoral dissertation, University of California, Berkeley.

Campbell, D. T. (1950). The indirect assessment of social attitudes. *Psychological Bulletin, 47,* 15–38.

Campbell, D. T. (1963). Social attitudes and other acquired behavioral dispositions. In S. Koch (Ed.), *Psychology: A study of a science.* New York: McGraw-Hill.

Campbell, D. T., & Stanley, J. C. (1963). *Experimental and quasi-experimental designs for research.* Chicago: Rand-McNally.

Cantor, J., Zillmann, D., & Bryant, J. (1975). Enhancement of experienced sexual arousal in response to erotic stimuli through misattribution of unrelated residual excitation. *Journal of Personality and Social Psychology, 32,* 69–75.

Cappella, J. N. (1981). Mutual influence in expressive behavior: Adult-adult and infant-adult dyadic interaction. *Psychological Bulletin, 89,* 101–132.

Carbonell, J. L. (1984). Sex roles and leadership revisited. *Journal of Applied Psychology, 69,* 44–49.

Carlopio, J., Adair, J. G., Lindsay, R. C. L., & Spinner, B. (1983). Avoiding artifact in search of bias: The importance of assessing subjects' perceptions of the experiment. *Journal of Personality and Social Psychology, 44,* 693–701.

Carlsmith, J. M., & Anderson, C. A. (1979). Ambient temperature and the occurrence of collective behavior: A new analysis. *Journal of Personality and Social Psychology, 37,* 337–344.

Carlston, D. E., & Cohen, J. L. (1980). A closer examination of subject roles. *Journal of Personality and Social Psychology, 38,* 857–870.

Carlyle, T. (1841). *On heroes, hero-worship, and the heroic.* London: Fraser.

Carnegie, D. (1937). *How to win friends and influence people.* New York: Simon & Schuster.

"Carnegie fund honors heroism of 21 people." (1984). *Richmond Times Dispatch,* Dec. 15, p. A-7.

Carroll, J. S. (1979). Judgments by parole boards. In I. H. Frieze, D. Bar-Tal, & J. S. Carroll (Eds.), *New approaches to social problems: Applications of attribution theory.* San Francisco: Jossey-Bass.

Carroll, J. S., & Coates, D. (1980). Parole decisions: Social psychological research in applied settings. In L. Bickman (Ed.), *Applied social psychology annual* (Vol. 1). Beverly Hills, Calif.: Sage.

Carroll, J. S., & Payne, J. W. (1977). Crime seriousness, recidivism risk, and causal attributions in judgments of prison term by students and experts. *Journal of Applied Psychology, 62,* 595–602.

Carroll, J. S., & Ruback, R. B. (1980). Sentencing by parole board: The parole revocation decision. In B. D. Sales (Ed.), *Perspectives in law and psychology: The jury, trial, and judicial process* (Vol. 2). New York: Plenum.

Cartwright, D. (1979). Contemporary social psychology in historical perspective. *Social Psychology Quarterly, 42,* 82–93.

Cartwright, D., & Zander, A. (Eds.). (1968). *Group dynamics: Research and theory* (3rd ed.). New York: Harper & Row.

Carver, C. S., Blaney, P. H., & Scheier, M. F. (1979). Reassertion and giving up: The interactive role of self-directed attention and outcome expectancy. *Journal of Personality and Social Psychology, 37,* 1859–1870.

Carver, C. S., & Scheier, M. F. (1981). *Attention and self-regulation: A control-theory approach to human behavior.* New York: Springer-Verlag.

Carver, C. S., & Scheier, M. F. (1983). Two sides of the self: One for you and one for me. In J. Suls & A. G. Greenwald (Eds.), *Psychological perspectives on the self* (Vol. 2). Hillsdale, N.J.: Erlbaum.

Carver, C. S., & Scheier, M. F. (1984). Self-focused attention in test anxiety: A general theory applied to a specific phenomenon. In H. van der Ploeg, R. Schwarzer, & C. D. Spielberger (Eds.), *Advances in test anxiety research* (Vol. 3). Hillsdale, N.J.: Erlbaum.

Cash, T. F., & Janda, L. H. (1984). The eye of the beholder. *Psychology Today, 18*(5), 46–52.

Ceci, S. J., Peters, D., & Plotkin, J. (1985). Human subjects review, personal values, and the regulation of social science research. *American Psychologist, 40,* 994–1006.

Central Intelligence Agency. (1981). *Patterns of international terrorism: 1980.* Springfield, Va.: National Technical Information Service.

Chaikin, A., & Derlega, V. (1974). Variables affecting the appropriateness of self-disclosure. *Journal of Consulting and Clinical Psychology, 42,* 588–593.

Chaiken, A. L., & Darley, J. M. (1973). Victim or perpetrator? Defensive attribution of responsibility and the need for order and justice. *Journal of Personality and Social Psychology, 25,* 268–275.

Chaiken, S. (1979). Communicator physical attractiveness and persuasion. *Journal of Personality and Social Psychology, 37,* 1387–1397.

Chaiken, S., & Baldwin, M. W. (1981). Affective-cognitive consistency and the effect of salient behavioral information on the self-perception of attitudes. *Journal of Personality and Social Psychology, 41,* 1–12.

Chave, E. J. (1928). A new type scale for measuring attitudes. *Religious Education, 23,* 364–369.

Cheek, J. M., & Buss, A. H. (1981). Shyness and sociability. *Journal of Personality and Social Psychology, 41,* 330–339.

Chemers, M. M., & Skrzypek, G. J. (1972). Experimental test of the contingency model of leadership effectiveness. *Journal of Personality and Social Psychology, 24,* 173–177.

Chen, S. C. (1937). Social modification of the activity of ants in nest-building. *Physiological Zoology, 10,* 420–436.

Cherry, F., & Byrne, D. (1977). Authoritarianism. In T. Blass (Ed.), *Personality variables in social behavior.* Hillsdale, N.J.: Erlbaum.

Cherry, F., Byrne, D., & Mitchell, H. E. (1976). Clogs in the bogus pipeline: Demand characteristics and social desirability. *Journal of Research in Personality, 10,* 69–75.

Chesterfield, Earl of (Philip Dormer Stanhope) (1774/1901). *Letters to his son.* Walter M. Dunne, (Ed.). New York: Wiley.

Christensen, L. (1982). A critique of Carlston and Cohen's examination of subject roles. *Personality and Social Psychology Bulletin, 8,* 579–582.

Christian, J. J. (1963). Pathology of overpopulation. *Military Medicine, 128,* 571–603.

Christian, J. J., Flyger, V., & Davis, D. E. (1960). Factors in the mass mortality of a herd of Silka deer, *Cervus nippon. Chesapeake Science, 1,* 79–95.

Christie, R., & Geis, F. L. (Eds.). (1970). *Studies in Machiavellianism.* New York: Academic Press.

Cialdini, R. B. (1985). *Influence: Science and practice.* Glenview, Ill.: Scott, Foresman.

Cialdini, R. B., Borden, R., Thorne, A., Walker, M., Freeman, S., & Sloane, L. T. (1976). Basking in reflected glory: Three (football) field studies. *Journal of Personality and Social Psychology, 34,* 366–375.

Cialdini, R. B., Cacioppo, J. T., Bassett, R., & Miller, J. A. (1978). Low-ball procedure for producing compliance: Commitment then cost. *Journal of Personality and Social Psychology, 36,* 463–476.

Cialdini, R. B., Darby, B. L., & Vincent, J. E. (1973). Transgression and altruism: A case for hedonism. *Journal of Experimental Social Psychology, 9,* 502–516.

Cialdini, R. B., & Kenrick, D. T. (1976). Altruism as hedonism: A social development perspective on the relationship of negative mood state and helping. *Journal of Personality and Social Psychology, 34,* 907–914.

Cialdini, R. B., Vincent, J. E., Lewis, S. K., Catalan, J., Wheeler, D., & Darby, B. L. (1975). Reciprocal concessions procedure for inducing compliance: The door-in-the-face technique. *Journal of Personality and Social Psychology, 31,* 206–215.

Clark, L. F., & Woll, S. B. (1981). Stereotype biases: A reconstructive analysis of their role in reconstructive memory. *Journal of Personality and Social Psychology, 41,* 1064–1072.

Clark, M. S. (1984). Record keeping in two types of relationships. *Journal of Personality and Social Psychology, 47,* 549–557.

Clark, M. S., Milberg, S., & Erber, R. (1984). Effects of arousal on judgments of others' emotions. *Journal of Personality and Social Psychology, 46,* 551–560.

Clark, M. S., & Mills, J. (1979). Interpersonal attraction in exchange and communal relationships. *Journal of Personality and Social Psychology, 37,* 12–24.

Clark, R. D., III. (1971). Group-induced shift toward risk: A critical appraisal. *Psychological Bulletin, 76,* 251–270.

Clark, R. D., III. (1976). On the Piliavin & Piliavin model of helping behavior: Costs are in the eye of the beholder. *Journal of Applied Social Psychology, 6,* 322–328.

Clark, R. D., III, & Word, L. E. (1972). Why don't bystanders help? Because of ambiguity? *Journal of Personality and Social Psychology, 24,* 392–400.

Clark, R. D., III, & Word, L. E. (1974). Where is the apathetic bystander? Situational characteristics of the emergency. *Journal of Personality and Social Psychology, 29,* 279–287.

Clary, E. G., & Tesser, A. (1983). Reactions to unexpected events: The naive scientist and interpretive activity. *Personality and Social Psychology Bulletin, 9,* 609–620.

Cline, V. B., Croft, R. G., & Courrier, S. (1973). Desensitization of children to television violence. *Journal of Personality and Social Psychology, 27,* 360–365.

Clore, G. L., Wiggins, N. H., & Itkin, S. (1975). Gain and loss in attraction: Attributions from nonverbal behavior. *Journal of Personality and Social Psychology, 31,* 706–712.

Cloward, R. A., & Ohlin, L. E. (1960). *Delinquency and opportunity: A theory of delinquent gangs.* Glencoe, Ill.: Free Press.

Cohen, C. E. (1981). Person categories and social perception: Testing some boundaries of the processing effects of prior knowledge. *Journal of Personality and Social Psychology, 40,* 441–452.

Cohen, C. E. (1983). Inferring the characteristics of other people: Categories and attribute accessibility. *Journal of Personality and Social Psychology, 44,* 34–44.

Cohen, S. (1980). Aftereffects of stress on human performance and social behavior: A review of research and theory. *Psychological Bulletin, 87,* 578–604.

Cohen, S., Evans, G. W., Krantz, D. S., & Stokols, D. (1980). Physiological, motivation, and cognitive effects of aircraft noise on children: Moving from the laboratory to the field. *American Psychologist, 35,* 231–243.

Cohen, S., Evans, G. W., Krantz, D. S., Stokols, D., & Kelly, S. (1981). Aircraft noise and children: Longitudinal and cross-sectional evidence on adaptation to noise and the effectiveness of noise abatement. *Journal of Personality and Social Psychology, 40,* 331–345.

Cohen, S., Glass, D. C., & Singer, J. E. (1973). Apartment noise, auditory discrimination, and reading ability in children. *Journal of Experimental Social Psychology, 9,* 407–422.

Cohen, S., Krantz, D. S., Evans, G. W., & Stokols, D. (1981). Cardiovascular and behavioral effects of community noise. *American Scientist, 69,* 528–535.

Cohen, S., & Weinstein, N. (1981). Nonauditory effects of noise on behavior and health. *Journal of Social Issues, 37,* 36–70.

Cohen, S., & Wills, T. A. (1985). Stress, social support, and the buffering hypothesis. *Psychological Bulletin, 98,* 310–357.

Coke, J. S., Batson, C. D., & McDavis, K. (1978). Empathic mediation of helping: A two-stage model. *Journal of Personality and Social Psychology, 36,* 752–766.

Coleman, J. F., Blake, R. R., & Mouton, J. S. (1958). Task difficulty and conformity pressures. *Journal of Abnormal and Social Psychology, 57,* 120–122.

Coleman, S. R., & Gormezano, I. (1979). Classical conditioning and the "law of effect:" Historical and empirical assessment. *Behaviorism, 7,* 1–33.

Collins, R. W., Dmitruk, V. M., & Ranney, J. T. (1977). Personal validation: Some empirical and ethical considerations. *Journal of Consulting and Clinical Psychology, 45,* 70–77.

Condry, J. (1977). Enemies of exploration. *Journal of Personality and Social Psychology, 35,* 459–477.

Cone, J. D., & Hayes, S. C. (1980). *Environmental problems/behavioral solutions.* Monterey, Calif.: Brooks/Cole.

Conner, R. C., & Norris, K. S. (1982). Are dolphins and whales reciprocal altruists? *American Naturalist, 119,* 358–374.

Conroy, J., & Sundstrom, E. (1977). Territorial dominance in a dyadic conversation as a function of similarity of opinion. *Journal of Personality and Social Psychology, 35,* 570–576.

Constantian, C. A. (1981/1982). Solitude: Attitudes, beliefs, and behavior in regard to spending time alone. Unpublished doctoral dissertation. Cambridge, Mass.: Harvard University.

Constantinople, A. (1973). Masculinity-femininity: An exception to the famous dictum? *Psychological Bulletin, 80,* 389–407.

Converse, J., Jr., & Cooper, H. (1979). The importance of decisions and free-choice attitude change: A curvilinear finding. *Journal of Experimental Social Psychology, 15,* 48–61.

Conway, M., & Ross, M. (1985). Getting what you want by revising what you had. *Journal of Personality and Social Psychology, 47,* 738–748.

Cook, S. W. (1984). The 1954 social science statement and school desegregation: A reply to Gerard. *American Psychologist, 39,* 819–832.

Cook, S. W. (1985). Experimenting on social issues: The case of school desegregation. *American Psychologist, 40,* 452–460.

Cook, T. D., & Campbell, D. T. (1979). *Quasi-experimentation.* Chicago: Rand-McNally.

Cook, T. D., & Flay, B. R. (1978). The temporal persistence of experimentally induced attitude change: An evaluative review. In L. Berkowitz (Ed.), *Advances in experimental social psychology* (Vol. 11). New York: Academic Press.

Cook, T. D., Gruder, C. L., Hennigan, K. M., & Flay, B. R. (1979). History of the sleeper effect: Some logical pitfalls in accepting the null hypothesis. *Psychological Bulletin, 86,* 662–679.

Cook, T. D., Leviton, L. C., & Shadish, W. R., Jr. (1985). Program evaluation. In G. Lindzey & E. Aronson (Eds.), *Handbook of social psychology* (Vol. 1, 3rd ed.). New York: Random House.

Cooley, C. H. (1902). *Human nature and the social order.* New York: Scribner.

Cooper, H. M. (1979). Statistically combining independent studies: Meta-analysis of sex differences in conformity research. *Journal of Personality and Social Psychology, 37,* 131–146.

Cooper, J., Fazio, R. H., & Rhodewalt, F. (1978). Dissonance and humor: Evidence for the undifferentiated nature of dissonance arousal. *Journal of Personality and Social Psychology, 36,* 280–285.

Cooper, J., Zanna, M. P., & Taves, P. A. (1978). Arousal as a necessary condition for attitude change following induced compliance. *Journal of Personality and Social Psychology, 36,* 1101–1106.

Cooper, W. H. (1981). Ubiquitous halo. *Psychological Bulletin, 90,* 218–244.

Corrigan, J. D., Dell, D. M., Lewis, K. N., & Schmidt, L. D. (1980). Counseling as a social influence process: A review. *Journal of Counseling Psychology, 27,* 395–441.

Cottrell, N. B. (1972). Social facilitation. In C. G. McClintock (Ed.), *Experimental social psychology.* New York: Holt, Rinehart, & Winston.

Cottrell, N. B. (1972). Social facilitation. In C. G. McClintock (Ed.), *Experimental social psychology.* New York: Holt, Rinehart & Winston.

cesses. Washington, D.C.: Hemisphere.

Courtney, A. E., & Whipple, T. W. (1974). Women in TV commercials. *Journal of Communication, 24,* 110–118.

Courtright, J. A. (1978). A laboratory investigation of groupthink. *Communication Monographs, 43,* 229–246.

Covington, M. V., & Omelich, C. L. (1979). Are causal attributions causal? A path analysis of the cognitive model of achievement motivation. *Journal of Personality and Social Psychology, 37,* 1487–1504.

Cozby, P. C. (1973). Self-disclosure: A literature review. *Psychological Bulletin, 79,* 73–91.

Crocker, J. (1981). Judgment of covariation by social perceivers. *Psychological Bulletin, 90,* 272–292.

Crocker, J. (1982). Biased questions in judgment of covariation studies. *Personality and Social Psychology Bulletin, 8,* 214–220.

Crooks, R., & Baur, K. (1980). *Our sexuality.* Menlo Park, Calif.: Benjamin/Cummings.

Crosby, F., Bromley, S., & Saxe, L. (1980). Recent unobtrusive studies of black and white discrimination and prejudice: A literature review. *Psychological Bulletin, 87,* 546–563.

Cross, H. A., Halcomb, C. G., & Matter, W. W. (1967). Imprinting or exposure learning in rats given early auditory stimulation. *Psychonomic Sciences, 7,* 233–234.

Crutchfield, R. S. (1955). Conformity and character. *American Psychologist, 10,* 191–198.

Csikszentmihalyi, M., & Rochberg-Halton, E. (1981). Object lessons. *Psychology Today, 15(12),* 79–85.

Cunningham, M. R. (1979). Weather, mood, and helping behavior: Quasi-experiments with the sunshine Samaritan. *Journal of Personality and Social Psychology, 37,* 1947–1956.

Cunningham, M. R. (1981). Sociobiology as a supplementary paradigm for social psychological research. In L. Wheeler (Ed.), *Review of personality and social psychology* (Vol. 2). Beverly Hills, Calif.: Sage.

Cunningham, M. R., Steinberg, J., & Grev, R. (1980). Wanting to help and having to help: Separate motivations for positive moods and guilt-induced helping. *Journal of Personality and Social Psychology, 38,* 181–190.

Curtiss, S. (1977): *Genie: A psycholinguistic study of a modern-day "wild child."* New York: Academic Press.

Cutrona, C. E. (1982). Transition to college: Loneliness and the process of social adjustment. In L. A. Peplau & D. Perlman (Eds.), *Loneliness: A sourcebook of current theory, research, and therapy.* New York: Wiley-Interscience.

Darley, J. M., & Aronson, E. (1966). Self-evaluation vs. direct anxiety reduction as determinants of the fear-affiliation relationship. *Journal of Personality and Social Psychology* (Supplement 1), 66–79.

Darley, J. M., & Batson, C. D. (1973). "From Jerusalem to Jericho:" A study of situational and dispositional variables in helping behavior. *Journal of Personality and Social Psychology, 27,* 100–108.

Darley, J. M., & Berscheid, E. (1967). Increased liking as a result of the anticipation of personal contact. *Human Relations, 20,* 29–40.

Darley, J. M., & Fazio, R. H. (1980). Expectancy confirmation processes arising in the social interaction sequence. *American Psychologist, 35,* 867–881.

Darley, J. M., & Gilbert, D. T. (1985). Social psychological aspects of environmental psychology. In G. Lindzey & E. Aronson (Eds.), *Handbook of social psychology* (Vol. 2, 3rd ed.). New York: Random House.

Darley, J. M., & Gross, P. H. (1983). A hypothesis-confirming bias in labeling effects. *Journal of Personality and Social Psychology, 44,* 20–33.

Darley, J. M., & Latané, B. (1968). Bystander intervention in emergencies: Diffusion of responsibility. *Journal of Personality and Social Psychology, 8,* 377–383.

Darley, J. M., & Latané, B. (1970). Norms and normative behavior: Field studies of social interdependence. In J. Macaulay & L. Berkowitz (Eds.), *Altruism and helping behavior: Social psychological studies of some antecedents and consequences.* New York: Academic Press.

Dart, R. A. (1953). The predatory transition from ape to man. *International Anthropological and Linguistic Review, 1,* 201–208

Dashiell, J. F. (1930). An experimental analysis of some group effects. *Journal of Abnormal and Social Psychology, 25,* 190–199.

Davage, R. (1958). Effect of achievement-affiliation motive patterns on yielding behavior in two-person groups. *Dissertation Abstracts, 18,* 1506.

Davidson, A. R., & Jaccard, J. J. (1979). Variables that moderate the attitude-behavior relation: Results of a longitudinal study. *Journal of Personality and Social Psychology, 37,* 1364–1376.

Davidson, A. R., Yantis, S., Norwood, M., & Montano, D. E. (1985). Amount of information about the attitude object and attitude-behavior consistency. *Journal of Personality and Social Psychology, 49,* 1184–1198.

Davis, K. E. (1985). Near and dear: Friendship and love compared. *Psychology Today, 19(2),* 22–30.

Davis, K. E., & Roberts, M. K. (1985). Relationships in the real world: The descriptive psychology approach to personal relationships. In K. J. Gergen & K. E. Davis (Eds.), *The social construction of the person.* New York: Springer-Verlag.

Davison, R., & Jones, S. C. (1976). Similarity in real-life friendship pairs. *Journal of Personality and Social Psychology, 34,* 313–317.

Dawes, R. M., & Smith, T. L. (1985). Attitude and opinion measurement. In G. Lindzey & E. Aronson (Eds.), *Handbook of social psychology* (Vol. 1, 3rd ed.). New York: Random House.

Dean, L. M., Willis, F. N., & Hewitt, J. (1975). Initial interaction distance among individuals equal and unequal in military rank. *Journal of Personality and Social Psychology, 32,* 294–299.

Deaux, K. (1976). Sex: A perspective on the attribution process. In J. H. Harvey, W. J. Ickes, & R. F. Kidd (Eds.), *New directions in attribution research* (Vol. 1), Hillsdale, N.J.: Erlbaum.

Deaux, K. (1978). Sex-related patterns of social interaction. Paper presented at the Annual Meeting of the Midwestern Psychological Association, Chicago.

Deaux, K. (1984). From individual differences to social categories: Analysis of a decade's research on gender. *American Psychologist, 39,* 105–116.

Deaux, K., & Lewis, L. L. (1984). Structure of gender components: Interrelationships among components and gender labels. *Journal of Personality and Social Psychology, 46,* 991–1004.

Deci, E. L., & Ryan, R. M. (1985). *Intrinsic motivation and self-determination in human behavior.* New York: Plenum.

DeFleur, M. L., & Westie, F. R. (1958). Verbal attitudes and overt acts: An experiment on the salience of attitudes. *American Sociological Review, 23,* 667–673.

Dengerink, H. A., Schnedler, R. W., & Covey, M. K. (1978). Role of avoidance in aggressive responses to attack and no attack. *Journal of Personality and Social Psychology, 36,* 1044–1053.

DePaulo, B. M., Nadler, A., & Fisher, J. D. (Eds.). (1983). *New directions in helping: Help-seeking.* New York: Academic Press.

Derlega, V. J., & Grzelak, J. (Eds.). (1982). *Cooperation and helping behavior.* New York: Academic Press.

Dermer, M., & Pyszczynski, T. A. (1978). Effects of erotica upon men's loving and liking responses for women they love. *Journal of Personality and Social Psychology, 36,* 1302–1309.

Deutsch, M. (1949a). A theory of cooperation and competition. *Human Relations, 2,* 129–152.

Deutsch, M. (1949b). An experimental study of the effects of cooperation and competition upon group process. *Human Relations, 2,* 199–231.

Deutsch, M. (1973). *The resolution of conflict.* New Haven, Conn.: Yale University Press.

Deutsch, M. (1980). Fifty years of conflict. In L. Festinger (Ed.), *Retrospections on social psychology.* New York: Oxford University Press.

Deutsch, M., & Gerard, H. B. (1955). A study of normative and informational social influences upon individual judgment. *Journal of Abnormal and Social Psychology, 51,* 629–636.

Deutsch, M., & Hornstein, H. A. (Eds.). (1975). *Applying social psychology: Implications for research, practice, and training.* Hillsdale, N.J.: Erlbaum.

Deutsch, M., & Solomon, L. (1959). Reactions to evaluations by others as influenced by self-evaluations. *Sociometry, 22,* 93–112.

Dewey, J. (1922) *Human nature and conduct: An introduction to social psychology.* New York: Henry Holt.

Diener, C. I., & Dweck, C. S. (1978). An analysis of learned helplessness: Continuous changes in performance, strategy, and achievement cognitions following failure. *Journal of Personality and Social Psychology, 36,* 451–462.

Diener, C. I., & Dweck, C. S. (1980). An analysis of learned helplessness: II. The processing of success. *Journal of Personality and Social Psychology, 39,* 940–952.

Diener, E. (1980). Deindividuation: The absence of self-awareness and self-regulation in group members. In P. B. Paulus (Ed.), *The psychology of group influence.* Hillsdale, N.J.: Erlbaum.

Diener, E., Fraser, S. C., Beaman, A. L., & Kelem, R. (1976). Effects of deindividuation on stealing among Halloween trick or treaters. *Journal of Personality and Social Psychology, 33,* 178–183.

Dill, C. A., Gilden, E. R., Hill, P. C., & Hanselka, L. L. (1982). Federal human subjects regulations: A methodological artifact? *Personality and Social Psychology Bulletin, 8,* 417–425.

Dillon, W. R., & Kumar, A. (1985). Attitude organization and the attitude-behavior relation: A critique of Bagozzi and Burnkrant's reanalysis of Fishbein and Ajzen. *Journal of Personality and Social Psychology, 49,* 33–46.

Dion, K. K., Berscheid, E., & Walster, E. (1972). What is beautiful is good. *Journal of Personality and Social Psychology, 24,* 285–290.

Dion, K. K., & Stein, S. (1978). Physical attractiveness and interpersonal influence. *Journal of Experimental Social Psychology, 14,* 97–108.

Dion, K. L., Berscheid, E., & Walster, E. (1972). What is beautiful is good. *Journal of Personality and Social Psychology, 24,* 285–290.

Dion, K. L., & Dion, K. K. (1973). Correlates of romantic love. *Journal of Consulting and Clinical Psychology, 41,* 51–56.

Dodge, R. W., Lentzner, H. R., & Shenk, F. (1976). Crime in the United States: A report on the National Crime Survey. In W. G. Skogan (Ed.), *Sample surveys of the victims of crime.* Cambridge, Mass.: Ballinger.

Doise, W. (1969). Intergroup relations and polarization of individual and collective judgments. *Journal of Personality and Social Psychology, 12,* 136–143.

Dollard, J. R., Doob, L. W., Miller, N. E., Mowrer, O. H., & Sears, R. R. (1939). *Frustration and aggression.* New Haven, Conn.: Yale University Press.

Dominick, J. R., & Rauch, G. E. (1972). The image of women in network TV commercials. *Journal of Broadcasting, 16,* 259–265.

Donnerstein, E. I. (1983). Erotica and human aggression. In R. G. Geen & E. I. Donnerstein (Eds.), *Aggression: Theoretical and empirical reviews* (Vol. 2). New York: Academic Press.

Donnerstein, E. I., & Berkowitz, L. (1981). Victim reactions in aggressive erotic films as a factor in violence against women. *Journal of Personality and Social Psychology, 41,* 710–724.

Donnerstein, E. I., & Wilson, D. W. (1976). The effects of noise and perceived control upon ongoing and subsequent aggressive behavior. *Journal of Personality and Social Psychology, 34,* 774–781.

Dovidio, J. F. (1984). Helping and altruism: An empirical and conceptual overview. In L. Berkowitz (Ed.), *Advances in experimental social psychology* (Vol. 17). New York: Academic Press.

Doyle, A. C. (1938). *The complete Sherlock Holmes.* Garden City, N.Y.: Garden City Publishing.

Drabman, R. S., & Thomas, M. H. (1974). Does media violence increase children's toleration of real-life aggression? *Developmental Psychology, 10,* 418–421.

Drabman, R. S., & Thomas, M. H. (1976). Does watching violence on television cause apathy? *Pediatrics, 57,* 329–331.

Driscoll, R., Davis, K. W., & Lipetz, M. E. (1972). Parental influence and romantic love: The Romeo and Juliet effect. *Journal of Personality and Social Psychology, 24,* 1–10.

DSM-III: Diagnostic and statistical manual of mental disorders (1980). Washington, D.C.: American Psychiatric Association.

Dubos, R. (1965). *Man adapting*. New Haven, Conn.: Yale University Press.

Dutton, D. G. (1971). Reactions of restauranteurs to blacks and whites violating restaurant dress regulations. *Canadian Journal of Behavioral Science, 3*, 298–302.

Dutton, D. G., & Aron, A. P. (1974). Some evidence for heightened sexual attraction under conditions of high anxiety. *Journal of Personality and Social Psychology, 30*, 510–517.

Dutton, D. G., & Lake, R. A. (1973). Threat of own prejudice and reverse discrimination in interracial situations. *Journal of Personality and Social Psychology, 28*, 94–100.

Duval, S. (1976). Conformity on a visual task as a function of personal novelty on attitudinal dimensions and being reminded of the object status of the self. *Journal of Experimental Social Psychology, 12*, 87–98.

Duval, S., & Wicklund, R. A. (1972). *A theory of objective self-awareness*. New York: Academic Press.

Dweck, C. S. (1975). The role of expectations and attributions in the alleviation of learned helplessness. *Journal of Personality and Social Psychology, 31*, 674–685.

Dweck, C. S., & Bush, E. S. (1976). Sex differences in learned helplessness: I. Differential debilitation with peer and adult evaluators. *Developmental Psychology, 12*, 147–156.

Dweck, C. S., & Licht, B. G. (1980). Learned helplessness and intellectual achievement. In M. E. P. Seligman & J. Barger (Eds.), *Human helplessness: theory and application*. New York: Academic Press.

Dweck, C. S., & Reppucci, N. D. (1973). Learned helplessness and reinforcement of responsibility in children. *Journal of Personality and Social Psychology, 25*, 109–116.

Eagly, A. H. (1978). Sex differences in influenceability. *Psychological Bulletin, 85*, 86–116.

Eagly, A. H., & Carli, L. L. (1981). Sex of researchers and sex-typed communications as determinants of sex differences in influenceability: A meta-analysis of social influence studies. *Psychological Bulletin, 90*, 1–20.

Eagly, A. H., & Chaiken, S. (1975). An attribution analysis of the effect of communicator characteristics on opinion change: The case of communicator attractiveness. *Journal of Personality and Social Psychology, 32*, 136–144.

Eagly, A. H., & Warren, R. (1976). Intelligence, comprehension, and opinion change. *Journal of Personality, 44*, 226–242.

Eagly, A. H., Wood, W., & Chaiken, S. (1978). Causal inferences about communicators and their effect on opinion change. *Journal of Personality and Social Psychology, 36*, 424–435.

Eagly, A. H., Wood, W., & Fishbaugh, L. (1981). Sex differences in conformity: Surveillance by the group as a determinant of male nonconformity. *Journal of Personality and Social Psychology, 40*, 384–394.

Earle, H. H. (1973). *Police recruit training: Stress vs. nonstress*. Springfield, Ill.: Charles C Thomas.

Ebbesen, E., Kjos, G., & Konečni, V. (1976). Spatial ecology: Its effects on the choice of friends and enemies. *Journal of Experimental Social Psychology, 12*, 505–518.

Edinger, J. A., & Patterson, M. L. (1983). Nonverbal involvement and social control. *Psychology Bulletin, 93*, 30–56.

Edney, J. (1975). Territoriality and control: A field experiment. *Journal of Personality and Social Psychology, 31*, 1108–1115.

Edney, J. (1976). Human territories: Comment on functional properties. *Environment and Behavior, 8*, 31–48.

Edney, J. J. (1980). The commons problem. *American Psychologist, 35*, 131–150.

Edwards, D. J. A. (1972). Approaching the unfamiliar: A study of human interaction distances. *Journal of Behavioral Sciences, 1*, 249–250.

Ehlert, J., Ehlert, N., & Merrens, M. (1973). The influence of ideological affiliation on helping behavior. *Journal of Social Psychology, 89*, 315–316.

Eibl-Eibesfeldt, I. (1972). Similarities and differences between cultures in expressive movements. In R. A. Hinde (Ed.), *Nonverbal communication and movement*. New York: Academic Press.

Einhorn, H. J. (1980). Overconfidence in judgment. In R. A. Shweder & D. Fiske (Eds.), *New directions for methodology of behavioral science: Fallible judgment in behavioral research* (Vol. 4). San Francisco: Jossey-Bass.

Ekman, P. (1985). *Telling lies: Clues to deceit in the marketplace, politics, and marriage*. New York: Norton.

Ekman, P., & Friesen, W. V. (1975). *Unmasking the face*. Englewood Cliffs, N.J.: Prentice-Hall.

Ekman, P., Friesen, W. V., & Bear, J. (1984). The international language of gestures. *Psychology Today, 18*(5), 64–69.

Ekman, P., Friesen, W. V., O'Sullivan, M., & Scherer, K. (1980). Relative importance of face, body, and speech in judgments of personality and affect. *Journal of Personality and Social Psychology, 38*, 270–277.

Elig, T. W., & Frieze, I. H. (1979). Measuring causal attributions for success and failure. *Journal of Personality and Social Psychology, 37*, 621–634.

Elliott, G. C. (1979). Some effects of deception and level of self-monitoring on planning and reacting to a self-presentation. *Journal of Personality and Social Psychology, 37*, 1282–1290.

Ellsworth, P. C., Carlsmith, J. M., & Hensen, A. (1972). The stare as a stimulus to flight in human subjects: A series of field experiments. *Journal of Personality and Social Psychology, 21*, 302–311.

Elms, A. C. (1972). *Social psychology and social relevance.* Boston: Little, Brown.

Emerson, R. W. (1926). *On civil disobedience and other essays.* New York: Henry Holt.

Enzle, M. E., & Schopflocher D. (1978). Instigation of attribution processes by attribution questions. *Personality and Social Psychology Bulletin, 4,* 595–599.

Erber, R., & Fiske, S. T. (1984). Outcome dependency and attention to inconsistent information. *Journal of Personality and Social Psychology, 47,* 709–726.

Erikson, M. (1968). The inhumanity of ordinary people. *International Journal of Psychiatry, 6,* 278–279.

Eron, L. D. (1980). Prescription for reduction of aggression. *American Psychologist, 35,* 244–252.

Eron, L. D. (1982). Parent-child interaction, TV violence, and aggression in children. *American Psychologist, 37,* 197–211.

Eron, L. D., Huesmann, L. R., Lefkowitz, M. M., & Walder, L. O. (1972). Does television violence cause aggression? *American Psychologist, 27,* 253–263.

Esser, A. H. (1970). Interactional hierarchy and power structure on a psychiatric ward. In S. J. Hutt & C. Hutt (Eds.), *Behavior studies in psychiatry.* New York: Oxford University Press.

Etzioni, A. (1968). A model of significant research. *International Journal of Psychiatry, 6,* 279–280.

Evans, G. W. (1979). Behavioral and physiological consequences of crowding in humans. *Journal of Applied Social Psychology, 9,* 27–46.

Evans, R. I. (1980). Behavioral medicine: A new applied challenge to social psychologists. In L. Bickman (Ed.), *Applied social psychology annual* (Vol. 1). Beverly Hills, Calif.: Sage.

Exline, R. (1962). Need affiliation and initial communication behavior in problem-solving groups characterized by low interpersonal visibility. *Psychological Reports, 10,* 79–89.

Exline, R., & Messick, D. (1967). The effects of dependency and social reinforcement upon visual behavior during an interview. *British Journal of Social and Clinical Psychology, 6,* 256–266.

Fairweather, G. W., & Tornatzky, L. G. (1977). *Experimental methods for social policy research.* New York: Pergamon.

Falbo, T. (1977). The multidimensional scaling of power strategies. *Journal of Personality and Social Psychology, 35,* 537–548.

Falbo, T., & Peplau, L. A. (1980). Power strategies in intimate relationships. *Journal of Personality and Social Psychology, 38,* 618–628.

Fazio, R. H. (1979). Motives for social comparison: The construction-validation distinction. *Journal of Personality and Social Psychology, 37,* 1683–1698.

Fazio, R. H., Effrein, E. A., & Falender, V. J. (1981). Self-perceptions following social interaction. *Journal of Personality and Social Psychology, 41,* 232–242.

Fazio, R. H., Powell, M. C., & Herr, P. M. (1983). Toward a process model of the attitude-behavior relation: Accessing one's attitude upon mere observation of the attitude object. *Journal of Personality and Social Psychology, 44,* 723–735.

Fazio, R. H., Sanbonmatsu, D. M., Powell, M. C., & Kardes, F. R. (1986). On the automatic activation of attitudes. *Journal of Personality and Social Psychology, 50,* 229–238.

Fazio, R. H., Sherman, S. J., & Herr, P. M. (1982). The feature-positive effect in the self-perception process: Does not doing matter as much as doing? *Journal of Personality and Social Psychology, 42,* 404–411.

Fazio, R. H., Zanna, M. P., & Cooper, J. (1977). Dissonance and self-perception: An integrative view of each theory's proper domain of application. *Journal of Experimental Social Psychology, 13,* 464–479.

Feather, N. T., & Simon, J. G. (1971). Attribution of responsibility and valence of outcome in relation to initial confidence and success and failure of self and other. *Journal of Personality and Social Psychology, 18,* 173–188.

Feldman, N. S., Higgins, E. T., Karlovac, M., & Ruble, D. N. (1976). Use of consensus information in causal attributions as a function of temporal presentation and availability of direct information. *Journal of Personality and Social Psychology, 34,* 694–698.

Feldman, N. S., & Ruble, D. N. (1981). Social comparison strategies: Dimensions offered and options taken. *Personality and Social Psychology Bulletin, 7,* 11–16.

Felipe, N. J., & Sommer, R. (1966). Invasions of personal space. *Social Problems, 14,* 206–214.

Fellner, C. H., & Marshall, J. R. (1981). Kidney donors revisited. In J. P. Rushton & R. M. Sorrentino (Eds.), *Altruism and helping behavior.* Hillsdale, N.J.: Erlbaum.

Felson, R. B. (1978). Aggression as impression management. *Social Psychology Quarterly, 41,* 205–213.

Felson, R. B. (1981a). Self and reflected appraisals among football players: A test of the Meadian hypothesis. *Social Psychology Quarterly, 44,* 116–126.

Felson, R. B. (1981b). An interactionist approach to aggression. In J. T. Tedeschi (Ed.), *Impression management theory and social psychological research.* New York: Academic Press.

Felson, R. B. (1984). The effect of self-appraisals of ability on academic performance. *Journal of Personality and Social Psychology, 47,* 944–955.

Felson, R. B. (1985). Reflected appraisal and the development of self. *Social Psychology Quarterly, 48,* 71–78.

Fenigstein, A., Scheier, M. F., & Buss, A. H. (1975). Public and private self-consciousness: Assessment and theory. *Journal of Consulting and Clinical Psychology, 43,* 522–527.

Ferguson, T. J., & Rule, B. G. (1983). An attributional analysis of anger and aggression. In R. G. Geen & E. I.

Donnerstein (Eds.), *Aggression: Theoretical and empirical reviews* (Vol. 1). New York: Academic Press.

Feshbach, S. (1956). The catharsis hypothesis and some consequences of interaction with aggressive and neutral play objects. *Journal of Personality, 24*, 449–461.

Feshbach, S. (1971). Dynamics and morality of violence and aggression: Some psychological considerations. *American Psychologist, 26*, 281–292.

Feshbach, S., & Singer, R. D. (1971). *Television and aggression*. San Francisco: Jossey-Bass.

Festinger, L. (1950). Informal social communication. *Psychological Review, 57*, 271–282.

Festinger, L. (1951). Architecture and group members. *Journal of Social Issues, 1*, 152–163.

Festinger, L. (1954). A theory of social comparison processes. *Human Relations, 7*, 117–140.

Festinger, L. (1957). *A theory of cognitive dissonance*. Stanford, Calif.: Stanford University Press.

Festinger, L. (Ed.). (1980). *Retrospections on social psychology*. New York: Oxford University Press.

Festinger, L. (1980). Looking backward. In L. Festinger (Ed.), *Retrospections on social psychology*. New York: Oxford University Press.

Festinger, L., & Carlsmith, J. M. (1959). Cognitive consequences of forced compliance. *Journal of Abnormal and Social Psychology, 58*, 203–210.

Festinger, L., Riecken, H. W., & Schachter, S. (1956). *When prophecy fails*. Minneapolis: University of Minnesota Press.

Festinger, L., Schachter, S., & Back, K. (1950). *Social pressures in informal groups: A study of human factors in housing*. New York: Harper.

Fiedler, F. E. (1978). The contingency model and the dynamics of the leadership process. In L. Berkowitz (Ed.), *Advances in experimental social psychology* (Vol. 12). New York: Academic Press.

Fiedler, F. E. (1981). Leadership effectiveness. *American Behavioral Scientist, 24*, 619–632.

Fischhoff, B. (1977). Perceived informativeness of acts. *Journal of Experimental Psychology: Human Perception and Performance, 3*, 349–358.

Fishbein, M., & Ajzen, I. (1975). *Belief, attitude, intention, and behavior: An introduction to theory and research*. Reading, Mass.: Addison-Wesley.

Fisher, B. A. (1980). *Small group decision making* (2nd ed.). New York: McGraw-Hill.

Fisher, J. D., Bell, P. A., & Baum, A. (1984). *Environmental psychology* (2nd ed.). New York: Holt, Rinehart & Winston.

Fisher, J. D., & Byrne, D. (1975). Too close for comfort: Sex differences in response to invasions of personal space. *Journal of Personality and Social Psychology, 32*, 15–21.

Fisher, J. D., DePaulo, B. M., & Nadler, A. (1981). Extending altruism beyond the altruistic act: The mixed effects of aid on the help recipient. In J. P. Rushton & R. M. Sorrentino (Eds.), *Altruism and helping behavior*. Hillsdale, N.J.: Erlbaum.

Fisher, J. D., Nadler, A., & Whitcher-Alagna, S. W. (1982). Recipient reactions to aid. *Psychological Bulletin, 91*, 27–54.

Fishman, C. (1966). Need for approval and the expression of aggression under varying conditions of frustration. *Journal of Personality and Social Psychology, 4*, 155–164.

Fiske, S. T. (1980). Attention and weight in person perception: The impact of negative and extreme behavior. *Journal of Personality and Social Psychology, 38*, 889–906.

Fiske, S. T., & Taylor, S. E. (1984). *Social cognition*. Reading, Mass.: Addison-Wesley.

Fleming, J. S., & Courtney, B. E. (1984). The dimensionality of self-esteem: II. Hierarchical facet model for revised measurement scales. *Journal of Personality and Social Psychology, 46*, 404–421.

Fletcher, G. J. O. (1984). Psychology and common sense. *American Psychologist, 39*, 203–213.

Foa, U. G. (1961). Convergences in the analysis of the structure of interpersonal behavior. *Psychological Review, 68*, 341–353.

Foa, U. G., & Foa, E. B. (1974). *Societal structures of the mind*. Springfield, Ill.: Charles C Thomas, 1974.

Fogelman, E., & Wiener, V. L. (1985). The few, the brave, the noble. *Psychology Today, 19(8)*, 60–65.

Folkes, V. S. (1985). Mindlessness or mindfulness: A partial replication and extension of Langer, Blank, and Chanowitz. *Journal of Personality and Social Psychology, 48*, 600–604.

Forer, B. R. (1949). The fallacy of personal validation: A classroom demonstration of gullibility. *Journal of Abnormal and Social Psychology, 44*, 118–123.

Forgas, J. P., & Dobosz, B. (1980). Dimensions of romantic involvment: Towards a taxonomy of heterosexual relationships. *Social Psychology Quarterly, 43*, 290–300.

Forsterling, F. (1985). Attribution retraining: A review. *Psychological Bulletin, 98*, 495–512.

Forsyth, D. R. (1980). The functions of attributions. *Social Psychology Quarterly, 43*, 184–189.

Forsyth, D. R. (1981). A psychological perspective on ethical uncertainties in research. In A. J. Kimmel (Ed.), *New directions for methodology of social and behavioral science: Ethics of human subject research* (Vol. 10). San Francisco: Jossey-Bass.

Forsyth, D. R. (1983). *An introduction to group dynamics*. Monterey, Calif.: Brooks/Cole.

Forsyth, D. R. (1985). Individual differences in information integration during moral judgment. *Journal of Personality and Social Psychology, 49*, 264–272.

Forsyth, D. R., & McMillan, J. H. (1981a). Attributions, affect, and expectations: A test of Weiner's three-dimensional model. *Journal of Educational Psychology, 73*, 393–403.

Forsyth, D. R., & McMillan, J. H. (1981b). The attribution cube and reactions to educational outcomes. *Journal of Educational Psychology, 73*, 632–641.

Forsyth, D. R., & Pope, W. R. (1983). The attribution cube and moral evaluations. *Bulletin of the Psychonomic Society, 21*, 117–118.

Forsyth, D. R., & Pope, W. R. (1984). Ethical ideology and judgments of social psychology research: Multidimensional analysis. *Journal of Personality and Social Psychology, 46*, 1365–1375.

Forsyth, D. R., Pope, W. R., & McMillan, J. H. (1985). Students' reactions after cheating: An attributional analysis. *Contemporary Educational Psychology, 10*, 72–82.

Forsyth, D. R., & Schlenker, B. R. (1977). Attributing the causes of group performance: Effects of performance quality, task importance, and future testing. *Journal of Personality, 45*, 220–236.

Forsyth, D. R., Schlenker, B. R., Leary, M. R., & McCown, N. E. (1985). Self-presentational determinants of sex differences in leadership behavior. *Small Group Behavior, 16*, 197–210.

Forsyth, D. R., & Strong, S. R. (1986). The scientific study of counseling and psychotherapy: A unificationist view. *American Psychologist, 41*, 113–119.

Forsyth, N. L., & Forsyth, D. R. (1982). Internality, controllability, and the effectiveness of attributional interpretations in counseling. *Journal of Counseling Psychology, 29*, 140–150.

Foti, R. J., Fraser, S. L., & Lord, R. G. (1982). Effects of leadership labels and prototypes on perceptions of political leaders. *Journal of Applied Psychology, 67*, 326–333.

Fox, S. (1984). *The mirror makers.* New York: Morrow.

Frable, D. E. S., & Bem, S. L. (1985). If you are gender schematic, all members of the opposite sex look alike. *Journal of Personality and Social Psychology, 49*, 459–468.

Frager, R. (1970). Conformity and anticonformity in Japan. *Journal of Personality and Social Psychology, 15*, 203–210.

Frazzini, S. F. (1981). Review of eyewitness testimony. *Yale Review, 70*, xviii–xx.

Freedman, J. L. (1965). The long-term behavioral effects of cognitive dissonance. *Journal of Experimental Social Psychology, 1*, 145–155.

Freedman, J. L. (1973). The effects of population density on humans. In James T. Fawcett (Ed.), *Psychological perspectives on population.* New York: Basic Books.

Freedman, J. L. (1975). *Crowding and human behavior.* San Francisco: Freeman.

Freedman, J. L. (1979). Reconciling apparent differences between responses of humans and other animals to crowding. *Psychological Review, 86*, 80–85.

Freedman, J. L. (1984). Effect of television violence on aggressiveness. *Psychological Bulletin, 96*, 227–246.

Freedman, J. L., & Doob, A. N. (1968). *Deviancy: The psychology of being different.* New York: Academic Press.

Freedman, J. L., & Fraser, S. C. (1966). Compliance without pressure: The foot-in-the-door technique. *Journal of Personality and Social Psychology, 4*, 195–202.

French, J. R. P., Jr., & Raven, B. (1959). The bases of social power. In D. Cartwright (Ed.), *Studies in social power.* Ann Arbor, Mich.: Institute for Social Research.

Freud, S. (1961). *A general introduction to psychoanalysis.* New York: Washington Square Press.

Freuh, T., & McGhee, P. E. (1975). Traditional sex-role development and amount of time spent watching television. *Child Development, 11*, 109.

Frey, D. (1978). Reactions to success and failure in public and private conditions. *Journal of Experimental Social Psychology, 14*, 172–179.

Frey, D. (1981). Postdecisional preferences for decision-relevant information as a function of the competence of its source and the degree of familiarity with this information. *Journal of Experimental Social Psychology, 17*, 51–67.

Frey, D. (1982). Different levels of cognitive dissonance, information seeking, and information avoidance. *Journal of Personality and Social Psychology, 43*, 1175–1183.

Frey, D., & Wicklund, R. A. (1978). A clarification of selective exposure: The impact of choice. *Journal of Experimental Social Psychology, 14*, 132–139.

Fried, R., & Berkowitz, L. (1979). Music hath charms . . . and can influence helpfulness. *Journal of Applied Social Psychology, 9*, 199–208.

Friedman, M., & Rosenman, R. H. (1974). *Type A behavior and your heart.* New York: Knopf.

Gaertner, S. L., & Bickman, L. (1971). Effects of race on the elicitation of helping behavior: The wrong number technique. *Journal of Personality and Social Psychology, 20*, 218–222.

Gaertner, S. L., & Dovidio, J. F. (1977). The subtlety of white racism, arousal, and helping behavior. *Journal of Personality and Social Psychology, 35*, 691–707.

Gaes, G. G., Kalle, R. J., & Tedeschi, J. T. (1978). Impression management in the forced compliance situation: Two studies using the bogus pipeline. *Journal of Experimental Social Psychology, 14*, 579–582.

Gaes, G. G., Quigley-Fernandez, B., & Tedeschi, J. T. (1978). Unclogging the bogus pipeline: A critical reanalysis of the Cherry, Byrne, and Mitchell study. *Journal of Research in Personality, 12*, 189–192.

Galle, O. R., Gove, W. R., & McPherson, J. M. (1972). Population density and pathology: What are the relationships for man? *Science, 176*, 23–30.

Gallup, G. G. (1977). Self-recognition in primates: A comparative approach in bidirectional properties of consciousness. *American Psychologist, 32*, 329–338.

Gallup, G. H. (1978). *The gallup poll: Public opinion 1978.* Wilmington, Del.: Scholarly Resources.

Gallup, G. H. (1980). *The Gallup poll.* August 28, pp. 215–216.

Gallup, G. H. (1983). Gallup poll on mixed marriages. *Parade Magazine,* August 21, p. 8.

Gangestad, S., & Snyder, M. (1985). "To carve nature at its joints": On the existence of discrete classes in personality. *Psychological Review, 92,* 317–349.

Gardner, G. T. (1978). The effects of human subject regulations on data obtained in environmental stressor research. *Journal of Personality and Social Psychology, 36,* 628–634.

Garfinkel, H. (1967). *Studies in ethnomethodology.* Englewood Cliffs, N.J.: Prentice-Hall.

Geen, R. G. (1980). The effects of being observed on performance. In P. B. Paulus (Ed.), *Psychology of group influence.* Hillsdale, N.J.: Erlbaum.

Geen, R. G. (1981). Evaluation apprehension and social facilitation: A reply to Sanders. *Journal of Experimental Social Psycholgy, 17,* 252–256.

Geen, R. G., & Berkowitz, L. (1967). Some conditions facilitating the occurrence of aggression after the observation of violence. *Journal of Personality, 35,* 666–676.

Geen, R. G., & Donnerstein, E. I. (Eds.). (1982). *Aggression: Theoretical and empirical reviews* (Vol. 1). New York: Academic Press.

Gelfand, D. M., & Hartmann, D. P. (1982). Response consequences and attributions: Two contributors to prosocial behavior. In N. Eisenberg (Ed.), *The development of prosocial behavior.* New York: Academic Press.

Geller, D. M. (1982). Alternatives to deception: Why, what, and how. In J. E. Sieber (Ed.), *The ethics of social research: Surveys and experiments.* New York: Springer-Verlag.

Geller, E. S. (1981). Evaluating energy conservation programs: Is verbal report enough? *Journal of Consumer Research, 8,* 331–335.

Geller, E. S., Winnett, R. A., & Everett, P. B. (1982). *Preserving the environment: New strategies for behavior change.* New York: Pergamon.

Gelles, R. J. (1980a). A profile of violence toward children in the United States. In G. Gerbner, C. J. Ross, & E. Zigler (Eds.), *Child abuse: An agenda for action.* New York: Oxford University Press.

Gelles, R. J. (1980b). Violence in the family: A review of research in the seventies. *Journal of Marriage and the Family, 42,* 873–885.

Gerard, H. B. (1983). School desegregation: The social science role. *American Psychologist, 38,* 869–877.

Gerard, H. B., & Mathewson, G. C. (1966). The effects of severity of initiation on liking for a group: A replication. *Journal of Experimental Social Psychology, 2,* 278–287.

Gerard, H. B., & Miller, N. (1975). *School desegregation.* New York: Plenum.

Gerard, H. B., Wilhelmy, R. A., & Conolley, E. S. (1968). Conformity and group size. *Journal of Personality and Social Psychology, 8,* 79–82.

Gerbner, G. (1978). The dynamics of cultural resistance. In G. Tuchman, A. K. Daniels, & J. Benet (Eds.), *Hearth and home: Images of women in the mass media.* New York: Oxford University Press.

Gerbner, G., Gross, L., Morgan, M., & Signorielli, N. (1980). The "mainstreaming" of America: Violence profile No. 11. *Journal of Communication, 30(3),* 10–29.

Gerbner, G., Gross, L., Signorielli, N., Morgan, M., & Jackson-Beeck, M. (1979). The demonstration of power: Violence profile No. 10. *Journal of Communication, 29(3),* 177–195.

Gerdes, E. P. (1979). College students' reactions to social psychological experiments involving deception. *Journal of Social Psychology, 107,* 99–110.

Gergen, K. J. (1984). Theory of the self: Impasse and evolution. In L. Berkowitz (Ed.), *Advances in experimental social psychology* (Vol. 15). New York: Academic Press.

Gergen, K. J., Gergen, M. M., & Meter, K. (1972). Individual orientations to prosocial behavior. *Journal of Social Issues, 28,* 105–130.

Gewirtz, J. L., & Kurtines, W. M. (Eds.). (1984). *Morality, moral behavior, and moral development.* New York: Wiley Interscience.

Gibb, C. A. (1969). Leadership. In G. Lindzey & E. Aronson (Eds.), *The handbook of social psychology* (Vol. 4, 2nd ed.). Reading, Mass.: Addison-Wesley.

Gibbons, F. X. (1978). Sexual standards and reactions to pornography: Enhancing behavioral consistency through self-focused attention. *Journal of Personality and Social Psychology, 36,* 976–987.

Gibbons, F. X., Smith, T. W., Ingram, R. E., Pearce, K., Brehm, S. S., & Schroeder, D. J. (1985). Self-awareness and self-confrontation: Effects of self-focused attention on members of a clinical population. *Journal of Personality and Social Psychology, 48,* 662–675.

Gibbons, F. X., & Wicklund, R. A. (1982). Self-focused attention and helping behavior. *Journal of Personality and Social Psychology, 43,* 462–474.

Giesen, M., & McClaren, H. A. (1976). Discussion, distance, and sex: Changes in impressions and attraction during small group interaction. *Sociometry, 1976, 39,* 60–70.

Gilbert, D. T., & Jones, E. E. (1986). Perceiver-induced constraint: Interpretations of self-generated reality. *Journal of Personality and Social Psychology, 50,* 269–280.

Gilbert, S. J. (1981). Another look at the Milgram obedience studies: The role of the graduated series of shocks. *Personality and Social Psychology Bulletin, 7,* 690–695.

Gillig, P. M., & Greenwald, A. G. (1974). Is it time to lay the sleeper effect to rest? *Journal of Personality and Social Psychology, 29,* 132–139.

Gilmour, D. R., & Walkey, F. H. (1981). Identifying violent offenders using a video measure of interpersonal distance. *Journal of Consulting and Clinical Psychology, 49,* 287–291.

Gilovich, T. (1983). Biased evaluation and persistence in gambling. *Journal of Personality and Social Psychology, 44,* 1110–1126.

Glass, D. C. (1977). Stress, behavior patterns, and coronary disease. *American Scientist, 65(2),* 177–187.

Glass, D. C., & Singer, J. E. (1972). *Urban stress: Experiments on noise and social stressors.* New York: Academic Press.

Glass, D. C., Singer, J. E., & Friedman, L. W. (1969). Psychic cost of adaptation to an environmental stressor. *Journal of Personality and Social Psychology, 12,* 200–210.

Glass, D. C., Singer, J. E., & Pennebaker, J. W. (1977). Behavioral and physiological effects of uncontrollable environmental events. In D. Stokols (Ed.), *Perspectives on environment and behavior.* New York: Plenum.

Goethals, G. R., & Zanna, M. P. (1979). The role of social comparison in choice shifts. *Journal of Personality and Social Psychology, 37,* 1469–1476.

Goetz, T. E., & Dweck, C. S. (1980). Learned helplessness in social situations. *Journal of Personality and Social Psychology, 39,* 246–255.

Goffman, E. (1959). *The presentation of self in everyday life.* Garden City, N.Y.: Doubleday.

Goffman, E. (1961). *Asylums.* Garden City, N.Y.: Doubleday.

Goffman, E. (1963). *Stigma.* Englewood Cliffs, N.J.: Prentice-Hall.

Goffman, E. (1971). *Relations in public.* New York: Basic Books.

Goldberg, C. (1974). Sex roles, task competence, and conformity. *Journal of Psychology, 86,* 157–164.

Goldberg, C. (1975). Conformity to majority as a function of task type and acceptance of sex-related stereotypes. *Journal of Psychology, 89,* 25–37.

Goldstein, A. P. (1983). United States: Causes, controls, and alternatives to aggression. In A. P. Goldstein & M. H. Segall (Eds.), *Aggression in global perspective.* New York: Pergamon.

Goldstein, A. P., & Keller, H. R. (1983). Aggression prevention and control: Multitargeted, multichannel, multiprocess, multidisciplinary. In A. P. Goldstein (Ed.), *Prevention and control of aggression.* New York: Pergamon.

Goldstein, J. H., Rosnow, R. L., Raday, T., Silverman, I., & Gaskell, G. D. (1975). Punitiveness in response to films varying in content: A cross-national field study of aggression. *European Journal of Social Psychology, 5,* 149–165.

Goldstein, M., Kilroy, M. C., & Van de Voort, D. (1976). Gaze as a function of conversation and degree of love. *Journal of Psychology, 92,* 227–234.

Gollob, H. F., Rossman, B. B., & Abelson, R. P. (1973). Social inference as a function of the number of instances and consistency of information presented. *Journal of Personality and Social Psychology, 27,* 19–35.

Gollwitzer, P. M., & Wicklund, R. A. (1985). Self-symbolizing and the neglect of others' perspectives. *Journal of Personality and Social Psychology, 48,* 702–715.

Gonzales, M. H., Davis, J. M., Loney, G. L., Lukens, C. K., & Junghans, C. H. (1983). Interactional approach to interpersonal attraction. *Journal of Personality and Social Psychology, 44,* 1192–1197.

Gordon, W. (1961). *Synectics: The development of creative capacity.* New York: Harper & Row.

Gorn, G. J. (1982). The effects of music in advertising on choice behavior: A classical conditioning approach. *Journal of Marketing, 46,* 94–101.

Graen, G. B., Orris, J. B., & Alvares, K. M. (1971). Contingency model of leadership effectiveness: Some experimental results. *Journal of Applied Psychology, 55,* 196–201.

Green, B. F. (1954). Attitude measurement. In G. Lindzey (Ed.), *Handbook of social psychology* (Vol. 1). Reading, Mass.: Addison-Wesley.

Green, J. A. (1972). Attitudinal and situational determinants of intendent behavior toward blacks. *Journal of Personality and Social Psychology, 22,* 13–17.

Green, S. G., & Mitchell, T. R. (1979). Attributional processes of leaders in leader-member interactions. *Organizational Behavior and Human Performance, 23,* 249–258.

Greenberg, J., & Pyszczynski, T. (1985). The effect of an overheard ethnic slur on evaluations of the target: How to spread a social disease. *Journal of Experimental Social Psychology, 21,* 61–72.

Greenberg, J., Pyszczynski, T., & Solomon, S. (1982). The self-serving attributional bias: Beyond self-presentation. *Journal of Experimental Social Psychology, 18,* 56–67.

Greenberg, M. S., & Shapiro, S. (1971). Indebtedness: An adverse aspect of asking for and receiving help. *Sociometry, 34,* 290–301.

Greene, D., & Lepper, M. R. (1974). Effects of extrinsic rewards on children's subsequent intrinsic interest. *Child Development, 45,* 1141–1145.

Greenwald, A. G. (1975). On the inconclusiveness of "crucial" cognitive tests of dissonance versus self-perception theories. *Journal of Experimental Social Psychology, 11,* 490–499.

Greenwald, A. G. (1980). The totalitarian ego: Fabrication and revision of personal history. *American Psychologist, 35,* 603–618.

Greenwald, A. G. (1981). Self and memory. In G. H. Bower (Ed.), *The psychology of learning and motivation* (Vol. 15). New York: Academic Press.

Greenwald, A. G., & Pratkanis, A. R. (1984). The self. In R. S. Wyer, Jr., & T. K. Srull (Eds.), *Handbook of social cognition* (Vol 3). Hillsdale, N.J.: Erlbaum.

Greenwald, A. G., & Ronis, D. L. (1978). Twenty years of cognitive dissonance: Case study of the evolution of a theory. *Psychological Review, 85*, 53–57.

Greer, D. L. (1983). Spectator booing and the home advantage: A study of social influence in the basketball arena. *Social Psychology Quarterly, 46*, 252–261.

Griffith, C. R. (1921). A comment upon the psychology of the audience. *Psychological Mongraphs, 30(136)*, 36–47.

Gross, A. E., & Fleming, I. (1982). Twenty years of deception in social psychology. *Personality and Social Psychology Bulletin, 8*, 402–408.

Gruder, C. L., Cook, T. D., Hennigan, K. M., Flay, B. R., Alessis, C., & Halamaj, J. (1978). Empirical tests of the absolute sleeper effect predicted from the discounting cue hypothesis. *Journal of Personality and Social Psychology, 36*, 1061–1074.

Grush, J. E. (1980). Impact of candidate expenditures, regionality, and prior outcomes on the 1976 Democratic presidential primaries. *Journal of Personality and Social Psychology, 38*, 337–347.

Grush, J. E., McKeough, K. L., & Ahlering, R. F. (1978). Extrapolating laboratory exposure research to actual political elections. *Journal of Personality and Social Psychology, 36*, 257–270.

Guttman, L. (1950). The basis for scalogram analysis. In S. A. Stouffer (Ed.), *Measurement and prediction*. Princeton, N.J.: Princeton University Press.

Haber, G. M. (1980). Territorial invasion in the classroom: Invadee response. *Environment and Behavior, 12*, 17–31.

Haber, G. M. (1982). Spatial relations between dominants and marginals. *Social Psychology Quarterly, 45*, 219–228.

Hackman, J. R., & Morris, C. G. (1975). Group tasks, group interaction process, and group performance effectiveness: A review and proposed integration. In L. Berkowitz (Ed.), *Advances in experimental social psychology* (Vol. 8). New York: Academic Press.

Hakmiller, K. L. (1966). Threat as a determinant of downward comparison. *Journal of Experimental Social Psychology* (Supplement 1), *2*, 32–39.

Hall, E. T. (1966) *The hidden dimension*. New York: Doubleday.

Halpin, A. W., & Winer, B. J. (1952). *The leadership behavior of the airplane commander*. Columbus: Ohio State University Research Foundation.

Hamachek, D. E. (1978). *Encounters with the self*. New York: Holt, Rinehart & Winston.

Hamill, R., Wilson, T. D., & Nisbett, R. E. (1980). Insensitivity to sample bias: Generalizing from atypical cases. *Journal of Personality and Social Psychology, 39*, 578–589.

Hamilton, D. L. (1979). A cognitive–attributional analysis of stereotyping. In L. Berkowitz (Ed.), *Advances in experimental social psychology* (Vol. 12). New York: Academic Press.

Hamilton, D. L. (1981). Cognitive representations of persons. In E. T. Higgins, C. P. Herman, & M. P. Zanna (Eds.), *Social cognition: The Ontario Symposium* (Vol. 1). Hillsdale, N.J.: Erlbaum.

Hamilton, D. L., & Rose, T. L. (1980). Illusory correlation and the maintenance of stereotypic beliefs. *Journal of Personality and Social Psychology, 39*, 832–845.

Hamilton, D. L., & Zanna, M. P. (1974). Context effects in impression formation: Changes in connotative meaning. *Journal of Personality and Social Psychology, 29*, 649–654.

Hamilton, W. D. (1964). The genetical evolution of social behaviour: I and II. *Journal of Theoretical Biology, 7*, 1–52.

Haney, C., Banks, C., & Zimbardo, P. (1973). Interpersonal dynamics in a simulated prison. *International Journal of Criminology and Penology, 1*, 69–97.

Hansen, R. D., & Donoghue, J. M. (1977). The power of consensus: Information derived from one's own and others' behavior. *Journal of Personality and Social Psychology, 35*, 294–302.

Hansen, R. D., & Lowe, C. A. (1976). Distinctiveness and consensus: The influence of behavioral information on actors' and observers' attributions. *Journal of Personality and Social Psychology, 34*, 425–433.

Hansen, W. B., & Altman, I. (1976). Decorating personal places: A descriptive analysis. *Environment and Behavior, 8*, 491–504.

Hardin, G. (1968). The tragedy of the commons. *Science, 162*, 1243–1248.

Hardyck, J. A., & Braden, M. (1962). Prophecy fails again: A report of a failure to replicate. *Journal of Abnormal and Social Psychology, 65*, 136–141.

Hare, A. P. (1976). *Handbook of small group research* (2nd ed.). New York: Free Press.

Harkins, S. G., Latané, B., & Williams, K. (1980). Social loafing: Allocating effort or taking it easy. *Journal of Experimental Social Psychology, 16*, 457–465.

Harkins, S. G., & Petty, R. E. (1982). Effects of task difficulty and task uniqueness on social loafing. *Journal of Personality and Social Psychology, 43*, 1214–1229.

Harootunian, B., & Apter, S. J. (1983). Violence in school. In A. P. Goldstein (Ed.), *Prevention and control of aggression*. New York: Pergamon.

Harrell, A. W. (1978). Physical attractiveness, self-disclosure, and helping behavior. *Journal of Social Psychology, 104*, 15–17.

Harris, B., & Harvey, J. H. (1975). Self-attributed choice as a function of the consequences of a decision. *Journal of Personality and Social Psychology, 31*, 1013–1019.

Harris, B., Luginbuhl, J. R., & Fishbein, J. E. (1978). Density and personal space in a field setting. *Social Psychology, 41*, 350–353.

Harris, M. B., & Huang, L. C. (1973). Helping and the attribution process. *Journal of Social Psychology, 90*, 291–297.

Harris, M. J., & Rosenthal, R. (1985). Mediation of interpersonal expectancy effects. *Psychological Bulletin, 97,* 363–386.

Harrison, A. A., Hwalek, M., Raney, D. F., & Fritz, J. G. (1978). Cues to deception in an interview situation. *Social Psychology, 41,* 156–161.

Hartshorne, H., & May, M. A. (1928). *Studies in the nature of character: Studies in deceit (Vol. 1); Studies in self-control (Vol. 2); Studies in the organization of character (Vol. 3).* New York: Macmillan.

Hartup, W. W. (1974). Aggression in childhood: Developmental perspectives. *American Psychologist, 29,* 336–341.

Harvey, J. H., Ickes, W. J., & Kidd, R. F. (1978). A conversation with Edward E. Jones and Harold H. Kelley. In J. H. Harvey, W. J. Ickes, & R. F. Kidd (Eds.), *New directions in attribution research* (Vol. 2). Hillsdale, N.J.: Erlbaum.

Harvey, J. H., & McGlynn, R. P. (1982). Matching words to phenomena: The case of the fundamental attribution error. *Journal of Personality and Social Psychology, 43,* 345–346.

Harvey, J. H., Town, J. P., & Yarkin, K. L. (1981). How fundamental is "The fundamental attribution error?" *Journal of Personality and Social Psychology, 40,* 346–349.

Harvey, J. H., & Weary, G. (1981). *Perspectives on attributional processes.* Dubuque, Iowa: Wm. C. Brown.

Harvey, O. J., Hunt, D. E., & Schroeder, H. M. (1961). *Conceptual systems and personality organization.* New York: Wiley.

Hass, R. G. (1984). Perspective taking and self–awareness: Drawing an E on your forehead. *Journal of Personality and Social Psychology, 46,* 788–798.

Hastie, R. (1984). Causes and effects of causal attribution. *Journal of Personality and Social Psychology, 46,* 44–56.

Hastie, R., Ostrom, T. M., Ebbesen, E. B., Wyer, R. S., Hamilton, D. L., Carlston, D. E. (Eds.). (1980). *Person memory: The cognitive basis of social perception.* Hillsdale, N.J.: Erlbaum.

Hastie, R., Penrod, S. D., & Pennington, N. (1983). *Inside the jury.* Cambridge, Mass.: Harvard University Press.

Hayduk, L. (1978). Personal space: An evaluative and orienting overview. *Psychological Bulletin, 85,* 117–134.

Hayduk, L. (1983). Personal space: Where we now stand. *Psychological Bulletin, 94,* 293–335.

Hays, R. B. (1985). A longitudinal study of friendship development. *Journal of Personality and Social Psychology, 48,* 909–924.

Hays, R. B., & Oxley, D. (1986). Social network development and functioning during a life transition. *Journal of Personality and Social Psychology, 50,* 304–313.

Heider, F. (1958). *The psychology of interpersonal relations.* New York: Wiley.

Heller, J. F., Groff, B. D., & Solomon, S. H. (1977). Toward an understanding of crowding: The role of physical interaction. *Journal of Personality and Social Psychology, 35,* 183–190.

Hendrick, C. (1977). Role-taking, role-playing, and the laboratory experiment. *Personality and Social Psychology Bulletin, 3,* 467–478.

Hendrick, C., & Hendrick, S. (1983). *Liking, loving, and relating.* Monterey, Calif.: Brooks/Cole.

Hendrick, C., & Hendrick, S. (1986). A theory and method of love. *Journal of Personality and Social Psychology, 50,* 392–402.

Hendrick, S., Hendrick, C., Slapion-Foote, M. J., & Foote, F. H. (1985). Gender differences in sexual attitudes. *Journal of Personality and Social Psychology, 48,* 1630–1642.

Hendrick, S. S. (1981). Self-disclosure and marital satisfaction. *Journal of Personality and Social Psychology, 40,* 1150–1159.

Henley, N. M. (1977). *Body politics: Power, sex, and nonverbal communication.* Englewood Cliffs, N.J.: Prentice Hall.

Heppner, P. P., & Dixon, D. N. (1981). A review of the interpersonal influence process in counseling. *Personnel and Guidance Journal, 59,* 542–550.

Hersey, P., & Blanchard, K. H. (1976). Leadership effectiveness and adaptability description (LEAD). In J. W. Pfeiffer & J. E. Jones (Eds.), *The 1976 annual handbook for group facilitators* (Vol. 5). La Jolla, Calif.: University Associates.

Hersey, P., & Blanchard, K. H. (1977). *Management of organization behavior: Utilizing human resources* (3rd ed.). Englewood Cliffs, N.J.: Prentice-Hall.

Heshka, S., & Nelson, Y. (1972). Interpersonal speaking distance as a function of age, sex, and relationship. *Sociometry, 25,* 491–498.

Heslin, R., & Patterson, M. L. (1982). *Nonverbal behavior and social psychology.* New York: Plenum.

Higbee, K. L. (1969). Fifteen years of fear arousal: Research on threat appeals: 1953–1968. *Psychological Bulletin, 72,* 426–444.

Higbee, K. L., Millard, R. J., & Folkman, J. R. (1982). Social psychology research during the 1970s: Predominance of experimentation and college students. *Personality and Social Psychology Bulletin, 8,* 180–183.

Higgins, E. T., King, G. A., & Mavin, G. H. (1982). Individual construct accessibility and subjective impression and recall. *Journal of Personality and Social Psychology, 43,* 35–47.

Higgins, E. T., Rhodewalt, F., & Zanna, M. P. (1979). Dissonance motivation: Its nature, persistence, and reinstatement. *Journal of Experimental Social Psychology, 15,* 16–34.

Higgins, E. T., Rholes, W. S., & Jones, C. R. (1977). Category accessibility and impression formation. *Journal of Experimental Social Psychology, 13,* 141–154.

Hill, C. T., Rubin, Z., & Peplau, L. A. (1976). Breakups before marriage: The end of 103 affairs. *Journal of Social Issues, 32(1),* 147–167.

Hill, C. T., & Stull, D. E. (1981). Sex differences in effects of social and value similarity in same–sex friendship. *Journal of Personality and Social Psychology, 41,* 488–502.

Hirokawa, R. Y. (1980). A comparative analysis of communication patterns within effective and ineffective decision-making groups. *Communication Monographs, 47,* 312–321.

Hirokawa, R. Y. (1984). Does consensus really result in higher quality group decisions? In G. M. Phillips & J. T. Wood (Eds.), *Emergent issues in human decision making.* Carbondale, Ill.: Southern Illinois University Press.

Hoelter, J. W. (1983). The effects of role evaluation and commitment on identity salience. *Social Psychology Quarterly, 46,* 140–147.

Hoelter, J. W. (1984). Relative effects of significant others on self-evaluation. *Social Psychology Quarterly, 47,* 255–262.

Hoffman, M. L. (1981). Is altruism part of human nature? *Journal of Personality and Social Psychology, 40,* 121–137.

Hokanson, J. E. (1970). Psychophysiological evaluation of the catharsis hypothesis. In E. I. Megargee & J. E. Hokanson (Eds.), *The dynamics of aggression: Individual, group, and international analyses.* New York: Harper & Row.

Hokanson, J. E., & Burgess, M. (1962a). The effects of three types of aggression on vascular processes. *Journal of Abnormal and Social Psychology, 64,* 446–449.

Hokanson, J. E., & Burgess, M. (1962b). The effects of status, type of frustration and aggression on vascular processes. *Journal of Abnormal and Social Psychology, 65,* 232–237.

Hokanson, J. E., & Shetler, S. (1961). The effect of overt aggression on physiological arousal. *Journal of Abnormal and Social Psychology, 63,* 446–448.

Hokanson, J. E., Willers, K. R., & Koropsak, E. (1968). The modification of autonomic responses during aggressive interchange. *Journal of Personality, 36,* 386–404.

Hollander, E. P. (1958). Conformity, status, and idiosyncrasy credit. *Psychological Review, 65,* 117–127.

Hollander, E. P. (1960). Competence and conformity in the acceptance of influence. *Journal of Abnormal and Social Psychology, 61,* 365–369.

Hollander, E. P. (1961). Some effects of perceived status on responses to innovative behavior. *Journal of Abnormal and Social Psychology, 63,* 247–250.

Hollander, E. P. (1978). *Leadership dynamics: A practical guide to effective relationships.* New York: Free Press.

Hollander, E. P. (1981). *Principles and methods of social psychology.* New York: Oxford University Press.

Hollander, E. P. (1985). Leadership and power. In G. Lindzey & E. Aronson (Eds.), *Handbook of social psychology* (Vol. 2, 3rd ed.). New York: Random House.

Holmes, D. S. (1981). Existence of classical projection and the stress-reducing function of attributive projection: A reply to Sherwood. *Psychological Bulletin, 90,* 460–466.

Homans, G. C. (1961). *The human group.* New York: Harcourt, Brace, & World.

Horai, J., Naccari, N., & Fatoullah, E. (1974). The effects of expertise and physical attractiveness upon opinion agreement and liking. *Sociometry, 37,* 601–606.

Hornstein, H. A. (1982). Promotive tension: Theory and research. In V. J. Derlega & J. Grzelak (Eds.), *Cooperation and helping behavior.* New York: Academic Press.

Hornstein, H. A., Masor, H., Sole, K., & Heilman, M. (1971). Effects of sentiment and completion of a helping act on observer helping. *Journal of Personality and Social Psychology, 17,* 107–112.

Hovland, C. I., Janis, I. L., and Kelley, H. H. (1953). *Communication and persuasion.* New Haven: Yale University Press.

Hovland, C. I., Lumsdaine, A. A., & Sheffield, F. D. (1949). *Experiments on mass communication.* Princeton, N.J.: Princeton University Press.

Hovland, C. I., & Mandell, W. (1952). An experimental comparison of conclusion-drawing by the communicator and by the audience. *Journal of Abnormal and Social Psychology, 47,* 581–588.

Hovland, C. I., & Weiss, W. (1951). The influence of source credibility on communication effectiveness. *Public Opinion Quarterly, 15,* 635–650.

Howard, J., & Rothbart, M. (1980). Social categorization and memory for ingroup and outgroup behavior. *Journal of Personality and Social Psychology, 38,* 301–308.

Hrdy, S. B. (1977). Infanticide as a primate reproductive strategy. *American Scientist, 65,* 40–49.

Huesmann, L. R. (1982). TV violence and aggressive behavior. In D. Pearl, L. Bouthilet, & J. Lazar (Eds.), *Television and behavior, ten years of scientific progress and implications for the eighties.* Rockville, Md.: NIMH.

Huff, D. (1954). *How to lie with statistics.* New York: Norton.

Hunt, M. (1974). *Sexual behavior in the 1970s.* New York: Dell.

Huston, T., Ruggiero, M., Conner, E. R., & Geis, G. (1981). Bystander intervention into crime: A study based on naturally occurring episodes. *Social Psychology Quarterly, 44,* 14–23.

Huston, T. L., & Burgess, R. L. (1979). Social energy in developing relationships: An overview. In R. L. Burgess & T. L. Huston (Eds.), *Social exchange in developing relationships.* New York: Academic Press.

Hyman, H. H., & Sheatsley, P. B. (1954). "The authoritarian personality"—a methodological critique. In R. Christie & M. Jahoda (Eds.), *Studies in the scope and method of "The Authoritarian Personality."* New York: Free Press.

Ingham, A. G., Levinger, G., Graves, J., & Peckham, V. (1974). The Ringelmann effect: Studies of group size and group performance. *Journal of Personality and Social Psychology, 10,* 371–384.

Ingram, R. E., Smith, T. W., & Brehm, S. S. (1983). Depression and information processing: Self-schemata and the encoding of self-referent information. *Journal of Personality and Social Psychology, 45,* 412–420.

Insko, C. A. (1965). Verbal reinforcement of attitude. *Journal of Personality and Social Psychology, 2,* 621–623.

Insko, C. A., & Schopler, J. (1972). *Experimental social psychology.* New York: Academic Press.

Insko, C. A., & Wilson, M. (1977). Interpersonal attraction as a function of social interaction. *Journal of Personality and Social Psychology, 35,* 903–911.

Institute for Social Research (1983a). Black Americans surveyed. *ISR Newsletter, 11(1),* 3, 7.

Institute for Social Research (1983b). Why do women earn less? *ISR Newsletter, 11(1),* 4–5, 8.

Institute for Social Research (1985). Racial attitudes. *ISR Newletter, 13(2),* 6–7.

Isen, A. M. (1970). Success, failure, attention, and reaction to others: The warm glow of success. *Journal of Personality and Social Psychology, 15,* 294–301.

Isen, A. M., Clark, M., & Schwartz, M. F. (1976). Duration of the effect of good mood on helping: "Footprints in the sands of time." *Journal of Personality and Social Psychology, 34,* 385–393.

Isen, A. M., Horn, N., & Rosenhan, D. L. (1973). Effects of success and failure on children's generosity. *Journal of Personality and Social Psychology, 27,* 239–248.

Isen, A. M., & Levin, P. F. (1972). Effect of feeling good on helping: Cookies and kindness. *Journal of Personality and Social Psychology, 21,* 384–388.

Isen, A. M., Shalker, T. F., Clark, M., & Karp, L. (1978). Affect, accessibility of material in memory, and behavior: A cognitive loop? *Journal of Personality and Social Psychology, 36,* 1–12.

Isen, A. M., & Simmonds, S. (1978). The effect of feeling good on a helping task that is incompatible with good mood. *Social Psychology, 41,* 346–349.

Izard, C. E. (1977). *Human emotions.* New York: Plenum.

Jackson, J. M. (1986). In defense of social impact theory: Comment on Mullen. *Journal of Personality and Social Psychology, 50,* 511–513.

Jackson, J. M., & Latané, B. (1981). All alone in front of all those people: Stage fright as a function of number and type of co-performers and audience. *Journal of Personality and Social Psychology, 40,* 73–85.

Jackson, J. M., & Williams, K. D. (1985). Social loafing on difficult tasks: Working collectively can improve performance. *Journal of Personality and Social Psychology, 49,* 937–942.

Jacobs, R. C., & Campbell, D. T. (1961). The perpetuation of an arbitrary tradition through several generations of a laboratory microculture. *Journal of Abnormal and Social Psychology, 62,* 649–658.

Jacobson, M. B., & Effertz, J. (1974). Sex roles and leadership perceptions of the leaders and the led. *Organizational Behavior and Human Performance, 12,* 383–396.

James, R. (1959). Status and competency of jurors. *American Journal of Sociology, 64,* 563–570.

James, W. (1961). *Psychology.* New York: Harper & Row. (First published 1892 by Henry Holt and Co.).

Janis, I. L. (1982). *Victims of groupthink* (2nd ed.). Boston, Mass.: Houghton-Mifflin.

Janis, I. L. (1983). Groupthink. In H. H. Blumberg, A. P. Hare, V. Kent, & M. F. Davis (Eds.), *Small groups and social interaction* (Vol. 2). New York: Wiley.

Janis, I. L., & Feshbach, S. (1953). Effects of fear-arousing communications. *Journal of Abnormal and Social Psychology, 48,* 78–92.

Janis, I. L., & Mann, L. (1977). *Decision making: A psychological analysis of conflict, choice, and commitment.* New York: Free Press.

Janisse, M. P., & Peavler, W. S. (1974). Pupillary research today: Emotion in the eye. *Psychology Today, 8(2),* 60–63.

Janoff-Bulman, R. (1979). Characterological versus behavioral self-blame: Inquiries into depression and rape. *Journal of Personality and Social Psychology, 37,* 1798–1809.

Janoff-Bulman, R., Timko, C., & Carli, L. L. (1985). Cognitive biases in blaming the victim. *Journal of Experimental Social Psychology, 21,* 161–177.

Javornisky, G. (1979). Task context and sex differences in conformity. *Journal of Social Psychology, 108,* 213–220.

Jenni, D. A., & Jenni, M. A. (1976). Carrying behavior in humans: Analysis of sex differences. *Science, 194,* 859–860.

Jennings [Walstedt], J., Geis, F. L., & Brown, V. (1980). Influence of television commercials on women's self-confidence and independent judgment. *Journal of Personality and Social Psychology, 38,* 203–210.

Jessor, R., Costa, F., Jessor, L., & Donovan, J. E. (1983). Time of first intercourse: A prospective study. *Journal of Personality and Social Psychology, 44,* 608–626.

Johnson, H. G., Ekman, P., & Friesen, W. V. (1975). Communicative body movements: American emblems. *Semiotica, 15,* 335–353.

Johnson, J. A., Hogan, R., Zonderman, A. B., Callens, C., & Rogolsky, S. (1981). Moral judgment, personality, and attitudes toward authority. *Journal of Personality and Social Psychology, 40,* 370–373.

Johnson, J. T., Cain, L. M., Falke, T. L., Hayman, J., & Perillo, E. (1985). The "Barnum effect" revisited: Cognitive and motivational factors in the acceptance of personality descriptions. *Journal of Personality and Social Psychology, 49,* 1378–1391.

Johnson, R. N. (1972). *Aggression in man and animals.* Philadelphia: Saunders.

Johnson, T. E., & Rule, B. G. (1986). Mitigating circumstances information, censure, and aggression. *Journal of Personality and Social Psychology, 50,* 537–542.

Johnson, T. J., Feigenbaum, R., & Weiby, M. (1964). Some determinants and consequences of the teacher's perception of causation. *Journal of Educational Psychology, 55,* 237–246.

Jones, C., & Aronson, E. (1973). Attribution of fault to a rape victim as a function of respectability of the victim. *Journal of Personality and Social Psychology, 26,* 415–419.

Jones, E. E. (1964). Ingratiation. New York: Appleton-Century-Crofts.

Jones, E. E. (1978). Update of "From acts to dispositions: The attribution process in person perception." In L. Berkowitz (Ed.), *Cognitive theories in social psychology.* New York: Academic Press.

Jones, E. E. (1979). The rocky road from acts to dispositions. *American Psychologist, 34,* 107–117.

Jones, E. E. (1985). Major developments in social psychology during the past five decades. In G. Lindzey & E. Aronson (Eds.), *Handbook of social psychology* (Vol. 1, 3rd ed.). New York: Random House.

Jones, E. E., & Berglas, S. (1978). Control of attributions about the self through self-handicapping strategies: The appeal of alcohol and the role of underachievement. *Personality and Social Psychology Bulletin, 4,* 200–206.

Jones, E. E., & Davis, K. E. (1965). From acts to dispositions: The attribution process in person perception. In L. Berkowitz (Ed.), *Advances in experimental social psychology* (Vol. 2). New York: Academic Press.

Jones, E. E., Davis, K. E., & Gergen, K. J. (1961). Role playing variations and their informational value for person perception. *Journal of Abnormal and Social Psychology, 63,* 302–310.

Jones, E. E., Kanouse, D. E., Kelley, H. H., Nisbett, R. E., Valins, S., & Weiner, B. (Eds.). (1972). *Attribution: Perceiving the causes of behavior.* Morristown, N.J.: General Learning Press.

Jones, E. E., & McGillis, D. (1976). Correspondent inferences and the attribution cube: A comparative reappraisal. In J. H. Harvey, W. J. Ickes, & R. F. Kidd (Eds.), *New directions in attribution research* (Vol. 1). Hillsdale, N.J.: Erlbaum.

Jones, E. E., & Nisbett, R. E. (1971). The actor and the observer: Divergent perceptions of the causes of behavior. In E. E. Jones, D. E. Kanouse, H. H. Kelley, R. E. Nisbett, S. Valins, & B. Weiner (Eds.), *Attribution: Perceiving the causes of behavior.* Morristown, N.J.: General Learning Press.

Jones, E. E. & Pittman, T. S. (1982). Towards a general theory of strategic self-presentation. In J. Suls (Ed.), *Psychological perspectives on the self* (Vol. 1). Hillsdale, N.J.: Erlbaum.

Jones, E. E., Rhodewalt, F., Berglas, S., & Skelton, J. A. (1981). Effects of strategic self-presentation on subsequent self-esteem. *Journal of Personality and Social Psychology, 41,* 407–421.

Jones, E. E., & Sigall, H. (1971). The bogus pipeline: A new paradigm for measuring affect and attitude. *Psychological Bulletin, 76,* 349–364.

Jones, E. E., & Wortman, C. (1973). *Ingratiation: An attributional approach.* Morristown, N.J.: General Learning Press.

Jones, J. M. (1972). *Prejudice and racism.* Reading, Mass.: Addison-Wesley.

Jones, J. M. (1983). The concept of race in social psychology: From color to culture. In L. Wheeler & P. Shaver (Eds.), *Review of personality and social psychology* (Vol. 4). Beverly Hills, Calif.: Sage.

Jones, R. A. (1982). Perceiving other people: Stereotyping as a process of social cognition. In A. G. Miller (Ed.), *In the eye of the beholder: Contemporary issues in stereotyping.* New York: Praeger.

Jones, S. C. (1973). Self- and interpersonal evaluations: Esteem theories versus consistency theories. *Psychological Bulletin, 79,* 185–199.

Jones, W. H. (1985). Interview with J. Meer. *Psychology Today, 19(7),* 33.

Jones, W. H., Freemon, J. E., & Goswick, R. A. (1981). The persistence of loneliness: Self and other determinants. *Journal of Personality, 49,* 27–48.

Jones, W. H., Hobbs, S. A., & Hockenbury, D. (1982). Loneliness and social skill deficits. *Journal of Personality and Social Psychology, 42,* 682–689.

Kadish, S. H., & Paulsen, M. G. (1975). *Criminal law and its processes.* Boston: Little, Brown.

Kahle, L. R., & Berman, J. J. (1979). Attitudes cause behaviors: A cross-lagged panel analysis. *Journal of Personality and Social Psychology, 37,* 315–321.

Kahle, L. R., & Page, M. M. (1976). The deprivation-satiation effect in attitude conditioning without deprivation but with deviant characteristics. *Personality and Social Psychology Bulletin, 2,* 470–473.

Kahneman, D., & Tversky, A. (1972). Subjective probability: A judgment of representativeness. *Cognitive Psychology, 3,* 430–454.

Kahneman, D., & Tversky, A. (1973). On the psychology of prediction. *Psychological Review, 80,* 237–251.

Kahneman, D., & Tversky, A. (1984). Choices, values, and frames. *American Psychologist, 39,* 341–350.

Kalven, H., Jr., & Zeisel, H. (1966). *The American jury.* Boston: Little, Brown.

Kandel, D. B. (1978). Similarity in real-life adolescent friendship pairs. *Journal of Personality and Social Psychology, 36,* 306–312.

Kanouse, D. E., & Hanson, L. R., Jr. (1971). Negativity in evaluations. In E. E. Jones, D. E. Kanouse, H. H. Kelley, R. E. Nisbett, S. Valins, & B. Weiner (Eds.), *Attribution: *Perceiving the causes of behavior.* Morristown, N.J.: General Learning Press.

Kaplan, M. F. (1975). Evaluative judgments are based on evaluative information: Evidence against meaning change in evaluative context effects. *Memory and Cognition, 3,* 375–380.

Kaplan, M. F., & Schershing, C. (1981). Juror deliberation: An information integration analysis. In B. D. Sales (Ed.), *The trial process.* New York: Plenum.

Kassin, S. M. (1979). Consensus information, prediction, and causal attribution: A review of the literature and issues. *Journal of Personality and Social Psychology, 37,* 1966–1981.

Katz, D. (1960). The functional approach to the study of attitudes. *Public Opinion Quarterly, 24,* 163–204.

Katz, I., Cohen, S., Glass, D. (1975). Some determinants of cross-racial helping. *Journal of Personality and Social Psychology, 32,* 964–970.

Katz, P. A. (1978). Attitude change in children: Can the twig be straightened? In P. A. Katz (Ed.), *Towards the elimination of racism.* New York: Pergamon.

Katz, R. (1977). The influence of group conflict on leadership effectiveness. *Organizational Behavior and Human Performance, 20,* 265–286.

Keating, C. F., Mazur, A., Segall, M. H., Cysneiros, P. G., Divale, W. T., Kilbride, J. E., Komin, S., Leahy, P., Thurman, B., & Wirsing, R. (1981). Culture and the perception of social dominance from facial cues. *Journal of Personality and Social Psychology, 40,* 615–626.

Kelley, H. H. (1952). Two functions of reference groups. In G. E. Swanson, T. M. Newcomb, & E. L. Hartley (Eds.), *Readings in social psychology* (2nd ed.). New York: Holt.

Kelley, H. H. (1967). Attribution theory in social psychology. *Nebraska Symposium on Motivation, 15,* 192–241.

Kelley, H. H. (1971a). Attribution in social interaction. In E. E. Jones, D. E. Kanouse, H. H. Kelley, R. E. Nisbett, S. Valins, & B. Weiner (Eds.), *Attribution: Perceiving the causes of behavior.* Morristown, N.J.: General Learning Press.

Kelley, H. H. (1971b). Causal schemata and the attribution process. In E. E. Jones, D. E. Kanouse, H. H. Kelley, R. E. Nisbett, S. Valins, & B. Weiner (Eds.), *Attribution: Perceiving the causes of behavior.* Morristown, N.J.: General Learning Press.

Kelley, H. H. (1979). *Personal relationships: Their structures and processes.* Hillsdale, N.J.: Erlbaum.

Kelley, H. H. (1982). The two major facets of attribution research: An overview of the field. In H. Hiebsch (Ed.), *Social psychology.* New York: North-Holland.

Kelley, H. H. (1983). Love and commitment. In H. H. Kelley, E. Berscheid, A. Christensen, J. H. Harvey, T. L. Huston, G. Levinger, E. McClintock, L. A. Peplau, & D. R. Peterson, *Close relationships.* New York: Freeman.

Kelley, H. H., Berscheid, E., Christensen, A., Harvey, J. H., Huston, T. L., Levinger, G., McClintock, E., Peplau, L. A., & Peterson, D. R. (1983). *Close relationships.* New York: Freeman.

Kelley, H. H., & Stahelski, A. J. (1970a). Errors of perception of intentions in a mixed-motive game. *Journal of Experimental Social Psychology, 6,* 379–400.

Kelley, H. H., & Stahelski, A. J. (1970b). The inference of intentions from moves in the Prisoner's Dilemma Game. *Journal of Experimental Social Psychology, 6,* 401–419.

Kelley, H. H., & Stahelski, A. J. (1970c). Social interaction basis of cooperators' and competitors' beliefs about others. *Journal of Personality and Social Psychology, 16,* 66–91.

Kelley, H. H., & Thibaut, J. W. (1978). *Interpersonal relations: A theory of interdependence.* New York: Wiley.

Kelman, H. C. (1982). Ethical issues in different social science methods. In T. L. Beauchamp, R. R. Faden, R. J. Wallace, Jr., & L. Walters (Eds.), *Ethical issues in social science research.* Baltimore: The Johns Hopkins University Press.

Kelman, H. C., & Hovland, C. I. (1953). "Reinstatement" of the communicator in delayed measurement of opinion change. *Journal of Abnormal and Social Psychology, 48,* 327–335.

Kenny, D. A., & Nasby, W. (1980). Splitting the reciprocity correlation. *Journal of Personality and Social Psychology, 38,* 249–260.

Kenrick, D. T., & Cialdini, R. B. (1977). Romantic attraction: Misattribution versus reinforcement explanations. *Journal of Personality and Social Psychology, 35,* 381–391.

Kenrick, D. T., Cialdini, R. B., & Linder, D. E. (1979). Misattribution under fear-producing circumstances: Four failures to replicate. *Personality and Social Psychology Bulletin, 5,* 329–334.

Kenrick, D. T., & Johnson, G. A. (1979). Interpersonal attraction in aversive environments: A problem for the classical conditioning paradigm? *Journal of Personality and Social Psychology, 37,* 572–579.

Kerckhoff, A. C., & Davis, K. E. (1962). Value consensus and need complementarity in mate selection. *American Sociological Review, 27,* 295–303.

Kerr, N. L., & Bruun, S. E. (1981). Ringelmann revisited: Alternative explanations for the social loafing effect. *Personality and Social Psychology Bulletin, 7,* 224–231.

Kerr, S., Schriesheim, C. A., Murphy, C. J., & Stogdill, R. M. (1974). Toward a contingency theory based upon the consideration and initiating structure literature. *Journal of Personality and Social Psychology, 12,* 62–82.

Kidder, L. H. (1981). *Research methods in social relations.* New York: Holt, Rinehart & Winston.

Kiesler, C. A., Nisbett, R. E., & Zanna, M. P. (1969). On inferring one's beliefs from one's behavior. *Journal of Personality and Social Psychology, 11,* 321–327.

Kiesler, C. A., & Pallak, M. S. (1976). Arousal properties of dissonance manipulations. *Psychological Bulletin, 83,* 1014–1025.

Kihlstrom, J. F., & Cantor, N. (1984). Mental representations of the self. In L. Berkowitz (Ed.), *Advances in experimental social psychology* (Vol. 15). New York: Academic Press.

Kilham, W., & Mann, L. (1974). Level of destructive obedience as a function of transmitter and executant roles in the Milgram obedience paradigm. *Journal of Personality and Social Psychology, 29,* 696–702.

Kim, M. P., & Rosenberg, S. (1980). Comparison of two structural models of implicit personality theory. *Journal of Personality and Social Psychology, 38,* 375–389.

Kimmel, A. J. (Ed.). (1981). *New directions for methodology of social and behavioral science: Ethics of human subject research* (No. 10). San Francisco: Jossey-Bass.

Kinder, D. R., & Sears, D. O. (1985). Public opinion and political action. In G. Lindzey & E. Aronson (Eds.), *Handbook of social psychology* (Vol. 2, 3rd ed.). New York: Random House.

Kingdon, J. W. (1967). *Congressmen's voting decisions.* New York: Harper & Row.

Kipnis, D. (1974). *The powerholders.* Chicago: University of Chicago Press.

Kipnis, D., & Schmidt, S. M. (1983). An influence perspective on bargaining within organizations. In M. H. Bazerman & R. J. Lewicki (Eds.), *Negotiating in organizations.* Beverly Hills, Calif.: Sage.

Kleinke, C. (1977). Compliance to requests made by gazing and touching experimenters in field settings. *Journal of Experimental Social Psychology, 13,* 218–223.

Kleinmuntz, B., & Szucko, J. J. (1984). Lie detection in ancient and modern times. *American Psychologist, 39,* 766–776.

Klentz, B., & Beaman, A. L. (1981). The effects of type of information and method of dissemination on the reporting of a shoplifter. *Journal of Applied Social Psychology, 11,* 64–82.

Klinger, E. (1977). *Meaning and void: Inner experience and the incentives in people's lives.* Minneapolis: University of Minnesota Press.

Knapp, M. L. (1978). *Nonverbal communication in human interaction* (2nd ed.). New York: Holt, Rinehart & Winston.

Knowles, E. (1980). An affiliative-conflict theory of personal and group spatial behavior. In P. B. Paulus (Ed.), *Psychology of group influence.* Hillsdale, N.J.: Erlbaum.

Knowles, E. (1982). A comment on the study of classroom ecology. *Personality and Social Psychology Bulletin, 8,* 357–361.

Knowles, E. S. (1983). Social physics and the effects of others: Tests of the effects of audience size and distance on social judgments and behavior. *Journal of Personality and Social Psychology, 45,* 1263–1279.

Knox, R. E., & Inkster, J. A. (1968). Postdecision dissonance at post time. *Journal of Personality and Social Psychology, 8,* 310–323.

Kohlberg, L. (1969). The cognitive-developmental approach to socialization. In D. A. Goslin (Ed.), *Handbook of socialization theory and research.* Chicago: Rand-McNally.

Kohlberg, L., & Candee, D. (1984). The relationship of moral judgment to moral action. In W. M. Kurtines & J. L. Gewirtz (Eds.), *Morality, moral behavior, and moral development.* New York: Wiley.

Konečni, V. J. (1975a). Annoyance, type, and duration of post-annoyance activity, and aggression: The "cathartic" effect. *Journal of Experimental Psychology: General, 104,* 76–102.

Konečni, V. J. (1975b). The mediation of aggressive behavior: Arousal level versus anger and cognitive labeling. *Journal of Personality and Social Psychology, 32,* 706–712.

Konečni, V. J., & Ebbesen, E. B. (1976). Disinhibition versus the cathartic effect. Artifact and substance. *Journal of Personality and Social Psychology, 34,* 352–365.

Konečni, V. J., Libuser, L., Morton, H., & Ebbesen, E. B. (1975). Effects of violation of personal space on escape and helping responses. *Journal of Experimental Social Psychology, 11,* 288–299.

Koocher, G. P. (1977). Bathroom behavior and human dignity. *Journal of Personality and Social Psychology, 35,* 120–121.

Korte, C. (1970). Effects of individual responsibility and group communication on help-giving in an emergency. *Human Relations, 24,* 149–159.

Korte, C. (1978). Helpfulness in the urban environment. In A. Baum, J. E. Singer, & S. Valins (Eds.), *Advances in environmental psychology* (Vol. 1). Hillsdale, N.J.: Erlbaum.

Korte, C. (1981). Constraints on helping in an urban environment. In J. P. Rushton & R. M. Sorrentino (Eds.), *Altruism and helping behavior.* Hillsdale, N.J.: Erlbaum.

Korte, C., & Kerr, N. (1975). Response to altruistic opportunities in urban and nonurban settings. *Journal of Social Psychology, 95,* 183–184.

Kothandapani, V. (1971). Validation of feeling, belief, and intention to act as three components of attitude and their contribution to prediction of contraceptive behavior. *Journal of Personality and Social Psychology, 19,* 321–333.

Krauss, R. M., Apple, W., Morency, N., Wenzel, C., & Winton, W. (1981). Verbal, vocal, and visible factors in judgments of another's affect. *Journal of Personality and Social Psychology, 40,* 312–320.

Kraut, R. E., & Lewis, S. H. (1982). Person perception and self-awareness: Knowledge of influences on one's own judgments. *Journal of Personality and Social Psychology, 42,* 448–460.

Kraut, R. E., & Poe, D. (1980). Behavioral roots of person perception: The deception judgments of customs inspectors and laymen. *Journal of Personality and Social Psychology, 39,* 784–798.

Krebs, D. L., & Miller, D. T. (1985). Altruism and aggression. In G. Lindzey & E. Aronson (Eds.), *Handbook of social psychology* (Vol. 2, 3rd ed.). New York: Random House.

Kremer, J. F., & Stephens, L. (1983). Attributions and arousal as mediators of mitigation's effect on retaliation. *Journal of Personality and Social Psychology, 45,* 335–343.

Kruglanski, A. W., Friedland, N., & Farkash, E. (1984). Lay persons' sensitivity to statistical information: The case of high perceived applicability. *Journal of Personality and Social Psychology, 46,* 503–518.

Krupat, E. (1977). A re-assessment of role-playing as a technique in social psychology. *Personality and Social Psychology Bulletin, 3,* 498–504.

Kruuk, H. (1972). *The spotted hyena.* Chicago: University of Chicago Press.

Kudoh, T., & Matsumoto, D. (1985). Cross-cultural examination of the semantic dimensions of body postures. *Journal of Personality and Social Psychology, 48,* 1440–1446.

Kuhn, M. H. (1960). Self attitudes by age, sex, and professional training. *Sociological Quarterly, 1,* 39–55.

Kuhn, M. H., & McPartland, T. S. (1954). An empirical investigation of self attitudes. *American Sociological Review, 19,* 68–76.

Kuhn, T. (1962). *The structure of scientific revolutions.* Chicago: University of Chicago Press. (Revised ed. 1970).

Kunst-Wilson, W. R., & Zajonc, R. B. (1980). Affective discrimination of stimuli that cannot be recognized. *Science, 207,* 557–558.

Kutash, I. L., Kutash, S. B., & Schlesinger, L. B. (Eds.). (1978). *Violence: Perspectives on murder and aggression.* San Francisco: Jossey-Bass.

Kutash, S. B. (1978). Psychoanalytic theories of aggression. In I. L. Kutash, S. B. Kutash, & L. B. Schlesinger (Eds.), *Violence: Perspectives on murder and aggression.* San Francisco: Jossey-Bass.

Kutner, B., Wilkins, C., & Yarrow, P. R. (1952). Verbal attitudes and overt behavior involving racial prejudice. *Journal of Abnormal and Social Psychology, 47,* 642–649.

Lakatos, I., & Musgrave, A. (Eds.). (1970). *Criticism and the growth of knowledge.* New York: Cambridge University Press.

Landis, C. (1924). Studies of emotional reactions, II. General behavior and facial expression. *Journal of Comparative Psychology, 4,* 447–509.

Langer, E. J. (1982). Automated lives. *Psychology Today, 16(4),* 60–71.

Langer, E. J. (1983). *The psychology of control.* Beverly Hills, Calif.: Sage.

Langer, E. J., Blank, A., & Chanowitz, B. (1978). The mindlessness of ostensibly thoughtful action. *Journal of Personality and Social Psychology, 36,* 635–642.

Langer, E. J., Chanowitz, B., & Blank, A. (1985). Mindlessness-mindfulness in perspective: A reply to Valerie Folkes. *Journal of Personality and Social Psychology, 48,* 605–607.

Langer, E. J., Janis, I. L., & Wolfer, J. A. (1975). Reduction of psychological stress in surgical patients. *Journal of Experimental Social Psychology, 11,* 155–165.

Langer, E. J., & Newman, H. M. (1979). The role of mindlessness in a typical social psychology experiment. *Personality and Social Psychology Bulletin, 5,* 295–298.

Langer, E. J., & Rodin, J. (1976). The effects of choice and enhanced personal responsibility for the aged: A field experiment in an institutional setting. *Journal of Personality and Social Psychology, 34,* 191–198.

LaPiere, R. T. (1934). Attitudes vs. action. *Social Forces, 13,* 230–237.

Larsen, R. J., & Seidman, E. (1986). Gender schema theory and sex role inventories: Some conceptual and psychometric considerations. *Journal of Personality and Social Psychology, 50,* 205–211.

Latané, B. (1981). The psychology of social impact. *American Psychologist, 36,* 343–356.

Latané, B., & Bidwell, L. D. (1977). Sex and affiliation in college cafeterias. *Personality and Social Psychology Bulletin, 3,* 571–574.

Latané, B., & Darley, J. M. (1968). Group inhibition of bystander intervention in emergencies. *Journal of Personality and Social Psychology, 10,* 215–221.

Latané, B., & Darley, J. M. (1970). *The unresponsive bystander: Why doesn't he help?* New York: Appleton-Century-Crofts.

Latané, B., & Darley, J. M. (1976). Help in a crisis: Bystander response to an emergency. In J. W. Thibaut, J. T. Spence, & R. C. Carson (Eds.), *Contemporary topics in social psychology.* Morristown, N.J.: General Learning Press.

Latané, B., & Nida, S. A. (1981). Ten years of research on group size and helping. *Psychological Bulletin, 89,* 308–324.

Latané, B., Williams, K., & Harkins, S. (1979). Many hands make light the work: The causes and consequences of social loafing. *Journal of Personality and Social Psychology, 37,* 822–832.

Latané, B., & Wolf, S. (1981). The social impact of majorities and minorities. *Psychological Review, 88,* 438–453.

Lau, R. R. (1984). Dynamics of the attribution process. *Journal of Personality and Social Psychology, 46,* 1017–1028.

Lau, R. R., & Russell, D. (1980). Attributions in the sports pages: A field test of some current hypotheses about attribution research. *Journal of Personality and Social Psychology, 39,* 29–38.

Lauer, J., & Lauer, R. (1985). Marriages made to last. *Psychology Today, 19(6),* 22–26.

Lazarus, R. S. (1984). On the primacy of cognition. *American Psychologist, 39,* 124–129.

Leary, M. R. (1982). Hindsight distortion and the 1980 presidential election. *Personality and Social Psychology Bulletin, 8,* 257–263.

Leary, M. R. (1983). *Understanding social anxiety.* Beverly Hills, Calif.: Sage.

Lee, J. A. (1977). A typology of styles of loving. *Personality and Social Psychology Bulletin, 3,* 173–182.

Lepper, M. R., Greene, D., & Nisbett, R. E. (1973). Undermining children's intrinsic interest with external rewards: A test of the overjustification hypothesis. *Journal of Personality and Social Psychology, 28,* 129–137.

Lerner, M. J. (1970). The desire for justice and reactions to victims. In J. Macaulay & L. Berkowitz (Eds.), *Altruism and helping behavior: Social psychological studies of some antecedents and consequences.* New York: Academic Press.

Lerner, M. J., & Miller, D. T. (1978). Just world research and the attribution process: Looking back and ahead. *Psychological Bulletin, 85,* 1030–1051.

Levenson, R. W., & Gottman, J. M. (1983). Marital interaction: Physiological linkage and affective exchange. *Journal of Personality and Social Psychology, 45,* 587–597.

Levenson, R. W., & Gottman, J. M. (1985). Physiological and affective predictors of change in relationship satisfaction. *Journal of Personality and Social Psychology, 49,* 85–94.

Leventhal, H., Singer, R., & Jones, S. (1965). Effects of fear and specificity of recommendation upon attitudes and behavior. *Journal of Personality and Social Psychology, 2,* 20–29.

Levine, D. W., McDonald, P. J., O'Neal, E. C., Garwood, S. G. (1982). Classroom seating effects: Environment or self-selection—neither, either, or both. *Personality and Social Psychology Bulletin, 8,* 365–369.

Levine, D. W., O'Neal, E. C., Garwood, S. G., & McDonald, P. J. (1980). Classroom ecology: The effects of seating position on grades and participation. *Personality and Social Psychology Bulletin, 6,* 409–412.

Levine, J. M. (1980). Reaction to opinion deviance in small groups. In P. B. Paulus (Ed.), *Psychology of group influence.* Hillsdale, N.J.: Erlbaum.

Levine, J. M., & Ranelli, C. J. (1978). Majority reactions to shifting and stable attitudinal deviates. *European Journal of Social Psychology, 8,* 55–70.

Levine, J. M., & Ruback, R. B. (1980). Reaction to opinion deviance: Impact of a fence-straddler's rationale on majority evaluation. *Social Psychology Quarterly, 43,* 73–81.

Levine, J. M., Saxe, L., & Harris, H. J. (1976). Reaction to attitudinal deviance: Impact of deviate's directions and distance of movement. *Sociometry, 39,* 97–107.

Levine, J. M., Sroka, K. R., & Snyder, H. N. (1977). Group support and reaction to stable and shifting agreement/disagreement. *Sociometry, 40,* 214–224.

LeVine, R. A., & Campbell, D. T. (1972). *Ethnocentrism: Theories of conflict, ethnic attitudes, and group behavior.* New York: Wiley.

Levine, S. V. (1984). Radical departures. *Psychology Today, 18(8),* 20–27.

Levinger, G. (1980). Toward the analysis of close relationships. *Journal of Experimental Social Psychology, 16,* 510–544.

Levinger, G., Senn, D. J., & Jorgensen, B. W. (1970). Progress toward permanence in courtship: A test of the Kerckhoff–Davis hypothesis. *Sociometry, 33,* 427–433.

Levinger, G., & Snoek, D. J. (1972). *Attraction in relationship: A new look at interpersonal attraction.* Morristown, N.J.: General Learning Press.

Lewicki, P. (1983). Self-image bias in person perception. *Journal of Personality and Social Psychology, 45,* 384–393.

Lewin, K. (1936). *A dynamic theory of personality.* New York: McGraw-Hill.

Lewin, K. (1951). *Field theory in social science.* New York: Harper.

Lewin, K., Lippitt, R., & White, R. K. (1939). Patterns of aggressive behavior in experimentally created "social climates." *Journal of Social Psychology, 10,* 271–299.

Lewis, H. S. (1974). *Leaders and followers: Some anthropological perspectives.* Reading, Mass.: Addison-Wesley.

Lewis, M., & Kreitzberg, V. S. (1979). Effects of birth order and spacing on mother-infant interactions. *Developmental Psychology, 15,* 617–625.

Leyens, J. P., & Parke, R. D. (1975). Aggressive slides can induce a weapons effect. *European Journal of Social Psychology, 5,* 229–236.

Liebert, R. M., & Baron, R. A. (1972). Short-term effects of televised aggression on children's aggressive behavior. In J. P. Murray, E. A. Rubinstein, & G. A. Comstock (Eds.), *Television and social behavior (Vol. 2): Television and social learning.* Washington, D.C.: Government Printing Office.

Liebert, R. M., Sprafkin, J. N., & Davidson, E. S. (1982). *The early window: Effects of television on children and youth* (2nd ed.). New York: Pergamon.

Likert, R. (1932). A technique for the measurement of attitudes. *Archives of Psychology,* No. 140.

Lindgren, H. C. (1974). Political conservatism and its social environment: An appraisal of the American presidential election of 1972. *Psychological Reports, 34,* 55–62.

Lindzey, G., & Aronson, E. (Eds.). (1985). *Handbook of social psychology* (3rd ed.). New York: Random House.

Lingle, J. H., Dukerich, J. M., & Ostrom, T. M. (1983). Accessing information in memory-based impression judgments: Incongruity versus negativity in retrieval selectivity. *Journal of Personality and Social Psychology, 44,* 262–272.

Linville, P. W. (1982). The complexity-extremity effect and age-based stereotyping. *Journal of Personality and Social Psychology, 42,* 193–211.

Linville, P. W., & Jones, E. E. (1980). Polarized appraisals of out-group members. *Journal of Personality and Social Psychology, 38,* 689–703.

Lippa, R. (1977). Androgyny, sex typing, and the perception of masculinity-femininity in handwriting. *Journal of Research in Personality, 12,* 1–14.

Liska, A. E. (Ed.). (1975). *The consistency controversy.* Cambridge, Mass.: Schenkman.

Livesley, W. J., & Bromley, D. B. (1973). *Person perception in childhood and adolescence.* New York: Wiley.

Loftus, E. F. (1979). *Eyewitness testimony.* Cambridge, Mass.: Harvard University Press.

Loftus, E. F. (1983a). Silence is not gold. *American Psychologist, 38,* 564–572.

Loftus, E. F. (1983b). Whose shadow is crooked? *American Psychologist, 38,* 576–577.

London, P. (1970). The rescuers: Motivational hypotheses about Christians who saved Jews from the Nazis. In J. Macaulay & L. Berkowitz (Eds.), *Altruism and helping behavior: Social psychological studies of some antecedents and consequences.* New York: Academic Press.

Lopez, S. (1986). Brothers short-circuit crime. *Centre Daily Times,* State College, Penn., January 7, p. B–10.

Lord, C. G. (1980). Schemas and images as memory aids: Two modes of processing social information. *Journal of Personality and Social Psychology, 38,* 257–269.

Lord, C. G., & Saenz, D. S. (1985). Memory deficits and memory surfeits: Differential cognitive consequences of tokenism for tokens and observers. *Journal of Personality and Social Psychology, 49,* 918–926.

Lord, R. G. (1977). Functional leadership behavior: Measurement and relation to social power and leadership perceptions. *Administrative Science Quarterly, 22,* 114–133.

Lorenz, K. (1966). *On aggression.* New York: Harcourt, Brace & World.

Lorge, I. (1936). Prestige, suggestion, and attitudes. *Journal of Social Psychology, 7,* 386–402.

Lott, A. J., & Lott, B. E. (1974). The role of reward in the formation of positive interpersonal attitudes. In T. L. Huston (Ed.), *Foundations of interpersonal attraction.* New York: Academic Press.

Lott, B. E., & Lott, A. J. (1985). Learning theories in contemporary social psychology. In G. Lindzey & E. Aronson (Eds.), *Handbook of social psychology* (Vol. 1, 3rd ed.). New York: Random House.

Lowery, C. R., Denney, D. R., & Storms, M. D. (1979). Insomnia: A comparison of the effects of pill attributions and nonpejorative self-attributions. *Cognitive Therapy Research, 3,* 161–164.

Luce, T. S. (1974). Blacks, whites, and yellows: They all look alike to me. *Psychology Today, 8(2),* 105–108.

Lurigio, A. J., & Carroll, J. S. (1985). Probation officers' schemata of offenders: Content, development, and impact on treatment decisions. *Journal of Personality and Social Psychology, 48,* 1112–1126.

Lykken, D. T. (1979). The detection of deception. *Psychological Bulletin, 86,* 47–53.

Lynch, J. J. (1977). *The broken heart: The medical consequences of loneliness.* New York: Basic Books.

Maass, A., & Clark, R. D., III. (1984). Hidden impact of minorities: Fifteen years of minority influence research. *Psychological Bulletin, 95,* 428–450.

McAdams, D. P. (1982). Experiences of intimacy and power: Relationships between social motives and autobiographical memory. *Journal of Personality and Social Psychology, 42,* 292–301.

McAdams, D. P., & Constantian, C. A. (1983). Intimacy and affiliation motives in daily living: An experience sampling analysis. *Journal of Personality and Social Psychology, 45,* 851–861.

McArthur, L. Z. (1972). The how and what of why: Some determinants and consequences of causal attribution. *Journal of Personality and Social Psychology, 22,* 171–193.

McArthur, L. Z. (1981). What grabs you? The role of attention in impression formation and causal attribution. In E. T. Higgins, C. P. Herman, & M. P. Zanna (Eds.), *Social cognition: The Ontario symposium* (Vol. 1). Hillsdale, N.J.: Erlbaum.

McArthur, L. Z. (1982). Physical distinctiveness and self-attribution. *Personality and Social Psychology Bulletin, 8,* 460–467.

McArthur, L. Z., & Baron, R. M. (1983). Toward an ecological theory of social perception. *Psychological Review, 90,* 215–238.

McArthur, L. Z. & Friedman, S. (1980). Illusory correlation in impression formation: Variations in the shared distinctiveness effect as a function of the distinctive person's age, race, and sex. *Journal of Personality and Social Psychology, 39,* 615–624.

McCallum, R. C., Rusbult, C., Hong, C., Walden, T., & Schopler, J. (1979). The effects of resource availability and importance of behavior upon the experience of crowding. *Journal of Personality and Social Psychology, 37,* 1304–1313.

McCarthy, E. D., Langner, T. S., Gerstein, J. C., Eisenberg, J. G., & Orzeck, L. (1975). Violence and behavior disorders. *Journal of Communication, 25,* 71–85.

McCauley, C. C., Stitt, L., & Segal, M. (1980). Stereotyping: From prejudice to prediction. *Psychological Bulletin, 87,* 195–208.

McClelland, D. C. (1980). Motive dispositions: The merits of operant and respondent measures. In L. Wheeler (Ed.), *Review of personality and social psychology* (Vol. 1). Beverly Hills, Calif.: Sage.

McClelland, D. C. (1985). How motives, skills, and values determine what people do. *American Psychologist, 40,* 812–825.

McCloskey, M., & Egeth, H. E. (1983a). Eyewitness identification: What can a psychologist tell a jury? *American Psychologist, 38,* 550–563.

McCloskey, M., & Egeth, H. E. (1983b). A time to speak, or a time to keep silence? *American Psychologist, 38,* 573–575.

McDougall, W. (1908). *Introduction to social psychology.* London: Methuen.

McGovern, L. P. (1976). Dispositional social anxiety and helping behavior under three conditions of threat. *Journal of Personality, 44,* 84–97.

McGrath, J. E. (1984). *Groups: Interaction and performance.* Englewood Cliffs, N.J.: Prentice-Hall.

McGuire, W. J. (1964). Inducing resistance to persuasion. In L. Berkowitz (Ed.), *Advances in experimental social psychology* (Vol. 1). New York: Academic Press.

McGuire, W. J. (1968). Personality and susceptibility to social influence. In E. F. Borgatta & W. W. Lambert (Eds.), *Handbook of personality theory and research.* Chicago: Rand McNally.

McGuire, W. J. (1969). The nature of attitudes and attitude change. In G. Lindzey & E. Aronson (Eds.), *Handbook of social psychology* (Vol. 3, 2nd ed.). Reading, Mass.: Addison Wesley.

McGuire, W. J. (1985). Attitudes and attitude change. In G. Lindzey & E. Aronson (Eds.), *Handbook of social psychology.* (Vol. 2, 3rd ed.). New York: Random House.

McGuire, W. J., & McGuire, C. V. (1981). The spontaneous self-concept as affected by personal distinctiveness. In M. D. Lynch, A. A. Norem-Hebeisen, & K. J. Gergen (Eds.), *Self-concept: Advances in theory and research.* Cambridge, Mass.: Ballinger.

McGuire, W. J., & McGuire, C. V. (1982). Significant others in self-space: Sex differences and developmental trends in the social self. In J. Suls (Ed.), *Psychological perspectives on the self* (Vol. 1). Hillsdale, N.J.: Erlbaum.

McGuire, W. J., & Padawer-Singer, A. (1976). Trait salience in the spontaneous self-concept. *Journal of Personality and Social Psychology, 33,* 743–754.

McGuire, W. J., & Papageorgis, D. (1961). The relative efficacy of various types of prior belief-defense in producing immunity from persuasion. *Journal of Abnormal and Social Psychology, 62,* 327–337.

McHugh, M., Beckman, L., & Frieze, I. H. (1979). Analyzing alcoholism. In I. H. Frieze, D. Bar-Tal, & J. S. Carroll (Eds.), *New approaches to social problems: Applications of attribution theory.* San Francisco: Jossey-Bass.

MacLachlan, J. (1979). What people really think of fast talkers. *Psychology Today, 13(11),* 113–117.

McMahon, J. T. (1972). The contingency model: Logic and method revisited. *Personnel Psychology, 25,* 697–710.

McNeil, J. C. (1975). Feminism, femininity, and the television series: A content analysis. *Journal of Broadcasting, 19,* 259–271.

McNeill, D. (1985). So you think gestures are nonverbal? *Psychological Review, 92,* 350–371.

Maier, N. R. F., & Solem, A. R. (1952). The contribution of a discussion leader to the quality of group thinking: The effective use of minority opinions. *Human Relations, 5,* 277–288.

Major, B. (1981). Gender patterns in touching behavior. In C. Mayo & N. M. Henley (Eds.), *Gender and nonverbal behavior.* New York: Springer-Verlag.

Maki, J. E., Thorngate, W. B., & McClintock, C. G. (1979). Prediction and perception of social motives. *Journal of Personality and Social Psychology, 37,* 203–220.

Malamuth, N. M. (1985). The mass media and aggression against women: Research findings and prevention. In A. W. Burgess (Ed.), *Rape and sexual assault.* New York: Garland.

Malamuth, N. M., Check, J. V. P., & Briere, J. (1986). Sexual arousal in response to aggression: Ideological, aggressive, and sexual correlates. *Journal of Personality and Social Psychology, 50,* 330–340.

Malamuth, N. M., & Donnerstein, E. (1982). The effects of aggressive-pornographic mass media stimuli. In L. Berkowitz (Ed.), *Advances in experimental social psychology* (Vol. 15). New York: Academic Press.

Malamuth, N. M., & Donnerstein, E. (Eds.). (1984). *Pornography and sexual aggression.* New York: Academic Press.

Mallick, S. K., & McCandless, B. R. (1966). A study of catharsis of aggression. *Journal of Personality and Social Psychology, 4,* 591–596.

Malpass, R. S., & Devine, P. G. (1984). Research on suggestion in lineups and photospreads. In G. L. Wells & E. F. Loftus (Eds.), *Eyewitness testimony: Psychological perspectives.* New York: Cambridge University Press.

Manicas, P. T., & Secord, P. F. (1982). Implications for psychology of the new philosophy of science. *American Psychologist, 38,* 399–413.

Manis, M. (1955). Social interaction and the self-concept. *Journal of Abnormal and Social Psychology, 51,* 362–370.

Manis, M., Gleason, T. C., & Dawes, R. M. (1966). The evaluation of complex social stimuli. *Journal of Personality and Social Psychology, 3,* 404–419.

Mann, L. (1979). Sports crowds viewed from the perspective of collective behavior. In J. H. Goldstein (Ed.), *Sports, games, and play: Social and psychological viewpoints.* Hillsdale, N.J.: Erlbaum.

Mann, L. (1981). The baiting crowd in episodes of threatened suicide. *Journal of Personality and Social Psychology, 41,* 703–709.

Mann, R. D. (1967). *Interpersonal styles and group development.* New York: Wiley.

Manning, M. M., & Wright. T. L. (1983). Self-efficacy expectancies, outcome expectancies, and the persistence of pain control in childbirth. *Journal of Personality and Social Psychology, 45,* 421–431.

Mantell, D. M. (1971). The potential for violence in Germany. *Journal of Social Issues, 27(4),* 101–112.

Manucia, G. K., Baumann, D. J., & Cialdini, R. B. (1984). Mood influences on helping: Direct effects or side effects? *Journal of Personality and Social Psychology, 46,* 357–364.

Markus, H. (1977). Self-schemata and processing information about the self. *Journal of Personality and Social Psychology, 35,* 63–78.

Markus, H. (1978). The effect of mere presence on social facilitation: An unobtrusive test. *Journal of Experimental Social Psychology, 14,* 380–397.

Markus, H. (1980). The self in thought and memory. In D. M. Wegner & R. R. Vallacher (Eds.), *The self in social psychology.* New York: Oxford University Press.

Markus, H. (1981). The drive for integration: Some comments. *Journal of Experimental Social Psychology, 17,* 257–261.

Markus, H., Crane, M., Berstein, S., & Siladi, M. (1982). Self-schemas and gender. *Journal of Personality and Social Psychology, 42,* 38–50.

Markus, H., & Zajonc, R. B. (1985). The cognitive perspective in social psychology. In G. Lindzey & E. Aronson (Eds.), *Handbook of social psychology* (Vol. 1, 3rd. ed.). New York: Random House.

Marsh, H. W. (1980). The influence of student, course, and instructor characteristics on evaluations of university teaching. *American Educational Research Journal, 197,* 219–237.

Marsh, H. W. (1982). SEEQ: A reliable, valid, and useful instrument for collecting students' evaluations of university teaching. *British Journal of Educational Psychology, 52,* 77–95.

Marsh, H. W., Barnes, J., & Hocevar, D. (1985). Self-other agreement on multidimensional self-concept ratings: Factor analysis and multitrait-multimethod analysis. *Journal of Personality and Social Psychology, 49,* 1360–1377.

Marsh, H. W., & Parker, J. W. (1984). Determinants of student self-concept: Is it better to be a relatively large fish in a small pond even if you don't learn to swim as well? *Journal of Personality and Social Psychology, 47,* 213–231.

Marsh, H. W., Relich, J. D., & Smith, I. D. (1983). Self-concept: The contruct validity of interpretations based upon the SDQ. *Journal of Personality and Social Psychology, 45,* 173–187.

Marshall, G. D., & Zimbardo, P. G. (1979). Affective consequences of inadequately explained physiological arousal. *Journal of Personality and Social Psychology, 37,* 970–988.

Martin, J., Lobb, B., Chapman, G. C., & Spillane, R. (1976). Obedience under conditions demanding self-immolation. *Human Relations, 29,* 345–356.

Martin, J., & Westie, F. (1959). The tolerant personality. *American Sociological Review, 24,* 521–528.

Maruyama, G., Fraser, S. C., & Miller, N. (1982). Personal responsibility and altruism in children. *Journal of Personality and Social Psychology, 42,* 658–664.

Maruyama, G., Rubin, R. A., & Kingsbury, G. G. (1981). Self-esteem and educational achievement: Independent constructs with a common cause? *Journal of Personality and Social Psychology, 40,* 962–975.

Maslach, C. (1979). Negative emotional biasing of unexplained arousal. *Journal of Personality and Social Psychology, 37,* 953–969.

Masling, J. (1966). Role-related behavior of the subject and psychologist and its effects upon psychological data. *Nebraska Symposium on Motivation, 14,* 67–103.

Matthews, K. A., Glass, D. C., Rosenman, R. H., & Bortner, R. W. (1977). Competitive drive, pattern A, and coronary heart disease: A further analysis of some data from the collaborative group study. *Journal of Chronic Diseases, 30,* 489–498.

Maynard Smith, J. (1964). Group selection and kin selection. *Nature, 201,* 1145–1147.

Maynard Smith, J. (1976). Evolution and the theory of games. *American Scientist, 64,* 41–45.

Mead, G. H. (1934). *Mind, self, and society.* Chicago: University of Chicago Press.

Meddin, J. (1979). Chimpanzees, symbols, and the reflective self. *Social Psychology Quarterly, 42,* 99–109.

Meer, J. (1984). Civil rights indicators. *Psychology Today, 18(6),* 49–50.

Meer, J. (1985). Loneliness. *Psychology Today, 19(7),* 28–33.

Mehrabian, A. (1972). *Nonverbal communication.* Chicago: Aldine-Atherton.

Mehrabian, A. (1976). Questionnaire measures of affiliation tendency and sensitivity to rejection. *Psychological Reports, 38,* 199–209.

Mehrabian, A., & Ksionsky, S. (1974). *A theory of affiliation.* Lexington, Mass.: Heath.

Merton, R. (1948). The self-fulfilling prophecy. *Antioch Review, 8,* 193–210.

Mettee, D. R., & Aronson, E. (1974). Affective reactions to appraisal from others. In T. L. Huston (Ed.), *Foundations of interpersonal attraction.* New York: Academic Press.

Meumann, E. (1904). Haus- und Schularbeit: Experimente an Kindern der Volkschule. *Die Deutsche Schule, 8,* 278–303, 337–359, 416–431.

Meyer, J. P., & Mulherin, A. (1980). From attribution to helping: An analysis of the mediating of affect by expectancy. *Journal of Personality and Social Psychology, 39*, 201–210.

Meyer, J. P., & Pepper, S. (1977). Need compatibility and marital adjustment in young married couples. *Journal of Personality and Social Psychology, 35*, 331–342.

Meyer, P. (1970). If Hitler asked you to electrocute a stranger, would you? Probably. *Esquire Magazine, 73(2)*, 128–132.

Middlemist, R. D., Knowles, E. S., & Matter, C. F. (1976). Personal space invasions in the lavatory: Suggestive evidence for arousal. *Journal of Personality and Social Psychology, 33*, 541–546.

Midlarsky, E., & Midlarsky, M. (1973). Some determinants of aiding under experimentally induced stress. *Journal of Personality, 41*, 305–327.

Midlarsky, M., & Midlarsky, E. (1976). Status inconsistency, aggressive attitude, and helping behavior. *Journal of Personality, 44*, 371–391.

Milavsky, J. R., Stipp, H. H., Kessler, R. C., & Rubens, W. S. (1982). *Television and aggression: A panel study.* New York: Academic Press.

Milgram, S. (1963). Behavioral study of obedience. *Journal of Abnormal and Social Psychology, 67*, 371–378.

Milgram, S. (1965). Some conditions of obedience and disobedience to authority. *Human Relations, 18*, 57–76.

Milgram, S. (1970). The experience of living in cities: A psychological analysis. *Science, 167*, 1461–1468.

Milgram, S. (1974). *Obedience to authority.* New York: Harper & Row.

Milgram, S. (1977). *The individual in a social world.* Reading, Mass.: Addison-Wesley.

Milgram, S., & Sabini, J. (1978). On maintaining urban norms: A field experiment in the subway. In A. Baum, J. E. Singer, & S. Valins (Eds.), *Advances in environmental psychology* (Vol. 1). Hillsdale, N.J.: Erlbaum.

Milgram, S., & Shotland, R. L. (1973). *Television and antisocial behavior: Field experiments.* New York: Academic Press.

Miller, A. G. (Ed.). (1972a). *The social psychology of psychological research.* New York: Free Press.

Miller, A. G. (1972b). Role playing: An alternative to deception: A review of the evidence. *American Psychologist, 27*, 623–636.

Miller, A. G. (1982). Historical and contemporary perspectives on stereotyping. In A. G. Miller (Ed.), *In the eye of the beholder: Contemporary issues in stereotyping.* New York: Praeger.

Miller, C. T. (1984). Self-schemas, gender, and social comparison: A clarification of the related attributes hypothesis. *Journal of Personality and Social Psychology, 46*, 1222–1229.

Miller, D. T. (1976). Ego involvement and attributions for success and failure. *Journal of Personality and Social Psychology, 34*, 901–906.

Miller, D. T., & Ross, M. (1975). Self-serving biases in the attribution of causality: Fact or fiction? *Psychological Bulletin, 82*, 213–255.

Miller, E., & Tejwani, G. A. (1984). Effects of music on exercise. Reported by R. J. Trotter, *Psychology Today, 18(5)*, 8.

Miller, N., & Brewer, M. (Eds.). (1984). *Groups in contact: The psychology of desegregation.* New York: Academic Press.

Miller, N., & Campbell, D. T. (1959). Recency and primacy in persuasion as a function of the timing of speeches and measurement. *Journal of Abnormal and Social Psychology, 59*, 1–9.

Miller, N., Maruyama, G., Beaber, R. J., & Valone, K. (1976). Speed of speech and persuasion. *Journal of Personality and Social Psychology, 34*, 615–625.

Miller, N., Rogers, M., & Hennigan, K. (1983). Increasing interracial acceptance: Using cooperative games in desegregated elementary schools. In L. Bickman (Ed.), *Applied social psychology annual* (Vol. 4). Beverly Hills, Calif.: Sage.

Miller, N. E. (1941). The frustration-aggression hypothesis. *Psychological Review, 48*, 337–342.

Miller, N. E., & Dollard, J. R. (1941). *Social learning and imitation.* New Haven, Conn.: Yale University Press.

Mills, C. J. (1983). Sex-typing and self-schemata effects on memory and response latency. *Journal of Personality and Social Psychology, 45*, 163–172.

Minard, R. D. (1952). Race relationships in the Pocahontas coal field. *Journal of Social Issues, 8*, 29–44.

Miolardo, R. M., Johnson, M. P., & Huston, T. L. (1983). Developing close relationships: Changing patterns of interaction between pair members and social networks. *Journal of Personality and Social Psychology, 44*, 964–976.

Mischel, W. (1984). Convergences and challenges in the search for consistency. *American Psychology, 39*, 351–364.

Mita, T. H., Dermer, M., & Knight, J. (1977). Reversed facial images and the mere-exposure hypothesis. *Journal of Personality and Social Psychology, 35*, 597–601.

Mixon, D. (1977). Why pretend to deceive? *Personality and Social Psychology Bulletin, 3*, 647–653.

Mixon, D. (1979). Understanding shocking and puzzling conduct. In G. P. Ginsberg (Ed.), *Emerging strategies in social psychological research.* New York: Wiley.

Moine, D. J. (1982). To trust, perchance to buy. *Psychology Today, 16(8)*, 50–54.

Moine, D. J. (1984). Going for the gold in the selling game. *Psychology Today, 18(3)*, 36–44.

Monahan, J., & Loftus, E. F. (1982). The psychology of law. *Annual Review of Psychology, 33*, 441–476.

Monson, T. C., & Snyder, M. (1977). Actors, observers, and the attribution process: Toward a reconceptualization. *Journal of Experimental Social Psychology, 13,* 89–111.

Mook, D. G. (1983). In defense of external validity. *American Psychologist, 38,* 379–387.

Moore, B., Underwood, B., & Rosenhan, D. L. (1973). Affect and altruism. *Developmental Psychology, 8,* 99–104.

Moore, T. E. (1982). Subliminal advertising: What you see is what you get. *Journal of Marketing, 46,* 38–47.

Morasch, B., Groner, N., & Keating, J. (1979). Type of activity and failure as mediators of perceived crowding. *Personality and Social Psychology Bulletin, 5,* 223–226.

Moreland, R. L., & Zajonc, R. B. (1977). Is stimulus recognition a necessary condition for the occurrence of exposure effects? *Journal of Personality and Social Psychology, 35,* 191–199.

Moreland, R. L., & Zajonc, R. B. (1979). Exposure effects may not depend on stimulus recognition. *Journal of Personality and Social Psychology, 37,* 1085–1089.

Morgan, M. (1982). Television and adolescents' sex role stereotypes: A longitudinal study. *Journal of Personality and Social Psychology, 43,* 947–955.

Moriarty, T. (1975). Crime, commitment, and the unresponsive bystander: Two field experiments. *Journal of Personality and Social Psychology, 31,* 370–376.

Morris, W. N., & Miller, R. S. (1975a). The effects of consensus-breaking and consensus-preempting partners on reduction of conformity. *Journal of Experimental Social Psychology, 11,* 215–223.

Morris, W. N., & Miller, R. S. (1975b). Impressions of dissenters and conformers: An attributional analysis. *Sociometry, 38,* 327–339.

Morris, W. N., Worchel, S., Bois, J. L., Pearson, J. A., Rountree, C. A., Samaha, G. M., Wachtler, J., & Wright, S. L. (1976). Collective coping with stress: Group reactions to fear, anxiety, and ambiguity. *Journal of Personality and Social Psychology, 33,* 674–679.

Moscovici, S. (1976). *Social influence and change.* London: Academic Press.

Moscovici, S. (1980). Toward a theory of conversion behavior. In L. Berkowitz (Ed.), *Advances in experimental social psychology* (Vol. 13). New York: Academic Press.

Moscovici, S. (1985). Social influence and conformity. In G. Lindzey & E. Aronson (Eds.), *Handbook of social psychology* (Vol. 2, 3rd ed.). New York: Random House.

Moscovici, S., & Faucheaux, C. (1972). Social influence, conformity biases, and the study of active minorities. In L. Berkowitz (Ed.), *Advances in experimental social psychology* (Vol. 6). New York: Academic Press.

Moscovici, S., & Nemeth, C. (1974). Minority influence. In C. Nemeth (Ed.), *Social psychology: Classic and contemporary integrations.* Chicago: Rand McNally.

Moscovici, S., & Zavalloni, M. (1969). The group as a polarizer of attitudes. *Journal of Personality and Social Psychology, 12,* 125–135.

Mueller, C. W. (1983). Environmental stressors and aggressive behavior. In R. G. Geen & E. I. Donnerstein (Eds.), *Aggression: Theoretical and empirical reviews* (Vol. 1). New York: Academic Press.

Mueser, K. T., Grau, B. W., Sussman, S., & Rosen, A. J. (1984). You're only as pretty as you feel: Facial expression as a determinant of physical attractiveness. *Journal of Personality and Social Psychology, 46,* 469–478.

Mullen, B. (1983). Operationalizing the effect of the group on the individual: A self-attention perspective. *Journal of Experimental Social Psychology, 19,* 295–322.

Mullen, B. (1985). Strength and immediacy of sources: A meta-analytic evaluation of the forgotten elements of social impact theory. *Journal of Personality and Social Psychology, 48,* 1458–1466.

Mullen, B. (1986). Effects of strength and immediacy in group contexts: Reply to Jackson. *Journal of Personality and Social Psychology, 50,* 514–516.

Mullen, B., Atkins, J. L., Champion, D. S., Edwards, C., Hardy, D., Story, J. E., & Vanderlok, M. (1985). The false consensus effect: A meta-analysis of 115 hypothesis tests. *Journal of Experimental Social Psychology, 21,* 262–283.

Mulvihill, D. J., & Tumin, M. M. (1969). *Crimes of violence. A publication of the National Commission on the Causes and Prevention of Violence.* Washington, D.C.: Government Printing Office.

Murphy, G., & Murphy, L. B. (1931). *Experimental social psychology.* New York: Harper.

Murphy-Berman, V., & Berman, J. (1978). Importance of choice and sex invasions of personal space. *Personality and Social Psychology Bulletin, 4,* 424–428.

Murray, H. G. (1983). Low-inference classroom teaching behaviors and student ratings of college teaching effectiveness. *Journal of Educational Psychology, 75,* 138–149.

Murstein, B. I. (1976). *Who will marry whom? Theories and research in marital choice.* New York: Springer.

Myers, A. M., & Gonda, G. (1982). Empirical validation of the Bem Sex Role Inventory. *Journal of Personality and Social Psychology, 43,* 304–318.

Myers, D. G. (1978). The polarizing effects of social comparison. *Journal of Experimental Social Psychology, 14,* 554–563.

Myers, D. G. (1982). Polarizing effects of social interaction. In H. Brandstatter, J. H. Davis, & G. Stocker-Kreichgauer (Eds.), *Group decision making.* New York: Academic Press.

Myers, D. G., & Bishop, G. D. (1970). Discussion effects on racial attitudes. *Science, 169,* 778–789.

Myers, D. G., & Lamm, H. (1975). The polarizing effect of group discussion. *American Scientist, 63,* 297–303.

Myers, D. G., & Lamm, H. (1976). The group polarization phenomenon. *Psychological Bulletin, 83,* 602–627.

Napolitan, D. A., & Goethals, G. R. (1979). The attribution of friendliness. *Journal of Experimental Social Psychology, 15,* 105–113.

Nelson, E. (1939). Attitudes. *Journal of General Psychology, 21,* 367–436.

Nemeth, C., & Wachtler, J. (1974). Creating the perceptions of consistency and confidence: A necessary condition for minority influence, *Sociometry, 37,* 529–540.

Newcomb, T. M. (1943). *Personality and social change.* New York: Dryden.

Newcomb, T. M. (1953). An approach to the study of communicative acts. *Psychological Review, 60,* 393–404.

Newcomb, T. M. (1960). Varieties of interpersonal attraction. In D. Cartwright and A. Zander (Eds.), *Group dynamics: Research and theory* (2nd ed.). Evanston, Ill.: Row, Peterson.

Newcomb, T. M. (1961). *The acquaintance process.* New York: Holt, Rinehart & Winston.

Newcomb, T. M. (1979). Reciprocity of interpersonal attraction: A nonconfirmation of a plausible hypothesis. *Social Psychology Quarterly, 42,* 299–306.

Newcomb, T. M. (1981). Heiderean balance as a group phenomenon. *Journal of Personality and Social Psychology, 40,* 862–867.

Newman, O. (1972). *Defensible space.* New York: Macmillan.

Newman, O. (1980). *Community of interest.* New York: Doubleday.

Newtson, D. L., & Pennebaker, J. W. (1981). Misattribution after the eruption of Mount St. Helens. Paper presented at the 1981 Meeting of the Capital Area Social Psychological Association, Washington, D.C.

NIMH (National Institute of Mental Health). (1972). *Television and social behavior.* G. A. Comstock & E. A. Rubinstein (Eds.). Washington, D.C.: Government Printing Office.

NIMH (National Institute of Mental Health). (1982). *Television and behavior, ten years of scientific progress and implications for the eighties.* D. Pearl, L. Bouthilet, & J. Lazar (Eds.). Rockville, Md.: NIMH.

Nisbett, R. E., & Bellows, N. (1977). Verbal reports about causal inferences on social judgments: Private access versus public theories. *Journal of Personality and Social Psychology, 35,* 613–624.

Nisbett, R. E., & Borgida, E. (1975). Attribution and the psychology of prediction. *Journal of Personality and Social Psychology, 32,* 932–943.

Nisbett, R. E., Borgida, E., Crandall, R., & Reed, H. (1976). Popular induction: Information is not necessarily informative. In J. S. Carroll & J. W. Payne (Eds.), *Cognition and social behavior.* Hillsdale, N.J.: Erlbaum.

Nisbett, R. E., Caputo, C., Legant, P., & Marecek, J. (1973). Behavior as seen by the actor and as seen by the observer. *Journal of Personality and Social Psychology, 27,* 154–165.

Nisbett, R. E., & Ross, L. (1980). *Human inference: Strategies and shortcomings in social judgment.* Englewood Cliffs, N.J.: Prentice-Hall.

Nisbett, R. E., & Wilson, T. D. (1977). Telling more than we can know: Verbal reports on mental processes. *Psychological Review, 84,* 231–259.

Nisbett, R. E., Zukier, H., & Lemley, R. (1981). The dilution effect: Nondiagnostic information weakens the effect of diagnostic information. *Cognitive Psychology, 13,* 248–277.

Nord, W. R. (1969). Social exchange theory: An integrative approach to social conformity. *Psychological Bulletin, 71,* 174–208.

Normoyle, J., & Lavrakas, P. J. (1984). Fear of crime in elderly women: Perceptions of control, predictability, and territoriality. *Personality and Social Psychology Bulletin, 10,* 191–202.

Northcott, H. J., Seggar, J. F., & Hinton, J. L. (1975). Trends in TV portrayal of blacks and women. *Journalism Quarterly, 52,* 741–744.

Norvell, N., & Forsyth, D. R. (1984). The impact of inhibiting or facilitating causal factors on group members' reactions after success and failure. *Social Psychology Quarterly, 47,* 293–297.

Notz, W. W. (1975). Work motivation and the negative effects of extrinsic rewards. *American Psychologist, 30,* 884–891.

Oflofsky, J. L. (1981). Relationship between sex role attributes and personality traits and the Sex Role Behavior Scale—1: A new measure of masculine and feminine role behaviors and interests. *Journal of Personality and Social Psychology, 40,* 927–940.

O'Riordan, T. (1976). Attitudes, behavior, and environmental policy issues. In I. Altman & J. F. Wohlwill (Eds.), *Human behavior and environment: Advances in theory and research* (Vol 1). New York: Plenum.

Orne, M. T. (1962). On the social psychology of the psychological experiment: With particular reference to demand characteristics and their implications. *American Psychologist, 17,* 776–783.

Orne, M. T., & Evans, F. J. (1965). Social control in the psychological experiment: Antisocial behavior and hypnosis. *Journal of Personality and Social Psychology, 1,* 189–200.

Orne, M. T., & Holland, C. C. (1968). On the ecological validity of laboratory deceptions. *International Journal of Psychiatry, 6,* 282–293.

Osborn, A. F. (1957). *Applied imagination.* New York: Scribner.

Osgood, C. E., Suci, G. J., & Tannenbaum, P. H. (1957). *The measurement of meaning.* Urbana: University of Illinois Press.

Osgood, C. E., & Tannenbaum, P. H. (1955). The principle of congruity in the prediction of attitude change. *Psychological Review, 62,* 42–55.

Oskamp, S. (1984). *Applied social psychology.* Englewood Cliffs, N.J.: Prentice-Hall.

O'Sullivan, M., Ekman, P., Friesen, W. V., & Scherer, K. (1985). What you say and how you say it: The contribution of speech content and voice quality to judgments of others. *Journal of Personality and Social Psychology, 48,* 54–62.

Overmier, J. B., & Seligman, M. E. P. (1967). Effects of inescapable shock upon subsequent escape and avoidance learning. *Journal of Comparative and Physiological Psychology, 63,* 23–33.

Page, M. M. (1969). Social psychology of a classical conditioning of attitudes experiment. *Journal of Personality and Social Psychology, 11,* 177–186.

Page, M. M., & Scheidt, R. (1971). The elusive weapons effect: Demand awareness, evaluation apprehension, and the slightly sophisticated subject. *Journal of Personality and Social Psychology, 20,* 304–318.

Pagel, M. D., & Davidson, A. R. (1984). A comparison of three social-psychological models of attitude and behavioral plan: Prediction of contraceptive behavior. *Journal of Personality and Social Psychology, 47,* 517–533.

Pallak, M. S., Cook, D. A., & Sullivan, J. J. (1980). Commitment and energy conservation. In L. Bickman (Ed.), *Applied social psychology annual* (Vol. 1). Beverly Hills, Calif.: Sage.

Pallak, M. S., & Cummings, W. (1976). Commitment and voluntary energy conservation. *Personality and Social Psychology Bulletin, 2,* 27–30.

Palmer, D. L., & Kalin, R. (1985). Dogmatic responses to belief dissimilarity in the "bogus stranger" paradigm. *Journal of Personality and Social Psychology, 48,* 171–179.

Pantin, H. M., & Carver, C. S. (1982). Induced competence and the bystander effect. *Journal of Applied Social Psychology, 12,* 100–111.

Park, B., & Rothbart, M. (1982). Perception of out-group homogeneity and levels of social categorization: Memory for the subordinate attributes of in-group and out-group members. *Journal of Personality and Social Psychology, 42,* 1051–1068.

Parke, R., Berkowitz, L., Leyens, J., West, S., & Sebastian, R. (1977). Some effects of violent and nonviolent movies on the behavior of juvenile delinquents. In L. Berkowitz (Ed.), *Advances in experimental social psychology* (Vol. 10). New York: Academic Press.

Parkinson, B. (1985). Emotional effects of false autonomic feedback. *Psychological Bulletin, 98,* 471–494.

Passer, M. W., Kelley, H. H., & Michela, J. L. (1978). Multidimensional scaling of the causes for negative interpersonal behavior. *Journal of Personality and Social Psychology, 36,* 951–962.

Patten, S. C. (1977). Milgram's shocking experiments. *Philosophy, 52,* 425–440.

Patterson, M. L. (1975). Personal space—Time to burst the bubble? *Man-Environment Systems, 5,* 67.

Patterson, M. L. (1976). An arousal model of interpersonal intimacy. *Psychological Review, 83,* 235–245.

Patterson, M. L. (1982). A sequential function model of verbal exchange. *Psychological Review, 89,* 231–249.

Paulus, P. B. (1980). Crowding. In P. B. Paulus (Ed.), *Psychology of group influence.* Hillsdale, N.J.: Erlbaum.

Paulus, P. B., Annis, A. B., Seta, J. J., Schkade, J. K., & Matthews, R. W. (1976). Density does affect task performance. *Journal of Personality and Social Psychology, 34,* 248–253.

Paulus, D., Shaffer, D., & Downing, L. (1977). Effects of making blood donor motives salient upon donor retention: A field experiment. *Personality and Social Psychology Bulletin, 3,* 99–102.

Pearce, P. L., & Amato, P. R. (1980). A taxonomy of helping: A multidimensional scaling analysis. *Social Psychology Quarterly, 43,* 363–371.

Pempus, E., Sawaya, C., & Cooper, R. E. (1975). "Don't fence me in." Personal space depends on architectural enclosure. Paper presented at the Annual Meetings of the American Psychological Association, Chicago.

Pennebaker, J. W., & Sanders, D. Y. (1976). American graffiti: Effects of authority and reactance arousal. *Personality and Social Psychology Bulletin, 2,* 264–267.

Penrod, S., & Hastie, R. (1980). A computer simulation of jury decision making. *Psychological Review, 87,* 133–159.

Peplau, L. A., & Perlman, D. (1982). Perspectives on loneliness. In L. A. Peplau & D. Perlman (Eds.), *Loneliness: A sourcebook of current theory, research, and therapy.* New York: Wiley-Interscience.

Peplau, L. A., Rubin, Z., & Hill, C. T. (1977). Sexual intimacy in dating relationships. *Journal of Social Issues, 33,* 86–109.

Peplau, L. A., Russell, D., & Heim, M. (1979). The experience of loneliness. In I. H. Frieze, D. Bar-Tal, & J. S. Carroll (Eds.), *New approaches to social problems: Application of attribution theory.* San Francisco: Jossey-Bass.

Perrin, F. A. C. (1921). Physical attractiveness and repulsiveness. *Journal of Experimental Psychology, 4,* 203–217.

Pessin, J. (1933). The comparative effects of social and mechanical stimulation on memorizing. *American Journal of Psychology, 45,* 263–270.

Peters, L. H., Hartke, D. D., & Pohlmann, J. T. (1985). Fiedler's contingency theory of leadership: An application of the meta-analysis procedures of Schmidt and Hunter. *Psychological Bulletin, 97,* 247–285.

Peterson, C., & Seligman, M. E. P. (1984). Causal explanations as a risk factor for depression: Theory and evidence. *Psychological Review, 91,* 347–374.

Pettigrew, T. (1975). *Racial discrimination in the United States*. New York: Harper & Row.

Petty, R. E., & Cacioppo, J. T. (1981). *Attitudes and persuasion: Classic and contemporary approaches*. Dubuque, Iowa: Wm. C. Brown.

Petty, R. E., Cacioppo, J. T., & Heesacker, M. (1981). The use of rhetorical questions in persuasion: A cognitive response analysis. *Journal of Personality and Social Psychology, 40*, 432–440.

Petty, R. E., Harkins, S. G., & Williams, K. D. (1980). The effects of group diffusion of cognitive effort on attitudes. An information-processing view. *Journal of Personality and Social Psychology, 38*, 81–92.

Petty, R. E., Harkins, S. G., Williams, K. D., & Latané, B. (1977). The effects of group size on cognitive effort and evaluation. *Personality and Social Psychology Bulletin, 4*, 579–582.

Phares, E. J., & Wilson, K. G. (1972). Responsibility attribution: Role of outcome severity, situational ambiguity and internal-external control. *Journal of Personality, 40*, 392–406.

Philipsen, G., Mulac, A., & Dietrich, D. (1979). The effects of social interaction on group idea generation. *Communication Monographs, 46*, 119–125.

Phillips, D. (1974). The influence of suggestion on suicide: Substantive and theoretical implications of the Werther effect. *American Sociological Review, 39*, 340–354.

Phillips, D. (1979). Suicide, motor vehicle fatalities, and the mass media: Evidence toward a theory of suggestion. *American Journal of Sociology, 84*, 1150–1174.

Phillips, D. (1980). Airplane accidents, murder, and the mass media: Towards a theory of imitation and suggestion. *Social Forces, 58*, 1001–1024.

Phillips, D. (1982). The impact of fictional television stories on U.S. adult fatalities: New evidence on the effect of mass media on violence. *American Journal of Sociology, 87*, 1340–1359.

Phillips, D. (1983). The impact of mass media violence on U.S. homicides. *American Sociological Review, 48*, 560–568.

Piaget, J. (1934). *The moral judgment of the child*. New York: Harcourt, Brace.

Piliavin, I. M., Piliavin, J. A., & Rodin, J. (1975). Costs, diffusion, and the stigmatized victim. *Journal of Personality and Social Psychology, 32*, 429–438.

Piliavin, I. M., Rodin, J., & Piliavin, J. A. (1969). Good Samaritanism: An underground phenomenon? *Journal of Personality and Social Psychology, 13*, 289–299.

Piliavin, J. A., Callero, P. L., & Evans, D. E. (1982). Addiction to altruism? Opponent-process theory and habitual blood donation. *Journal of Personality and Social Psychology, 43*, 1200–1213.

Piliavin, J. A., Dovidio, J. F., Gaertner, S. L., & Clark, R. D., III. (1981). *Emergency intervention*. New York: Academic Press.

Piliavin, J. A., & Piliavin, I. M. (1972). Effects of blood on reactions to a victim. *Journal of Personality and Social Psychology, 23*, 353–361.

Pines, M. (1981). The civilizing of Genie. *Psychology Today, 15(9)*, 28–34.

Podlesny, J. A., & Raskin, D. C. (1977). Psychophysiological measures and the detection of deception. *Psychological Bulletin, 84*, 782–799.

Podsakoff, P. M., & Schriesheim, C. A. (1985). Field studies of French and Raven's bases of power: Critique, reanalysis, and suggestions for future research. *Psychological Bulletin, 97*, 387–411.

Pollis, N. P., Montgomery, R. L., & Smith, T. G. (1975). Autokinetic paradigms: A reply to Alexander, Zucker, and Brody. *Sociometry, 38*, 358–373.

Pomazal, R. J., & Clore, G. L. (1973). Helping on the highway: The effects of dependency and sex. *Journal of Applied Social Psychology, 3*, 150–164.

Post-Kammer, P., & Smith, P. L. (1985). Sex differences in career self-efficacy, consideration, and interests of eighth and ninth graders. *Journal of Counseling Psychology, 32*, 551–559.

Prasad, J. (1950). A comparative study of rumours and reports in earthquakes. *British Journal of Psychology, 41*, 129–144.

Prentice-Dunn, S., & Rogers, R. W. (1983). Deindividuation and aggression. In R. G. Geen & E. I. Donnerstein (Eds.), *Aggression: Theoretical and empirical reviews* (Vol. 1). New York: Academic Press.

Prince, G. (1975). The mind spring theory. *Journal of Creative Behavior, 9(3)*, 159–181.

Pryor, J., Gibbons, F. X., Wicklund, R. A., Fazio, R., & Hood, R. (1977). Self-focused attention and self-report validity. *Journal of Personality, 45*, 513–527.

Pyszczynski, T. A., & Greenberg, J. (1981). Role of disconfirmed expectancies in the instigation of attributional processing. *Journal of Personality and Social Psychology, 40*, 31–38.

Pyszczynski, T. A., & Greenberg, J. (1985). Depression and preference for self-focusing stimuli after success and failure. *Journal of Personality and Social Psychology, 49*, 1066–1075.

Quattrone, G. A. (1986). On the perception of a group's variability. In S. Worchel & W. G. Austin (Eds.), *Psychology of intergroup relations* (2nd ed.). Chicago: Nelson-Hall.

Quattrone, G. A., & Jones, E. E. (1980). The perception of variability within in-groups and out-groups: Implications for the law of small numbers. *Journal of Personality and Social Psychology, 38*, 141–150.

Rabbie, J. (1963). Differential preference for companionship under stress. *Journal of Abnormal and Social Psychology, 67*, 643–648.

Rajecki, D. W. (1982). *Attitudes*. Sunderland, Mass.: Sinauer.

Rankin, R. E., & Campbell, D. T. (1955). Galvanic skin response to Negro and white experimenters. *Journal of Abnormal and Social Psychology, 51,* 30–33.

Raven, B. H. (1965). Social influence and power. In I. D. Steiner & M. Fishbein (Eds.), *Current studies in social psychology.* New York: Holt, Rinehart & Winston.

Raven, B. H., & Rubin, J. Z. (1976). *Social psychology: People in groups.* New York: Wiley.

Reeder, G. D. (1982). Let's give the fundamental attribution error another chance. *Journal of Personality and Social Psychology, 43,* 341–344.

Regan, D., & Totten, J. (1975). Empathy and attribution: Turning observers into actors. *Journal of Personality and Social Psychology, 32,* 850–856.

Regan, J. W. (1976). Liking for evaluators: Consistency and self-esteem theories. *Journal of Experimental Social Psychology, 12,* 159–169.

Reich, J. W. (1981). An historical analysis of the field. In L. Bickman (Ed.), *Applied social psychology annual* (Vol. 2). Beverly Hills, Calif.: Sage.

Reich, J. W., & Robertson, J. L. (1979). Reactance and normal appeal in antilittering messages. *Journal of Applied Social Psychology, 9,* 91–101.

Reis, H. T., Senchak, M., & Solomon, B. (1985). Sex differences in the intimacy of social interaction: Further examination of potential explanations. *Journal of Personality and Social Psychology, 48,* 1204–1217.

Reis, H. T., Wheeler, L., Spiegel, N., Kernis, M. H., Nezlek, J., & Perri, M. (1982). Physical attractiveness in social interaction: II. Why does appearance affect social experience? *Journal of Personality and Social Psychology, 43,* 979–996.

Reisenzein, R. (1983). The Schachter theory of emotion: Two decades later. *Psychological Bulletin, 94,* 239–264.

Rempel, J. K., & Holmes, J. G. (1986). How do I trust thee? *Psychology Today, 20(2),* 28–34.

Rempel, J. K., Holmes, J. G., & Zanna, M. P. (1985). Trust in close relationships. *Journal of Personality and Social Psychology, 49,* 95–112.

Ressler, R. K., Burgess, A. W., & Douglas, J. E. (1985). Rape and rape murder: One offender and twelve victims. In A. W. Burgess (Ed.), *Rape and sexual assault.* New York: Garland.

Reston, J. (1975). Proxmire on love. *New York Times,* March 14.

Revitch, E., & Schlesinger, L. B. (1978). Murder: Evaluation, classification, and prediction. In I. L. Kutash, S. B. Kutash, & L. B. Schlesinger (Eds.), *Violence: Perspectives on murder and aggression.* San Francisco: Jossey-Bass.

Reyes, R. M., Thompson, W. C., & Bower, G. H. (1980). Judgmental biases resulting from differing availabilities of arguments. *Journal of Personality and Social Psychology, 39,* 2–12.

Reynolds, P. D. (1979). *Ethical dilemmas and social science research.* San Francisco: Jossey-Bass.

Rhodewalt, F., & Agustsdottir, S. (1986). Effects of self-presentation on the phenomenal self. *Journal of Personality and Social Psychology, 50,* 47–55.

Rhodewalt, F., & Comer, R. (1979). Induced-compliance attitude change: Once more with feeling. *Journal of Experimental Social Psychology, 15,* 35–47.

Rhodewalt, F., Saltzman, A. T., & Wittmer, J. (1984). Self-handicapping among competitive athletes: The role of practice in self-esteem protection. *Basic and Applied Social Psychology, 5,* 197–209.

Rice, B. (1974). Rattlesnakes, french fries, and pupillometric oversell. *Psychology Today, 8(2),* 55–59.

Rice, B. (1985). Performance review: The job nobody likes. *Psychology Today, 19(9),* 30–36.

Rice, R. W. (1978a). Psychometric properties of the Esteem for Least Preferred Co-worker (LPC) Scale. *Academy of Management Review, 3,* 106–118.

Rice, R. W. (1978b). Construct validity of the Least Preferred Co-worker (LPC) score. *Psychological Bulletin, 85,* 1199–1237.

Rice, R. W. (1979). Reliability and validity of the LPC scale: A reply. *Academy of Management Review, 4,* 291–294.

Ridgeway, C. L. (1981). Nonconformity, competence, and influence in groups: A test of two theories. *American Sociological Review, 46,* 333–347.

Ridgeway, C. L. (1982). Status in groups: The importance of motivation. *American Sociological Review, 47,* 76–88.

Ridley, M., & Dawkins, R. (1980). The natural selection of altruism. In J. P. Rushton & R. M. Sorrentino (Eds.), *Altruism and helping behavior.* Hillsdale, N.J.: Erlbaum.

Riecken, H. W., & Boruch, R. F. (1975). *Social experimentation: A method for planning and evaluating social intervention.* New York: Academic Press.

Riess, M., Rosenfeld, P., Melburg, V., & Tedeschi, J. T. (1981). Self-serving attributions: Biased private perceptions and distorted public descriptions. *Journal of Personality and Social Psychology, 41,* 224–231.

Riess, M., & Salzer, S. (1981). Individuals avoid invading the space of males but not females. Paper presented at the Annual Meetings of the American Psychological Association, Los Angeles.

Rigby, K., & Rump, E. E. (1979). The generality of attitude to authority. *Human Relations, 32,* 469–487.

Riggio, R. E., & Friedman, H. S. (1986). Impression formation: The role of expressive behavior. *Journal of Personality and Social Psychology, 50,* 421–427.

Riordan, C., & Riggiero, J. (1980). Producing equal-status interracial interaction: A replication. *Social Psychology Quarterly, 43,* 131–136.

Riordan, C. A., & Tedeschi, J. T. (1983). Attraction in aversive environments: Some evidence for classical conditioning and negative reinforcement. *Journal of Personality and Social Psychology, 44,* 683–691.

Rodin, J. (1985). The application of social psychology. In G. Lindzey & E. Aronson (Eds.), *Handbook of social psychology* (Vol. 2, 3rd ed.). New York: Random House.

Rodin, J., & Langer, E. J. (1980). Aging labels: The decline of control and the fall of self-esteem. *Journal of Social Issues, 36,* 12–29.

Rofé, Y. (1984). Stress and affiliation: A utility theory. *Psychological Review, 91,* 235–250.

Rogers, M., & Miller, N. (1981). The effect of school setting on cross-racial interaction. Paper presented at the Annual Meetings of the American Psychological Association, Montreal.

Rogers, R. W. (1975). A protection motivation theory of fear appeals and attitude change. *Journal of Psychology, 91,* 93–114.

Rogers, R. W., & Mewborn, R. (1976). Fear appeals and attitude change: Effects of a threat's noxiousness, probability of occurrence, and the efficacy of coping responses. *Journal of Personality and Social Psychology, 34,* 54–61.

Rogers, T. B., Kuiper, N. A., & Kirker, W. S. (1977). Self-reference and the encoding of personal information. *Journal of Personality and Social Psychology, 35,* 677–688.

Rogers, T. B., Rogers, P. J., & Kuiper, N. A. (1979). Evidence for the self as a cognitive prototype: The "false alarms effect." *Personality and Social Psychology Bulletin, 5,* 53–56.

Rokeach, M. (1960). *The open and closed mind.* New York: Basic Books.

Ronis, D. L., & Greenwald, A. G. (1979). Dissonance theory revised again: Comment on the paper by Fazio, Zanna, and Cooper. *Journal of Experimental Social Psychology, 15,* 62–69.

Ronis, D. L., & Lipinski, E. R. (1985). Value and uncertainty as weighting factors in impression formation. *Journal of Experimental Social Psychology, 21,* 47–60.

Rook, K. S., & Peplau, L. A. (1982). Perspectives on helping the lonely. In L. A. Peplau & D. Perlman (Eds.), *Loneliness: A sourcebook of current theory, research, and therapy.* New York: Wiley-Interscience.

Rosen, B., & Jerdee, T. H. (1973). The influence of sex-role stereotypes on evaluations of male and female supervisory behavior. *Journal of Applied Psychology, 57,* 44–48.

Rosen, B., & Jerdee, T. H. (1978). Perceived sex differences in managerially relevant characteristics. *Sex Roles, 4,* 837–843.

Rosenberg, M. (1979). *Conceiving the self.* New York: Basic Books.

Rosenberg, M., & Kaplan, H. B. (Eds.). (1982). *Social psychology of the self-concept.* Arlington Heights, Ill.: Harlan Davidson.

Rosenberg, M. J. (1965). When dissonance fails: On eliminating evaluation apprehension from attitude measurement. *Journal of Personality and Social Psychology, 1,* 28–42.

Rosenberg, M. J., & Hovland, C. I. (1960). Cognitive, affective, and behavioral components of attitude. In M. J. Rosenberg, C. I. Hovland, W. J. McGuire, R. P. Abelson, & J. W. Brehm (Eds.), *Attitude organization and change: An analysis of consistency among attitude components.* New Haven, Conn.: Yale University Press.

Rosenhan, D. L. (1970). The natural socialization of altruistic autonomy. In J. Macaulay & L. Berkowitz (Eds.), *Altruism and helping behavior: Social psychological studies of some antecedents and consequences.* New York: Academic Press.

Rosenhan, D. L., Karylowski, J., Salovey, P., & Hargis, K. (1981). Emotion and altruism. In J. P. Rushton & R. M. Sorrentino (Eds.), *Altruism and helping behavior.* Hillsdale, N.J.: Erlbaum.

Rosenhan, D. L., Underwood, B., & Moore, B. S. (1974). Affect moderates self-gratification and altruism. *Journal of Personality and Social Psychology, 30,* 546–552.

Rosenthal, R. (1966). *Experimenter effects in behavioral research.* New York: Appleton-Century-Crofts.

Rosenthal, R. (1969). Interpersonal expectations: Effects of the experimenter's hypothesis. In R. Rosenthal & R. L. Rosnow (Eds.), *Artifact in behavioral research.* New York: Academic Press.

Rosenthal, R. (1973). The mediation of Pygmalion effects: A four-factor "theory." *Papua New Guinea Journal of Education, 9,* 1–12.

Rosenthal, R., & DePaulo, B. M. (1979). Sex differences in eavesdropping on nonverbal cues. *Journal of Personality and Social Psychology, 37,* 273–285.

Rosenthal, R., & Fode, K. L. (1963). Three experiments in experimenter bias. *Psychological Reports, 12,* 491–511.

Rosenthal, R., & Jacobson, L. (1968). *Pygmalion in the classroom: Teacher expectation and pupils' intellectual development.* New York: Holt, Rinehart & Winston.

Rosenthal, R., & Rosnow, R. L. (1974). *The volunteer subject.* New York: Wiley.

Rosenthal, R., & Rosnow, R. L. (1984). *Essentials of behavioral research.* New York: McGraw-Hill.

Rosnow, R. L. (1980). Psychology of rumor reconsidered. *Psychological Bulletin, 87,* 578–591.

Rosnow, R. L. (1981). *Paradigms in transition: The methodology of social inquiry.* New York: Oxford University Press.

Rosnow, R. L., & Kimmel, A. J. (1979). Lives of a rumor. *Psychology Today, 13(6),* 88–92.

Ross, A. S., & Braband, J. (1973). Effect of increased responsibility on bystander intervention: II. The cue value of a blind person. *Journal of Personality and Social Psychology, 25,* 254–258.

Ross, E. A. (1908). *Social psychology.* New York: Macmillan.

Ross, L. (1977). The intuitive psychologist and his shortcomings: Distortions in the attribution process. In L. Berkowitz (Ed.), *Advances in experimental social psychology* (Vol. 10). New York: Academic Press.

Ross, L., & Anderson, C. A. (1982). Shortcomings in attribution processes: On the origins and maintenance of erroneous social assessments. In D. Kahneman, P. Slovic, & A. Tversky (Eds.), *Judgment under uncertainty: Heuristics and biases.* New York: Cambridge University Press.

Ross, L., Bierbrauer, G., & Hoffman, S. (1976). The role of attribution processes in conformity and dissent: Revisiting the Asch situation. *American Psychologist, 31,* 148–157.

Ross, L., Greene, D., & House, P. (1977). The false consensus phenomenon: An attributional bias in self-perception and social perception processes. *Journal of Experimental Social Psychology, 13,* 279–301.

Ross, L., & Lepper, M. R. (1980). The perseverence of beliefs: Empirical and normative considerations. In R. A. Shweder & D. Fiske (Eds.), *New directions for methodology of behavioral science: Fallible judgment in behavioral research* (Vol. 4). San Francisco: Jossey-Bass.

Ross, L., Lepper, M. R., & Hubbard, M. (1975). Perseverance in self-perception and social perception: Biased attribution processes in the debriefing paradigm. *Journal of Personality and Social Psychology, 32,* 880–892.

Rothbart, M., Evans, M., & Fulero, S. (1979). Recall for confirming events: Memory processes and the maintenance of social stereotypes. *Journal of Experimental Social Psychology, 15,* 343–356.

Ruback, R. B., Dabbs, J. M., Jr., & Hopper, C. H. (1984). The process of brainstorming: An analysis with individual and group vocal parameters. *Journal of Personality and Social Psychology, 47,* 558–567.

Rubenstein, C. M., & Shaver, P. (1982). The experience of loneliness. In L. A. Peplau & D. Perlman (Eds.), *Loneliness: A sourcebook of current theory, research, and therapy.* New York: Wiley-Interscience.

Rubin, D. C. (1985). The subtle deceiver: Recalling our past. *Psychology Today, 19(9),* 39–46.

Rubin, Z. (1973). *Liking and loving: An invitation to social psychology.* New York: Holt, Rinehart & Winston.

Rubin, Z. (1985). Deceiving ourselves about deception: Comment on Smith and Richardson's "Amelioration of deception and harm in psychological research". *Journal of Personality and Social Psychology, 48,* 252–253.

Rubin, Z., & Mitchell, C. (1976). Couples research as couples counseling: Some unintended effects of studying close relationships. *American Psychologist, 31,* 17–25.

Ruble, D. N., & Feldman, N. S. (1976). Order of consensus, distinctiveness, and consistency information and causal attribution. *Journal of Personality and Social Psychology, 34,* 930–937.

Ruble, D. N., & Ruble, T. L. (1982). Sex stereotypes. In A. G. Miller (Ed.), *In the eye of the beholder: Contemporary issues in stereotyping.* New York: Praeger.

Rule, B. G., & Nesdale, A. R. (1976). Emotional arousal and aggressive behavior. *Psychological Bulletin, 83,* 851–863.

Rusbult, C. E. (1983). A longitudinal test of the investment model: The development (and deterioration) of satisfaction and commitment in heterosexual involvements. *Journal of Personality and Social Psychology, 45,* 101–117.

Rusbult, C. E., Zembrodt, I. M., & Gunn, L. K. (1982). Exit, voice, loyalty, and neglect: Responses to dissatisfaction in romantic involvements. *Journal of Personality and Social Psychology, 43,* 1230–1242.

Rushton, J. P. (1980). *Altruism, socialization, and society.* Englewood Cliffs, N.J.: Prentice-Hall.

Rushton, J. P. (1981). The altruistic personality. In J. P. Rushton & R. M. Sorrentino (Eds.), *Altruism and helping behavior.* Hillsdale, N.J.: Erlbaum.

Rushton, J. P., & Sorrentino, R. M. (Eds.) (1981). *Altruism and helping behavior.* Hillsdale, N.J.: Erlbaum.

Russell, D. (1982). The causal dimension scale: A measure of how individuals perceive causes. *Journal of Personality and Social Psychology, 42,* 1137–1145.

Russell, D., Cutrona, C. E., Rose, J., & Yurko, K. (1984). Social and emotional loneliness: An examination of Weiss's typology of loneliness. *Journal of Personality and Social Psychology, 46,* 1313–1321.

Russell, D. E. H. (1984). *Sexual exploitation.* Beverly Hills, Calif.: Sage.

Saegert, S. (1978). High-density environments: Their personal and social consequences. In A. Baum & Y. M. Epstein (Eds.), *Human response to crowding.* Hillsdale, N.J.: Erlbaum.

Saegert, S., Swap, W., & Zajonc, R. B. (1973). Exposure, context, and interpersonal attraction. *Journal of Personality and Social Psychology, 25,* 234–242.

Safer, M. A. (1980). Attributing evil to the subject, not the situation: Student reaction to Milgram's film on obedience. *Personality and Social Psychology Bulletin, 6,* 205–209.

Sagar, H. A., & Schofield, J. W. (1980). Racial and behavioral cues in black and white children's perceptions of ambiguously aggressive acts. *Journal of Personality and Social Psychology, 39,* 590–598.

St. John, N. (1975). *School desegregation: Outcomes for children.* New York: Wiley.

Saks, M. J. (1977). *Jury verdicts.* Lexington, Mass.: Heath.

Salovey, P., & Rodin, J. (1984). Some antecedents and consequences of social-comparison jealousy. *Journal of Personality and Social Psychology, 47,* 780–792.

Salovey, P., & Rodin, J. (1985). The heart of jealousy. *Psychology Today, 19(9),* 22–29.

Samerotte, G. C., & Harris, M. B. (1976). Some factors influencing helping: The effects of a handicap, responsibility, and requesting help. *Journal of Social Psychology, 98,* 39–45.

Sampson, E. E. (1985). The decentralization of identity: Toward a revised concept of personal and social order. *American Psychologist, 40,* 1203–1211.

Sanders, G. S. (1981a). Driven by distraction: An integrative review of social facilitation theory and research. *Journal of Experimental Social Psychology, 17,* 227–251.

Sanders, G. S. (1981b). Toward a comprehensive account of social facilitation: Distraction/conflict does not mean theoretical conflict. *Journal of Experimental Social Psychology, 17,* 262–265.

Sanders, G. S., & Baron, R. S. (1975). The motivating effects of distraction on task performance. *Journal of Personality and Social Psychology, 32,* 956–963.

Sanders, G. S., Baron, R. S., & Moore, D. L. (1978). Distraction and social comparison as mediators of social facilitation effects. *Journal of Experimental Social Psychology, 14,* 291–303.

Santee, R. T., & Maslach, C. (1982). To agree or not to agree: Personal dissent amid social pressure to conform. *Journal of Personality and Social Psychology, 42,* 690–700.

Sarnoff, I., & Zimbardo, P. G. (1961). Anxiety, fear, and social affiliation. *Journal of Abnormal and Social Psychology, 62,* 356–363.

Sawyer, A. G. (1973). The effects of repetition of refutational and supportive advertising appeals. *Journal of Marketing Research, 10,* 23–33.

Saxe, L., Dougherty, D., & Cross, T. (1983). *Scientific validity of polygraph testing: A research review and evaluation.* Washington, D.C.: U.S. Congress, Office of Technology Assessment, OTA-TM-H-15.

Saxe, L., & Fine, M. (1981). *Social experiments: Methods for evaluation and design.* Beverly Hills, Calif.: Sage.

Schachter, S. (1951). Deviation, rejection, and communication. *Journal of Abnormal and Social Psychology, 46,* 190–207.

Schachter, S. (1959). *The psychology of affiliation.* Stanford, Calif.: Stanford University Press.

Schachter, S., & Singer, J. (1962). Cognitive, social, and physiological determinants of emotional state. *Psychological Review, 65,* 379–399.

Schachter, S., & Wheeler, L. (1962). Epinephrine, chlorpromazine, and amusement. *Journal of Abnormal and Social Psychology, 65,* 121–128.

Scheier, M. F. (1976). Self-awareness, self-consciousness, and angry aggression. *Journal of Personality, 44,* 627–644.

Scheier, M. F. (1980). Effects of public and private self-consciousness on the public expression of personal beliefs. *Journal of Personality and Social Psychology, 39,* 514–521.

Scheier, M. F., & Carver, C. S. (1977). Self-focused attention and the experience of emotion: Attraction, repulsion, elation, and depression. *Journal of Personality and Social Psychology, 35,* 625–636.

Schein, E. H. (1956). The Chinese indoctrination program for prisoners of war: A study of attempted "brainwashing." *Psychiatry, 19,* 149–172.

Schein, E. H. (1961). *Coercive persuasion.* New York: Norton.

Schifter, D. E., & Ajzen, I. (1985). Intention, perceived control, and weight loss: An application of the theory of planned behavior. *Journal of Personality and Social Psychology, 49,* 843–851.

Schlenker, B. R. (1980). *Impression management: The self-concept, social identity, and interpersonal relations.* Monterey, Calif.: Brooks/Cole.

Schlenker, B. R. (Ed.). (1985). *The self and social life.* New York: McGraw-Hill.

Schlenker, B. R., Bonoma, T. V., Hutchinson, D., & Burns, L. (1976). The bogus pipeline and stereotypes towards blacks. *Journal of Psychology, 93,* 319–329.

Schlenker, B. R., Forsyth, D. R., Leary, M. R., & Miller, R. W. (1980). A self-presentational analysis of the effects of incentives and attitude change following counterattitudinal behavior. *Journal of Personality and Social Psychology, 39,* 553–577.

Schlenker, B. R., & Leary, M. R. (1982). Social anxiety and self presentation: A conceptualization and model. *Psychological Bulletin, 92,* 641–669.

Schlenker, B. R., Nacci, P., Helm, B., & Tedeschi, J. T. (1976). Reactions to coercive and reward power: The effects of switching influence modes on target compliance. *Sociometry, 39,* 316–323.

Schlesinger, A. M., Jr., (1965). *A thousand days.* Boston: Houghton Mifflin.

Schmidt, D. E., & Keating, J. P. (1979). Human crowding and personal control: An integration of the research. *Psychological Bulletin, 86,* 680–700.

Schneider, D. J. (1973). Implicit personality theory: A review. *Psychological Bulletin, 79,* 294–319.

Schneider, D. J., & Blankmeyer, B. L. (1983). Prototype salience and implicit personality theories. *Journal of Personality and Social Psychology, 44,* 712–722.

Schneider, D. J., Hastorf, A. H., & Ellsworth, P. C. (1979). *Person perception* (2nd ed.). Reading, Mass.: Addison-Wesley.

Schneider, D. J., & Miller, R. S. (1975). The effects of enthusiasm and quality of arguments on attitude attribution. *Journal of Personality, 43,* 693–708.

Schofield, J. W. (1978). School desegregation and intergroup relations. In D. Bar-Tal & L. Saxe (Eds.), *The social psychology of education.* Washington, D.C.: Halstead.

Schofield, J. W. (1979). The impact of positively structured contact on intergroup behavior: Does it last under adverse conditions? *Social Psychology Quarterly, 42,* 280–284.

Schramm, W., Lyle, J., & Parker, E. B. (1961). *Television in the lives of our children.* Stanford: Stanford University Press.

Schriesheim, C. A., Bannister, B. D., & Money, W. H. (1979). Psychometric properties of the LPC Scale: An extension of Rice's review. *Academy of Management Review, 4,* 287–290.

Schriesheim, C. A., & Kerr, S. (1977). Theories and measures of leadership: A critical appraisal of current and future directions. In J. G. Hunt and L. L. Larson (Eds.), *Leadership: The cutting edge.* Carbondale, Ill.: Southern Illinois University Press.

Schul, Y. (1983). Integration and abstraction in impression formation. *Journal of Personality and Social Psychology, 44,* 45–54.

Schuman, H., Steeh, C., & Bobo, L. (1985). *Racial attitudes in America: Trends and interpretations.* Cambridge, Mass.: Harvard University Press.

Schwartz, S. H. (1968). Awareness of consequences and the influence of moral norms on interpersonal behavior. *Sociometry, 31,* 355–369.

Schwartz, S. H. (1970). Elicitation of moral obligation and self-sacrificing behavior. *Journal of Personality and Social Psychology, 15,* 283–293.

Schwartz, S. H. (1974). Awareness of interpersonal consequences, responsibility denial and volunteering. *Journal of Personality and Social Psychology, 30,* 57–63.

Schwartz, S. H. (1977). Normative influences on altruism. In L. Berkowitz (Ed.), *Advances in experimental social psychology* (Vol. 10). New York: Academic Press.

Schwartz, S. H., & Clausen, G. T. (1970). Responsibility, norms, and helping in an emergency. *Journal of Personality and Social Psychology, 16,* 299–310.

Schwartz, S. H., & Fleishman, J. A. (1978). Personal norms and the mediation of legitimacy effects on helping. *Social Psychology, 41,* 306–315.

Schwartz, S. H., & Gottlieb, A. (1976). Bystander reactions to a violent theft: Crime in Jerusalem. *Journal of Personality and Social Psychology, 34,* 1188–1199.

Schwartz, S. H., & Howard, J. A. (1980). Explanations for the moderating effect of responsibility denial on the personal norms-behavior relationship. *Social Psychology Quarterly, 43,* 441–446.

Schwartz, S. H., & Howard, J. A. (1981). A normative decision making model of altruism. In J. P. Rushton & R. M. Sorrentino (Eds.), *Altruism and helping behavior.* Hillsdale, N.J.: Erlbaum.

Schwartz, S. H., & Howard, J. A. (1982). Helping and cooperation: A self-based motivational model. In V. J. Derlega & J. Grzelak (Eds.), *Cooperation and helping behavior.* New York: Academic Press.

Scully, D., & Marolla, J. (1984). Convicted rapists' vocabulary of motive: Excuses and justifications. *Social Problems, 31,* 530–544.

Scully, D., & Marolla, J. (1985). Rape and vocabularies of motive: Alternative perspectives. In A. W. Burgess (Ed.), *Rape and sexual assault.* New York: Garland.

Sears, D. O. (1983). The person-positivity bias. *Journal of Personality and Social Psychology, 44,* 233–250.

Sears D. O., & Kinder, D. R. (1985). Whites' opposition to busing: On conceptualizing and operationalizing group conflict. *Journal of Personality and Social Psychology, 48,* 1141–1147.

Sechrest, L., & Belew, J. (1983). Nonreactive measures of social attitudes. In L. Bickman (Ed.), *Applied social psychology annual* (Vol 4). Beverly Hills, Calif.: Sage.

Secord, P. F., & Backman, C. W. (1961). Personality theory and the problem of stability and change in individual behavior: An interpersonal approach. *Psychological Review, 68,* 21–32.

Segal, H. A. (1954). Initial psychiatric findings of recently repatriated prisoners of war. *American Journal of Psychiatry, 111,* 358–363.

Segal, M. W. (1979). Varieties of interpersonal attraction and their interrelationships in natural groups. *Social Psychology Quarterly, 42,* 253–261.

Seligman, M. E. P. (1975). *Helplessness.* San Francisco: Freeman.

Seligman, M. E. P., & Maier, S. F. (1967). Failure to escape traumatic shock. *Journal of Experimental Psychology, 74,* 1–9.

Semmell, A. K. (1976). Group dynamics and the foreign policy process: The choice-shift phenomenon. Paper presented at the Annual Meetings of the Southern Political Science Association.

Senneker, P., & Hendrick, C. (1983). Androgyny and helping behavior. *Journal of Personality and Social Psychology, 45,* 916–925.

Severy, L. J., Forsyth, D. R., & Wagner, P. J. (1979). A multimethod assessment of personal space development in female and male, black and white children. *Journal of Nonverbal Behavior, 4,* 68–86.

Shaffer, D. R., Rogel, M., & Hendrick, D. (1975). Intervention in the library: The effect of increased reponsibility on bystanders' willingness to prevent a theft. *Journal of Applied Social Psychology, 5,* 303–319.

Shaffer, D. R., & Sadowski, C. (1975). This table is mine: Respect for marked barroom tables as a function of gender of spatial marker and desirability of locale. *Sociometry, 38,* 408–419.

Shanab, M. E., & Yahya, K. A. (1977). A behavioral study of obedience in children. *Journal of Personality and Social Psychology, 35,* 530–536.

Shanteau, J., & Nagy, G. F. (1979). Probability of acceptance in dating choice. *Journal of Personality and Social Psychology, 37,* 522–533.

Shavelson, R. J., Hubner, J. J., & Stanton, G. C. (1976). Self-concept: Validation of construct interpretations. *Review of Educational Research, 46,* 407–441.

Shaver, K. G. (1970a). Redress and conscientiousness in the attribution of responsibility for accidents. *Journal of Experimental Social Psychology, 6,* 100–110.

Shaver, K. G. (1970b). Defensive attributions: Effects of severity and relevance on the responsibility assigned for an accident. *Journal of Personality and Social Psychology, 14,* 101–113.

Shaw, M. E., & Costanzo, P. R. (1982). *Theories of social psychology* (2nd ed.). New York: McGraw-Hill.

Shaw, M. E., & Sulzer, J. L. (1964). An empirical test of Heider's levels in attribution of responsibility. *Journal of Abnormal and Social Psychology, 69,* 39–46.

Sheatsley, P. B., & Feldman, J. J. (1964). The assassination of President Kennedy: A preliminary report on public attitudes and behavior. *Public Opinion Quarterly, 28,* 189–215.

Sheridan, C. L., & King, R. G., Jr. (1972). Obedience to authority with an authentic victim. Proceedings of the 80th Annual Convention of the American Psychological Association, 165–166.

Sherif, C. W., Sherif, M., & Nebergall, R. E. (1965). *Attitude and attitude change: The social judgment approach.* Philadelphia: Saunders.

Sherif, M. (1936). *The psychology of social norms.* New York: Harper & Row.

Sherif, M. (1966). *In common predicament: Social psychology of intergroup conflict and cooperation.* Boston: Houghton Mifflin.

Sherif, M., Harvey, O. J., White, B. J., Hood, W. E., & Sherif, C. W. *Intergroup conflict and cooperation: The Robber's Cave experiment.* Norman, Okla.: Institute of Group Relations.

Sherif, M., & Hovland, C. I. (1961). *Social judgment: Assimilation and contrast effects in communication and attitude change.* New Haven: Yale University Press.

Sherif, M., & Sherif, C. W. (1967). Attitude as the individual's own categories: The social judgment-involvement approach to attitude and attitude change. In C. W. Sherif and M. Sherif (Eds.), *Attitude, ego-involvement, and change.* New York: Wiley.

Sherman, P. (1980). The limits of ground squirrel nepotism. In G. Barlow & J. Silverberg (Eds.), *Sociobiology: Beyond nature/nurture?* Boulder, Colo.: Westview.

Sherwood, G. G. (1981). Self-serving biases in person perception: A reexamination of projection as a mechanism of defense. *Psychological Bulletin, 90,* 445–459.

Sherwood, G. G. (1982). Consciousness and stress reduction in defensive projection: A reply to Holmes. *Psychological Bulletin, 91,* 372–375.

Shifflet, S. C. (1973). The contingency model of leadership effectiveness: Some implications of its statistical and methodological properties. *Behavioral Science, 18,* 429–440.

Shotland, R. L. (1985). When bystanders just stand by. *Psychology Today 19(6),* 50–55.

Shotland, R. L., & Heinold, W. D. (1985). Bystander response to arterial bleeding: Helping skills, the decision-making process, and differentiating the helping responses. *Journal of Personality and Social Psychology, 49,* 347–356.

Shotland, R. L., & Huston, T. L. (1979). Emergencies: What are they and do they influence bystanders to intervene? *Journal of Personality and Social Psychology, 37,* 1822–1824.

Shrauger, J. S. (1975). Responses to evaluation as a function of initial self-perceptions. *Psychological Bulletin, 82,* 581–596.

Shrauger, J. S., & Schoeneman, T. J. (1979). Symbolic interactionist view of the self-concept: Through the looking-glass darkly. *Psychological Bulletin, 86,* 549–573.

Shugan, S. M. (1980). The cost of thinking. *Journal of Consumer Research, 7,* 99–111.

Shure, G. H., Meeker, R. J., & Hansford, E. A. (1965). The effectiveness of pacifist strategies in bargaining games. *Journal of Conflict Resolution, 9,* 106–117.

Sieber, J. E. (Ed.). (1982). *The ethics of social research: Surveys and experiments.* New York: Springer-Verlag.

Sigall, H., & Aronson, E. (1967). Opinion change and the gain-loss model of interpersonal attraction. *Journal of Experimental Social Psychology, 3,* 178–188.

Sigall, H., & Page, R. (1971). Current stereotypes: A little fading, a little faking. *Journal of Personality and Social Psychology, 18,* 247–255.

Signorielli, N., Gross, L., & Morgan, M. (1982). Violence in television programs: Ten years later. In D. Pearl, L. Bouthilet, & J. Lazar (Eds.). *Television and behavior, ten years of scientific progress and implications for the eighties.* Rockville, Md.: NIMH.

Silverman, I., & Shaw, M. (1973). Effects of sudden mass desegregation on interracial interaction and attitudes in one southern city. *Journal of Social Issues, 29(4),* 133–142.

Simon, R. J. (1980). *The jury: Its role in American society.* Lexington, Mass.: Heath.

Simons, H. (1976). *Persuasion: Understanding, practice, and analysis.* Reading, Mass.: Addison-Wesley.

Simonton, D. K. (1980). Land battles, generals, and armies: Individual and social determinants of victory and casualties. *Journal of Personality and Social Psychology, 38,* 110–119.

Simonton, D. K. (1981). The library laboratory: Archival data in personality and social psychology. In L. Wheeler (Ed.), *Review of personality and social psychology* (Vol. 2). Beverly Hills, Calif.: Sage.

Sinclair, W. J. (1909). *Semmelweis: His life and his doctrine.* Manchester, England: Manchester University Press.

Singer, D. G., & Singer, J. L. (1980). *Television, imagination, and aggression: A study of preschoolers.* Hillsdale, N.J.: Erlbaum.

Sistrunk, F., & McDavid, J. W. (1971). Sex variable in conforming behavior. *Journal of Personality and Social Psychology, 17,* 200–207.

Sivacek, J., & Crano, W. D. (1982). Vested interest as a moderator of attitude-behavior consistency. *Journal of Personality and Social Psychology, 43,* 210–221.

Skinner, B. F. (1975). The steep and thorny way to a science of behavior. *American Psychologist, 30,* 42–49.

Skinner, E. A. (1985). Action, control judgments, and the structure of control experience. *Psychological Review, 92,* 39–58.

Skolnick, A. (1978). *The intimate environment: Exploring marriage and the family* (2nd ed.). Boston: Little Brown.

Skrypnek, B. J., & Snyder, M. (1982). On the self-perpetuating nature of stereotypes about women and men. *Journal of Experimental Social Psychology, 18,* 277–291.

Sloan, L. R., & Ostrom, T. M. (1974). Amount of information and interpersonal judgment. *Journal of Personality and Social Psychology, 29,* 23–29.

Slonim, M. J. (1960). *Sampling.* New York: Simon & Schuster.

Slovic, P., Fischhoff, B., & Lichtenstein, S. C. (1977). Behavioral decision theory. *Annual Review of Psychology, 28,* 1–39.

Smart, R. (1965). Social-group membership, leadership, and birth order. *Journal of Social Psychology, 67,* 221–225.

Smith, E. R., & Miller, F. D. (1978). Limits on perception of cognitive processes: A reply to Nisbett and Wilson. *Psychological Review, 85,* 355–362.

Smith, E. R., & Miller, F. D. (1983). Mediation among the attributional inferences and comprehension processes: Initial findings and a general method. *Journal of Personality and Social Psychology, 44,* 492–505.

Smith, M. B. (1947). The personal setting of public opinions: A study of attitudes toward Russia. *Public Opinion Quarterly, 11,* 507–523.

Smith, R. J., & Knowles, E. S. (1978). Attributional consequences of personal space invasions. *Personality and Social Psychology Bulletin, 4,* 429–433.

Smith, S. S., & Richardson, D. (1983). Amelioration of deception and harm in psychological research: The important role of debriefing. *Journal of Personality and Social Psychology, 44,* 1075–1082.

Smith, S. S., & Richardson, D. (1985). On deceiving ourselves about deception: A reply to Rubin. *Journal of Personality and Social Psychology, 48,* 254–255.

Smith, T. W. (1980). *A compendium of trends on general social survey questions.* Chicago, Ill.: National Opinion Research Center.

Smyth, L. D. (1982). Psychopathology as a function of neuroticism and a hypnotically implanted aggressive conflict. *Journal of Personality and Social Psychology, 43,* 555–564.

Snyder, C. R. (1984). Excuses, excuses. *Psychology Today, 18(9),* 50–55.

Snyder, C. R., & Fromkin, H. L. (1980). *Uniqueness: The human pursuit of difference.* New York: Plenum.

Snyder, C. R., Higgins, R. L., & Stucky, R. J. (1983). *Excuses: Masquerades in search of grace.* New York: Wiley.

Snyder, C. R., Shenkel, R. J., & Lowery, C. R. (1977). Acceptance of personality interpretations: The "Barnum effect" and beyond. *Journal of Consulting and Clinical Psychology, 45,* 104–114.

Snyder, C. R., Smith, T. W., Augelli, R. W., & Ingram, R. E. (1985). On the self-serving function of social anxiety: Shyness as a self-handicapping strategy. *Journal of Personality and Social Psychology, 48,* 970–980.

Snyder, M. (1974). The self-monitoring of expressive behavior. *Journal of Personality and Social Psychology, 30,* 526–537.

Snyder, M. (1979). Self-monitoring processes. In L. Berkowitz (Ed.), *Advances in experimental social psychology* (Vol. 12). New York: Academic Press.

Snyder, M. (1982). When believing means doing: Creating links between attitude and behavior. In M. P. Zanna, E. T. Higgins, & C. P. Herman (Eds.), *Consistency in social behavior: The Ontario Symposium* (Vol. 2). Hillsdale, N.J.: Erlbaum.

Snyder, M., & Campbell, B. H. (1982). Self-monitoring: The self in action. In J. Suls (Ed.), *Psychological perspectives on the self* (Vol. 1). Hillsdale, N.J.: Erlbaum.

Snyder, M., & DeBono, K. G. (1985). Appeals to image and claims about quality: Understanding the psychology of advertising. *Journal of Personality and Social Psychology, 49,* 586–597.

Snyder, M., & Ickes, W. (1985). Personality and social behavior. In G. Lindzey & E. Aronson (Eds.), *Handbook of social psychology* (Vol. 2, 3rd ed.). New York: Random House.

Snyder, M., & Kendzierski, D. (1982). Acting on one's attitudes: Procedures for linking attitude and behavior. *Journal of Experimental Social Psychology, 18,* 165–183.

Snyder, M., & Monson, T. C. (1975). Persons, situations, and the control of social behavior. *Journal of Personality and Social Psychology, 32,* 637–644.

Snyder, M., & Swann, W. B., Jr. (1976). When actions reflect attitudes: The politics of impression management. *Journal of Personality and Social Psychology, 34,* 1034–1042.

Snyder, M., & Swann, W. B., Jr. (1978). Hypothesis-testing processes in social interaction. *Journal of Personality and Social Psychology, 36,* 1202–1212.

Snyder, M., Tanke, E. D., & Berscheid, E. (1977). Social perception and interpersonal behavior: On the self-fulfilling nature of social stereotypes. *Journal of Personality and Social Psychology, 35,* 656–666.

Snyder, M., & Uranowitz, S. W. (1978). Reconstructing the past: Some cognitive consequences of person perception. *Journal of Personality and Social Psychology, 36,* 941–950.

Snyder, M. L., & Jones, E. E. (1974). Attitude attribution when behavior is constrained. *Journal of Experimental Social Psychology, 10,* 585–600.

Snyder, M. L., Stephan, W. G., & Rosenfield, D. (1976). Egotism and attribution. *Journal of Personality and Social Psychology, 33,* 435–441.

Solomon, R. (1980). The opponent-process theory of acquired motivation: The costs of pleasure and the benefits of pain. *American Psychologist, 35,* 691–712.

Solomon, R., & Corbit, J. D. (1974). An opponent-process theory of motivation: I. Temporal dynamics of affect. *Psychological Review, 81,* 119–145.

Sommer, R. (1969). *Personal space.* Englewood Cliffs, N.J.: Prentice-Hall.

Spence, J. T. (1983). Comment on Lubinski, Tellegen, and Butcher's "Masculinity, femininity, and androgyny viewed and assessed as distinct concepts." *Journal of Personality and Social Psychology, 44,* 440–446.

Spence, J. T. (1985). Gender identity and its implications for the concepts of masculinity and femininity. *Nebraska Symposium on Motivation, 32,* 59–96.

Spence, J. T., Helmreich, R., & Stapp, J. (1974). The Personal Attributes Questionnaire: A measure of sex-role stereotypes and masculinity-femininity. *JSAS Catalog of Selected Documents in Psychology, 4,* 43.

Spence, J. T., Helmreich, R., & Stapp, J. (1975). Ratings of self and peers on sex-role attributes and their relation to self-esteem and conceptions of masculinity and femininity. *Journal of Personality and Social Psychology, 32,* 29–39.

Spitzer, C. E., & Davis, J. H. (1978). Mutual social influence in dynamic groups. *Social Psychology, 41,* 24–33.

Srull, T. K. (1983). Organizational and retrieval processes in person memory: An examination of processing objectives, presentation format, and possible role of self-generated retrieval cues. *Journal of Personality and Social Psychology, 44,* 1157–1170.

Staats, A. W. (1975). *Social behaviorism.* Homewood, Ill.: Dorsey.

Staats, A. W., & Staats, C. K. (1958). Attitudes established by classical conditioning. *Journal of Abnormal and Social Psychology, 57,* 37–40.

Stang, D. J. (1974). Intuition as artifact in mere exposure studies. *Journal of Personality and Social Psychology, 30,* 647–653.

Stang, D. J., & Wrightsman, L. S. (1981). *Dictionary of social behavior and social research methods.* Monterey, Calif.: Brooks/Cole.

Stanovich, K. E. (1986). *How to think straight about psychology.* Glenview, Ill.: Scott, Foresman.

Stasser, G., Kerr, N. L., & Davis, J. H. (1980). Influence processes in decision-making groups: A modeling approach. In P. B. Paulus (Ed.), *Psychology of group influence.* Hillsdale, N.J.: Erlbaum.

Staub, E. (1974). Helping a distressed person: Social, personality, and stimulus determinants. In L. Berkowitz (Ed.), *Advances in experimental social psychology* (Vol. 7). New York: Academic Press.

Staub, E. (Ed.). (1978). *Positive social behavior and morality: Social and personal influences* (Vol. 1). New York: Academic Press.

Staub, E., Erkut, S., & Jaquette. D. (1978). Personality variation in the permissibility of action and response to another's need for help. Unpublished manuscript, Harvard University.

Steck, L., Levitan, D., McLaine, D., & Kelley, H. H. (1982). Care, need, and conceptions of love. *Journal of Personality and Social Psychology, 43,* 481–491.

Steckler, C. (1957). Authoritarian ideology in Negro college students. *Journal of Abnormal and Social Psychology, 54,* 396–399.

Steele, C. M., Southwick, L. L., & Critchlow, B. (1981). Dissonance and alcohol: Drinking your troubles away. *Journal of Personality and Social Psychology, 41,* 831–846.

Stein, R. T., & Heller, T. (1979). An empirical analysis of the correlations between leadership status and participation rates reported in the literature. *Journal of Personality and Social Psychology, 37,* 1993–2002.

Steiner, I. D. (1972). *Group process and productivity.* New York: Academic Press.

Stephan, W. G. (1975). Actor vs. observer: Attributions to behavior with positive or negative outcomes and empathy for the other role. *Journal of Experimental Social Psychology, 11,* 205–214.

Stephan, W. G. (1985). Intergroup relations. In G. Lindzey & E. Aronson (Eds.), *Handbook of social psychology* (Vol. 2, 3rd ed.). New York: Random House.

Stephan, W. G., & Rosenfield, D. (1978). Effects of desegregation on racial attitudes. *Journal of Personality and Social Psychology, 36,* 795–804.

Stephan, W. G., & Rosenfield, D. (1982). Racial and ethnic stereotypes. In A. G. Miller (Ed.), *In the eye of the beholder: Contemporary issues in stereotyping.* New York: Praeger.

Stephenson, B., & Wicklund, R. A. (1983). Self-directed attention and taking the other's perspective. *Journal of Experimental Social Psychology, 19,* 58–77.

Stephenson, B., & Wicklund, R. A. (1984). The contagion of self-focus within a dyad. *Journal of Personality and Social Psychology, 46,* 163–168.

Stern, L. D., Marrs, S., Millar, M. G., & Cole, E. (1984). Processing time and the recall of inconsistent and consistent behaviors of individuals and groups. *Journal of Personality and Social Psychology, 47,* 253–262.

Sternberg, R. J. (1985). Implicit theories of intelligence, creativity, and wisdom. *Journal of Personality and Social Psychology, 49,* 607–627.

Sternberg, R. J., & Grajek, S. (1984). The nature of love. *Journal of Personality and Social Psychology, 47,* 312–329.

Stier, D. S., & Hall, J. A. (1984). Gender differences in touch: An empirical and theoretical review. *Journal of Personality and Social Psychology, 47,* 440–459.

Stiles, W. B. (1978). Verbal response modes and dimensions of interpersonal roles: A method of discourse analysis. *Journal of Personality and Social Psychology, 36,* 693–703.

Stiles, W. B. (1980). Comparison of dimensions derived from rating versus coding of dialogue. *Journal of Personality and Social Psychology, 38,* 359–374.

Stires, L. (1980). Classroom seating location, student grades, and attitudes: Environment or selection? *Environment and Behavior, 12,* 241–254.

Stires, L. (1982). Classroom seating location, order effects, and reactivity. *Personality and Social Psychology Bulletin, 8,* 362–364.

Stogdill, R. M. (1974). *Handbook of leadership.* New York: Free Press.

Stokols, D. (1972). On the distinction between density and crowding: Some implications for future research. *Psychological Review, 79,* 275–278.

Stoner, J. A. F. (1961). *A comparison of individual and group decisions involving risk.* Unpublished master's thesis, Massachusetts Institute of Technology.

Storms, M. D. (1973). Videotape and the attribution process: Reversing actors' and observers' points of view. *Journal of Personality and Social Psychology, 27,* 165–175.

Storms, M. D., Denney, D. R., McCaul, K. D., & Lowery, C. R. (1979). Insomnia and attributions. In I. H. Frieze, D. Bar-Tal, & J. S. Carroll (Eds.), *New approaches to social problems: Applications of attribution theory.* San Francisco: Jossey-Bass.

Storms, M. D., & McCaul, K. D. (1976). Attribution processes and emotional exacerbation of dysfunctional behavior. In J. H. Harvey, W. J. Ickes, & R. F. Kidd (Eds.), *New directions in attribution research* (Vol. 1). Hillsdale, N.J.: Erlbaum.

Storms, M. D., & Nisbett, R. E. (1970). Insomnia and the attribution process. *Journal of Personality and Social Psychology, 16,* 319–328.

Storms, M. D., & Thomas, G. C. (1977). Reactions to physical closeness. *Journal of Personality and Social Psychology, 35,* 412–418.

Straus, M., Gelles, R., & Steinmetz, S. (1980). *Behind closed doors: Violence in the American family.* Garden City, N.Y.: Doubleday.

Stricker, L. J., Messick, S., & Jackson, D. N. (1970a). Conformity, anticonformity, and independence: Their dimensionality and generality. *Journal of Personality and Social Psychology, 16,* 494–507.

Stricker, L. J., Messick, S., & Jackson, D. N. (1970b). You can't get there from here. *Journal of Personality and Social Psychology, 16,* 509.

Strodtbeck, F. L., & Hook, L. H. (1961). The social dimensions of a twelve-man jury table. *Sociometry, 24,* 397–415.

Strodtbeck, F. L., James, R. M., & Hawkins, C. (1957). Social status in jury deliberation. *American Sociological Review, 22,* 713–719.

Strodtbeck, F. L., & Mann, R. D. (1956). Sex role differentiation in jury deliberations. *Sociometry, 19,* 3–11.

Strohmer, D. C, & Chiodo, A. L. (1984). Counselor hypothesis testing strategies: The role of initial impressions and self-schema. *Journal of Counseling Psychology, 31,* 510–519.

Strom, J. C., & Buck, R. W. (1979). Staring and participants' sex: Physiological and subjective reactions. *Personality and Social Psychology Bulletin, 5,* 114–117.

Strong, S. R. (1968). Counseling: An interpersonal influence process. *Journal of Counseling Psychology, 15,* 215–224.

Strong, S. R. (1982). Emerging integrations of clinical and social psychology: A clinician's perspective. In G. Weary and H. Mirels (Eds.), *Integrations of clinical and social psychology.* New York: Oxford University Press.

Strong, S. R. (1984). Interpersonal influence processes in counseling and psychotherapy. *SASP Newsletter, 10(1),* 17–24.

Strong, S. R., & Claiborn, C. D. (1982). *Change through interaction.* New York: Wiley.

Strube, M. J., & Garcia, J. E. (1981). A meta-analytic investigation of Fiedler's contingency model of leadership effectiveness. *Psychological Bulletin, 90,* 307–321.

Suls, J. (Ed.). (1982). *Psychological perspectives on the self* (Vol. 1). Hillsdale, N.J.: Erlbaum.

Suls, J., & Greenwald, A. G. (Eds.). (1983). *Psychological perspectives on the self* (Vol. 2). Hillsdale, N.J.: Erlbaum.

Suls, J., & Greenwald, A. G. (Eds.). (1986). *Psychological perspectives on the self* (Vol. 3). Hillsdale, N.J.: Erlbaum.

Suls, J. M., & Fletcher, B. (1983). Social comparison in the social and physical sciences: An archival study. *Journal of Personality and Social Psychology, 44,* 575–580.

Suls, J., & Miller, R. L. (Eds.). (1977). *Social comparison processes.* Washington, D.C.: Hemisphere.

Sundstrom, E. (1975). An experimental study of crowding: Effects of room size, intrusion, and goal-blocking on nonverbal behavior, self-disclosure, and self-reported stress. *Journal of Personality and Social Psychology, 32,* 645–654.

Sundstrom, E., & Altman, I. (1974). Field study of dominance and territorial behavior. *Journal of Personality and Social Psychology, 30,* 115–125.

Suppe, P. (1974). *The structure of scientific theories.* Urbana: University of Illinois Press.

Surra, C. A. (1985). Courtship types: Variations in interdependence between partners and social networks. *Journal of Personality and Social Psychology, 49,* 357–375.

Sussman, S., Gavriel, Z. A., & Romer, D. (1983). Attractiveness matching is good: Physical attractiveness and stereotypes about marriage. Paper presented at the Annual Meetings of the Midwestern Psychological Association, Chicago.

Swann, W. B., Jr. (1983). Self-verification: Bringing social reality into harmony with the self. In J. Suls & A. G. Greenwald (Eds.), *Psychological perspectives on the self* (Vol. 2). Hillsdale, N.J.: Erlbaum.

Swann, W. B., Jr. (1984). Quest for accuracy in person perception: A matter of pragmatics. *Psychological Review, 91,* 457–477.

Swann, W. B., Jr., & Ely, R. J. (1984). A battle of wills: Self-verification versus behavioral confirmation. *Journal of Personality and Social Psychology, 46,* 1287–1302.

Swann, W. B., Jr., & Hill, C. A. (1982). When our identities are mistaken: Reaffirming self-conceptions through social interaction. *Journal of Personality and Social Psychology, 43,* 59–66.

Swann, W. B., Jr., & Read, S. J. (1981a). Self-verification processes: How we sustain our self-conceptions. *Journal of Experimental Social Psychology, 17,* 351–372.

Swann, W. B., Jr., & Read, S. J. (1981b). Acquiring self-knowledge: The search for feedback that fits. *Journal of Personality and Social Psychology, 41,* 1119–1128.

Szasz, T. S. (1974). *The myth of mental illness* (Rev. ed.). New York: Harper & Row.

Szybillo, G. J., & Heslin, R. (1973). Resistance to persuasion: Inoculation theory in a marketing context. *Journal of Marketing Research, 10,* 396–403.

Tabachnik, N., Crocker, J., & Alloy, L. B. (1983). Depression, social comparison, and the false-consensus effect. *Journal of Personality and Social Psychology, 45,* 688–699.

Tajfel, H. (Ed.). (1978). *Differentiation between social groups: Studies in the social psychology of intergroup relations.* London: Academic Press.

Tajfel, H., & Turner, J. C. (1979). An integrative theory of intergroup conflict. In W. Austin & S. Worchel (Eds.), *The social psychology of intergroup relations.* Monterey, Calif.: Brooks/Cole.

Tajfel, H., & Turner, J. C. (1986). The social identity theory of intergroup behavior. In S. Worchel & W. G. Austin (Eds.), *Psychology of intergroup relations* (2nd ed.). Chicago: Nelson-Hall.

Tanford, S., & Penrod, S. (1984). Social influence model: A formal integration of research on majority and minority influence processes. *Psychological Bulletin, 95,* 189–225.

Tavris, C. (1982). *Anger: The misunderstood emotion.* New York: Simon & Schuster.

Taylor, D. A. (1984). Toward the promised land. *Psychology Today, 18*(6), 46–48.

Taylor, M. C., & Hall, J. A. (1982). Psychological androgyny: A review and reformulation of theories, methods, and conclusions. *Psychological Bulletin, 92,* 347–366.

Taylor, R. B., & Brower, S. (1985). Home and near-home territories. In I. Altman & C. M. Werner (Eds.), *Home environments.* New York: Plenum.

Taylor, R. B., Gottfredson, S. D., & Brower, S. (1980). The defensibility of defensible space: A critical review and a synthetic framework for future research. In T. Hirshi & M. Gottfredson (Eds.), *Understanding crime.* Beverly Hills, Calif.: Sage.

Taylor, R. B., Gottfredson, S. D., & Brower, S. (1984). Understanding block crime and fear. *Journal of Research in Crime and Delinquency, 21,* 303–331.

Taylor, R. B., & Lanni, J. C. (1981). Territorial dominance: the influence of the resident advantage in triadic decision making. *Journal of Personality and Social Psychology, 41,* 909–915.

Taylor, S. E. (1975). On inferring one's attitudes from one's behavior: Some limiting conditions. *Journal of Personality and Social Psychology, 31,* 126–131.

Taylor, S. E. (1983). Adjustment to threatening events: A theory of cognitive adaptation. *American Psychologist, 38,* 1161–1173.

Taylor, S. E., & Crocker, J. (1981). Schematic bases of social information processing. In E. T. Higgins, C. P. Herman, & M. P. Zanna (Eds.), *Social cognition: The Ontario Symposium* (Vol. 1). Hillsdale, N.J.: Erlbaum.

Taylor, S. E., & Fiske, S. T. (1975). Point of view and perceptions of causality. *Journal of Personality and Social Psychology, 32,* 439–445.

Taylor, S. E., Lichtman, R. R., & Wood, J. V. (1984). Attributions, beliefs in control, and adjustment to breast cancer. *Journal of Personality and Social Psychology, 46,* 489–502.

Taylor, S. E., & Thompson, S. C. (1982). Stalking the elusive "vividness" effect. *Psychological Review, 89,* 155–181.

Taylor, S. E., Wood, J. V., & Lichtman, R. R. (1983). It could be worse: Selective evaluation as a response to victimization. *Journal of Social Issues, 39,* 19–40.

Taylor, S. P., & Leonard, K. E., Jr. (1983). Alcohol and human physical aggression. In R. G. Geen & E. I. Donnerstein (Eds.), *Aggression: Theoretical and empirical reviews* (Vol. 1). New York: Academic Press.

Taylor, S. P., Vadaris, R. M., Rawtich, A. B., Gammon, C. B., Cranston, J. W., & Lubetkin, A. I. (1976). The effects of alcohol and delta-9-tetrahydrocannabinol on human physical aggression. *Aggressive Behavior, 2,* 153–161.

Tedeschi, J. T. (Ed.). (1981). *Impression management theory and social psychological research.* New York: Academic Press.

Tedeschi, J. T., Melburg, V., & Rosenfeld, P. (1981). Is the concept of aggression useful? In P. E. Brain & D. Denton (Eds.), *Multidisciplinary approach to aggression research.* New York: Elsevier/North Holland Biomedical Press.

Tedeschi, J. T., & Riess, M. (1981). Identities, the phenomenal self, and laboratory research. In J. T. Tedeschi (Ed.), *Impression management theory and social psychological research*. New York: Academic Press.

Tedeschi, J. T., Schlenker, B. R., & Bonoma, T. V. (1973). *Conflict, power, and games*. Chicago: Aldine.

Tedeschi, J. T., Smith, R. B., III., & Brown, R. C., Jr. (1974). A reinterpretation of research on aggression. *Psychological Bulletin, 81*, 540–563.

Teger, A. (1980). *Too much invested to quit*. New York: Pergamon.

Teichman, Y. (1973). Emotional arousal and affiliation. *Journal of Experimental Social Psychology, 9*, 591–605.

Tellegen, A., & Lubinski, D. (1983). Some methodological comments on labels, traits, interaction, and types in the study of "femininity" and "masculinity": Reply to Spence. *Journal of Personality and Social Psychology, 44*, 447–455.

Tesser, A., & Campbell, J. (1983). Self-definition and self-evaluation maintenance. In J. Suls & A. G. Greenwald (Eds.), *Psychological perspectives on the self* (Vol. 2). Hillsdale, N.J.: Erlbaum.

Tetlock, P. E. (1981). The influence of self-presentation goals on attributional reports. *Social Psychology Quarterly, 44*, 300–311.

Tetlock, P. E. (1985). Toward an intuitive politician model of attribution processes. In B. R. Schlenker (Ed.), *The self and social life*. New York: McGraw Hill.

Tetlock, P. E., & Levi, A. (1982). Attribution bias: On the inconclusiveness of the cognition-motivation debate. *Journal of Experimental Social Psychology, 18*, 68–88.

Tetlock, P. E., & Manstead, A. S. R. (1985). Impression management versus intrapsychic explanations in social psychology: A useful dichotomy? *Psychological Review, 92*, 59–77.

Thibaut, J. W., & Kelley, H. H. (1959). *The social psychology of groups*. New York: Wiley.

Thomas, M. H., Horton, R. W., Lippincott, E. C., & Drabman, R. S. (1977). Desensitization to portrayals of real-life aggression as a function of exposure to TV violence. *Journal of Personality and Social Psychology, 35*, 450–458.

Thompson, S. C. (1981). Will it hurt less if I can control it? A complex answer to a simple question. *Psychological Review, 90*, 89–101.

Thompson, W. C., Cowan, C. L., & Rosenhan, D. L. (1980). Focus of attention mediates the impact of negative affect on altruism. *Journal of Personality and Social Psychology, 38*, 291–300.

Thoreau, H. D. (1962). *Walden and other writings*. New York: Bantam.

Thrasher, F. M. (1927). *The gang*. Chicago: University of Chicago Press.

Thurstone, L. L. (1928). Attitudes can be measured. *American Journal of Sociology, 33*, 529–554.

Thurstone, L. L. (1931). *The measurement of social attitudes*. Chicago, Ill.: University of Chicago Press.

Tice, D. M., & Baumeister, R. F. (1985). Masculinity inhibits helping in emergencies: Personality does predict the bystander effect. *Journal of Personality and Social Psychology, 49*, 420–428.

Tinbergen, L. (1951). *The study of instinct*. Oxford: Oxford University Press.

Toch, H. (1969). *Violent men*. Chicago: Aldine.

Tognoli, J., & Kiesner, R. (1972). Gain and loss of esteem as determinants of interpersonal attraction: A replication and extension. *Journal of Personality and Social Psychology, 23*, 201–204.

Toi, M., & Batson, C. D. (1982). More evidence that empathy is a source of altruistic motivation. *Journal of Personality and Social Psychology, 43*, 281–292.

Tolman, C. W. (1968). The role of the companion in social facilitation of animal behavior. In E. C. Simmel, R. A. Hoppe, & G. A. Milton (Eds.), *Social facilitation and imitative behavior*. Boston: Allyn & Bacon.

Tolstedt, B. E., & Stokes, J. P. (1984). Self-disclosure, intimacy, and the depenetration process. *Journal of Personality and Social Psychology, 46*, 84–90.

Tolstoy, L. (1869/1952). *War and peace*. Chicago: Encylopaedia Britannica.

Toulmin, S. (1953). *The philosophy of science*. New York: Harper & Row.

Traupmann, J., & Hatfield, E. (1981). Love: Its effects on mental and physical health. In J. March, S. Kiesler, R. Fegel, E. Hatfield, & E. Shana (Eds.), *Aging: Stability and change in the family*. New York: Academic Press.

Triplett, N. (1897). The dynamogenic factors in pacemaking and competition. *American Journal of Psychology, 9*, 507–533.

Trivers, R. (1985). *Social evolution*. Reading, Mass.: Benjamin/Cummings.

Trope, Y. (1979). Uncertainty-reducing properties of achievement tasks. *Journal of Personality and Social Psychology, 37*, 1505–1518.

Trope, Y. (1980). Self-assessment, self-enhancement, and task preference. *Journal of Experimental Social Psychology, 16*, 116–129.

Trope, Y. (1983). Self-assessment in achievement behavior. In J. Suls & A. G. Greenwald (Eds.), *Psychological perspectives on the self* (Vol. 2). Hillsdale, N.J.: Erlbaum.

Trope, Y., & Bassok, M. (1982). Confirmatory and diagnosing strategies in social information gathering. *Journal of Personality and Social Psychology, 43*, 22–34.

Trope, Y., & Ben-Yair, E. (1982). Task construction and persistence as a means for self-assessment of abilities. *Journal of Personality and Social Psychology, 42*, 637–645.

Trope, Y., & Brickman, P. (1975). Difficulty and diagnosticity as determinants of choice among tasks. *Journal of Personality and Social Psychology, 31*, 918–925.

Tuchman, G. (1978). The symbolic annihilation of women by the mass media. In G. Tuchman, A. K. Daniels, & J. Benet (Eds.), *Hearth and home: Images of women in the mass media.* New York: Oxford University Press.

Turk, A., Turk, J., Wittes, J. T., & Wittes, R. (1974). *Environmental science.* Philadelphia: Saunders.

Turner, C. W., Layton, J. F., & Simons, L. S. (1975). Naturalistic studies of aggressive behavior: Aggressive stimuli, victim visibility, and horn honking. *Journal of Personality and Social Psychology, 31,* 1098–1107.

Turner, C. W., Simons, L. S., Berkowitz, L., & Frodi, A. (1977). The stimulating and inhibiting effects of weapons on aggressive behavior. *Aggressive Behavior, 3,* 355–378.

Tversky, A., & Kahneman, D. (1973). Availability. A heuristic for judging frequency and probability. *Cognitive Psychology, 5,* 207–232.

Tversky, A., & Kahneman, D. (1981). The framing of decisions and the psychology of choice. *Science, 211,* 453–458.

Tybout, A. M., & Scott, C. A. (1983). Availability of well-defined internal knowledge and the attitude formation process: Information aggregation versus self-perception. *Journal of Personality and Social Psychology, 44,* 474–491.

Tyler, T. R., & Sears, D. O. (1977). Coming to like obnoxious people when we must live with them. *Journal of Personality and Social Psychology, 35,* 200–211.

Ullian, D. Z. (1981). The child's construction of gender: Anatomy is destiny. In E. K. Shapiro & E. Weber (Eds.), *Cognitive and affective growth: Developmental interaction.* Hillsdale, N.J.: Erlbaum.

Underwood, B., & Moore, B. S. (1982). The generality of altruism in children. In N. Eisenberg (Ed.), *The development of prosocial behavior.* New York: Academic Press.

U.N. (1974). *Committee on the Definition of Aggression.* New York: The U.N. Printing Office.

Valins, S. (1966). Cognitive effects of false heart rate feedback. *Journal of Personality and Social Psychology, 4,* 400–408.

Valzelli, L. (1981). *Psychobiology of aggression and violence.* New York: Raven.

Vecchio, R. P. (1977). An empirical examination of the validity of Fiedler's model of leadership effectiveness. *Organizational Behavior and Human Performance, 19,* 180–206.

Veitch, R., Dewood, R., & Bosko, K. (1977). Radio news broadcasts: Their effects on interpersonal helping. *Sociometry, 40,* 383–386.

Vinokur, A., & Burnstein, E. (1974). The effects of partially shared persuasive arguments on group-induced shifts: A group-problem-solving approach. *Journal of Personality and Social Psychology, 29,* 305–315.

Vinokur, A., & Burnstein, E. (1978). Depolarization of attitudes in groups. *Journal of Personality and Social Psychology, 36,* 872–885.

Vinsel, A., Brown, B., Altman, I., & Foss, C. (1980). Privacy regulation, territorial displays, and effectiveness of individual functioning. *Journal of Personality and Social Psychology, 39,* 1104–1115.

Vreven, R., & Nuttin, J. (1976). Frequency perception of successes as a function of results previously obtained by others and by oneself. *Journal of Personality and Social Psychology, 34,* 734–743.

Walden, T. A., & Forsyth, D. R. (1981). Close encounters of the stressful kind: Affective, physiological, and behavioral reactions to the experience of crowding. *Journal of Nonverbal Behavior, 6,* 46–64.

Wallach, M. A., Kogan, N., & Bem, D. J. (1962). Group influence on individual risk taking. *Journal of Abnormal and Social Psychology, 65,* 75–86.

Waller, W. (1938). *The family: A dynamic interpretation.* New York: Dryden.

Walster, E. (1966). The assignment of responsibility for an accident. *Journal of Personality and Social Psychology, 3,* 73–79.

Walster, E. (1968). Postdecision dissonance. In R. P. Abelson, E. Aronson, W. J. McGuire, T. M. Newcomb, M. J. Rosenberg, & P. H. Tannenbaum (Eds.), *Theories of cognitive consistency: A sourcebook.* Chicago: Rand McNally.

Walster, E., Aronson, V., Abrahams, D., & Rottman, L. (1966). The importance of physical attractiveness in dating behavior. *Journal of Personality and Social Psychology, 4,* 508–516.

Walster, E., & Berscheid, E. (1974). A little bit about love: A minor essay on a major topic. In T. L. Huston (Ed.), *Foundations of interpersonal attraction.* New York: Academic Press.

Walster, E., & Walster, G. W. (1978). *A new look at love.* Reading, Mass.: Addison-Wesley.

Walster, E., Walster, G. W., & Berscheid, E. (1978). *Equity: Theory and research.* Boston, Mass.: Allyn & Bacon.

Walster, E., Walster, G. W., Piliavin, J., & Schmidt, L. (1973). "Playing hard to get": Understanding an elusive phenomenon. *Journal of Personality and Social Psychology, 26,* 113–122.

Warner, L. G., & DeFleur, M. L. (1969). Attitude as an interactional concept: Social constraint and social distance as intervening variables between attitudes and action. *American Sociological Review, 34,* 153–169.

Warren, J. R. (1966). Birth order and social behavior. *Psychological Bulletin, 65,* 38–49.

Watkins, M. J., & Peynircioğlu, Z. F. (1984). Determining perceived meaning during impression formation: Another look at the meaning change hypothesis. *Journal of Personality and Social Psychology, 46,* 1005–1016.

Watzlawick, P., Beavin, J. H., & Jackson, D. D. (1967). *Pragmatics of human communication: A study of interactional patterns, pathologies, and paradoxes.* New York: Norton.

Weary, G. (1980). Affect and egotism as mediators of bias in causal attributions. *Journal of Personality and Social Psychology, 38,* 348–357.

Webb, E. J., Campbell, D. T., Schwartz, R. D., Sechrest, L., & Grove, J. B. (1981). *Nonreactive measures in the social sciences.* Boston: Houghton Mifflin.

Weeks, D. G., Michela, J. L., Peplau, L. A., & Bragg, M. E. (1980). The relation between loneliness and depression: A structural equation analysis. *Journal of Personality and Social Psychology, 39,* 1238–1244.

Wegner, D. M., & Crano, W. D. (1975). Racial factors in helping behavior in an unobtrusive field experiment. *Journal of Personality and Social Psychology, 32,* 901–905.

Weick, K. E. (1985). Systematic observational methods. In G. Lindzey & E. Aronson (Eds.), *Handbook of social psychology* (Vol. 1, 3rd ed.). New York: Random House.

Weigel, R. H., Loomis, J. W., & Soja, M. J. (1980). Race relations on prime time television. *Journal of Personality and Social Psychology, 39,* 884–893.

Weigel, R. H., Vernon, D. T. A., & Tognacci, L. N. (1974). Specificity of the attitude as a determinant of attitude behavior congruence. *Journal of Personality and Social Psychology, 30,* 724–728.

Weiner, B. (1980a). A cognitive (attribution)-emotion-action model of motivated behavior: An analysis of judgments of help-giving. *Journal of Personality and Social Psychology, 39,* 186–200.

Weiner, B. (1980b). May I borrow your class notes? An attributional analysis of judgments of help giving in an achievement-related context. *Journal of Educational Psychology, 72,* 676–681.

Weiner, B. (1980c). *Human motivation.* New York: Holt, Rinehart & Winston.

Weiner, B. (1983). Some methodological pitfalls in attributional research. *Journal of Educational Psychology, 75,* 530–543.

Weiner, B. (1985a). "Spontaneous" causal thinking. *Psychological Bulletin, 97,* 74–84.

Weiner, B. (1985b). An attributional theory of achievement motivation and emotion. *Psychological Review, 92,* 548–573.

Weiner, B., & Brown, J. (1984). All's well that ends well. *Journal of Educational Psychology, 76,* 169–171.

Weiss, R. S. (1973). *Loneliness: the experience of emotional and social isolation.* Cambridge, Mass.: MIT Press.

Weitz, S. (1972). Attitude, voice, and behavior: A repressed affect model of interracial interaction. *Journal of Personality and Social Psychology, 24,* 14–21.

Wells, G. L., & Harvey, J. H. (1977). Do people use consensus information in making causal attributions? *Journal of Personality and Social Psychology, 35,* 279–293.

Wells, G. L., & Harvey, J. H. (1978). Naive attributors' attributions and prediction: What is informative and when is an effect an effect? *Journal of Personality and Social Psychology, 36,* 483–490.

Wells, G. L., & Loftus, E. F. (Eds.). (1984). *Eyewitness testimony: Psychological perspectives.* New York: Cambridge University Press.

Wells, G. L., & Murray, D. M. (1984). Eyewitness confidence. In G. L. Wells & E. F. Loftus (Eds.), *Eyewitness testimony: Psychological perspectives.* New York: Cambridge University Press.

Wells, L. E., & Marwell, G. (1976). *Self-esteem: Its conceptualization and measurement.* Beverly Hills, Calif.: Sage.

Wenz, F. V. (1977). Seasonal suicide attempts and forms of loneliness. *Psychological Reports, 40,* 807–810.

Wertham, F. (1978). The catathymic crisis. In I. L. Kutash, S. B. Kutash, & L. B. Schlesinger (Eds.), *Violence: Perspectives on murder and aggression.* San Francisco: Jossey-Bass.

West, S. G., Gunn, S. P., & Chernicky, P. (1975). Ubiquitous Watergate: An attributional analysis. *Journal of Personality and Social Psychology, 32,* 55–65.

West, S. G., Whitney, G., & Schnedler, R. (1975). Helping a motorist in distress: The effects of sex, race, and neighborhood. *Journal of Personality and Social Psychology, 31,* 691–698.

West, S. G., & Wicklund, R. A. (1980). *A primer of social psychological theories.* Monterey, Calif.: Brooks/Cole.

West Eberhard, M. J. (1975). The evolution of social behavior by kin selection. *The Quarterly Review of Biology, 50,* 1–33.

Weyant, J. M. (1978). Effects of mood states, costs, and benefits on helping. *Journal of Personality and Social Psychology, 36,* 1169–1176.

Wheeler, H. (1985). Pornography and rape: A feminist perspective. In A. W. Burgess (Ed.), *Rape and sexual assault.* New York: Garland.

Wheeler, L., & Nezlek, J. (1977). Sex differences in social participation. *Journal of Personality and Social Psychology, 35,* 742–754.

White, G. L., Fishbein, S., & Rutstein, J. (1981). Passionate love and the misattribution of arousal. *Journal of Personality and Social Psychology, 41,* 56–62.

White, J. D., & Carlston, D. E. (1983). Consequences of schemata for attention, impressions, and recall in complex social interactions. *Journal of Personality and Social Psychology, 45,* 538–549.

White, J. W., & Gruber, K. J. (1982). Instigative aggression as a function of past experience and target characteristics. *Journal of Personality and Social Psychology, 42,* 1065–1075.

White, L. A. (1979). Erotica and aggression: The influence of sexual arousal, positive affect, and negative affect on aggressive behavior. *Journal of Personality and Social Psychology, 37,* 591–601.

White, M. (1975). Interpersonal distance as affected by room size, status, and sex. *Journal of Social Psychology, 95,* 241–249.

White, P. (1980). Limitations on verbal reports of internal events: A refutation of Nisbett and Wilson and Bem. *Psychological Review, 87,* 105–112.

White, R. K. (1977). Misperception in the Arab-Israeli conflict. *Journal of Social Issues, 33(1),* 190–221.

Whyte, W. F. (1943). *Street corner society.* Chicago: University of Chicago Press.

Wicker, A. W. (1969). Attitudes versus actions: The relationship between verbal and overt behavioral responses to attitude objects. *Journal of Social Issues, 25,* 41–78.

Wicker, A. W. (1979). *An introduction to ecological psychology.* Monterey, Calif.: Brooks/Cole.

Wicklund, R. A. (1975). Objective self-awareness. In L. Berkowitz (Ed.), *Advances in experimental social psychology* (Vol. 8). New York: Academic Press.

Wicklund, R. A. (1978). Three years later. In L. Berkowitz (Ed.), *Cognitive theories in social psychology.* New York: Academic Press.

Wicklund, R. A. (1982). Self-focused attention and the validity of self-reports. In M. P. Zanna, E. T. Higgins, & C. P. Herman (Eds.), *Consistency in social behavior: The Ontario Symposium* (Vol. 2). Hillsdale, N.J.: Erlbaum.

Wicklund, R. A., & Brehm, J. W. (1976). *Perspectives on cognitive dissonance.* Hillsdale, N.J.: Erlbaum.

Wiley, M. G., Crittenden, K. S., & Birg, L. D. (1979). Why a rejection? Causal attribution of a career achievement event. *Social Psychology Quarterly, 42,* 214–222.

Williams v. Florida (1970). 399 U.S. 78.

Williams, K., Harkins, S., & Latané, B. (1981). Identifiability as a deterrent to social loafing: Two cheering experiments. *Journal of Personality and Social Psychology, 40,* 303–311.

Willis, F. N. (1966). Initial speaking distance as a function of the speakers' relationship. *Psychonomic Science, 5,* 221–222.

Willis, R. H. (1970). The conscientious cartographers: A fable inspired by Stricker, Messick, and Jackson. *Journal of Personality and Social Psychology, 16,* 508.

Willis, R. H., & Hollander, E. P. (1964). An experimental study of three responses modes in social influence situations. *Journal of Abnormal and Social Psychology, 69,* 150–156.

Wills, T. A. (1981). Downward comparison principles in social psychology. *Psychological Bulletin, 90,* 245–271.

Wilson, D. W. (1981). Is helping a laughing matter? *Psychology, 18,* 6–9.

Wilson, D. W., & Donnerstein, E. (1976). Legal and ethical aspects of nonreactive social psychological research: An excursion into the public mind. *American Psychologist, 31,* 765–784.

Wilson, E. O. (1975). *Sociobiology and the new synthesis.* Cambridge, Mass.: Harvard University Press.

Wilson, T. D. (1985). Strangers to ourselves: The origins and accuracy of beliefs about one's own mental states. In J. H. Harvey & G. Weary (Eds.), *Attribution: Basic issues and applications.* New York: Academic Press.

Wilson, T. D., & Linville, P. W. (1982). Improving the academic performance of college freshmen: Attribution therapy revisited. *Journal of Personality and Social Psychology, 42,* 367–376.

Wilson, T. D., & Linville, P. W. (1985). Improving the performance of college freshmen with attributional techniques. *Journal of Personality and Social Psychology, 49,* 287–293.

Wilson, W. R. (1979). Feeling more than we can know: Exposure effects without learning. *Journal of Personality and Social Psychology, 37,* 811–821.

Wimer, S., & Kelley, H. H. (1982). An investigation of the dimensions of causal attribution. *Journal of Personality and Social Psychology, 43,* 1142–1162.

Winston, B. V. (1983). Vestiges of racism remain, psychologist says. *Richmond Times-Dispatch,* February 22, p. D–3.

Winter, L., Uleman, J. S., & Cunniff, C. (1985). How automatic are social judgments? *Journal of Personality and Social Psychology, 49,* 904–917.

Wish, M., D'Andrade, R. G., & Goodnow, J. E., II. (1980). Dimensions of interpersonal communication: Correspondences between structures for speech acts and bipolar scales. *Journal of Personality and Social Psychology, 39,* 848–860.

Wish, M., & Kaplan, S. J. (1977). Toward an implicit theory of interpersonal communication. *Sociometry, 40,* 234–246.

Wispé, L. (1986). The distinction between sympathy and empathy: To call forth a concept, a word is needed. *Journal of Personality and Social Psychology, 50,* 314–321.

Wittgenstein, L. (1965). *The blue and brown books.* New York: Barnes & Noble.

Wolf, S. (1985). Manifest and latent influence of majorities and minorities. *Journal of Personality and Social Psychology, 48,* 899–908.

Wolf, S., & Latané, B. (1983). Majority and minority influence on restaurant preferences. *Journal of Personality and Social Psychology, 45,* 282–292.

Wollman, N. (Ed.). (1985). *Working for peace: A handbook of practical psychology and other tools.* San Luis Obispo, Calif.: Impact.

Wong, P. T. P., & Weiner, B. (1981). When people ask "why" questions and the heuristics of attributional search. *Journal of Personality and Social Psychology, 40,* 650–663.

Wood, G. (1978). The knew-it-all-along effect. *Journal of Experimental Psychology: Human Perception and Performance, 4,* 345–353.

Wood, J. V., Taylor, S. E., & Lichtman, R. R. (1985). Social comparison in adjustment to breast cancer. *Journal of Personality and Social Psychology, 49,* 1169–1183.

Wood, W., & Eagly, A. H. (1981). Stages in the analysis of persuasive messages: The role of causal attributions and message comprehension. *Journal of Personality and Social Psychology, 40,* 246–255.

Woodmansee, J. J. (1970). The pupil response as a measure of social attitude. In G. F. Summers (Ed.), *Attitude measurement.* Chicago: Rand McNally.

Worchel, S. (1978). The experience of crowding: An attributional analysis. In A. Baum & Y. M. Epstein (Eds.), *Human response to crowding.* Hillsdale, N.J.: Erlbaum.

Worchel, S., & Austin, W. G. (Eds.). (1986). *Psychology of intergroup relations* (2nd ed.). Chicago: Nelson-Hall.

Worchel, S., & Brehm, J. W. (1971). Direct and implied social restoration of freedom. *Journal of Personality and Social Psychology, 18,* 294–304.

Worchel, S., & Teddlie, C. (1976). The experience of crowding: A two-factor theory. *Journal of Personality and Social Psychology, 34,* 30–40.

Worchel, S., & Yohai, S. (1979). The role of attribution in the experience of crowding. *Journal of Experimental Social Psychology, 15,* 91–104.

Word, C. O., Zanna, M. P., & Cooper, J. (1974). The nonverbal mediation of self-fulfilling prophecies in interracial interaction. *Journal of Experimental Social Psychology, 10,* 109–120.

Wortman, C. B., Addesman, P., Herman, E., & Greenberg, R. (1976). Self-disclosure: An attributional analysis. *Journal of Personality and Social Psychology, 33,* 184–191.

Wortman, C. B., Costanzo, P. R., & Witt, T. R. (1973). Effects of anticipated performance on the attribution of causality to self and others. *Journal of Personality and Social Psychology, 27,* 372–381.

Wortman, P. (1983). Evaluation research: A methodological perspective. *Annual Review of Psychology, 34,* 223–260.

Wrightsman, L. S., O'Connor, J., & Baker, N. J. (Eds.). (1972). *Cooperation and competition: Readings on mixed-motive games.* Belmont, Calif.: Wadsworth.

Wrong, D. H. (1979). *Power: Its forms, bases, and uses.* New York: Harper & Row.

Wyer, R. S. (1974). *Cognitive organization and change.* Hillsdale, N.J.: Erlbaum.

Wyer, R. S., & Srull, T. K. (Eds.). (1984). *Handbook of social cognition.* Hillsdale, N.J.: Erlbaum.

Yablonsky, L. (1962). *The violent gang.* New York: Macmillan.

Yamagishi, T., & Hill, C. T. (1981). Adding versus averaging models revisited. A test of a path-analytic integration model. *Journal of Personality and Social Psychology, 41,* 13–25.

Yancey, W. L. (1971). Architecture, interaction, and social control: The case of large-scale housing projects. In J. F. Wohlwill & D. H. Carson (Eds.), *Environment and the social sciences: Perspectives and applications.* Washington, D.C.: American Psychological Association.

Yates, J. (1985). The content of awareness is a model of the world. *Psychological Review, 92,* 249–284.

Yinon, Y., & Bizman, A. (1980). Noise, success, and failure as determinants of helping behavior. *Personality and Social Psychology Bulletin, 6,* 125–130.

Younger, J. C., Walker, L., & Arrowood, A. J. (1977). Postdecision dissonance at the fair. *Personality and Social Psychology Bulletin, 3,* 284–287.

Zacker, J. (1973). Authoritarian avoidance of ambiguity. *Psychological Reports, 33,* 901–902.

Zajonc, R. B. (1965). Social facilitation. *Science, 149,* 269–274.

Zajonc, R. B. (1968). Attitudinal effects of mere exposure. *Journal of Personality and Social Psychology* (Monograph), *9,* 1–29.

Zajonc, R. B. (1980). Compresence. In P. B. Paulus (Ed.), *Psychology of group influence.* Hillsdale, N.J.: Erlbaum.

Zajonc, R. B. (1984). On the primacy of affect. *American Psychologist, 39,* 117–123.

Zajonc, R. B., Heingartner, A., & Herman, E. M. (1969). Social enhancement and impairment of performance in the cockroach. *Journal of Personality and Social Psychology, 13,* 83–92.

Zajonc, R. B., Markus, H., & Markus, G. B. (1979). The birth order puzzle. *Journal of Personality and Social Psychology, 37,* 1325–1341.

Zander, A. (1982). *Making groups effective.* San Francisco: Jossey-Bass.

Zanna, M. P., & Cooper, J. (1976). Dissonance and the attribution process. In J. H. Harvey, W. J. Ickes, & R. F. Kidd (Eds.), *New directions in attribution research* (Vol. 1). Hillsdale, N.J.: Erlbaum.

Zanna, M. P., Goethals, G., & Hill, J. (1975). Evaluating a sex-related ability: Social comparison with similar others and standard setters. *Journal of Experimental Social Psychology, 11,* 86–93.

Zanna, M. P., & Hamilton, D. L. (1977). Further evidence for meaning change in impression formation. *Journal of Experimental Social Psychology, 13,* 224–228.

Zanna, M. P., Higgins, E. T., & Herman, C. P. (Eds.). (1982). *Consistency in social behavior: The Ontario Symposium* (Vol. 2). Hillsdale, N.J.: Erlbaum.

Zanna, M. P., Kiesler, C. A., & Pilkonis, P. A. (1970). Positive and negative attitudinal affect established by classical conditioning. *Journal of Personality and Social Psychology, 14,* 321–328.

Zanna, M. P., Olson, J. M., & Fazio, R. H. (1980). Attitude-behavior consistency: An individual difference perspective. *Journal of Personality and Social Psychology, 38,* 432–440.

Zillmann, D. (1972). Rhetorical elicitation of agreement in persuasion. *Journal of Personality and Social Psychology, 21,* 159–165.

Zillmann, D. (1983). Arousal and aggression. In R. G. Geen & E. I. Donnerstein (Eds.), *Aggression: Theoretical and empirical reviews* (Vol. 1). New York: Academic Press.

Zillmann, D., Bryant, J., Comsky, P., & Medoff, N. J. (1981). Excitation and hedonic valence in the effect of erotica on motivated intermale aggression. *Journal of European Social Psychology, 11,* 233–252.

Zillmann, D., & Cantor, J. R. (1974). Rhetorical elicitation of concession in persuasion. *Journal of Personality and Social Psychology, 94,* 223–236.

Zillmann, D., & Cantor, J. R. (1976). Effect of timing of information about mitigating circumstances on emotional responses to provocation and retaliatory behavior. *Journal of Experimental Social Psychology, 12,* 38–55.

Zimbardo, P. G. (1969). The human choice: Individuation, reason, and order versus deindividuation, impulse, and chaos. *Nebraska Symposium on Motivation, 17,* 237–307.

Zimbardo, P. G. (1975). Transforming experimental research into advocacy for social change. In M. Deutsch & H. A. Hornstein (Eds.), *Applying social psychology.* Hillsdale, N.J.: Erlbaum.

Zimbardo, P. G. (1977). *Shyness: What it is and what to do about it.* New York: Jones.

Zimbardo, P. G., Ebbesen, E. B., & Maslach, C. (1977). *Influencing attitudes and changing behavior.* Reading, Mass.: Addison-Wesley.

Zimbardo, P. G., Weisenberg, M., Firestone, I., & Levy, B. (1965). Communicator effectiveness in producing public conformity and private opinion change. *Journal of Personality, 33,* 233–256.

Zucker, P., Worthington, E., & Forsyth, D. R. (1985). Empathy skills training in structured groups. *Human Relations, 38,* 247–255.

Zuckerman, M., Amidon, M. D., Bishop, S. E., & Pomerantz, S. D. (1982). Face and tone of voice in the communication of deception. *Journal of Personality and Social Psychology, 43,* 347–357.

Zuckerman, M., DePaulo, B. M., & Rosenthal, R. (1981). Verbal and nonverbal communication of deception. In L. Berkowitz (Ed.), *Advances in experimental social psychology* (Vol. 14). New York: Academic Press.

Zuckerman, M., Koestner, R., Colella, M. J., & Alton, A. O. (1984). Anchoring in the detection of deception and leakage. *Journal of Personality and Social Psychology, 47,* 301–311.

Zukier, H. (1982). The dilution effect: The role of the correlation and the dispersion of predictor variables in the use of nondiagnostic information. *Journal of Personality and Social Psychology, 43,* 1163–1174.

GLOSSARY

Actor-observer difference: The tendency for actors (the people who actually perform the behavior) to explain their behavior in terms of situational causes and observers to explain the actors' behavior in terms of dispositional causes.

Affiliation: The act of joining together with members of one's own species.

Aggression: An action performed with the deliberate intention of harming or injuring another person.

Altruism: Helpful behaviors that are motivated solely by the other person's need rather than the desire for personal gain; also the motive underlying self-sacrificing actions.

Anchoring/adjustment: A cognitive heuristic that involves making an initial judgment (which serves as a reference point or anchor) and then adjusting this estimate as more information is obtained.

Applied science: Research conducted to increase scientists' understanding of practical and social problems and to identify possible solutions.

Archival analysis: A type of nonreactive measurement method that involves the collection and analysis of existing records and public archives.

Arousal-aggression hypothesis: A motivational explanation of aggressive behavior that argues aversive events lead to arousal, which in turn can prompt aggression.

Assumed similarity bias: The tendency for individuals to assume that they are similar to most other people.

Attitude: An affective feeling of liking or disliking toward an object. According to the tricomponent model, attitudes include affective, cognitive, and behavioral components.

Attitude scale: A series of fixed-response questions pertaining to a single attitudinal topic that have been selected using scaling methods.

Attribution: An inference about the cause of a behavior or event; also, the cognitive processes underlying these inferences.

Attribution retraining: Helping individuals cope with stressful life events by training them to formulate attributions that promote healthy psychological functioning.

Authentic self-presentations: Impression management tactics that individuals use to convey accurate information about their personal qualities to others.

Authoritarian personality: An overall system of values, beliefs, and preferences characterized by a submissive, uncritical acceptance of authority, condemnation of anyone who violates conventional norms, and negative attitudes toward the members of other social groups.

Availability: A cognitive heuristic that prompts perceivers to base their judgments on information readily accessible in memory.

$B = f(P, E)$: Kurt Lewin's interactionism formula that states behavior is a function of the person and the environment.

Balance theory: A theoretical framework advanced by Fritz Heider that assumes interpersonal relationships can be either balanced (integrated units with elements that fit together without stress) or unbalanced (inconsistent units with elements that conflict with one another). Heider believed that unbalanced relationships create an unpleasant tension that must be relieved by changing some element of the system.

Basic science: Research conducted to increase scientists' understanding of theoretically significant hypotheses.

Behavioral measures: Any measurement method that involves the direct assessment of behavior.

Behaviorism: A theoretical account of learning processes that stresses association and reinforcement.

Belief perseverance: The tendency for individuals who have generated an explanation for a social event or phenomenon to continue to accept this explanation even when the evidence that initially supported the explanation has been shown to be false.

Brainstorming: A method for enhancing creativity in groups that calls for heightened expressiveness, inhibited evaluation, quantity rather than quality, and deliberate attempts to build on earlier ideas.

Bystander effect: The tendency for people to help less in groups than when they are alone.

Catharsis: The discharge of hostile impulses and urges that is often achieved by behaving aggressively.

Change-of-meaning hypothesis: Solomon Asch's prediction that perceivers formulate coherent impressions of other people by changing the meaning of some of the available perceptual information. According to Asch, central traits, such as warmth or coldness, do not just add new information but act by changing the meaning of other information available to the perceiver.

Classical conditioning: A learning process that takes place when a neutral stimulus is paired repeatedly with a stimulus that already evokes a response. After sufficient pairings, the formerly neutral stimulus will evoke the response when presented by itself.

Close relationships: Enduring, often intensely emotional relationships characterized by frequent and diverse interdependence.

Coercive persuasion: Psychologically compelling techniques designed to change individuals' attitudes against their wills.

Cognitive consistency: A psychological state in which an individual's attitudes, beliefs, and other cognitions are logically compatible with one another. Many theorists believe that individuals will change their attitudes in order to maximize consistency among their various cognitions.

Cognitive dissonance: An aversive psychological state that occurs when an individual simultaneously accepts two conflicting cognitions.

Cognitive response theory: A theory of attitude change that assumes persuasion is most likely to occur when receivers' internal cognitive responses support the message, and least likely to occur when receivers' cognitive responses are inconsistent with or irrelevant to the message.

Cohesiveness: The strength of the relationships linking the members of a group to one another and to the group as whole.

Compliance: Change that occurs when the targets of social influence publicly accept the influencer's position, but privately continue to maintain their original beliefs.

Conceptually-driven cognitive processes: Inferential processes that are guided by the perceiver's cognitive structures and expectations; also known as "top-down" processes.

Conflict: Disagreement, discord, and friction that occur when the actions and/or beliefs of one individual or group of individuals are incompatible with and hence are resisted by another individual or group of individuals.

Conformity: A change in beliefs and/or behaviors brought about through social influence.

Contact hypothesis: The prediction that equal-status contact between the members of different groups will reduce intergroup conflict.

Contingency theory of leadership: Any model that predicts that leadership depends on the interaction of personal characteristics of the leader and the nature of the group situation; usually used in reference to the leadership theory developed by Fred Fiedler and based on leadership style and the favorability of the group situation.

Correlation coefficient: A statistic that measures the strength and direction of a relationship between two variables; often symbolized by r, correlations can range from -1.0 to $+1.0$.

Correspondent inference theory: A theoretical framework developed by Edward E. Jones that proposes that individuals make attributions when they believe that a person's actions correspond to his or her disposition.

Cost-reward model of helping: An extension of the Latané-Darley decision model of helping that argues that individuals also consider the costs and rewards they might experience if they help or do not help.

Counterconformist: An individual who deliberately adopts views that run counter to others' views.

Covariation principle: The commonsense assumption that prescribes attributing an effect to one of its possible causes with which, over time, it varies.

Crowding: A psychological reaction that occurs when individuals feel that the amount of space available to them is insufficient for their needs.

Cube model: A three-dimensional theory developed by Harold H. Kelley that posits individuals formulate attributions by considering the covariation of an effect and its possible cause across objects (distinctiveness), time (consistency), and people (consensus).

Data-driven cognitive processes: Inferential processes that rely more on incoming perceptual data than the perceiver's existing cognitive structures; also known as "bottom-up" processes.

Debriefing: A session, held after the subjects have participated in the research project, in which the experimenter asks subjects about their reactions to the experience and provides information about the purpose of the research.

Decision model of helping: A theoretical framework developed by Bibb Latané and John Darley that proposes individuals make a series of decisions before they offer a victim help, including noticing the event, interpreting the event as an emergency, taking responsibility, identifying a way to help, and implementing the chosen form of help.

Defensible space: Semipublic areas surrounding private dwellings that residents can territorialize.

Defensive attribution: The tendency to blame individuals for actions that yield negative outcomes, even when the outcomes were unintended and unforeseeable.

Deindividuation: A process by which individuals lose their sense of personal identity when they become too submerged in a group; also, the psychological state produced by this process.

Demand characteristics: Implicit and explicit cues that convey information about the type of response expected in the situation.

Density: The number of individuals per unit of space.

Dependent variable: The responses of the subject measured by the researcher; the effect variable in a cause-effect relationship.

Dominant responses: Well-learned or instinctive behaviors that the organism has practiced and is primed to perform.

Door-in-the-face: An influence technique in which influencers first make a very large request that the target will likely refuse. After they are turned down, influencers then make the more reasonable request they actually want.

Downward social comparison: The tendency to compare ourselves to others who are performing less effectively.

Emotional loneliness: Feelings of isolation and depression that occur when individuals desire, but cannot achieve, a meaningful, intimate relationship with another person.

Equity norm: A societal standard suggesting individuals should receive outcomes in proportion to their inputs.

Ethology: A branch of biology devoted to the study of animal behavior in natural surroundings.

Evaluation apprehension: An anxiety-creating concern to appear normal; often used to describe subjects' reactions when taking part in psychological research.

Excitation transfer: The process by which arousal produced by nonviolent stimuli or events, such as high temperatures or pornography, energizes aggression when misattributed to an unrelated source.

Expectancy effects: The unintentional tendency for researchers to obtain responses from subjects that confirm their initial expectancies.

Experiment: A research design in which the investigator manipulates at least one variable, systematically measures at least one other variable, and maintains control over other influential variables.

Explanatory attributions: Causal inferences that enable attributors to achieve an intellectual understanding of their social experiences.

External validity: The degree to which findings can be generalized to other populations and settings.

Extrinsic motivation: A psychological motive aroused by factors that are external to the individual; the desire to earn good grades is an example of extrinsic motivation.

False-consensus effect: Perceivers' tendency to assume that their personal qualities and characteristics are common in the general population.

Field study: Scientific experimentation or research performed in a natural setting.

Foot-in-the-door principle: An influence technique in which influencers first make a very small request that the target will probably agree to. Once the target agrees to the minor request, influencers then make the more important request.

Frustration-aggression hypothesis: An early motivational model that argued individuals become aggressive whenever external conditions prevent them from reaching their goals; eventually subsumed by the arousal-aggression hypothesis.

F-scale: A self-report measure of authoritarianism, so named because high scorers tend to adopt extremely conservative (fascistic) political views.

Fundamental attribution error: The tendency to overestimate the causal influence of dispositional factors while underemphasizing the causal influence of situational factors.

Gain-loss hypothesis: The prediction that evaluators who are negative initially but gradually become positive are liked more than consistently positive evaluators, whereas evaluators who are positive initially but gradually become negative are disliked more than consistently negative evaluators.

Group: Two or more individuals who influence one another through social interaction.

Group polarization: The tendency for groups to polarize members' opinions and beliefs in the direction of the average of the group members' prediscussion opinions.

Groupthink: A distorted style of thinking that renders group members incapable of making a rational decision.

Halo effect: Allowing an overall positive or negative impression of a person to influence one's perceptions of that person's specific characteristics.

Helping behavior: Rendering aid to another person.

Heuristics: Inferential principles or rules of thumb that perceivers use to reach conclusions when the amount of available information is limited. Heuristics enable the perceiver to process information efficiently, but they can bias judgments.

Hindsight bias: Perceivers' tendency to overestimate the accuracy of their original beliefs once these beliefs have been confirmed or disconfirmed; also termed the I-knew-it-all-along phenomenon.

Idiosyncrasy credits: Psychological credits or bonuses earned when an individual makes a contribution to the group.

Illusory correlations: Assumed relationships between two variables that are not actually related to one another; also, overestimations of the strength of the relationship between unrelated characteristics possessed by the members of a particular group.

Implicit personality theory: The perceiver's personal assumptions about the naturally occurring relationships among various traits and attributes.

Impression management: The display of social behaviors that establish, maintain, or refine the impression that others have of us; also known as self-presentation.

Inclusive fitness: A species member's ability to ensure the survival of its genes in future generations.

Incompatible response strategy: Reducing aggression by creating emotions that are not compatible with anger.

Independent variable: The aspect of the situation manipulated by the researcher in an experimental study; the causal variable in a cause-effect relationship.

Individual differences: Variations among people, including differences in personality traits, intelligence, age, gender, and race.

Information integration theory: A conceptual framework that assumes perceivers combine bits of information about other people to form overall impressions.

Informed consent: An accurate description of the nature of the study given to subjects prior to the solicitation of their agreement to participate.

In-group/out-group bias: The tendency to view people who are members of one's own group more favorably than those who are not members.

Innovation: Influencing others by adopting a staunch, unyielding position on the issue from the outset of the discussion.

Inoculation theory: A theoretical position that hypothesizes resistance to persuasion can be developed by exposing individuals to weak versions of the arguments that will be used by a persuasive communicator.

Interactionism: A theoretical framework based on the assumption that individuals' personal qualities interact with aspects of the social situation to determine social behavior.

Interaction model of leadership: A theory of leadership that assumes the leader's qualities, the nature of the situation, and the group members' qualities interact to determine leadership emergence and effectiveness.

Internal validity: The degree to which the results obtained in a study are produced by the independent variable manipulated by the researcher rather than some uncontrolled factor.

Interpersonal attributions: Statements about the causes of behavior or events that serve a self-presentational function.

Interpersonal model of perception: A theoretical framework that, in rejecting the notion that perceivers passively observe others, proposes perceivers and those who are observed influence one another in a dynamic, interpersonal process.

Intrinsic motivation: A psychological motive aroused by factors that are inside the individual. Actions performed for their own sake rather than to achieve some external goal or reward are said to be intrinsically motivated.

Just-world hypothesis: The prediction that most people assume the world is a just place where individuals receive what they deserve.

Kinesic cues: Movements of the body that convey information to others, including gestures, postures, facial expressions, gazes, and touch.

Laboratory study: Scientific experimentation or research carried out in a room or building designed for research or normally used for this purpose.

Learned helplessness: A psychological state that occurs when individuals believe that important events in their lives are uncontrollable. According to Martin E. P. Seligman, this belief can lead to emotional, cognitive, and motivational deficits.

Least preferred co-worker (LPC) scale: A self-report method for assessing leadership style developed by Fred Fiedler; those individuals who give relatively high ratings to their least preferred co-worker tend to adopt a relationship-oriented leadership style, whereas those who give low ratings to their least preferred co-worker tend to adopt a task-oriented style.

Loneliness: Feelings of desperation, boredom, self-deprecation, and depression experienced when individuals feel their personal relationships are too few or too unsatisfying.

Love: An emotion-laden state of intense interest in another person (passionate love); also, a strong commitment to support and care for another person that develops gradually over time (companionate love).

Low-ball technique: An influence technique in which the influencer first exacts agreement from the target before revealing hidden costs or the unexpected lack of benefits.

Mere exposure: The formation of a positive attitude through repeated exposure to the object.

Mindlessness: A state of reduced cognitive activity in which individuals respond without considering the meaning of their behavior or its possible consequences.

Misattribution: The attribution of an event to a source with which it has little or no connection.

***n*Affiliation:** The need for affiliation; the dispositional tendency to seek out others.

Negative state relief model: A theory of helping that suggests individuals who are in bad moods help others in order to improve their negative mood states.

Noise: Unwanted sound.

Nonconformity: Refusing to change one's beliefs and/or behaviors despite social pressures.

Nondominant responses: Novel, complicated, or untried behaviors that the organism has never performed before or has performed only infrequently.

Nonexperimental design: A research technique that involves systematically measuring all variables of interest and then examining the relationship among measures.

Nonreactive measures: Measurement methods that have little or no impact on the participants in the research.

Nonverbal cues: Qualities or actions that communicate without words; facial expressions, style of dress, and body postures are examples.

Norms: Implicit social standards that describe what behaviors should and should not be performed in a social setting; guidelines for actions.

Observational methods: Any measurement method that involves an individual who watches and records another individual's actions.

Operant conditioning: A learning process based on the principle that actions that are immediately followed by a reinforcer will occur more frequently in the future.

Opponent-process theory: A theoretical framework that proposes that, after individuals experience an emotion, they begin to experience the opposing emotional reaction after a short period of time.

Overattribution: The tendency for observers to make attributions about an individual even though the individual's actions are constrained by the situation.

Overjustification: Undermining the intrinsic motivation for a behavior by providing an extrinsic reason for the action.

Overload: An excessive number of inputs that come so rapidly that the information cannot be processed effectively.

Paradigm: Scientists' shared assumptions about the phenomena they study; also, a set of research procedures.

Paralanguage: Voice cues, such as intonation, pitch, and pauses that accompany spoken language; how something is said, rather than what is said.

Participant observation: An observational method that involves making observations while taking part in the social process.

Personal norm: A personal standard for specific behavior generated by one's own internalized values.

Personal space: The area individuals maintain around themselves into which others cannot intrude without arousing discomfort.

Person-positivity bias: The tendency to evaluate human beings more positively than nonhuman objects.

Persuasion: The communication of facts, arguments, and information calculated to change another person's attitudes.

Predictive attributions: Causal inferences that increase the attributor's ability to make predictions about future actions and events.

Prejudice: An attitude toward an ethnic, racial, or other social group.

Prisoner's dilemma game (PDG): A laboratory procedure in which players must make either cooperative or competitive choices in order to earn points or money; used in the study of cooperation, competition, and the development of mutual trust.

Private acceptance: Change that occurs when the targets of social influence personally accept the influencer's position.

Projection: The tendency for perceivers to attribute their socially undesirable qualities to other people.

Prosocial behavior: Actions that benefit other people, such as helping, cooperation, and common courtesy.

Proxemic cues: The physical distances individuals maintain between one another that convey information about the interactants and their interrelationships.

Psychoanalytic theory: A theoretical framework proposed by Sigmund Freud that argues individuals' thoughts and actions are often motivated by internal and possibly unknown personality processes.

Psychological reactance: A complex emotional and cognitive reaction that occurs when individuals feel that their freedom to make choices has been threatened or eliminated.

Random assignment: A research technique used in experiments that involves placing various people in various conditions at random.

Realistic-group-conflict theory: The view that prejudice stems from competition between groups for scarce resources.

Reciprocity norm: A societal standard enjoining individuals to pay back in kind what they receive from others.

Representativeness: A cognitive heuristic that enables the perceiver to classify others into social categories by examining the extent to which their qualities match, or resemble, the qualities generally associated with members of the category.

Ringelmann effect: The tendency for group members to become less productive as the size of their group increases.

Risk-benefit approach: An approach to ethical decision making that prescribes enumerating the risks created for participants as well as the possible gains for subjects, society, and science.

Risky shift: The tendency for groups to make riskier decisions than individuals.

Role-play studies: A research technique that involves describing a social situation to subjects and then asking them to describe how they think they would respond.

Schema: A network of cognitive generalizations that organizes and guides the processing and recall of social information; the plural form is schemas or schemata.

Selective exposure: The tendency for people to seek out information that is consistent with their choices while avoiding information that is inconsistent with their choices.

Self: One's sense of personal identity; the individual as viewed by himself or herself.

Self-assessment: Testing one's conception of oneself by performing tasks that will provide the clearest information concerning abilities and shortcomings.

Self-awareness: The psychological state in which one's attention is focused on the self, personal standards, or inner experiences.

Self-concept: An individual's perception of his or her personal qualities and characteristics; the individual's answer to the question "Who am I?"

Self-consciousness: The dispositional tendency to be in a state of self-awareness. Individuals who are high in self-consciousness tend to be more self-focused across all situations.

Self-consistency: Seeking out information that confirms preconceptions about the self.

Self-disclosure: The process of revealing information about oneself to another person.

Self-efficacy: The belief that one can personally produce and regulate one's outcomes.

Self-enhancement: The processes by which individuals protect and increase their self-esteem; also, the result of such processes.

Self-esteem: Individuals' personal appraisal or evaluation of their attributes; the evaluative component of the self-concept.

Self-evaluation: Acquiring veridical, diagnostic information about personal qualities.

Self-fulfilling prophecy: A perceiver's inaccurate belief that can evoke new behaviors in the person being observed that confirm the perceiver's original inaccurate conception.

Self-handicapping: Actively seeking or creating impediments for performance.

Self-monitoring: The degree to which individuals monitor and regulate their behavior to fit the situation. High self-monitors tend to regard themselves as shrewd, adaptable individuals who alter their actions to fit a given situation, whereas low self-monitors value congruence between their private attributions and public actions.

Self-perception theory: A theoretical model that assumes individuals come to know their own attitudes, emotions, and other internal states by inferring them from observations of their own overt behavior.

Self-presentation: The display of social behaviors that establish, maintain, or refine the impression that others have of us; also known as impression management.

Self-report measures: Assessment devices, such as questionnaires, tests, or interviews, that ask respondents to describe their feelings, attitudes, or beliefs.

Self-schemata: Cognitive generalizations about the self that organize and guide the processing of self-related information.

Self-serving attributions: Causal inferences that protect, maintain, or extend beliefs about the self.

Self-serving bias: The general tendency to attribute positive outcomes to personal factors but negative outcomes to external factors. Although the term *self-serving* suggests this bias stems from a desire to maintain and enhance self-esteem, cognitive and self-presentational processes also sustain this attributional tendency.

Sex role: Individuals' beliefs and expectations about themselves that are based on their biological gender.

Shyness: A pronounced form of social anxiety that is characterized by disabling emotional (feelings of tension, awkwardness, fear of evaluation by others), physiological (blushing, perspiration), and behavioral (reticence, withdrawal from others) symptoms.

Similarity-helping effect: The tendency for bystanders to render aid to others who are similar to them in some way.

Sleeper effect: A delayed increase in the persuasiveness of noncredible sources that generally occurs when the source of the message is forgotten before the message itself is forgotten.

Social anxiety: Generalized feelings of apprehension and embarrassment experienced when anticipating or actually interacting with other people.

Social categorization: The perceptual classification of people into various social groups.

Social cognition: The inferential processes perceivers rely on to organize, structure, and integrate perceptual information.

Social comparison: Evaluating the accuracy of personal beliefs and attitudes by comparing oneself to others.

Social desirability bias: The tendency to give socially acceptable responses when answering self-report questionnaires and surveys.

Social exchange theory: An economic model of interpersonal relationships that argues individuals seek out relationships that offer them many rewards while exacting few costs.

Social facilitation: The enhancement of an individual's performance when that person works in the presence of other people.

Social impact theory: An analysis of social influence processes that proposes the impact of any source of influence depends on the strength, immediacy, and number of influencers involved.

Social influence: A change in beliefs or behaviors in response to social pressure.

Socialization: The gradual acquisition of language, attitudes, and other socially approved values through reinforcement, observation, and other learning processes.

Social judgment theory: A theoretical analysis of attitude change that emphasizes the receiver's perception and appraisal of the persuasive message. This theory predicts that communications that fall in the latitude of acceptance are more persuasive than communications that fall in the latitude of rejection.

Social learning: A model of learning that argues new behaviors are acquired by observing and imitating the actions displayed by models, such as parents and peers.

Social loafing: The reduction of individual effort exerted when people work in groups compared to when they work alone.

Social loneliness: Feelings of isolation and depression that occur when individuals believe that their relationships with friends and acquaintances are too few or unsatisfying.

Social perception: The perceptual process by which individuals gather information about and form initial impressions of other people.

Social power: The ability to produce intended and foreseen changes in others.

Social psychology: The scientific study of the way individuals' thoughts, feelings, and behaviors are influenced by the actual, imagined, or implied presence of others.

Social responsibility norm: A societal standard prescribing socially commendable actions, such as helping others in need.

Social trap: A situation in which an action that is personally advantageous is damaging to society as a whole.

Sociobiology: A biological approach to understanding social behavior that assumes recurring patterns of behavior in animals ultimately stem from evolutionary pressures that increase the likelihood of adaptive social actions while extinguishing nonadapative practices.

Stereotypes: Cognitive generalizations about the qualities and characteristics of the members of a particular group or social category.

Strategic self-presentations: Impression management tactics that individuals use to deliberately create, shape, and control another person's perceptions of their personal qualities; examples include ingratiation, self-promotion, basking in reflected glory, and excuses.

Stressor: An environmental event that threatens an individual's existence or sense of well-being.

Structured observation: An observational method that involves classifying (coding) the subject's actions into clearly defined categories. In many cases, the observer simply notes the occurrence and frequency of each targeted behavior.

Subject role: The behavior characteristic of subjects when they take part in research. An individual who adopts a good subject role may be very conscientious, while an individual who adopts a bad subject role may try to ruin the study.

Symbolic interactionism: A sociologically oriented theory that assumes our conception of self develops as we interpret and selectively internalize others' symbolic gestures.

Territory: A specific area that an individual or group of individuals claims and defends for personal use.

Tricomponent theory of attitudes: A theoretical perspective that argues an attitude forms when three components—affect, cognition, and behavior—become linked in an organized structure. According to this theory, an attitude is an affective feeling of liking or disliking based on beliefs about an object which leads to a readiness to behave in a certain manner.

Two-factor theory of emotions: A framework that argues emotions are based on arousal and attributions about the cause of that arousal.

Two-factor theory of love: An attributional theory of love that traces passionate love to increases in an individual's level of arousal and the individual's attribution of this arousal to feelings of attraction for another person.

Type A personality: A constellation of personal traits and behavioral tendencies that has been linked to heart disease. In contrast to the Type B personality, Type As are competitive, time-oriented, and hostile and experience stress when faced with a loss of control.

Unconscious: A portion of the mind that actively directs actions and thoughts while remaining hidden from conscious awareness.

Unweighted models: Information-integration theories that argue social perceivers form impressions of others by combining information about other people without giving extra weight to any specific bit of information. In consequence, all information has an equal impact on impressions.

Upward social comparison: Comparing oneself to others who are performing more effectively.

Vivid data: Novel, interesting, and/or unexpected perceptual information and events that dominate our perceptual attention.

Weighted models: Information-integration theories that argue social perceivers form impressions of others by combining information about other people after first giving extra weight to certain bits of information.

AUTHOR INDEX

Abbey, A., 124, 129
Abel, G., 400
Abeles, N., 407
Abelson, R. P., 116, 262
Abrahams, D., 298
Abramson, L. Y., 177
Ackerman, P., 364
Adair, J. G., 34, 35
Adams, G. R., 298
Adams, S., 369
Addesman, P., 317
Adorno, T. W., 227
Agustsdottir, S., 89
Ahlering, R. F., 217
Aiello, J. R., 528, 532, 538
Ajzen, I., 162, 192, 193, 209, 211, 212–214, 234, 235
Akert, R. M., 100, 224
Alessis, C., 248–249
Alexander, C. N., 440
Allen, H., 358
Allen, V. L., 447
Alloy, L. B., 84
Allport, F. H., 44, 45, 237, 475
Allport, G. W., 15, 16, 44, 45, 208, 225, 229, 235, 288
Altman, I., 316, 518, 520, 521, 523–525, 527, 528, 530, 531, 548, 549
Alton, A. O., 109
Alvares, K. M., 505
Amabile, T. M., 158
Amato, P. R., 334, 343, 344
Amidon, M. D., 109–110
Andersen, S. M., 69, 71, 94
Anderson, C. A., 547
Anderson, D. A., 131
Anderson, D. C., 547
Anderson, N. H., 116, 118
Annis, A. B., 540
Antaki, C., 184
Appelman, A. J., 167

Apple, W., 108, 250
Apter, S. J., 388
Archer, D., 100, 224
Archer, R. L., 349, 364
Argyle, M., 106, 107, 530
Arkin, R. M., 81, 89, 167, 175, 207, 298, 302
Aron, A. P., 313–314
Aronoff, J., 17, 349
Aronson, E., 39, 43, 141, 173, 235, 239, 268, 276, 288, 305–307
Aronson, V., 298
Asch, S. E., 120, 121, 140, 430–434, 437, 440, 441, 450, 462, 465
Ashmore, R. D., 231
Ashour, A. S., 505
Atkins, J. L., 129
Atkinson, J. W., 290
Atwood, R. W., 206
Augelli, R. W., 81
Austin, W., 355
Austin, W. G., 236
Averill, J. R., 315
Azuma, H., 54
Back, K., 297
Backman, C. W., 82
Backstrom, C. H., 196, 235
Bagozzi, R. P., 194
Bailey, K. D., 18
Baker, N. J., 420
Baldwin, M. W., 70–71
Bales, R. F., 112, 504, 509
Ball, R. L., 415
Bandura, A., 55, 222, 234, 399, 401–403, 406, 418
Banks, C., 427
Bannister, B. D., 504
Barash, D. P., 295, 374, 378, 393, 411
Barber, T. X., 36
Bargh, J. A., 125, 131, 152
Barker, R. G., 540

Barlow, G., 400
Barnes, J., 122
Baron, R. A., 39, 385, 394, 402, 415, 416, 535, 546, 547
Baron, R. M., 99
Baron, R. S., 480, 482
Barrios, M., 224
Barrow, J. C., 500
Barsaloux, J., 40, 497
Bar-tal, D., 154, 335, 364, 368
Basow, S. A., 235
Bass, B. M., 499
Bassett, R., 462
Bassok, M., 131
Batson, C. D., 264–266, 348, 351–352, 358, 363–364
Baum, A., 525–526, 530–531, 536–538, 541, 550
Baum, C., 536–537, 541
Baumann, D. J., 366–367
Baumeister, R. F., 85, 347, 522
Baumgardner, A. H., 81, 89
Baumrind, D., 38
Baur, K., 324
Beaber, R. J., 250
Beaman, A. L., 355, 410, 460
Bear, J., 102
Beavin, J. H., 112
Becker, H. S., 65
Becker, L., 554
Beckman, L., 154
Belew, J., 22
Bell, P. A., 415, 530, 541, 546–547, 550
Bellezza, F. S., 53, 125
Bellows, N., 119
Bem, D. J., 69, 71, 156–159, 163, 272, 511
Bem, S., 92, 94
Benne, K. D., 503
Benson, P. L., 345

Bentler, P. M., 215
Ben-Yair, E., 74
Berg, J. H., 317, 321
Berger, J., 502
Berger, J. M., 167
Berger, S. M., 478
Berglas, S., 81, 89
Berkowitz, L., 366, 370, 384, 396–398, 400, 402–403, 407, 418
Berlyne, D. E., 218
Berman, J., 535
Berman, J. J., 215
Bernbach, W., 257
Berscheid, E., 88, 101, 296, 298, 299, 302, 306, 308, 309, 313, 315, 316, 320, 325, 369
Berstein, S., 94
Bettelheim, B., 21
Bettman, J. R., 153
Betz, N. E., 55
Beuf, A., 224
Beyth-Marom, R., 135
Biaggio, M. K., 387
Bickman, L., 18–19, 33, 200–201, 234, 339, 345–346, 355
Bidwell, L. D., 285
Biederman, M. F., 358
Bierbrauer, G., 441
Birch, K., 364
Birchler, G. R., 320
Birg, L. D., 165
Birnbaum, M. H., 116, 118, 218, 219
Bishop, G. D., 512
Bishop, S. E., 109–110
Bither, S. W., 260
Bizman, A., 366
Blake, R. R., 437
Blanchard, D. H., 400
Blanchard, K. H., 507, 510
Blanck, P. D., 109
Blaney, N., 239
Blaney, P. H., 60
Blank, A., 10, 442
Blankmeyer, B. L., 125, 131
Blass, T., 17
Blosser, J. L., 358
Blumberg, H. H., 510
Bobo, L., 205
Bochner, S., 246
Bogardus, E. S., 198–199
Boice, R., 98, 128
Bois, J. L., 289
Bolen, M. H., 348
Bond, C. F., 478
Bonoma, T. V., 456
Boothroyd, P., 315
Borden, R., 85
Borgida, E., 162, 173, 211
Borofsky, G. L., 358
Bortner, R. W., 179
Boruch, R. F., 33

Bosko, K., 366
Bouchard, T. J., 40, 497
Bower, G. H., 125, 133, 134
Bowerman, W. R., 166
Braband, J., 339
Braden, M., 264
Bradley, G. W., 166
Brady, J. J., 478
Bragg, M. E., 293
Braginsky, B. M., 65
Braginsky, D. D., 65
Bramel, D. A., 128
Bray, R. M., 449
Breckler, S. J., 192, 194
Bredemeier, B. J., 408
Brehm, J., 252, 266–267
Brehm, S. S., 53, 60, 296, 324, 329
Brekke, N., 162
Brenner, M., 34
Brent, E., 302
Brewer, M., 39, 237
Brewin, C., 184
Brewin, C. R., 177
Brickman, P., 74–75
Briere, J., 400
Brigham, J. C., 226–227
Brinberg, D., 304
Brock, T. C., 247
Brockner, J., 54, 55, 297
Brodt, S. E., 187
Bromley, D. B., 50
Bromley, D. G., 281
Bromley, S., 202, 346
Brothen, T., 307
Brower, S., 527
Brown, B., 520–521, 524–525
Brown, B. B., 527
Brown, D., 69
Brown, J., 155
Brown, R. C., 384, 386, 408
Brown, S. M., 502
Brown, V., 224
Brownmiller, S., 173
Bruun, S. E., 486
Bryan, J. H., 346, 370
Bryant, J., 313, 400, 416
Buchwald, A., 79
Buck, R., 103
Buck, R. W., 106
Buckley, T., 364
Bugental, J., 50
Buller, D. B., 106
Bulman, R. J., 177
Bungard, W., 34
Bunge, M., 33
Burger, J. M., 172, 298, 302, 462
Burgess, A. W., 390, 419
Burgess, M., 413
Burgess, R. L., 318
Burgoon, J. K., 106, 530
Burke, P. A., 52

Burke, P. J., 502
Burn, S. M., 553
Burnkrant, R. E., 194
Burns, J. M., 498
Burns, R. B., 50, 54
Burnstein, E., 121, 513
Burt, M. R., 173
Bush, E. S., 177
Buss, A. H., 59, 62, 294, 387
Buss, D. M., 302–304
Byrne, D., 207, 247, 291, 301–302, 532
Cacioppo, J. T., 209, 244, 250–251, 256, 277, 339, 462
Cain, L. M., 80
Calder, B. J., 502
Caldwell, M. A., 317
Calesnick, L. E., 525
Calhoun, J. B., 516–517, 540–541
Callaway, M. R., 493
Callens, C., 12
Callero, P. L., 365
Campbell, A., 198, 284, 299
Campbell, B., 211
Campbell, B. H., 87
Campbell, D. T., 22, 26, 27, 191, 193, 203, 214, 225, 231, 253, 437
Campbell, J., 77
Candee, D., 17
Cantor, J., 313, 415–416
Cantor, J. R., 251
Cantor, N., 51
Cappella, J. N., 112
Caputo, C., 174
Carbonell, J. L., 502
Carli, L. C., 478
Carli, L. L., 173, 256, 445, 447–478
Carlopio, J., 35
Carlsmith, J. M., 39, 107, 269–271, 274, 276, 547
Carlston, D. E., 35, 125
Carlyle, T., 499
Carnegie, D., 324
Carroll, J. S., 150–151, 184
Cartwright, D., 44–45, 491, 500, 510
Carver, C. S., 56, 58, 60, 62, 91, 356
Cash, T. F., 102
Castell, P., 304
Catalan, J., 461
Ceci, S. J., 37
Chaiken, A. L., 172
Chaiken, S., 70–71, 246–247
Chaikin, A., 317
Champion, D. S., 129
Chanowitz, B., 10, 442
Chapman, G. C., 28
Chave, E. J., 191
Check, J. V. P., 400
Cheek, J. M., 294
Chein, I., 237
Chemers, M. M., 507, 523
Chen, J., 224

Chen, S. C., 475
Chernicky, P., 28, 35
Cherry, F., 207, 227
Chesterfield, E., 309
Chilstrom, J. T., 449
Chiodo, A. L., 131
Christensen, A., 308, 309, 325
Christensen, L., 35
Christian, J. J., 541
Christie, R., 458
Cialdini, R. B., 12, 85, 314, 366–368, 372, 443, 459, 461–462, 464
Claiborn, C. D., 455
Clark, K. B., 205, 237
Clark, L. F., 125
Clark, M., 366
Clark, M. S., 134, 318
Clark, R. D., 341, 345, 356, 358–362, 366, 375, 449, 464, 512
Clary, E. G., 153
Clausen, G. T., 339, 346, 356
Cline, V. B., 404
Clore, G. L., 106, 346
Cloward, R. A., 409
Coates, D., 150, 184
Cochran, P. J., 358
Cohen, A. R., 267
Cohen, C. E., 125, 129
Cohen, J. L., 35
Cohen, S., 293, 346, 542–545
Coke, J. S., 363–364
Cole, C. M., 460
Cole, E., 125, 131
Colella, M. J., 109
Coleman, J. F., 437
Coleman, S. R., 220
Collins, R. W., 79
Comer, R., 273
Comsky, P., 400
Condry, J., 158
Cone, J. D., 549, 551
Conner, E. R., 356
Conner, R. C., 376
Connor, W. H., 370
Conolley, E. S., 435
Conroy, J., 522
Constantian, C. A., 292
Constantinople, A., 92
Converse, J., 267
Converse, P. E., 284
Conway, M., 78
Cook, D. A., 553
Cook, M., 107
Cook, S. W., 26–27, 237–239
Cook, T. D., 33, 248
Cook, T. K., 249
Cooley, C. H., 64
Cooper, H., 267
Cooper, H. M., 256
Cooper, J., 202, 233, 272, 273
Cooper, R. E., 531

Cooper, W. H., 127
Corbit, J. D., 365
Corrigan, J. D., 455
Costa, F., 327
Costanzo, P. R., 43, 167
Cottrell, N. B., 73, 290, 475, 479, 481–482
Courrier, S., 404
Courtney, A. E., 224
Courtney, B. F., 54
Courtright, J. A., 494–495
Covey, M. K., 408
Covington, M. V., 166
Cowan, C. L., 367
Cozby, P. C., 317
Crandall, R., 162
Crane, M., 94
Crano, W. D., 211, 346
Cranston, J. W., 414
Critchlow, B., 274
Crittenden, K. S., 165
Crocker, J., 84, 124, 135
Croft, R. G., 404
Crooks, R., 324
Crosby, F., 202, 346
Cross, H. A., 217
Cross, J. A., 348
Cross, T., 206
Crutchfield, R. S., 444
Csikszentmihalyi, M., 242
Cummings, W., 553
Cunniff, C., 152
Cunningham, M. R., 366, 378
Curtiss, S., 61
Cutrona, C. E., 292–293
Cysneiros, P. G., 107
Dabbs, J. M., 497
D'Andrade, R. G., 111
Daniels, L. R., 370
Darby, B. L., 367, 461
Darley, J. M, 14, 40, 130, 142, 172, 288, 302, 333, 337–339, 341, 346, 350–354, 357, 358, 360, 373
Dart, R. A., 392
Dashiell, J. F., 475
Davage, R., 291
Davenport, M., 370
Davidson, A. R., 211, 214
Davidson, E. S., 403, 417, 419
Davis, D. E., 541
Davis, G. E., 525, 538
Davis, J. H., 444, 513
Davis, J. M., 301–302
Davis, K. E., 156–157, 304, 310–311, 327
Davis, K. W., 310, 314
Davis, M. F., 510
Davis, M. H., 364
Davison, R., 302
Dawes, R. M., 118, 194, 235
Dawkins, R., 378

Dean, J., 106, 530
Dean, L. M., 530
Deaux, K., 230, 235, 285, 345
DeBono, K. G., 257
Deci, E. L., 158, 184
DeFleur, M. L., 209, 214
DelBoca, F. K., 231
Dell, D. M., 455
Dengerink, H. A., 408
Denney, D. R., 181–182
DePaulo, B. M., 369, 374
Derlega, V., 317, 374
Dermer, M., 88, 216, 313
deTurck, M. A., 106
Deutsch, M., 33, 84, 305, 419–420, 423, 437
Devine, P. G., 137
Dewey, J., 64
DeWood, R., 366
Diaz-Loving, R., 364
Diener, C. I., 177–178
Diener, E., 409–410
Dietrich, D., 497
Dill, C. A., 544
Dillon, W. R., 194
Dion, K. K., 101, 315, 456
Dion, K. L., 299, 315
Divale, W. T., 107
Dixon, D. N., 455
Dmitruk, V. M., 79
Dobosz, B., 327
Dockett, D., 527
Dodge, R. W., 386
Doise, W., 511
Dolich, I. J., 260
Dollard, J. R., 45, 394, 396
Dominick, J. R., 224
Donath, C. H., 478
Donnerstein, E. I., 39, 398, 400, 419, 545
Donoghue, J. M., 162
Donovan, J. E., 327
Doob, A. N., 441
Doob, L. W., 45, 394
Dougherty, D., 206
Douglas, J. E., 390
Dovidio, J. F., 345–346, 359–362, 375
Downing, L., 370
Doyle, A. C., 100, 114, 120, 129, 131, 141
Drabman, R. S., 404
Drauden, G., 40, 497
Driscoll, R., 310, 314
Dubos, R., 541
Dukerich, J. M., 131
Duncan, B. D., 364
Durkee, A., 387
Dutton, D. G., 313, 314, 346
Duval, S., 56, 58, 62, 175
Dweck, C. S., 177–180, 184
Dworkin, R. H., 52

Eagly, A. H., 246, 247, 256, 445, 447
Earle, H. H., 33
Ebbesen, E. B., 125, 277, 297, 412, 532
Edinger, J. A., 106
Edney, J., 522, 523, 551
Edwards, C., 129
Edwards, D. J. A., 532
Effertz, J., 502
Effrein, E. A., 142
Egeth, H. E., 138
Ehlert, J., 345
Ehlert, N., 345
Eibl-Eibesfeldt, I., 106
Einhorn, H. J., 132
Eisenberg, J. G., 406
Ekman, P., 102, 103, 108, 110, 141, 206
Elig, T. W., 155, 165
Elliot, G. C., 88
Ellsworth, P. C., 107, 122, 141
Elms, A. C., 17
Ely, R. J., 86
Emerson, R. W., 437
Enzle, M. E., 153
Epley, S. W., 73, 290
Epstein, Y. M., 532
Erber, R., 131, 134
Erikson, M., 28
Erkut, S., 349
Eron, L. D., 407, 417
Ervin, C. F., 302
Esser, A. H., 522
Esser, J. K., 493
Etzioni, A., 28
Evans, D. E., 365
Evans, F. J., 35
Evans, G. W., 532, 545
Evans, M., 232
Evans, R. I., 260
Everett, P. B., 553
Exline, R., 104, 291
Fairweather, G. W., 33
Falbo, T., 456, 458
Falender, V. J., 142
Falke, T. L., 80
Farkash, E., 136
Fatoullah, E., 247
Faucheaux, C., 448
Fazio, R. H., 60, 69, 142, 211, 272, 273, 286, 288
Feather, N. T., 84
Feigenbaum, R., 165
Feldman, J. J., 289
Feldman, N. S., 76, 162
Felipe, N. J., 532
Fellner, C. H., 370, 371
Felson, R. B., 55, 66, 386
Fenigstein, A., 59, 62
Ferguson, T. J., 396, 415
Feshbach, S., 254, 384, 407, 412
Feshbaugh, L., 447

Festinger L., 12, 43, 45, 262–265, 269–271, 273–274, 276, 279, 286, 297, 428
Fiedler, F., 501, 504–505, 509
Fine, M., 33
Firestone, I., 35, 271
Fischhoff, B., 135, 139
Fisek, M. H., 502
Fishbaugh, L., 445
Fishbein, J. E., 532, 533
Fishbein, M., 192–193, 209, 212–214, 234, 235
Fishbein, S., 313, 314
Fisher, B. A., 502
Fisher, J. D., 369, 374, 530, 532, 541, 550
Fishman, C., 291
Fiske, S. T., 11, 118, 124–125, 131, 133–135, 141, 152, 175
Flay, B. R., 248–249
Fleishman, J. A., 371
Fleming, I., 38
Fleming, J. S., 54
Fletcher, B., 74
Fletcher, G., 40
Flyger, V., 541
Foa, E. B., 304
Foa, U. G., 112, 304
Fode, K. L., 35
Fogelman, E., 349
Folkes, V. S., 442
Folkman, J. R., 31
Foote, F. H., 328, 329
Forer, B. R., 80
Forgas, J. P., 327
Forsyth, D. R., 12, 33, 39, 81, 119, 149, 156, 161, 165, 167, 181, 275, 502, 510, 528, 532
Forsyth, N. L., 181
Foss, C., 520, 521, 524, 525
Fosterling, F., 181
Foti, R. J., 124, 502
Foushee, H. C., 364
Fox, S., 257
Frable, D., 94
Frager, R., 445
Fraser, S. C., 355, 410, 459–460
Fraser, C., 124, 502
Frazzini, S. F., 139
Freedman, J. L., 271, 407, 441, 459–460, 541
Freeman, S., 85
Freemon, J. E., 293
Freidman, S., 232
French, J. R. P., 452–455, 459, 463
Frenkel-Brunswick, E., 227
Freud, S., 44, 389, 410, 412–413, 417–418
Freuh, T., 224
Frey, D., 167, 267
Fried, R., 366

Friedland, N., 136
Friedman, H. S., 106
Friedman, L. W., 542, 543
Friedman, M., 178, 179, 184
Friesen, W. V., 102–103, 110
Frieze, I. H., 154, 155, 165
Fritz, J. G., 109
Frodi, A., 398
Fromkin, H. L., 441
Fulero, S., 232
Fultz, J., 364
Gaertner, S. L., 200–201, 234, 345–346, 359–362, 375
Gaes, G. G., 207
Galle, O. R., 541
Gallup, G. G., 57
Gallup, G. H., 168, 170, 205, 215
Gammon, C. B., 414
Gangestad, S., 289
Garcia, J. E., 506
Garcia, R., 478
Gardner, G. T., 544
Garfinkel, H., 430
Garwood, S. G., 519
Gaskell, G. D., 406
Gatchel, R. J., 525
Gavriel, Z. A., 299
Geen, R. G., 397–398, 419, 480, 482
Geis, F. L., 224, 458
Geis, G., 356
Gelfand, D. M., 335
Geller, E. S., 38, 39, 553
Gelles, R. J., 388, 413
Gerard, H. B., 237, 268, 435, 437
Gerbner, G., 224, 405
Gerdes, E. P., 39
Gergen, K. J., 53, 157, 348
Gergen, M. M., 348
Gerstein, J. C., 406
Gewirtz, J. L., 375
Gibb, C. A., 499
Gibbons, F. X., 60, 351
Giesen, M., 528
Gilbert, D. T., 14
Gilbert, S. J., 28, 172
Gilden, E. R., 544
Gillig, P. M., 248
Gilmour, D. R., 528
Gilovich, T., 165
Glass, D., 346
Glass, D. C., 177, 178, 179, 542–545
Gleason, T. C., 118
Goethals, G. R., 76, 171, 513
Goetz, T. E., 177
Goffman, E., 65, 83–84, 87–88, 194, 274, 430, 441
Goldberg, C., 446
Goldberg, M., 154
Goldstein, A. P., 388, 417, 419
Goldstein, J. H., 406
Goldstein, M., 311

Gollob, H. F., 116
Gollwitzer, P. M., 89, 364
Gonda, G., 94
Gonzales, M. H., 301, 302
Goodnow, J. E., 111
Gordon, W., 497
Gormezano, I., 220
Gormley, F., 538
Gorn, G. J., 218, 220
Goswick, R. A., 293
Gottfredson, S. D., 527
Gottlieb, A., 339
Gottman, J. M., 320
Gove, W. R., 541
Graen, G. B., 505
Grajek, S., 311
Granberg, D., 302
Grandmaison, P. S., 478
Grau, B. W., 106
Graves, J., 484
Graziano, W., 88
Green, B. F., 191
Green, J. A., 214
Green, S. G., 502
Greenberg, J., 60, 84, 153, 222
Greenberg, M. S., 368
Greenberg, R., 317
Greenberg, T., 167
Greene, D., 129, 159
Greene, T. C., 546
Greenwald, A. G., 10, 50, 51, 78, 91, 248, 272
Greer, D. L., 522
Grev, R., 366
Griffith, C. R., 519
Groff, B. D., 540
Groner, N., 540
Gross, A. E., 38
Gross, L., 402, 405
Gross, P. G., 130
Grossman, B. S., 158
Grove, J. B., 22
Gruber, K. J., 408
Gruder, C. L., 248, 249
Grush, J. E., 217
Grzelak, J., 374
Guild, D., 400
Gunn, L. K., 322
Gunn, S. P., 28, 35
Guttman, L., 198
Haber, G. M., 519
Hackett, G., 55
Hackman, J. R., 498
Hakmiller, K. L., 77
Halamaj, J., 248, 249
Halcomb, C. G., 217
Hale, J. L., 106
Hall, E. T., 527–531, 534, 549
Hall, J. A., 94
Hall, M. A., 106
Halpin, A. W., 503

Hamill, R., 136
Hamilton, D. L., 121, 124, 125, 192, 232
Hamilton, J. C., 522
Hamilton, W. D., 376, 377
Hampton, K. L., 478
Haney, C., 427
Hanselka, L. L., 544
Hansen, R. D., 162
Hansen, W. B., 520, 521
Hansford, E. A., 422
Hanson, L. R., 118
Hardin, G., 551
Hardy, D., 129
Hardyck, J. A., 264
Hare, A. P., 445, 447, 510
Hare, M., 497
Hargis, K., 367
Harkins, S. G., 251, 484–486
Harootunian, B., 388
Harpin, R. E., 525
Harrell, A. W., 345
Harris, B., 81, 532, 533
Harris, H. J., 440
Harris, M. B., 345, 463
Harris, M. J., 142
Harris, R., 370
Harrison, A. A., 109
Hartke, D. D., 506
Hartmann, D. P., 335
Hartshorne, H., 348, 349
Hartup, W. W., 408
Harvey, J. H., 81, 99, 161, 162, 170, 184, 308, 309, 325
Harvey, O. J., 227, 238
Hass, R. G., 62
Hastie, R., 125, 153, 464, 465, 467
Hastorf, A. H., 122, 141
Hatfield, E., 296, 298, 299, 306, 310, 313, 315, 325
Hawkins, C., 467
Hayduck, L. A., 528, 531–533, 550
Hayes, S. C., 549, 551
Hayman, J., 80
Hays, R. B., 308
Hays, R. E., 317, 321
Haythorne, W. W., 527
Heesacker, M., 251
Heider, F., 11, 45, 81, 148, 151, 152, 184, 262, 302, 345
Heim, M., 293
Heingartner, A., 477, 478
Heinold, W. D., 356
Heller, J. F., 540
Heller, T., 502
Helm, B., 202, 452
Helmreich, R., 92
Hendrick, C., 39, 296, 310, 329
Hendrick, D., 355
Hendrick, S., 296, 310, 317, 328, 329, 347, 348

Henley, N., 141, 533
Henley, N. M., 104, 106
Hennessey, B. A., 158
Hennigan, K., 238
Hennigan, K. M., 248–249
Henson, A., 107
Herman, C. P., 209, 236
Herman, E., 317
Herman, E. M., 477, 478
Herr, P. M., 69, 211
Herschlag, L. R., 478
Hersey, P., 507
Heshka, S., 532
Heslin, R., 100, 260
Hess, E., 203, 204
Hewitt, J., 530
Heyns, R. W., 291
Higbee, K. L., 31, 254
Higgins, E. T., 125, 162, 209, 236, 273
Higgins, R. L., 91
Hill, C. A., 67, 84, 86
Hill, C. T., 116, 311, 317, 328
Hill, J., 76
Hill, P. C., 544
Hinton, J. L., 224
Hirokawa, R. Y., 498
Hobbs, S. A., 293
Hocevar, D., 122
Hockenbury, D., 293
Hoelter, J. W., 65, 79
Hoffman, M. L., 378
Hoffman, S., 441
Hogan, R., 12
Hokanson, J. E., 413
Holland, C. C., 27
Hollander, E. P., 445, 447–449, 500
Holmes, D. S., 128
Holmes, J. G., 317
Homans, G. C., 318
Hong, C., 540
Hood, R., 60
Hood, W. E., 238
Hook, L. H., 467
Hooper, C. H., 497
Horai, J., 247
Horn, N., 366
Hornstein, H. A., 33, 345
Horton, R. W., 404
House, P., 129
Hovland, C. I., 45, 193, 244, 245, 248, 252–253, 256, 258, 275
Howard, J., 129
Howard, J. A., 371
Howell, R. J., 206
Hrdy, S. B., 392
Huang, L. C., 363
Hubbard, M., 131
Hubner, J. J., 54
Huesmann, L. R., 407

Huff, D., 31
Hunt, D. F., 227
Hunt, M., 327
Hursh-César, G., 196, 235
Huston, T. L., 308, 309, 318, 319, 325, 353, 354, 356
Hwalek, M., 109
Hyman, H. H., 227
Ickes, W. J., 17, 80, 161, 336
Ingham, A. G., 484
Ingram, R. E., 53, 60, 81
Inkster, J. A., 267
Insko, C. A., 222, 246, 297, 302
Iritani, B., 224
Isen, A. M., 364–366
Itkin, S., 106
Izard, C. E., 103
Jaccard, J. J., 214
Jackson, D. D., 112
Jackson, D. N., 445
Jackson, J. M., 435, 484
Jackson-Beeck, M., 405
Jacobs, R. C., 437
Jacobson, L., 142
Jacobson, M. B., 502
James, R. M., 467
James, W., 49, 53, 56, 64, 185
Janda, L. H., 102
Janis, I. L., 45, 181, 244–245, 248, 254, 487–496, 509, 510
Janisse, M. P., 204
Janoff-Bulman, R., 173
Jaquette, D., 349
Javornisky, G., 446
Jenni, D. A., 532
Jenni, M. A., 532
Jennings, J., 224
Jerdee, T. H., 502
Jessor, R., 327
Jessor, L., 327
Johnson, D., 449
Johnson, G. A., 297, 314
Johnson, H. G., 102
Johnson, J. A., 12
Johnson, J. T., 80
Johnson, M. P., 319
Johnson, R. N., 384
Johnson, S., 507, 510
Johnson, T. E., 415
Johnson, T. J., 165
Jones, C. R., 125
Jones, E. E., 17, 44, 81, 84, 85, 89, 156, 157, 159, 171–173, 175, 184, 228, 296, 308, 309
Jones, J. M., 231, 236
Jones, R. A., 230
Jones, S., 254
Jones, S. C., 302, 305
Jones, W. H., 293
Jorgensen, B. W., 304
Junghans, C. H., 301, 302

Kadish, S. H., 465
Kahle, L. R., 215, 220
Kahneman, D., 132, 134, 136
Kalin, R., 301
Kalle, R. J., 207
Kalven, H., 465
Kandel, D. B., 302, 305
Kanouse, D. E., 118
Kaplan, H. B., 50
Kaplan, M. F., 121, 513
Kaplan, S. J., 112
Karabenick, S. A., 345
Kardes, F. R., 211
Karlin, R. A., 532
Karlovac, M., 162
Karp, L., 366
Karylowski, J., 367
Kassin, S. M., 162
Katz, D., 191
Katz, I., 346
Katz, P. A., 233
Katz, R., 500
Keating, C. F., 107
Keating, J., 540
Keating, J. P., 538
Kelem, R., 410
Keller, H. R., 417
Kelley, H. H., 45, 149, 155, 156, 159, 160, 163, 174, 175, 183, 244–245, 248, 308–310, 311, 317, 318, 321, 325, 408, 422, 423, 437
Kelly, S., 545
Kelman, H. C., 37, 38, 245
Kendzierski, D., 211
Kenny, D. A., 305
Kenrick, D. T., 297, 314, 367
Kent, V., 510
Kepner, C. R., 416
Kerckhoff, A. C., 304
Kernis, M. H., 299
Kerr, N., 343
Kerr, N. L., 486, 504, 513
Kerr, S., 504
Kessler, R. C., 406
Kidd, R. F., 161
Kidder, L. H., 18
Kiesler, C. A., 220, 272, 273
Kiesner, R., 307
Kihlstrom, J. F., 51
Kilbride, J. E., 107
Kilham, W., 28
Kilroy, M. C., 311
Kim, M. P., 112, 122
Kimes, D. D., 224
Kimmel, A. J., 38, 288
Kinder, D. R., 243, 276
Kinder, P. R., 223
King, G. A., 125
King, R. G., 28, 35
Kingdon, J. W., 165
Kingsberry, G. G., 55

Kipnis, D., 456, 464
Kirker, W. S., 53
Kjos, G., 297
Klanderman, S. B., 370
Kleinke, C., 345, 346
Kleinmuntz, B., 206
Klemp, G., 69
Klentz, B., 355, 460
Klinger, E., 284
Knaani, A., 154
Knapp, M. L., 101, 141
Knight, J., 216
Knowles, E. S., 433, 519, 532, 535
Knox, R. E., 267
Koestner, R., 109
Kogan, N., 511
Kohlberg, L., 17
Komin, S., 107
Konečni, V. J., 297, 412, 532
Koocher, G. P., 532
Koropsak, E., 413
Korte, C., 339, 342, 343, 351
Kothandapani, V., 194
Krantz, D. S., 545
Krauss, R. M., 108, 250
Kraut, R. E., 52, 109, 119
Krebs, D. L., 10, 336, 349, 362
Kreitzberg, V. S., 289
Kremer, J. F., 415
Kruglanski, A. W., 136
Krupat, E., 39
Kruuk, H., 392
Ksionsky, S., 291
Kudoh, T., 106
Kuhn, M. H., 50
Kuhn, T., 15
Kuiper, N. A., 53
Kumar, A., 194
Kunst-Wilson, W. R., 218
Kurtines, W. M., 375
Kutash, I. L., 390
Kutash, S. B., 390
Kutner, B., 209
Lakatos, I., 32
Lake, E. A., 207
Lake, R. A., 346
Lamberth, J., 302
Lamm, H., 494, 511–513
Landis, C., 35
Langer, E. J., 10, 181, 184, 441, 442
Langner, T. S., 406
Lanni, J. C., 522
Larsen, R. J., 94
LaPiere, R. T., 208, 212, 234
Latané, B., 40, 285, 333, 337–339, 341, 346, 350–354, 357, 358, 360, 373, 433, 434, 435, 449, 464, 484–486
Lau, R. R., 153, 155, 165
Lauderdale, P., 440
Lauer, J., 318–319

Lauer, R., 318–319
Lavrakas, P. J., 527
Layton, J. F., 398
Lazarus, R. S., 187
Leahy, P., 107
Leary, M. R., 139, 275, 293–294, 325, 502
Lebetkin, A. I., 414
Lee, J. A., 310
Lefkowitz, M. M., 407
Legant, P., 174
Lemley, R., 137
Lentzner, H. R., 386
Leonard, K. E., 414
LePage, A., 398
Lepper, M. R., 131, 159
Lerner, M. J., 172, 173
Lerner, R. M., 345
Levenson, R. W., 69, 320
Leventhal, H., 254
Levi, A., 167
Levin, P. F., 366
Levine, D. W., 519
Levine, J. M., 440, 449
LeVine, R. A., 225, 231
Levine, S. V., 281
Levinger, G., 284, 304, 308, 309, 325, 484
Levinson, D., 227
Levitan, D., 311
Leviton, L. C., 33
Levy, B., 35, 271
Lewicki, P., 79
Lewin, K., 4 5, 17, 262, 452
Lewis, H. S., 498
Lewis, K. N., 455
Lewis, L. L., 230
Lewis, M., 289
Lewis, S. H., 119
Lewis, S. K., 461
Leyens, J. P., 398, 407
Libuser, L., 532
Licht, B. G., 177, 178
Lichtenstein, S. D., 135
Lichtman, R. R., 77
Liebert, R. M., 402, 403, 417, 419
Likert, R., 199
Linder, D., 306, 307
Linder, D. E., 314
Lindgren, H. C., 227
Lindsay, R., 35
Lindzey, G., 43, 141, 235, 276
Lingle, J. H., 131
Linville, P. W., 181, 228, 229
Lipetz, M. E., 310, 314
Lipinski, E. R., 118
Lippa, R., 94
Lippincott, E. C., 404
Lippitt, R., 45
Liska, A. E., 209
Livesley, W. J., 50

Lobb, B., 28
Loftus, E. F., 133, 138, 150
London, P., 349
Loney, G. L., 301, 302
Lopez, S., 347
Lord, C. G., 53, 233
Lord, R. G., 124, 502, 504
Lorenz, K., 391–392, 410, 412
Lorge, I., 245
Losch, M., 339
Lott, A. J., 221, 304
Lott, B. E., 221, 304
Lowe, C. A., 162
Lowery, C. R., 80, 181, 182
Lubinski, D., 94
Luce, T. S., 227, 228
Luginbuhl, J. R., 531, 532
Lukens, C. K., 301, 302
Lumsdaine, A. A., 248, 253, 256
Lurigio, A. J., 150
Lykken, D. T., 206
Lyle, J., 402
Lynch, J. J., 292
Maass, A., 226, 449, 464
MacLachlan, J., 250
Maier, N. R. F., 444
Maier, S. F., 176
Major, B., 106
Maki, J. E., 423
Malamuth, N. M., 400
Mallick, S. K., 412
Malpass, R. S., 137
Mandell, W., 252
Manicas, P. T., 32
Manis, M., 66, 118
Mann, L., 28, 408, 409, 492
Mann, R. D., 20, 467
Manning, M. M., 55
Manstead, A. S. R., 89, 167
Mantell, D. M., 28
Manucia, G. K., 366, 367
Marecek, J., 174
Markus, G. B., 289
Markus, H., 11, 52, 53, 75, 93, 94, 141, 289, 480–482
Marolla, J., 390
Marriott, R. G., 493
Marrs, S., 125, 131
Marsh, H. W., 54, 122, 128
Marshall, G. D., 187
Marshall, J. R., 370, 371
Martin, J., 28, 227
Maruyama, G., 55, 250, 355
Marwell, G., 54
Maslach, C., 187, 277, 447, 449
Masling, J., 35
Masor, H., 345
Mathewson, G. C., 268
Matsumoto, D., 106
Matter, C. F., 533
Matter, W. W., 217

Matthews, K. A., 179
Matthews, R. W., 540
Mavin, G. H., 125
May, M. A., 348, 349
Maynard Smith, J., 377, 393
Mazur, A., 107
McAdams, D. P., 291, 292
McArthur, L. Z., 99, 100, 152, 161, 162, 232
McCallum, R. C., 540
McCandless, B. R., 412
McCarthy, E. D., 406
McCaul, K. D., 181, 182
McCauley, C. C., 230
McClaren, H. A., 528
McClelland, D. C., 290, 292
McClintock, C. G., 423
McClintock, E., 308, 309, 325
McCloskey, M., 138
McCown, N. E., 502
McDavid, J. W., 446
McDavis, K., 363, 364
McDonald, P. J., 519
McDougall, W., 44
McGhee, P. E., 224
McGillis, D., 156
McGlynn, R. P., 170
McGovern, L. P., 358
McGrath, J. E., 510
McGuire, C. V., 50, 52
McGuire, W. J., 12, 50, 52, 216, 256, 260, 277
McHugh, M., 154
McKeough, K. L., 217
McLaine, D., 311
McMahon, J. T., 505
McMillan, J. H., 81, 156, 161, 162, 165
McNeil, J. C., 224
McNeill, D., 103
McPartland, T. S., 50
McPherson, J. M., 541
Mead, G. H., 64
Meddin, J., 57
Medoff, N. J., 400
Meeker, R. J., 422
Meer, J., 205, 293
Mehrabian, A., 106, 291, 532
Melburg, V., 167, 386
Mellers, B. A., 218, 219
Merrens, M., 345
Merton, R., 142
Messe, L. A., 358
Messick, D., 104
Messick, S., 445
Meter, K., 348
Mettee, D. R., 305, 306
Meumann, E., 474, 480
Mewborn, R., 254
Meyer, J. P., 5, 304, 363
Michela, J. L., 175, 293
Middlemist, R. D., 533

Midlarsky, E., 356, 358
Midlarsky, M., 356, 358
Milavsky, J. R., 406
Milberg, S., 134
Milgram, S., 5–14, 17–22, 24–32, 34–36, 39, 41, 43, 202, 227, 342, 343, 407, 416, 430, 454, 464, 537
Millar, M. G., 125, 131
Millard, R. J., 31
Miller, A. G., 34, 39, 230
Miller, C. T., 76
Miller, D. T., 10, 39, 166, 167, 173, 336, 349, 362
Miller, E., 543
Miller, F. D., 119, 152
Miller, J. A., 462
Miller, N., 237, 238, 250, 253, 355
Miller, N. E., 45, 394, 396
Miller, R. L., 73
Miller, R. S., 172, 433, 440
Miller, R. W., 275
Mills, C. J., 94
Mills, J., 268, 318
Minard, R. D., 212–213
Miolardo, R. M., 319
Mischel, W., 40
Mita, T. H., 216
Mitchell, C., 311
Mitchell, H. E., 207
Mitchell, T. R., 502
Mixon, D., 27, 39
Moine, D. J., 459
Monahan, J., 150
Money, W. H., 504
Monson, T. C., 88, 175
Montano, D. E., 211
Montgomery, R. L., 436, 437
Mook, D. G., 19
Moore, B., 366, 367
Moore, B. S., 349
Moore, D. L., 480, 482
Moore, T. E., 218, 219
Morasch, B., 540
Moreland, R. L., 218, 219
Morency, N., 108
Morgan, M., 224, 402, 405
Moriarty, T., 355
Morris, C. G., 498
Morris, W. N., 289, 433, 440
Morton, H., 532
Moscovici, S., 12, 448–449, 511–512
Mouton, J. S., 437
Mowrer, O. H., 45, 394
Mueller, C. W., 396
Mueser, K. T., 106
Mulac, S., 497
Mulherin, A., 363
Mullen, B., 129, 433, 435
Mulvihill, D. J., 388
Murphy, C. J., 504
Murphy, G., 44

Murphy, L. B., 44
Murphy-Berman, V., 535
Murray, D. M., 137
Murray, H. G., 128
Murstein, B. I., 302
Musgrave, A., 32
Myers, A. M., 94
Myers, D. G., 494, 511–513
Naccari, N., 247
Nacci, P., 202, 452
Nadler, A., 369, 374
Nagy, G. F., 302
Napolitan, D. A., 171
Nasby, W., 305
Nebergall, R. E., 258
Nell, E. B., 260
Nelson, D., 301
Nelson, E., 191
Nelson, Y., 532
Nemeth, C., 448, 502
Nesdale, A. R., 399
Neuringer-Benefiel, H. E., 348
Newcomb, T. M., 45, 262, 280, 295–298, 300, 303, 305
Newman, H. M., 10
Newman, O., 526–527
Newton, D. L., 181
Nezlek, J., 285, 299
Nida, S. A., 339
Nisbett, R. E., 68, 119, 136, 137, 141, 159, 162, 174, 175, 181, 272
Nord, W. R., 445
Norman, A., 118
Norman, R. Z., 502
Normoyle, J., 527
Norris, K. S., 376
Northcott, H. J., 224
Norvell, N., 165
Norwood, M., 211
Notz, W. W., 158
Nuttin, J., 78
O'Connor, J., 420
Oflofsky, J. L., 94
O'Hara, J., 531
Ohlin, L. E., 409
Olson, J. M., 211
Omelich, C. L., 166
O'Neal, E. C., 519
O'Quin, K., 364
O'Riordan, T., 551
Orne, M. T., 27, 35
Orris, J. B., 505
Orzeck, L., 406
Osborn, A. F., 497
Osgood, C. E., 112, 262
Oskamp, S., 43, 553
Ostrom, T. M., 116, 125, 131
O'Sullivan, M., 110
Overmier, J. B., 176
Oxley, D., 308
Padawer-Singer, A., 52

Page, M. M., 220, 398
Page, R., 202, 207
Pagel, M. D., 214
Pallak, M. S., 273, 553
Palmer, D. L., 301
Pantin, H. M., 356
Papageorgis, D., 260
Park, B., 129, 228
Parke, R. D., 398, 407
Parker, E. B., 402
Parker, J. W., 54
Parkinson, B., 187
Passer, M. W., 175
Patten, S. C., 27
Patterson, M. L., 100, 106, 530, 535
Paulsen, M. H., 465
Paulus, D., 370
Paulus, P. B., 540, 541
Pavlov, I., 219
Payne, J. W., 150
Pearce, K., 60
Pearce, P. L., 334
Pearson, J. A., 289
Peavler, W. S., 204
Peckham, V., 484
Pempus, E., 531
Pennebaker, J. W., 22, 181, 544
Pennington, N., 464, 465, 467
Penrod, S. D., 433, 449, 464, 465, 467
Peplau, L. A., 292–293, 308–309, 311, 317, 325, 328, 456
Pepper, S., 304
Perillo, E., 80
Perlman, D., 292–293
Perri, M., 299
Perrin, F. A. C., 102
Pessin, J., 475
Peters, D., 37
Peters, L. H., 506
Peterson, C., 177
Peterson, D. R., 308, 309, 325
Pettigrew, T., 238
Petty, R., 209, 227, 244, 250–251, 256, 277, 339, 462, 484, 486
Peynircioglu, Z. F., 121
Phares, E. J., 172
Philipsen, G., 497
Phillips, D., 403
Piaget, J., 163
Pietromonaco, P., 125, 131
Piliavin, I. M., 340, 341, 345, 346, 357, 359
Piliavin, J. A., 39, 296, 306, 340, 341, 345, 346, 357, 359–362, 365, 375
Pilkonis, P. A., 220
Pines, M., 61
Pittman, T. S., 85
Plotkin, J., 37
Podlesny, J. A., 206
Podsakoff, P. M., 452

Poe, D., 109
Pohlman, J. T., 506
Pollis, N. P., 436, 437
Pomazal, R. J., 346
Pomerantz, S. D., 109, 110
Pope, W. R., 39, 81, 162
Post-Krammer, P., 55
Postman, L. J., 288
Powell, M. C., 211
Prasad, J., 288
Pratkanis, A. R., 50, 51, 91
Prentice-Dunn, S., 409
Preston, M., 460
Prince, G., 497
Pryor, J., 60
Pych, V., 364
Pyszczynski, T. A., 60, 84, 153, 167, 222, 313
Quattrone, G. A., 226, 228
Quigley-Fernandez, B., 207
Rabbie, J., 288
Raday, T., 406
Rajecki, D. W., 39, 192, 236
Ranelli, C. J., 440
Raney, D. F., 109
Rankin, R. E., 203
Ranney, J. T., 79
Ransberger, V. M., 547
Raskin, D. C., 206
Rauch, G. E., 224
Raven, B. H., 452–455, 459, 463
Raviv, A., 364
Rawtich, A. B., 414
Read, S. J., 82
Reed, M., 162
Reeder, G. D., 170
Regan, D., 175
Regan, J. W., 84, 305
Reich, J. W., 45, 553
Reis, H. T., 299, 317
Reisenzein, R., 187
Relich, J. D., 54
Rempel, J. K., 317
Reppucci, N. D., 177, 178
Ressler, R. K., 390
Reston, J., 296
Revitch, E., 390
Reyes, R. M., 133
Reynolds, P. D., 37
Rhodewalt, F., 81, 89, 273
Rholes, W. S., 125
Rice, B., 128, 203
Rice, R. W., 504
Richardson, D., 39
Ridgeway, C. L., 449
Ridley, M., 378
Riecken, H. W., 33, 262, 264, 265, 276
Riess, M., 87, 167, 531, 533
Rigby, K., 17
Riggiero, J., 237

Riggio, R. E., 106
Ring, K., 65
Riordan, C., 237
Riordan, C. A., 297, 315
Roberts, M. K., 311
Robertson, J. L., 553
Rochberg-Halton, E., 242
Rodgers, W. L., 284
Rodin, J., 33, 77, 181, 340, 341, 345, 346
Rofé, Y., 288
Rogel, M., 355
Rogers, M., 238
Rogers, P. J., 53
Rogers, R. W., 237, 254, 409
Rogers, T. B., 53
Rogolosky, S., 12
Rokeach, M., 227
Romer, D., 299
Ronis, D. L., 118, 272
Rook, K. S., 293
Rose, J., 292
Rose, T. L., 232
Rosen, A. J., 106
Rosen, B., 502
Rosenbaum, D. P., 355
Rosenberg, M. J., 34, 262
Rosenberg, M. S., 193
Rosenberg, S., 112, 122
Rosenburg, M., 50–51
Rosenfeld, P., 167, 386
Rosenfield, D., 165, 230, 231, 238
Rosenhan, D. L., 349, 366, 367
Rosenman, R. H., 178, 179, 184
Rosenthal, R., 18, 28, 35, 36, 108, 109, 142, 143
Rosnow, R. L., 18, 28, 34, 36, 43, 288, 406
Ross, A. S., 339
Ross, E. A., 44
Ross, L., 11, 71, 129–131, 141, 441
Ross, M., 39, 78, 166, 169
Ross, R., 401
Ross, S., 401
Rossman, B. B., 116
Rothbart, M., 129, 228, 232
Rottman, L., 298
Rountree, C. A., 289
Ruback, R. B., 150, 440, 497
Rubens, W. S., 406
Rubenstein, C. M., 292, 293
Rubin, D. C., 78
Rubin, J. Z., 452
Rubin, R. A., 55
Rubin, Z., 38, 40, 310–313, 324, 325, 328
Ruble, D. N., 76, 162, 230, 231
Ruble, T. L., 230, 231
Ruggiero, M., 356
Rule, B. G., 396, 399, 415
Rump, E. E., 17

Rusbult, C. E., 319, 321, 322, 540
Rushton, J. P., 335, 348, 349, 375
Russell, D., 153, 155, 292, 293
Russell, D. E., 400
Rutstein, J., 313, 314
Ryan, M. J., 358
Ryan, R. M., 158, 184
Sabini, J., 430
Sadow, J. S., 478
Sadowski, C., 520
Saegert, S., 297, 537
Saenz, D. S., 233
Safer, M. A., 11
Sagar, H. A., 231
St. John, 237
Saks, M. J., 467, 468
Salovey, P., 77, 367
Saltzman, A. T., 81
Salzer, S., 533
Samaha, G. M., 289
Samerotte, G. C., 345
Sampson, E. E., 53, 91
Sanbonmatsu, D. M., 211
Sanders, D. Y., 22
Sanders, G. S., 480–482
Sanford, N., 227
Santee, R. T., 447, 449
Sarnoff, I., 289
Sawaya, C., 531
Sawyer, A. G., 261
Saxe, L., 33, 202, 206, 346, 440
Schachter, S., 185, 186, 187, 262, 264, 265, 276, 286–290, 297, 323, 325, 438, 439, 491
Scheidt, R., 398
Scheier, M. F., 56, 58, 59, 60, 62, 91
Schein, E. H., 277, 278, 445
Scherer, K., 110
Schershing, C., 513
Schifter, D. E., 214
Schkade, J. K., 540
Schlenker, B. R., 83, 86, 87, 91, 165, 202, 275, 293, 294, 452, 456, 502
Schlesinger, A. M., 490
Schlesinger, L. B., 390
Schmidt, D. E., 538
Schmidt, L., 39, 296, 306
Schmidt, D. L., 455
Schmidt, S. M., 456
Schnedler, R., 346
Schnedler, R. W., 408
Schneider, D. J., 122, 125, 131, 141, 172
Schoeneman, T. J., 66
Schofield, J. W., 231, 237, 238
Schopflocher, D., 153
Schopler, J., 302, 540
Schramm, W., 402
Schriesheim, C. A., 452, 504
Schroeder, D. J., 60
Schroeder, H. M., 227

Schul, Y., 121
Schuman, H., 205
Schunk, D. H., 55
Schwartz, M. F., 366
Schwartz, R. D., 22
Schwartz, S. H., 339, 346, 356, 371
Scott, C. A., 70
Scully, D., 390
Sears, D. O., 45, 127, 128, 223, 243, 276, 297, 298, 302
Sears, R. R., 394
Sebastian, R., 407
Sechrest, L., 22
Secord, P. F., 32, 82
Segal, H. A., 280
Segal, M., 230
Segal, M. W., 305
Segall, M. H., 107
Seggar, J. F., 224
Seidman, E., 94
Seligman, C., 554
Seligman, M. E. P., 176, 177, 183
Semmell, A. K., 513
Senchak, M., 317
Senn, D. J., 304
Senneker, P., 347, 348
Seta, J. J., 540
Severy, L. J., 528
Shadish, W. R., 33
Shaffer, D., 370
Shaffer, D. R., 355, 520
Shalker, T. F., 366
Shanab, M. E., 28
Shanteau, J., 302
Shapiro, S., 368
Sharabany, R., 364
Shavelson R. J., 54
Shaver, K. G., 172
Shaver, P., 292, 293
Shaw, M., 238
Shaw, M. E., 43, 172
Sheats, P., 503
Sheatsley, P. B., 227, 289
Sheffield, F. D., 248, 253, 256
Shenk, F., 386
Shenkel, R. J., 80
Sheridan, C. L., 28, 35
Sherif, C. W., 238, 259
Sherif, M., 45, 238, 259, 436, 437
Sherman, P., 376
Sherman, S. J., 69
Sherwood, G. G., 128
Shetler, S., 413
Shields, D. L., 408
Shifflet, S. C., 507
Shotland, R. L., 342, 353, 354, 356, 407
Shrauger, J. S., 66, 84, 305
Shugan, S. M., 132
Shure, G. H., 422
Sieber, J. E., 38

Sigall, H., 202, 207, 307
Signorielli, N., 402, 405
Sikes, J., 239
Siladi, M., 94
Silver, M. J., 36
Silverman, I., 238, 406
Simmonds, S., 366
Simon, J. G., 84
Simon, R. J., 465
Simons, H., 247
Simons, L. S., 398
Simonton, D. K., 22, 499
Sinclair, W. J., 146
Singer, D. G., 407
Singer, J., 536–537, 541
Singer, J. E., 177, 185–187, 542–545
Singer, J. L., 407
Singer, R., 254
Sistrunk, F., 446
Sivacek, J., 211
Skelton, J. A., 89
Skinner, B. F., 221
Skinner, E. A., 177
Skolnick, A., 328
Skrypnek, B. J., 233
Skrzypek, G. J., 507
Slapion-Foote, M. J., 328, 329
Sloan, L. R., 116
Sloane, L. T., 85
Slonim, M. J., 196
Slovic, P., 135
Smart, R., 291
Smith, E. R., 119, 152
Smith, I. D., 54
Smith, M. B., 192
Smith, P. L., 55
Smith, R. B., 384, 386, 408
Smith, R. J., 532
Smith, S. S., 39
Smith, T. G., 436, 437
Smith, T. L., 194, 235
Smith, T. W., 53, 60, 81
Smyth, L. D., 412
Snapp, M., 239
Snodgrass, S. E., 109
Snoek, D. J., 284
Snyder, C. R., 80, 81, 91, 441
Snyder, H. N., 440
Snyder, L. D., 226
Snyder, M., 17, 86, 87, 88, 125, 130, 175, 210, 211, 257, 289, 299, 336
Snyder, M. L., 165, 172
Sole, K., 345
Solem, A. R., 444
Solomon, B., 317
Solomon, L., 84, 305
Solomon, R., 365
Solomon, S., 167
Solomon, S. H., 540
Sommer, R., 520, 521, 522, 532, 550
Sorrentino, R. M., 335, 375

Southwick, L. L., 273
Spaulding, K., 226
Speckart, G., 215
Spence, J. T., 92, 94
Spiegel, N., 299
Spillane, R., 28
Spinner, B., 35
Spitzer, C. E., 444
Sprafkin, J. N., 403, 417, 419
Sroka, K. R., 440
Srull, T. K., 125, 131
Staats, A. W., 220
Staats, C. K., 220
Stahelski, A. J., 408, 422, 423
Stang, D. J., 218, 384
Stanley, J. C., 27
Stanovich, K. E., 30, 43
Stanton, G. C., 54
Stapp, J., 92
Stasser, G., 513
Staub, E., 335, 349
Steblay, N. M., 460
Steck, L., 311
Steckler, C., 200
Steeh, C., 205
Steele, C. M., 273
Stein, R. T., 502
Stein, S., 456
Steinberg, J., 366
Steiner, I. D., 483, 484
Steinhilber, A., 522
Steinmetz, S., 388, 413
Stephan, C., 239
Stephan, W. G., 165, 175, 230, 231, 233, 238
Stephens, L., 415
Stephenson, B., 62
Stern, L. D., 125, 131
Sternberg, R. J., 122, 311
Stier, D. S., 106
Stiles, W. B., 111
Stipp, H. H., 406
Stires, L., 519
Stitt, L., 230
Stogdill, R. M., 499, 500, 502, 504
Stokes, J. P., 320
Stokols, D., 537, 545
Stollak, G. E., 358
Stoner, J. A. F., 511
Storms, M. D., 175, 181–182, 535
Story, J. E., 129
Straus, M., 388, 413
Streeter, L. A., 250
Stricker, L. J., 445
Strodtbeck, F. L., 465, 467
Strohmer, D. C., 131
Strom, J. C., 106
Strong, S. R., 33, 455
Strube, M. J., 506
Stucky, R. J., 91
Stull, D. E., 317

Suci, G. J., 112
Sullivan, J. J., 553
Suls, J., 10, 73, 74, 91
Sulzer, J. L., 172
Sundstrom, E., 522, 540
Suppe, P., 32
Surra, C. A., 319
Sussman, S., 106, 299
Swann, W. B., 66, 67, 82, 84, 86, 130, 141, 143, 211
Swap, W. C., 297
Szasz, T. S., 65
Szucko, J. J., 206
Szybillo, G. J., 260
Tabachnik, N., 84
Tajfel, H., 226, 235
Tanford, S., 433, 449
Tanke, E. D., 299
Tannenbaum, P. H., 112, 262
Taves, P. A., 273
Tavris, C., 398, 413, 419
Taylor, D. A., 202, 316, 527
Taylor, M. C., 94
Taylor, R., 527
Taylor, R. B., 522, 527
Taylor, S. E., 11, 69, 77, 118, 124, 125, 133–135, 141, 152, 175
Taylor, S. P., 414
Teasdale, J. D., 177
Teddlie, C., 538
Tedeschi, J. T., 83, 87, 167, 202, 207, 297, 315, 384, 386, 408, 452, 456
Teger, A., 268
Teichman, Y., 289
Tejwani, G. A., 543
Tellegen, A., 94
Tesser, A., 77, 153
Test, M. A., 346
Tetlock, P. E., 85, 89, 167
Thibaut, J., 45, 317, 321
Thomas, G. C., 535
Thomas, M. H., 404
Thompson, D. E., 528
Thompson, S. C., 135, 538
Thompson, S. L., 40
Thompson, W. C., 133, 367
Thoreau, H. D., 292
Thorne, A., 85
Thorngate, W. B., 423
Thrasher, F. M., 409
Thurman, B., 107
Thurstone, L. L., 44, 45, 191, 194, 199
Tice, D. M., 347, 522
Timko, C., 173, 211
Tinbergen, L., 391
Titus, L. J., 478
Toch, H., 409
Tognacci, L. N., 212–213
Tognoli, J., 307
Toi, M., 364

Tolman, C. W., 475
Tolstedt, B. E., 320
Tolstoy, L., 499
Tornatzky, L. G., 33
Totten, J., 175
Toulmin, S., 32
Town, J. P., 170
Traupmann, J., 310
Triplett, N., 44, 45, 474
Trivers, R., 377
Trope, Y., 74, 75, 131
Tuchman, G., 223
Tumin, M. M., 388
Turk, A., 542
Turk, J., 542
Turner, C. W., 398
Turner, J. C., 226
Tversky, A., 132, 134, 136
Tybout, A. M., 70
Tyler, T. R., 297, 298, 302
Uleman, J. S., 152
Ullian, D. Z., 92
Underwood, B., 349, 366, 367
Uranowitz, S. W., 125
Vadaris, R. M., 414
Valins, S., 187, 314, 525–526, 538
Valone, K., 250
Valzelli, L., 390
Vanderlok, M., 129
Vanderplas, M., 364
Van de Voort, D., 311
Vecchio, R. P., 505
Veitch, R., 366
Vernon, D. T., 212–213
Veroff, J., 291
Vincent, J. E., 367, 461
Vincent, J. P., 320
Vinokur, A., 513
Vinsel, A., 520–521, 524–525, 531
Vogt, B., 358
Vreven, R., 78
Wachtler, J., 289, 502
Wagner, D. G., 502
Wagner, P. J., 528
Walden, T. A., 532, 540
Walder, L. O., 407
Walker, M., 85
Walkey, F. H., 528
Wallach, M. A., 511
Waller, W., 315
Walster, G. W., 39, 101, 296, 310, 313, 315, 325, 369
Walster-Hatfield, E., 39, 172, 266, 296, 298, 299, 306, 310, 313, 315, 325, 369
Warner, L. G., 214
Warren, J. R., 290
Warren, R., 256
Watkins, M. J., 121
Watzlawick, P., 112
Weary, G., 162, 167, 184

Webb, E. J., 22
Weeks, D. G., 293
Wegner, D. M., 346
Weiby, M., 165
Weick, K. E., 20
Weigel, R. H., 213
Weiner, B., 148, 153–156, 363
Weinstein, N., 542
Weisenberg, M., 35, 271
Weiss, R. L., 320
Weiss, R. S., 292
Weiss, W., 245
Weitz, B. A., 153
Weitz, S., 202
Wells, G. L., 137, 138, 162
Wells, L. E., 54
Wenz, F. V., 293
Wenzel, C., 108
Wertham, F., 390
West, S. G., 28, 35, 43, 346, 407
West Eberhard, M. J., 376
Westie, F. R., 209, 227
Weyant, J. M., 366
Wheeler, D., 461
Wheeler, H., 400
Wheeler, L., 187, 285, 299, 527
Whipple, T. W., 224
Whitcher-Alagna, S. W., 369
White, B. J., 238
White, G. L., 313–314
White, J. B., 211
White, J. D., 125
White, J. W., 408
White, L. A., 400
White, M., 531
White, P., 119
White, R. K., 45
Whitney, G., 346
Whittmer, J., 81
Whyte, W. F., 45, 423, 522
Wicker, A. W., 209, 540, 550
Wicklund, R. A., 43, 56, 58, 60, 62, 89, 267, 351
Wiener, V. L., 349
Wiggins, N. H., 106
Wiley, M. G., 165
Wilhelmy, R. A., 435
Wilkins, C., 209
Willers, K. R., 413
Williams, K. D., 251, 484–486
Williams, M., 71
Williamson, N. L., 227
Williamson, S. A., 509
Willis, R. H., 445, 530, 535
Wills, T. A., 77, 293
Wilson, D. W., 39, 218, 366, 545
Wilson, E. O., 376, 392
Wilson, J. P., 17, 349
Wilson, K. G., 172
Wilson, M., 297
Wilson, T. D., 68, 119, 136, 141, 181

Wimer, S., 155
Winer, B. J., 503
Winnett, R. A., 553
Winston, B. V., 205
Winter, L., 152
Winton, W., 108
Wirsing, R., 107
Wish, M., 111, 112
Wispe, L., 375
Witt, T. R., 167
Wittes, J. T., 542
Wittes, R., 542
Wittgenstein, L., 110
Wohlers, A. J., 231
Wolf, S., 433, 434, 435, 449
Wolfer, J. A., 181
Woll, S. B., 125
Wollman, N., 419
Wong, P. T. P., 153
Wood, G., 139
Wood, J. V., 77
Wood, W., 246, 247, 445, 447
Woodmansee, J. J., 204
Worchel, S., 236, 252, 289, 538, 539
Word, C. O., 202, 233
Word, L. E., 341, 356, 361
Wortman, C. B., 167, 177, 308, 317
Wortman, P., 33
Wright, S. L., 289
Wright, T. L., 55
Wrightsman, L. S., 384, 420
Wrong, D. H., 452, 464
Wyer, R. S., 116, 125
Yablonsky, L., 409
Yahya, K. A., 28
Yamagishi, T., 116
Yancey, W. L., 526
Yantis, S., 211
Yarkin, K. L., 170
Yarrow, P. R., 209
Yates, J., 49
Yinon, Y., 366
Yohai, S., 538, 539
Yurko, K., 292
Zacker, J., 227
Zajonc, R. B., 11, 141, 187, 216, 218, 219, 289, 297, 476–481, 508
Zander, A., 500, 510
Zanna, M. P., 76, 121, 202, 209, 211, 220, 233, 236, 272, 273, 317, 513
Zavalloni, M., 511, 512
Zeisel, H., 465
Zelditch, M., 502
Zelen, S. L., 50
Zembrodt, I. M., 322
Zillmann, D., 251, 313, 396, 399, 400, 415, 416
Zimbardo, P. G., 35, 187, 271, 277, 289, 294, 409, 418, 426–427, 429, 437, 441–443, 462
Zonderman, A. B., 12
Zuckerman, M., 109–110
Zukier, H., 121, 137

SUBJECT INDEX

Achievement:
    academic performance, 177–178, 478, 519
    attributions and, 179–180
    intrinsic motivation and, 158–159
    self-efficacy and, 54–55
    self-fulfilling prophecies about, 142–143
    Type A personality and, 178–179
Activism:
    attitudes and political, 211
    conservationism, 212–213, 551–554
    controlling conflict, 237–239, 417–418
    eliminating prejudice, 237–239
    instigating social change, 447–449
Actor-observer differences, 174–175
Adjustment, social and psychological:
    androgyny and, 94
    attributions and, 176–181
    self-esteem and, 54–56
    shyness and, 291–293
    social comparison and, 77
Advertising:
    classical conditioning and, 218–220
    face-ism, 220, 223
    hard sell versus soft sell, 257
    inoculation and, 260–261
    persuasive messages used in, 246, 255
    sexism in, 223–224
    as social influence, 458–459
    subliminal, 218–219
Affect (*see also* Emotions):
    classical conditioning and, 218–220
    as a component of attitudes, 192
    mere exposure and, 216
    and relationship dissolution, 319–320
Affiliation:
    biological determinants of, 294
    embarrassment and, 288–289
    individual differences in, 289–295
    nature of, 285–286
    Schachter's studies of, 286–287
    situational determinants of, 286–289

Aggression (*see also* Violence):
    anger and, 393–399
    arousal-aggression hypothesis, 394–396
    competition and, 420–423
    controlling aggression, 411–417
    definition of, 383–385
    ethological models of, 390–392
    frustration-aggression theory of, 394–396
    individual differences in, 387
    irritable versus instrumental, 385–386
    learning theories of, 399–401
    legitimate versus illegitimate, 386
    motivational approaches to, 393–399
    normative models of, 408–411
    pornography and, 400
    psychodynamic approaches to, 389–390
    sociobiological theory of, 393
    televised violence and, 401–407
    violence and, 386–388
    the weapons effect, 397–398
Air pollution, 551–554
Alcohol:
    aggression and, 414
    attitudes about, 211
Altruism (*see also* Helping behavior):
    definition of, 333–334
    personality traits associated with, 348–349
    sociobiological theory of, 376–378
Androgyny:
    Bem's theory of, 92–94
    cognitive schemata theory of, 93–94
    conformity and, 446
    definition of, 92
    helping and, 347–348
Anger:
    aggression and, 396–397
    controlling aggression by venting, 412
    displacement of, 413
    incompatible responses and, 414
    mitigating circumstances and, 415–416
    relationship dissolution and, 320

Anxiety:
   insomnia and, 181–182
   social, 293–294
   social comparison and, 286–288
Applied science:
   origins within social psychology, 45
   versus basic science, 33
Applied social psychology:
   in athletic settings, 66, 81, 165, 408, 474–477
   in business settings, 157, 218–219, 257, 260–261, 459–462
   in clinical settings, 54–56, 65, 77, 94, 176–182, 390, 455
   criminology, 355, 390, 400, 402–403, 408–409, 426–428, 446–447, 526–527, 541
   in educational settings, 54–55, 73, 78, 81, 101, 128, 142–143, 158–159, 177–188, 239, 478, 519
   in industrial/organizational settings, 128, 472–508
   in judicial settings, 137–139, 150–151, 156, 172–173, 204–205, 211, 237, 465–468
   opinion polling, 196–197
   origins of, 45
   in political settings, 85–86, 109, 165, 216–217, 243, 369, 487–490, 492
   preventing drug abuse, 259–260
   program evaluation, 33
   social experimentation, 33
   understanding social problems, 65, 173, 190, 192–193, 202–205, 209–210, 225–233, 281, 292–293, 315, 319–322, 326–329, 386–388, 390, 400–404, 450–451, 526–527, 542–547, 551–554
Aquino, Corazon, 200
Archival analysis, 22
Aristotle, 44, 285
Arousal:
   aggression and, 394–396
   attitudes and, 202—204
   crowding and, 538–540
   helping and, 361
   passionate love and, 312–316
   personal space violations and, 531–535
   polygraph as a measure of, 205–206
   pupil dilation during, 203–205
   social anxiety and, 292
   social facilitation and, 478–479
Arousal-aggression hypothesis, 396
Assumed similarity bias, 127–128
Attention:
   attributional processing and, 152–154
   nature of, 56–58
   self-focused, 58–62
   social perception and, 134
Attitude(s):
   and behavior, 208–215
   changes in prejudicial, 202–205
   definition of, 11, 191–193
   measurement of, 194–208
   prejudicial, 190, 192–193
   racist, 190, 192–193
   sexist, 192, 202–205, 209–210
   sources of, 215–225
   tricomponent theory of, 191–193

Attitude-behavior correspondence, 208–215
Attitude change:
   coercive, 278–281
   cognitive consistency approaches to, 261–275
   and desegregation, 237–239
   increasing resistance to, 260–261
   persuasion and, 243–260
Attitude scaling, 198–200
Attraction:
   beauty and, 298–299
   complementarity and, 303–304
   criticisms of research dealing with, 296
   gain-loss theory of, 306–307
   ingratiation, 308–309
   interpersonal distance and, 530, 535–536
   Newcomb's studies of, 295–297
   nonverbal behavior and, 105–106
   overattribution and, 170–171
   personal characteristics and, 299–304
   persuasion and, 247
   playing hard to get, 305–306
   proximity and, 297–298
   reciprocity of, 304–305
   rewards and, 304–307
   similarity-attraction effect, 300–303
Attribution(s):
   about the cause of crime, 150–151
   cognitive biases and, 163–175
   conflict and, 174–175
   definition of, 11, 146–147
   dimensions of, 154–155
   and emotions, 185–187
   functions of, 149–152
   and health, 179–182
   and helping, 361–363
   instigating attributional thought, 152–154
   stressful events and, 176–178
   theories of, 156–164
Attributional biases:
   actor-observer difference, 174–175
   causes of, 165–167
   conflict caused by, 175, 423
   defensive attribution, 172–173
   explanations of obedience and, 11
   fundamental attribution error, 168–170
   overattribution, 170–172
   self-serving, 80–81, 164–165
Attributional theories:
   of adjustment, 179–182
   of crowding, 538–540
   of helping, 361–363
   of insomnia, 181–182
   of love, 313–315
Attribution retraining, 179–181
Attribution theory:
   Bem's self-perception theory, 157–158
   description of, 147
   Jones' correspondent inference theory, 156–157
   Kelley's cube theory, 159–161
Authoritarianism, 17, 226–227

Awareness (*see also* Self-awareness), 49
B = f(P, E), 17
Balance theory, 302–303
Barnum effect, 80
Base-rate data, social cognition and, 135–136
Basic science, 33
Basking in reflected glory, 85
Behavioral intention, 193, 214–215
Behavioral measures, 200–201
Behavioral medicine, *see* Adjustment, Health, Stress
Behavioral sink, 541
Behaviorism, 44
Belief(s):
    attitudes and, 192–193
    and helping, 345
    inconsistency among, 261–263
    about leadership, 499–500
    perseverance, 130–131
    persuasion and change in, 244–261
    polarization of, 511–513
    about romantic love, 315–316
    self-beliefs, 10, 50–51
    as self-fulfilling prophecies, 142–143
    about sexuality, 328
    similarity of, 300–303
    about violence, 404–405
Birth order, 289–290
Blaming the victim, 173
Body language, 102–107
Bottom-up cognitive processes, 126
Brainstorming, 497
Brainwashing, 278–281
Brown, H. Rap, 202
Browning, Elizabeth Barrett, 311
Brown v. Board of Education of Topeka, 237
Buchwald, Art, 79
Bystander effect, 337–339
Carlyle, Thomas, 499
Carnegie, Dale, 308–309
Carnegie Hero Fund Commission, 360
Carter, Jimmy, 242–243
Case data, social cognition and, 135–136
Catharsis, 389–390, 411–413
Central traits, 121–122
Chamberlain, Neville, 108
Change-of-meaning hypothesis, the, 120
Chesterfield, Lord, 309
Classical conditioning of attitudes, 218–220
Close relationships:
    attributional conflict in, 174–175
    companionate versus passionate, 309–312
    definition of, 308–309
    dissolution of, 319–322
    self-disclosure in, 316–317
    social exchange theory of, 317–318
Coalition formation, 449
Coercive persuasion, 278–281
Cognition (*see also* Social cognition):
    access to cognitive processes, 119
    as source of self-information, 69–71

Cognitive consistency:
    attitude change and, 261–275
    attraction and, 297
    similarity and, 302–303
Cognitive dissonance:
    alternative explanations for, 272–275
    arousal properties of, 273
    attitude change and, 261–275
    choices and, 266–267
    counterattitudinal behavior and, 269–271
    definition of, 12
    following destructive obedience, 12
    Festinger's theory of, 263
    following initiation to join a group, 267–269
    public commitment and, 273–275
    reactions to disconfirmed expectations, 261–262
    selective exposure and, 267
Cognitive response theory, 250–251
Cohesiveness in groups, 491–492, 494–495
Colson, Charles E., 488
Communal relationships, 318
Communication:
    deviance and, 438–439
    expressive versus semantic, 111–113
    nonverbal, 100–110
    one-sided versus two-sided, 253
    persuasion, 244–259
    relationship dissolution and, 320
    self-disclosure, 316–317
    self-presentation as, 83–89
    speech rate and persuasion, 249–250
    verbal, 110–112
Common-sense reasoning, 37–40
Competition, 420–423
Compliance:
    door-in-the-face technique, 460–461
    foot-in-the-door technique, 459–460
    individual differences in, 444–445
    low-balling, 461–462
    mindlessness and, 441–442
    versus private acceptance, 439–440
Conceptually driven cognitive processes, 126
Confirmatory cognitive biases, 129–131
Conflict:
    attributional, 174–175
    competition and, 420–423
    exploitation during, 422–423
    loss of trust during, 422–423
    perceptions during, 422–423
Conflict, between groups:
    causes of, 225–233
    contact and, 237–239
    ingroup/outgroup biases, 226–227
    social categorization and, 225–226
    stereotyping and, 230–232
    superordinate goals and, 238
Conformity:
    Asch's studies of, 430–433
    compliance versus private acceptance, 439–440
    fear of dissent and, 441

Conformity *continued*
  group size and, 433–435
  informational influence and, 435–436
  mindlessness and, 441–442
  normative influence and, 437
  opinion conformity, 308
  self-awareness and, 62
  social pressure and, 437–440
  unanimous majorities and, 431–432
Confusion of responsibility, 339
Consciousness, 49
Conservation, environmental, 551–554
Consistency theories of attitude change, 261–275
Contact cultures, 529–530
Contact hypothesis, 237–238
Contingency model of leadership, 501–506
Controllability:
  as an attributional dimension, 155
  learned helplessness and loss of, 176–177
  and reactions to crowding, 538
  and reactions to failure, 177–178
  and reactions to noise, 542–544
Cool Hand Luke, 427
Cooperation:
  competition versus, 420
  Prisoner's Dilemma Game and, 420–423
  reducing prejudice by encouraging, 237–239
Correlation coefficient, 29–30
Correspondent inference theory, 156–157
Cost-reward model of helping, 357–360
Counterattitudinal behavior and attitude change, 269–271
Counterconformity, 445
Covariation:
  attributional principle of, 159–160
  biases in the perception of, 134–135
  illusory correlations, 232
Crime:
  attributions about cause of, 150–151
  attributions about victims of, 173
  criminal violence, 386–388
  and defensible space, 526–527
  in housing projects, 526–527
  and overcrowding, 541
  polygraph as a means of detecting, 205–206
  prevention programs, 355–357
  vandalism, 526–527
Criminal justice:
  accuracy of eyewitness testimony, 138–139, 226–228
  criminal insanity and violence, 390
  parole decisions, 150–151
  prisoner and guard roles, 426–429
  pupillometrics and, 206
  reactions to rape, 172–173
  use of polygraph tests, 205–206
Cross-cultural differences:
  in conceptions of love, 315
  in personal space needs, 528–530
  in recognizing emotions, 103
  in self-conception, 53–54
  in use of gestures, 103

Crowding:
  attributional theory of, 538–540
  controllability and, 538
  density versus, 537
  density-intensity theory, 541
  overcrowded cities, 541
  overload theory of, 537
  performance and, 540
  rats, studies of, 516–517, 541
  sex differences in, 532
  social pathology and, 541
  staffing theory of, 540
Crutchfield apparatus, 444
Cube model of attributions, 159–164
Cults:
  attributions about, 168–170
  commitment to, 261–263
  influence techniques used by, 281, 368
  leadership power in, 450–451
  People's Temple, 450–452
  recruitment tactics, 281
Cupid, 312–313
Darwin, Charles, 443
Data-driven cognitive processes, 126
Dean, J., 488
Debriefing, 37
Deception, detection of:
  bogus pipeline and the, 206–207
  polygraphy, 205–206
Deception research, 36–39
  alternatives to, 38
  Baumrind's reaction to, 38
  controversy over ethics of, 38–39
  debriefing and, 37
Decision-making:
  dissonance reduction following, 266–267
  effective, in groups, 496, 498
  during groupthink, 490
Decision model of helping:
  identifying a way to help, 356
  interpreting the event, 352–353
  noticing the event, 351–352
  taking responsibility, 339, 354–356
Defensible space, 526–527
Defensive attribution, 172–173
Deindividuation, 409–410
DeLorean, John Z., 156
Demand characteristics, 25–36
Depression and loneliness, 292–293
Desegregation, 237–239
Developmental processes, *see* Social development
Deviance:
  attraction and, 440
  communication and, 439
  fear of, 441
  Moscovici's studies of, 448–449
  nonconformity versus anticonformity, 444–445
  reactions to, 438–439
  reactions to "sliders," 440
  Schachter's study of attitudinal, 438–439
  social influence and, 448–449

Diffusion of responsibility:
   and helping, 339
   and polarization in groups, 512
Dilution effect, 136–137
Discounting cue hypothesis, 248–249
Discrimination, see Prejudice
Distinctiveness postulate, 52–53
Door-in-the-face technique, 460–461
Dormitories, effects of living in, 524–526
Drug abuse, prevention of, 259–260
Educational performance:
   attributions and, 177–178
   self-efficacy and, 55
   self-esteem and, 54–55
   self-fulfilling prophecies and, 142–143
   social comparison and, 75–77
   social facilitation and, 478
Ehrlichman, J., 488
Einstein, A., 33
Embarrassment:
   affiliation and, 288–289
   norm violations and, 430
   size of audience and, 435
   social anxiety and, 292
Emblems, 102–103
Emergencies:
   impulsive helping and, 361
   nature of, 353–354
Emergency intervention, see Helping behavior
Emerson, R. W., 437
Emotions:
   attitude change and, 253
   as component of an attitude, 192
   expression of, 103
   fear and affiliation, 286–289
   fear appeals and attitude change, 253–255
   helping and emotional arousal, 360–364
   James' theory of, 185
   loneliness, 292
   opponent process theory of, 365
   passionate love and, 313–315, 320
   perception of, 103
   during relationship dissolution, 319–320
   Schachter-Singer two-factor theory of, 185–187
   self-awareness and, 60–61
Empathy:
   actor/observer differences and, 175
   altruistic personality and, 349
   compared to sympathy, 375
   helping and, 363–364
Energy conservation, 551, 553–554
Environment, and social behavior:
   crowding, 536–541
   interpersonal distance, 528–536
   noise, 542–545
   personal space, 527–536
   stressors, 536–547
   temperature, 546–548
   territoriality, 517–527
Environmentally constructive actions, 551–554
Environmental stressors, and aggression, 394–396

Equilibrium model, 530
Equity:
   actual versus psychological, 369
   in close relationships, 317–318
   and helping, 368–369
   and reactions to help, 369
Erotica, 60, 400
Ethics of research:
   deception and, 38–39
   institutional review boards, 37
   risk-benefit approach, 36–37
   safeguards, 37
Ethology, 390–392
Evaluation apprehension:
   in experiments, 34
   helping behavior and, 339
   social anxiety and,
   social facilitation and, 479
Excitation transfer, 398–399
Experimenter effects, 35–36
Experiments:
   characteristics of, 24–27
   strengths and limitations of, 30–31
   variables in, 25
External validity, 27–28
Extrinsic motivation, 158
Eye-contact:
   equilibrium theory of, 530
   social perception and, 103–106
Eyewitness testimony, 138–139
Face-ism, 220, 223
Facial expressions, 103–104
False-consensus effect, 128
Field studies:
   advantages of, 19
   of aggression and televised violence, 406–407
   of crowding, 541
   of helping behavior, 342–344
   versus laboratory research, 19
   of televised violence, 406–407
Foot-in-the-door technique, 459–460
Friendship (see also Close relationships):
   nature of, 316–319
   and social comparison, 77
Frustration-aggression hypothesis, 394–396
F-scale, 227
Fundamental attribution error, 11, 169–170
Gain-loss hypothesis, 306–307
Galileo, 443
Gambler's fallacy, 135
Gandhi, Mohandas K., 443
Gender differences, see Sex differences
Genovese, Catherine ("Kitty"), 332–333, 335, 341, 372
Gestalt psychology, 120
Goetz, Bernhard, 382–384, 410
Group performance:
   brainstorming and, 497
   crowding and, 540
   groupthink and, 487–498
   process loss and, 483–484
   Ringelmann effect and, 483–484

Group performance *continued*
  social facilitation and, 474–480
  staffing and, 540
Groups:
  conflict between, 225–233
  conformity pressures in, 429–450
  decision-making in, 488–496
  definition of, 508
  individual performance in, 483–487
  leadership in, 499–507
  learning, 478
  obedience in, 13–14
  polarization in, 493–494, 511–513
  social impact of, 434–435
Groupthink:
  during Bay of Pigs invasion planning, 487
  biased perceptions and, 489–490
  causes of, 490–495
  closed-mindedness, 489
  cohesiveness and, 491–492, 494–495
  conformity and dissent during, 489–490
  decisional stress and, 492
  defective decision making during, 490, 494
  definition of, 488
  isolation and, 492
  leadership and, 492
  mindguards and, 490–491
  overestimation of the group, 489
  polarization processes and, 493–494
  pressures toward uniformity, 489–490
  symptoms of, 487–490
  ways to avoid, 495–496, 498
Halo effect, 127
Hamlet, 67–69
Hard-to-get phenomenon, 305–306
Hare Krishnas, 268
Health (*see also* Adjustment, Stress):
  attributional processes and, 178–181
  exposure to uncontrollable noise and, 543–544
  insomnia, treatment of, 181–182
  loneliness and, 292–293
  mental illness and the self, 65
  and social comparison, 77
  Type A personality and, 178–179
Helping behavior:
  altruism as a form of, 333–334
  in animals, 376–377
  cost-reward model of, 357–360
  emotional models of, 360–364
  impulsive, 361
  individual differences in, 344–349
  Latane-Darley decision model of, 350–357
  moods and, 364–367
  normative approaches to, 367–371
  situational determinants of, 335–344
  sociobiological theories of, 376–378
  types of, 334
Heuristics:
  social cognition and, 133–135
  types of, 131–132

Hindsight biases:
  blaming the victim and, 173
  perceivers' overconfidence and, 138–139
  reactions to social psychological research and, 40
Hitler, Adolf, 108, 450
Hobbes, Thomas, 388
Holmes, Sherlock, 98–100, 110, 113, 120, 122, 127, 131
Home field advantage, 522
Idiosyncrasy credits, 447–448
Illness:
  loneliness and, 292–293
  mental, 65
  noise and, 544–545
  Type A personality and, 178–179
Illustrators, 102–103
Implicit personality theory, 121–122
Impression formation, *see* Social perception
Impression management, *see* Self-presentation
Impulsive helping, 361
Inclusive fitness, 376–377, 393
Incompatible response theory, 414
Individual differences:
  in aggressiveness, 387
  in authoritarianism, 17, 226–227
  definition of, 17
  in empathy, 349
  in helping, 348–349
  in information integration, 119
  in leadership style, 502–504
  in masculinity and femininity, 92–94
  in moral development, 349
  in need for affiliation, 289–295
  in nonconformity, 444–445
  persuasion and, 256–259
  in self-awareness, 59
  in self-efficacy, 55–56
  in self-esteem, 54–55
  in self-monitoring, 87–88
  in shyness, 292–294
  in social anxiety, 292–294
  in use of social influence tactics, 456–458
  and the Type A personality, 178–179
Informational influence, 339, 435–436
Information integration:
  determinants of weights, 118–119
  primacy/recency effects, 118
  unweighted models, 115–116
  weighted models, 117–118
Informed consent, 37
Ingratiation:
  attraction and, 308–309
  the ingratiator's dilemma, 308
  self-presentation via, 85–86
  social influence and, 455–456
In-group/out-group bias, 226
  complexity bias, 228
  extremity bias, 229
Innovation, 448–449
Inoculation theory, 260–261
Insomnia, attributional treatment of, 181–182

Interactionism:
    aggression and, 410–411
    definition of, 17
    helping behavior and, 336
    leadership and, 500
Internal validity, 27–28
Interpersonal circle, 113
Interpersonal distance (*see also* Crowding, Personal space):
    determinants of, 527–531
    obedience and, 14–15
    social perception and, 108–110
Interpersonal zones, 531, 534
Intrinsic motivation, 158
Jealousy, 77
Jefferson, Thomas, 245, 296
Jigsaw method, 239
Johnson, Lyndon B., 488
Jones, Jim, 450–451
Juries:
    acceptance of eyewitness testimony, 138–139
    attitudes of jurors and verdicts, 211–212
    blaming victims of crimes, 172–173
    decision-making in, 465–468
    sex differences in, 467
    size of, 467–468
    social pressure in, 465–467
    status in, 465–466
    supports for nonconformity in, 446–447
Just-world hypothesis, 172–173
Kennedy, John F., 289, 488, 490
Kimmel, Admiral H. E., 488
Kinesic cues, 102–107
King, Martin Luther, Jr., 443, 547
Kin selection, 377
Laboratory research:
    advantages of, 19
    versus field research, 19
Landon, Alfred E., 196
Law of small numbers, 228–229
Leaders:
    behaviors of, 502–504
    emergence of, 502–503
    task versus relationship, 502–505
Leadership (*see also* Leadership effectiveness):
    definition of, 498
    emergence, 502
    interactionist approach to, 500
    risky shift and, 512
    situational approach to, 499–500
    style, 502–504
    trait approach to, 499
Leadership effectiveness:
    Fiedler's contingency theory of, 501–506
    "great leader" theory of, 499
    life-cycle theory of, 507
    Least Preferred Coworker (LPC) and, 504
    sex differences in, 502
Learned helplessness, 176–177
Learning (*see also* Social learning theory):
    aggression and, 399

Learning *continued*
    applied to pro-environment actions, 551–554
    classical conditioning, 218–220
    mere exposure and, 218–219
    operant conditioning, 220–222
    social learning, 222–224
Legal system, *see* Crime, Criminal justice
Lenin, Vladimir Ilyich, 245
Life-cycle theory of leadership, 507
Likert attitude scales, 199
Literary Digest, 196
Littering, 551–552
Locke, John, 289
Loneliness:
    causes of, 293
    overcoming, 293
    social and emotional, 292
Love:
    companionate versus passionate, 309–312
    determinants of companionate, 316–319
    friendship, 311
    measurement of, 311–312
    two-factor theory of, 313–315
    types of, 310
Love Scale, 311–312
Low-balling technique, 461–462
Manipulators, 102–103
Marijuana, and aggression, 414
Marketing, *see* Advertising
Marriage:
    belief similarity and, 302
    commitment to, 318–319
    based on companionate love, 316–319
    complementarity in, 303–304
    dissolution of, 319–322
    based on passionate love, 315–316
    physical attractiveness and, 299
    sex outside of, 326–329
Martin, Billy, 385
Measurement:
    attitudes, 194–208
    behavioral, 19
    bogus pipeline method, 206–207
    nonreactive, 21–22
    observational, 20
    physiological, 202–206
    selecting method of, 22
    self-report, 21
Memory:
    mere exposure and, 218–219
    persuasion and, 248–249
    schematic biases in, 125, 129
    selective forgetting, 77–78
    self-attention and, 60
Mental health:
    crowded living conditions and, 541
    loneliness and, 292–293
Mental illness:
    aggression and, 390
    personal space and, 528
    the self and, 65

Mere exposure:
    attitude formation through, 216–217
    attraction and, 297
    mediators of, 218–219
Mindlessness, 441–442
Mirror-image thinking, 423
Misattribution:
    aggression and, 398–399
    cognitive dissonance and, 273
    crowding and, 538–540
    emotions and, 187
    helping and, 362–363
    passionate love and, 313–315
    reactions to stressful events and, 181–182
Mitigating circumstances and aggression, 415
Moods and helping, 364–367
Moral development, and obedience, 17
Motives:
    aggressive, 394–396
    egoistic motives and helping, 363–364
    intrinsic versus extrinsic, 158–159
    n Affiliation, 290–291
    Type A and achievement, 178–179
    unconscious drives, 389
Mount St. Helens, 181
Natural selection, 376
Nature-nurture controversy, 389, 410–411
Need for affiliation (nAffiliation), 290–291
Negative state relief model of helping, 367
Neighborhood Watch, 355
Nixon, Richard M., 488
Noise:
    adapting to, 543–545
    aggression and, 545
    controllability and, 544
    definition of, 542
    psychological effects of, 542–543
Nonconformity:
    idiosyncrasy credits and, 447–448
    individual differences in, 444–445
    innovation and, 448–449
    sex differences in, 445–446
    situational supports for, 446–447
    as social influence, 447–449
Nonexperimental designs:
    causality and, 30
    characteristics of, 27–30
    correlational studies, 29–30
    strengths and limitations of, 30–31
Nonreactive measures, 21–22
Nonverbal behavior:
    during deception, 108–109
    dissynchrony in, 108–109
    eye contact, 103–107
    kinesic cues, 102–107
    paralanguage, 107–110
    physical appearance as, 100–102
    proxemics, 110
    types of, 100–101
Nonverbal leakage, 108–109
Normative social influence, 437

Norm of reciprocity:
    aggression and, 408
    conflict and, 422
    helping and, 368
Norm of social responsibility, 370–371
Norms:
    aggression and, 408–410, 416–417
    attitude-behavior relationship and, 213–214
    conformity to, 427, 437–438
    desegregation and, 238
    emergent, 408–409
    equity, 368–369
    experimental creation of, 437
    helping and, 367–371
    personal, 367
Obedience:
    causes of, 32, 454
    ethics of research on, 36–39
    in groups, 13–14
    individual differences in, 17
    Milgram's studies of, 5–15
    power and, 13, 454
    prods and, 9
    situational determinants of, 13–15
    validity of studies of, 27–28
Observational measurement, 20–21
    compared to other types of measures, 22
    participant, 20–21
    structured, 20
Operant conditioning of attitudes, 220–222
Opponent process theory, 365
Out-group homogeneity bias, 226–228
Overattribution, 170–171
Overcrowding, see Crowding
Overjustification effect, 158–159
Overload:
    crowding and, 537
    helping and, 342–344
    in urban environments, 344
Ovid, 305
Paradigm, 15, 73–74
Paralanguage, 107–110
Participant observation, 20–21
People's Temple, 168, 450–452
Performance:
    brainstorming and, 497
    causal explanations after, 165
    crowding and, 540
    enhancing creativity, 497
    groupthink, 487–498
    improving academic, 179–181
    Ringelmann effect, 483–487
    self-efficacy and, 55–56
    self-handicapping and, 81
    social facilitation, 473–482
    social loafing, 483–487
Performance reviews, 128
Personality (see also Individual differences):
    authoritarian, 17
    and social behavior, 17
Personal norms, 371

Personal relationships:
　affiliation and, 285–295
　close, 308–319
　dissolution of, 319–322
　interpersonal attraction and, 295–307
　stages in, 284–285
Personal space:
　cognitive labeling and, 535–536
　cross-cultural studies of, 528–530
　definition of, 528
　determinants of, 528–535
　eye contact and, 530
　Hall's theory of interpersonal zones, 531, 534
　interpersonal zones and, 532–533
　reactions to invasion of, 532–535
　in restrooms, 532–533
　sex differences in, 528, 532–533
Person perception (see also Social perception):
　attributions and, 146–147
　impression formation, 98–114
　racial differences in, 227–228
　social cognition and, 114–134
Person-positivity bias, 127
Persuasion:
　coercive, 278–281
　cognitive response theory of, 250–251
　credibility and, 225–227
　fear and, 253–255
　inoculation against, 260–261
　message variables, 247–256
　psychological reactance and, 252
　receiver variables, 256–261
　as a social influence strategy, 455
　social judgment theory of, 258–259
　source variables, 244–247
　Yale communication model of, 244–260
Persuasive arguments hypothesis, 513
Philosophy of science:
　applied and basic science, 33
　paradigms, 15, 73–74
　scientific process, 32
　value of scientific research, 37–40, 296
Physical appearance:
　attraction and, 298–299
　helping and, 344–345
Physiological arousal, see Arousal
Plato, 44
Polarization processes:
　causes of, 512–513
　cultural value hypothesis, 512–513
　early theories of, 512
　history of research on, 511
　and choice dilemma questionnaire, 511
　risky shift versus cautious shift, 493–494
Politics:
　authoritarianism and conservative politics, 227
　persuasion and, 242–243
　self-presentation and, 85–86
　voting behavior, 214–215
Polls, public opinion, 196–197
Pollution, 551–554

Pope Urban, II, 450
Pornography, 400
Power, see Social power
Prejudice (see also Racism, Sexism):
　attitudes and, 190, 192–193
　changes in, 202–205
　discrimination, 200–202, 208–215
　intergroup attitudes and, 225–226
　measurement of, 194–208
　perceptual biases and, 226–229
　principles-implementation gap, 205
　reducing, 237–239
　sources of, 215–225
　stereotypes and, 124, 192, 230–233
Premarital sex, 326–328
Primacy-recency:
　in impression formation, 118
　in persuasion, 253
Prisoner's dilemma game, 420–423
Privacy:
　Altman's theory of, 523–524
　mechanisms for maintaining, 524–426
　residential satisfaction and, 524–525
Program evaluation, 33
Projection, 128
Propaganda, 248
Prosocial behavior (see also Helping behavior):
　altruism, 333–334
　cooperation as a form of, 420–423
　doctrine of specificity and, 348–349
　television and, 417
　types of, 333–334
Proxemics, 110, 528–536
Proximity-attraction effect, 297–298
Proxmire, William, 296
Pruitt-Igoe, 526
Psychoanalytic theory, 44
Pygmalion effect, see Self-fulfilling prophecy
Pupillometrics, 203–204
Psychodynamic theory:
　aggression and, 389–390
　catharsis and aggression, 389–390, 411–413
　displacement of aggression, 413
Psychotherapy:
　as applied social influence, 455
　attributions and, 179–182
Racial differences:
　in classroom territoriality, 519
　in helping, 201, 346
　in identification of faces, 226–228
　in personal space needs, 528
Racism (see also Prejudice):
　authoritarianism and, 226–227
　changes in, 202–205
　discrimination and, 208–215
　eliminating, 237–239
　helping and, 346
　intergroup conflict and, 225–233
　measurement of, 194–207
　nature of, 190, 192–193
　sources of, 222–225

Rape:
   blaming the victim, 173
   incidence of, 388
   myths about, 173
   pornography and, 400
   psychopathology and, 390
   self-blame following, 177
   television and, 402–403
Reactance:
   attitude change and, 252
   attraction and, 314–315
Reagan, Ronald, 243
Realistic group conflict theory, 225
Reasoned action, theory of, 214–215
Reciprocal altruism, 377
Reciprocity:
   aggression and, 408
   helping and, 368–369
   negative, 422–423
   norm of, 368
   principle of attraction, 305
Regulators, 102–103
Research methods:
   contrasting approaches, 19, 22, 30–31
   correlational versus experimental, 26–27, 30–31
   historical advances in, 44
   laboratory versus field methods, 18–19
   measurement methods, 19–22
Research process, 33
Reward theory of attraction, 307–308
Ringelmann effect, the, 483–488
   avoiding, 486–487
   coordination losses and, 484–485
   identifiability and, 486–487
   social loafing and, 484–487
Risk-benefit approach to ethics, 36–37
Risky shift, *see* Polarization processes
Rogers, Will, 127
Role-play methods, 39
Roles:
   in experimental studies, 34–35
   and the self, 50, 64–67, 79
   sex roles, 92–94
Role-taking, 64
Romeo-and-Juliet effect, 314–315
Roosevelt, F. D., 196
Rumors, 288
Rusk, D., 490
Schemata:
   biases caused by, 93–94
   definition of, 123
   impact on memory, 125
   impact on perceptions, 124–125
   information processing and, 52–54, 123–125
   person, 124
   priming of, 125
   self-schemata, 51–54
   sex roles and, 92–94
   stereotypes as, 124
Selective exposure, 267
Selective forgetting, 77–78

Self:
   awareness of, 56–61
   definition of, 10, 49
   evaluation of, 54–56, 75–81
   multiple selves, 53
   nature of, 50–53
   organization of, 51–54
   presentation of, 83–89
   self-concept, 49–56
   self-processes, 72–89
   social basis of the, 61–63
   sources of, 63–72
Self-assessment, 74–75
Self-awareness:
   consequences of, 59–61
   definition of, 56
   determinants of, 57–59
   in nonhuman animals, 57
   public versus private, 62
   self-consciousness and, 59
Self-concept:
   contents of, 50–56
   evaluation of the, 54–56
   self-schemata and, 51–54
   spontaneous, 52–53
Self-confirmation:
   acceptance of feedback, 66–67, 82–84
   versus self-enhancement, 84
Self-consciousness:
   dispositional self-awareness, 59
   shyness and, 294
Self-consistency, 82–84
Self-disclosure, 316–317
Self-efficacy, 55–56
Self-enhancement:
   compensatory biases and, 79–80
   reactions to feedback and, 78–80, 84
   selective forgetting and, 77–78
   self-handicapping and, 81
   self-serving attributions and, 80–81, 164–168
   social comparison and, 73–74
Self-esteem:
   compared to self-efficacy, 55
   enhancement processes, 75–81
   impact on social behavior, 55–56
   measurement of, 55
   and performance, 54–55
   and self-serving attributional bias, 164–167
Self-evaluation:
   biases in, 75–81
   selective acceptance of feedback, 78–79
   via self-assessment, 74–75
   via social comparison, 73–74
Self-fulfilling prophecy:
   and expectancy effects, 35–36
   and prejudice, 232–233
   and physical beauty, 299
   theory of, 142–143
Self-handicapping, 81
Self-monitoring:
   definition of, 87

Self-monitoring *continued*
   impression management and, 87–88
   persuasion and, 257
Self-perception:
   attitude change and, 272
   attributional processes and, 157–159
   Bem's theory of, 67–69
   overjustification and, 158–159
Self-presentation:
   after behaving counterattitudinally, 273–275
   consequences of, 88–89
   ingratiation and, 85, 308–309
   interpersonal attributions, 152
   polarization in groups and, 513
   self-monitoring and, 87–88
   self-serving attributional biases and, 166–167
   social anxiety and, 292–295
   strategic versus authentic, 84–86
   tactics, 85–86
Self-reference effect, 53
Self-report measures:
   of attitudes, 194–200
   definition of, 21
   fixed versus free responses, 195–197
   of public opinion, 196–197
Self-schemata:
   nature of, 51–54
   the self-reference effect and, 53
   sex-roles and, 92–94
Self-serving attributional biases:
   causes of, 165–167
   field studies of, 165
   nature of, 80–81, 164–168
Sex differences:
   in aggression, 387
   in conformity, 445–446
   determinants of, 94
   in helping, 346
   in jury behavior, 467
   in leadership emergence, 502
   in marking territories, 521, 532–533
   in nonverbal behavior, 106
   in perceptions of sexuality, 124
   in personal space, 528, 532–533
   in persuadability, 256–257
   sex-role socialization and, 92–94
   in sexual beliefs, 328
   in strength of friendships, 317
Sexism (*see also* Prejudice):
   attitudes and, 192
   changes in, 202–205
   discrimination against female leaders, 502–503
   discrimination against women, 209–210
   face-ism, 220, 223
   myths about rape, 173
   sources of, 222–225
Sex roles:
   aggression and, 417
   conformity in face-to-face settings and, 446
   helping and, 347–348
   origin of, 92–95

Sex roles *continued*
   and social cognition, 93–95
Sexuality:
   biased perceptions of, 124
   Boston Couples Study of, 328–329
   changes in, 326
   in long-term relationships, 326–328
   reinforcement model of, 314–315
   sex differences in beliefs about, 328
   two-factor theory of, 313–315
Shyness, 292–294
Sierra Club, 212–213
Significant others, 65
Similarity:
   of beliefs and attraction, 300–303
   helping and, 345–346
   interpersonal distance and, 530
   persuasion and, 247
   social comparison and, 76
Sleeper effect, 247–249
Social anxiety, 292–294
Social categorization, 226–227
   perceptual biases and, 226–229
   Tajfel's studies of, 226
Social cognition:
   access to cognitive processes, 119
   attributional biases, 164–175
   belief perseverance and, 130–131
   change-of-meaning hypothesis, 120–121
   confirmatory biases, 129–130
   data-driven processes vs. conceptually-driven processes, 125–127
   definition of, 11
   dilution effect, 136–137
   gambler's fallacy, 135
   heuristics and, 131–133
   hindsight bias, 138–139
   impact of base-rate data, 135–136
   impact of case data, 135–136
   impact of irrelevant information, 136–137
   impact of salient data, 152
   impact of statistical data, 134–135
   impact of vivid data, 134, 152
   implicit personality theories, 121–122
   inferential biases, 133–137
   integrating information, 115–119
   leadership emergence and, 502–503
   processing self-relevant information, 51–53
   schemata, 123–126
Social comparison:
   affiliation and, 286–288
   downward and upward, 75–76
   jealousy and, 77
   polarization in groups and, 513
   rumors and, 288
   self-evaluation and, 73–74
   uncertainty and, 73–74
Social desirability bias, 200–201
Social development:
   changes in personal space needs, 528
   empathy and helping in children, 364

Social development *continued*
  impact of television on children, 402–407, 416
  moral development, 349
  school children's reactions to noise, 544–545
  self-concept formation, 61–62
  self-perceptions of intrinsic motivation, 158–159
  sexual development, 326, 328
  socialization and aggression, 417
  socialization of attitudes, 222–224
Social distance scale, 198
Social exchange theory, 317–318, 321–322
Social experimentation, 33
Social facilitation:
  before an audience, 474
  during coaction, 474
  definition of, 474
  early studies of, 474–475
  in educational settings, 478
  historical roots of, 44
  in nonhuman species, 474–475
  theories of, 477–480
  Zajonc's explanation of, 476–477
Social impact theory, 434–435
Social influence (*see also* Conformity, Social Power):
  coalition formation and, 450
  informational, 435–437
  in juries, 446–447, 465–468
  nonconformity as, 447–449
  normative, 437
  obedience and, 13, 450–452, 454
  power and, 450–454
  psychotherapy as, 455
  and reactions to deviancy, 438–439
  social pressure and, 437–440
  specialized strategies, 458–462
  status and, 447–448
  tactics, 453–458
Socialization, 222–224
Social judgment theory, 258–259
Social learning theory:
  of aggression, 399–402
  of attitudes, 222–224
  modeling nonaggression, 416
  punishing aggression, 416
  suicide and, 403–404
  violent television programming and, 402–407
Social loafing, 484–487
  avoiding, 486–487
  causes of, 485
  definition of, 484
Social perception:
  attributional processes, 147–148
  biases in, 127–129
  interpersonal model of, 143
  nonverbal cues and, 100–110
  verbal cues and, 110–112
Social phobia, 294
Social power:
  coalition formation and, 449
  coercive, 452
  definition of, 451–452

Social power *continued*
  expert, 453
  legitimate, 452–453
  obedience and, 13
  referent, 453
  reward, 452
  in therapeutic settings, 455
  verbal communication and, 111–113
Social problems:
  aggression, 383–417
  air pollution, 551–554
  child abuse, 388
  collective violence, 388
  criminal violence, 386
  cults, 281, 168–170, 450–451
  destructive obedience, 5–15
  divorce, 315, 319–322
  domestic violence, 386
  extramarital and premarital sex, 326–329
  intergroup conflict, 225–233
  littering, 551–552
  loneliness, 292–293
  mental illness, 65, 390
  murder, 390
  noise pollution, 542–544
  overcrowding, 537–541
  pollution, 551, 553–554
  pornography, 400
  prejudice, 190, 192–193
  racism, 190, 192–193
  rape, 173, 388, 390, 402–403
  riots, 546–547
  sexism, 192, 202–205, 209–210
  suicide, 292–293, 403–404
  terrorism, 388
  vandalism, 526–527
  violent crime, 386–388
Social psychology:
  areas within, 10–14
  criticisms of, 34, 37–40, 296
  definition of, 4, 15–16
  history of, 44–45
  methods used in, 16–40
  value of research in, 37–40
Social psychophysiology:
  attitudes and, 202–203
  personal space violations and, 531–535
  polygraphy, 205–206
  pupil dilation, 203–205
Social traps, 541
Sociobiology:
  and affiliation, 294
  and aggression, 393
  and helping behavior, 376–378
Socrates, 305
Source:
  attractiveness of, 247
  credibility, 245–246
  similarity and persuasion, 247
Spontaneous self-concept, 52
Spreading, of alternatives, 266–267

Stanford County Prison Study, 426–429
Status:
    emergence as leader and, 502
    influence in juries, 467
    nonverbal behavior and, 106
    personal space and, 530–534
Stereotypes:
    cognitive schemata, 124
    definition of, 192
    prejudice and, 230–231
    self-fulfilling prophecies and, 232–233
Stress:
    attributions and reactions to, 176–182
    coping with, 77
    decisional, 492–494
    environmental stressors, 536–547
    exposure to uncontrollable noise and, 543–544
    learned helplessness and, 176–177
    social anxiety and, 292
    social comparison and reactions to, 77
    Type A personality and, 178–179
Stressors, environmental, 536–547
Structured observation, 20
Subject roles, 34–35
Subliminal advertising, 218–219
Suicide:
    loneliness and, 292–293
    social learning and, 404
Supreme Court, 237, 467–468
Symbolic interactionism:
    actual versus perceived appraisals, 66
    labeling theory of mental illness, 65
    looking-glass theory of the self, 64
    role-taking, 64
    self as process, 64–65
Television:
    aggression and, 402–407
    prejudicial attitudes and, 223–225
    prosocial behavior and, 417
    values and, 405
Temperature and aggression, 546–547
Territoriality:
    in the aged, 526–527
    competition and, 522
    defensible space and, 526–527
    dominance and, 523
    dropping out of college and, 524–526
    educational performance and, 519
    in groups, 523
    home field advantage and, 522
    isolated groups and, 526–527
    privacy and, 523–524
    racial differences in, 519
    in university dormitories, 524–526
Territories:
    architectural determinants of, 525–527
    in classrooms, 519

Territories *continued*
    defense of, 521–522
    defensible space, 526–527
    definition of, 518
    examples of, 517–518
    functions of, 522–524
    marking of, 520–521
    sex differences in marking, 521, 532–533
    types of, 518–519
Thatcher, Margaret, 200
Thematic Apperception Test, 290
Thoreau, Henry David, 292–293
Three Mile Island, 288
Thurstone attitudes scales, 198
Tolstoy, Leo, 499
Top-down cognitive processes, 126
Tragedy of the commons, 551
Tricomponent theory of attitudes, 191–193
Truman, Harry S, 196, 488
Trust:
    attraction and, 316
    conflict and loss of, 422–423
    erosion of, after deception, 37
    loss of, during competition, 422–423
Type A personality, 178–179
U.S. Riot Commission, 546
U.S.S. Pueblo, 104
Validity:
    demand characteristics and, 35
    evaluational apprehension and, 34
    experimenter effects and, 35–36
    subject roles and, 34–35
    types of, 27–28
Verbal behavior (*see also* Communication):
    dimensions of, 112–113
    expressive versus semantic, 110–113
    verbal aggression, 387
Violence (*see also* Aggression):
    child abuse, 388
    collective violence, 388
    criminal violence, 386
    desensitization to, 403–404
    domestic violence, 386
    terrorism, 388
Vividness, 133–134, 152
"Warm glow of success," 365–366
"Weapons" effect, the, 398
"What is beautiful is good" stereotype:
    attraction and, 298–299
    impression formation and, 101–102
    as self-fulfilling prophecy, 299
Wittgenstein, Ludwig, 110–111
Wrong-number technique:
    description of, 201
    and helping behavior, 343
Zeigarnik effect, 78

PHOTO CREDITS

This page constitutes an extension of the copyright page.

Chapter One
2: Eric Kroll, Taurus Photos, Inc.; **6 and 7:** © Stanley Milgram, 1965; **31:** (top) Susan Lapides, Design Conceptions; (left) Ellis Herwig, Stock Boston, Inc.; (right) Judy Blamer, Brooks/Cole; (bottom) James Holland, Stock Boston, Inc.

Chapter Two
46: Michael Weisbrot, Stock Boston, Inc.; **51:** Peter Vandermark, Stock Boston, Inc.; **56:** Alan Carey, The Image Works, Inc.; **85:** M. Rangell, The Image Works, Inc.; **93:** Alan Carey, The Image Works, Inc.

Chapter Three
96: Joel Gordon; **104:** AP/Wide World Photos, Inc.; **105:** (top) Frank Siteman, Taurus Photos, Inc.; (middle) Charles Gatewood, The Image Works, Inc.; (bottom left and right) Robert Kalman, The Image Works, Inc.; **114:** AP/Wide World Photos, Inc.; **118:** Nicholas Sapieha, Stock Boston, Inc.; **139:** (both) AP/Wide World Photos, Inc.

Chapter Four
114: Frank Siteman, Taurus Photos, Inc.; **149:** Frank Siteman, EKM-Nepenthe; **151:** Cathy Cheney, EKM-Nepenthe; **164:** Robert Kalman, The Image Works, Inc.; **169:** AP/Wide World Photos, Inc.

Chapter Five
188: Michale Grecco, Stock Boston, Inc.; **193:** Christopher Brown, Stock Boston, Inc.; **202:** AP/Wide World Photos, Inc.; **217:** Judy Blamer, Brooks/Cole; **220:** Rick Smolan, Stock Boston, Inc.; **230:** Shirley Zeiberg, Taurus Photos, Inc.

Chapter Six
240: Mark Antman, The Image Works, Inc.; **243:** AP/Wide World Photos, Inc.; **269:** Christopher Morrow, Stock Boston, Inc.; **274:** Alan Carey, The Image Works, Inc.

Chapter Seven
282: Mark Antman, The Image Works, Inc.; **291:** Harvard University Press; **292:** Charles Gatewood, Stock Boston, Inc.: **309:** Judy Gelles, Stock Boston, Inc.; **319:** Cleo Freelance Photos; **327:** Frank Siteman, EKM-Nepenthe.

Chapter Eight
330: Jack Prelutsky, Stock Boston, Inc.; **335:** Tom Ballard, EKM-Nepenthe; **354:** Frank Keillor; **360 and 369:** AP/Wide World Photos, Inc.

Chapter Nine
380: Anestis Diakopoulos, Stock Boston, Inc.; **383, 385,** and **391:** AP/Wide World Photos, Inc.; **394:** (left) Mark Antman, The Image Works, Inc.; (right and bottom) Ellis Herwig, Stock Boston, Inc.; **401:** Photo from "Imitation of Film-Mediated Aggressive Models," by A. Bandura, D. Ross and S. A. Ross, in *Journal of Abnormal and Social Psychology,* 1963, *66,* 3–11. Copyright 1963 by the American Psychological Association. Reprinted by permission.

Chapter Ten
424: Owen Franken, Stock Boston, Inc.; **428:** (all) Philip Zimbardo, Department of Psychology, Stanford University; **438:** Bonnie Hawthorne; **451:** AP/Wide World Photos, Inc.; **460:** Jerry Berndt, Stock Boston, Inc.

Chapter Eleven
470: Peter Southwick, Stock Boston, Inc.; **475:** Anestis Diakopoulos, Stock Boston, Inc.; **485:** Hazel Hankin, Stock Boston, Inc.; **491:** Arthur Grace, Stock Boston, Inc.; **503:** (all) Judy Blamer, Brooks/Cole.

Chapter Twelve
514: Charles Gatewood, Stock Boston, Inc.; **520:** Donald Patterson, Stock Boston, Inc.; **534:** (top left, middle, and bottom) Alan Carey, The Image Works, Inc.; (top right) Mark Antman, The Image Works, Inc.; **535:** Jeffrey Meyers, Stock Boston, Inc.; **543:** Mark Antman, The Image Works, Inc.; **552:** Owen Franken, Stock Boston, Inc.

CREDITS

This page constitutes an extension of the copyright page.

Chapter One
6, (Figure 1–1), **7,** (Figure 1–2), **9,** (Table 1–1), **14,** (Figure 1–3), **15,** (Figure 1–4), **21,** (Figure 1–5), and **24,** (Table 1–4), all adapted from *Obedience to Authority: An Experimental View,* by Stanley Milgram. Copyright © 1974 by Stanley Milgram. Reprinted by permission of Harper & Row Publishers, Inc. **38,** (Table 1–8): From "Twenty Years of Deception in Social Psychology," by A. E. Gross and I. Fleming. In *Personality and Social Psychology Bulletin,* 1982, *8,* 402–408. Copyright 1982 by Sage Publications, Inc. Reprinted by permission.

Chapter Two
54, (Table 2–1): From "The Dimensionality of Self-Esteem: II. Hierarchical Facet Model for Revised Measurement Scales," by J. S. Fleming and B. E. Courtney. In *Journal of Personality and Social Psychology,* 1984, *46,* 404–421. Copyright 1984 by the American Psychological Association. Reprinted by permission. **57,** (Figure 2–3): From "Self-Recognition in Primates: A Comparative Approach in Bidirectional Properties of Consciousness," by G. G. Gallup. In *American Psychologist,* 1977, *32,* 329–338. Copyright 1977 by the American Psychological Association. Reprinted by permission. **62,** (Table 2–2): From "Public and Private Self-Consciousness: Assessment and Theory," by A. Fenigstein, M. F. Scheier, and A. H. Buss. In *Journal of Consulting and Clinical Psychology,* 1975, *43,* 522–527. Copyright 1975 by the American Psychological Association. Reprinted by permission. **66,** (Figure 2–7): From "Reflected Appraisal and the Development of Self," by R. B. Felson. In *Social Psychology Quarterly,* 1985, *48,* 71–78. Copyright 1986 by the American Psychological Association. Reprinted by permission. **67,** (Table 2–3): From "When Our Identities Are Mistaken: Reaffirming Self-Conceptions through Social Interaction," by W. B. Swann, Jr., and C. A. Hill. *In Journal of Personality and Social Psychology,* 1982, *43,* 59–66. Copyright 1982 by the American Psychological Association. Reprinted by permission. **70,** (Figure 2–9): From "Affective-Cognitive Consistency and the Effect of Salient Behavioral Information on the Self-Perception of Attitudes," by S. Chaiken and M. W. Baldwin. In *Journal of Personality and Social Psychology,* 1981, *41,* 1–12. Copyright 1981 by the American Psychological Association. Reprinted by permission. **71,** (Table 2–4): From "Self-Knowledge and Social Inference: I. The Impact of Cognitive/Affective and Behavioral Data," by S. M. Anderson and L. Ross. In *Journal of Personality and Social Psychology,* 1984, *46,* 280–293. Copyright 1984 by the American Psychological Association. Reprinted by permission. **75,** (Figure 2–10): From "Difficulty and Diagnosticity as Determinants of Choice among Tasks," by Y. Trope and P. Brickman. In *Journal of Personality and Social Psychology,* 1975, *31,* 918–925. Copyright 1975 by the American Psychological Association. Reprinted by permission. **80,** (Focus 2–6): From "The Fallacy of Personal Validation: A Classroom Demonstration of Gullibility," by B. R. Forer. In *Journal of Personality and Social Psychology,* 1949, *44,* 118–123. Copyright 1949 by the American Psychological Association. Reprinted by permission. **83,** (Figure 2–13): From "Self-Verification Processes: How We Sustain Our Self-Conceptions," byW. B. Swann, Jr., and S. J. Read. In *Journal of Personality and Social Psychology,* 1981, *41,* 1119–1128. Copyright 1981 by the American Psychological Association. Reprinted by permission. **87,** (Table 2–6): From "The Self-Monitoring of Expressive Behavior," by M. Snyder. In *Journal of Personality and Social Psychology,* 1974, *30,* 526–537. Copyright 1974 by the American Psychological Association. Reprinted by permission.

Chapter Three
108, (Figure 3–3): From "Verbal, Vocal, and Visible Factors in Judgments of Another's Affect," by R. M. Krauss, W. Apple, N. Morency, C. Wenzell, and W. Winton. In *Journal of Personality and Social Psychology,* 1981, *40,* 312–320. Copyright 1981 by the American Psychological Association. Reprinted by permission. **113,** (Figure 3–6): From "Interpersonal Communication Rating Scale," by S. R. Strong and H. I. Hills. Unpublished manuscript, Virginia Commonwealth University. **116,** (Figure 3–7): From "Averaging Versus Adding as a Stimulus Combination Rule in Impression Formation," by N. H. Anderson. In

Journal of Experimental Psychology, 1965, 70, 394–400. Copyright 1965 by the American Psychological Association. Reprinted by permission. **143,** (Table 3–8): From "Expectancy Confirmation Processes Arising in the Social Interaction Sequence," by J. M. Darley and R. H. Fazio. In *American Psychologist*, 1980, 35, 867–881. Copyright 1980 by the American Psychological Association. Reprinted by permission.

Chapter Four

154, (Figure 4–2): From "Role of Disconfirmed Expectancies in the Instigation of Attributional Processing," T. A. Pyszczynski and J. Greenberg. In *Journal of Personality and Social Psychology*, 1981, 40, 31–38. Copyright 1981 by the American Psychological Association. Reprinted by permission. **171,** (Figure 4–7): From "The Attribution of Friendliness," by D. A. Napolitan and G. R. Goethals. In *Journal of Experimental Psychology*, 1979, 15, 104–113. Copyright 1979 by the American Psychological Association. Reprinted by permission. **177,** (Figure 4–9): From "Learned Helplessness in Humans: Critique and Reformulation," by L. Y. Abramson, M. E. P. Seligman, and J. D. Teasdale. In *Journal of Abnormal and Social Psychology*, 1978, 87, 49–74. Copyright 1978 by the American Psychological Association. Reprinted by permission. **180,** (Figure 4–10): From "The Role of Expectations and Attributions in the Alleviation of Learned Helplessness," by C. S. Dweck. In *Journal of Personality and Social Psychology*, 1975, 31, 674–785. Copyright 1975 by the American Psychological Association. Reprinted by permission. **185,** (Figure 4–11): From "The Schachter Theory of Emotion: Two Decades Later," by R. Reisenzein. In *Psychological Bulletin*, 1983, 94, 239–264. Copyright 1983 by the American Psychological Association. Reprinted by permission.

Chapter Five

189, (Figure 5–3): Cartoon by Stayskal. © 1984. Reprinted by permission: Tribune Media Services. **195,** (Table 5–1): From *Whites' Attitudes Toward Black People*, by A. Campbell. Copyright © 1971 by the Institute for Social Research, Ann Arbor. **199,** (Figure 5–4): From *The Measurement of Social Attitudes*, by L. L. Thurstone. © 1931 by The University of Chicago Press. **199,** (Table 5–2): From "Measuring Social Distance," by E. S. Bogardus. In *Journal of Applied Sociology*, 1925, 9, 299–308. Copyright 1925 by The American Sociological Society. **200,** (Figure 5–5): From "Authoritarianism Ideology in Negro College Students," by C. Steckler. In *Journal of Abnormal and Social Psychology*, 1957, 54, 396–399. Copyright 1957 by the American Psychological Association. **201,** (Table 5–3): From "Effects of Race on the Elicitation of Helping Behavior," by S. Gaertner and L. Bickman. In *Journal of Personality and Social Psychology*, 1971, 20, 218–222. Copyright 1971 by the American Psychological Association. Reprinted by permission. **203** and **204,** (Figures 5–6 and 5–7): From *A Compendium of Trends on General Social Survey Questions*, by T. W. Smith. Copyright 1980 by the National Opinion Research Center. **206,** (Figure 5–8): From "Pupillometric and Personality Test Score Differences of Female Aggressing Pedophiliacs and Normals," by R. W. Atwood and R. J. Howell. In *Psychonomic Science*, 1971, 22, 115–116. Copyright 1971 by the Psychonomic Society. Reprinted by permission. **207,** (Table 5–4): From "Current Stereotypes: A Little Fading, a Little Faking," by H. Sigall and R. Page. In *Journal of Personality and Social Psychology*, 1971, 18, 247–255. Copyright 1971 by the American Psychological Association. Reprinted by permission. **212,** (Figure 5–10): From "Specificity of the Attitude as a Determinant of Attitude-Behavior Congruence," by R. H. Wiegel, D. T. A. Vernon, and L. N. Tognacci. In *Journal of Personality and Social Psychology*, 1974, 30, 724–738. Copyright 1974 by the American Psychological Association. Reprinted by permission. **213,** (Table 5–5): From "Attitude-Behavior Relations: A Theoretical Analysis and Review of Empirical Research," by I. Ajzen and M. Fishbein. In *Psychological Bulletin*, 1977, 84, 888–918. Copyright 1977 by the American Psychological Association. Reprinted by permission. **215,** (Figure 5–11): From *Understanding Attitudes and Predicting Social Behavior*, by I. Ajzen and M. Fishbein. Copyright 1980 by Prentice-Hall, Publishers. Reprinted by permission. **219,** (Figure 5–12): From "Exposure Effects May Not Depend on Stimulus Recognition," by R. L. Moreland and R. B. Zajonc. In *Journal of Personality and Social Psychology*, 1979, 37, 1085–1089. Copyright 1979 by the American Psychological Association. Reprinted by permission. **229,** (Figure 5–17): Adapted from "Blacks, Whites, and Yellows: They All Look Alike to Me," by T. S. Luce. In *Psychology Today*, 1974, 8(2), 105–108.

Chapter Six

249, (Figure 6–2): Adapted from "Empirical Tests of the Absolute Sleeper Effect Predicted from the Discounting Cue Hypothesis," by C. L. Gruder, T. D. Cook, K. M. Hennigan, B. R. Flay, C. Alessis, and J. Halamaj. In *Journal of Personality and Social Psychology*, 1978, 36, 1061–1074. Copyright 1978 by the American Psychological Association. Reprinted by permission. **252,** (Figure 6–4): From "The Use of Rhetorical Questions in Persuasion: A Cognitive Response Analysis," by R. E. Petty, J. T. Cacioppo, and J. Heesacker. In *Journal of Personality and Social Psychology*, 1981, 40, 432–440. Copyright 1981 by the American Psychological Association. Reprinted by permission. **254,** (Figure 6–5): Adapted from "Fear Appeals and Attitude Change: Effects of a Threat's Noxiousness, Probability of Occurrence, and the Efficacy of Coping Responses," by R. W. Rogers and R. Newborn. In *Journal of Personality and Social Psychology*, 1976, 34, 54–61. Copyright 1976 by the American Psychological Association. Reprinted by permission. **257,** (Table 6–2): From "Appeals to Image and Claims about Quality: Understanding the Psychology of Advertising," by M. Snyder. In *Journal of Personality and Social Psychology*, 1985, 49, 586–597. Copyright 1985 by the American Psychological Association. Reprinted by permission. **261,** (Table 6–3): Adapted from "The Effects of Repetition of Refutational and Supportive Advertising Appeals," by A. G. Sawyer. In *Journal of Marketing Research*, 1973, 10, 23–33. Copyright 1973 by the American Marketing Association. **264,** (Table 6–4): Adapted from *A Theory of Cognitive Dissonance*, by Leon Festinger. Copyright 1957 by the Board of Trustees of the Leland Stanford Junior University. **265,** (Table 6–5): Adapted from "Rational Processing or Rationalization? The Effect of Disconfirming Information on a Stated

Religious Belief," by C. D. Batson. In *Journal of Personality and Social Psychology,* 1975, *32,* 176–184. Copyright 1975 by the American Psychological Association. Reprinted by permission. **268,** (Figure 6–8): Adapted from "The Effects of Severity of Initiation on Liking for a Group," by E. Aronson and J. Mills. In *Journal of Personality and Social Psychology,* 1959, 177–181. Copyright 1959 by the American Psychological Association. **271,** (Table 6–6): Adapted from "Cognitive Consequences of Forced Compliance," by L. Festinger and J. M. Carlsmith. In *Journal of Abnormal and Social Psychology,* 1959, *58,* 203–210. Copyright 1959 by the American Psychological Association.

Chapter Seven

290, (Figure 7–3): Adapted from *The Psychology of Affiliation,* by S. Schachter. Copyright 1959 by the Board of Trustees of the Leland Stanford Junior University. **293,** (Table 7–2): Items from the Cheek-Buss Shyness Inventory. From "Shyness and Sociability," by J. M. Cheek and A. H. Buss. In *Journal of Personality and Social Psychology,* 1981, *41,* 330–339. Copyright 1981 by the American Psychological Association. Reprinted by permission. **301,** (Figure 7–6): From "Interactional Approach to Interpersonal Attraction," by M. H. Gonzales, J. M. Davis, G. L. Loney, C. K. Lukens, and C. H. Junghans. In *Journal of Personality and Social Psychology,* 1983, *44,* 1192–1197. Copyright 1983 by the American Psychological Association. Reprinted by permission. **307,** (Figure 7–8): From "Gain and Loss of Esteem as Determinants of Interpersonal Attractiveness," by E. Aronson and D. Linder. In *Journal of Experimental Social Psychology,* 1965, *1,* 156–172. Copyright 1965 by Academic Press. Reprinted by permission. **310,** (Table 7–3): From "A Typology of Styles of Loving," by J. A. Lee. In *Journal of Personality and Social Psychology,* 1977, *3,* 173–182. Copyright 1977 by the Society for Personality and Social Psychology, Inc. **311,** (Table 7–4): From "Measurement of Romantic Love," by Z. Rubin. In *Journal of Personality and Social Psychology,* 1970, *16,* 265–273. Copyright 1970 by the American Psychological Association. Reprinted by permission. **314,** (Table 7–5): From "Passionate Love and the Misattribution of Arousal," by G. L. White, S. Fishbein, and J. Rutstein. In *Journal of Personality and Social Psychology,* 1981, *41,* 56–62. Copyright 1981 by the American Psychological Association. Reprinted by permission. **317,** (Figure 7–10): BLOOM COUNTY Cartoon © 1983, Washington Post Writers Group. Reprinted with permission. **329,** (Table 7–6): From "Gender Differences in Sexual Attitudes," by S. Hendrick, C. Hendrick, M. J. Slapion-Foote, and F. H. Foote. In *Journal of Personality and Social Psychology,* 1985, *48,* 1630–1642. Copyright 1985 by the American Psychological Association. Reprinted by permission.

Chapter Eight

334, (Table 8–1): From "A Taxonomy of Helping: A Multidimensional Scaling Analysis," by P. L. Pearce and P. R. Amato. In *Social Psychology Quarterly,* 1980, *43,* 363–371. Copyright 1980 by the American Sociological Association. Reprinted by permission. **338,** (Figure 8–2): From "Bystander Intervention in Emergencies: Diffusion of Responsibility," by J. M. Darley and B. Latane. In *Journal of Personality and Social Psychology,* 1968, *8,* 377–383. Copyright 1968 by the American Psychological Association. Reprinted by permission. **340,** (Figure 8–3) and **341,** (Table 8–2): From "Good Samaritanism: An Underground Phenomenon?", by I. M. Piliavin, J. Rodin, and J. A. Piliavin. In *Journal of Personality and Social Psychology,* 1969, *13,* 289–299. Copyright 1969 by the American Psychological Association. Reprinted by permission. **342,** (Figure 8–4): From "Why Don't Bystanders Help? Because of Ambiguity," by R. D. Clark, III, and L. E. Ward. In *Journal of Personality and Social Psychology,* 1972, *24,* 392–400. Copyright 1972 by the American Psychological Association. Reprinted by permission. **347,** (Figure 8–4): From "Androgyny and Helping Behavior," by P. Senneker and C. Hendrick. In *Journal of Personality and Social Psychology,* 1983, *45,* 916–925. Copyright 1983 by the American Psychological Association. Reprinted by permission. **352,** (Figure 8–5) and **358,** (Table 8–6): From B. Latane and J. M. Darley, *The Unresponsive Bystander: Why Doesn't He Help?,* © 1970. Reprinted by permission of Appleton-Century-Crofts. **357,** (Figure 8–7): From "Bystander Intervention into Crime: A Study Based on Naturally Occurring Episodes," by T. Huston, M. Ruggiero, E. R. Conner, and G. Geis. In *Social Psychology Quarterly,* 1981, *44,* 14–23. Copyright 1981 by the American Sociological Association. Reprinted by permission. **362,** (Figure 8–9): From "On the Piliavin and Piliavin Model of Helping Behavior: Costs Are in the Eye of the Beholder," by R. D. Clark, III. In *Journal of Applied Social Psychology,* 1976, *6,* 322–328. Copyright 1976 by V. H. Winston & Sons, Inc. Reprinted by permission.

Chapter Nine

387, (Table 9–1): From "Inventory for Assessing Different Kinds of Hostility," by A. H. Buss and A. Durkee. In *Journal of Consulting Psychology,* 1957, *21,* 343–349. Copyright 1957 by the American Psychological Association. Reprinted by permission. **397,** (Table 9–2): From "Some Conditions Facilitating the Occurrence of Aggression after the Observation of Violence," by R. G. Green and L. Berkowitz. In *Journal of Personality,* 1967, *35,* 666–676. Copyright 1967 by Duke University Press. Reprinted by permission. **401,** (Figure 9–4): From "Imitation of Film-Mediated Aggressive Models," by A. Bandura, D. Ross, and S. A. Ross. In *Journal of Abnormal and Social Psychology,* 1963, *66,* 3–11. Copyright 1963 by the American Psychological Association. Reprinted by permission. **403,** (Figure 9–5): DOONESBURY, by Gary Trudeau. Copyright, 1985, G. B. Trudeau. Reprinted with permission of Universal Press Syndicate. All rights reserved. **404,** (Figure 9–6): From "Imitative Suicides: A National Study of the Effects of Television News Stories," by K. A. Bollen and D. P. Phillips. In *American Sociological Review,* 1982, *47,* 802–809. Copyright 1982 by the American Sociological Association. Reprinted by permission. **405,** (Table 9–3): Adapted from "The Demonstration of Power: Violence Profile No. 10," by G. Gerbner, L. Gross, N. Signorielli, M. Morgan, and M. Jackson-Beeck. In *Journal of Communication,* 1979, *29*(3), 177–195. Copyright 1979 by the Journal of Communication. **406,** (Figure 9–7): ZIGGY, by Tom Wilson. Copyright, 1985, Universal Press Syndicate. Reprinted with permission. All rights reserved. **410,** (Table 9–4): From "Effects of Deindividuation on Stealing Among Halloween Trick or Treaters," by E. Diener, S. C. Fraser, A. L. Beaman, and R. Kelem. In

Journal of Personality and Social Psychology, 1976, *33,* 178–183. Copyright 1976 by the American Psychological Association. Reprinted by permission. **414,** (Figure 9–8): From "The Effects of Alcohol and Delta-9-Tetrahydrocaccabinol on Human Physical Aggression," by S. P. Taylor, R. M. Vardaris, A. B. Rawtich, C. B. Gammon, J. W. Cranston, and A. I. Lubetkin. In *Aggressive Behavior,* 1976, *2,* 153–161. Copyright 1976 by Alan R. Liss, Inc. Reprinted by permission.

Chapter Ten
427, (Table 10–1): From "Stanford Prison Experiment," a slide show written and narrated by Philip Zimbardo. **432,** (Figure 10–2): Adapted from "An Experimental Investigation of Group Influence," by S. E. Asch. In *Symposium on Preventive and Social Psychiatry,* April 15–17, 1957, Walter Reed Army Institute of Research. Washington, D.C.: Government Printing Office. **433,** (Figure 10–3): From "Opinions and Social Pressure," by S. W. Asch. In *Scientific American,* 1955, *193*(5), 31–35. Copyright © by Scientific American, Inc. All rights reserved. **435,** (Figure 10–4): From "The Psychology of Social Impact," by B. Latane. In *American Psychologist,* 1981, *36,* 343–356. Copyright 1981 by the American Psychological Association. Reprinted by permission. **436,** (Figure 10–5): From *The Psychology of Social Norms,* by M. Sherif. Copyright © 1936 by Harper & Row, Publishers, Inc.; renewed by Muzafer Sherif. **439,** (Figure 10–6): From "Deviance, Rejection, and Communication," by S. Schachter. In *Journal of Abnormal and Social Psychology,* 1951, *46,* 190–207. Copyright 1951 by the American Psychological Association. **440,** (Table 10–2): From "Reaction to Attitudinal Deviance: Impact of Deviate's Direction and Distance of Movement," by J. M. Levine, L. Saze, and H. J. Harris. In *Sociometry,* 1976, *36,* 97–107. Copyright 1976 by the American Sociological Association. Reprinted by permission. **442,** (Table 10–3): From "The Mindlessness of Ostensibly Thoughtful Action," by E. J. Langer, A. Blank, and B. Chanowitz. In *Journal of Personality and Social Psychology,* 1978, *36,* 635–642. Copyright 1978 by the American Psychological Association. Reprinted by permission. **457,** (Figure 10–8) and (Table 10–6): From "The Multidimensional Scaling of Power Strategies," by T. Falbo. In *Journal of Personality and Social Psychology,* 1977, *35,* 537–538. Copyright 1977 by the American Psychological Association. Reprinted by permission. **466,** (Figure 10–9): From *Inside the Jury* by R. Hastie, S. D. Penrod, and N. Pennington. Copyright © 1983 by the President and Fellows of Harvard College.

Chapter Eleven
478, (Table 11–1): From "Social Enhancement and Impairment of Performance in the Cockroach," by R. B. Zajonc, A. Heingartner, and E. M. Herman. In *Journal of Personality and Social Psychology,* 1969, *13,* 83–92. Copyright 1962 by the American Psychological Association. Reprinted by permission. **479,** (Figure 11–3): From "Social Facilitation," by R. B. Zajonc, Science, *149,* 1965, 269–274. Copyright 1965 by the AAAS. **479,** (Figure 11–4): From "Social Facilitation," by N. B. Cottrell. In C. G. McClintock (Ed.), *Experimental Social Psychology.* Copyright 1972 by Holt, Rinehart and Winston, Inc. Reprinted by permission of Holt, Rinehart & Winston. **482,** (Table 11–3): From "The Drive for Integration: Some Comments," by H. Markus. In *Journal of Experimental Social Psychology,* 1981, *17,* 257–261. Copyright 1981 by Academic Press. Reprinted by permission. **483,** (Figure 11–6): From *Group Process and Productivity,* by I. D. Steiner. Copyright 1972 by Academic Press. Reprinted by permission. **485,** (Figure 11–8): From "Many Hands Make Light the Work: The Causes and Consequences of Social Loafing," by B. Latane, K. Williams, and S. Harkins. In *Journal of Personality and Social Psychology,* 1979, *37,* 822–832. Copyright 1979 by the American Psychological Association. Reprinted by permission. **486,** (Table 11–4): From "Identifiability as a Deterrent to Social Loafing: Two Cheering Experiments," by K. Williams, S. Harkins, and B. Latane. In *Journal of Personality and Social Psychology,* 1981, *40,* 303–311. Copyright 1981 by the American Psychological Association. Reprinted by permission. **488,** (Table 11–6): From *Victims of Groupthink,* 2nd Edition, by I. L. Janis. Copyright © 1982 by Houghton-Mifflin Company. Reprinted by permission. **493,** (Figure 11–9): From "The Group Polarization Phenomenon," by D. G. Myers and H. Lamm. In *Psychological Bulletin,* 1976, *83,* 602–627. Copyright 1976 by the American Psychological Association. Reprinted by permission. **496,** (Figure 11–10): From "Groupthink," by I. L. Janis. In H. H. Blumberg, A. P. Hare, V. Kent, and M. F. Davies (Eds.), *Small Groups and Social Interaction,* (Vol. 2). Copyright 1983 by John Wiley & Sons, Inc. Reprinted by permission. **497,** (Table 11–7): From *Applied Imagination,* by A. F. Osborn. Copyright 1957 by Charles Scribner's Sons. Reprinted by permission of The Scribner Book Companies, Inc. **501,** (Figure 11–11): From *Group Dynamics: Research and Theory,* 3rd Ed., by D. Cartwright and A. Zander (Eds.). Copyright 1968 by Harper & Row Publishers, Inc. Reprinted by permission. **504,** (Table 11–8) and **505,** (Table 11–9): From "The Contingency Model and the Dynamics of the Leadership Process," by F. E. Fiedler. In L. Berkowitz (Ed.), *Advances in Experimental Social Psychology* (Vol. 12). Copyright © 1978 by Academic Press. Reprinted by permission. **507,** (Figure 11–14): From "Leadership Effectiveness and Adaptability Description (LEAD)." In J. W. Pfeiffer and J. E. Jones (Eds.), *The 1976 Annual Handbook for Group Facilitators* (Vol. 5).

Chapter Twelve
519, (Table 12-1): From "Territorial Invasion in the Classroom: Invadee Response," by G. M. Haber. In *Environment and Behavior,* 1980, *12,* 17–31. Copyright 1969 by Sage Publications, Inc. Reprinted by permission. **524,** (Figure 12–1): From *The Environment and Social Behavior,* by I. Altman. Copyright © 1976 by Wadsworth Publishing Company, Inc. Reprinted by permission of Brooks/Cole Publishing Company, Monterey, California. **525,** (Table 12–2): From R. Sommer, *Personal Space,* © 1969. Reprinted by permission of Prentice-Hall, Inc., Englewood Cliffs, N.J. **527,** (Table 12–4): From *Defensible Space* by O. Newman. Copyright © 1972 by Macmillan, Inc. Reprinted by permission. **529,** (Figure 12–2): From "Personal Space: Where We Now Stand," by L. Hayduk. In *Psychological Bulletin,* 1983, *94,* 293–335. Copyright 1983 by the American Psychological Association. Reprinted by permission. **533,** (Table 12–5): From *The Hidden Dimension,* by E.

T. Hall. Copyright © 1966 by Doubleday & Co., Inc. Reprinted by permission. **533,** (Figure 12–3): From "Personal Space: An Evaluative and Orienting Overview," by L. Hayduk. In *Psychological Bulletin, 85,* 117–134. Copyright 1978 by the American Psychological Association. Reprinted by permission. **536,** (Figure 12–6): From "Reactions to Physical Closeness," by M. D. Storms and G. C. Thomas. In *Journal of Personality and Social Psychology,* 1977, *35,* 412–418. Copyright 1977 by the American Psychological Association. Reprinted by permission. **538,** (Table 12–6): From "Social Determinants of Residential Crowding Stress," by J. R. Aiello, A. Baum, and F. Gormley. In *Personality and Social Psychology Bulletin,* 1981, *7,* 643–644. Copyright 1981 by the American Psychological Association. Reprinted by permission. **539,** (Figure 12–7): From "The Role of Attribution in the Experiences of Crowding," by S. Worchel and S. Yohai. In *Journal of Experimental Social Psychology,* 1979, *34,* 91–104. Copyright 1979 by Academic Press. Reprinted by permission. **541,** (Table 12–7): From "The Effects of Density on Humans," by J. L. Freedman. In James T. Fawcett (Ed.), *Psychological Perspectives on Population.* Copyright © 1973 by Basic Books, Inc. Reprinted by permission of Harper & Row, Publishers, Inc. **542,** (Table 12–8): From *Environmental Science,* by A. Turk, J. Turk, J. T. Wittes, and R. Wittes. Copyright © 1974 by W. B. Saunders Company. Reprinted by permission. **545,** (Figure 12–9): From "The Effects of Noise and Perceived Control upon Ongoing and Subsequent Aggressive Behavior," by E. T. Donnerstein and D. E. Wilson. In *Journal of Personality and Social Psychology,* 1976, *34,* 774–781. Copyright 1976 by the American Psychological Association. Reprinted by permission. **547,** (Figure 12–10): From "Ambient Temperature and Violent Crime: Tests of the Linear and Curvilinear Hypothesis," by C. A. Anderson and D. C. Anderson. In *Journal of Personality and Social Psychology,* 1984, *46,* 91–97. Copyright 1984 by the American Psychological Association. Reprinted by permission.